AF512981

AutoCAD 2021 for Engineers and Designers

(3D and Advanced)

Sham Tickoo
Professor
Purdue University Northwest
Hammond, Indiana, USA

Contributing Author
Tickoo Institute of Emerging Technologies(TIET)
Gurugram, India

CADCIM Technologies
Indiana, USA

BPB PUBLICATIONS

ISBN: 978-93-89898-97-2
REPRINT 2023

Limits of Liability and Disclaimer of Warranty

Distributors

COMPUTER BOOK CENTRE
12, Shrungar Shopping Centre
M.G. Road
BENGALURU–56000
Ph: 25587923/25584641

DECCAN AGENCIES
4-3-329, Bank Street
HYDERABAD-500195
Ph: 24756967/24756400

MICRO MEDIA
Shop No. 5, Mahendra Chambers
150 DN Rd. Next to Capital Cinema
V.T (C.S.T.) Station
MUMBAI-400001

BPB BOOK CENTRE
376 Old Lajpat Rai Market
DELHI-110006
Ph: 23861747

INFOTECH
G-2, Sidhartha Building, 96 Nehru Place
NEW DELHI-110019
Ph: 26438245

BPB PUBLICATIONS
20, Ansari Road, Darya Ganj
New Delhi-110002
Ph: 23254990/23254991

Published by Manish Jain for BPB Publications, 20 Ansari Road, Darya Ganj
New Delhi-110002 and Printed by Manipal Technologies Limited, Manipal

DEDICATION

To teachers, who make it possible to disseminate knowledge
to enlighten the young and curious minds
of our future generations

To students, who are dedicated to learning new technologies
and making the world a better place to live in

THANKS

To employees of CADCIM Technologies and
Tickoo Institute of Emerging Technologies (TIET)
for their valuable help

This page is intentionally left blank

Table of Contents

Chapter 4: Editing 3D Objects-I

Chapter 5: Editing 3D Objects-II

Chapter 6: Surface Modeling

Chapter 7: Mesh Modeling

Chapter 8: Rendering and Animating Designs

Chapter 9: AutoCAD on Internet and 3D Printing

Chapter 10: Script Files and Slide Shows

Chapter 11: Creating Linetypes and Hatch Patterns

Chapter 12: Customizing the acad.pgp File

Chapter 13: Conventional Dimensioning and Projection Theory Using AutoCAD

Chapter 14: Isometric Drawings

Student Projects

This page is intentionally left blank

Preface

AutoCAD 2021

AutoCAD, developed by Autodesk Inc., is the most popular PC-CAD system available in the market. Today, over 7 million people use AutoCAD and other AutoCAD-based design products. 100% of the Fortune 100 firms and 98% of the Fortune 500 firms are Autodesk customers. AutoCAD's open architecture allows third-party developers to write application software that has significantly added to its popularity. For example, the author of this book has developed a software package "**SMLayout**" for sheet metal products that generates a flat layout of various geometrical shapes such as transitions, intersections, cones, elbows, tank heads, and so on. Several companies in Canada and United States are using this software package with AutoCAD to design and manufacture various products. AutoCAD also facilitates customization that enables the users to increase their efficiency and improve their productivity.

The **AutoCAD 2021 for Engineers and Designers - 3D and Advanced** textbook contains detailed explanation of AutoCAD commands and their applications to solve design problems. Every AutoCAD command is thoroughly explained with the help of examples and illustrations. This makes it easy for the users to understand the functions and applications of the tools and commands.

After reading this textbook, you will be able to create 3D objects, apply materials to objects, generate drafting views of a model, create surface or mesh objects, and render and animate designs.

The book covers designing concepts in detail as well as provides elaborative description of technical drawing in AutoCAD including orthographic projections, dimensioning principles, sectioning, auxiliary views, and assembly drawings. While going through this textbook, you will discover some new unique applications of AutoCAD that will have a significant effect on your drawings and designs. In addition, you will be able to understand why AutoCAD has become such a popular software package and an international standard in PC-CAD.

Symbols Used in the Textbook

Note

The author has provided additional information to the users about the topic being discussed in the form of notes.

Tip

Special information and techniques are provided in the form of tips that will increase the efficiency of the users.

New

This symbol indicates that the command or tool being discussed is new.

Enhanced

This symbol indicates that the command or tool being discussed has been enhanced in AutoCAD 2021.

Formatting Conventions Used in the Textbook

Refer to the following list for the formatting conventions used in this textbook.

- Command names are capitalized and written in boldface letters.

  Example: The **MOVE** command

- A key icon appears when you have to respond by pressing the ENTER or the RETURN key.

  Enter

- Command sequences are indented. The responses are indicated in boldface. The directions are indicated in italics and the comments are enclosed in parentheses.

  Command: **MOVE**
  Select object: **G**
  Enter group name: *Enter a group name (the group name is group1)*

- The methods of invoking a tool/option from the **Ribbon, Menu Bar, Quick Access Toolbar, Tool Palettes, Application menu**, toolbars, Status Bar, and Command prompt are enclosed in a shaded box.

Ribbon:	Draw > Line
Menu Bar:	Draw > Line
Tool Palettes:	Draw > Line
Toolbar:	Draw > Line
Command:	LINE or L

Naming Conventions Used in the Textbook

Tool

If you click on an item in a toolbar or a panel of the **Ribbon** and a command is invoked to create/edit an object or perform some action, then that item is termed as **tool**, refer to Figure 1.

For example:
To Create: **Line** tool, **Circle** tool, **Extrude** tool
To Edit: **Fillet** tool, **Array** tool, **Stretch** tool
Action: **Zoom** tool, **Move** tool, **Copy** tool

If you click on an item in a toolbar or a panel of the **Ribbon** and a dialog box is invoked wherein you can set the properties to create/edit an object, then that item is also termed as **tool**, refer to Figure 1.

For example:
To Create: **Define Attributes** tool, **Create** tool, **Insert** tool
To Edit: **Edit Attributes** tool, **Block Editor** tool

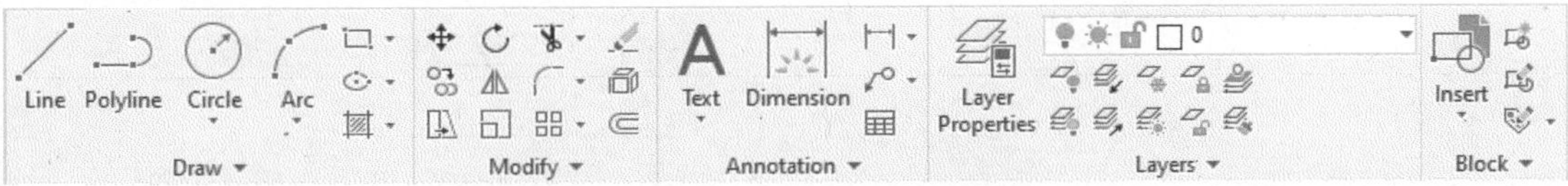

Figure 1** Various tools in the **Ribbon

Button

If you click on an item in a toolbar or a panel of the **Ribbon** and the display of the corresponding object is toggled on/off, then that item is termed as **Button**. For example, **Grid** button, **Snap** button, **Ortho** button, **Properties** button, **Tool Palettes** button, and so on; refer to Figure 2.

Figure 2** Various buttons displayed in the **Status Bar** and **Ribbon

The item in a dialog box that has a 3d shape like a button is also termed as **Button**. For example, **OK** button, **Cancel** button, **Apply** button, and so on.

Dialog Box

In this textbook, different terms are used for referring to the components of a dialog box. Refer to Figure 3 for the terminology used.

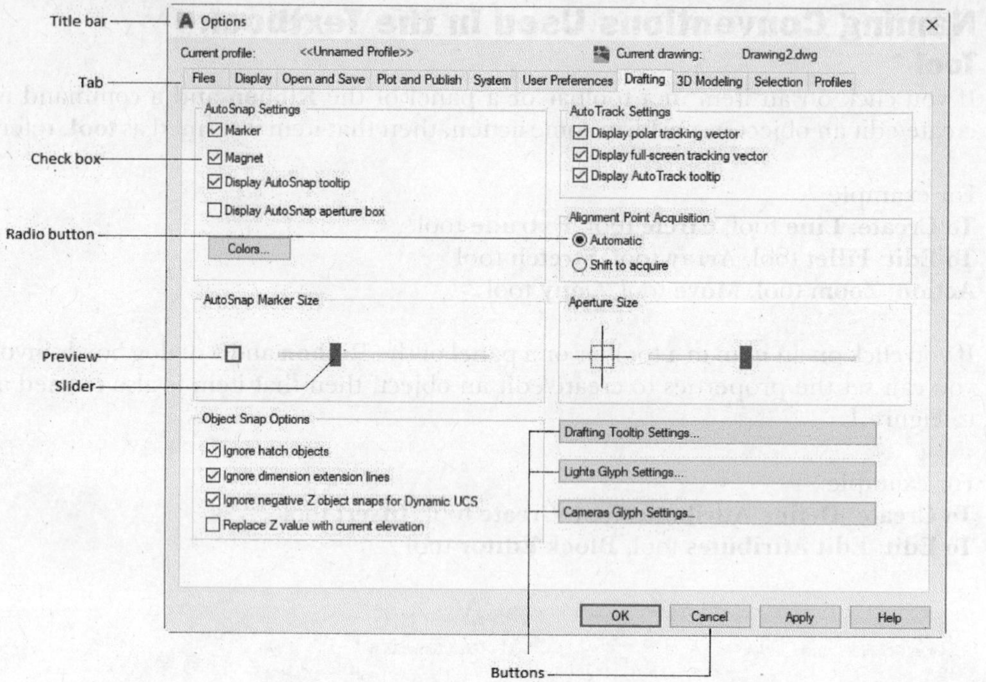

Figure 3 The components of a dialog box

Drop-down

A drop-down is the one in which a set of common tools are grouped together. You can identify a drop-down with a down arrow on it. These drop-downs are given a name based on the tools grouped in them. For example, **Circle** drop-down, **Fillet/Chamfer** drop-down, **Create Light** drop-down, and so on; refer to Figure 4.

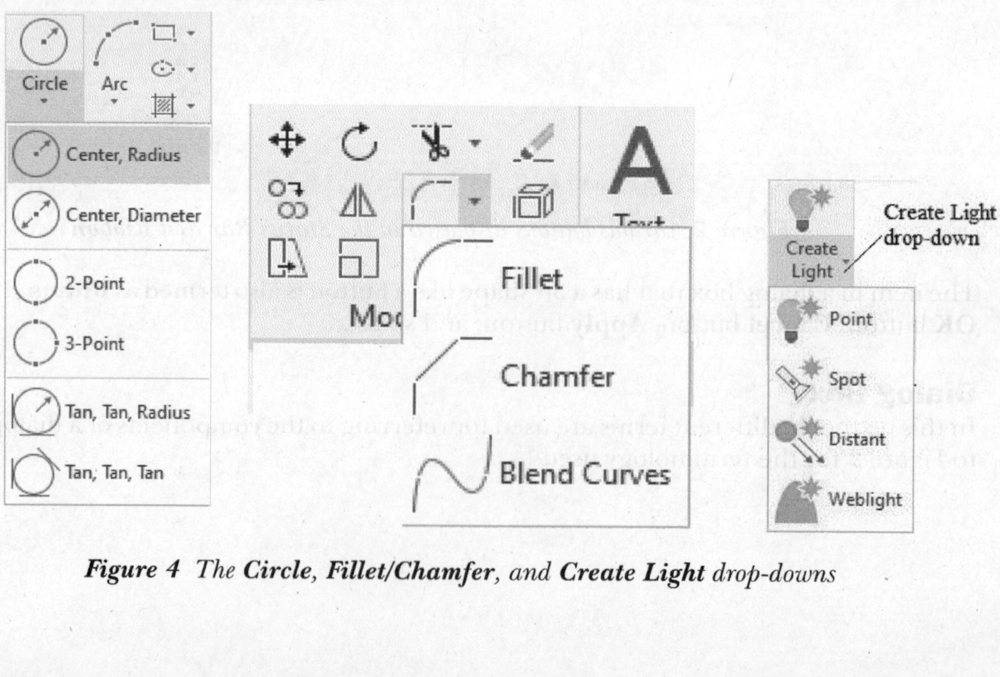

*Figure 4 The **Circle**, **Fillet/Chamfer**, and **Create Light** drop-downs*

Drop-down List

A drop-down list is the one in which a set of options are grouped together. You can set various parameters using these options. You can identify a drop-down list with a down arrow on it. To know the name of a drop-down list, move the cursor over it; its name will be displayed as a tool tip. For example, **Lineweight** drop-down list, **Linetype** drop-down list, **Object Color** drop-down list, **Visual Styles** drop-down list, and so on; refer to Figure 5.

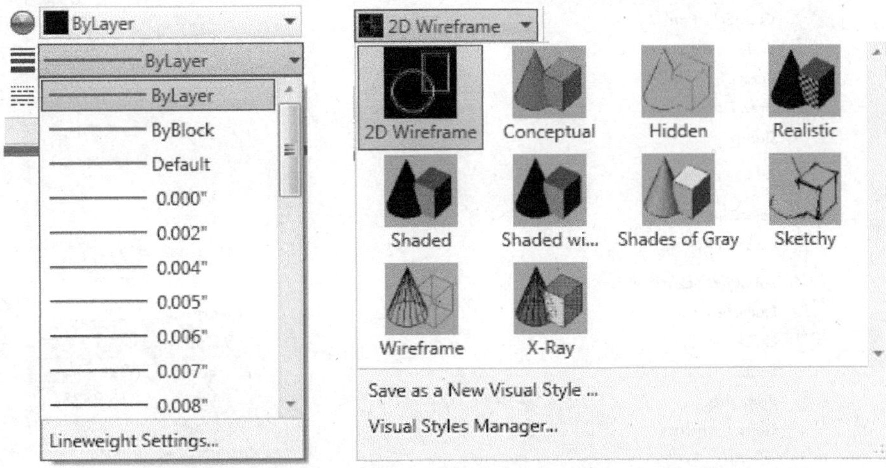

*Figure 5 The **Lineweight** and **Visual Styles** drop-down lists*

Options

Options are the items that are available in shortcut menu, drop-down list, Command prompt, **Properties** panel, and so on. For example, choose the **Properties** option from the shortcut menu displayed on right-clicking in the drawing area, refer to Figure 6.

Tools and Options in Menu Bar

A menu bar consists of both tools and options. As mentioned earlier, the term **tool** is used to create/edit something or to perform some action. For example, in Figure 7, the item Box has been used to create a box shaped surface, therefore it will be referred to as the **Box** tool.

Similarly, an option in the menu bar is the one that is used to set some parameters. For example, in Figure 7, the item Linetype has been used to set/load the linetype, therefore it will be referred to as an option.

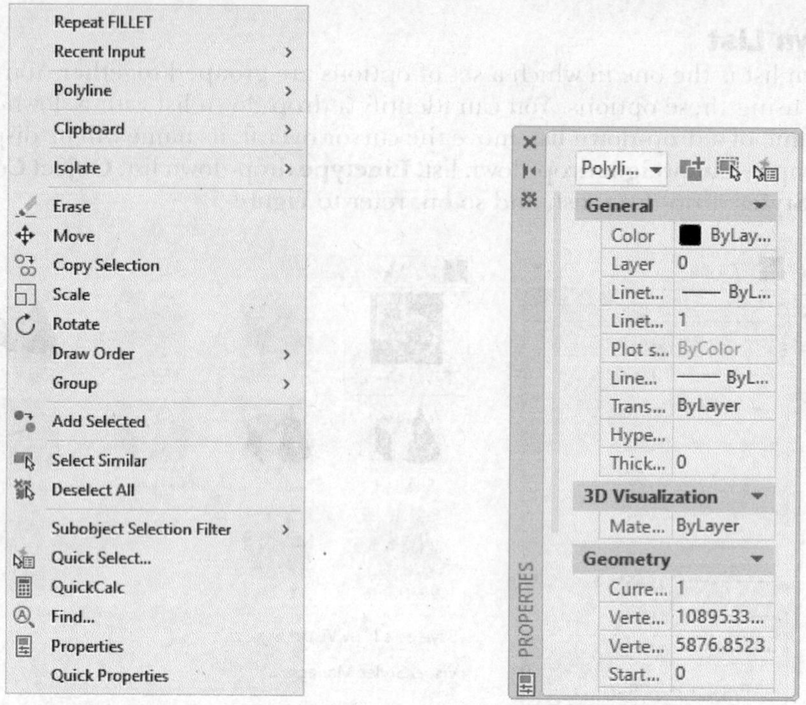

Figure 6 Options in the shortcut menu and the ***Properties*** *palette*

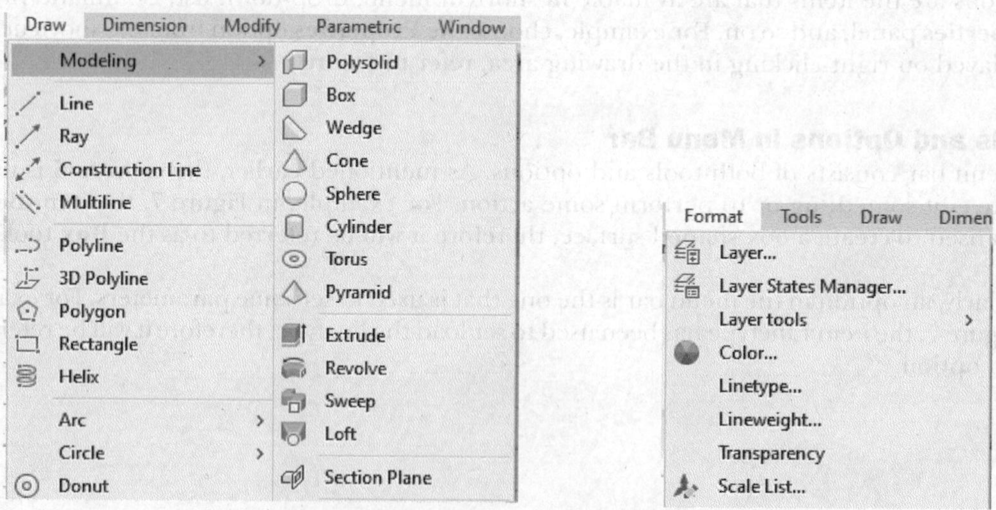

Figure 7 Tools and options in the menu bar

Free Companion Website

It has been our constant endeavor to provide you the best textbooks and services at affordable price. In this endeavor, we have come out with a Free Companion website that will facilitate the process of teaching and learning of AutoCAD 2021. If you purchase this textbook, you will get access to the files on the Companion website.

The following resources are available in this website:

- **Technical Support**
  You can get online technical support by contacting techsupport@cadcim.com.

- **Instructor Guide**
  Solutions to all review questions and exercises in the textbook are provided in this guide.

- **Part Files**
  The part files used in illustration, examples, tutorials, and exercises are available for free download.

You can access additional learning resources by visiting ***https://allaboutcadcam.blogspot.com***.

If you face any problem in accessing these files, please contact at ***sales@cadcim.com*** or the author at ***stickoo@pnw.edu*** or ***tickoo525@gmail.com***.

Video Courses

CADCIM offers video courses in CAD, CAE Simulation, BIM, Civil/GIS, and Animation domains on various e-Learning/Video platforms. To enroll for the video courses, please visit the CADCIM website using the link ***https://www.cadcim.com/video-courses***.

Stay Connected

You can now stay connected with us through Facebook and Twitter to get the latest information about our textbooks, videos, and teaching/learning resources. To stay informed of such updates, follow us on Facebook (***www.facebook.com/cadcim***) and Twitter (***@cadcimtech***). You can also subscribe to our You Tube channel (***www.youtube.com/cadcimtech***) to get the information about our latest video tutorials.

This page is intentionally left blank

Chapter 1

The User Coordinate System

Learning Objectives

After completing this chapter, you will be able to:

- *Understand the concept of World Coordinate System (WCS)*
- *Understand the concept of User Coordinate System (UCS)*
- *Control the display of UCS icon*
- *Change the current UCS icon type*
- *Use the UCS command*
- *Dynamically move and align the UCS*
- *Understand different options for changing UCS using the UCS tool*
- *Change UCS using the Dynamic UCS button*
- *Manage UCS through the UCS dialog box*
- *Understand different system variables related to the UCS and the UCS icon*

Key Terms

- *UCS Icon*
- *UCS*
- *UCS Manager*

THE USER COORDINATE SYSTEM (UCS)

When you start a new drawing in AutoCAD, the world coordinate system (WCS) is established by default. The objects you draw uses the WCS to locate itself in the drawing space. In WCS, the *X*, *Y*, and *Z* coordinates of any point are measured with respect to the fixed origin (0,0,0). By default this origin is located at the lower left corner of the screen, by nature this coordinate system is fixed and can not be moved. Generally 2D drawings, wireframe models, and surface models can be created in WCS but in the case of solid models it is not possible to keep the origin and the orientation of the *X*, *Y*, and *Z* axes at the same place every time. The reason for this is that in case you want to create a feature on the top face of an existing model you will need to shift the working plane to the top face of the model. This can be done by using the Elevation option of the **ELEV** command, refer to Figure 1-1. But, on using the **ELEV** command, it is not possible to create a feature on the faces other than the top and bottom faces of an existing model.

This problem can be solved by using the user coordinate system (UCS). Using the **UCS** command, you can relocate and reorient the origin and *X*, *Y*, and *Z* axes and establish your own coordinate system, depending on your requirement. The UCS is mostly used in 3D drawings, where you may need to specify points that vary from each other along the *X*, *Y*, and *Z* axes. It is also useful for relocating the origin or rotating the *X* and *Y* axes in 2D work, such as ordinate dimensioning, drawing auxiliary views, or controlling the hatch alignment. The UCS and its icon can be modified using the **UCSICON** and **UCS** commands. After reorienting the UCS, you can create a feature on any of the face of an existing model, refer to Figure 1-2.

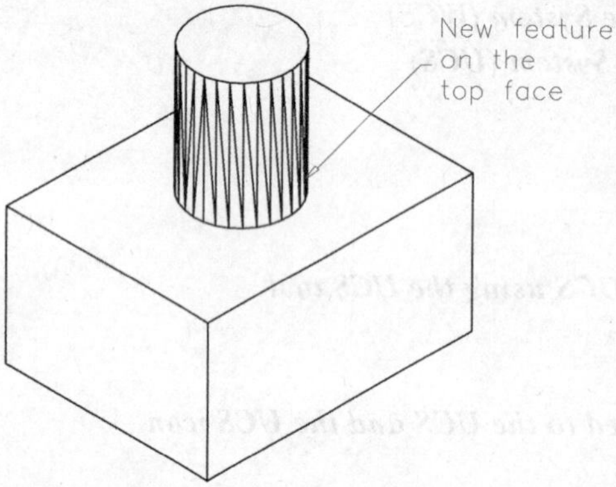

Figure 1-1 *Creating a new feature on the top face*

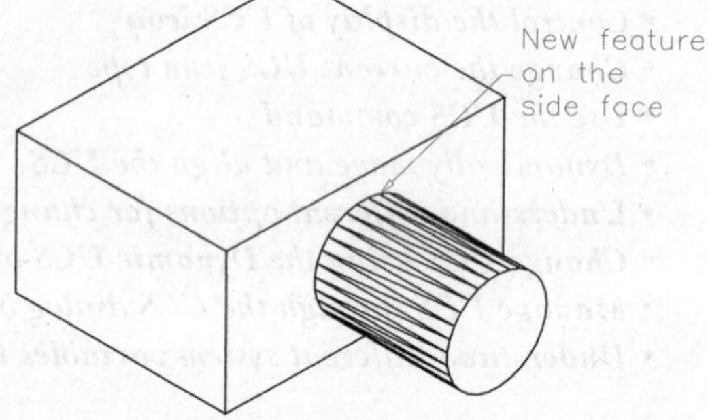

Figure 1-2 *Creating a new feature on the side face*

CONTROLLING THE VISIBILITY OF THE UCS ICON

Ribbon: View > Viewport Tools > UCS Icon
Menu Bar: View > Display > UCS Icon > On **Command:** UCSICON

The **UCS Icon** tool is used to control the visibility and location of the UCS icon, which is a geometric representation of the directions of the current *X*, *Y*, and *Z* axes. AutoCAD displays different UCS icons in model space and paper space, as shown in Figures 1-3 and 1-4. By default, the UCS icon is displayed near the bottom left corner of the drawing area. You can change the location and visibility of this icon using the **UCSICON** command. The prompt sequence for the **UCSICON** command is given next.

Enter an option [ON/OFF/All/Noorigin/ORigin/Selectable/Properties] <ON>: *You can specify any option or press ENTER to accept the default option.*

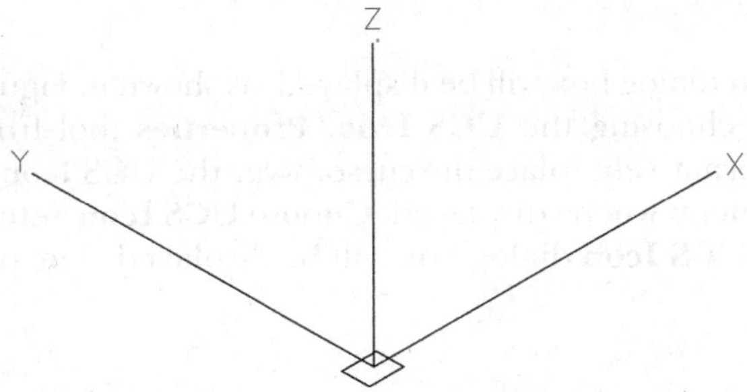

Figure 1-3 *The UCS icon in the Model space*

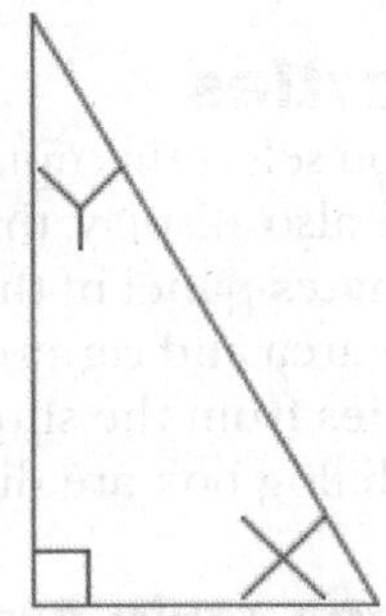

Figure 1-4 *The UCS icon in the Paper space*

ON

This option is used to display the UCS icon on the screen. You can also display the UCS icon by choosing the **Show UCS Icon** tool from the **Show UCS** drop-down list of **Coordinates** panel in the **Home** tab.

OFF

This option is used to make the UCS icon invisible from the screen. When you choose this option, the UCS icon will no longer be displayed on the screen. You can again turn on the display using the **ON** option of the **UCSICON** command. Alternatively, choose the **Hide UCS Icon** tool from the **Show UCS** drop-down list of **Coordinates** panel in the **Home** tab to make the UCS icon invisible.

All

This option is used to apply changes to the UCS icon in all active viewports. If this option is not used, the changes will be applied only to the current viewport.

Noorigin

This option is used to display the UCS icon at the lower left corner of the viewport, irrespective of the actual location of the origin of the current UCS.

ORigin

This option is used to place the UCS icon at the origin of the current UCS. You can also choose the **Show UCS Icon at Origin** tool from the **Show UCS** drop-down list of the **Coordinates** panel in the **Home** tab. Alternatively, type **UCSICON** at the command prompt and press enter. Next, select the **ORigin** option from the options displayed.

Note

*You can switch into different workspaces using the **Workspace** Switching drop-down list available at the right in the **Status Bar**.*

Selectable

This option allows you to control the selection of UCS. By default, UCS is selectable.

Properties

When you select this option, the **UCS Icon** dialog box will be displayed, as shown in Figure 1-5. You can also display this dialog box by choosing the **UCS Icon, Properties** tool from the **Coordinates** panel in the **Home** tab. Alternatively, place the cursor over the UCS Icon in the drawing area and right-click; a shortcut menu will be displayed. Choose **UCS Icon Settings > Properties** from the shortcut menu; the **UCS Icon** dialog box will be displayed. The options in this dialog box are discussed next.

UCS icon style Area

The options in this area are discussed next.

3D: This button is selected by default. As a result, the 3D UCS icon will be displayed in the model space.

2D: If this radio button is selected, the 2D UCS icon will be displayed instead of the 3D UCS icon, refer to Figure 1-6.

Line width. This drop-down list is used to specify the line width of the 3D UCS icon. The default value for the line width is 1. Note that this drop-down list will not be activated if the **2D** radio button is selected.

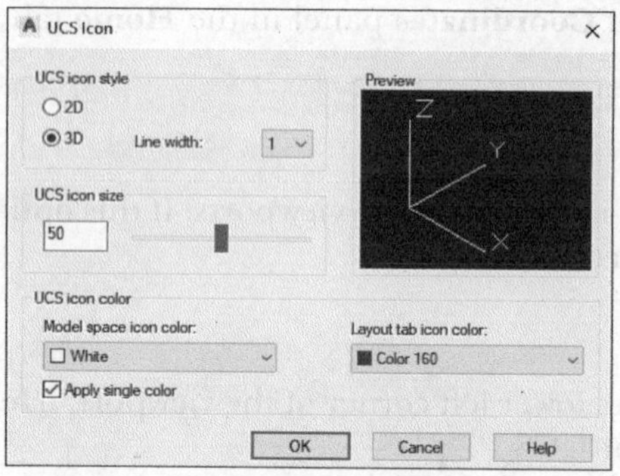

*Figure 1-5 The **UCS Icon** dialog box*

Figure 1-6 2D UCS icon at the World position

UCS icon size Area

The edit box and slider bar provided in this area are used to control the size of the UCS icon. You can enter values from ranging 5 to 95 in the edit box or by adjusting the sliding bar. The size of the UCS icon is proportional to the viewport size as the value entered is the percentage of the viewport size.

UCS icon color Area

The **UCS icon color** area has two drop-down lists, **Model space icon color** and **Layout tab icon color**. The options in these drop-down lists are used to change the color of the UCS icon. By default, the color in the **Model space icon color** drop-down list is white and in the **Layout tab**

icon color drop-down list is Color 160. You can assign any color to the UCS icon. By default, there are seven colors in first and eight colors in second drop-down list. However, you can also select a color from the **Select Color** dialog box which will be displayed after you select the **Select Color** option from the **Model space icon color** drop-down list or the **Layout tab icon color** drop-down list.

DEFINING THE NEW UCS

Ribbon: Visualize > Coordinates > UCS **Toolbar:** UCS
Menu Bar: Tools > New UCS **Command:** UCS

The **UCS** tool is used to set a new coordinate system by shifting the working plane (*XY* plane) to the desired location. For certain views of the drawing, it is better to have the origin of measurements at some other point on or relative to your drawing objects. This makes locating the features and dimensioning the objects easier. The change in the UCS can be viewed by the change in the position and orientation of the UCS icon, which is placed by default at the lower left corner of the drawing window. The origin and orientation of a coordinate system can be redefined by using the **UCS** command. Alternatively, choose the **UCS** tool from the **Coordinates** panel of the **Visualize** tab. The prompt sequence after choosing this tool is given next:

Current ucs name: *WORLD*
Specify origin of UCS or [Face/NAmed/OBject/Previous/View/World/X/Y/Z/ZAxis] <World>: *Select an option.*

If the **UCSFOLLOW** system variable is set to 0, any change in the UCS will not affect the drawing view.

If you choose the default option of the **UCS** tool, you can establish a new coordinate system by specifying a new origin point, a point on the positive side of the new *X* axis, and a point on the positive side of the new *Y* axis. The direction of the *Z* axis is determined by applying the right-hand rule, about which you will learn in the next chapter. This option changes the orientation of the UCS to any angled surface. The prompt sequence that will follow is given next.

Specify origin of UCS or [Face/NAmed/OBject/Previous/View/World/X/Y/Z/ZAxis] <World>: *Specify the origin point of the new UCS.*
Specify point on X-axis or <accept>: *Specify a point on the positive portion of the X axis.*
Specify point on the XY plane or <accept>: *Specify a point on the positive portion of the Y axis to define the orientation of the UCS completely.*

In AutoCAD, you can directly manipulate the UCS as per your requirement. This implies that you can easily move the origin of UCS, align the UCS with objects, or rotate it around X, Y, and Z axis without invoking the UCS command. You can also move the UCS and place it at the desired location without using any command. To do so, select the UCS; the grips are displayed on it. Place the cursor on the rectangular grip displayed at the intersection of three axes of UCS; a shortcut menu will be displayed, as shown in Figure 1-7.

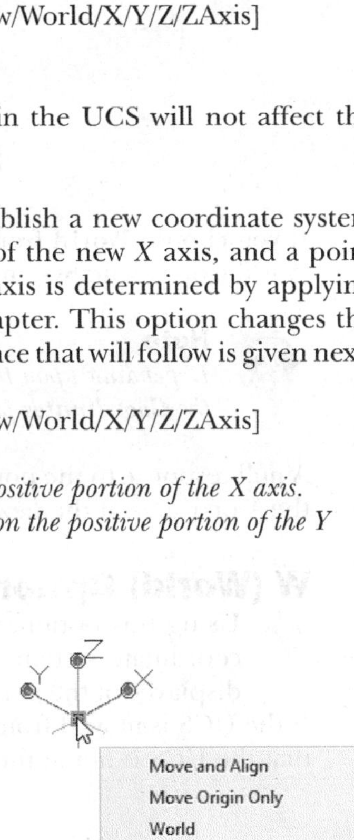

Figure 1-7 *UCS shortcut menu*

Choose the **Move and Align** option from the shortcut menu; the UCS will be displayed attached to the cursor. You can move the UCS to any point but you can align it only with the face of a 3D object, surface, or mesh. To align the UCS, move it to any point on the face of a 3D object, surface, or mesh; the face gets highlighted and the UCS automatically aligns with the orientation of that face, surface, or mesh, as shown in Figure 1-8.

In case of a curved surface, the UCS will get aligned in such a way that the Z-axis becomes normal to the surface at the specified point. After aligning the UCS to the selected face, you can change the direction of X axis, Y axis, or Z axis dynamically. You can also use the shortcut menu displayed on placing the cursor on the X, Y, or Z grip.

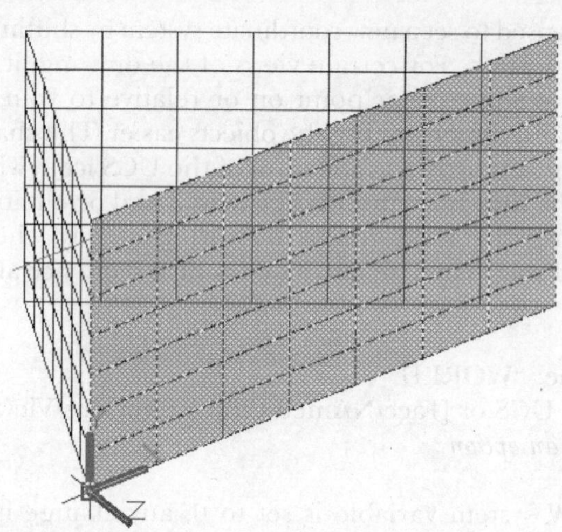

Figure 1-8 UCS aligned to the highlighted face

If you choose **World** from the UCS shortcut menu, then the UCS will move and align to the World Coordinate System. The World Coordinate System is discussed next.

Note
*Depending upon the type of UCS required, you can choose the corresponding tools available in the **Coordinates** panel of the **Home** tab.*

A null response to the point on the *X* or *Y* axis prompt will lead to a coordinate system, in which the *X* or *Y* axis of the new UCS is parallel to that of the previous UCS.

W (World) Option

Using this option, you can set the current UCS back to the WCS, which is the default coordinate system. When the UCS is placed at the world position, a small rectangle is displayed at the point where all the three axes meet in the UCS icon, refer to Figure 1-9 (a). If the UCS is moved from its default position, this rectangle is no longer displayed, indicating that the UCS is not at the world position, as shown in Figure 1-9(b).

Note

If 2D UCS icon is selected instead of 3D UCS icon and if the UCS is not at the world position; the W icon will not be displayed.

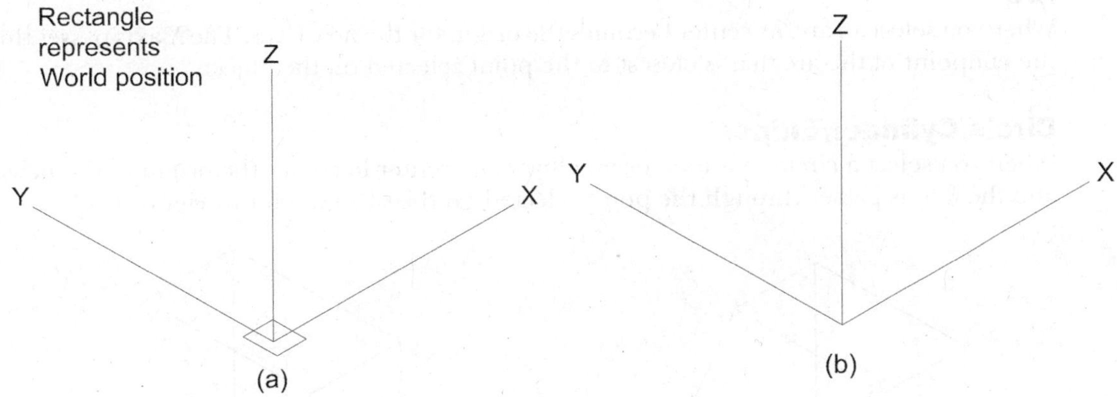

***Figure 1-9** UCS at the world position and UCS not at the world position*

F (Face) Option

This option is used to align a new UCS with the selected face of a solid object. You can invoke this option by choosing the **Face** tool from the Align UCS drop-down list in the **Coordinates** panel, as shown in Figure 1-10. The prompt sequence that will follow when you choose this tool is given next.

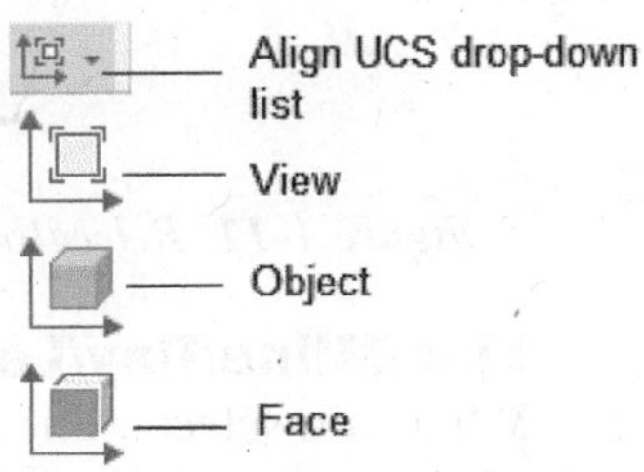

***Figure 1-10** The **Face** tool in the Align UCS drop-down list*

Select face of solid, surface, or mesh: *Select the face to align the UCS.*
Enter an option [Next/Xflip/Yflip] <accept>: *Select an option or accept the selected face to align.*

The **Next** option is used to locate the new UCS on the adjacent face or the back face of the selected edge. **Xflip** rotates the new UCS by 180 degrees about the *X* axis and **Yflip** rotates it about the *Y* axis. Pressing ENTER at the **Enter an option [Next/Xflip/Yflip] <accept>** prompt accepts the location of the new UCS as specified.

OB (OBject) Option

With the **OB** (**OBject**) option of the **UCS** tool, you can establish a new coordinate system by selecting an object in the drawing. However, some of the objects such as 3D polyline, 3D mesh, viewport object, or xline cannot be used for defining a UCS. The positive *Z* axis of the new UCS is in the same direction as the positive *Z* axis of the object selected. If the *X* and *Z* axes are given, the new *Y* axis is determined by the right-hand rule. You can also invoke this option by choosing the **Object** tool from the Align UCS drop-down list in the **Coordinates** panel. The prompt sequence that will follow when you choose this tool is given next.

Select object to align UCS: *Select the object to align the UCS.*

In Figure 1-11, the UCS is relocated using the **OBject** option and is aligned to the circle. The origin and the *X* axis of the new UCS are determined by using the following rules:

Arc

When you select an arc, its center becomes the origin for the new UCS. The *X* axis passes through the endpoint of the arc that is closest to the point selected on the object.

Circle/Cylinder/Ellipse

When you select a circle, cylinder, or an ellipse, its center becomes the origin of the new UCS, and the *X* axis passes through the point selected on the object, refer to Figure 1-12.

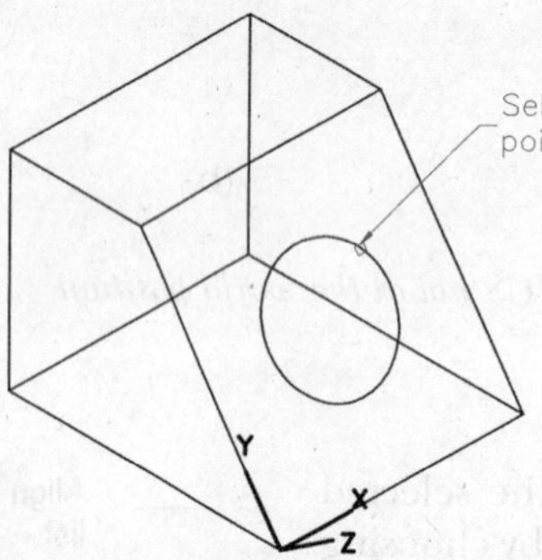

Figure 1-11 *Relocating the UCS using a circle*

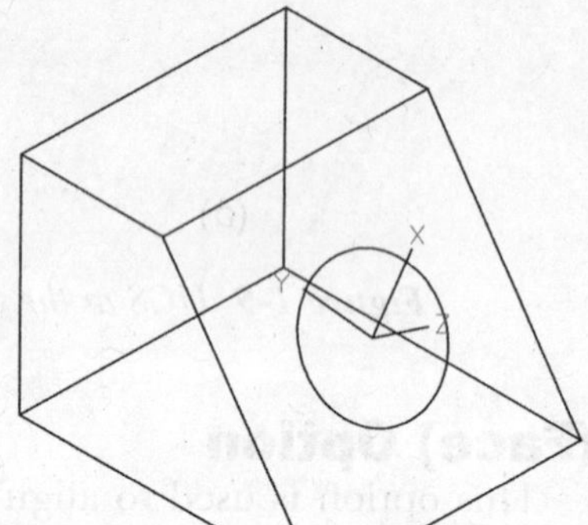

Figure 1-12 *UCS at a new location*

Line/Mline/Ray/Leader

When you select a line, mline, ray, or a leader, the endpoint nearest to the point selected on it becomes the origin of the new UCS. The *X* axis is defined so that the line lies on the *XY* plane of the new UCS. Therefore, in the new UCS, the *Y* coordinate of the second endpoint of the line is 0.

Note

The linear edges of solid models or regions are considered as individual lines when selected to align a UCS.

Spline

When you select a spline, the endpoint that is nearest to the point selected on the spline becomes the origin of the new UCS. An imaginary line will be drawn between the two endpoints of the spline and the *X* axis will be aligned along this imaginary line.

Dimension

When you select a dimension, the middle point of the dimension text becomes the origin of the new UCS. The *X* axis direction is identical to the direction of the *X* axis of the UCS that existed when the dimension was drawn.

Point

The position of the point is the origin of the new UCS. The directions of the *X*, *Y*, and *Z* axes will be same as those of the previous UCS.

Solid

When you select a solid, the first point selected on the solid becomes the origin of the new UCS. The *X* axis of the new UCS lies along the line between the first and second points of the solid.

2D Polyline

When you select a polyline, the end point nearest to the point selected on the polyline becomes the origin of the new UCS. The *X* axis extends from the start point to the next vertex.

3D Face

When you select a 3D face, its first point becomes the origin of the new UCS. The *X* axis is determined by using the first two points, and the positive side of the *Y* axis is determined by the first and fourth points for a flat rectangular face. For a flat planar face, the X axis will always be parallel to the edge through which the UCS is moved on the face. The *Z* axis is determined by applying the right-hand rule.

Shape/Text/Block/Attribute/Attribute Definition

When you select a shape, text, block, attribute, or a attribute definition, its insertion point becomes the origin of the new UCS. The new X axis is defined by the rotation of the object around its positive Z axis. Therefore, the object you select will have a rotation angle of zero in the new UCS.

Tip

Except for 3D faces, the XY plane of the new UCS will be parallel to the XY plane of the object when it was drawn. However, X and Y axes may be rotated.

V (View) Option

The **V (View)** option of the **UCS** tool is used to define a new UCS whose *XY* plane is parallel to the current viewing plane. The current viewing plane, in this case, is the screen of the monitor. Therefore, a new UCS is defined that is parallel to the screen of the monitor. The origin of the UCS defined in this option remains unaltered. This option is used mostly to view a drawing from an oblique viewing direction or to write text for the objects on the screen. You can also invoke this option by choosing the **View** tool from the **Align UCS** drop-down list in the **Coordinates** panel. As soon as you choose this tool, a new UCS is defined parallel to the screen of the monitor.

X/Y/Z

With these options, you can rotate the current UCS around the desired axis. You can specify the angle by entering the angle value at the required prompt or by selecting two points on the screen with the help of a pointing device. You can specify a positive or a negative angle. The new angle is taken relative to the *X* axis of the existing UCS. The **UCSAXISANG** system variable stores the default angle by which the UCS is rotated around the specified axis, by using the **X/ Y/ Z** options of the **UCS** tool. The right-hand thumb rule is used to determine the positive direction of rotation of the selected axis. You can also invoke the corresponding option by choosing the

X/Y/Z button from the Rotate UCS drop-down in the **Coordinates** panel, as shown in Figure 1-13. However, in AutoCAD, you can rotate the UCS dynamically using the grips and shortcut menu.

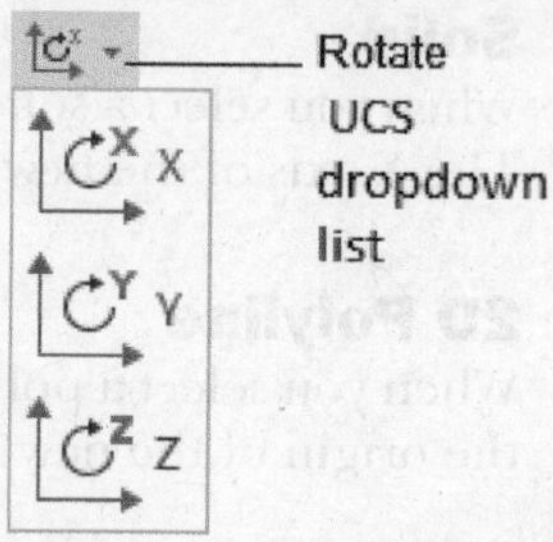

*Figure 1-13 Tools in the **Rotate UCS** drop-down list*

X

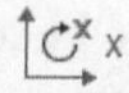

In Figure 1-14, the UCS is rotated using the **X** option by specifying an angle about the X axis at the command prompt. The first model shows the UCS setting before the UCS was relocated and the second model shows the relocated UCS.

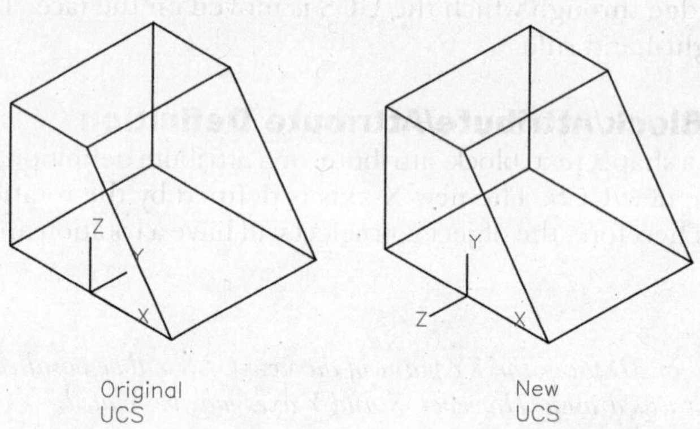

***Figure 1-14** Rotating the UCS about the X axis*

You can also choose the X tool from the Rotate UCS drop-down list in the **Coordinates** panel. The prompt sequence that will follow when you choose the **X** tool is given next.

Specify rotation angle about X axis <90>: *Specify the rotation angle.*

Alternatively, you can dynamically rotate the UCS about the X axis by following the steps given below:

1. Click on the UCS in the drawing area to select it.
2. Move the cursor to the grip of the Y or Z axis; a shortcut menu will be displayed, as shown in Figure 1-15.
3. Choose the **Rotate Around X Axis** option from the shortcut menu and then rotate the UCS dynamically. You can also enter the desired rotation angle in the edit box attached to the cursor.

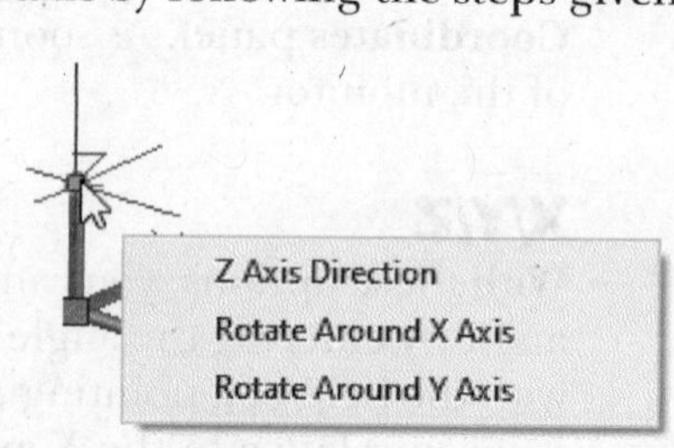

***Figure 1-15** Shortcut menu for UCS rotation*

Y

In Figure 1-16, the UCS is rotated using the **Y** option by specifying an angle about the Y axis. The first model shows the UCS setting before the UCS was relocated and the second model shows the relocated UCS. The prompt sequence that will follow when you choose the **Y** tool from the Rotate UCS drop-down list is given next.

Specify rotation angle about Y axis <90>: *Specify the angle.*

Alternatively, you can dynamically rotate the UCS about the Y axis by following the steps given below:

1. Click on the UCS in the drawing area to select it.
2. Move the cursor to the grip of the X or Z axis.
3. Choose the **Rotate Around Y Axis** option from the shortcut menu and rotate the UCS dynamically or specify the desired angle.

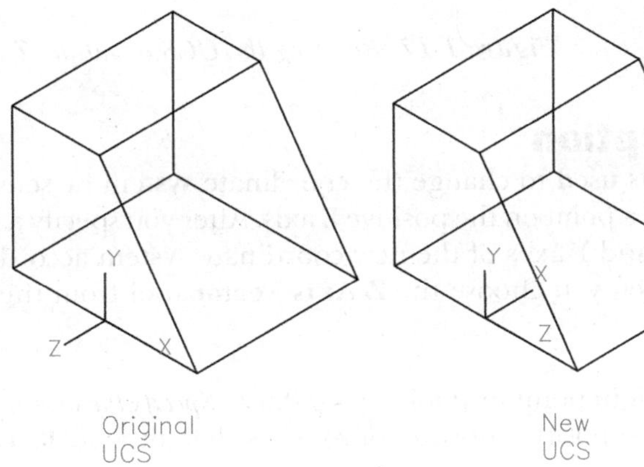

***Figure 1-16** Rotating the UCS about the Y axis*

Z

In Figure 1-17, the UCS is rotated using the **Z** option by specifying an angle about the Z axis. The first model shows the UCS setting before the UCS was rotated and the second model shows the rotated UCS. The prompt sequence that will follow when you choose the **Z** tool from the **Rotate UCS** drop-down is given next.

Specify rotation angle about Z axis <90>: *Specify the angle.*

Alternatively, you can dynamically rotate the UCS about the Z axis by following the steps given below:

1. Click on the UCS in the drawing area to select it.
2. Move the cursor to the grip of the X or Y axis.
3. Choose the **Rotate Around Z Axis** option from the shortcut menu and rotate the UCS dynamically or specify the desired rotation angle.

Note

*You can rotate the UCS about any axis also by using the options in the shortcut menu displayed on right-clicking on the UCS. To do so, move the cursor on the **Rotate Axis** sub-menu in the shortcut menu and then choose the required option.*

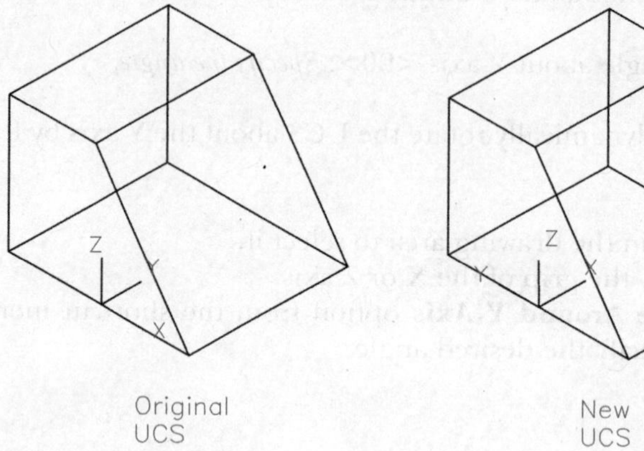

***Figure 1-17** Rotating the UCS about the Z axis*

ZA (ZAxis) Option

This option is used to change the coordinate system by selecting the origin point of the *XY* plane and a point on the positive *Z* axis. After you specify a point on the *Z* axis, AutoCAD determines the *X* and *Y* axes of the new coordinate system accordingly. The prompt sequence that will follow when you choose the **Z Axis Vector** tool from the **Coordinates** panel is given next.

Specify new origin point or [Object] <0,0,0>: *Specify the origin point, as shown in Figure 1-18.*
Specify point on positive portion of Z-axis <default>: **@ 0,-1,0**

Now, the front face of the model will become the new work plane, refer to Figure 1-19 and all the new objects will be oriented accordingly. If you give a null response to the **Specify point on positive portion of Z-axis <current>** prompt, the *Z* axis of the new coordinate system will be parallel to (in the same direction as) the *Z* axis of the previous coordinate system. Null responses to the origin point and the point on the positive *Z* axis establish a new coordinate system in which the direction of the *Z* axis is identical to that of the previous coordinate system; however, the *X* and *Y* axes may be rotated around the *Z* axis. The positive *Z* axis direction is also known as the extrusion direction.

When the **Object** option is selected at the **Specify new origin point or [Object] <0,0,0>** prompt, then you will be prompted to select an object. Select an open object and the UCS will be placed at the end point nearest to the point of the object selection, with its Z-axis along the tangent direction at that end point and pointing away from the object.

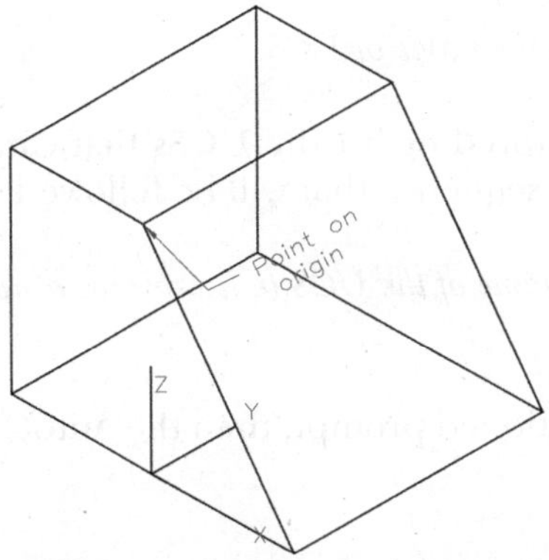

Figure 1-18 Specifying a point on the origin

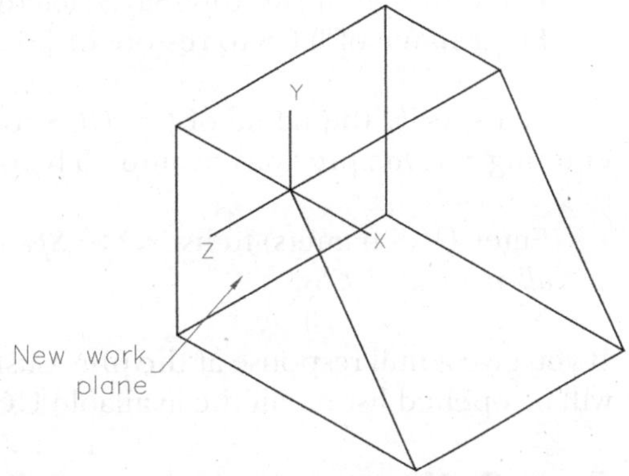

Figure 1-19 Relocating the UCS using the ZA option

Previous Option

The **Previous** option is used to restore the current UCS settings to the previous UCS settings. AutoCAD saves the last ten UCS settings. You can go back to the previous ten UCS settings in the current space using the **Previous** option. If the value of **TILEMODE** is 0, the last ten coordinate systems in paper space and in model space are saved. You can also invoke this option by choosing the **UCS, Previous** tool from the **Coordinates** panel. When you choose this tool, the previous UCS settings are automatically restored.

NAmed Option

This option is used to name and save the current UCS settings, restore a previously saved UCS setting, view a previously saved UCS list, and delete the saved UCS from the list. The prompt sequence for this option is given next.

Command: **UCS**
Current ucs name: *WORLD*
Specify origin of UCS or [Face/NAmed/OBject/Previous/View/World/X/Y/Z/ZAxis] <World>: **NA**
Enter an option [Restore/Save/Delete/?]: *Enter an option.*

Depending on your requirement, you can select any one of the following options:

Restore Option

The **Restore** option of the **UCS** command is used to restore a previously saved named UCS. Once it is restored, it becomes the current UCS. However, the viewing direction of the saved UCS is not restored. You can also restore a named UCS by selecting it from the **UCS** dialog box that appears when you invoke the **UCS, Named UCS** tool from the **Coordinates** panel. As this option does not have a button to restore the Named UCS, you need to choose this option by using the **UCS** command at the Command prompt. The prompt sequence that will follow when you invoke the **UCS** command is given next.

Enter an option [Restore/Save/Delete/?]: ***R***
Enter name of UCS to restore or [?]: *Specify the name of UCS.*

You can specify the name of the UCS to be restored or list the UCSs that can be restored by entering ? at the previous prompt. The prompt sequence that will be followed is given next.

Enter UCS name(s) to list <*>: *Specify the name of the UCS to list or give a null response to list all available UCSs.*

If you give a null response at the previously mentioned prompt, then the AutoCAD text window will be opened listing all the available UCSs.

Save Option

With this option, you can name and save the current UCS settings. The following points should be kept in mind while naming the UCS:

1. The name can be up to 255 characters long.
2. The name can contain letters, digits, blank spaces and the special characters $ (dollar), - (hyphen), and _ (underscore).

As this option does not have a tool, you can invoke this option using the Command prompt. The prompt sequence that will follow after entering the **UCS** command is given next.

Current ucs name: *WORLD*
Specify origin of UCS or [Face/NAmed/OBject/Previous/View/World/X/Y/Z/ZAxis]<WORLD>: **NA**
Enter an option [Restore/Save/Delete/?]: **S**
Enter name to save current UCS or [?]: *Specify a name to the UCS.*

Enter a valid name for the UCS at this prompt. AutoCAD saves it as a UCS. You can also list the previously saved UCSs by entering ? at this prompt. The next prompt sequence is:

Enter UCS name(s) to list <*>:

Enter the name of the UCS to list or give a null response to list all the available UCSs.

Delete Option

The **Delete** option is used to delete the selected UCS from the list of saved coordinate systems. As this option does not have a button, you can invoke this option using the Command prompt. The prompt sequence that will follow after entering the **UCS** command is given next.

Current ucs name: *WORLD*
Specify origin of UCS or [Face/NAmed/OBject/Previous/View/World/X/Y/Z/ZAxis]: **NA**
Enter an option [Restore/Save/Delete/?]: **D**
Enter UCS name(s) to delete <none>: *Specify the name of the UCS to delete.*

The UCS name you enter at this prompt is deleted. You can delete more than one UCS by entering the UCS names separated with commas.

? Option

By invoking this option, you can list the name of the specified UCS. This option gives you the name, origin, and *X*, *Y*, and *Z* axes of all the coordinate systems relative to the existing UCS. If the current UCS has no name, it is listed as WORLD or UNNAMED. The choice between these two names depends on whether the current UCS is the same as the WCS. The prompt sequence that will be displayed when you invoke this option using the Command prompt is given next.

Current ucs name: *WORLD*
Specify origin of UCS or [Face/NAmed/OBject/Previous/View/World/X/Y/Z/ZAxis] <WORLD>: **NA**
Enter an option [Restore/Save/Delete/?]: **?**
Enter UCS name(s) to list <*>:

Apply Option

The **Apply** option applies the current UCS settings to a specified viewport or to all the active viewports in a drawing session. If the **UCSVP** system variable is set to 1, each viewport saves its UCS settings. The **Apply** option is not displayed at the Command prompt as an option for the **UCS** command. Therefore, you have to choose the **Apply** button from the **UCS** toolbar. The prompt sequence that will follow when you choose this button is given next.

Pick viewport to apply current UCS or [All]<current>: *Pick inside the viewport or enter **A** to apply the current UCS settings to all viewports.*

Origin Option

This option is used to define a new UCS by changing the origin of the current UCS, without changing the directions of the X, Y, Z axes, refer to Figures 1-20 and 1-21. The new point defined becomes the origin point (0,0,0) for all the coordinate entries, until the origin is changed again. You can specify the coordinates of the new origin or click on the screen using the pointing device. The **Origin** option is not displayed at the Command prompt as an option for the **UCS** command. Therefore, you have to choose the **Origin** button from the **UCS** toolbar. Alternatively, choose the **Origin** tool from the **Coordinates** panel to specify the coordinates of the new origin. The prompt sequence that will follow when you choose this tool is given next.

Specify new origin point <0,0,0>: *Specify the origin point, as shown in Figure 1-20.*

> **Tip**
> *If you do not provide the Z coordinate for the origin, the current Z coordinate value will be assigned to the UCS.*

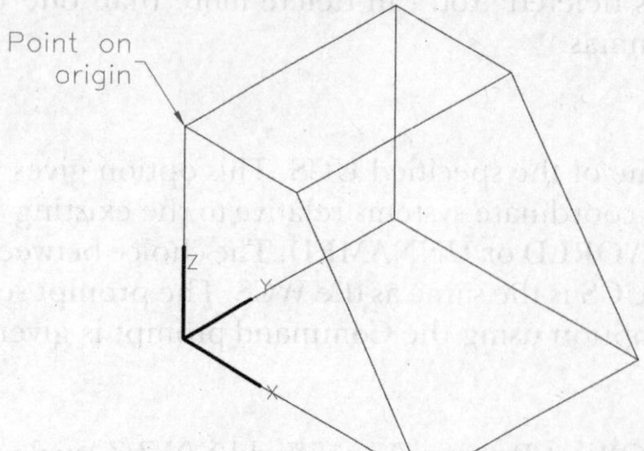

Figure 1-20 Defining a new origin for the UCS

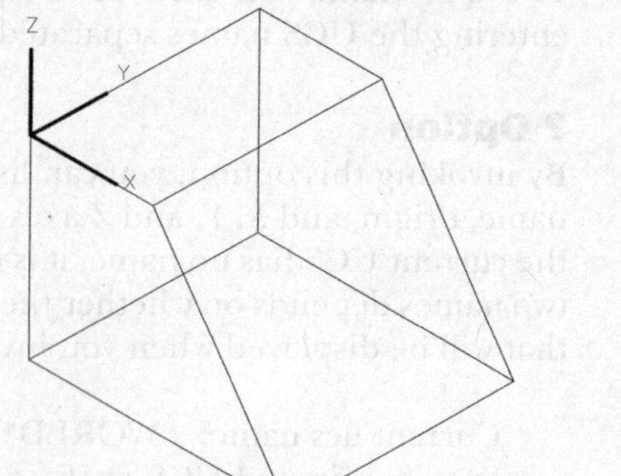

Figure 1-21 Relocating the UCS for the new origin

3-Point Option

The **3-Point** option is the default option of the **UCS** command. With this option, you can establish a new coordinate system by specifying a new origin point, a point on the positive side of the new *X* axis, and a point on the positive side of the new *Y* axis, refer to Figure 1-22. The direction of the *Z* axis is determined by applying the right-hand rule about which you will learn in the next chapter. This option can also be used to align the UCS at any angled surface. The prompt sequence that will follow when you choose the **3-Point** tool from the **Coordinates** panel is given next.

Specify new origin point <0,0,0>: *Specify the origin point of the new UCS.*
Specify point on positive portion of X-axis <default>: *Specify a point on the positive portion of the X axis.*
Specify point on positive-Y portion of the UCS XY plane<default>: *Specify a point on the positive portion of the Y axis.*

A null response to the **Specify new origin point <0,0,0>** prompt will lead to a coordinate system in which the origin of the new UCS is identical to that of the previous UCS. Similarly, null responses to the point on the *X* or *Y* axis prompt will lead to a coordinate system in which the *X* or *Y* axis of the new UCS is parallel to that of the previous UCS. In Figure 1-23, the UCS has been relocated by specifying three points (the origin point, a point on the positive portion of the *X* axis, and a point on the positive portion of the *Y* axis).

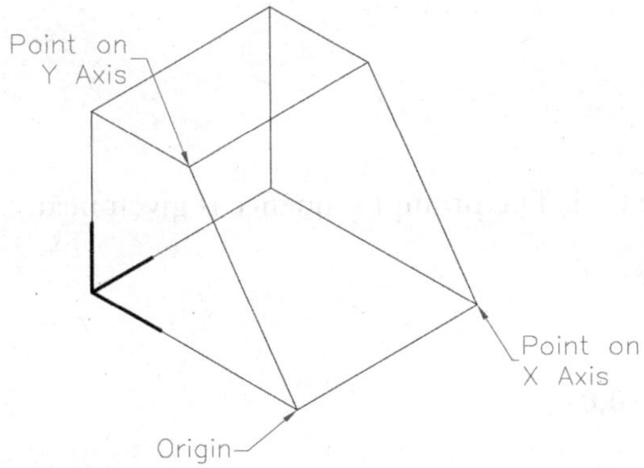

Figure 1-22 Relocating the UCS using the 3-Point option

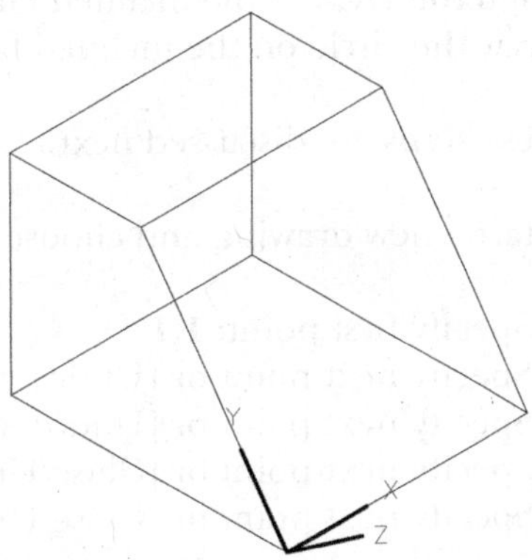

Figure 1-23 UCS at a new position

Example 1 — 3-Point

In this example, you will draw a tapered rectangular block. After drawing it, you will align the UCS with the inclined face of the block by using the dynamic alignment. Next, you will draw a circle on the inclined face. The dimensions for the block and the circle are shown in Figure 1-24.

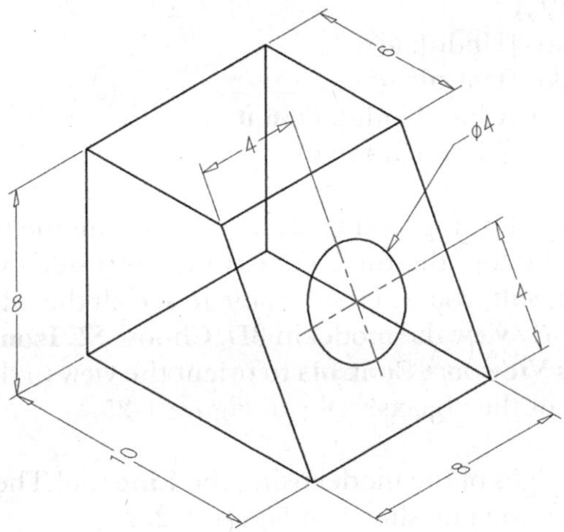

Figure 1-24 Model for Example 1

The steps to do this example are given next.

- Draw the edges of the bottom face of the tapered block.
- Specify a new origin.
- Draw the edges of the top face of the tapered block.
- Draw the remaining edges of the block.

- Align the UCS to the inclined face.
- Draw the circle on the inclined face.

These steps are discussed next.

1. Start a new drawing and choose the **Line** tool. The prompt sequence is given next.

   Specify first point: **1,1**
   Specify next point or [Undo]: **@10,0**
   Specify next point or [Undo]: **@0,8**
   Specify next point or [Close/Undo]: **@-10,0**
   Specify next point or [Close/Undo]: **C**

2. As the top face of the model is at a distance of 8 units from the bottom face in the positive *Z* direction, you need to define a UCS at a distance of 8 units to create the top face. To do so, select the UCS and then move the cursor to the rectangular grip displayed at the intersection of the three axes; a shortcut menu will be displayed. Choose the **Move Origin Only** option; AutoCAD will prompt you to specify a new origin point. The prompt sequence is as follows:

   Specify origin point : **0,0,8**

3. Choose the **Line** tool from the **Draw** panel. The prompt sequence is as follows:

   Specify first point: **1,1**
   Specify next point or [Undo]: **@6,0**
   Specify next point or [Undo]: **@0,8**
   Specify next point or [Close/Undo]: **@-6,0**
   Specify next point or [Close/Undo]: **C**

4. When you open a new drawing, you view the model from the top view by default. Therefore, when viewing from the top, the three edges of the top side overlap with the corresponding bottom edges. As a result, you will not be able to see all the edges. However, you can change the viewpoint to clearly view the model in 3D. Choose **SE Isometric** from the **View Controls** list in the **In-Canvas Viewport Controls** to orient the view to the SE isometric view. Now, you can see the 3D view of the objects, refer to Figure 1-25.

5. Join the remaining edges of the model using the **Line** tool.The model after joining all edges should look similar to the one shown in Figure 1-26.

Now, dynamic alignment of UCS can be done with a surface, a mesh, and a solid face but the inclined portion is a wire frame. So, you need to convert the wire frame into a surface by using the **Region** tool.

6. Invoke the **Region** tool from the **Draw** panel in the **Home** tab; AutoCAD will prompt you to select objects for generating a region. Next, select the four edges bounding the inclined face and press ENTER; a region will be generated.

7. Next, select the UCS and place the cursor on the rectangular grip; a shortcut menu will be displayed. Choose the **Move and Align** option from the shortcut menu; you will be prompted to select a face, surface, or mesh.

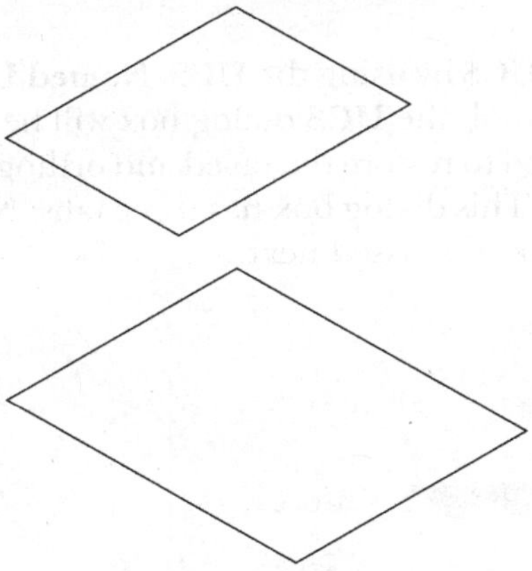

Figure 1-25 *3D view of the objects*

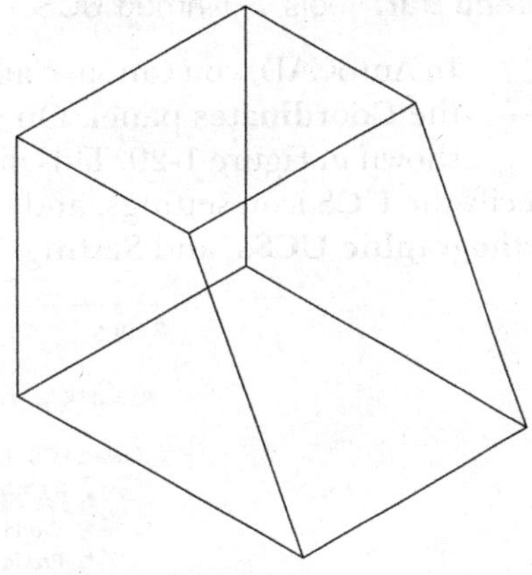

Figure 1-26 *Model after joining all the edges*

8. Select the inclined face by moving through the edge to which you want the X axis to be parallel or you can align the axes by dynamically rotating them. In this case, the X axis is parallel to P1P2 line, refer to Figure 1-27.

9. Choose the **Center, Radius** tool from the **Circle** drop-down in the **Draw** panel and draw the circle on the inclined face.

The final model should look similar to the one shown in Figure 1-28.

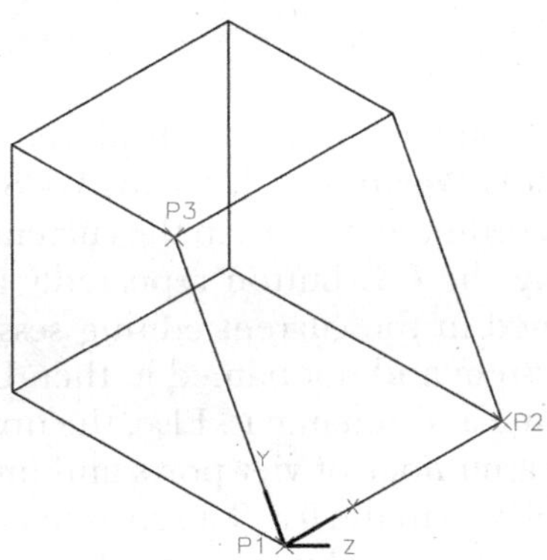

Figure 1-27 *Model after aligning the UCS on the inclined face*

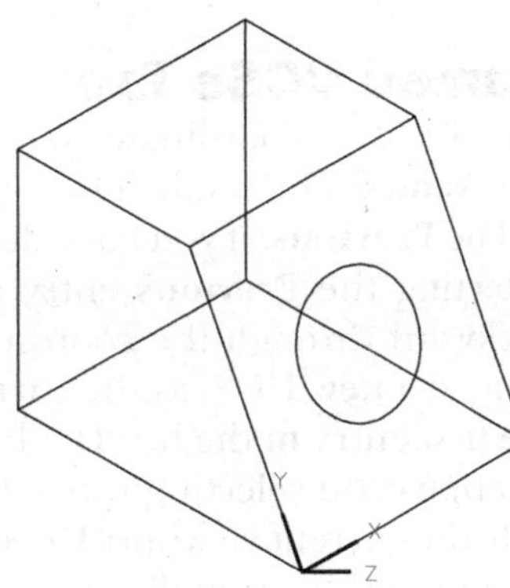

Figure 1-28 *Final model for Example 1*

MANAGING THE UCS THROUGH THE DIALOG BOX

Ribbon: Visualize > Coordinates > UCS, Named UCS **Command:** UCSMAN
Menu Bar: Tools > Named UCS

In AutoCAD, you can save and restore the UCS by using the **UCS, Named UCS** tool from the **Coordinates** panel. On choosing this tool, the **UCS** dialog box will be displayed, as shown in Figure 1-29. This dialog box is used to restore the saved and orthographic UCSs, specify the UCS icon settings, and rename UCSs. This dialog box has three tabs: **Named UCSs**, **Orthographic UCSs**, and **Settings**. These tabs are discussed next.

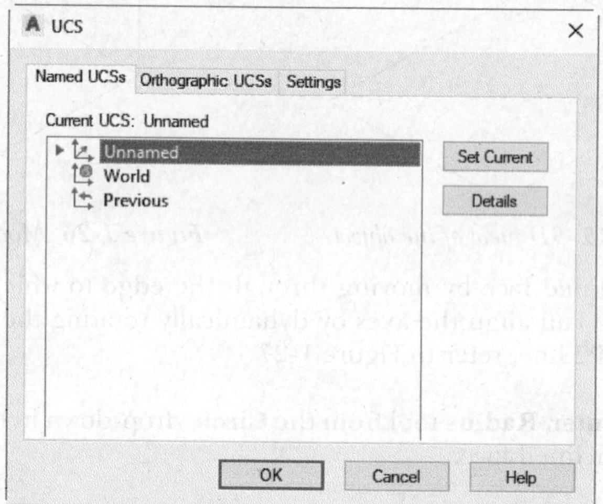

***Figure 1-29** The **Named UCSs** tab of the **UCS** dialog box*

Named UCSs Tab

The list of all coordinate systems defined (saved) on your system is displayed in the list box of the **Named UCSs** tab. The first entry in this list is **World**, which means WCS. The next entry will be **Previous**, if you have defined any other coordinate systems in the current editing session. Selecting the **Previous** entry and then choosing the **OK** button repeatedly allows you to go backward through the coordinate systems defined in the current editing session. If you have created a new UCS as the current coordinate system and not named it, then **Unnamed** will be the first entry in the list. Double-click on the name and rename it. Else, the unnamed UCS will disappear on selecting other UCS. If there are a number of viewports and unnamed settings, only the current viewport UCS name will be displayed in the list. The current coordinate system is indicated by a small pointer icon to the left of the coordinate system's name. The name of the current UCS is also displayed next to **Current UCS** on top of this list box. To make other coordinate system current, select its name in the list, choose the **Set Current** button, and choose the **OK** button. Alternatively, select the required UCS from the **Named UCS Combo Control** drop-down list available in the **Coordinates** panel of the **Visualize** tab. To delete a coordinate system created previously, select its name, and then right-click to display a shortcut menu. Choose the **Delete** option to delete the selected UCS name. To rename a coordinate system, select its name and then right-click to display a shortcut menu and choose **Rename**. Now, enter the new name. You can also double-click on the name you need to modify, and then change the name. The other options in the shortcut menu are **Set Current** and **Details**.

Tip

*All the changes and updating of the UCS information in the drawing are carried out only after you choose the **OK** button.*

If you want to check the current coordinate system's origin and *X*, *Y*, and *Z* axis values, select a UCS from the list and then choose the **Details** button; the **UCS Details** dialog box containing that information is displayed, refer to Figure 1-30. Alternatively, right click on the name of the specific UCS in the list box and then choose the **Details** option from the shortcut menu.

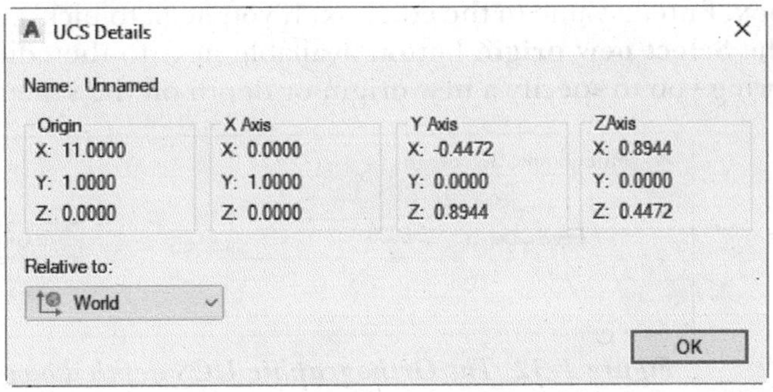

***Figure 1-30** The **UCS Details** dialog box*

Orthographic UCSs Tab

Different orthographic views are listed in the **Orthographic UCSs** tab, as shown in Figure 1-31. You can select any one of the six orthographic views of the WCS or the user defined coordinate system using the **UCS** dialog box. To define an orthographic coordinate system relative to a UCS, select it from the **Relative to** drop-down list. Next, select the orthographic view from the list of preset orthographic views, and then choose the **Set Current** button; the UCS icon is placed at the corresponding view. You can also right-click on the specific orthographic UCS name in the list and choose **Set Current** from the shortcut menu. The name of the current UCS is displayed above the list of orthographic view. If the current settings have not been saved and named, the **Current UCS** name displayed is **Unnamed**.

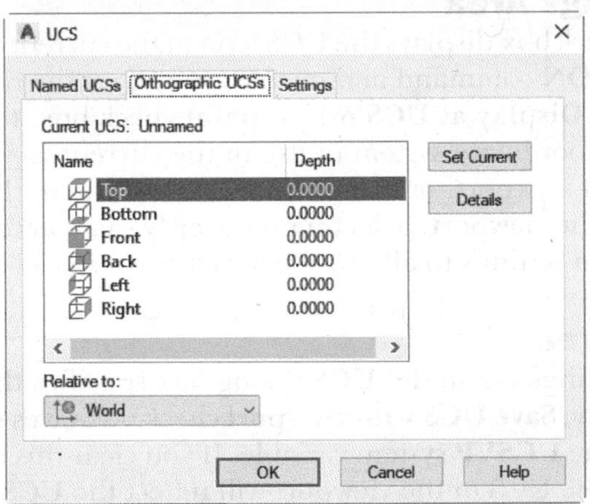

***Figure 1-31** The **Orthographic UCSs** tab of the **UCS** dialog box*

The **Depth** field in the list box of this dialog box displays the distance between the *XY* plane of the selected orthographic UCS setting and the parallel plane passing through the origin of the UCS base setting. The **UCSBASE** system variable stores the name of the UCS, which is considered as the base setting; that is, it defines the origin and orientation. You can enter or modify the values of depth by double-clicking on the depth value of the selected UCS in the list box.

On doing so, the **Orthographic UCS depth** dialog box will be displayed, where you can enter new depth values, refer to Figure 1-32. You can also right-click on a specific orthographic UCS in the list box to display a shortcut menu. Choose **Depth** to display the **Orthographic UCS depth** dialog box. Enter a value in the edit box. If you need to pick a position from the drawing area, choose the **Select new origin** button available next to the edit box; the dialog box will disappear allowing you to specify a new origin or depth on the screen.

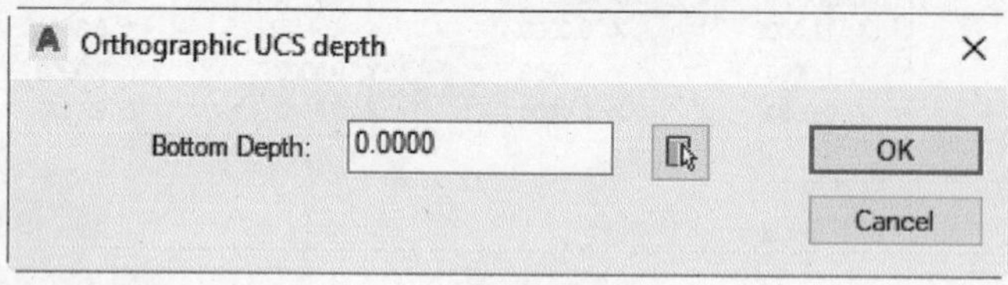

*Figure 1-32 The **Orthographic UCS depth** dialog box*

Choosing the **Details** button displays the **UCS Details** dialog box with the origin and the *X*, *Y*, *Z* coordinate values of the selected UCS. You can also choose **Details** from the shortcut menu that is displayed on right-clicking on a UCS in the list box. The shortcut menu also has the **Reset** option. Choosing **Reset** from the shortcut menu restores the selected UCS to its default settings. Also, the depth value, if assigned, becomes zero.

Settings Tab

The **Settings** tab of the **UCS** dialog box, refer to Figure 1-33, is used to display and modify the UCS and UCS icon settings of a specified viewport. If you choose the inclined arrow on the **Coordinates** panel, the **UCS** dialog box will be displayed with the **Settings** tab chosen. The options in this dialog box are discussed next.

UCS Icon settings Area

Selecting the **On** check box displays the UCS icon in the current viewport. This process is similar to using the **UCSICON** command and enables you to set the display of the UCS icon to on or off. If you select the **Display at UCS origin point** check box, the UCS icon is displayed at the origin point of the coordinate system in use in the current viewport. If the origin point is not visible in the current viewport, or if the check box is cleared, the UCS icon is displayed in the lower left corner of the viewport. Selecting the **Apply to all active viewports** check box applies the current UCS icon settings to all the active viewports in the current drawing.

UCS settings Area

This area of the **Settings** tab in the **UCS** dialog box specifies the UCS settings for the current viewport. Selecting the **Save UCS with viewport** check box saves the UCS with the viewport. This setting is stored in the **UCSVP** system variable. If you clear this check box, the **UCSVP** variable will be set to 0 and the UCS of the viewport will reflect the UCS of the current viewport. When you select the **Update view to Plan when UCS is changed** check box, the plan view is restored after the UCS in the viewport is changed. When the selected UCS is restored, the plan view is also restored. The value is stored in the **UCSFOLLOW** system variable.

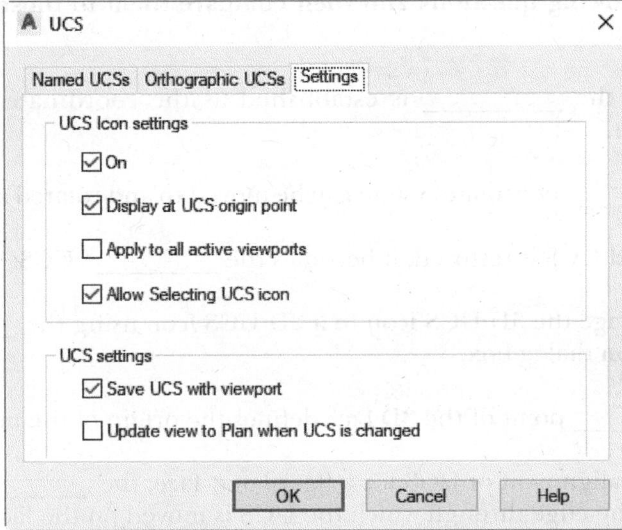

*Figure 1-33 The **Settings** tab of the **UCS** dialog box*

SYSTEM VARIABLES

The coordinate value of the origin of the current UCS is held in the **UCSORG** system variable. The *X* and *Y* axis directions of the current UCS are held in the **UCSXDIR** and **UCSYDIR** system variables, respectively. The name of the current UCS is held in the **UCSNAME** variable. All these variables are read-only. If the current UCS is identical to the WCS, the **WORLDUCS** system variable is set to 1; otherwise, it holds the value 0. The current UCS icon setting can be examined and manipulated with the help of the **UCSICON** command. This command defines the UCS icon setting of the current viewport. If more than one viewport is active, each one can have a different value for the **UCSICON** variable. If you are in paper space, the **UCSICON** variable will contain the setting for the UCS icon of the paper space. The **UCSFOLLOW** system variable controls the automatic display of a plan view when you switch from one UCS to another. If **UCSFOLLOW** is set to 1 and you switch from one UCS to another, a plan view is automatically displayed. The **UCSAXISANG** variable stores the default angle value for the *X*, *Y*, or *Z* axis around which the UCS is rotated using the ***X***, ***Y***, ***Z*** options of the **UCS** command. The **UCSBASE** variable stores the name of the UCS that acts as the base; that is, it defines the origin and orientation of the orthographic UCS setting. The **UCSVP** variable decides whether the UCS settings are stored with the viewport or not.

Self-Evaluation Test

Answer the following questions and then compare them to those given at the end of this chapter:

1. By default, the __________ is established as the coordinate system in the AutoCAD environment.

2. The __________ coordinate system can be moved to and rotated about any desired location.

3. Once a saved UCS is restored, it becomes the __________ UCS.

4. You can change the 3D UCS icon to a 2D UCS icon using the __________ radio button of the **UCS Icon** dialog box.

5. The __________ point of the 3D face defines the origin of the new UCS.

6. In dynamic alignment of UCS for a flat planar face, the __________ will always be parallel to the edge through which the UCS is moved on the face.

7. You can move the World Coordinate System from its original position. (T/F)

8. The **View** tool in the **Align UCS** drop-down of the **Coordinates** panel of the **Visualize** tab is used to define a new UCS whose *XY* plane is parallel to the current viewing plane. (T/F)

9. An ellipse cannot be used as an object for defining a new UCS. (T/F)

10. While moving the UCS, if you do not specify the *Z* coordinate of the new point, the previous *Z* coordinate will be taken for the new value. (T/F)

Review Questions

Answer the following questions:

1. Which of the following options is used to restore the previous UCS settings?

   (a) **ZAxis** (b) **Restore**
   (c) **Previous** (d) **Save**

2. Which of the following options is used to list names of all the saved UCSs?

   (a) **ZAxis** (b) **Restore**
   (c) ? (d) **Save**

3. Which of the following system variables is used to control the automatic display of the plan view when you switch to the new UCS?

(a) **UCSORG** (b) **UCSFOLLOW**
(c) **UCS** (d) **UCSBASE**

4. Which of the following system variables is used to store the coordinates of the origin of the current UCS?

(a) **UCSICON** (b) **UCSORG**
(c) **UCSVP** (d) **UCSFOLLOW**

5. Which of the following tools is used to manage the UCS using a dialog box?

(a) **UCS Icon, Properties** (b) **UCS, Named UCS**
(c) **UCS** (d) **UCS, World**

6. The __________ variable is used to control the *X* axis direction of the current UCS.

7. The __________ direction is known as the extrusion direction.

8. The lineweight of the UCS icon can be changed using the __________ option of the **UCS Icon** dialog box.

9. The __________ option of the **UCS** command is used to change the origin of the current UCS.

10. The __________ variable is used to control the *Y* axis direction of the current UCS.

11. The __________ variable is used to store the default angle value by which the UCS will be rotated.

12. You can change the line width of the UCS icon. (T/F)

13. The size of the UCS icon can vary between 5 and 100. (T/F)

14. The name of the current UCS is stored in the **UCSNAME** variable. (T/F)

15. The selection of the UCS can be controlled by using the options in the **Settings** tab of the **UCS** dialog box. (T/F)

Exercises 1 through 4

Draw the objects shown in Figures 1-34 through 1-37. Use the **UCS** tools to align the UCS icon and then draw the objects.

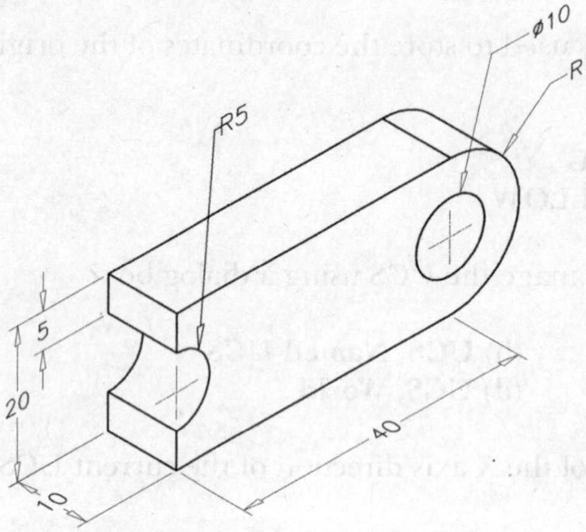

Figure 1-34 Drawing for Exercise 1

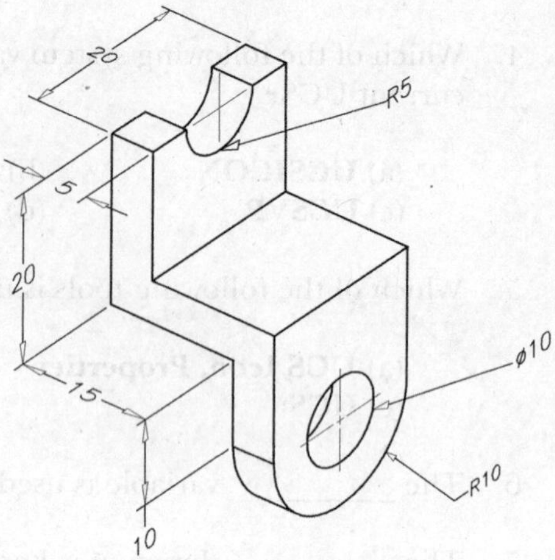

Figure 1-35 Drawing for Exercise 2

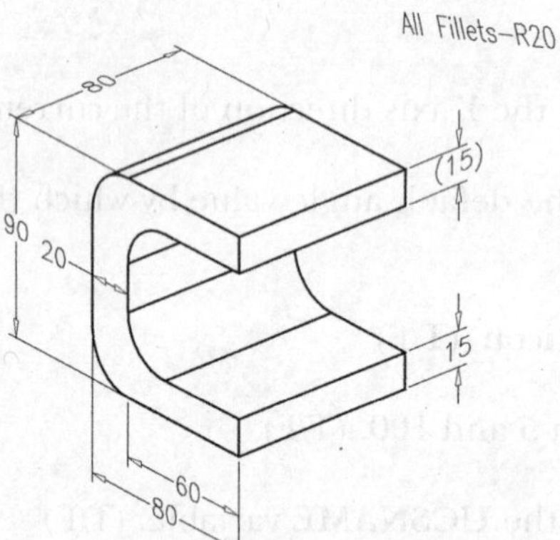

Figure 1-36 Drawing for Exercise 3

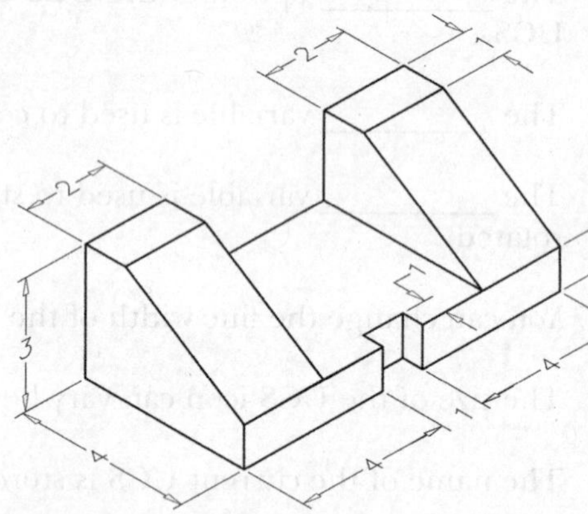

Figure 1-37 Drawing for Exercise 4

Exercise 5

Create the drawing shown in Figure 1-38. Align the UCS icon and then draw the objects. Note that in this drawing the left side of the transition should make a 90-degree angle with the bottom.

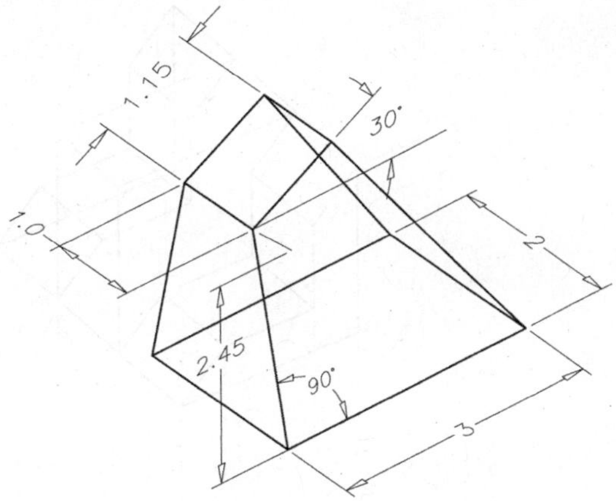

Figure 1-38 *Model for Exercise 5*

Exercise 6

Create the drawing shown in Figure 1-39. Position the UCS icon and then draw the objects. Note that in this drawing, the center of the top polygon is offset at 0.75 units from the center of the bottom polygon.

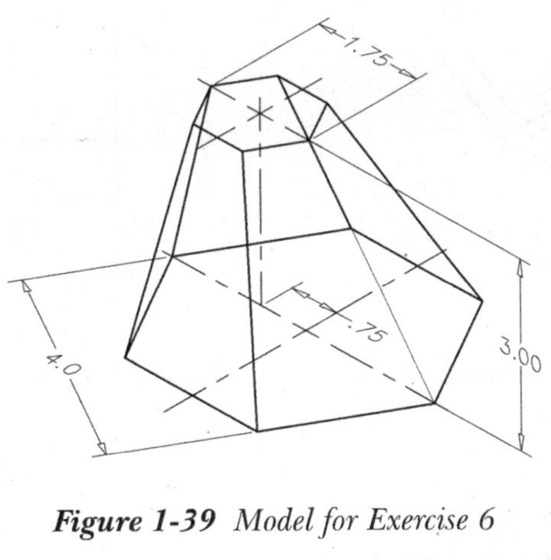

Figure 1-39 *Model for Exercise 6*

Exercises 7 and 8

In these exercises, you will create the drawing shown in Figures 1-40 and 1-41. Figure 1-42 shows the front view of the model for Exercise 8.

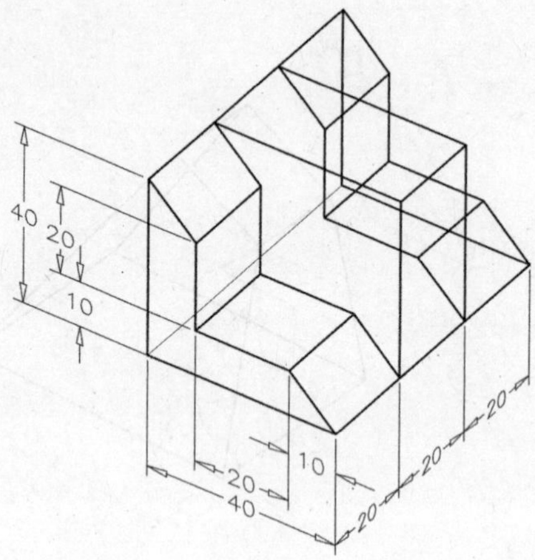

Figure 1-40 Model for Exercise 7

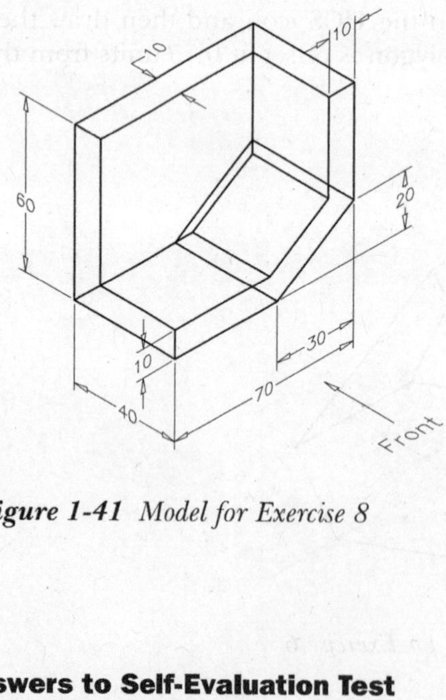

Figure 1-41 Model for Exercise 8

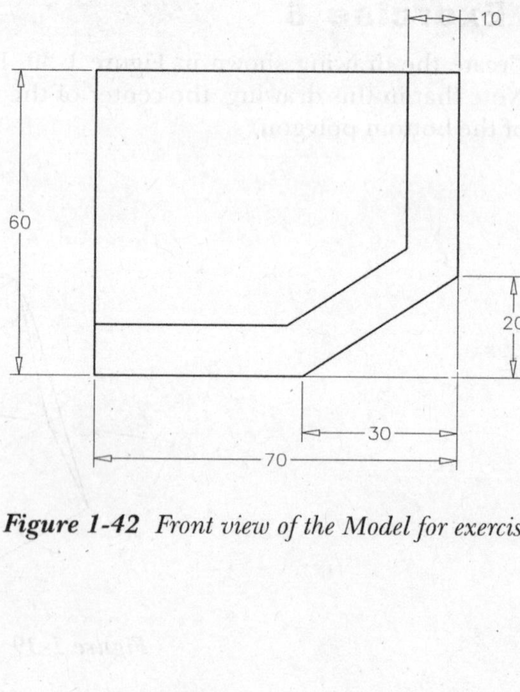

Figure 1-42 Front view of the Model for exercise 8

Answers to Self-Evaluation Test

1. World Coordinate System, **2.** user, **3.** current, **4.** 2D, **5.** first, **6.** X axis, **7.** F, **8.** T, **9.** F, **10.** T

Chapter 2

Getting Started with 3D

Learning Objectives

After completing this chapter, you will be able to:

- *Start 3D workspace in AutoCAD for creating models*
- *Use three-dimensional (3D) drawing*
- *Use various types of 3D models*
- *Know conventions used in AutoCAD*
- *Use the Viewpoint Presets tool to view objects in 3D space*
- *Use the ViewCube to view objects easily in 3D space*
- *Know various types of 3D coordinate systems*
- *Set thickness and elevation for objects*
- *Dynamically view 3D objects using the Orbit tool*
- *Use the SteeringWheel for viewing a model*

Key Terms

- *Wireframe*
- *Surface*
- *Solids*
- *ViewCube*
- *DDVPOINT*
- *3D Coordinate System*
- *ELEV*
- *Hide*
- *3D Polyline*
- *3D Face*
- *PFACE*
- *3DMESH*
- *Edit Polyline*
- *SteeringWheel*
- *Orbit*
- *3DCLIP*
- *Nudge*

STARTING THREE DIMENSIONAL (3D) MODELING IN AutoCAD

In AutoCAD, you can start the 3D Modeling in a separate workspace. All tools required to create the 3D design are displayed in this workspace by default. To start a new file in the 3D workspace, invoke the **Select template** dialog box and select the *acad3D.dwt* template. This template file supports the 3D environment. The other template files that support the 3D workspace are *acadiso3D.dwt, acad -Named Plot Styles3D.dwt,* and *acadISO -Named Plot Styles3D.dwt*. Next, select the **3D Modeling** option from the **Workspace** drop-down list available at the right in the **Status Bar**. Figure 2-1 shows the **3D Modeling** workspace of AutoCAD.

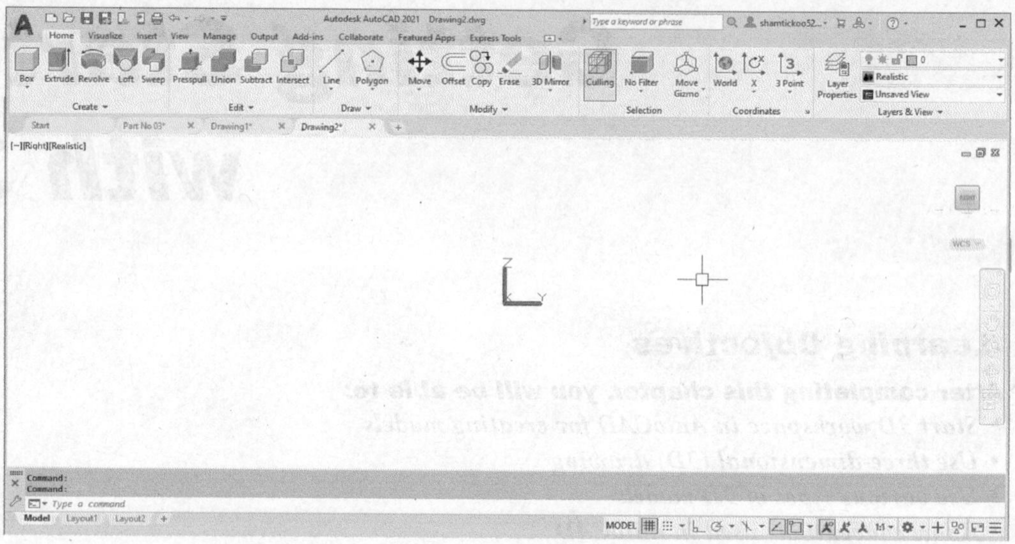

Figure 2-1 The ***3D Modeling*** *workspace of AutoCAD*

USE OF THREE-DIMENSIONAL DRAWING

The real world, and literally whatever you see around it, is three-dimensional (3D). Each and every design idea you think of is 3D. Before the development of 3D software packages, it was not possible to materialize these ideas in the design industry due to the lack of the third dimension. This is because the drawings were made on the drawing sheets, which are two dimensional objects with only *X* and *Y* coordinates. Therefore, it was not possible to draw the 3D objects. As prototyping is a very long and costly affair, therefore, the designers had to suppress their ideas and convert the 3D designs into 2D drawings.

The use of computers and the CADD (Computer Aided Design & Drafting) Technology has brought a significant improvement in materializing the design ideas and creating the engineering drawings. You can create a proper 3D object in the computer using the CADD Technology. This technology allows you to create models with the third coordinate called the *Z* coordinate, in addition to the *X* and *Y* coordinates. Apart from materializing the design ideas, the 3D models have the following advantages:

1. Generate the drawing views: Once you have created a 3D model, its 2D drawing views can be automatically generated.

2. Provide realistic effects: You can provide realistic effects to the 3D models by assigning a material and providing light effects to them. For example, an architectural drawing can be made more realistic and presentable by assigning the material to the walls and interiors and adding lights to it. You can also create its bitmap image and use it in presentations.

3. Create the assemblies and check them for interference: You can assemble various 3D models and create the assemblies. Once the components are assembled, you can check them for interference to reduce the errors and material loss during manufacturing. You can also generate the 2D drawing views of the assemblies.

4. Create an animation of the assemblies: You can animate the assemblies and view the animation to provide the clear display of the mating parts.

5. Apply Boolean operations: You can apply Boolean operations to the 3D models.

6. Calculate the mass properties: You can calculate the mass properties of the 3D models.

7. Cut Sections: You can cut sections through the solid models to view the shape at that cross-section.

8. NC Programs: You can generate an NC program with the help of 3D models by using a CAM software.

TYPES OF 3D MODELS

In AutoCAD, depending on their characteristics, the 3D models are divided into the following three categories:

Wireframe Models

Wireframe models are created using simple AutoCAD entities such as lines, polylines, rectangles, polygons, or some other entities such as 3D faces, and so on. To understand the wireframe models, consider a 3D model made up of match sticks or wires. These models consist of edges only, therefore you can see through them. You cannot apply the Boolean operations on these models and cannot calculate their mass properties. Wireframe models are generally used in frame building of vehicles. Figure 2-2 shows a wireframe model.

Surface Models

Surface models are made up of one or more surfaces. They have a negligible wall thickness and are hollow inside. To understand these models, consider a wireframe model with a cloth wrapped around it. You cannot see through it. These models are used in the plastic molding industry, such as shoe manufacturing, utensils manufacturing, and so on.

You can directly create a surface or a mesh. Alternatively, you can create wireframe model and then convert it into a mesh or surface model. Remember that you cannot perform the Boolean operations in surface models. Figure 2-3 shows a surface model created using a single surface or a mesh and Figure 2-4 shows a surface model created using a combination of surfaces.

Solid Models

Solid models are the solid filled models having mass properties. To understand a solid model, consider a model made up of metal or wood. You can perform Boolean operations on these models such as cutting a hole through them, or even cutting them into slices. Figure 2-5 shows a solid model.

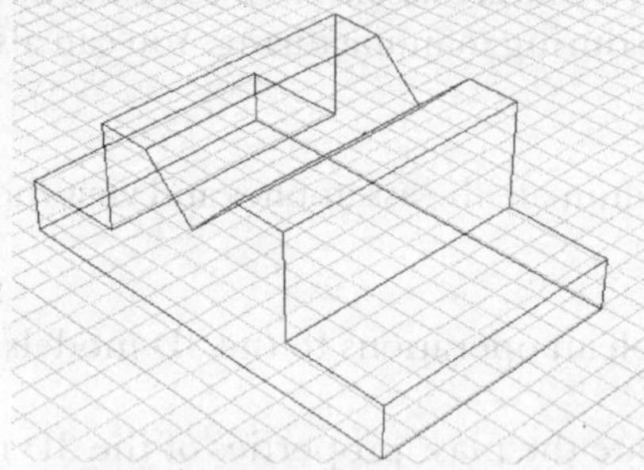

Figure 2-2 *A wireframe model*

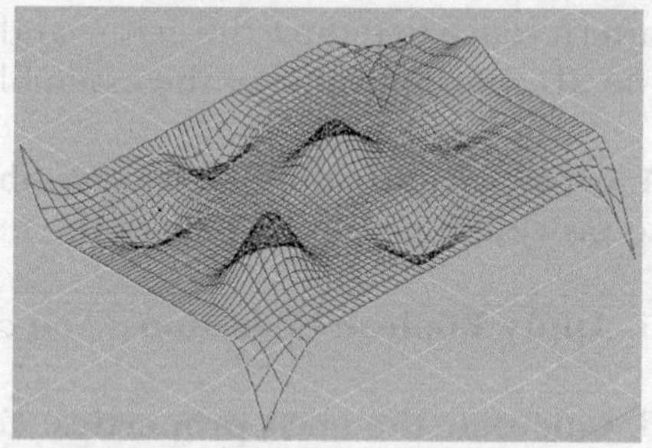

Figure 2-3 *A surface model created using a single surface*

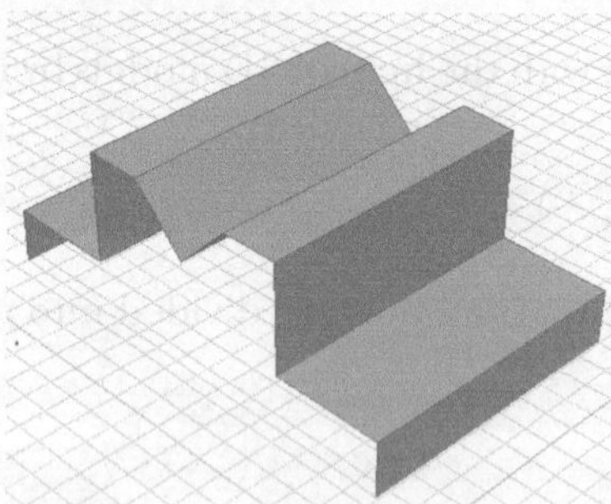

Figure 2-4 *A semi-finished surface model created using more than one surface*

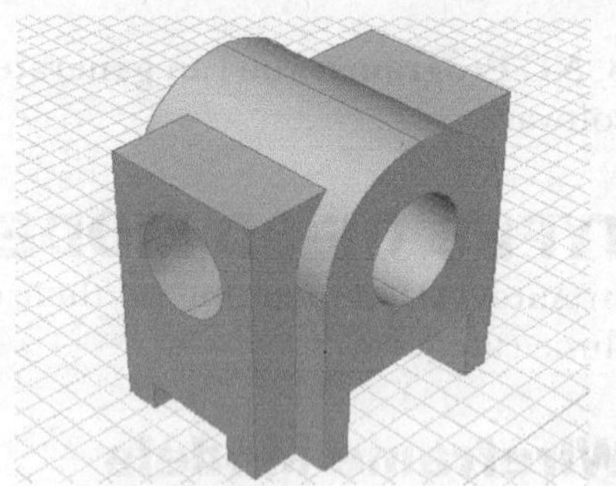

Figure 2-5 *A solid model*

CONVENTIONS FOLLOWED IN AutoCAD

It is important for you to know the conventions in AutoCAD before you proceed with 3D. AutoCAD follows these three conventions:

1. By default, any drawing you create in AutoCAD will be in the world XY plane.
2. The right-hand thumb rule is followed in AutoCAD to identify the *X*, *Y*, and *Z* axis directions. This rule states that if you keep the thumb, index finger, and middle finger of the right hand mutually perpendicular to each other, as shown in Figure 2-6(a), then the thumb of the right hand will represent the direction of the positive *X* axis, the index finger will represent the direction of the positive *Y* axis, and the middle finger of the right hand will represent the direction of the positive *Z* axis, refer to Figure 2-6(b).
3. The right-hand thumb rule is followed in AutoCAD to determine the direction of rotation or revolution in the 3D space. The right-hand thumb rule states that if the thumb of the

right hand points in the direction of the axis of rotation, then the direction of the curled fingers will define the positive direction of rotation, refer to Figure 2-6(c).

This rule will be used during the rotation of 3D models or the UCS and also, during the creation of revolved surfaces and revolved solids.

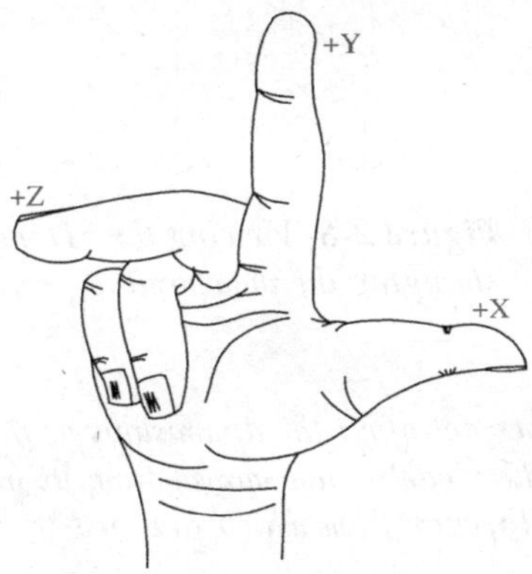

Figure 2-6(a) *The orientation of fingers as per the right-hand thumb rule*

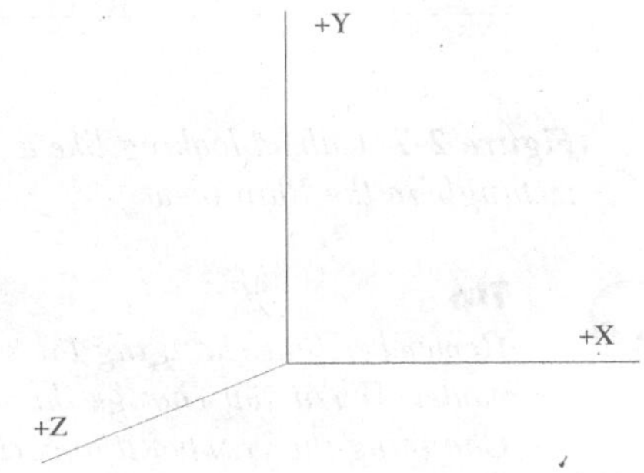

Figure 2-6(b) *Orientation of the X, Y, and Z axes*

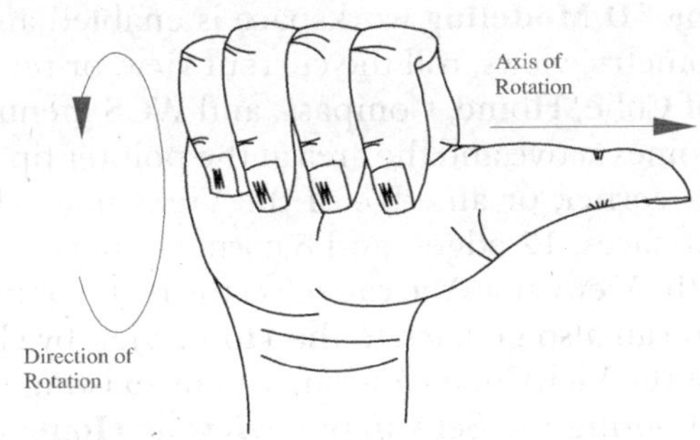

Figure 2-6(c) *Right-hand thumb rule showing the axis and direction of rotation*

CHANGING THE VIEWPOINT TO VIEW 3D MODELS

Until now, you have been drawing only the 2D entities in the *XY* plane and in the Plan view. But in the Plan view, it is very difficult to find out whether the object displayed is a 2D entity or a 3D model, refer to Figure 2-7. In this view, the cuboid displayed appears as a rectangle. The reason for this is that, by default, you view the objects in the Plan view from the direction of the positive *Z* axis. You can avoid this confusion by viewing the object from a direction that also displays the *Z* axis. In order to do that, you need to change the viewpoint so that the object is displayed in the space with all three axes, as shown in Figure 2-8. In this view, you can also see the *Z* axis of the model along with the *X* and *Y* axes. It will now be clear that the original object is not a rectangle but a 3D model. The viewpoint can be changed by using the ViewCube available in the drawing area or by using the options in the **View** panel.

Figure 2-7 Cuboid looking like a rectangle in the Plan view

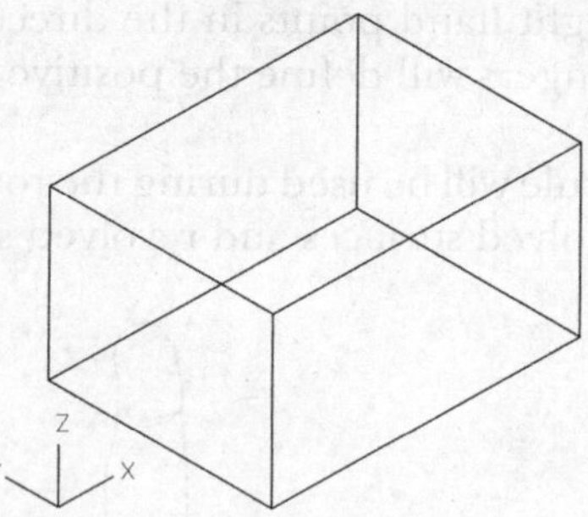

Figure 2-8 Viewing the 3D model after changing the viewpoint

Tip

Remember that changing the viewpoint does not affect the dimensions or the location of the model. When you change the viewpoint, the model is not moved from its original location. Changing the viewpoint only changes the direction from which you view the model.

Changing the Viewpoint Using the ViewCube

You can change the view of the models easily and quickly using the ViewCube. The ViewCube is displayed when the **3D Modeling** workspace is enabled and it allows you to switch between the standard and isometric views, roll the current view, or return to the **Home** view of a model. ViewCube consists of Cube, Home, Compass, and WCS menu. When you move the cursor over the ViewCube, it becomes active and the area at the pointer tip gets highlighted. The highlighted area can be a face, a corner, or an edge of the ViewCube. These highlighted areas are called hotspots. There are 6 faces, 12 edges, and 8 corners on a cube, refer to Figure 2-9. So, you can get 26 views by using the ViewCube. You can select the required hotspot to restore a view. You can also go back to the Home view by clicking on the Home icon of the ViewCube. You can set any existing view as the Home view by choosing the **Set Current View as Home** option from the shortcut menu that is displayed on right-clicking on the ViewCube. By default, a model is displayed in the perspective view. To display a model in parallel projection, right-click on the ViewCube and choose **Parallel** from the shortcut menu.

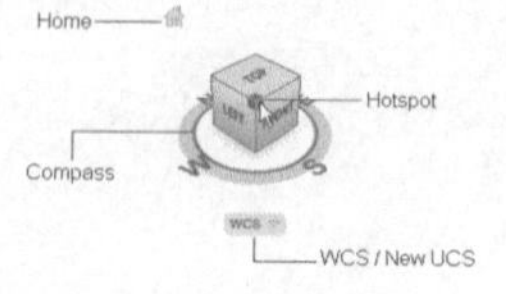

Figure 2-9 The ViewCube

The compass on the ViewCube indicates the geographic location of a model. The **N**, **E**, **S**, and **W** alphabets on the compass indicate the North, East, South, and West directions of a 3D model. You can pick and drag the compass ring to rotate the current view in the same plane. You can choose between the **UCS** and **WCS** from the WCS menu and even create a new UCS from the menu. When you right-click on the ViewCube, a shortcut menu will be displayed. Choose the **ViewCube Settings** option from it; the **ViewCube Settings** dialog box will be displayed, refer to Figure 2-10. This dialog box allows you to adjust the display of the compass ring and UCS menu, size, appearance, and location of the ViewCube.

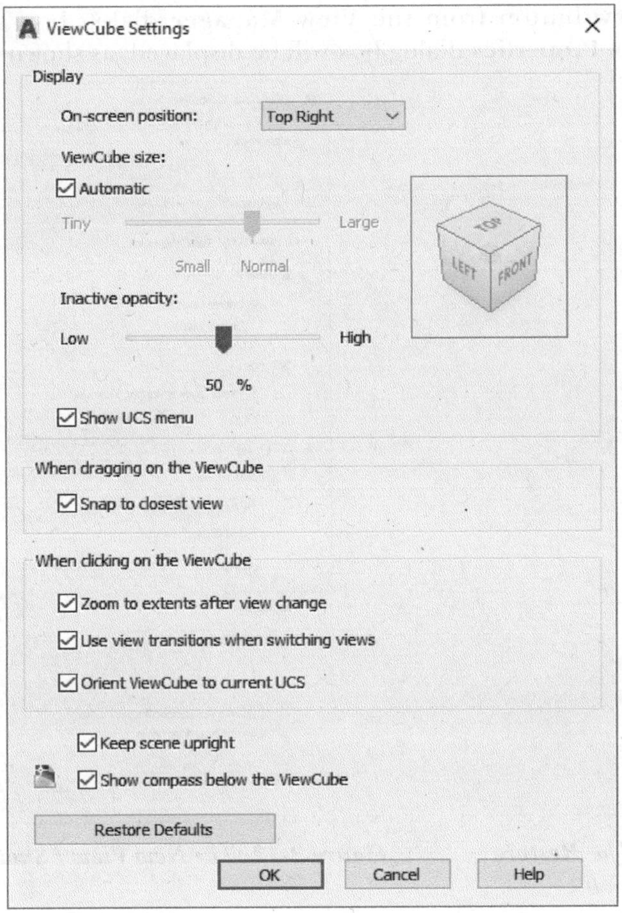

***Figure 2-10** The **ViewCube Settings** dialog box*

Note

*In AutoCAD, you can change the current viewport by using the **In-canvas Viewport controls**, displayed as **[-][Custom View][Realistic]**. It is available at the top left corner of the drawing area. When you choose the **[Custom View]** option, a flyout is displayed, refer to Figure 2-1. You can select the desired view from the flyout.*

Changing the Viewpoint Using the Ribbon or the Toolbar

You can also set the viewpoint either by using the **Named Views** panel in the **Visualize** tab of the **Ribbon** or by using the **View** toolbar.

The **Restore View** drop-down list in the **Named Views** panel consists of six preset orthographic views: **Top**, **Bottom**, **Left**, **Right**, **Front**, and **Back**; and four preset isometric views: **SW Isometric**, **SE Isometric**, **NE Isometric**, and **NW Isometric**, refer to Figure 2-11. This drop-down list also allows you to retrieve the previously set views or any previously created named views. All the above-mentioned controls are also available in the **View Manager** dialog box that is invoked on selecting the **View Manager** option from the **Restore View** drop-down list.

Choose the **New** button from the **View Manager** dialog box to create a new view; the **New View / Shot Properties** dialog box will be displayed, as shown in Figure 2-12.

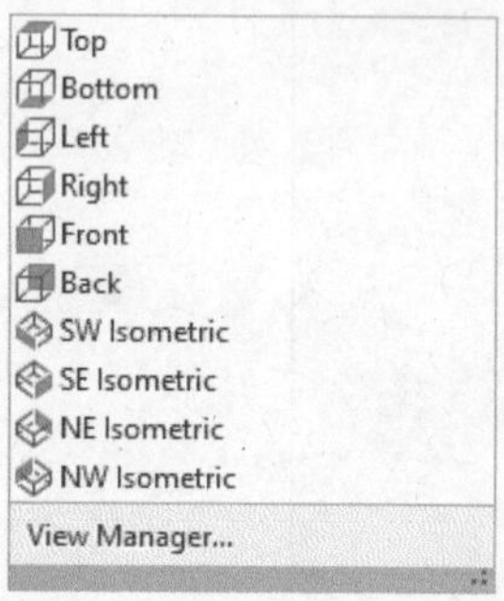

*Figure 2-11 The **Restore View** drop-down list*

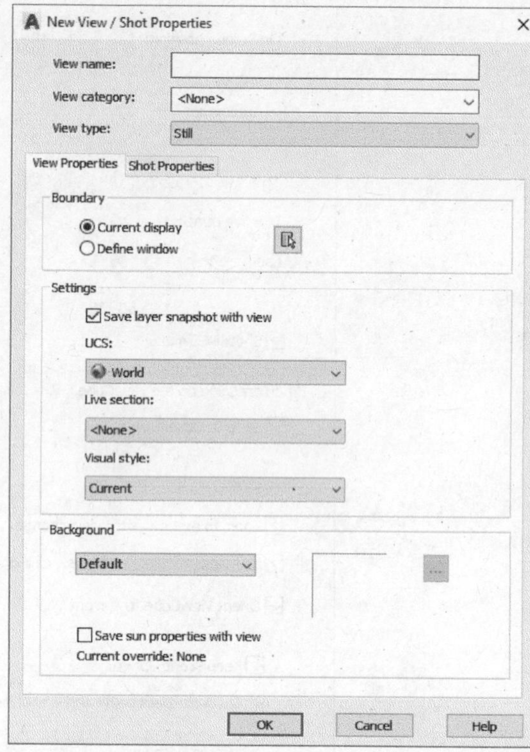

*Figure 2-12 The **New View / Shot Properties** dialog box*

Enter a name in the **View name** edit box to save the view. You can save different types of views into different categories using the options in this dialog box. The different types of views available in the **View type** drop-down list are **Still**, **Cinematic**, and **Recorded Walk**. But only **Still** is used for creating views and the other two are used for creating shots. The **View Properties** tab of this dialog box has three main areas: **Boundary**, **Settings,** and **Background**. The **Boundary** area allows you to save the current display or you can select an area of display by choosing the **Define window** radio button. In the **Settings** area, you can control the position of UCS to save the view, select the section of the view, and control the display of the model. The drop-down list in the **Background** area is used to select the type of background to save the view. The preview of the selected background is displayed in the preview area next to the drop-down list. You need to select the **Save sun properties with view** check box to save the view with the sun properties.

Tip

*When you select any of the preset orthographic views from the **View** drop-down list, the UCS is also aligned to that view.*

Changing the Viewpoint Using the Viewpoint Presets Dialog Box

Menu Bar: View > 3D Views > Viewpoint Presets	**Command:** DDVPOINT (VPOINT)

You can invoke the **Viewpoint Presets** dialog box using the **VPOINT** command for setting the viewpoint to view 3D models. The viewpoint is set with respect to the angle from the X axis and the angle from the XY plane. Figure 2-13 shows different view direction parameters.

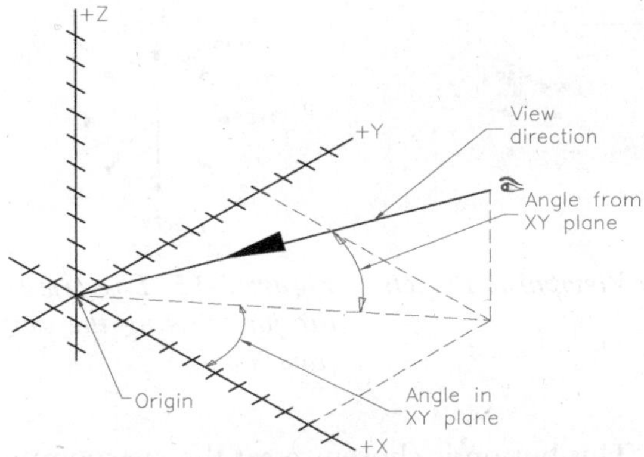

Figure 2-13 View direction parameters

Viewpoint Presets Dialog Box Options

The options in the **Viewpoint Presets** dialog box are discussed next, refer to Figure 2-14.

Absolute to WCS. This radio button is selected by default and used to set the viewpoint with respect to the world coordinate system (WCS).

Relative to UCS. This radio button is selected to set the viewpoint with respect to the current user coordinate system (UCS).

Note
The WCS and UCS have already been discussed in Chapter 1.

From: X Axis. This edit box is used to specify the angle in the *XY* plane from the *X* axis. You can directly enter the required angle in this edit box or select the desired angle from the image tile, refer to Figure 2-15. There are two arms in this image tile, and by default, they are placed one over the other. One arm displays current viewing angle and the other displays new viewing angle. On selecting a new angle from the image tile, it is automatically displayed in the **X Axis** edit box. This value can vary between **0** and **359.9**.

From: XY Plane. This edit box is used to specify the angle from the *XY* plane. You can directly enter the desired angle in it or select the angle from the image tile, as shown in Figure 2-16. This value can vary from -90 to +90.

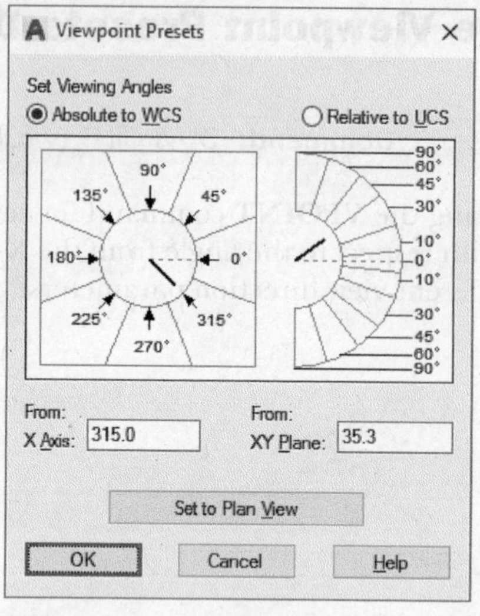

*Figure 2-14 The **Viewpoint Presets** dialog box*

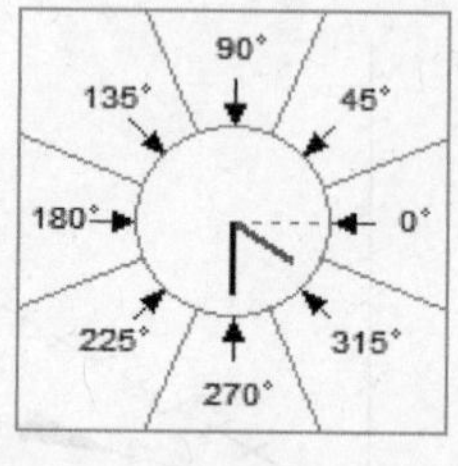

Figure 2-15 The image tile for selecting the angle from X axis

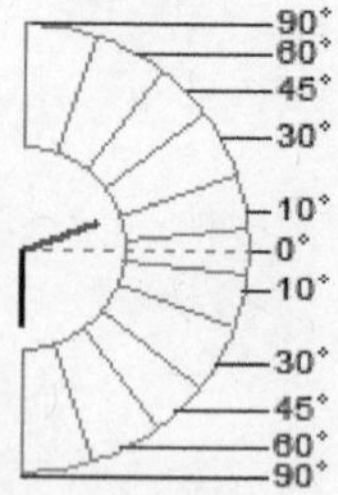

Figure 2-16 The image tile for selecting the angle from the XY plane

Set to Plan View. This button is chosen to set the viewpoint to the Plan view of the WCS or the UCS. If the **Absolute to WCS** radio button is selected, the viewpoint will be set to the Plan view of the WCS. If the **Relative to UCS** radio button is selected, the viewpoint will be set to the Plan view of the current UCS. Figures 2-17 and 2-18 show the 3D models from different viewing angles.

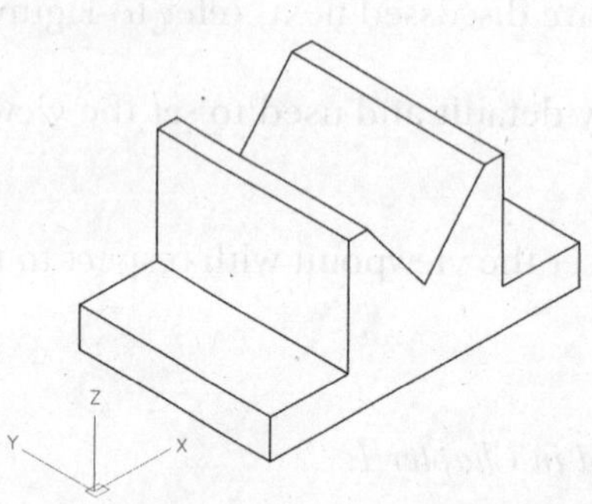

*Figure 2-17 Viewing the 3D model with the angle in the XY plane as **225** and the angle from the XY plane as **30***

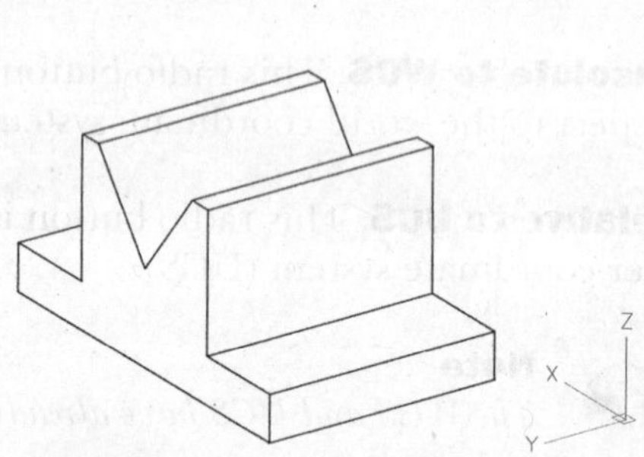

*Figure 2-18 Viewing the 3D model with the angle in the XY plane as **145** and the angle from the XY plane as **25***

Tip

1. If you set a negative angle from the XY plane, the Z axis will be displayed as a dotted line, indicating a negative Z direction, refer to Figures 2-19 and 2-20.

2. In case of confusion in identifying the direction of X, Y, and Z axes, use the right-hand thumb rule.

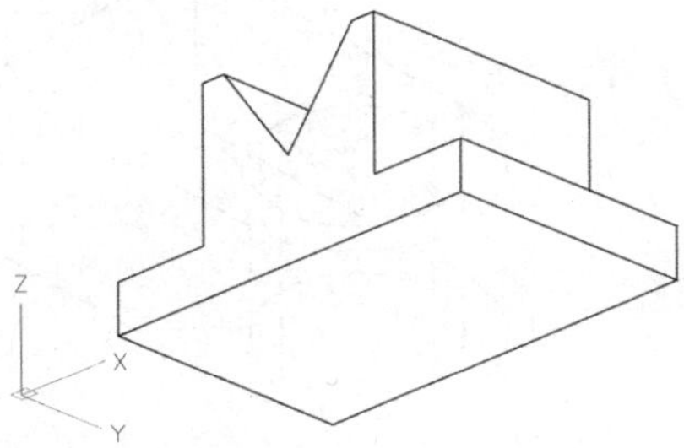

Figure 2-19 *Viewing the 3D model with the angle in the XY plane as **315** and the angle from the XY plane as **-25***

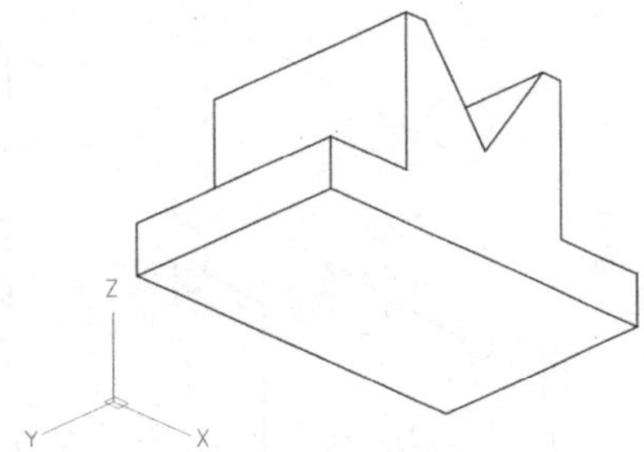

Figure 2-20 *Viewing the 3D model with the angle in the XY plane as **225** and the angle from the XY plane as **-25***

Changing the Viewpoint Using the -VPOINT Command

Menu Bar: View > 3D Views > Viewpoint **Command:** -VPOINT

The **-VPOINT** command is used to set the viewpoint for viewing the 3D models. Using this command, the users can specify a point in the 3D space that will act as the viewpoint.

Specifying a Viewpoint

This is the default option and is used to set a viewpoint by specifying its location (of viewer) using the *X*, *Y*, and *Z* coordinates of that particular point. AutoCAD follows a convention of the sides of the 3D model for specifying the viewpoint. The convention states that if the UCS is at the World position (default position), then

1. The side at the positive *X* axis direction will be taken as the right side of the model.
2. The side at the negative *X* axis direction will be taken as the left side of the model.
3. The side at the negative *Y* axis direction will be taken as the front side of the model.
4. The side at the positive *Y* axis direction will be taken as the back side of the model.
5. The side at the positive *Z* axis direction will be taken as the top side of the model.
6. The side at the negative *Z* axis direction will be taken as the bottom side of the model.

Some standard viewpoint coordinates and the view they display are given next.

Value	View	Value	View	Value	View
1,0,0	Right side	-1,0,0	Left side	0,1,0	Back
0,-1,0	Front	0,0,1	Top view	0,0,-1	Bottom view
1,1,1	NE Isometric	-1,1,1	NW Isometric	1,-1,1	SE Isometric
-1,-1,1	SW Isometric	1,1,-1	Right, Back, Bottom	-1,1,-1	Left, Back, Bottom
1,-1,-1	Right, Front, Bottom	-1,-1,-1	Left, Front, Bottom		

You can also enter the values in decimal, but the resultant views will not be the standard views. Figures 2-21 through 2-24 show a 3D model from different viewpoints.

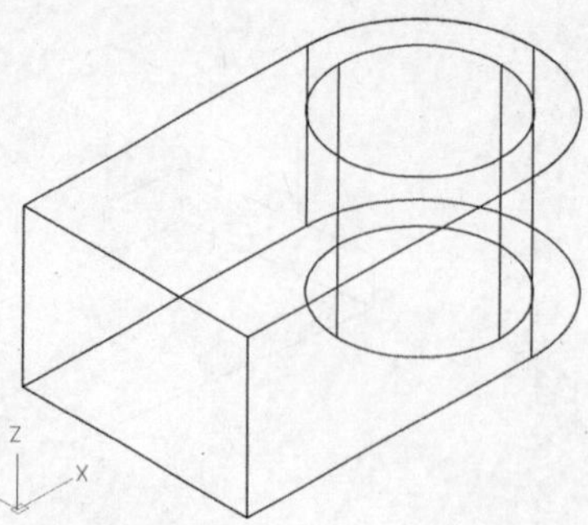

Figure 2-21 Viewing the model from the viewpoint -1,-1,1

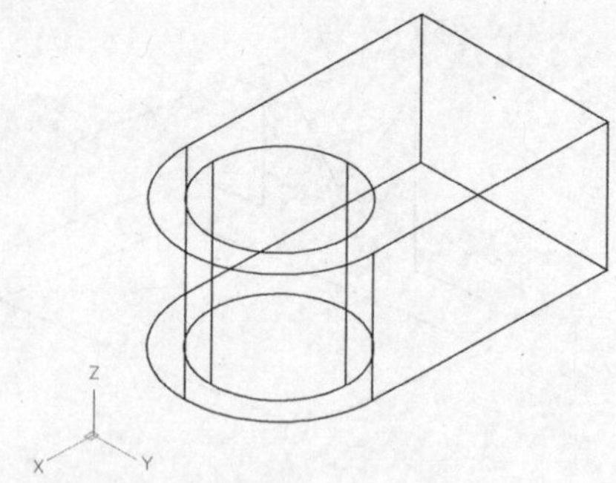

Figure 2-22 Viewing the model from the viewpoint 1,1,1

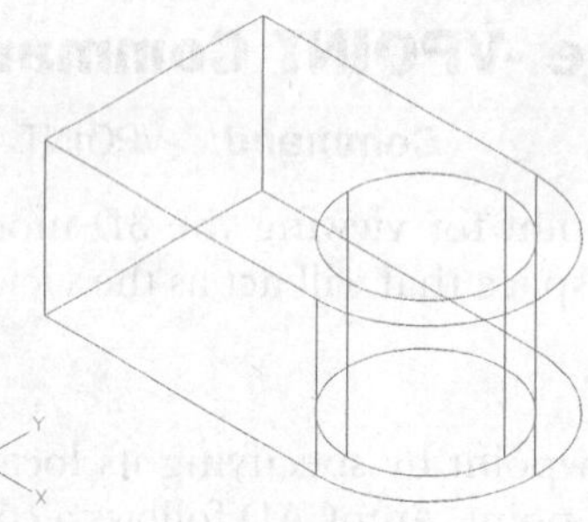

Figure 2-23 Viewing the model from the viewpoint 1,-1,1

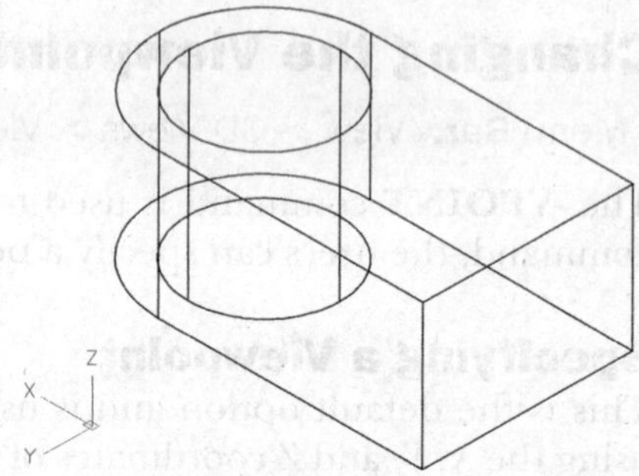

Figure 2-24 Viewing the model from the viewpoint -1,1,1

Compass and Tripod

When you choose **View > 3D Views > Viewpoint** from the menu bar, a compass and an axis tripod are displayed, as shown in Figure 2-25. You can directly set the viewpoint using this compass and can select any point on this compass to specify the viewpoint. The compass consists of two circles, a smaller circle and a bigger circle. Both these circles are divided into four quadrants: first, second, third, and fourth. The resultant view will depend upon the quadrant and the circle on which you select the point. In the first quadrant, both the X and Y axes are positive; in the second quadrant, the X axis is negative and the Y axis is positive; in the third quadrant, both the X and Y axes are negative; and in the fourth quadrant, the X axis is positive and the Y axis is negative. Now, if you select a point inside the inner circle, it will be in the positive Z axis direction. If you select the point outside the inner circle and inside the outer circle, it will be in the negative Z axis direction. Therefore, if the previously mentioned statements are added, the following is concluded.

1. If you select a point inside the smaller circle in the first quadrant, the resultant view will be the Right, Back, or Top view. If you select a point outside the smaller circle and inside the bigger circle in this quadrant, the resultant view will be the Right, Back, or Bottom view, refer to Figure 2-26.

2. If you select a point inside the smaller circle in the second quadrant, the resultant view will be the Left, Back, or Top view. If you select a point outside the smaller circle and inside

the bigger circle in this quadrant, the resultant view will be the Left, Back, or Bottom view, refer to Figure 2-26.

3. If you select a point inside the smaller circle in the third quadrant, the resultant view will be the Left, Front, or Top view. If you select a point outside the smaller circle and inside the bigger circle in this quadrant, the resultant view will be the Left, Front, or Bottom view, refer to Figure 2-26.

4. If you select a point inside the smaller circle in the fourth quadrant, the resultant view will be the Right, Front, or Top view. If you select a point outside the smaller circle and inside the bigger circle in this quadrant, the resultant view will be the Right, Front, or Bottom view, refer to Figure 2-26.

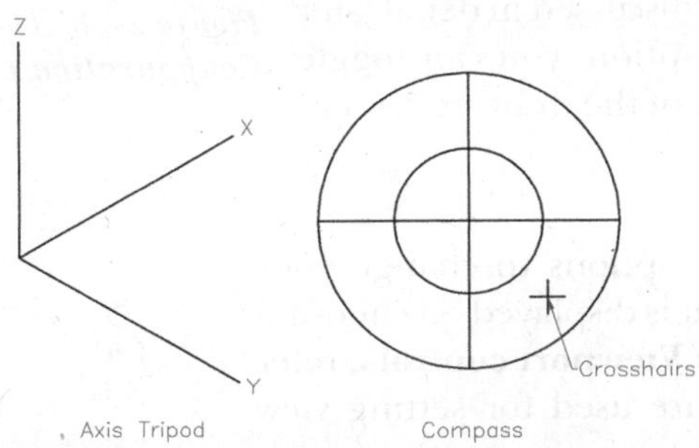

***Figure 2-25** The axis tripod and the compass*

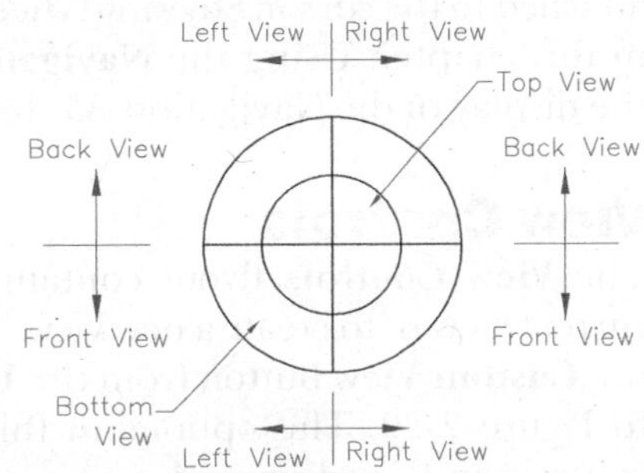

***Figure 2-26** The directions of the compass*

Rotate

This option is similar to setting the viewpoint in the **Viewpoint Presets** dialog box, which is displayed by invoking the **-VPOINT** command. When you select this option, you will be prompted to specify the angle in the *XY* plane and the angle from the *XY* plane. The angle in the *XY* plane will be taken from the *X* axis.

IN-CANVAS VIEWPORT CONTROL

The **In-canvas Viewport control** enables you to control the viewport as well as visual style. By default, the **In-canvas Viewport control** is displayed as **[-][Custom View][Realistic]** in the top left corner of the drawing area. The tools available in this viewport control are discussed next.

[-]

When you choose the [-] button in the **In-canvas Viewport control**, a flyout will be displayed, as shown in Figure 2-27. Options in this flyout are discussed next.

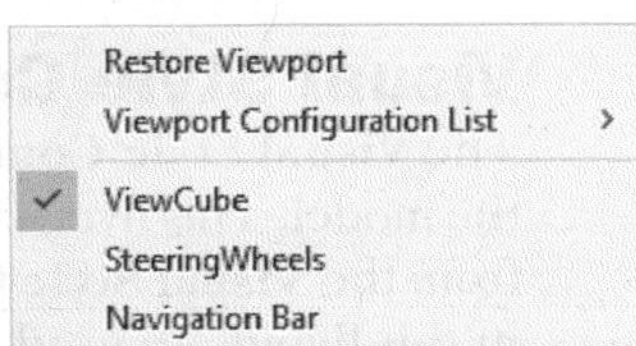

***Figure 2-27** Flyout displayed on choosing the [-] button*

Restore Viewport

When you choose this option, the drawing screen is displayed with four equal partitions. In each of these partitions, a [+] button is displayed in the upper left corner. When you click on the [+] button, a flyout will be displayed with the **Maximize Viewport** option. Using this option, you can maximize the partition window.

Viewport Configuration List

When you choose this option, a flyout will be displayed, as shown in the Figure 2-28. In this flyout, 12 options are available for viewport settings. Using these options, you can set as many partitions as needed to be created and their position in the drawing area.

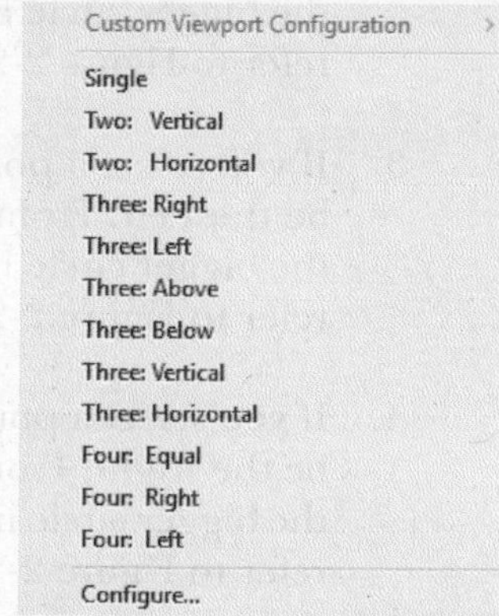

Figure 2-28 The Viewport Configuration List flyout

Viewcube, SteeringWheels, and Navigation Bar

ViewCube is used to minimize the time required in changing the view of the model, while the SteeringWheels and Navigation Bar are used to minimize the navigation time. Using the ViewCube from the Viewport Controls flyout, you can toggle the display of the ViewCube. As you choose the **SteeringWheels** option, SteeringWheels will get attached to the cursor. SteeringWheels will be discussed in detail later in this chapter. Using the **Navigation Bar** option, you can toggle the display of the Navigation Bar in the right of the drawing screen.

View Controls

The **View Controls** flyout contains various options to change your current view or to create a new view. This flyout is displayed on choosing the **Custom View** button from the **In-canvas Viewport controls**, refer to Figure 2-29. The options in this flyout are used for setting view controls and are discussed next.

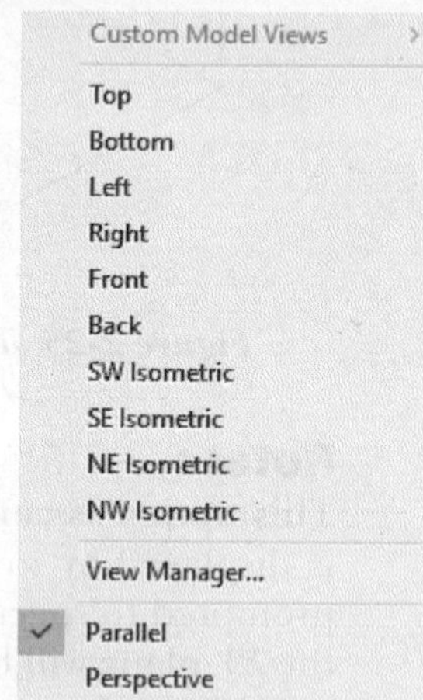

Figure 2-29 The View Controls flyout

- **Custom Model Views:** This flyout consists of custom views created by using the **View Manager**.
- **Views:** There are 10 view options available in this flyout to set 10 different views. When you change the view, the UCS gets reoriented according to the view selected.
- **View Manager:** Using this option, you can create a new view or edit the view settings of an existing view.
- **Parallel and Perspective:** These options are used to control the projection. If you choose the **Parallel** option, the drawing will be displayed parallel to the screen. If you choose the **Perspective** option, the drawing will be displayed in a perspective view.

Visual Style Controls

The **Visual Style Controls** flyout is used to control the visual style of the model. This flyout is displayed when you select the **Realistic** button from the **Visual Style Controls**, as shown in Figure 2-30. The options in this flyout are used for setting visual styles and are discussed next.

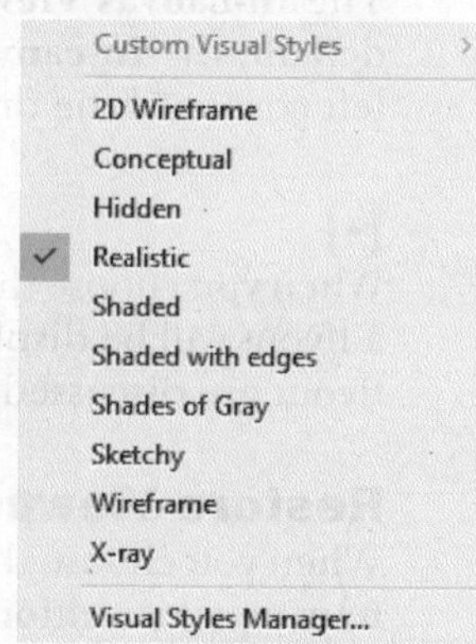

Figure 2-30 The Visual View Controls flyout

- **Custom Visual Styles**. When you click on this option, a flyout is displayed. This flyout displays the visual styles that you have created.

- **Visual Styles**. There are 10 options that enable you to select the required visual style.
- **Visual Styles Manager**. This option is used to create a new visual style as well as to change the settings of the current visual style.

3D COORDINATE SYSTEMS

Similar to 2D coordinate systems, there are two types of 3D coordinate systems. They are discussed next.

Absolute Coordinate System

This type of coordinate system is similar to the 2D absolute coordinate system in which the coordinates of the point are calculated from the origin (0,0). The only difference here is that, along with the *X* and *Y* coordinates, the *Z* coordinate is also included. For example, to draw a line in 3D space starting from the origin to a point say 10,6,6, the procedure to be followed is given next.

Command: *Choose the **Line** tool from the **Draw** panel.*
Specify first point: **0,0,0**
Specify next point or [Undo]: **10,6,6**
Specify next point or [Undo]: Enter

Figure 2-31 shows the model drawn using the absolute coordinate system.

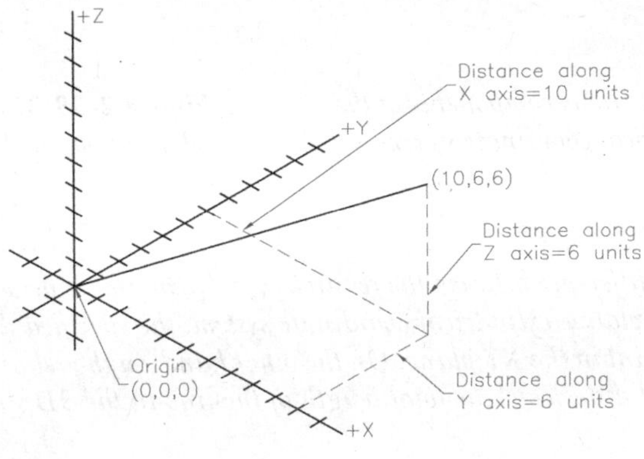

***Figure 2-31** Drawing a line from origin to 10,6,6*

Relative Coordinate System

The following are the three types of relative coordinate systems in 3D:

Relative Rectangular Coordinate System

This coordinate system is similar to the relative rectangular coordinate system of 2D, except that in 3D you also have to enter the *Z* coordinate along with the *X* and *Y* coordinates. The syntax of the relative rectangular system for the 3D is **@X coordinate, Y coordinate, Z coordinate**.

Relative Cylindrical Coordinate System

In this coordinate system, you can locate the point by specifying its distance from the reference point, the angle in the *XY* plane, and its distance from the *XY* plane. The syntax of the relative cylindrical coordinate system is **@Distance from the reference point in the XY plane < Angle in the XY plane from the X axis, Distance from the XY plane along the Z axis**. Figure 2-32 shows the components of the relative cylindrical coordinate system.

Relative Spherical Coordinate System

In this coordinate system, you can locate the point by specifying its distance from the reference point, the angle in the *XY* plane, and the angle from the *XY* plane. The syntax of the relative spherical coordinate system is **@Length of the line from the reference point < Angle in the XY plane from the X axis < Angle from the XY plane**. Figure 2-33 shows the components of the relative spherical coordinate system.

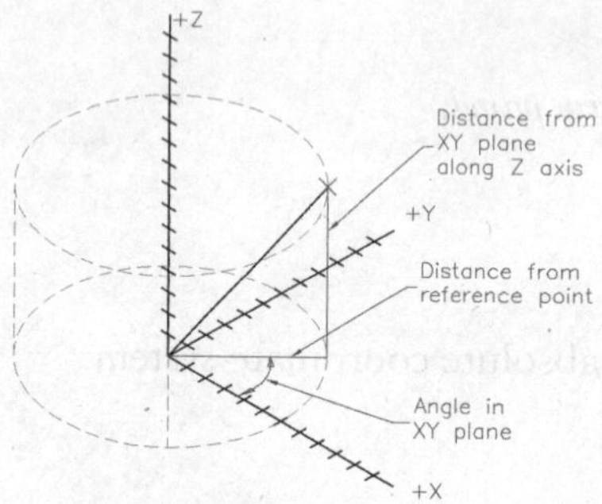

Figure 2-32 *Various components of the relative cylindrical coordinate system*

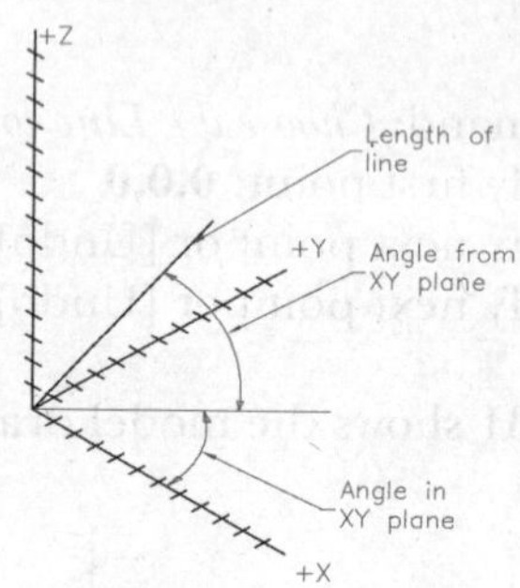

Figure 2-33 *Various components of the relative spherical coordinate system*

> **Tip**
>
> *The major difference between the relative cylindrical and relative spherical coordinate systems is that in the relative cylindrical coordinate system, the specified distance is the distance from the reference point in the XY plane. On the other hand, in the relative spherical coordinate system, the specified distance is the total length of the line in the 3D space.*

Example 1 — Relative Coordinate System

In this example, you will draw the 3D wireframe model shown in Figure 2-34. Its dimensions are given in Figure 2-35.

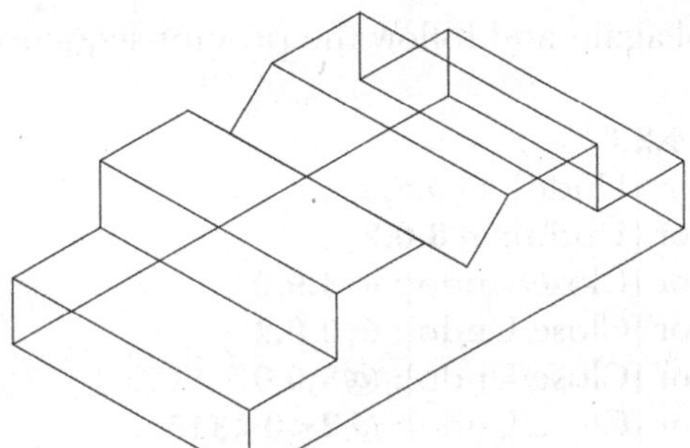

Figure 2-34 The 3D Wireframe model for Example 1

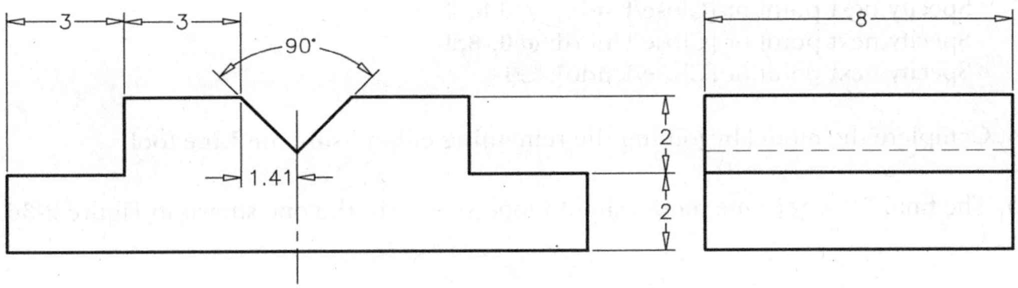

Figure 2-35 Orthographic views of the Wireframe model

1. Start a new *acad3D.dwt* file in the **3D Modeling** workspace and select the **SW Isometric** option from the **Restore View** drop-down list in the **View** panel of the **Home** tab. Alternatively, select the SouthWest top corner hotspot on the ViewCube, refer to the compass of the ViewCube to get the SouthWest view of the model.

2. As the start point of the model is not given, you can start the model from any point. Choose the **Line** tool from the **Draw** panel of the **Home** tab and follow the prompt sequence given next.

   Specify first point: **4,2,0**
   Specify next point or [Undo]: **@0,0,2**
   Specify next point or [Undo]: **@3,0,0**
   Specify next point or [Close/Undo]: **@0,0,2**
   Specify next point or [Close/Undo]: **@3,0,0**
   Specify next point or [Close/Undo]: **@2<0<315**
   Specify next point or [Close/Undo]: **@2<0<45**

Specify next point or [Close/Undo]: **@3,0,0**
Specify next point or [Close/Undo]: **@0,0,-2**
Specify next point or [Close/Undo]: **@3,0,0**
Specify next point or [Close/Undo]: **@0,0,-2**
Specify next point or [Close/Undo]: **C**

3. Choose the **Line** tool again and follow the prompt sequence given next.

Specify first point: **4,2,0**
Specify next point or [Undo]: **@0,8,0**
Specify next point or [Undo]: **@0,0,2**
Specify next point or [Close/Undo]: **@3,0,0**
Specify next point or [Close/Undo]: **@0,0,2**
Specify next point or [Close/Undo]: **@3,0,0**
Specify next point or [Close/Undo]: **@2<0<315**
Specify next point or [Close/Undo]: **@2<0<45**
Specify next point or [Close/Undo]: **@3,0,0**
Specify next point or [Close/Undo]: **@0,0,-2**
Specify next point or [Close/Undo]: **@3,0,0**
Specify next point or [Close/Undo]: **@0,0,-2**
Specify next point or [Close/Undo]: **@0,-8,0**
Specify next point or [Close/Undo]: Enter

4. Complete the model by joining the remaining edges using the **Line** tool.

5. The final 3D wireframe model should look similar to the one shown in Figure 2-36.

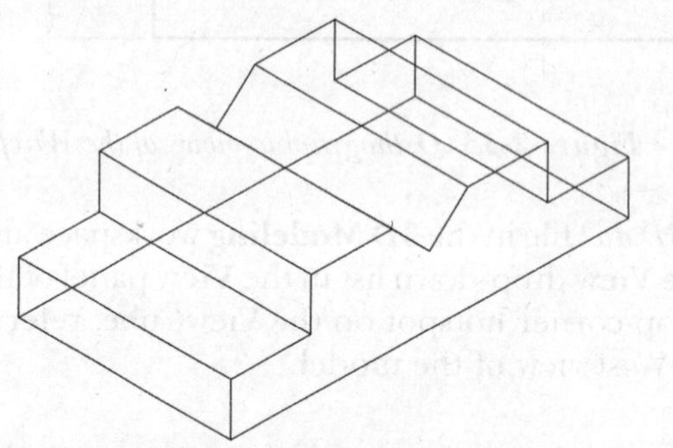

***Figure 2-36** The final 3D wireframe model for Example 1*

DIRECT DISTANCE ENTRY METHOD

In AutoCAD, you can directly create models in 3D space. This method is similar to that in 2D. The easiest way to draw a model by using the **Line** tool in 3D space of AutoCAD is by using the Direct Distance Entry method. Before drawing a model by using this method, ensure that the **Dynamic Input** button is chosen in the Status Bar. Next choose the **Line** tool; you will be prompted to specify the start point. Enter the coordinate values in the text box and press ENTER; you will be prompted to specify the next point. Move the cursor along the direction in which you need to draw the line and enter the absolute length of the line and its angle in the corresponding text boxes, with respect to the previous point. Note that you can use the TAB key to toggle between the text boxes.

To draw a line along the Z axis, move the cursor along the Z axis; you will notice that the tool tip displays **Ortho: (current length) < +Z**, if the ortho mode is on. Type the absolute distance and the angle, and press ENTER. If the ortho mode is not chosen, position the cursor at the desired angle, type the length at the Command prompt, and then press ENTER. If necessary change the UCS as discussed earlier.

Example 2 — *Direct Distance Entry*

In this example, you will draw the 3D wireframe model shown in Figure 2-37.

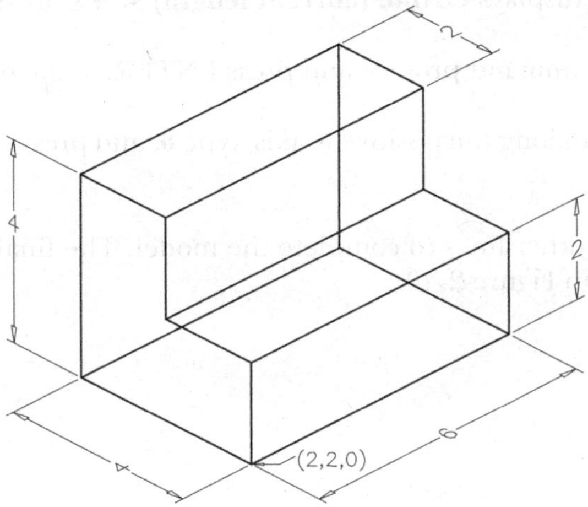

Figure 2-37 *3D wireframe model for Example 2*

1. Start a new *acad3D.dwt* file in the **3D Modeling** workspace and make sure the **Ortho Mode** and **Dynamic Input** buttons are chosen. Then, change the drawing view by using the ViewCube. The view needed is **SW Isometric**. The Southwest view of the ViewCube has three hotspots: bottom, edge, and top. You need to select the top hotspot to get the required view. Refer to Figure 2-38 for the SW Isometric hotspot. However, you can check different hotspots and view the model in different angles by using the ViewCube.

2. Choose the **Line** tool from the **Draw** panel and specify the start point at 2,2,0.

3. Move the cursor along the positive X axis. Then, type **6** and press ENTER; a line of length 6 units is drawn along the X axis.

4. Move the cursor along the positive Y axis, type **4**, and press ENTER; a line of length 4 units is drawn along the Y axis.

5. Draw the other two lines to create the closed profile at the bottom of the model.

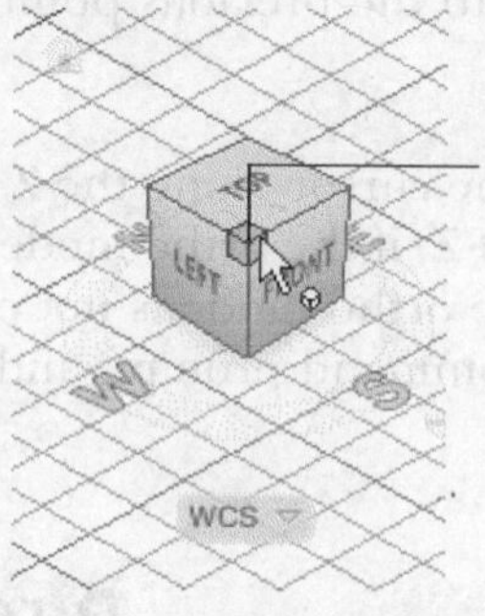

Figure 2-38 ViewCube showing the SW Isometric

6. From the start point of the model, move the cursor along the positive Z axis. You will notice that the tooltip displays **Ortho: (current length) < +Z**, as shown in Figure 2-39.

7. Type **2** at the Command prompt and press ENTER; a line of length 2 units is drawn.

8. Move the cursor along the positive X axis, type **6**, and press ENTER; a line of length 6 units is drawn.

9. Similarly, draw other lines to complete the model. The final model should look similar to the one shown in Figure 2-40.

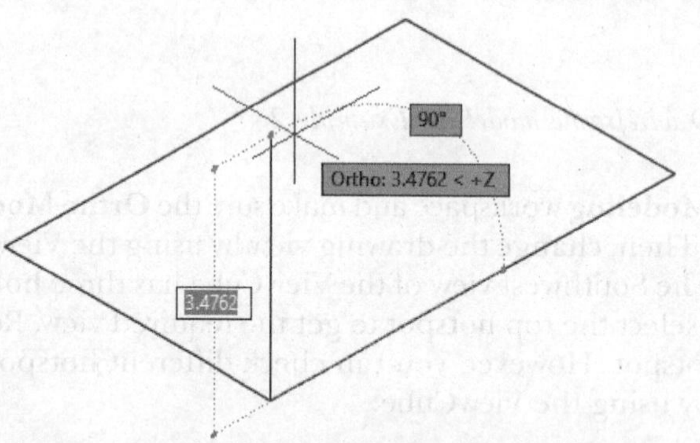

***Figure 2-39** Tooltip displayed on moving the cursor along the positive Z axis*

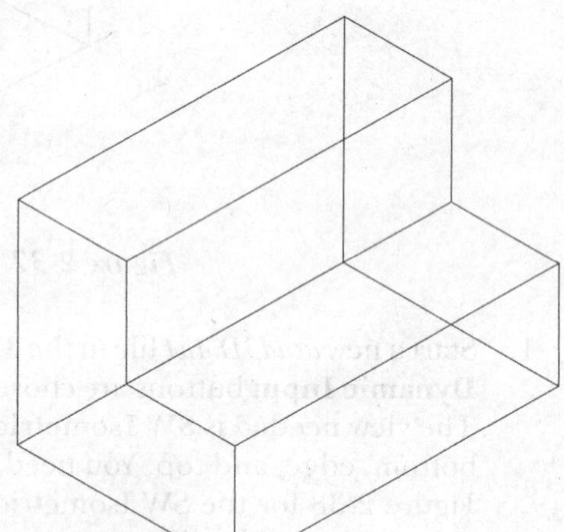

***Figure 2-40** Final 3D model for Example 2*

Exercise 1

In this exercise, you will draw the 3D wireframe model shown in Figure 2-41. Its dimensions are given in the same figure. You can start the model from any point.

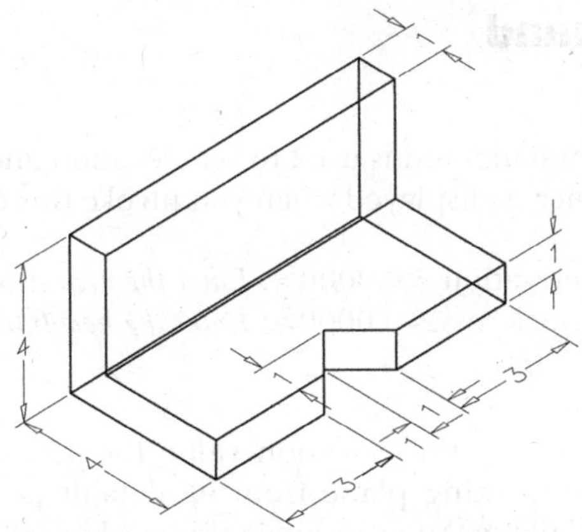

Figure 2-41 Wireframe model for Exercise 1

TRIM, EXTEND, AND FILLET TOOLS

In AutoCAD, you can use the trim, extend, and fillet tools in 3D workspace. You can also use the **PROJMODE** and **EDGEMODE** variables. The **PROJMODE** variable sets the projection mode for trimming and extending. The value of 0 implies **True 3D mode**, that is, no projection. In this case, the objects must intersect in 3D space to be trimmed or extended. It is similar to using the **None** option of the **Project** mode of the **Extend** and **Trim** tools. A value of 1 projects onto the *XY* plane of the current UCS and is similar to using the **UCS** option of the **Project** option of the **Trim** or **Extend** tools. A value of 2 projects onto the current view plane and is like using the **View** option of the **Project** option of the **Trim** or **Extend** tools. The value of the **EDGEMODE** system variable controls the cutting or trimming boundaries. A value of 0 considers the selected edge with no extension. You can also use the **No extend** option of the **Edge** option of the **Trim** or **Extend** tools. A value of 1 considers an imaginary extension of the selected edge. This is similar to using the **Extend** option of the **Edge** option of the **Trim** or **Extend** tools.

You can fillet coplanar objects whose extrusion directions are not parallel to the *Z* axis of the current UCS, by using the **Fillet** tool. The fillet arc exists on the same plane and has the same extrusion direction as the coplanar objects. If the coplanar objects to be filleted exist in opposite directions, the fillet arc will be on the same plane but will be inclined toward the positive *Z* axis.

SETTING THICKNESS AND ELEVATION FOR NEW OBJECTS

You can create the objects with a preset elevation or thickness using the **ELEV** command. This command is discussed next.

The ELEV Command

Command: ELEV

This is a transparent command and is used to set elevation and thickness for new objects. The following prompt sequence is displayed when you invoke this command:

Specify new default elevation <0.0000>: *Enter the new elevation value.*
Specify new default thickness <0.0000>: *Enter the new thickness value.*

Elevation

This option is used to specify the elevation value for new objects. Setting the elevation is nothing but moving the working plane from its default position. By default, the working plane is on the world *XY* plane. You can move this working plane by specifying the new value for elevation using the **ELEV** command. However, remember that the working plane can be moved only along the *Z* axis, refer to Figure 2-42. The default elevation value is 0.0 and you can set any positive or negative value. All objects that will be drawn hereafter will be with the specified elevation. The **ELEV** command sets the elevation only for the new objects and the existing objects are not modified using this option.

Thickness

This option is used to specify the thickness values for new objects. It can be considered as another method of creating surface models. Specifying the thickness creates extruded surface models. The thickness is always taken along the *Z* axis direction, refer to Figure 2-43. The 3D faces will be automatically applied on the vertical faces of the objects drawn with a thickness. The **Thickness** option sets the thickness only for the new objects and the existing objects are not modified.

Note

*By default, the model will be displayed in the **Realistic** visual style. To change it to wireframe, choose the **2D Wireframe** from the **Visual Style Controls** flyout in the **In-canvas Viewport Controls**. You can suppress the hidden edges in the model by using the **Hide** tool. The **Hide** tool is discussed in the next section.*

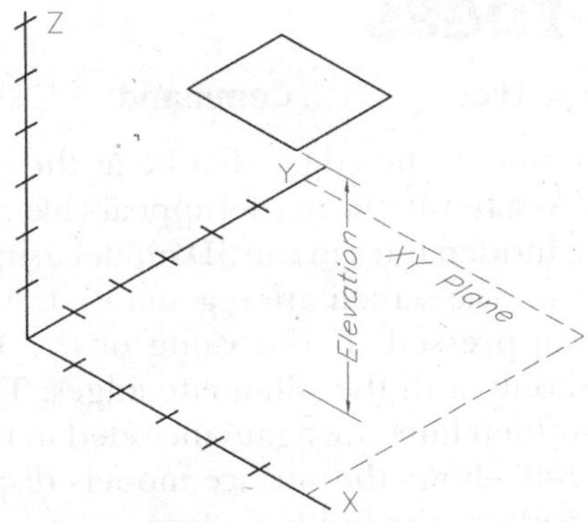

Figure 2-42 Object drawn with elevation

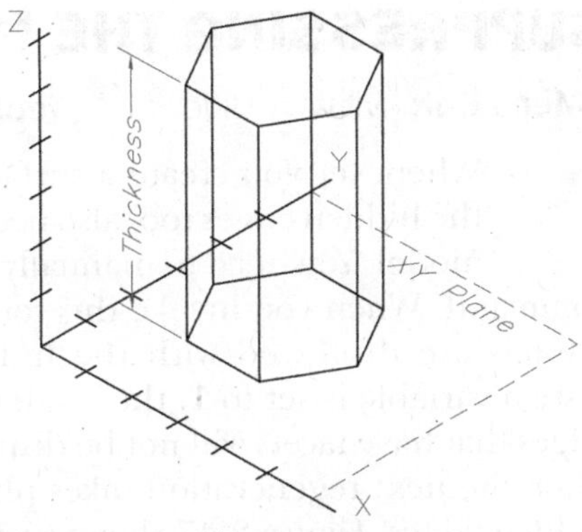

Figure 2-43 Object drawn with thickness

Tip

1 . The elevation value will be reset to 0.0 when you change the coordinate system to WCS.

*2. The rectangles drawn using the **Rectangle** tool do not consider the thickness value set by using the **ELEV** command. To draw a rectangle with thickness, use the **Thickness** option of the **Rectangle** tool.*

3. Figure 2-44 shows a point, line, polygon, circle drawn with a thickness of 5 units.

4. To write text with thickness, first write a single line text and then change its thickness using any of the commands that modify its property, refer to Figure 2-45.

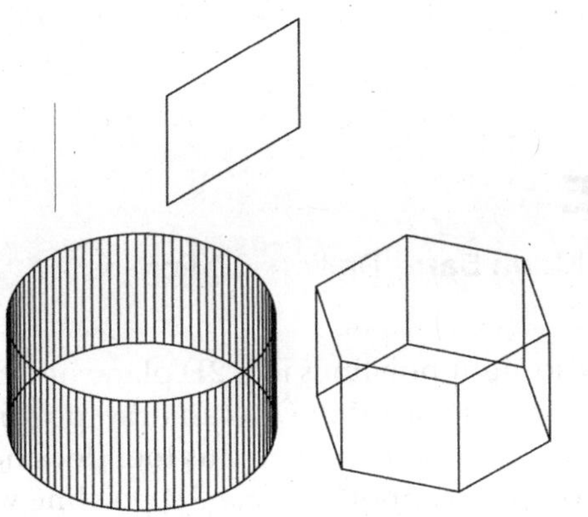

Figure 2-44 A point, line, polygon, and circle drawn with a thickness of 5 units

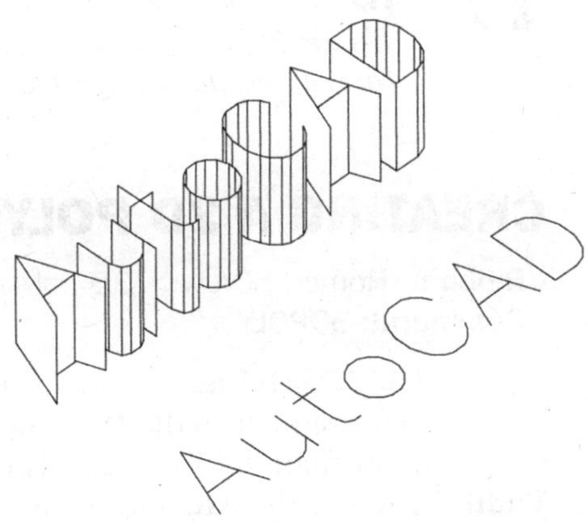

Figure 2-45 Text with and without thickness

SUPPRESSING THE HIDDEN EDGES

Menu Bar: View > Hide **Toolbar:** Render > Hide **Command:** HIDE

Whenever you create a surface or a solid model, the edges that lie at the back, called the hidden edges too, also become visible. As a result, the model appears like a wireframe model. You need to manually suppress the hidden lines in the 3D model using the **Hide** command. When you invoke this tool, all objects on the screen are regenerated. Also, the 3D models are displayed with the hidden edges suppressed. If the value of the **DISPSILH** system variable is set to **1**, the model is displayed only with the silhouette edges. The internal edges that have facets will not be displayed. The hidden lines are again included in the drawing when the next regeneration takes place. Figure 2-46 shows the surface models displaying the hidden edges. Figure 2-47 shows surface models without the hidden edges.

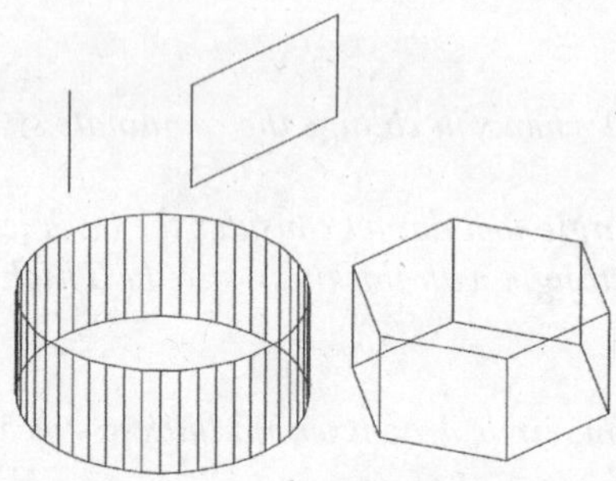

Figure 2-46 *3D models with hidden edges*

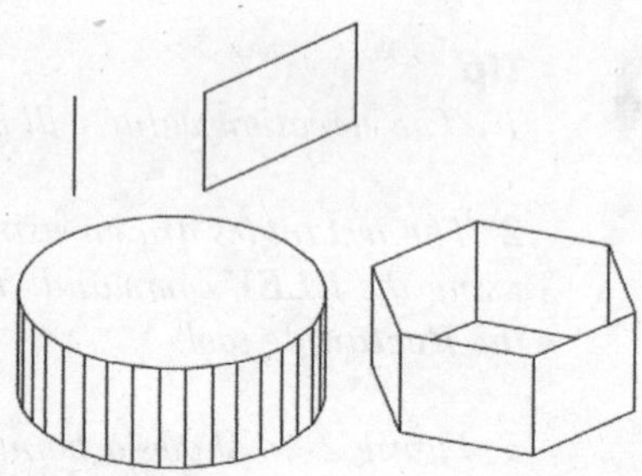

Figure 2-47 *Models without hidden edges*

Tip

*The **Hide** command considers Circles, Solids, Traces, Polylines with width, Regions, and 3D Faces as opaque surfaces that will hide objects.*

CREATING A 3D POLYLINE

Ribbon: Home > Draw > 3D Polyline **Menu Bar:** Draw > 3D Polyline
Command: 3DPOLY

The **3DPolyline** tool is used to draw straight polylines in a 2D plane or a 3D space. This tool is similar to the **Polyline** tool except the fact that you can draw polylines in a plane other than the *XY* plane also by using this tool. However, this tool does not provide the **Width** option or the **Arc** option; and therefore you cannot create a 3D polyline with a width or an arc. The **Close** and **Undo** options of this tool are similar to those of the **Polyline** tool.

Tip

*You can fit a spline curve about the 3D polyline using the **Edit Polyline** tool. Use the **Spline curve** option to fit the spline curve and the **Decurve** option to remove it.*

CONVERTING WIREFRAME MODELS INTO SURFACE MODELS

You can convert a wireframe model into a surface model using the **3DFACE** command and the **PFACE** command. These tools are discussed next.

Creating 3D Faces

Menu Bar: Draw > Modeling > Meshes > 3D Face	**Command:** 3DFACE

The **3D Face** tool is used to create 3D faces in space. You can create three-sided or four-sided faces using this tool. You can specify the same or a different Z coordinate value for each point of the face. On invoking this tool, you will be prompted to specify the first, second, third, and fourth points of the 3D face. Once you have specified the first four points, it will again prompt you to specify the third and fourth points. In this case, it will take the previous third and fourth points as the first and second points, respectively. This process will continue until you press ENTER at the **Specify third point or [Invisible] <exit>** prompt. Keep in mind that the points must be specified in the natural clockwise or the counterclockwise direction to create a proper 3D face. Figure 2-48 shows 3D faces created on the 3D wireframe model.

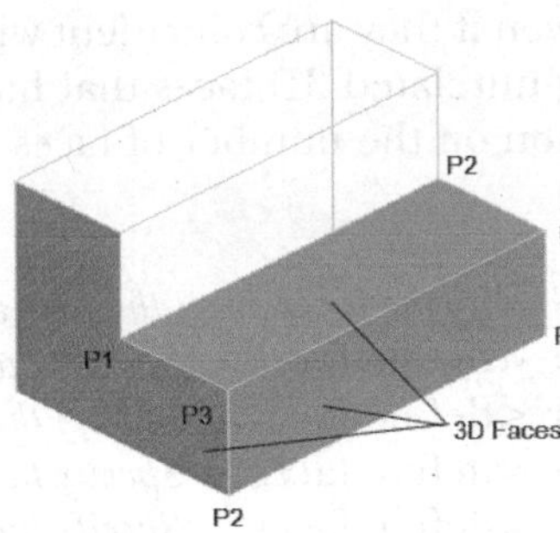

Figure 2-48 *3D faces created on the 3D wireframe model*

However, in case of complex wireframe models, refer to Figure 2-49, it is not easy to apply 3D faces. This is because when you apply a 3D face, it generates edges about all points that you specify. These edges will be displayed on the wireframe model, as shown in Figure 2-49. You can avoid these unwanted visible edges by applying the 3D faces with invisible edges using the **Invisible** option. It is very important to note here that the edge that will be created after you enter **I** at the **Specify next point or [Invisible] <exit>** prompt will not be the invisible edge. The edge that will be created after this edge will be the invisible edge. Therefore, to make the P3 edge and P4 edge invisible, specify P1 as the first point and P2 as the second point. Before specifying P3 as the third point, enter **I** at the **Specify third point or [Invisible] <exit>** prompt. Similarly, follow the same procedure for creating the other invisible edges, refer to Figure 2-50.

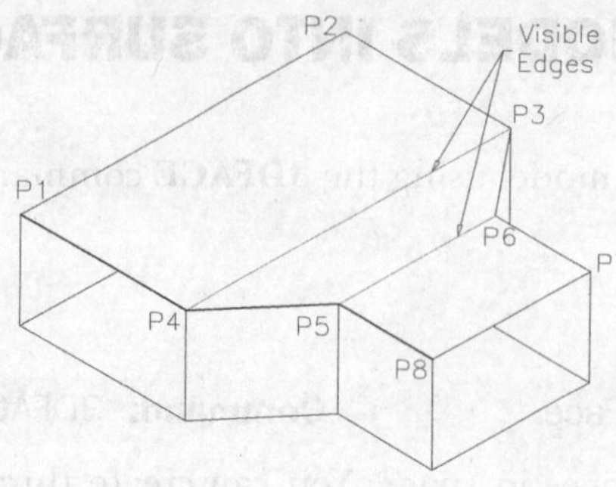

Figure 2-49 *Wireframe model with edges*

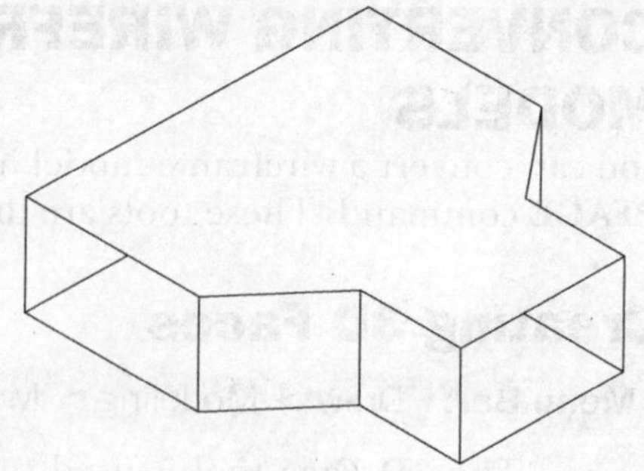

Figure 2-50 *Wireframe model without edges*

Creating Polyface Meshes

Command: PFACE

The **PFACE** command is similar to the **3D Face** tool. This command also allows you to create a mesh of any desired surface shape by specifying the coordinates of the vertices and assigning the vertices to the faces in the mesh. The difference between them is that on using the **3D Face** tool, you do not select the vertices that join another face twice. With the **PFACE** command, you need to select all the vertices of a face, even if they are coincident with the vertices of another face. In this way, you can avoid generating unrelated 3D faces that have coincident vertices. Also, with this command, there is no restriction on the number of faces and vertices the mesh can have.

Command: **PFACE**
Specify location for vertex 1: *Specify the location of the first vertex.*
Specify location for vertex 2 or <define faces>: *Specify the location of the second vertex.*
Specify location for vertex 3 or <define faces>: *Specify the location of the third vertex.*
Specify location for vertex 4 or <define faces>: *Specify the location of the fourth vertex.*
Specify location for vertex 5 or <define faces>: *Specify the location of the fifth vertex.*
Specify location for vertex 6 or <define faces>: *Specify the location of the sixth vertex.*
Specify location for vertex 7 or <define faces>: *Specify the location of the seventh vertex.*
Specify location for vertex 8 or <define faces>: *Specify the location of the eighth vertex.*
Specify location for vertex 9 or <define faces>: Enter

After defining the locations of all the vertices, press ENTER and assign vertices to the first face.

Face 1, vertex 1: *Specify the location of the first vertex.*
Enter a vertex number or [Color/Layer]: **1**
Face 1, vertex 2:
Enter a vertex number or [Color/Layer] <next face>: **2**
Face 1, vertex 3:
Enter a vertex number or [Color/Layer] <next face>: **3**
Face 1, vertex 4:
Enter a vertex number or [Color/Layer] <next face>: **4**

Once you have assigned the vertices to the first face, give a null response at the next prompt. Similarly, assign vertices to all faces, refer to Figure 2-51. To view the faces, select the **Realistic** option from the **Visual Styles** drop-down list in the **View** panel of the **Home** tab. To make an edge invisible, specify a negative number for its first vertex. The display of the invisible edges of 3D solid surfaces is governed by the **SPLFRAME** system variable. If **SPLFRAME** is set to 0, invisible edges are not displayed. If this variable is set to a number other than 0, all invisible edges are displayed after regeneration using the **REGENALL** command.

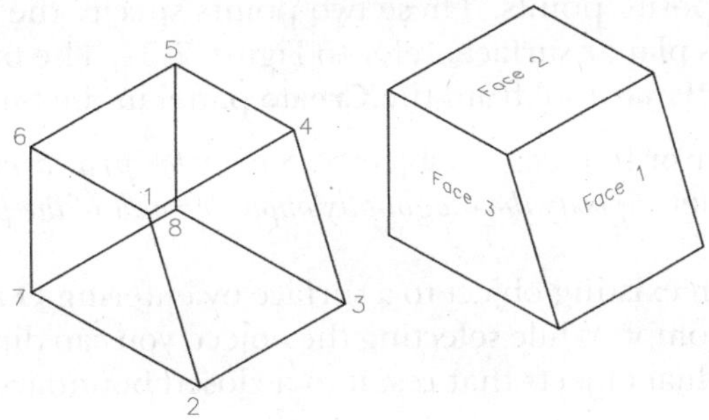

Figure 2-51 *Faces of block and assigned vertices*

Controlling the Visibility of the 3D Face Edges

Command: EDGE

The **EDGE** command is used to control the visibility of the edges created by using the **3D Face** tool. You can hide the edges of the 3D faces or display them using this command, refer to Figures 2-52 and 2-53. On invoking this command, you will be prompted to specify the 3D face edge to toggle its visibility or display. To hide an edge, select it. To display the edges, enter **D** at the **Specify edge of 3dface to toggle visibility or [Display]** prompt. You can display all invisible 3D face edges or the selected edges using this option.

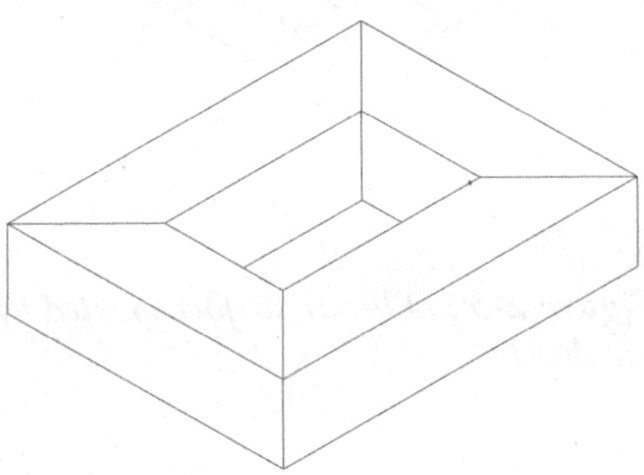

Figure 2-52 *Model with the visible 3D face edges*

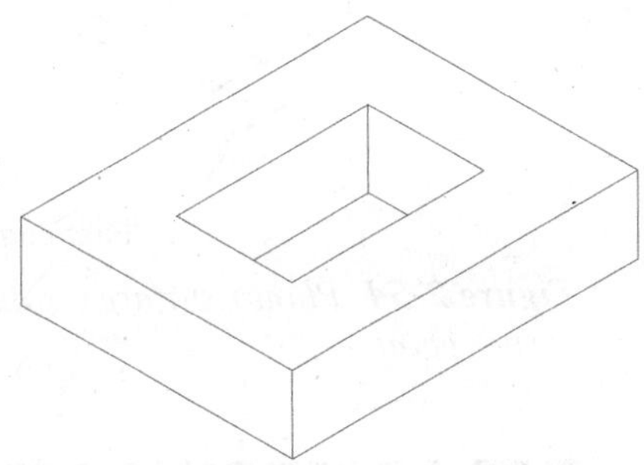

Figure 2-53 *Model after hiding the edges*

Exercise 2 — 3D Face

In this exercise, you will apply the 3D faces to the 3D wireframe model created in Example 2.

CREATING PLANAR SURFACES

Ribbon: Surface > Create > Planar **Toolbar:** Modeling > Planar Surface
Command: PLANESURF

The **Planar** tool is used to generate 2D surfaces on the working plane by specifying two diagonally opposite points. These two points specify the rectangular shape area to be covered by this planar surface, refer to Figure 2-54. The prompt sequence displayed on choosing the **Planar** tool from the **Create** panel in the **Surface** tab is discussed next.

Specify first corner or [Object] <Object>: *Specify the first corner point of the planar surface.*
Specify other corner: *Specify the diagonally opposite point of the planar surface.*

You can also convert an existing object to a surface by entering **O** at the **Specify first corner or [Object] <Object>** prompt. While selecting the object, you can directly select a closed boundary or a number of individual objects that result in a closed boundary, refer to Figure 2-55.

The number of lines displayed in the surface is controlled by the **SURFU** and **SURFV** system variables. The **SURFU** variable controls the number of lines to be displayed in the M direction and the **SURFV** variable controls the number of lines to be displayed in the N direction. These M and N directions are taken parallel to X and Y axis of the UCS respectively.

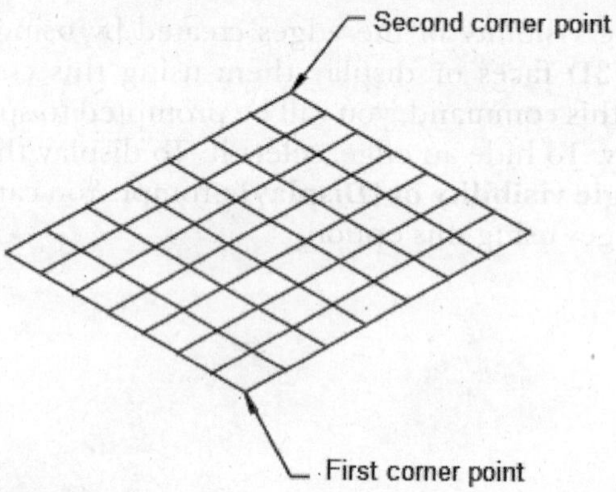

Figure 2-54 Planar surface created by specifying corner points

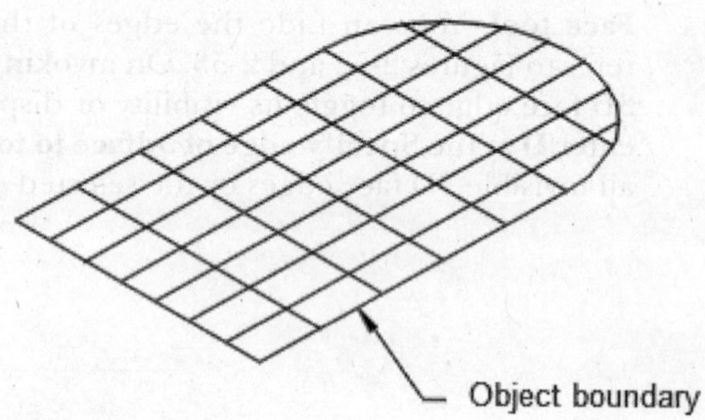

Figure 2-55 Planar surface created by selecting an object

THE 3DMESH COMMAND

Command: 3DMESH

The **3DMESH** command is used to create a free-form polygon mesh by using a matrix of M X N size. When you invoke this command, you will be prompted to specify the size of the mesh in the M direction and the N direction, where M X N is the total number of vertices in the mesh. The values of M and N can be 2 to 256. Once you have specified the size, you need to specify the coordinates of each and every vertex individually. For example, if the size of the mesh in the M and N directions is 12 X 12, then you will have to specify the coordinates of all the 144 vertices. You can specify any 2D or 3D coordinates for the vertices. Figure 2-54 shows a freeform mesh. This command is mostly used for programming. The 3D polygon mesh is always open in the M and N directions. You can edit the mesh created using the **3DMESH** command with the help of the **Edit Polyline** tool.

EDITING THE SURFACE MESH

The polyface or polygon meshes can be edited using the **Edit Polyline** tool as discussed next.

The Edit Polyline Tool

Ribbon: Home > Modify > Edit Polyline	**Menu Bar:** Modify > Object > Polyline
Toolbar: Modify II > Edit Polyline	**Command:** PEDIT

To edit a polyface or polygon mesh, invoke the **Edit Polyline** tool from the **Modify** panel. You can also select the **Polyline Edit** option from the shortcut menu displayed on selecting the surface mesh and right-clicking on it, to edit a polyface or polygon face. The prompt sequence that will be followed on choosing the **Edit Polyline** tool and selecting the mesh is given next.

Select polyline or [Multiple]: *Select the 3D mesh.*
Enter an option [Edit vertex/Smooth surface/Desmooth/Mclose/Nclose/Undo]: *Select an option.*

Edit Vertex

This option is used for the individual editing of vertices of the mesh in the M direction or the N direction. On invoking this option, a cross will appear on the first point of the mesh and the following sub-options will be provided. Change the visual style to Wireframe by selecting the **Wireframe** option from the **Visual Styles** drop-down list in the **View** panel of the **Home** tab, so that you can view the vertices clearly.

Next. This sub-option is used to move the cross to the next vertex.

Previous. This sub-option is used to move the cross to the previous vertex.

Left. This sub-option is used to move the cross to the previous vertex in the N direction of the mesh.

Right. This sub-option is used to move the cross to the next vertex in the N direction of the mesh.

Up. This sub-option is used to move the cross to the next vertex in the M direction of the mesh.

Down. This sub-option is used to move the cross to the previous vertex in the M direction of the mesh.

Move. This sub-option is used to redefine the location of the current vertex. You can define a new location by using any of the coordinate systems or can directly select the location on the screen, refer to Figures 2-56 and 2-57.

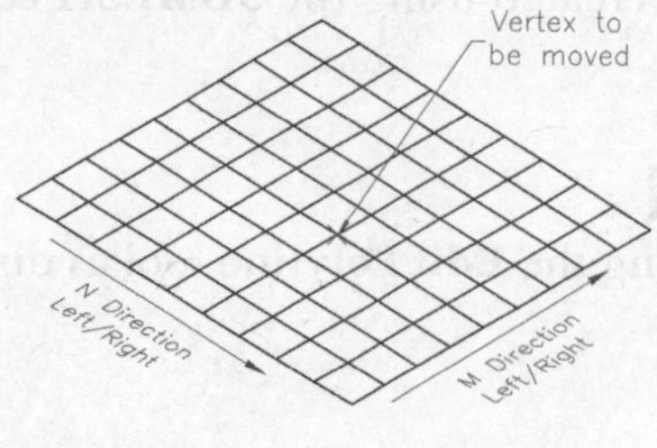

Figure 2-56 Vertex before moving

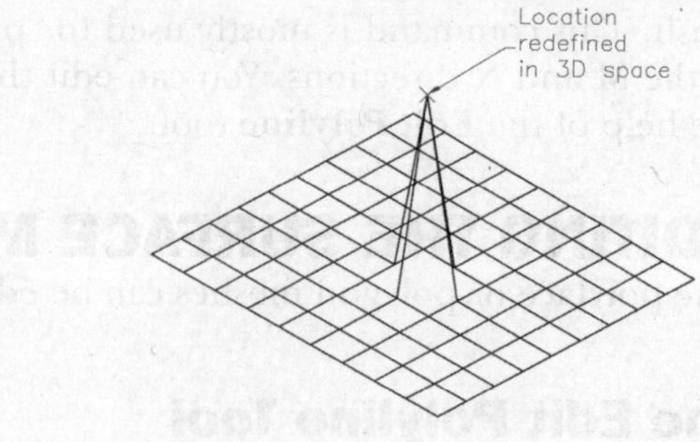

Figure 2-57 Vertex after moving

REgen. This sub-option is used to regenerate the 3D mesh.

eXit. This sub-option is used to exit the **Edit Vertex** option.

Smooth surface

This option is used to smoothen the surface of the 3D mesh by fitting a smooth surface, as shown in Figures 2-58 and 2-59. The smoothness of the surface will depend upon the **SURFU** and **SURFV** system variables. The value of these system variables can vary between 0 and 200.

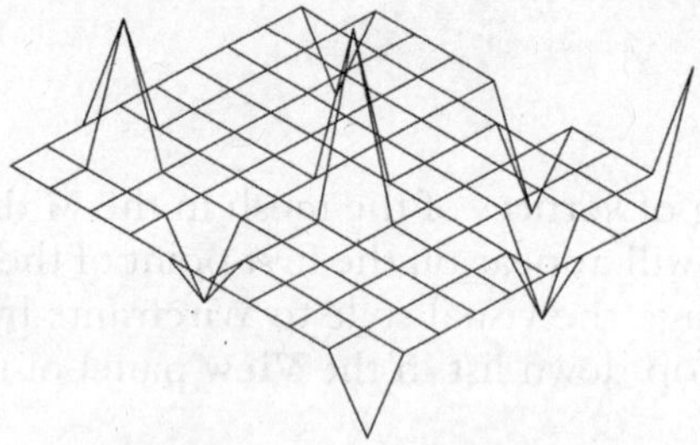

Figure 2-58 3D mesh before fitting the smooth surface

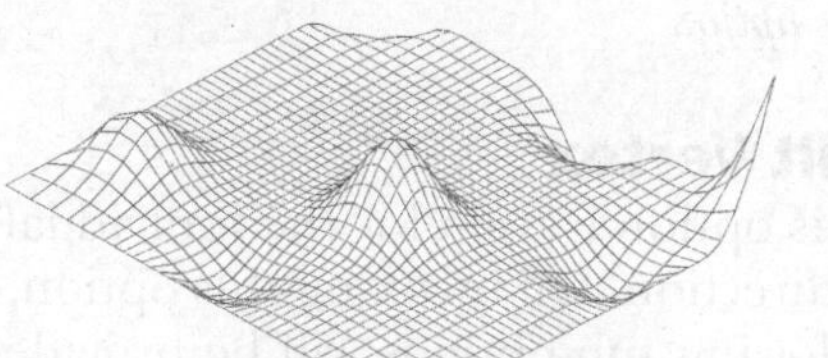

Figure 2-59 3D mesh after fitting the smooth surface

The type of the smooth surface to be fitted is controlled by the **SURFTYPE** system variable. If you set the value of the **SURFTYPE** system variable to 5, it will fit a Quadratic B-spline surface. If you set the value to 6, it will fit a Cubic B-spline surface. If you set the value to 8, it will fit a Bezier surface.

Desmooth

This option is used to remove the smooth surface that was fitted on the 3D mesh using the **Smooth surface** option and restore to the original mesh.

Mclose

This option is used to close the 3D mesh in the M direction, as shown in Figures 2-60 and 2-61.

Nclose

This option is used to close the 3D mesh in the N direction, as shown in Figures 2-60 and 2-61.

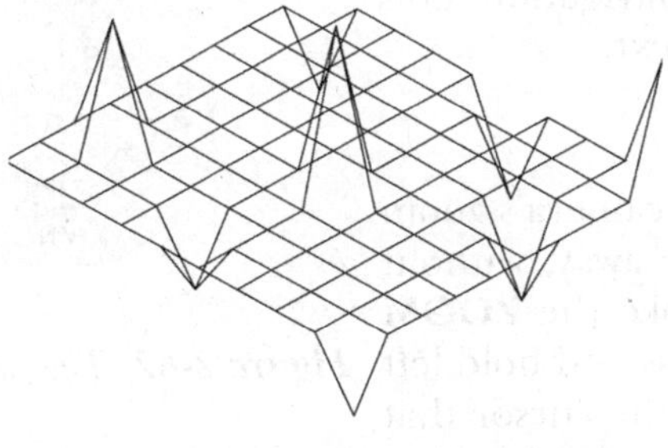

Figure 2-60 3D mesh open in the M and N directions

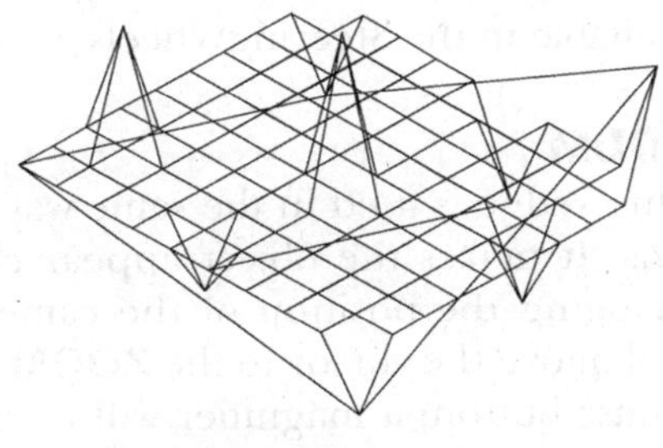

Figure 2-61 3D mesh closed in the M and N directions

Mopen

This option will be available if the 3D mesh is closed in the M direction. It is used to open the 3D mesh in the M direction, refer to Figures 2-60 and 2-61.

Nopen

This option will be available if the 3D mesh is closed in the N direction. It is used to open the 3D mesh in the N direction, refer to Figures 2-60 and 2-61.

Undo

This option is used to undo all the operations done by the **Edit Polyline** tool.

DYNAMIC VIEWING OF 3D OBJECTS

Ribbon: View > Navigate > SteeringWheels (Customize to add)
Navigator Bar: Full Navigation Wheel **Command:** NAVSWHEEL

The options available in the **Full Navigation Wheel** make the entire process of the solid modeling very interesting. You can dynamically rotate the solid models on the screen to view them from different angles. You can also define clipping planes and then rotate the solid models such that whenever the models pass through the cutting planes, they are sectioned just to be viewed. The original model can be restored as soon as you exit these commands or tools. The tools and their options that are used to perform all these functions are discussed next.

Using the SteeringWheels

The SteeringWheels enables you to easily view and navigate through your 3D models. It is an ideal tool for navigating through your models. It includes not only the common navigating tools such as **Zoom**, **Pan**, and **Orbit** but also an option to move the user specified center of the model to the center of the display window. Using this tool, you can also rewind and get back your previous views. It is a time saving tool, since it combines many common navigation tools into a single tool.

The SteeringWheel is divided into different sections known as Wedges. Each wedge on a wheel represents a command. You can activate a particular navigation option by clicking on the respective wedges and then modify the view of the model by dragging the cursor, refer to Figure 2-62. The navigation tools available in the SteeringWheels are discussed next.

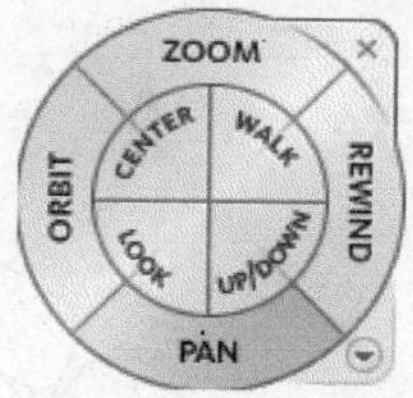

Figure 2-62 The SteeringWheel

ZOOM

This wedge is used in the same way as you use camera's zoom lens. It makes the object appear closer or far away, without changing the position of the camera. To invoke the **ZOOM** tool, move the cursor to the **ZOOM** wedge, press and hold left mouse button; a magnifier will be attached to the cursor that allows you to zoom in or out with reference to a base point. Now, drag to zoom in and zoom out. However, you can change the base point or pivot point to zoom in or zoom out of the model by choosing the **CENTER** wedge. You can even enable the incremental zoom of 25 percent on a single click from the **Zoom** area of the **SteeringWheels Settings** dialog box. To invoke this dialog box, right-click on the SteeringWheels; a shortcut menu will be displayed. Choose the **SteeringWheels Settings** option from the shortcut menu; the **SteeringWheels Settings** dialog box will be displayed. You can even choose the **Fit to Window** option from the shortcut menu of the SteeringWheels to view the entire drawing in the viewport.

REWIND

This wedge enables you to quickly restore the previous views. To invoke this tool, move the cursor to the **REWIND** wedge and click; a series of frames from the previous view orientation are displayed. You can now quickly pick the required view and control the thumbnail previews generated on changing various views using the **Rewind thumbnail** area of the **SteeringWheels Settings** dialog box.

PAN

This wedge allows you to drag the view to a new location in the drawing window. To invoke this tool, move the cursor to the **PAN** wedge, press and hold left mouse button; a plus arrow is attached to the cursor, enabling you to drag the view in any direction. Now, drag your mouse to pan in model space. You can choose the **Fit to Window** option from the shortcut menu of the SteeringWheels to view the entire drawing in the viewport.

ORBIT

This wedge allows you to visually maneuver around the 3D objects to obtain different views. When you move your cursor to the **ORBIT** wedge press and hold left mouse button; a circular arrow is attached to the cursor. Now, you can rotate the model with respect to a base point. Similar to the **ZOOM** option, in this case also, you can specify the required center point of the view and rotate the model using the **CENTER** wedge option. You can also set the viewpoint upside down using the options in the **SteeringWheels Settings** dialog box. Moreover, you can choose the **Fit to Window** option to view the full drawing view.

CENTER

This wedge helps you specify the pivot or center point of the view to orbit or zoom a model. When you move your cursor to this wedge and drag, a pivot ball is attached to the cursor. You can now adjust your center or target point by placing the cursor at the required point. However, you can restore the center of the viewport by choosing the **Restore Original Center** option from the shortcut menu of the SteeringWheels. You can also restore the home view of the model by choosing the **Go Home** option from the shortcut menu.

LOOK

This tool works similar to turning the camera on a tripod without changing the distance between the camera and the target. This means the source remains the same, but the target changes. To invoke this tool, move the cursor to the **LOOK** wedge; an arc is attached to the cursor which enables you to change your view direction. You can also invert the vertical direction of the **Look** tool by selecting the **Invert vertical axis for Look tool** check box from the **SteeringWheels Settings** dialog box. You can choose the **Fit to Window** option to view the entire drawing in the viewport.

WALK

This tool moves the camera around the model as if you are walking away or towards the focus direction of the camera. In the walk 3D navigation, the camera moves parallel to the XY plane and gives the effect as if you are walking. To invoke this tool, move the cursor to the **WALK** wedge. An arrow is attached to the cursor showing the direction of the camera. You can drag the cursor to move around the model and also control the walk speed using the options in the **Walk Tool** area of the **SteeringWheels Settings** dialog box. Using this dialog box, you can also constraint the walk angle to the ground plane.

UP/DOWN

This option slides the view along the Y-axis of the screen, which is like being in an elevator. When you move your cursor to the **UP/DOWN** wedge, a vertical slider is attached to the cursor. You can slide from up to down in the slider to view the model from up to down. Using the options in the shortcut menu of the SteeringWheels, you can go back to the original view, restore the original center, or fit the entire drawing in the viewport.

Modes of SteeringWheels

There are four working modes of SteeringWheels, refer to Figure 2-63. These working modes are discussed next.

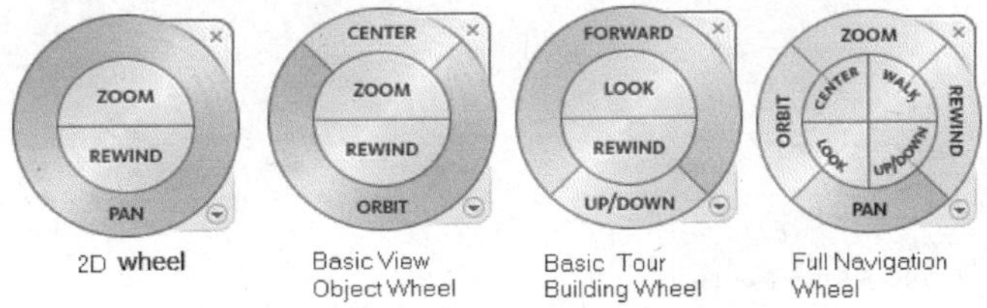

Figure 2-63 Different modes of the SteeringWheels

2D Wheel

You can invoke the SteeringWheel that has only the 2D navigation tools. To do so, choose the **2D** tool from **View > Navigate > SteeringWheels** drop-down; the 2D SteeringWheel with the **PAN**, **ZOOM**, and **REWIND** tools will be displayed.

Basic View Object Wheel

This mode contains only the viewing tools such as **CENTER**, **ZOOM**, **REWIND**, and **ORBIT**. You can invoke this mode by choosing **Basic Wheels > View Object Wheel** from the shortcut menu of the SteeringWheels or by choosing **Basic View Object Wheel** from the flyout that is displayed on clicking the down-arrow in the **SteeringWheels** group in the **Navigation bar**.

Basic Tour Building Wheel

This mode is ideal for navigating inside a building. It contains the **FORWARD, REWIND, LOOK,** and **UP/DOWN** tools. You can invoke this mode by choosing **Basic Wheels > Tour Building Wheel** from the shortcut menu of the SteeringWheels or by choosing **Mini Tour Building Wheel** from the flyout that is displayed on clicking on the down-arrow in the **SteeringWheels** group in the **Navigation bar**.

Full Navigation Wheel

This mode contains both the view and the navigating tools. It enables you to select a variety of tools from a single wheel. You can invoke this mode by choosing the **Full Navigation Wheel** option from the shortcut menu of the SteeringWheels or from the **Navigation bar**.

The SteeringWheels are of two types: Big Wheels and Mini Wheels. Both the wheels have the same functioning modes. The Big Wheels mode is displayed by default, whereas the Mini Wheels mode is invoked by choosing the **Mini View Object Wheel**, **Mini Tour Building Wheel**, or **Mini Full Navigation Wheel** option from the shortcut menu of the SteeringWheels or by choosing option from the **SteeringWheels** drop-down in the **Navigation bar** or by choosing option from the **SteeringWheels** drop-down in the **Navigate** panel of the **View** tab. You can customize the size, appearance, and behavior of the Steering Wheel using the **SteeringWheels Settings** dialog box, refer to Figure 2-64.

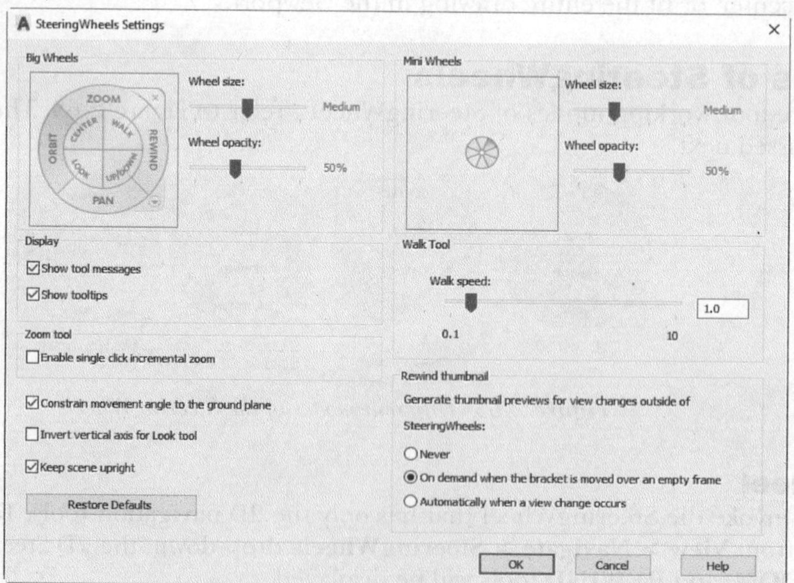

*Figure 2-64 The **SteeringWheels Settings** dialog box*

You can control the size and opacity of the Big Wheels and Mini Wheels with the help of a slider available next to the wheels. Also, using this dialog box you can control the tooltips and messages that are displayed when you move the cursor over any wedge.

Dynamically Rotating the View of a Model

Ribbon: View > Navigate > Orbit	**Navigation Bar:** Orbit
Toolbar: 3D Navigation > Constrained Orbit	**Command:** 3DO(3DORBIT)

The **Orbit** tool allows you to visually maneuver around 3D objects to obtain different views. This is one of the most important tools for the advanced 3D viewing options. All other advanced 3D viewing options can be invoked inside this tool or using the **3D Navigation** toolbar. This tool activates a 3D Orbit view in the current viewport. You can click and drag your pointing device to view the 3D object from different angles. In 3D orbit viewing, the target is considered stationary and the camera location is considered to be moving around it. The cursor looks like a sphere encircled by two arc shaped arrows. This is known as **Orbit mode** cursor, and clicking and dragging the pointing device allows you to rotate the view freely. You can move the **Orbit mode** cursor horizontally, vertically, and diagonally. If you drag the pointing device horizontally, the camera will move parallel to the XY plane of the WCS. If you move your pointing device vertically, then the camera will move along the Z axis. This tool is a transparent tool and can be invoked inside any other tool. You can select individual objects or the entire drawing to view before you invoke the **Orbit** tool.

Tip

Press and hold the SHIFT key and the middle mouse button to temporarily enter the constrained orbit mode.

You can invoke the other advanced viewing options using the shortcut menu that is displayed on right-clicking in the drawing window when you are inside the **Orbit** tool. The shortcut menu with other advanced viewing options is shown in Figure 2-65. The options of the shortcut menu are discussed next.

Exit

This option is used to exit the **Orbit** tool. You can also exit this tool by pressing ESC.

Current Mode

This option displays the currently active navigation mode in which you obtained this shortcut menu.

Other Navigation Modes

This option enables you to choose the other navigation modes of the **3D Navigation** toolbar. In this way, you can toggle between the navigation modes without exiting the tool. The sub-options provided by the **Other Navigation Modes** are as follows:

Free Orbit. This sub-option can be invoked by choosing the **Free Orbit** tool from **View > Navigate > Orbit** drop-down in the **View Tab** of the **Ribbon**, refer to Figure 2-66; 3D orbit view will be activated in the current viewport. When you invoke the **Free Orbit** tool, an arcball appears. This arcball is a circle with four smaller circles placed such that they divide the bigger circle into quadrants. The UCS icon is replaced by a shaded 3D UCS icon. In the 3D orbit viewing, the target is considered stationary and the camera location is considered to be moving around it. The target is the center of the arcball. The **Free Orbit** tool is a transparent tool and can be invoked inside any other tool.

The cursor icon changes as you move the cursor over the 3D Orbit view. The different icons indicate the different directions in which the view is being rotated. They are as follows.

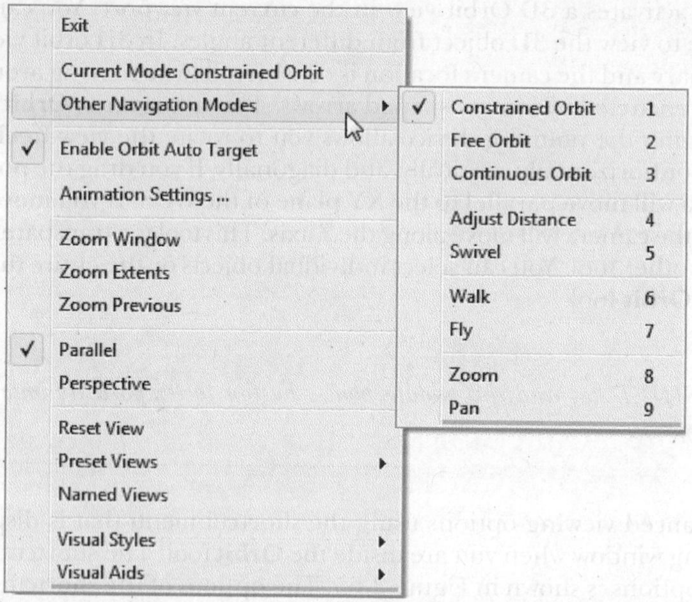

Figure 2-65 The shortcut menu displayed when the 3DORBIT command is active

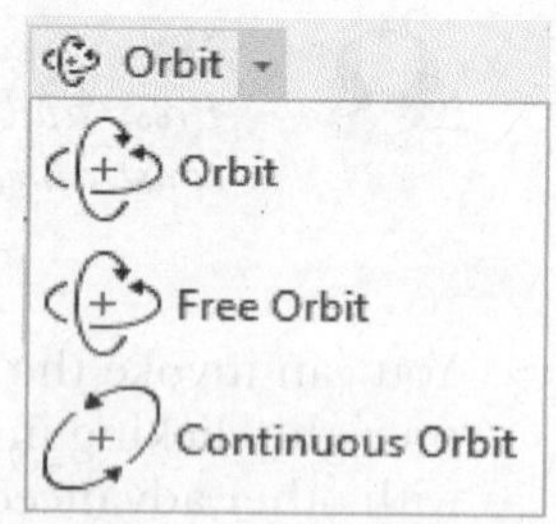

Figure 2-66 The tools in the ***Orbit*** *drop-down*

Orbit mode. When you move the cursor within the arcball, the cursor looks like a sphere encircled by two lines. This icon is the **Orbit mode** cursor, and clicking and dragging the pointing device allows you to rotate the view freely as if the cursor was grabbing a sphere surrounding the objects and moving it around the target point. You can move the **Orbit mode** cursor horizontally, vertically, and diagonally.

Roll mode. When you move the cursor outside the arcball, it changes to look like a sphere encircled by a circular arrow. When you click and drag, the view is rotated around an axis that extends through the center of the arcball, perpendicular to the screen.

Orbit Left-Right. When you move the cursor to the small circles placed on the left and right of the arcball, it changes into a sphere surrounded by a horizontal ellipse. When you click and drag, the view is rotated around the *Y* axis of the screen.

Orbit Up-down. When you move the cursor to the circles placed in the top or bottom of the arcball, it changes into a sphere surrounded by a vertical ellipse. Clicking and dragging the cursor rotates the view around the horizontal axis or the *X* axis of the screen, and passes it through the middle of the arcball.

Figure 2-67 shows a model being rotated using the **Free Orbit** tool.

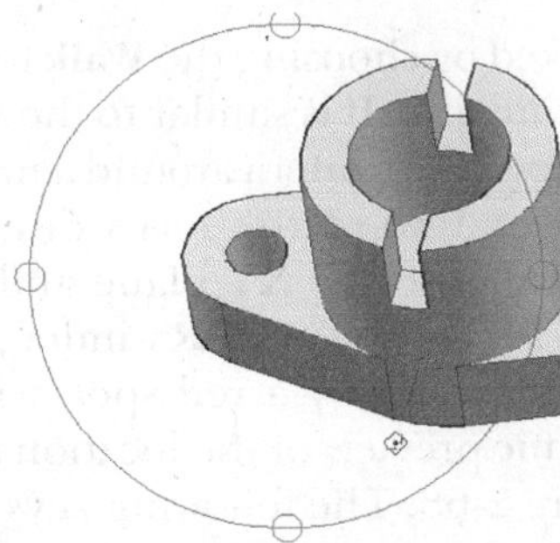

***Figure 2-67** Model being rotated using the **Free Orbit** tool*

Tip

*1 . Press and hold the SHIFT+CTRL keys and the middle button of the mouse to temporarily enter the **Free Orbit** navigation mode.*

*2 . If you are in the **3D Orbit** navigation mode, press and hold the SHIFT key to temporarily enter the **Free Orbit** navigation mode.*

Continuous Orbit. This tool allows you to set the objects you select in a 3D view into continuous motion in a free-form orbit. You can invoke this tool by choosing the **Continuous Orbit** tool from **View > Navigate > Orbit** drop-down. While using this tool, the cursor icon changes to the continuous orbit cursor. Clicking in the drawing area and dragging the pointing device in any direction starts to move the object(s) in the direction you have dragged it. When you release the pointing device button, that is, stop clicking and dragging, the object continues to move in its orbit in the direction you specified. The speed at which the cursor is moved determines the speed at which the objects spin. You can click and drag again to specify another direction for rotation in the continuous orbit. While using this sub-option, you can right-click in the drawing area to display the shortcut menu and choose the other sub-options without exiting the tool. Choosing **Pan**, **Zoom**, **Orbit**, **Adjust Clipping Plane** ends the continuous orbit.

Adjust Distance. This sub-option can be invoked by choosing **Other Navigation Modes > Adjust Distance** from the shortcut menu displayed on right-clicking in the drawing area. Alternatively, choose **View > Camera > Adjust Distance** from the menu bar. This sub-option is similar to taking the camera closer to or farther away from the target object. Therefore, it makes the object appear closer or farther away. You can press the left button and drag the mouse to adjust the distance between the target and the camera. This option is used to reduce the distance between the camera and the object when the object rotates by a large angle.

Swivel Camera. This sub-option can be invoked by choosing **View > Camera > Swivel** from the menu bar. It works similar to turning the camera on a tripod without changing the distance between the camera and the target. You can press the left mouse button and drag the mouse to swivel the camera.

Walk. This sub-option can be invoked by choosing the **Walk** tool from **Visualize > Animations> Walk** drop-down after customizing. It is similar to the **Walk** option in the SteeringWheel. This sub-option is used to move the camera around a model with the help of the keyboard, as if you are walking away or toward the focus direction of the camera. In walk 3D navigation, the camera moves parallel to the XY plane and this seems as if you are walking. Choose the **Walk** button; the **POSITION LOCATOR** window, showing the top view of the model with the location of the camera indicated by a red spot, will be displayed. The **POSITION LOCATOR** window shows a dynamic preview of the location and movement of the camera with respect to the object, refer to Figure 2-68. The following keys are used to control the location of the camera with respect to the object.

Motion Type	**Key**
Move the camera in the forward direction	UP ARROW or W key
Move the camera in the backward direction	DOWN ARROW or S key
Move the camera in the left direction	LEFT ARROW or A key
Move the camera in the right direction	RIGHT ARROW or D key
Change the focus direction of the camera	Press and hold the left mouse button in the drawing area and drag the mouse in the desired direction
Change the orientation of the XY plane	Press and hold the middle mouse button in the drawing area and drag the mouse in the desired direction
Change the distance of the camera	Move the cursor to the green triangular area in the **POSITION LOCATOR** window and pan to the desired location
Change the coverage area of the camera	Move the cursor onto the camera in the **POSITION LOCATOR** window and pan the camera

Fly. This sub-option can be invoked by choosing the **Fly** tool from **Visualize > Anima> Walk** drop-down after customizing. This sub-option is used to move the camera through a model with the help of the keyboard as if you are flying away or toward the focus direction, refer to Figure 2-68 of the camera. In the fly 3D navigation, the camera can even move at an inclination with the XY plane and this seems as if you are flying around the object. The **POSITION LOCATOR** window will be displayed on the screen while using the **Fly** tool also. The position of the camera with respect to the object can be controlled by using the same procedure as discussed in the **Walk** tool.

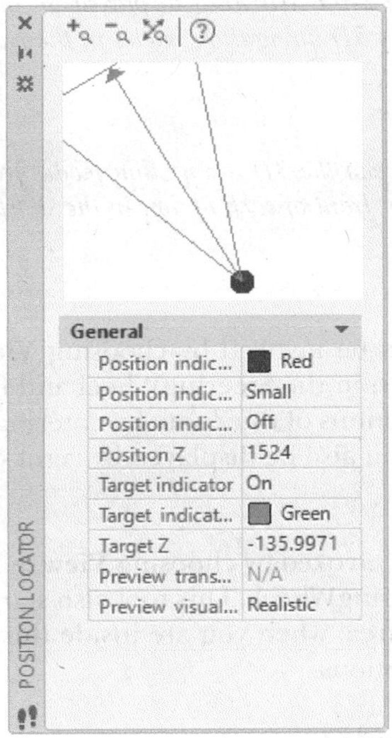

*Figure 2-68 The **POSITION LOCATOR** window*

Note

*1. To control the settings related to walk and fly, invoke the tool and right-click in the drawing area. Next, choose the **Walk and Fly Settings** option; the **Walk and Fly Settings** dialog box will be displayed. You can specify the settings in this dialog box.*

2. The Walk and Fly 3D navigation modes can be activated only in the perspective view. Activating the Walk or Fly 3D navigation mode in the parallel projection will display a warning window, as shown in Figure 2-69.

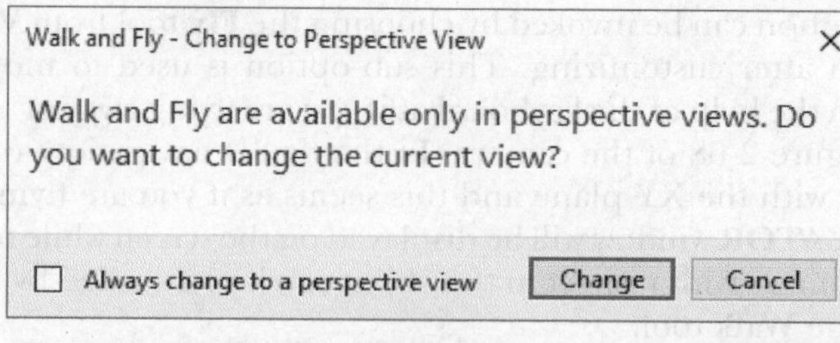

***Figure 2-69** Warning displayed on activating the Walk and Fly 3D navigation modes in the parallel projection*

Tip

You can toggle between the 3D navigation modes from the shortcut menu or by entering the number displayed in front of each option in the shortcut menu at the Command prompt.

Zoom. This sub-option can be invoked by choosing **View > Zoom** from the menu bar. It is similar to the **ZOOM** option in the SteeringWheel and functions like the camera's zoom lens. You can invoke the other options of the Zoom by entering **3DZOOM** at the Command prompt. Alternatively, the options can also be displayed by right-clicking in the drawing area when you are inside this tool.

Pan. The **Pan** sub-option is invoked by choosing **View > Pan** from the menu bar. It is similar to the **PAN** option in the SteeringWheel. This tool also starts the 3D interactive viewing. You can right-click in the drawing area, when you are inside this tool, to display a shortcut menu that displays all the 3D Orbit options.

Enable Orbit Auto Target

This option, if chosen, ensures that the target point is focused on the object while rotating the view. If this option is cleared, the target point is set at the center of the viewport, in which the **Orbit** tool is invoked.

Animation Settings

This option, if chosen, displays the **Animation Settings** dialog box, refer to Figure 2-70. Using this dialog box, you can change the settings for visual style, resolution, number of frames to be captured in one second, and the format in which you want to save the file while creating the animation of 3D navigation. Creating animations will be discussed in the next chapter.

Zoom Window/Extents/Previous

These options are used to zoom the solid model using a window, zoom the objects to the extents, or retrieve the previous zoomed views of the model.

Parallel

This option is chosen to display the selected model using the parallel projection method. It is the default method when a new AutoCAD file is started with 2D templates. In this method, no parallel lines in the model converge at any point.

Perspective

This option is chosen to use the one point perspective method to display a model. It is the default method when a new AutoCAD file is started with 3D templates. In this method, all parallel lines in the model converge at a single point, thus providing a realistic view of the model when viewed with the naked eye, refer to Figure 2-71.

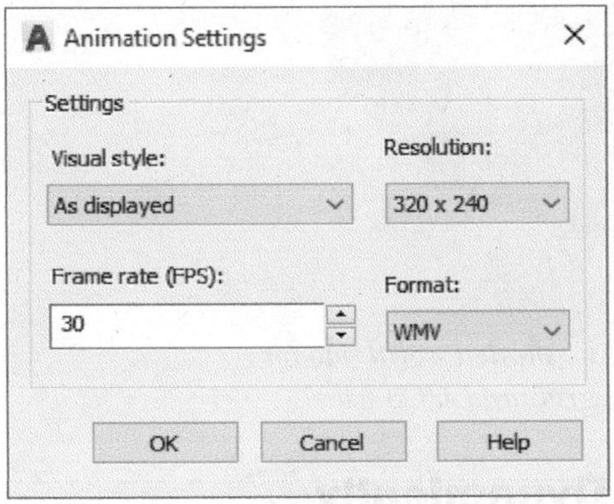

*Figure 2-70 The **Animation Settings** dialog box*

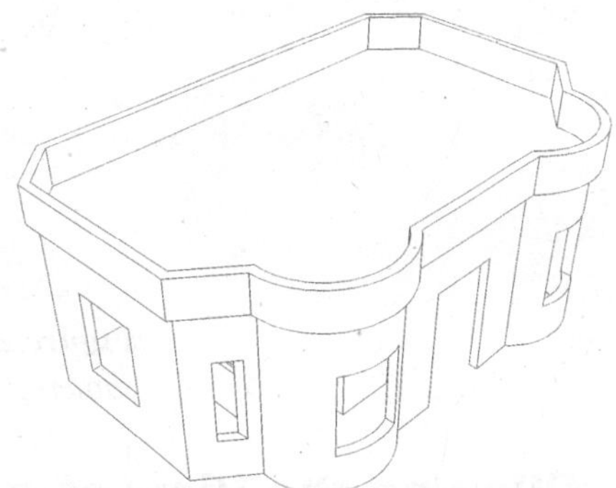

Figure 2-71 Viewing the model using the perspective projection

Reset View

This option, when chosen automatically, restores the view that was current when you started rotating the solid model in the 3D orbit. Note that you will not exit the **Orbit** tool if you choose this option.

Preset Views

This option is used to select any of the six standard orthogonal views or four isometric views.

Named Views

If you have created some views using the **VIEW** command, then the existing named views will be displayed as the sub-options under the **Named Views** option in the **3D Orbit** shortcut menu. Use this option to activate the saved view.

Visual Aids

The **Orbit** tool provides you with three visual aids for the ease of visualizing the solid model in the 3D orbit view. These visual aids are **Compass**, **Grid**, and **UCS Icon**. A check mark is displayed in front of the options you have selected. You can select none, one, two, or all three of the visual aids. Choosing **Compass** displays a sphere drawn within the arcball with three lines. These lines indicate the *X*, *Y*, and *Z* axis directions. Choosing the **Grid** displays a grid at the current *XY* plane. You can specify the height by using the **ELEVATION** system variable. The **GRID** system variable controls the display options of the **Grid** before using the **Orbit** tool. The size of the grid will depend upon the limits of the drawing. Choosing the **UCS Icon** displays the UCS icon. If this option is not selected, then AutoCAD turns off the display of the UCS icon. While using any of the 3D Orbit options, interactive 3D viewing is on and a shaded 3D view UCS icon is displayed. The *X* axis is red, the *Y* axis is green, and the *Z* axis is blue or cyan. Figure 2-72 shows a realistic shaded solid model displaying the compass, grid, and UCS icon.

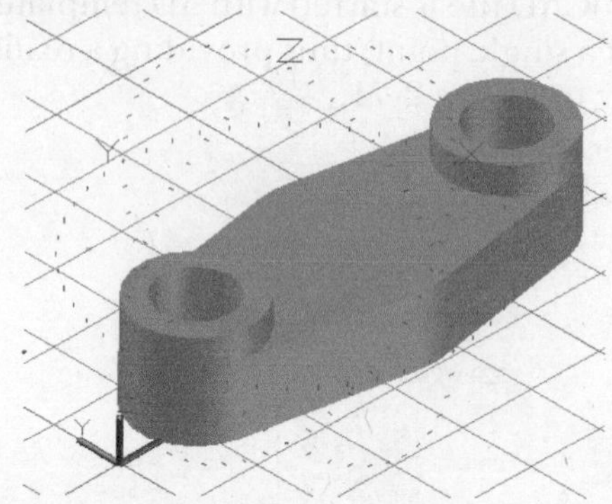

Figure 2-72 Realistic shaded solid model showing the compass, grid, and UCS icon

Clipping the View of a Model Dynamically

Command: 3DCLIP

The **3DCLIP** command is used to adjust the clipping planes for sectioning the selected solid model. Note that the actual solid model is not modified by this command. This command is used only for the purpose of viewing. The original solid model will be restored when you exit this command. With this option, you can adjust the location of the clipping planes. When you choose this option, the **Adjust Clipping Planes** window will be displayed, as shown in Figure 2-73. In this window, the object appears rotated at 90-degree to the top of the current view in the window. This facilitates the display of cutting planes. Setting the location of the front and back clipping planes in this window is reflected in the result in the current view. The various options of the **3DCLIP** command are displayed in the **Adjust Clipping Planes** toolbar in the window. There are seven buttons provided in this window. The functions of these buttons are discussed next.

Adjust Front Clipping. This button is chosen to locate the front clipping plane, which is defined by the line located in the lower end of the **Adjust Clipping Planes** window. You can see the result in the 3D Orbit view if the front clipping is on.

Adjust Back Clipping. This button is chosen to locate the back clipping plane, which is defined by the line located in the upper end of the **Adjust Clipping Planes** window. You can see the result in the 3D Orbit view if the back clipping is on.

Create Slice. Choosing this button causes both the front and back clipping planes to move together. The slice is created between the two clipping planes and is displayed in the current 3D view. You can first adjust the front and the back clipping planes individually by choosing the respective options. Next, by choosing the **Create Slice** button, activate both the clipping planes simultaneously and display the result in the current view.

Pan. Displays the pan cursor that you can use to pan the object in **Adjust Clipping Planes** window. Hold down the left mouse button and drag it in any direction. The pan cursor stays active until you click another button.

Zoom. Displays a magnifying-glass cursor that you can use to enlarge or reduce the clipping plane. To do so, choose the **Zoom** tool and hold the left mouse button and drag it in up or down direction.

Front Clipping On/Off. Turns on or off the sectioning of a solid model using the front clipping plane, refer to Figure 2-74.

Back Clipping On/Off. Turns on or off the sectioning of the solid model using the back clipping plane, refer to Figure 2-74.

Figure 2-73 The ***Adjust Clipping Planes*** *window*

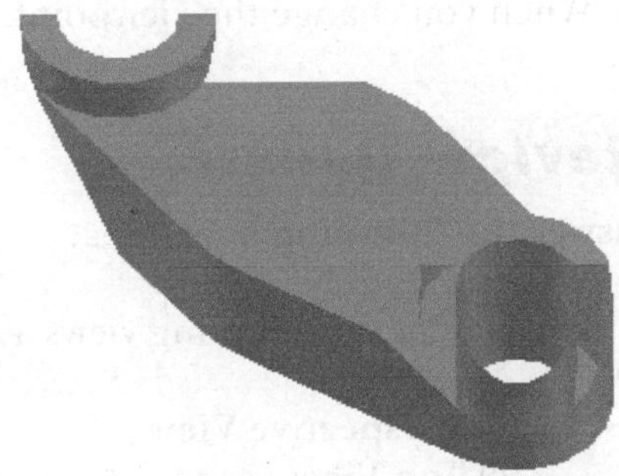

Figure 2-74 Model with the front and back clipping on

NUDGE FUNCTIONALITY

Nudge functionality gives you the freedom to move any kind of object by 2 pixels in any direction orthogonal to screen. When the snap mode is ON, the object moves to the distance specified in the **Snap spacing** edit box in the **Drafting Settings** dialog box. To nudge any object, select the object and press CTRL + arrow key corresponding to the direction in which you want to move the object.

Self-Evaluation Test

Answer the following questions and then compare them to those given at the end of this chapter:

1. The __________ and __________ commands can be used to change the viewpoint for viewing models in the 3D space.

2. Using the **Viewpoint Presets** dialog box, you can set the viewpoint with respect to __________ and __________.

3. The two types of 3D coordinate systems are __________ and __________.

4. To view 3D clipping on an object, the ________ command is used.
5. The **VPOINT** command is used to change the viewpoint to view a solid model. (T/F)
6. The wireframe models can be converted into surface models as well as solid models. (T/F)
7. In AutoCAD, the right-hand thumb rule is followed to identify the direction of the X, Y, and Z axes. (T/F)
8. In AutoCAD, the right-hand thumb rule is followed to find the direction of rotation in the 3D space. (T/F)
9. Once you exit the 3DCLIP command, the original solid model is restored. (T/F)
10. When you change the viewpoint, the 3D model moves from its default position. (T/F)

Review Questions

Answer the following questions:

1. In which of the following views a model is displayed by default in 3D Modeling workspace?

   (a) **Perspective View** (b) **Parallel View**
   (c) **Top View** (d) None of these

2. Which of the following tools is used to create a 3D polyline?

   (a) **Polyline** (b) **3D Poly**
   (c) **3D Polyline** (d) **Polyline 3D**

3. Which of the following commands is used to set the elevation and thickness for new objects?

   (a) **ELEVATION** (b) **THICKNESS**
   (c) **ELEV** (d) **THICK**

4. Which of the following commands is used to suppress the hidden edges in a 3D model?

   (a) **SUPPRESS** (b) **HIDE**
   (c) **3DHIDE** (d) **EDGE**

5. Which of the following views is set by default when you open a new drawing?

   (a) SE Isometric View (b) SW Isometric View
   (c) Custom View (d) Bottom View

6. For the **Sphere** and **Torus** meshes if the **MESHTYPE** system variable is set to 0, the resulting surface will be a ________ mesh.

7. The highlighted area in a ViewCube that is used to change a view is called ________.

8. A 3D model can be rotated continuously using the **3D Orbit** tool. (T/F)

9. The **ELEV** command is a transparent command. (T/F)

10. You can directly write a text with thickness. (T/F)

Exercises 3 and 4

In these exercises, you will create the models shown in Figures 2-75 and 2-76. Assume the missing dimensions.

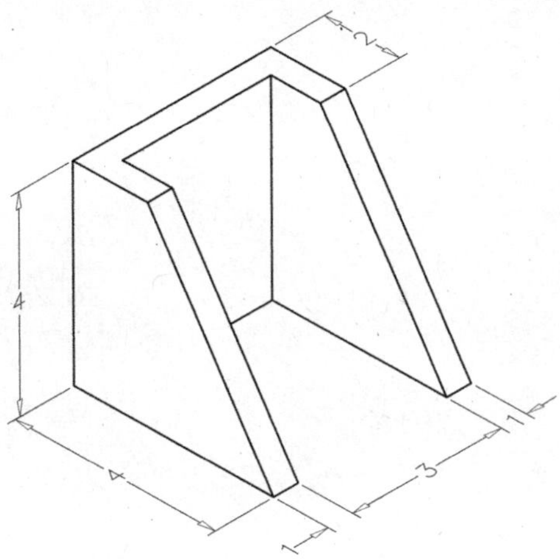

Figure 2-75 *Model for Exercise 3*

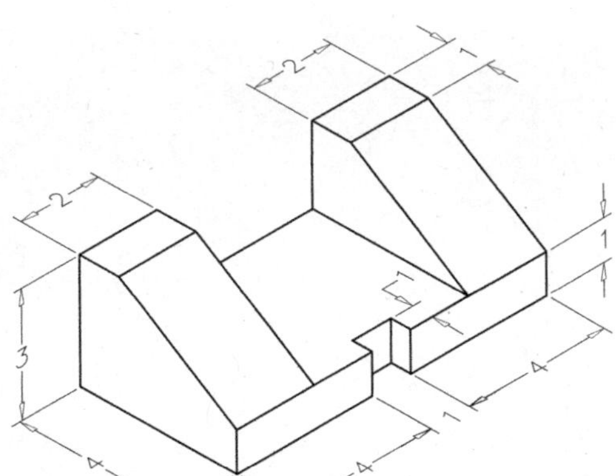

Figure 2-76 *Model for Exercise 4*

Answers to Self-Evaluation Test

1. **VPOINT, -VPOINT**, **2**. the angle in the *XY* plane from the *X* axis, angle from the *XY* plane, **3**. absolute, relative coordinate systems **4**. **3DCLIP**, **5**. T, **6**. F, **7**. T, **8**. T, **9**. T, **10**. F

Chapter 3

Creating Solid Models

Learning Objectives

After completing this chapter, you will be able to:

- *Create standard solid primitives and polysolids*
- *Create regions*
- *Use Boolean operations*
- *Modify the visual styles of solids*
- *Define new UCS using the Dynamic UCS, DDUCS, ViewCube, and Ribbon*
- *Use the Extrude and Revolve tools to create solid models*
- *Create complex solid models using the Sweep and Loft tools*
- *Use the Presspull tool*

Key Terms

- ***Solid Primitives***
- ***Box***
- ***Cone***
- ***Cylinder***
- ***Sphere***
- ***Torus***
- ***Wedge***
- ***Pyramid***
- ***Polysolid***
- ***Helix***
- ***Visual Styles***
- ***Region***
- ***Union***
- ***Intersect***
- ***INTERFERE***
- ***3D Snap***
- ***Dynamic UCS***
- ***Extrude***
- ***Mode***
- ***Revolve***
- ***Sweep***
- ***Loft***
- ***Solid***
- ***Surface***
- ***Presspull***

WHAT IS SOLID MODELING?

Solid modeling is the process of building objects that have all the attributes of an actual solid object. For example, if you draw a wireframe or a surface model of a bushing, it is sufficient to define the shape and size of the object. However, in engineering, the shape and size alone are not enough to describe an object. For engineering analysis, you need more information such as volume, mass, moment of inertia, and material properties (density, Young's modulus, Poisson's ratio, thermal conductivity, and so on). When you know these physical attributes of an object, it can be subjected to various tests to make sure that it performs as required by the product specifications. It eliminates the need for building expensive prototypes and makes the product development cycle shorter. Solid models also make it easy to visualize the objects because you always think of and see the objects as solids. With computers getting faster and software getting more sophisticated and affordable, solid modeling has become the core of the manufacturing process. AutoCAD solid modeling is based on the ACIS solid modeler, which is a part of the core technology.

CREATING PREDEFINED SOLID PRIMITIVES

The Solid primitives form the basic building blocks for a complex solid. ACIS has seven predefined solid primitives that can be used to construct a solid model such as Box, Cylinder, Cone, Sphere, Pyramid, Wedge, and Torus. The number of lines in a solid primitive is controlled by the value assigned to the **ISOLINES** variable. These lines are called tessellation lines. The number of lines determine the number of computations needed to generate a solid. If the value is high, it will take significantly more time to generate a solid on the screen. Therefore, the value assigned to the **ISOLINES** variable should be realistic. When you invoke tools for creating solid primitives, AutoCAD Solids will prompt you to enter information about the part geometry. The height of the primitive is always along the positive *Z* axis and perpendicular to the construction plane. Similar to surface meshes, solids are also displayed as wireframe models unless you hide, render, or shade them. The **FACETRES** system variable controls the smoothness in the shaded and rendered objects and its value can go up to 10. The tools to create solid primitives are grouped in the **Solid Primitives** drop-down in the **Modeling** panel, as shown in Figure 3-1.

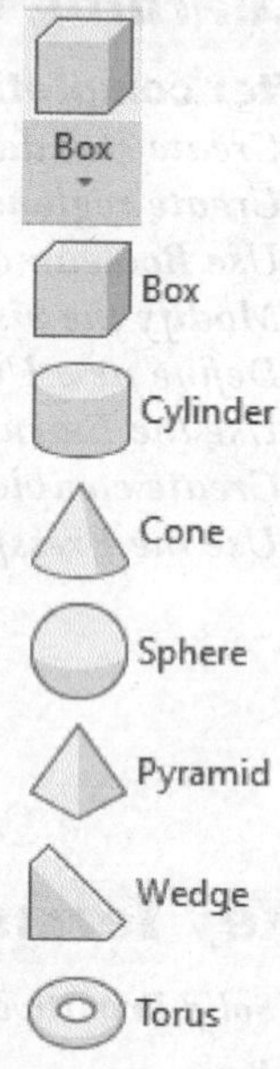

***Figure 3-1** Tools in the **Solid Primitives** drop-down*

Creating a Solid Box

Ribbon: Home > Modeling > Solid Primitives Drop-down > Box
Menu Bar: Draw > Modeling > Box **Toolbar:** Modeling > Box
Command: BOX

The **Box** tool is used to create a solid rectangular box or a cube. Start a new file using the *acad3D.dwt* template. In 3D drawing templates, you can dynamically preview the operations that you perform. The methods to create a solid box are discussed next.

Creating a Box Dynamically

To create a box dynamically, choose the **Box** tool from the **Modeling** panel. Specify the first corner point of the box and then specify the diagonally opposite corner point for defining the base of the box, refer to Figure 3-2. Now, specify the height of the box by moving the cursor away from the base. After getting the desired height, click in the drawing window to create the box or specify the height of the box in the dynamic input box, refer to Figure 3-2.

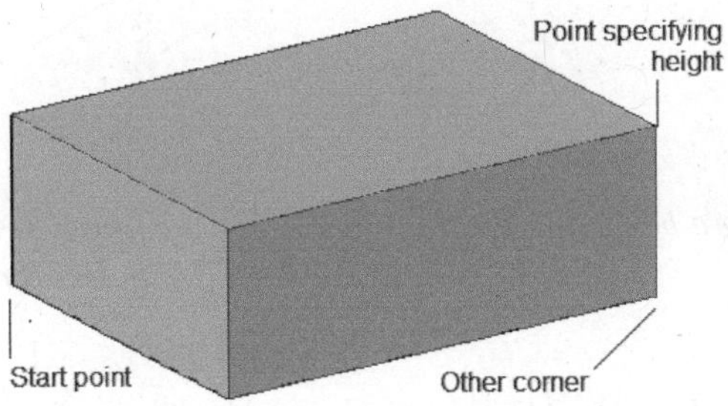

Figure 3-2 Box created dynamically

Two Corner Option

This option is selected by default. You can use this option to create a solid box by defining the first corner of the box and then its other corner, refer to Figure 3-3. Note that the length of the box will always be taken along the *X* axis, the width along the *Y* axis, and the height along the *Z* axis. Therefore, in this case, when you specify the other corner, the value along the *X* axis will be taken as the length of the box, the value along the *Y* axis will be taken as the width of the box, and the value along Z axis will be taken as height of the box. Given below is the prompt sequence to draw a box of length 5 units and height 4 units.

Specify first corner or [Center] : *Specify start point.*
Specify other corner or [Cube/Length]: *Drag the cursor in any one of the quadrants and type* ***5*** *(Planar face of length 5 units is displayed).*
Specify height or [2Point]: *4*

Center-Length Option

The center of the box is the point where the center of gravity of the box lies. This option is used to create a box by specifying the center of the box followed by the length, width, and height of the box, refer to Figure 3-4. The following prompt sequence is displayed when you choose the **Box** tool:

Specify first corner or [Center] : **C**
Specify center : **4,4**
Specify corner or [Cube/Length]: **L**
Specify length: **8** Enter
Specify width: **6** Enter
Specify height or [2point]: **3** Enter

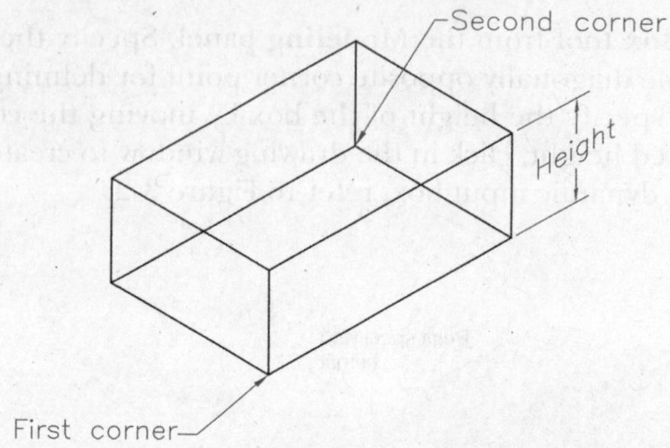

*Figure 3-3 Creating a box using the **Two Corner** option*

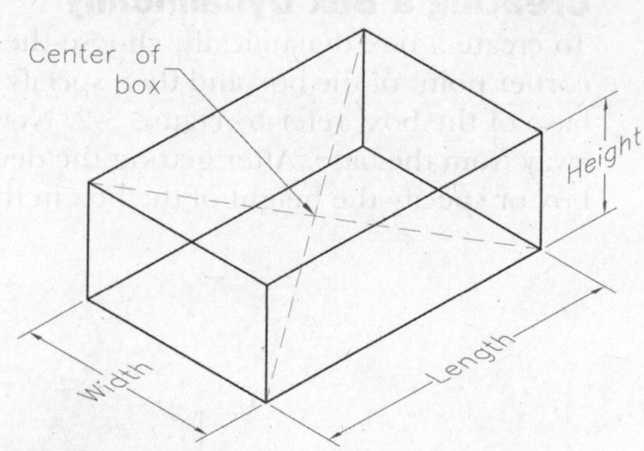

*Figure 3-4 Creating a box using the **Center-Length** option*

Note

1. The Corner-Length option is similar to the Center-Length option with the only difference that in the Corner-Length option, you will define the first corner of the box and then the length, width, and height of the box.

2. In the Two Corner option, you need to specify the height of the box by specifying 2 points using the pointing device.

Corner-Cube Option

This option is used to create a cube starting from a specified corner, as shown in Figure 3-5. As you are creating a cube, you will be prompted to enter the length of the cube that will also act as the width and height. The prompt sequence for creating the cube using the **Corner-Cube** option is given next.

Specify first corner or [Center] : **2,2**
Specify other corner or [Cube/Length]: **C**
Specify length: **5**

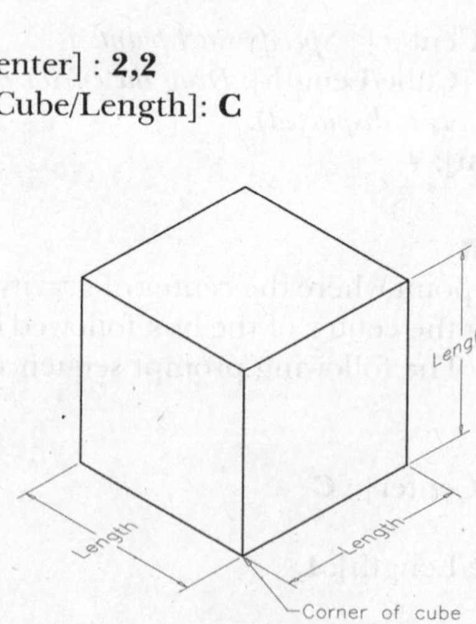

*Figure 3-5 Creating a cube using the **Corner-Cube** option*

Note

*The **Center-Cube** option is similar to the **Corner-Cube** option with the only difference that in the **Center-Cube** option you will have to define the center and the length of the cube.*

Creating a Solid Cone

Ribbon: Home > Modeling > Solid Primitives drop-down > Cone
Menu Bar: Draw > Modeling > Cone **Toolbar:** Modeling > Cone
Command: CONE

The **Cone** tool creates a solid cone with an elliptical or circular base. This tool provides you the option of defining the cone height or the location of the cone apex. Defining the location of the apex will also define the height of the cone and the orientation of the cone base from the *XY* plane.

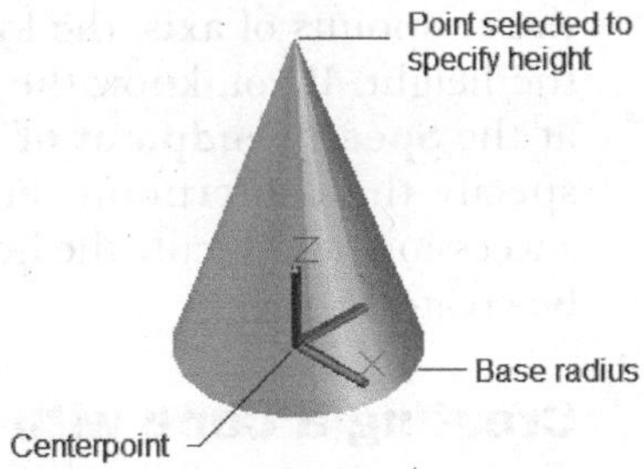

***Figure 3-6** Cone created dynamically*

To create a cone, start a new file using the *acad3D.dwt* template file and choose the **Cone** tool from the **Modeling** panel and specify the center point and the radius of the base, as shown in Figure 3-6. Next, specify the height of the cone by moving the cursor away from the base. After getting the desired height, click in the drawing window to create the cone. You can also enter all parameters defining the cone in the dynamic input box. Figure 3-6 shows a cone created dynamically.

Different methods to create a cone are discussed next.

Creating a Cone with Circular Base

The options for defining the circular base are Center Radius, Center Diameter, 3 Point, 2 Point, and Tangent tangent radius. The prompt sequence that will be displayed when you choose the **Cone** tool is given next.

Specify center point of base or [3P/2P/Ttr/Elliptical]: *Specify the center of the base.*

The default option to define a cone with circular base is Center Radius. In this option, after specifying the center point, enter the radius value and then the height of the cone. If you need to enter the diameter value, then enter **D** at the **Specify base radius or [Diameter]** prompt and specify the diameter value followed by the height. The prompt sequence for using this option is given below.

Specify center point of base or [3P/2P/Ttr/Elliptical]: *Specify the center of the base.*
Specify base radius or [Diameter] <default>: *Specify the radius or enter **D** to specify the diameter of the cone.*
Specify height or [2Point/Axis endpoint/Top radius]<default>: *Specify the height of the cone or enter an option or press the ENTER key to accept the default value.*

If you want to create a cone by specifying two ends of the circular base, then type **2P** at the **Specify center point of base or [3P/2P/Ttr/Elliptical]** prompt and then specify the two ends of the diameter. Similarly, if the base of the cone is tangent to two circles, choose **Ttr** at the **Specify center point of base or [3P/2P/Ttr/Elliptical]** prompt, select the circles in succession, and then specify the radius.

Creating a Cone with Elliptical Base

To create a cone with elliptical base as shown in Figure 3-7, choose the **Elliptical** option at the **Specify center point of base of cone or [3P/2P/Ttr/Elliptical]** prompt. On selecting this option, the **Specify endpoint of first axis or [Center]** prompt will be displayed. Now, you can create the elliptical base by specifying the endpoints of axis, the location of the minor axis, and then the height. If you know the centerpoint of the ellipse, enter **C** at the **Specify endpoint of first axis or [Center]** prompt and specify the centerpoint, endpoint of the other two axes in succession, and finally the height; a cone with elliptical base will be created.

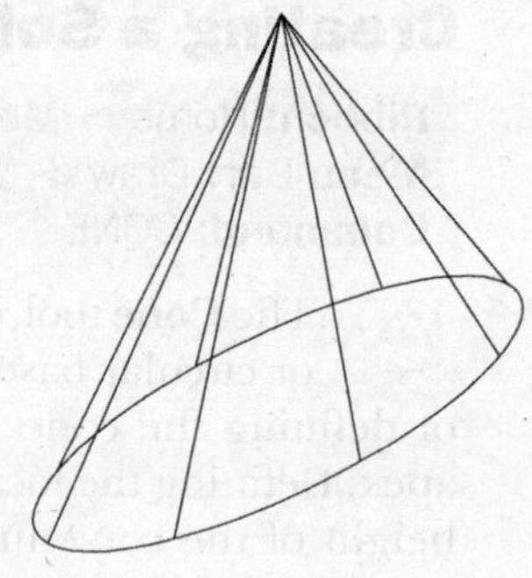

Figure 3-7 *An elliptical cone*

Creating a Cone with Apex

To create a cone with apex, first specify the base of the cone. Then, specify the height of the cone by choosing an option at the **Specify height or [2Point/Axis endpoint/Top radius]** prompt. By default, you will be prompted to specify the height of the cone. Enter the height of the cone or specify a location in the drawing area; the cone will be created.

To specify the height using the **2Point** option, enter **2P** at this prompt and specify two points in the drawing area. The distance between these two specified points will be considered as the height of the cone. The prompt sequence that will follow is given next.

> Specify height or [2Point/Axis endpoint/Top radius] <current>: **2P**
> Specify first point: *Specify the first point.*
> Specify second point: *Specify the second point on the screen.*

To specify the height using the **Axis endpoint** option, choose the **Axis endpoint** option at the **Specify height or [2Point/Axis endpoint/Top radius]** prompt. On selecting this option, you can specify the endpoint of the axis, whose start point is the center of the base. Apart from fixing the height of the cone, this option is also used to specify the orientation of the cone in 3D space. This means you can also create an inclined cone, refer to Figure 3-8. The prompt sequence is as follows:

> Specify axis endpoint: *Specify the location of the apex or axis endpoint of the right circular cone in 3D space.*

Creating the Frustum of a Cone

To create the frustum of a cone, choose the **Top radius** option at the **Specify height or [2Point/Axis endpoint/Top radius]** prompt; you will be prompted to specify the top radius. Specify the radius of the top of the frustum as the top radius; you will be prompted to specify the height. Specify the height as discussed earlier; a frustum of a cone will be created, refer to Figure 3-9. The prompt to create a frustum of a cone is given next.

Specify top radius <default>: *Specify the radius for the top of the cone frustum.*
Specify height or [2Point/Axis endpoint] <default>: *Specify the height of the frustum or choose an option.*

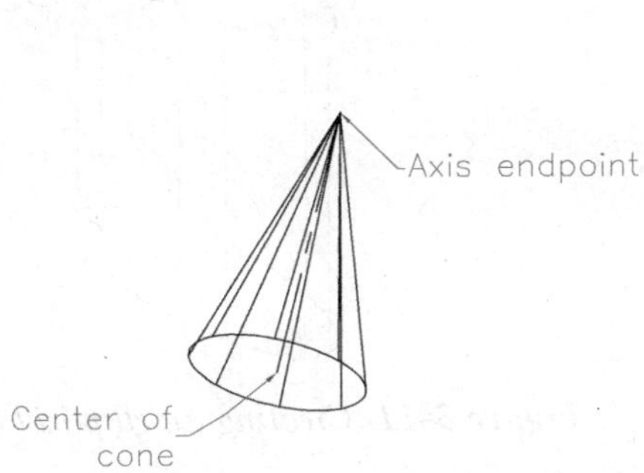

Figure 3-8 *Creating a cone using the **Axis endpoint** option*

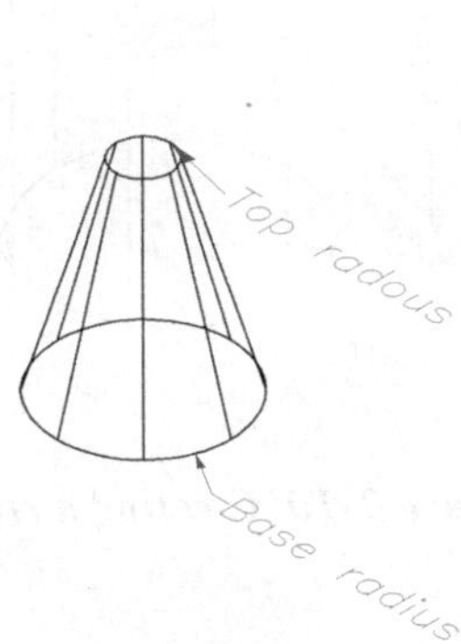

Figure 3-9 *Creating a cone using the **Top radius** option*

> **Tip**
> *In AutoCAD, when you select a primitive shape, grips are displayed on it. You can modify the dimensions of the primitive by dragging these grips.*

Creating a Solid Cylinder

Ribbon: Home > Modeling > Solid Primitives drop-down > Cylinder
Menu Bar: Draw > Modeling > Cylinder **Toolbar:** Modeling > Cylinder
Command: CYL (CYLINDER)

To create a cylinder, start a new drawing using the *acad3D.dwt* template file and choose the **Cylinder** tool from the **Solid Primitives** drop-down of the **Modeling** panel. Next, specify the center point of the base and then specify the radius of the base, as shown in Figure 3-10. Now, specify the height of the cylinder by moving the cursor away from the base. After getting the desired height, click in the drawing window to create the cylinder. You can also enter all parameters in the dynamic input box to define the cylinder.

Similar to the **Cone** tool, this tool provides you two options for creating the cylinder: circular cylinder and elliptical cylinder, refer to Figures 3-10 and 3-11. This tool also allows you to define the height of a cylinder dynamically or specify the height by using the **2Point** or **Axis endpoint** options. On selecting the **Axis endpoint** option, you can specify the endpoint of the axis, whose start point is the center of the base. Apart from fixing the height of the cylinder, this option is also used to specify the orientation of the cylinder in 3D space. This means you can also create an inclined cylinder, as shown in Figures 3-12 and 3-13.

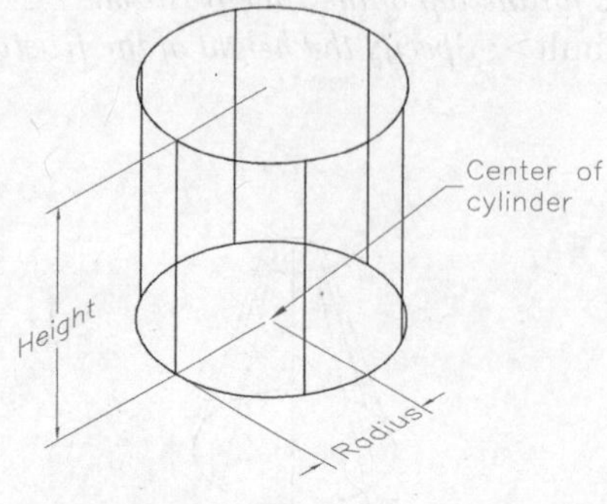

Figure 3-10 *Creating a circular cylinder*

Figure 3-11 *Creating an elliptical cylinder*

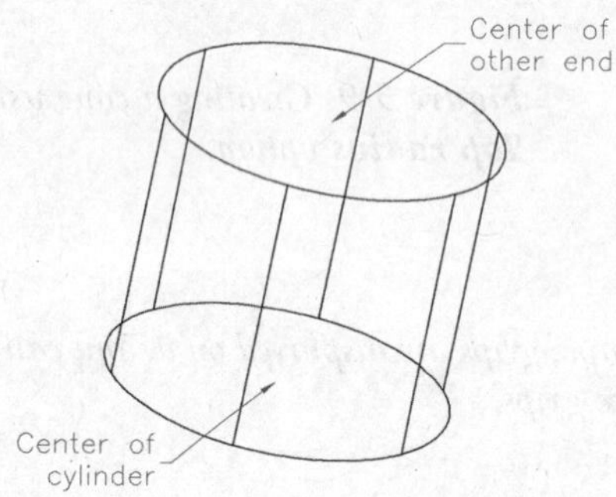

Figure 3-12 *Creating an inclined cylinder with circular base*

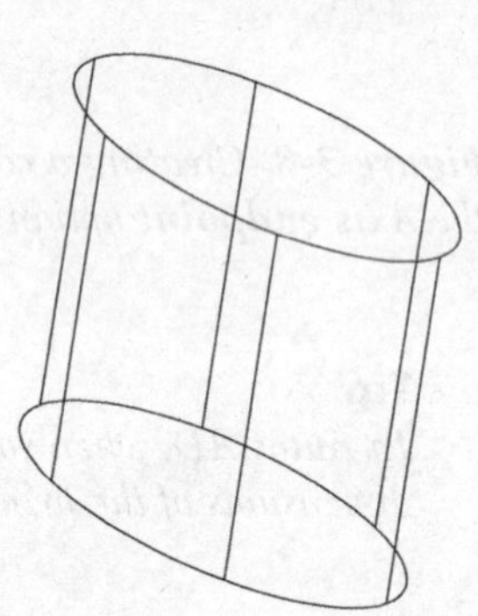

Figure 3-13 *Creating an inclined cylinder with elliptical base*

Creating a Solid Sphere

Ribbon: Home > Modeling > Solid Primitives drop-down > Sphere
Menu Bar: Draw > Modeling > Sphere **Toolbar:** Modeling > Sphere
Command: SPHERE

To create a sphere, choose the **Sphere** tool from the **Modeling** panel; you will be prompted to specify the center of the sphere. After specifying the center, you can create the sphere by defining its radius or diameter, as shown in Figure 3-14. Instead of specifying the center of the sphere, you can specify its circumference by choosing any one of the **3P/2P/Ttr** options as discussed earlier.

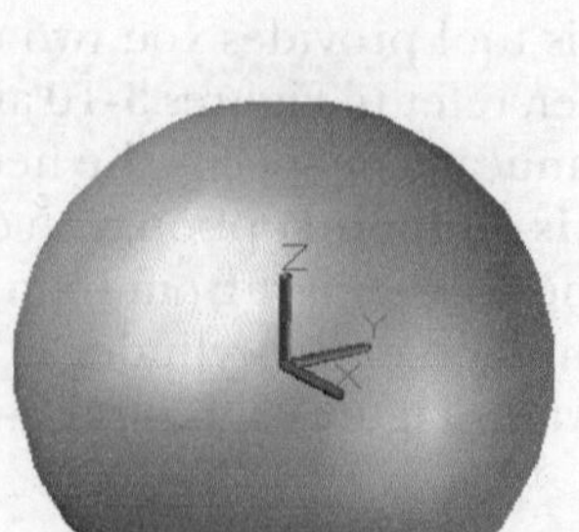

Figure 3-14 *Solid sphere created*

Creating a Solid Torus

Ribbon: Home > Modeling > Solid Primitives drop-down > Torus
Menu Bar: Draw > Modeling > Torus **Toolbar:** Modeling > Torus
Command: TOR (TORUS)

You can use the **Torus** tool to create a torus, refer to Figure 3-15. A torus is centered on the construction plane. The top half of the torus is above the construction plane and the other half is below it. To create a torus, choose the **Torus** tool from the **Modeling** panel; you will be prompted to enter the diameter or the radius of the torus and the diameter or the radius of tube, refer to Figure 3-16. The radius of torus is the distance from the center of the torus to the center-line of the tube. This radius can have a positive or a negative value. If the value is negative, the torus will have a rugby-ball like shape, refer to Figure 3-17. A torus can be self-intersecting. If both the radii of the tube and the torus are positive and the radius of the tube is greater than the radius of the torus, the resulting solid looks like an apple, refer to Figure 3-18. Instead of specifying the radius or diameter of the torus, you can specify the points through which the circumference of the torus will pass by choosing any one of the **3P**, **2P**, and **Ttr** options. These options are discussed earlier.

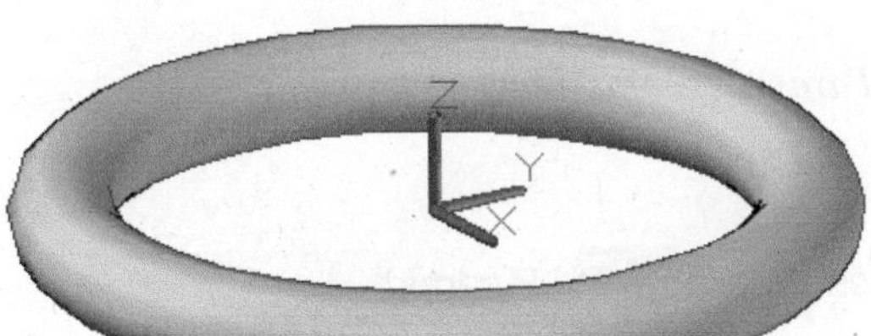

Figure 3-15 *Torus created dynamically*

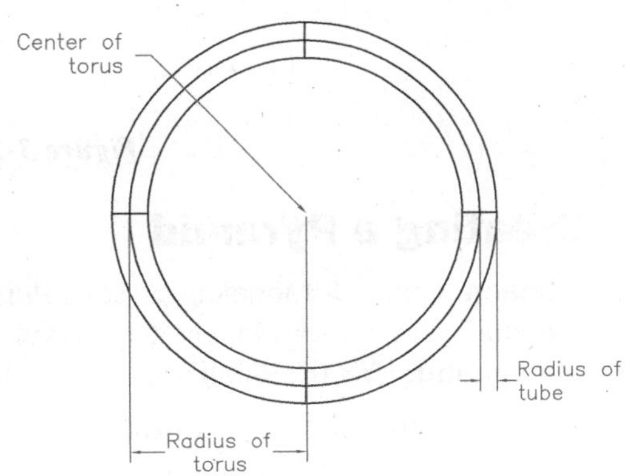

Figure 3-16 *Parameters associated with a torus*

Figure 3-17 *Torus with a negative radius value*

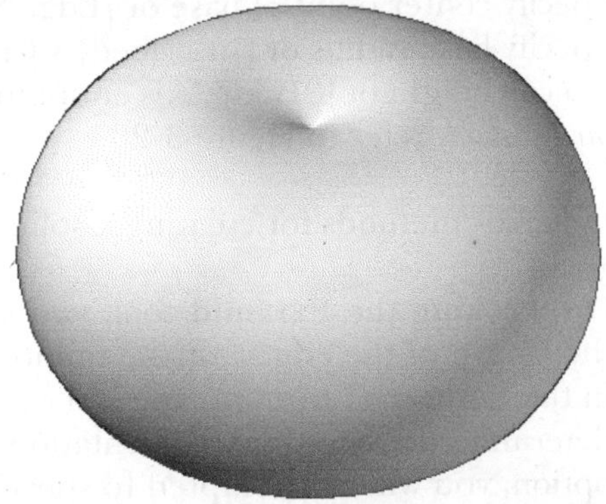

Figure 3-18 *Torus with radius of tube more than the radius of torus*

Creating a Solid Wedge

Ribbon: Home > Modeling > Solid Primitives drop-down > Wedge
Menu Bar: Draw > Modeling > Wedge **Toolbar:** Modeling > Wedge
Command: WEDGE

You can create a solid wedge by using the **Wedge** tool. To create a wedge by using this tool, you need to specify the start point, the diagonally opposite point, and the height of the wedge, refer to Figure 3-19. The other options to create a wedge are similar to those that are used to create a box.

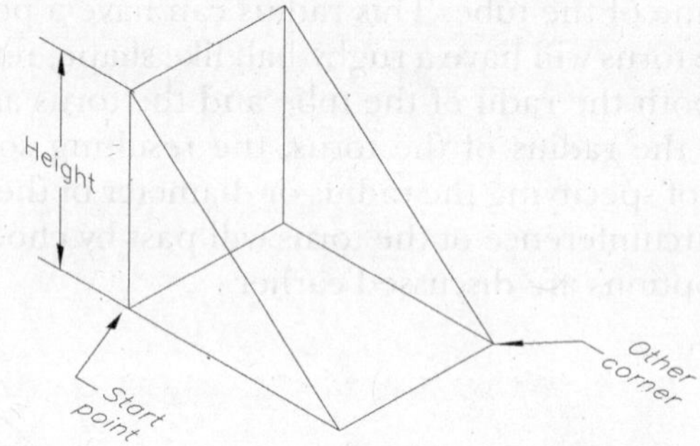

Figure 3-19 *Parameters of a wedge*

Creating a Pyramid

Ribbon: Home > Modeling > Solid Primitives drop-down > Pyramid
Menu Bar: Draw > Modeling > Pyramid **Toolbar:** Modeling > Pyramid
Command: PYR (PYRAMID)

The **Pyramid** tool is used to create a solid pyramid where all faces, other than the base, are triangular and converge at a point called apex, refer to Figure 3-20. The base of a pyramid can be any polygon but generally it is a square. To create a pyramid, choose the **Pyramid** tool from the **Modeling** panel and follow the prompt sequence given next.

Specify center point of base or [Edge/Sides]: *Specify the center point.*
Specify base radius or [Inscribed] <Current Value>: *Specify the base radius.*
Specify height or [2Point/Axis endpoint/Top radius] <Current Value>: *Specify the height to create the pyramid,* refer to Figure 3-20.

Different methods for creating a solid pyramid are discussed next.

On invoking the **Pyramid** tool, you need to specify the center point of the base polygon or the length of the edges, or the number of sides of the polygon. If you select the **Edge** option in the Command prompt, you will be prompted to pick two points from the drawing area that determine the length and orientation of the edge of the base polygon. If you select the **Sides** option, you will be prompted to specify the number of sides of the base polygon. Note that in AutoCAD, the number of sides of a pyramid can vary from 3 to 32.

Next, you need to specify the base radius of the circle in which the base polygon is created. The base polygon is either circumscribed around a circle or inscribed within a circle. By default, the base of the pyramid is circumscribed. After specifying the base radius, you need to specify the height of the pyramid or select an option.

The options to specify the height are same as for cone or cylinder.

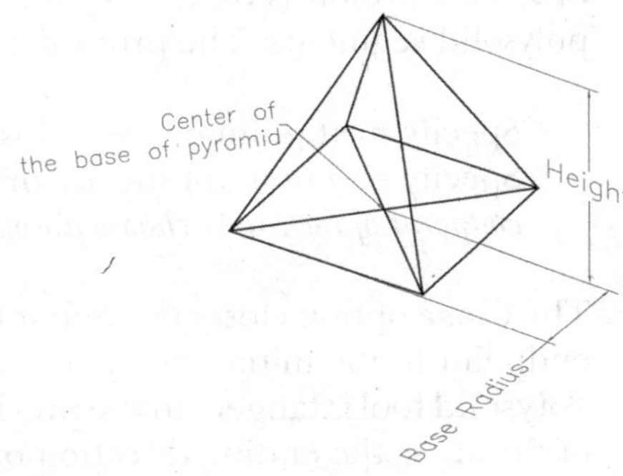

***Figure 3-20** Parameters associated with a pyramid*

You can also create the frustum of a pyramid by selecting the **Top radius** option at the **Specify height or [2Point/Axis endpoint/Top radius]** Command prompt. On selecting this option, you are prompted to specify the radius of the top of the pyramid frustum. Then, you need to specify the height of the frustum either dynamically or by selecting the **2Point** or the **Axis endpoint** option.

Creating a Polysolid

Ribbon: Home > Modeling > Polysolid **Menu Bar:** Draw > Modeling > Polysolid
Command: POLYSOLID or PSOLID

The **Polysolid** tool is similar to the **Polyline** tool with the only difference that this tool is used to create a solid with a rectangular cross-section of a specified width and height. This tool can also be used to convert existing lines, 2D polylines, arcs, and circles into a polysolid feature. To create a polysolid, choose the **Polysolid** tool from the **Modeling** panel and follow the prompt sequence given next.

Height = current, Width = current, Justification = current
Specify start point or [Object/Height/Width/Justify]<Object>: *Specify the start point for the profile of the polysolid. Else, press the ENTER key to select an object to convert it into a polysolid or enter an option.*

The options available at the Command prompt are discussed next.

Next Point of Polysolid

When you specify the start point for the profile of the solid, this option is displayed. This option is used to specify the next point of the current polysolid segment. If additional polysolid segments are added to the first polysolid, AutoCAD automatically makes the endpoint of the previous polysolid, the start point of the next polysolid segment. The prompt sequence is given next.

Specify start point or [Object/Height/Width/Justify] <Object>: *Specify the start point.*
Specify next point or [Arc/Undo]: *Specify the endpoint of the first polysolid segment.*
Specify next point or [Arc/Close/Undo]: *Specify the endpoint of the second polysolid segment or press the ENTER key to exit the tool.*

Arc. This option is used to switch from drawing linear polysolid segments to drawing curved polysolid segments. The prompt sequence that will follow is given next.

Specify next point or [Arc/Close/Undo]: **A** Enter
Specify end point of the arc or [Close/Direction/Line/Second point/Undo]: *Specify the endpoint of the arc or choose an option to create the arc.*

The **Close** option closes the polysolid by creating an arc shaped trajectory from the most recent endpoint to the initial start point and exits the **Polysolid** tool. Usually, the arc drawn with the **Polysolid** tool is tangent to the previous polysolid segment. This means that the starting direction of the arc is the ending direction of the previous segment. The **Direction** option allows you to specify the tangent direction of your choice for the arc segment to be drawn. You can specify the direction by specifying a point. The **Line** option switches the command to the **Line** mode. The **Second point** option selects the second point of the arc in the **3P** arc option. The **Undo** option reverses the changes made in the previously drawn polysolid.

Close. This option is available when at least two segments of the polysolid are drawn. It closes the polysolid segment by creating a linear polysolid from the recent endpoint to the initial point.

Undo. This option is used to erase the most recently drawn polysolid segment. You can use this option repeatedly until you reach the start point of the first polysolid segment.

Object

This option is used to convert an existing 2D object into a polysolid. The 2D objects that can be converted into a polysolid include lines, 2D polylines, arcs, and circles. Figure 3-21 shows a polysolid object created by converting a 2D polyline. Note that the polysolid is displayed in the **Realistic** visual style by default, but for clarity, it has been displayed in the **Wireframe** visual style. The prompt sequence for using this option is given next.

Specify start point or [Object/Height/Width/Justify]<Object>: Enter
Select object: *Select an object to convert it into a polysolid.*

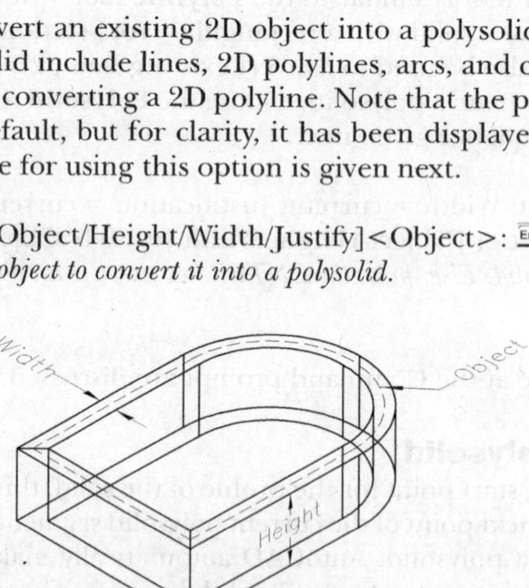

***Figure 3-21** Object converted to a polysolid by using the **Object** option*

Height

This option is used to specify the height of the rectangular cross-section of the polysolid. The value that you specify will be set as the default value for this tool. The prompt sequence for this option is given next.

Specify start point or [Object/Height/Width/Justify]<Object>: **H** Enter
Specify height <current>: *Specify the value of the height or press the ENTER key to accept the current value.*
Specify start point [Object/Height/Width/Justify]<Object>: *Specify the start point of the polysolid or choose an option.*

Width

This option is used to specify the width of the rectangular cross-section of a polysolid. The prompt sequence for this option is given next.

Specify start point [Object/Height/Width/Justify]<Object>: **W** Enter
Specify width <current>: *Specify the width or press the ENTER key to accept the current value.*
Specify start point [Object/Height/Width/Justify]<Object>: *Specify the start point of the polysolid or choose an option.*

Justify

The justification option determines the position of the created polysolid with respect to the starting point. The three justifications that are available for a **Polysolid** tool are **Left**, **Center**, and **Right**.

Left. This justification produces a polysolid with its left extent fixed at the start point and the width added to the right of the start point when the polysolid is viewed from the direction of its creation, refer to Figure 3-22.

Center. This justification produces a polysolid with its center fixed at the start point and the width added equally to both the sides of the start point when you view the polysolid from the direction of its creation, refer to Figure 3-22.

Right. This justification produces a polysolid with its right extent fixed at the start point and the width added to the left of the start point, when you view the polysolid from the direction of its creation, refer to Figure 3-22.

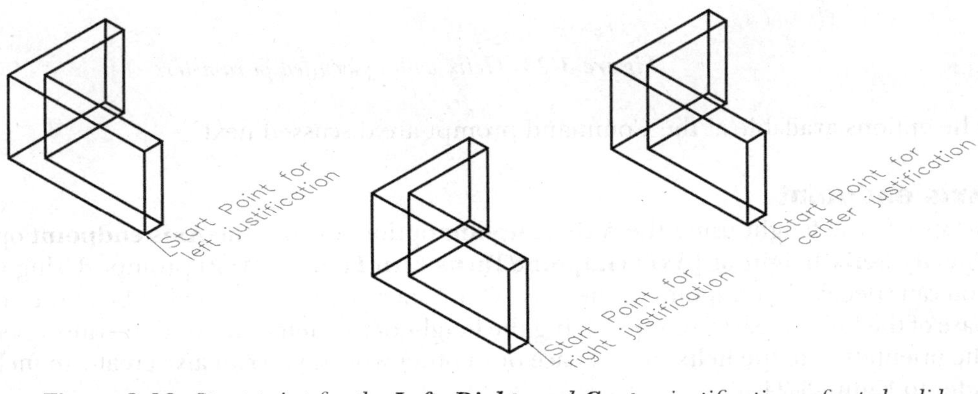

Figure 3-22 *Start point for the* ***Left***, ***Right***, *and* ***Center*** *justifications of a polysolid*

Creating a Helix

Ribbon: Home > Draw > Helix	**Toolbar:** Modeling > Helix
Menu Bar: Draw > Helix	**Command:** HELIX

The **Helix** tool is used to create a 3D helical curve. To generate a helical curve, you need to first specify the center for the base of the helix. Next, you need to specify the base radius, radius at the top of the helix, and height of the helix. A helix of converging or diverging shape can also be generated by specifying different values for the base and top radius. You can also control the number of turns in a helix and specify whether the twist will be in the clockwise direction or counter clockwise direction. Figure 3-23 shows a helix with the parameters to be defined.

The prompt sequence displayed on choosing the **Helix** tool is given next.

Specify center point of base: *Specify a point for the center of the helix base.*
Specify base radius or [Diameter] <default1.0000>: *Specify the value for the base radius, enter **D** to specify the diameter, or press the ENTER key to select the default value for the radius.*
Specify top radius or [Diameter] <current>: *Specify the value for the top radius of the helix, enter **D** to specify the diameter, or press the ENTER key to select the current value of the base radius.*
Specify helix height or [Axis endpoint/Turns/turn Height/tWist] <default>: *Specify the height of the helix and press the ENTER key to select the default value or choose an option.*

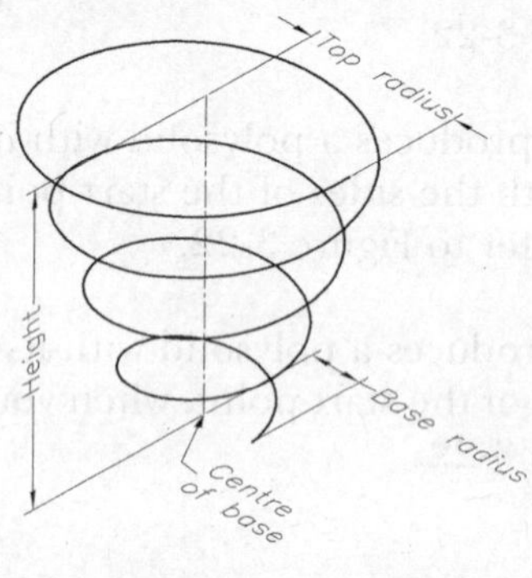

***Figure 3-23** Helix with associated parameters*

The options available at the Command prompt are discussed next.

Axis endpoint

To specify the height using the **Axis endpoint** option, choose the **Axis endpoint** option at the **Specify helix height or [Axis endpoint/Turns/turn Height/tWist]** prompt. Using this option, you can specify the endpoint of the axis, whose start point is assumed to be at the center of the base of the helix. Apart from specifying the height of the helix, this option is also used to specify the orientation of the helix in 3D space or in other words, you can also create an inclined helix, refer to Figure 3-24.

Turns

To specify the number of turns in the helix, choose the **Turns** option at the **Specify helix height or [Axis endpoint/Turns/turn Height/tWist]** prompt. Using this option, you can change the number of turns in the helical curve. The default number of turns for the **Helix** tool is three.

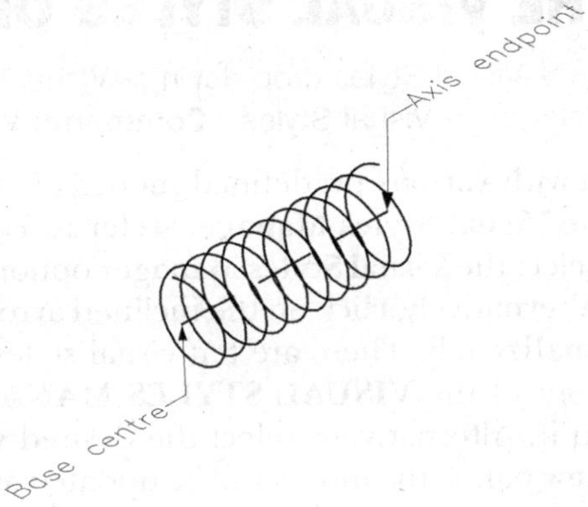

*Figure 3-24 Helix created using the **Axis endpoint** option*

Note

In a helical curve, the number of turns cannot be more than 500.

turn Height

To specify the pitch of the helix, choose the **turn Height** option at the **Specify helix height or [Axis endpoint/Turns/turn Height/tWist]** prompt. Using this option, instead of specifying the whole height of the helix, you can specify the height of one complete single turn of the helix. The helical curve will be generated with the total height equal to the turn height multiplied by the number of turns.

tWist

To specify the starting direction of the helical curve, choose the **tWist** option from the shortcut menu at the **Specify helix height or [Axis endpoint/Turns/turn Height/tWist]** prompt. By using this option, you can specify whether the curves will be generated in the clockwise or the counterclockwise direction. Figure 3-25 shows a helix with counterclockwise turns and Figure 3-26 shows a helix with clockwise turns. The default value for the starting direction of the helical curve is counterclockwise.

*Figure 3-25 Helix created using the **CCW** option*

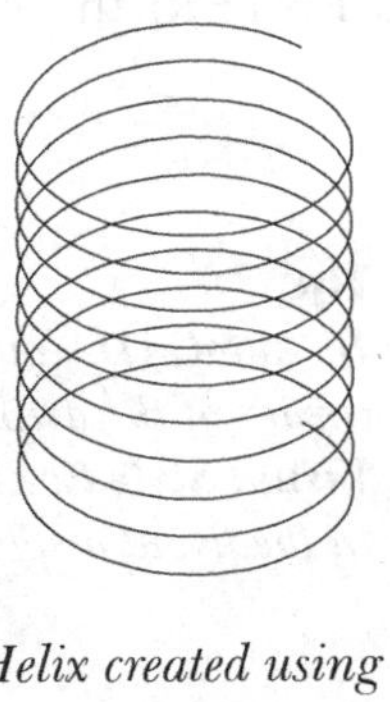

*Figure 3-26 Helix created using the **CW** option*

Tip

*You can use the generated helix as a trajectory for the **Sweep** tool. This tool will be discussed later in this chapter.*

MODIFYING THE VISUAL STYLES OF SOLIDS

Ribbon: Home > View > Visual Styles drop-down > Visual Styles Manager
Menu Bar: Tools > Palettes > Visual Styles **Command:** VISUALSTYLES

AutoCAD provides you with various predefined modes of visual styles. These visual styles are grouped together in the **Visual Styles Manager**, refer to Figure 3-27. To invoke the **VISUAL STYLES MANAGER**, select the **Visual Styles Manager** option from the **Visual Styles** drop-down list in the **View** panel. Alternatively, click on the inclined arrow at the bottom right of the **Visual Styles** panel in the **Visualize** tab. There are ten visual styles available in the **Available Visual Styles in Drawing** rollout of the **VISUAL STYLES MANAGER**. To apply a visual style, you need to double-click on it. Alternatively, select the desired visual style from the **Visual Styles** drop-down list in the **View** panel; the model will be updated automatically to the new visual style.

The properties of the selected visual style will be displayed below the **Available Visual Styles in Drawing** rollout. You can modify these properties depending upon your requirement. You can also create a user-defined visual style based on the current visual style applied to the model. To do so, choose the **Create New Visual Style** button from the tool strip at the bottom of the **Available Visual Styles in Drawing** rollout; the **Create New Visual Style** dialog box will be displayed. Enter a new name and description for the newly created visual style. Next, choose **OK**; a new visual style will be created. Set the properties of the new visual style by modifying the default properties. Alternatively, set the properties of the visual style and then select **Save as a New Visual Style** from the **Visual Styles** drop-down list in the **Visualize** tab; you will be prompted to specify a name to save the current visual style. Enter a name and press ENTER; the new visual style will be saved.

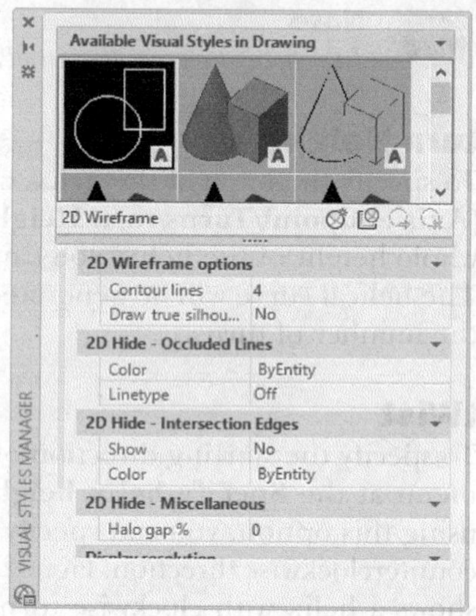

Figure 3-27** The **VISUAL STYLES MANAGER

Tip

*In AutoCAD, you can also use the **In-canvas Viewport controls** displayed on the top left corner of the drawing area for changing the visual style of a solid by simply clicking on the **Visual Style Controls** and selecting **Visual Styles Manager** which is the last option available in the flyout displayed.*

Available Visual Styles in Drawing

The options available in this rollout are discussed next.

2D Wireframe

On applying this visual style, all hidden lines will be displayed along with the visible lines in the model. Sometimes, it becomes difficult to recognize the visible lines and hidden lines if you set this visual style for complex models.

Conceptual

In this visual style, the model will be displayed as shaded and the edges of the visible faces of the model will also be displayed.

Hidden

On applying this visual style, the hidden lines in the model will not be displayed and only the edges of the faces that are visible in the current viewport will be displayed.

Realistic

This visual style is the same as **Conceptual** but with a more realistic appearance. Moreover, if materials are applied to a model, this visual style will display the model along with the materials applied.

Shaded

In this visual style, smooth shading is applied to the faces of a model. In this case, the edges of the visible faces are not visible.

Shaded with edges

In this visual style, smooth shading is applied to the faces of a model and the edges of the visible faces are visible.

Shades of Gray

In this visual style, a single shade (grey) is applied to all faces of a model.

Sketchy

In this visual style, a model appears as if it is hand sketched.

Wireframe

This visual style is used to display a solid model as a wireframe model. You can see through the solid model while the model is being rotated in the 3D orbit view.

X-Ray

This visual style is used to display the model with shading and mild transparency. In this case, the hidden lines will be visible.

2D Wireframe options

The options in this area are discussed next.

Contour Lines

The lines that are displayed on the curved surface of a solid are known as contour lines. The default value for the number of contours to be displayed on each curved surface is 4 and it is controlled by system variable **ISOLINES**. Figure 3-28 shows a cylinder with 4 contour lines and Figure 3-29 shows a cylinder with 8 contour lines.

Draw true silhouettes

This option is used to specify whether or not to display the true silhouette edges of a model when it is hidden by using the **Hide** tool. If you select **Yes** from this drop-down list, the silhouette edges will be displayed when you hide the model, refer to Figure 3-30. However, when you select **No** from this drop-down list, the silhouette edges will not be displayed when you hide the model, refer to Figure 3-31.

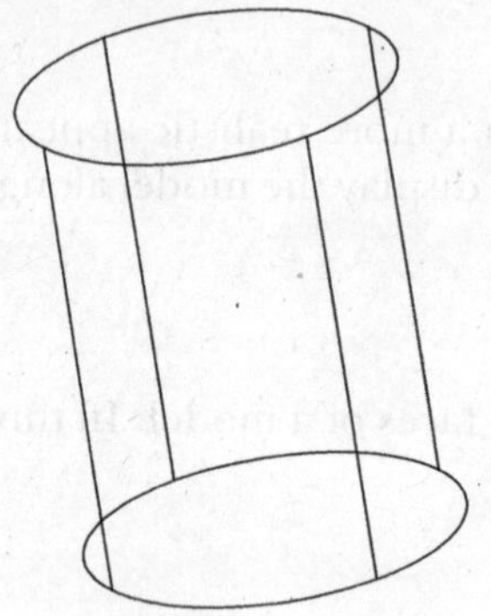

Figure 3-28 *Cylinder with 4 contour lines*

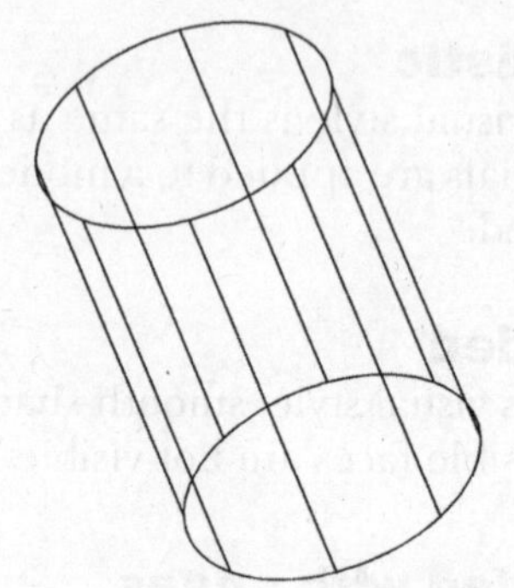

Figure 3-29 *Cylinder with 8 contour lines*

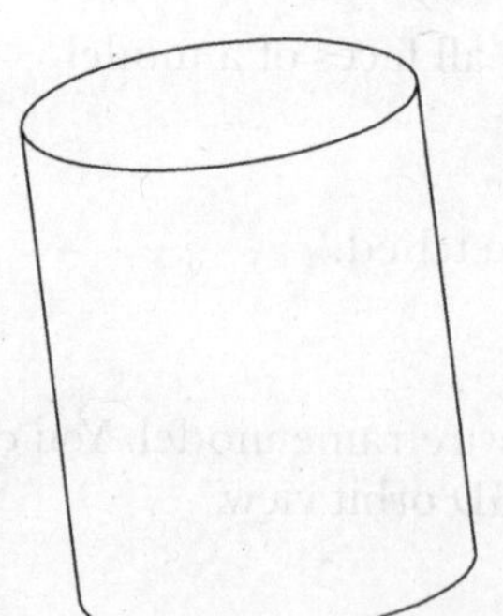

Figure 3-30 *Model with the true silhouette edges on*

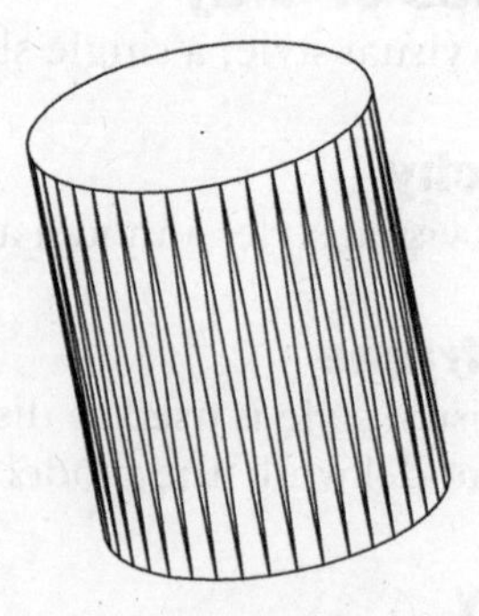

Figure 3-31 *Model with the true silhouette edges off*

2D Hide - Occluded Lines

The options in this area are used to set the linetype and color of the hidden lines (also called occluded lines).

Linetype

This drop-down list is used to set the linetype for the obscured lines. You can select the desired linetype from this drop-down list. The linetype of the hidden lines can also be modified using the **OBSCUREDLTYPE** system variable. The default value of this variable is 0. As a result, the hidden lines are suppressed when you invoke the **Hide** tool. You can set any value between 0 and 11 for this system variable. The following table gives the details of the different values of this system variable and the corresponding linetypes that will be assigned to the hidden lines:

Value	Linetype	Sample
0	Off	None
1	Solid	
2	Dashed	
3	Dotted	
4	Short Dash	
5	Medium Dash	
6	Long Dash	
7	Double Short Dash	
8	Double Medium Dash	
9	Double Long Dash	
10	Medium Long Dash	
11	Sparse Dot	

Figure 3-32 shows a model with a hidden linetype changed to dashed lines and Figure 3-33 shows the same model with hidden lines changed to dotted lines.

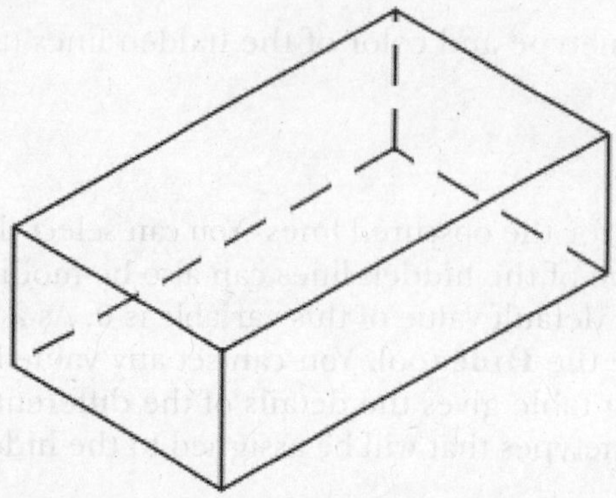

Figure 3-32 Model with hidden lines changed to dashed lines

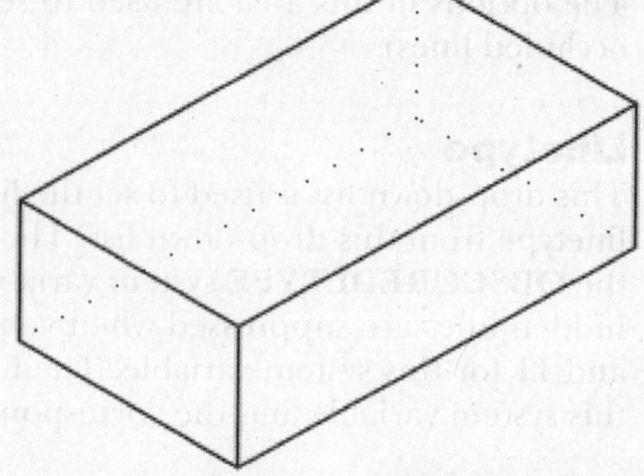

Figure 3-33 Model with hidden lines changed to dotted lines

Color

The **Color** drop-down list is used to define the color for the obscured lines. If you define a separate color, the hidden lines will be displayed with that color, when you invoke the **Hide** tool. You can select the required color from this drop-down list. This can also be done by using the **OBSCUREDCOLOR** system variable. Using this variable, you can define the color to be assigned to the hidden lines. The default value is 257. This value corresponds to the **ByEntity** color. You can enter the number of any color at the sequence that will follow when you enter this system variable. For example, if you set the value of the **OBSCUREDLTYPE** variable to **2**, and that of the **OBSCUREDCOLOR** to **1**, the hidden lines will appear in red dashed lines when you invoke the **Hide** tool.

Note

*The linetype and the color for the hidden lines defined using the previously mentioned variables are valid only when you invoke the **Hide** tool. They do not work if the model is regenerated.*

2D Hide - Intersection Edges

The options in this area are used to display a 3D curve at the intersection of two surfaces. Note that the 3D curve is displayed only after invoking the **Hide** tool. These options are discussed next.

Show

If you select **Yes** from the **Show** drop-down list, a 3D curve will define the intersecting portion of the 3D surfaces or solid models.

Color

The **Color** drop-down list is used to specify the color of the 3D curve that is displayed at the intersection of the 3D surfaces or solid models.

2D Hide - Miscellaneous

This head in the **Visual Styles Manager** is used to set the percentage for halo gap.

Halo gap %

The **Halo gap %** area is used to specify the distance in terms of percentage of unit length by which the edges that are hidden by a surface or solid model will be shortened, refer to Figures 3-34 and 3-35.

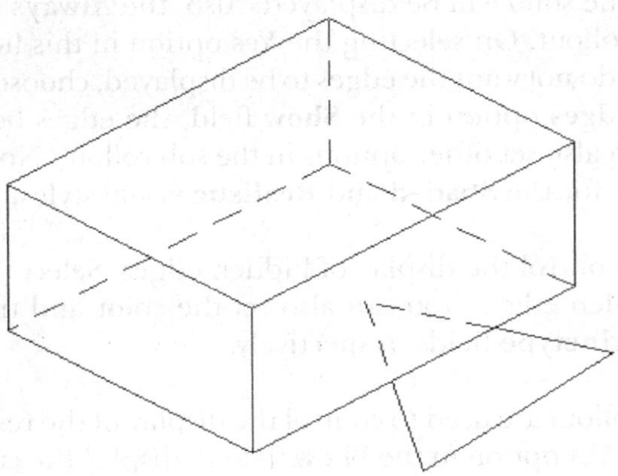

Figure 3-34 Hiding lines with halo gap % as ***0***

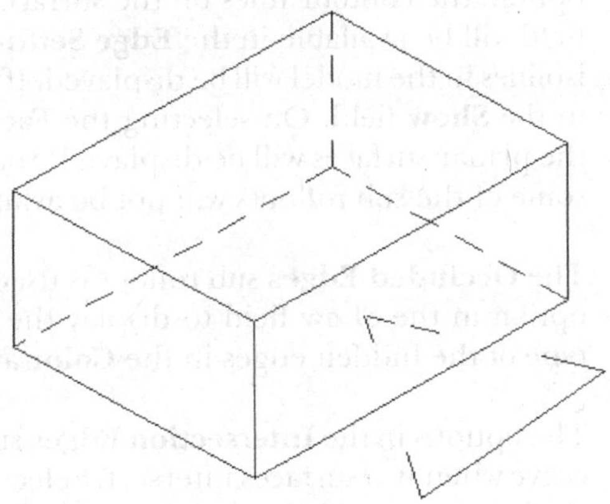

Figure 3-35 Hiding lines with halo gap % as ***40***

Note

The obscured linetype in Figures 3-34 and 3-35 has been changed to dashed.

Display resolution

The options in this area are used to set the resolutions for the curves, splines, and solids. These options are discussed next.

Arc/Circle Smoothing

This option is used to vary the smoothness of the curved surfaces of a 3D model. By default the value for smoothing of the curves or circles is 1000. You can change the value as per your requirement and this smoothness is controlled by the system variable **VIEWRES**.

Spline Segments

This option is used to set the number of segments in a polyline that can be fitted in the spline curve. By default, the number of segments that are displayed in a spline are 8. You can also set the number of segments by using the **SPLINESEGS** variable.

Solid Smoothness

The **Solid Smoothness** area is used to specify the smoothness of the surfaces of the 3D model. By default 0.5 is specified as the smoothness value for the surfaces and you can change this value from **0.1** to **10**. This solid smoothness can also be controlled by system variable **FACETRES**.

Similarly, you can specify the settings for faces, edges, and environment required for other visual styles. These settings are discussed next.

Controlling the Settings of Edges

You can control display settings of the edges by using the **Edge Settings** rollout in the **Available Visual Styles in Drawing** palette. Figure 3-36 shows different types of edge display. The **Show** field in this rollout has three options: **None**, **Isolines**, and **Facet Edges**. On selecting the **Isolines** option, the contour lines on the surface of the solid will be displayed. Also, the **Always on top** field will be available in the **Edge Settings** rollout. On selecting the **Yes** option in this field, all isolines in the model will be displayed. If you do not want the edges to be displayed, choose **None** in the **Show** field. On selecting the **Facet Edges** option in the **Show** field, the edges between the planar surfaces will be displayed. You can also set other options in the sub rollout. Note that some of the sub rollouts will not be available for the **Shaded** and **Realistic** visual styles.

The **Occluded Edges** sub rollout is used to control the display of hidden edges. Select the **Yes** option in the **Show** field to display the hidden edges. You can also set the color and the line type of the hidden edges in the **Color** and **Linetype** fields, respectively.

The options in the **Intersection Edges** sub rollout are used to control the display of the resulting curve when two surfaces intersect. Select the **Yes** option in the **Show** field to display the curve at the intersection. You can also set the color and the line type of the resulting curve in the **Color** and **Linetype** fields, respectively.

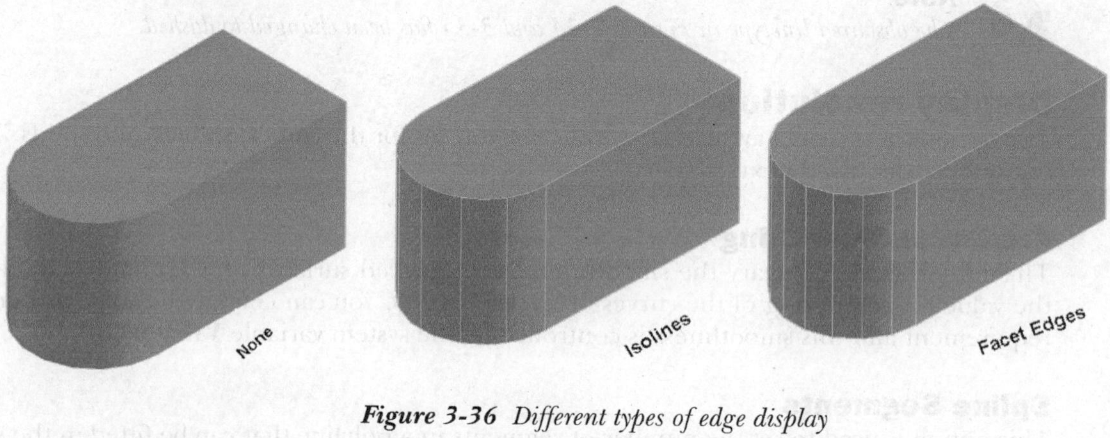

Figure 3-36 *Different types of edge display*

The **Silhouette Edges** sub rollout is used to control the display of the silhouette edges. Select the **Yes** option in the **Show** field to display the silhouette edges. You can set the width of the silhouette edges in the **Width** field. This value ranges from 1 to 25.

The **Edge Modifiers** sub rollout is used to assign special effects such as **Line Extensions** and **Jitter** to edges. Both the effects exhibit a hand-drawn effect with the only difference that the sketches drawn in **Line Extensions** extend beyond the model, whereas in **Jitter**, the edges look as if they were drawn using pencil and has multiple lines. Note that you need to choose the **Line Extension edges** and **Jitter edges** buttons from the title bar of the sub rollout to enable these options. You can set the value for the extension line from the vertices by using the **Line Extensions** spinner. Similarly, you can control the effect of jitter by using the options in the **Jitter** drop-down list. Figure 3-37 shows the effect of line extensions and jitter edges. The **Crease angle** field will be displayed only if you choose the **Facets Edges** option in the **Edge Settings** rollout.

Note that the Facets edges will be displayed only if the angle between the facets is smaller than the specified crease angle.

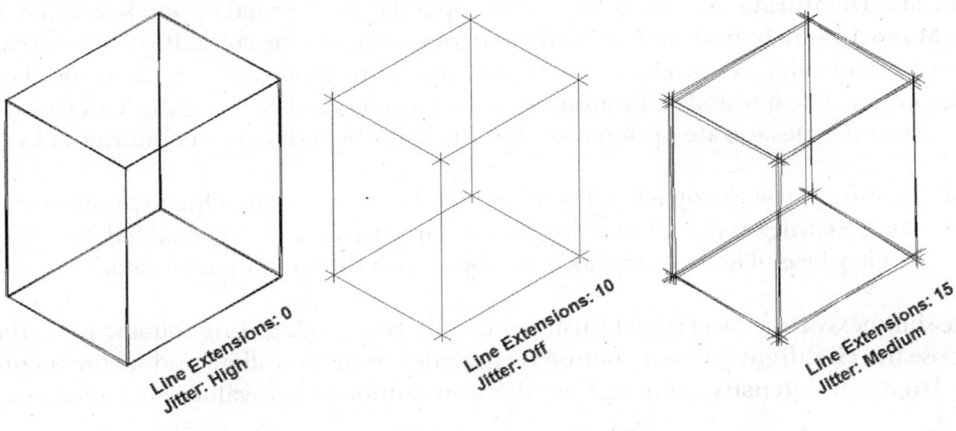

*Figure 3-37 The **Line Extensions** and **Jitter** effects of the edges*

Controlling the Face Display

AutoCAD enables you to control the display of faces by providing options to apply color effects and shading to solids or surfaces. The shading of models can be controlled by using the **Face style** field. The options in this field are **Realistic**, **Gooch**, and **None**, refer to Figure 3-38. By default, the **Realistic** option is chosen and therefore gives a real world effect to the model. The **Gooch** effect enhances the display by using light colors, instead of dark colors. If the **None** option is chosen, then no style will be applied to the model and only the edges will be displayed.

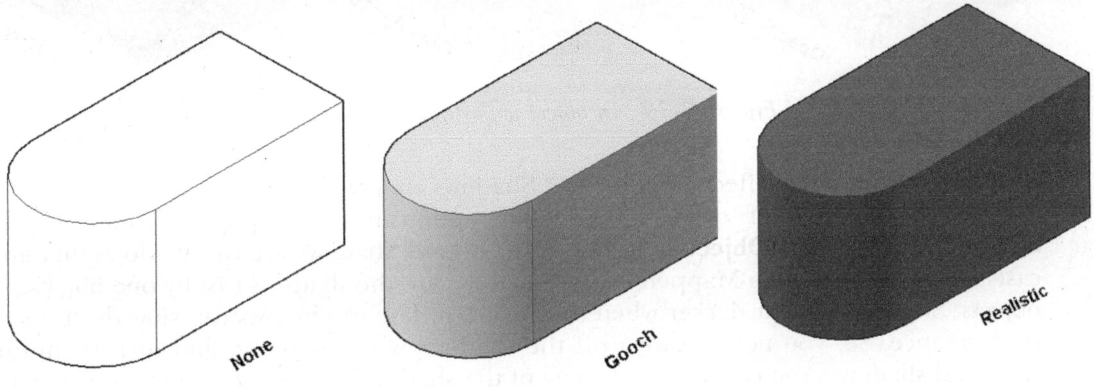

Figure 3-38 Different face styles

You can also control the appearance of faces in solids or surfaces using the **Lighting quality** field. The options available in this field are **Faceted**, **Smooth**, and **Smoothest**. On selecting the **Faceted** option, the color is applied to each face, thereby making the object to appear flat. On selecting the **Smooth** option, the color applied is the gradient between the two vertices of the face. This option is selected by default. On selecting the **Smoothest** option, the color is calculated for per pixel lighting.

You can apply different color settings to faces by selecting an option from the **Color** drop-down list in the **Face Settings** rollout. The options in this drop-down list are **Normal**, **Monochrome**, **Tint**, and **Desaturate**. No face color will be applied if the **Normal** option is selected. If you select the **Monochrome** option, all faces will be shaded with a single color. If you want to use the same color to shade all faces by changing the hue and saturation values of the color, then select the **Tint** option. The hue and saturation values can be changed by using the **Tint Color** drop-down list. Select the **Desaturate** option to soften the color by reducing the saturation by 30%.

You can also control the opacity of solid models by choosing the **Opacity** button in the title bar of the **Face Settings** rollout. On doing so, the **Opacity** field will be enabled. Specify the desired transparency level. Figure 3-39 shows an object with different opacity values.

The shininess of an object is set by using the options in the **Lighting** rollout. To set the shininess, choose the **Highlight intensity** button on the title bar of this rollout and set the required value in the **Highlight intensity** spinner. Note that you cannot set this value when a material is applied on it.

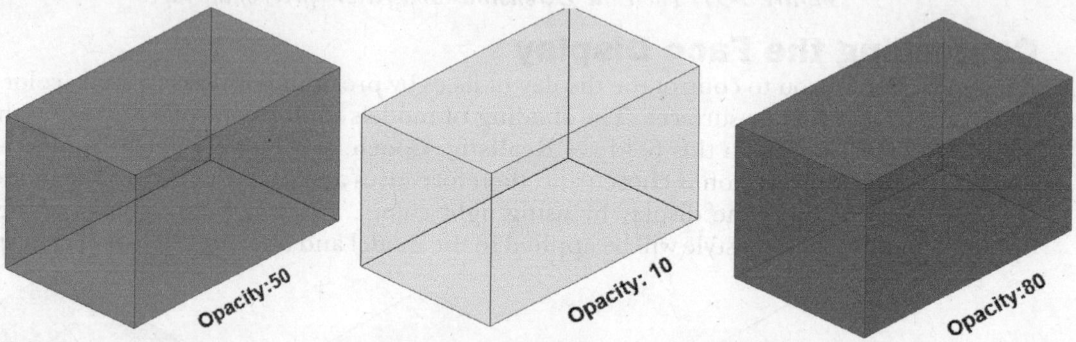

Figure 3-39 An object with different opacity values

Shadows provide a real effect at rendering. Shadows are generated when light is applied. Lights can be user-defined lights or the sunlight. The options in this drop-down list are **Off**, **Ground Shadow**, and **Mapped Object shadows**. The Ground Shadows are the shadows that an object casts on the ground. The Mapped Object shadows are the shadows cast by one object on other objects. Shadows appear darker when they overlap. Use of shadows can slow down the system performance. So, you need to turn off the shadows while working, and turn them on when you need shadows. You can set the display of the shadow by using the **Properties** palette. The shadows will be explained in detail in later chapters.

Controlling the Backgrounds

You can control the display of background by using the option in the **Environment Settings** rollout. You can turn on or off the background by using the **Backgrounds** drop-down list in this rollout. The background can be a single solid color, a gradient fill, an image, or the sun and the sky. This is explained in detail in Chapter 8 (Rendering and Animating Designs).

Note

*In AutoCAD, the default visual style applied to a model is **Realistic**. However, in this textbook, the **Wireframe** visual style is applied to models for clarity of printing.*

CREATING COMPLEX SOLID MODELS

Until now you have learned how to create simple solid models using the standard solid primitives. However, the real-time designs are not just the simple solid primitives but complex solid models. These complex solid models can be created by modifying the standard solid primitives with the boolean operations or directly by creating complex solid models by extruding or revolving the regions. All these options of creating complex solid models are discussed next.

Creating Regions

Ribbon: Home > Draw > Region **Menu Bar:** Draw > Region
Command: REG(REGION)

The **Region** tool is used to create regions from the selected loops or closed entities. Regions are the 2D entities with properties of 3D solids. You can apply the Boolean operation on the regions and you can also calculate their mass properties. Bear in mind that the 2D entity you want to convert into a region should be a closed loop. Once you have created regions, the original object is deleted automatically. However, if the value of the **DELOBJ** system variable is set to **0**, the original object is retained. The valid selection set for creating the regions are closed polylines, lines, arcs, splines, circles, or ellipses. The current color, layer, linetype, and lineweight will be applied to the regions.

CREATING COMPLEX SOLID MODELS BY APPLYING BOOLEAN OPERATIONS

You can create complex solid models by applying the Boolean operations on the standard solid primitives. The Boolean operations that can be performed are union, subtract, intersect, and interfere. The tools used to apply these Boolean operations are discussed next.

Combining Solid Models

Ribbon: Home > Boolean > Solid, Union **Menu Bar:** Modify > Solid Editing > Union
Command: UNI(UNION) **Toolbar:** Modeling / Solid Editing > Union

The **Solid, Union** tool is used to apply the Union Boolean operations on the selected set of solids or regions. You can create a composite solid or region by combining them using this tool. You can combine any number of solids or regions. When you invoke this tool, you will be prompted to select the solids or regions to be added. Figure 3-40 shows two solid models before union and Figure 3-41 shows the composite solid created after union.

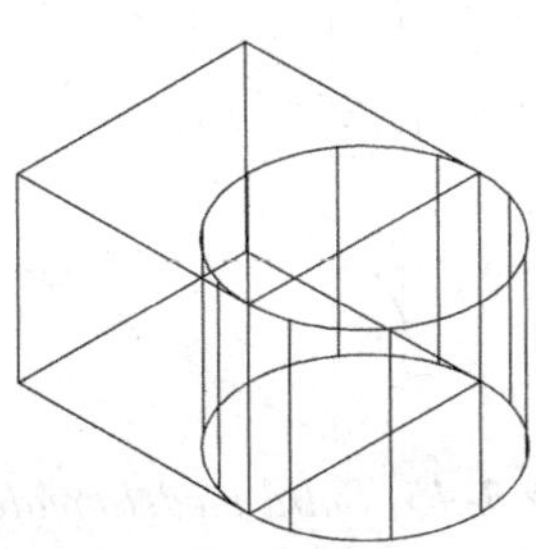

Figure 3-40 Solid models before union

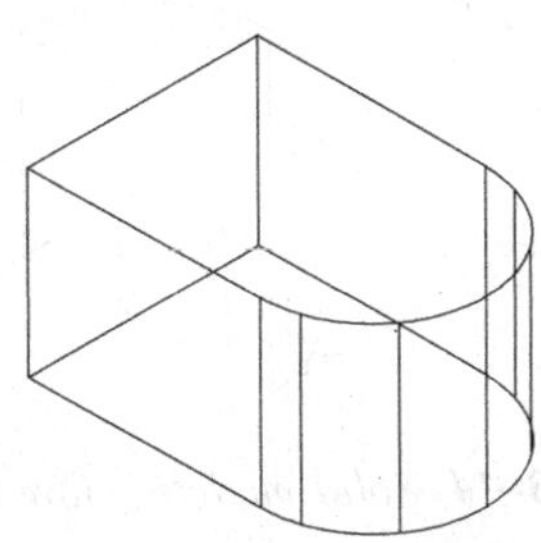

Figure 3-41 Composite solid created after union

Subtracting One Solid From the Other

Ribbon: Home > Boolean > Solid, Subtract
Menu Bar: Modify > Solid Editing > Subtract
Toolbar: Modeling / Solid Editing > Subtract **Command:** SUBTRACT

The **Subtract** tool is used to create a composite solid by removing the material common to the selected set of solids or regions. On invoking this tool, you will be prompted to select the set of solids or regions to subtract from. After selecting it, press ENTER; you will be prompted to select the solids or regions to subtract. After selecting it, press ENTER again.

The material common to the first selection set and the second selection set is removed from the first selection set. The resultant object will be a single composite solid, refer to Figures 3-42 and 3-43.

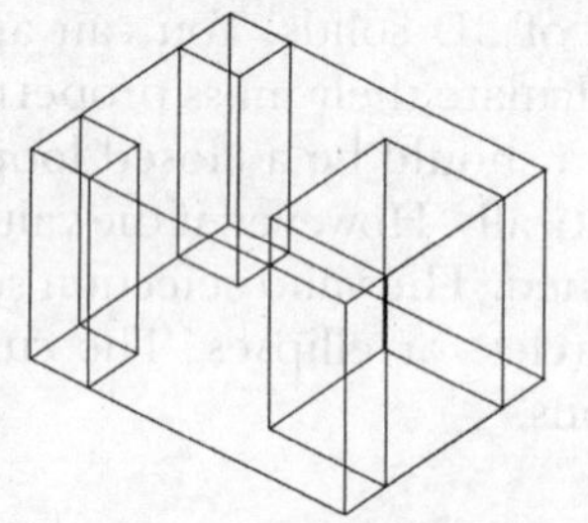

Figure 3-42 Solid models before subtracting

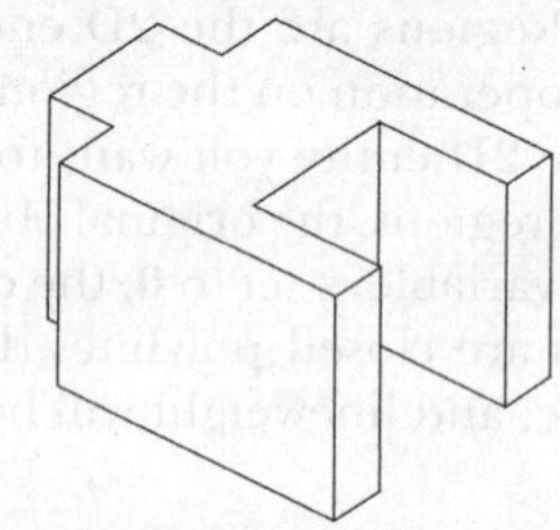

Figure 3-43 Composite solid created after subtracting

Intersecting Solid Models

Ribbon: Home > Boolean > Solid, Intersect
Menu Bar: Modify > Solid Editing > Intersect
Toolbar: Modeling / Solid Editing > Intersect **Command:** INTERSECT

The **Solid, Intersect** tool is used to create a composite solid or region by retaining the material common to the selected set of solids or regions. When you invoke this tool, you will be prompted to select the solids or regions to intersect. The material common to all the selected solids or regions will be retained to create a new composite solid, refer to Figures 3-44 and 3-45.

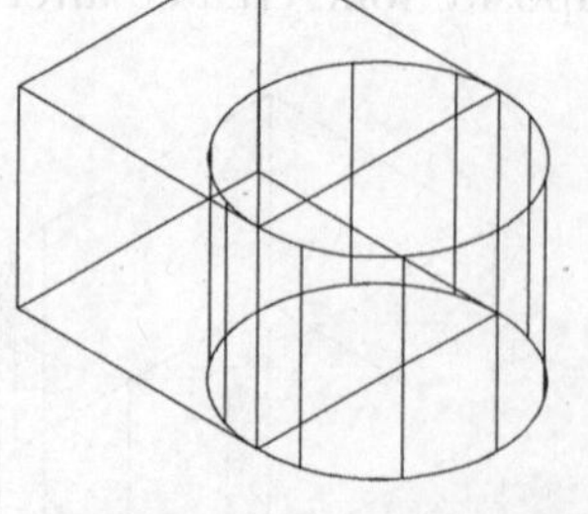

Figure 3-44 Solid models before intersecting

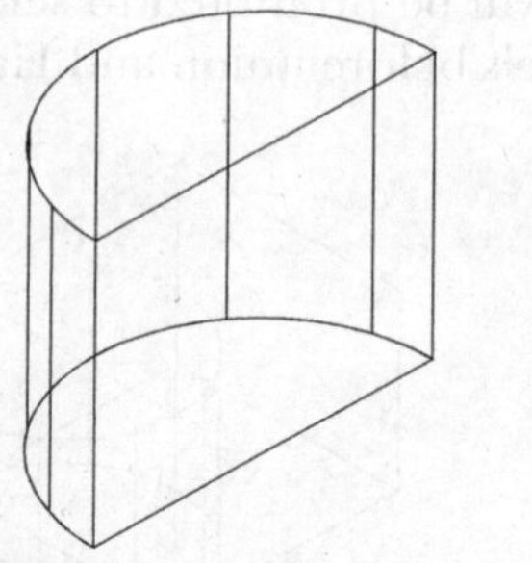

Figure 3-45 Solid model created after intersecting

Checking Interference in Solids

Ribbon: Home > Solid Editing > Interfere
Menu Bar: Modify > 3D Operations > Interference Checking **Command:** INTERFERE

The **Interfere** tool is used to create a composite solid model by retaining the material common to the selected sets of solids. This tool is generally used for analyzing interference between the mating parts of an assembly. On invoking this tool, you will be prompted to select the first set of objects. Once you have selected them, press ENTER; you will be prompted to select the second set of objects. Select the second set of objects and press ENTER; the **Interference Checking** dialog box will be displayed. Also, the interference will be highlighted in the drawing area. The **Interfering objects** area in this dialog box displays the number of objects selected in both the first and second sets and the number of interferences found between them. Choose the **Previous** or the **Next** button in the **Highlight** area to view the previous or next interferences. If the **Zoom to pair** check box is selected in this area, the interference is zoomed while cycling through the interference objects. You can also use the navigation tools in the **Interference Checking** dialog box to view the interfering area clearly. Clear the **Delete interference objects created on Close** check box, if you need to retain the interference objects after closing the dialog box. Close this dialog box by choosing the **Close** button.

If you clear the **Delete interference objects created on Close** check box and then close the **Interference Checking** dialog box, you can move the interfering objects by using the **Move** tool. Figure 3-46 shows two mating components of an assembly with interference between them and Figure 3-47 shows the interference solid created and moved out.

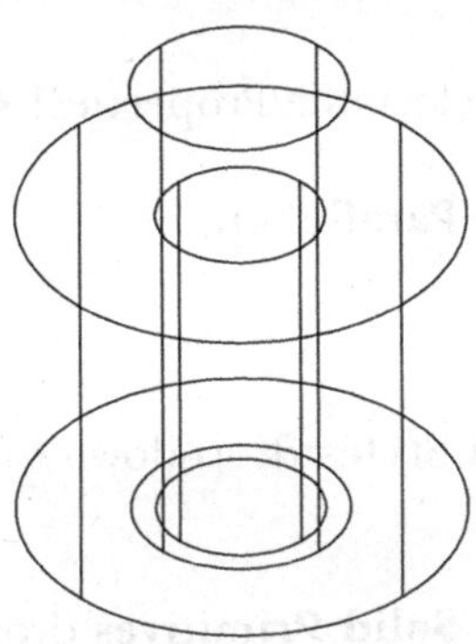

Figure 3-46 Two mating components with interference

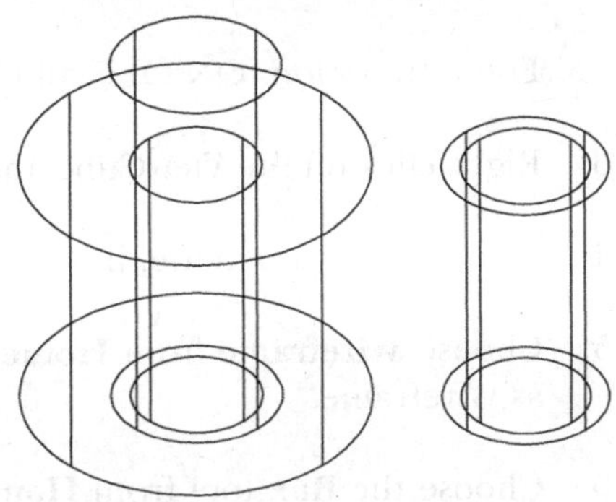

*Figure 3-47 Interference solid created using the **Interfere** tool*

You can also specify the visual style and color for the interfering objects. To do so, invoke the **Interfere** tool, type **S** at the **Select first set of Objects or [Nested selection/Settings]** prompt and press ENTER; the **Interference Settings** dialog box will be displayed. In this dialog box, specify the required parameters.

Example 1

In this example, you will create the solid model shown in Figure 3-48.

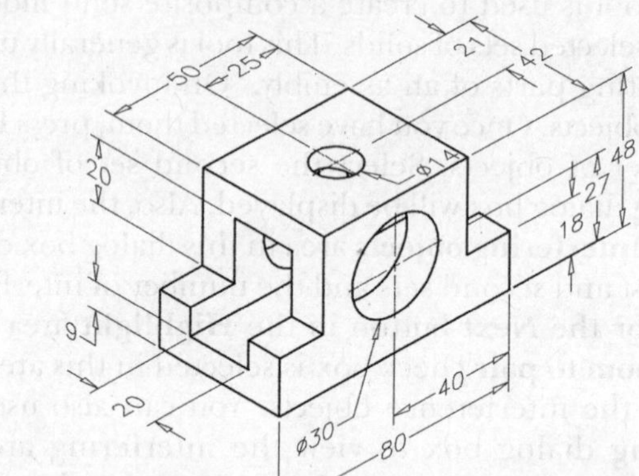

Figure 3-48 Solid model for Example 1

1. Increase the drawing limits to 100,100. Zoom to the limits of the drawing.

2. Enter **UCSICON** at the Command prompt. The following prompt sequence is displayed:

   Enter an option [ON/OFF/All/Noorigin/ORigin/Selectable/Properties] <ON>: **N**

3. Right-click on the ViewCube and then choose the **Parallel** option.

4. Invoke the ortho mode, if it is not turned on.

5. Choose **Wireframe** from **Home > View > Visual Styles** drop-down to set the visual style as Wireframe.

6. Choose the **Box** tool from **Home > Modeling > Solid Primitives** drop-down and follow the prompt sequence given next.

   Specify first corner or [Center] : **10, 10**
   Specify other corner or [Cube/Length]: **L**
   Specify length: *(Move the cursor along Y axis)* **80**
   Specify width: **42**
   Specify height: **48**

7. Again, invoke the **Box** tool and follow the prompt sequence given below.

   Specify first corner or [Center] : **10, 10, 18**
   Specify other corner or [Cube/Length]: **L**

Specify length: *(Move the cursor along X axis)* **42**
Specify width: **15**
Specify height: **30**

8. Right-click on the **3D Object Snap** button in the Status Bar and then choose the **Vertex** option. Clear the other options in this shortcut menu.

9. Turn **on** the **3D Object Snap** by choosing it, if it is not already turned **on**.

10. Move the new box inside the old box by snapping the midpoint on edge of both the boxes.

11. By using the **Copy** tool and the **Vertex** option of the **3D Object Snap**, copy the new box to the other side of the box, refer to Figure 3-49.

12. Choose the **Solid, Subtract** tool from the **Solid Editing** panel and follow the prompt sequence given next.

Select solids, surfaces, and regions to subtract from.
Select objects: *Select the bigger box.*
Select objects: Enter
Select solids, surfaces, and regions to subtract from.
Select objects: *Select one of the smaller boxes.*
Select objects: *Select other smaller boxes.*
Select objects: Enter

13. Change the visual style to **Hidden** from the **In-canvas Visual Style controls**. The model after subtracting the boxes should look similar to the one shown in Figure 3-50.

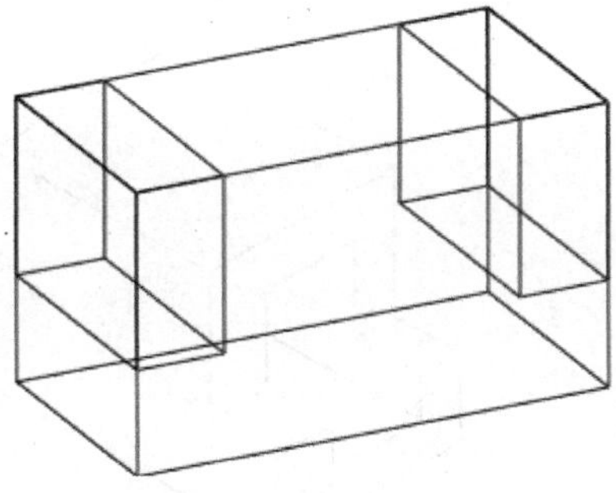

Figure 3-49 *Boxes moved inside the bigger box using midpoints*

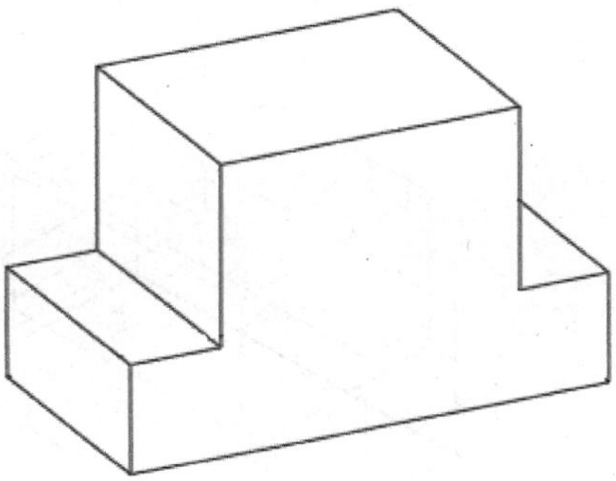

Figure 3-50 *Model after subtracting the smaller boxes*

14. Again, change the visual style to **Wireframe**. Then, choose the **Box** tool and follow the prompt sequence given next.

Specify first corner or [Center] : **21,10,9**
Specify other corner or [Cube/Length]: **L**
Specify length: *(Move the cursor along the X axis)* **20**

Specify width: **80**
Specify height: **29**
The box created is shown in Figure 3-51.

15. Invoke the **Move** tool and select the box created in the previous step.

16. Specify the midpoint of the lower edge as the base point; the **Specify second point or <use first point as displacement>** prompt is displayed.

17. Enter **From** and press ENTER; you are prompted to specify the base point.

18. Specify the midpoint of the lower edge of the solid created by using the **Subtract** tool.

19. Move the cursor vertically upward. Enter **9** at the Command prompt and press ENTER; the box is moved, as shown in Figure 3-51.

20. Choose the **Solid, Subtract** tool from the **Solid Editing** panel and follow the prompt sequence.

Select solids and regions to subtract from.
Select objects: *Select the model.*
Select objects: Enter
Select solids, surfaces, and regions to subtract.
Select objects: *Select the box.*
Select objects: Enter

The model after changing the visual style to Hidden should look similar to the one shown in Figure 3-52.

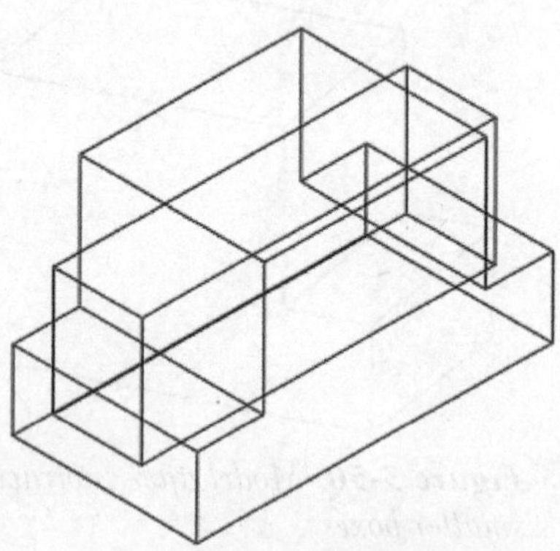

Figure 3-51 *Model before subtraction*

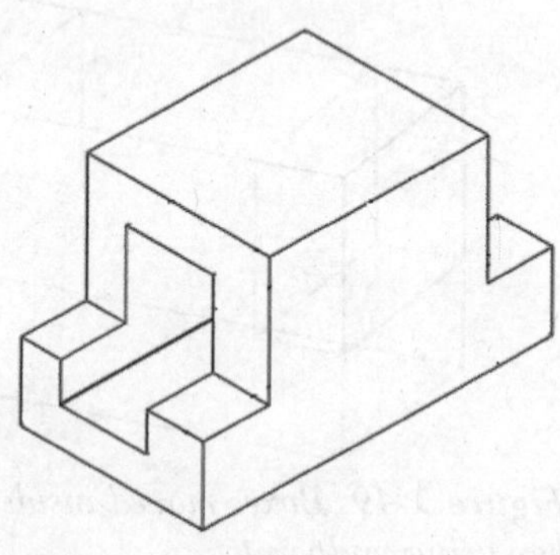

Figure 3-52 *Model after subtraction*

21. Right-click on the **3D Object Snap** button in the Status Bar and choose the **Center of face** option. Clear the other options in this shortcut menu.

22. Choose the **Cylinder** tool from **Home > Modeling > Solid Primitives** drop-down and follow the command sequence given next to create the cylinder, as shown in Figure 3-53.

    Specify center point of base or [3P / 2P / Ttr/ Elliptical]: *Move the cursor on top face of the model and snap the center of the top face.*
    Specify base radius or [Diameter]: **7**
    Specify height or [2Point / Axis endpoint]: *Move the cursor vertically downward and enter **10***

23. Subtract this cylinder from the existing model, refer to Figure 3-54.

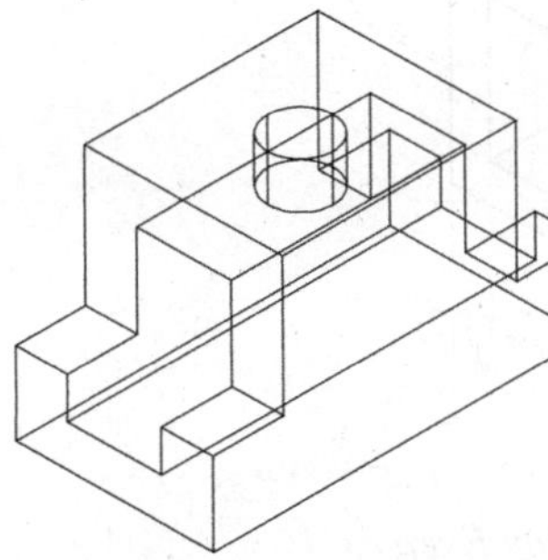

Figure 3-53 *Model before subtraction*

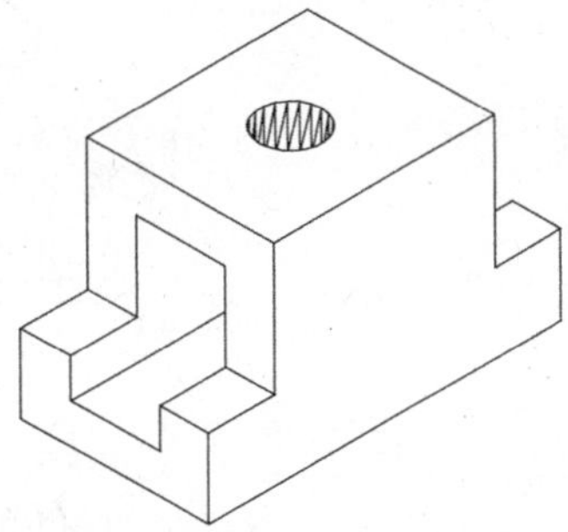

Figure 3-54 *Model after subtraction*

24. Create a new UCS on the left face of the model.

25. Choose **Cylinder** from **Home > Modeling > Solid Primitives** drop-down in the **Ribbon**. The following command sequence will be displayed:

    Specify center point of base or [3P / 2P / Ttr/ Elliptical]: *Use the **From** option to specify the center point of the cylinder at a distance of **27** units from the midpoint of the longer edge of the base.*
    Specify base radius or [Diameter]: **15**
    Specify height or [2Point / Axis endpoint]: **42**

26. Subtract this cylinder from the model and change the visual style to **Shades of Gray**. The final model should look similar to the one shown in Figure 3-55.

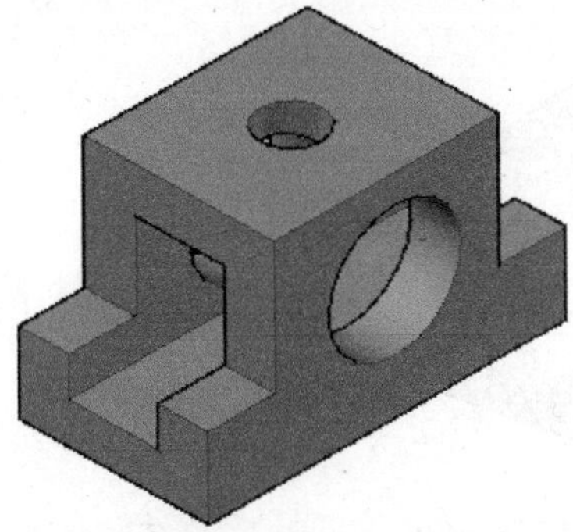

Figure 3-55 *Final solid model for Example 1*

Exercise 1

In this exercise, you will create the solid model shown in Figure 3-56. Save this drawing with the name *C-03_Exercise1.dwg*.

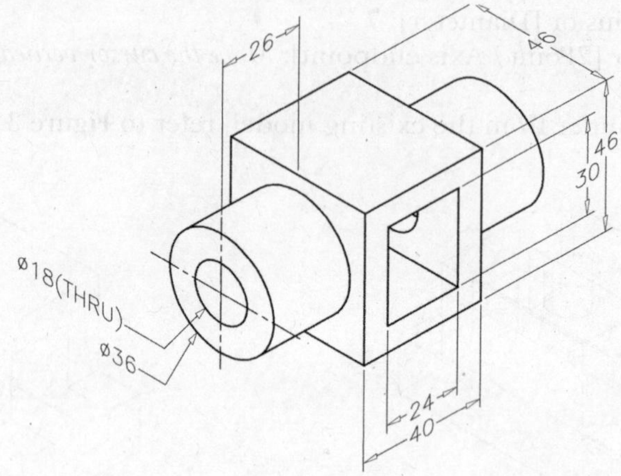

Figure 3-56 *Solid model for Exercise 1*

DYNAMIC UCS

This option is used to temporarily align the XY plane of the current UCS with the selected face of an existing solid. Choose the **Dynamic UCS** toggle button from the Status Bar to turn it on. Now, invoke a tool and move the cursor near the face on which you want to create the new sketch or solid; the face will be highlighted in dashed lines. Click the left mouse button on the desired face; the XY plane of the UCS will automatically be aligned with the selected face. Now, you can create the sketch or solid at the selected face. After the completion of the sketch or feature, the UCS will again move automatically to its original position.

For example, if you want to create a cylinder on the slant face of the model shown in Figure 3-57, choose the **Dynamic UCS** button from the Status Bar to turn it on. Then, choose the **Cylinder** tool from the **Solid Primitives** drop-down in the **Modeling** panel. Next, move the cursor near the slant face of the model; the slant face of the model will be highlighted. Next, left-click on that face and create the cylinder, as shown in Figure 3-58.

Figure 3-57 *Model with UCS at the origin*

Figure 3-58 *UCS dynamically moved on the slant face of the model*

If you want a better visualization of how the X, Y, and Z axes of the UCS will be oriented, right-click in the drawing area and choose **Options** from the shortcut menu; the **Options** dialog box will be displayed. Choose the **3D Modeling** tab from the dialog box and select the **Show labels for dynamic UCS** check box in the **3D Crosshairs** area. This will enable you to see the X, Y and Z labels attached with the axes and they will keep on changing as you move the cursor to different faces.

Note

*The option of **DUCS** works only when any tool is active.*

Tip

*To toggle between the ON and OFF states of the **Dynamic UCS** button, use the F6 function key.*

DEFINING THE NEW UCS USING THE ViewCube AND THE RIBBON

In the earlier chapters, you learned how to create new UCS using the **UCS** tool. You can also define a new UCS whose XY plane is parallel to the current viewing plane by using the ViewCube and the **Ribbon**. To define a new UCS whose XY plane is parallel to the current viewing plane, click on a hotspot in the ViewCube; the view corresponding to the hotspot will become normal to the screen. Next, choose **WCS > New UCS** from the **WCS** flyout in the ViewCube; you will be prompted to specify the origin. Enter **V** at the Command prompt and press ENTER; a new UCS will be created at the current viewing plane. Now, if you draw a sketch, it will be in the new UCS. To save the new UCS, choose the **UCS, Named UCS** tool from the **Coordinates** panel in the **Home** tab; the **UCS** dialog box will be displayed with the **Unnamed** option. Rename it and choose **OK**; the new name of the UCS will be saved and also displayed in the **WCS** flyout of the ViewCube.

To define a new UCS using the **Ribbon**, choose any one of the predefined orthographic views from the 3D Navigation drop-down list in the **View** panel of the **Home** tab; the model will orient to that view. Also, you will notice that the ViewCube is also oriented according to the selected view, but **Top** is displayed as the view and **Unnamed** is displayed at the **WCS** flyout. Now, if you draw a sketch, it will be in the new UCS. However, if there are different faces parallel to the new UCS, you can draw sketches on those faces.

CREATING EXTRUDED SOLIDS

Ribbon: Home > Modeling > Solid Creation drop-down > Extrude
Menu Bar: Draw > Modeling > Extrude **Toolbar:** Modeling > Extrude
Command: EXT (EXTRUDE)

Sometimes, the shape of a solid model is such that it cannot be created by just applying the Boolean operations on the standard solid primitives. In such cases, you can use the tools from the **Solid Creation** drop-down, as shown in Figure 3-59. These tools are also available in the **Solid** panel of the **Solid** tab. Using these tools, you can create solid models of any complex shape.

The **Extrude** tool is used to create a complex solid/surface model by extruding a 2D entity or a region along the *Z* axis or any specified direction or about a specified path. On invoking this tool, following prompt sequence will be displayed.

***Figure 3-59** Tools in the **Solid Creation** drop-down*

Select objects to extrude or [MOde]: _MO Closed profiles creation mode
[SOlid/SUrface] <Solid>: _SO
Select objects to extrude or [MOde]:

In AutoCAD, you can specify mode to extrude an object. There are two modes available: **Solid** and **Surface**. If you need to change the mode, enter **MO** at the **Select objects to extrude or [MOde]** prompt and specify the mode. Note that if the original entity is a closed loop or a region, you can extrude it as a solid/surface model. If the 2D entity is an open loop, then you can extrude it as a surface only. After specifying the mode, select the objects to be extruded and press ENTER; the **Specify height of extrusion or [Direction/Path/Taper angle/Expression]** prompt will be displayed. Specify the depth of extrusion or select other options to specify the depth. Different methods to extrude an object by using the options at the Command prompt are discussed next.

Extruding along the Normal

This is the default option and is used to create a model by extruding a 2D entity or a region along the normal. Figure 3-60 shows the region to be converted into an extruded solid and Figure 3-61 shows the solid created on extruding the region. The prompt sequence that will be displayed when you choose the **Extrude** tool is given next.

Select objects to extrude: *Select the region.*
Select objects to extrude: Enter
Specify height of extrusion or [Direction /Path /Taper angle/Expression]: *Specify the height.*

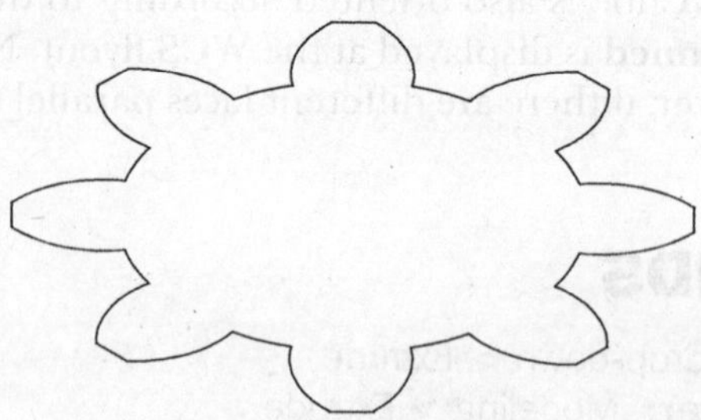

***Figure 3-60** Region for extruding*

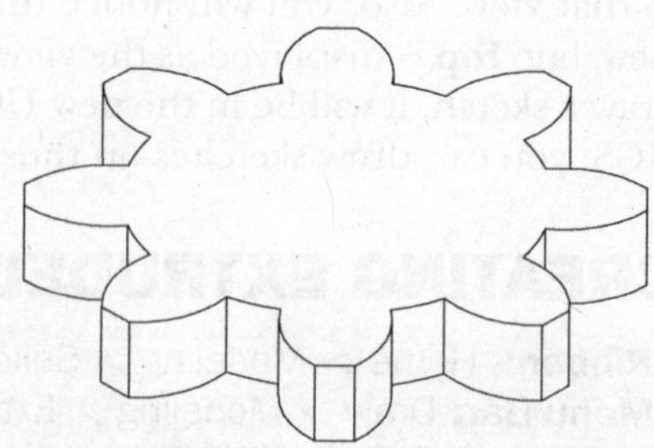

***Figure 3-61** Solid created on extruding*

Extruding with a Taper Angle

You can specify the taper angle for an extruded solid/surface by selecting the **Taper angle** option at the **Specify height of extrusion or [Direction/Path/Taper angle/Expression]** prompt. The positive value of the taper angle will taper in from the base object and the negative value will taper out of the base object, refer to Figure 3-62.

Extruding along a Direction

This option is used to create a solid by extruding a 2D entity or a region in any desired direction by specifying two points. You can create an inclined extruded object by selecting a start point and an endpoint. The distance between the start point and endpoint acts as the height of the extrusion. Figure 3-63 shows an object extruding along a direction.

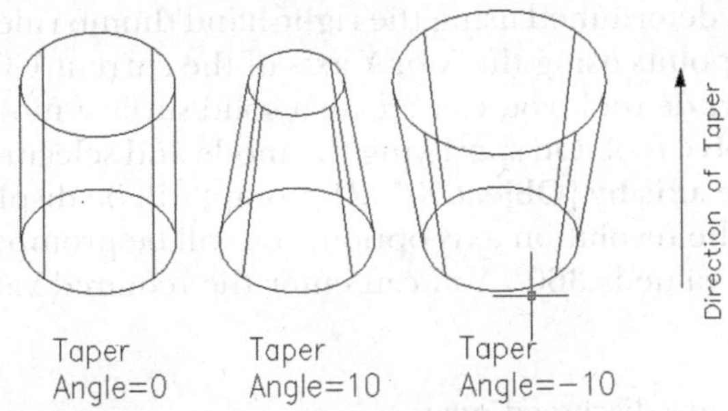

Figure 3-62 Results of various taper angles

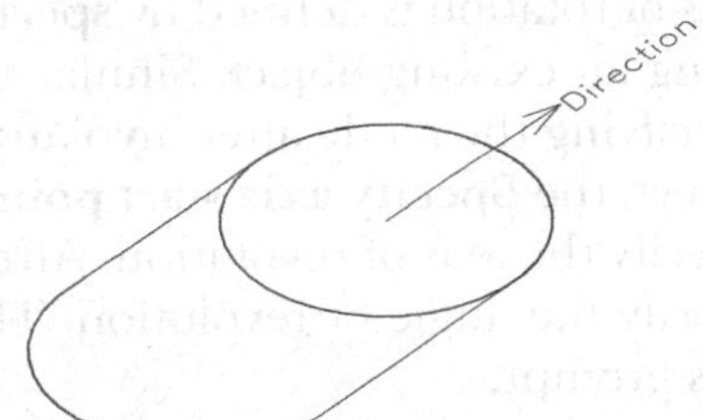

Figure 3-63 Object extruding along a direction

Extruding along a Path

This option is used to extrude a 2D entity or a region about a specified path. Bear in mind that the path of extrusion should be normal to the plane of the base object. If the path consists of more than one entity, all of them should be first joined using the **Edit Polyline** tool so that the path remains a single entity. This option is generally used for creating complex pipelines and also by architects and interior designers for creating beadings. The path used for extrusion can be a closed entity or an open entity and the valid entities that can be used as path are lines, circles, ellipses, polygons, arcs, polylines, or splines. You cannot specify the taper angle when you use a path. Figure 3-64 shows a base object and a path about which the base object has to be extruded and Figure 3-65 shows the solid created upon extruding the base entity about the specified path.

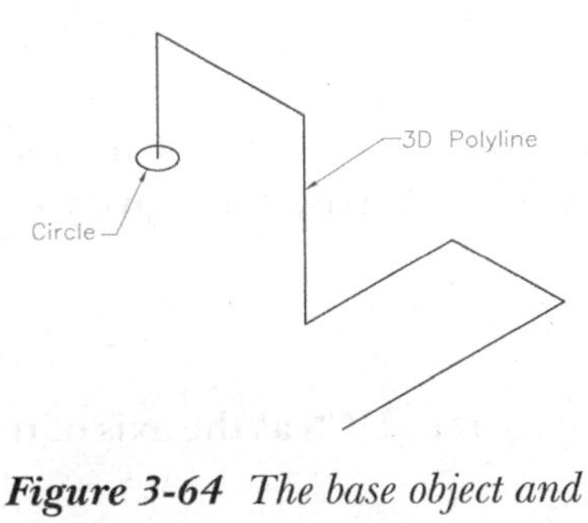

Figure 3-64 The base object and the path for extrusion

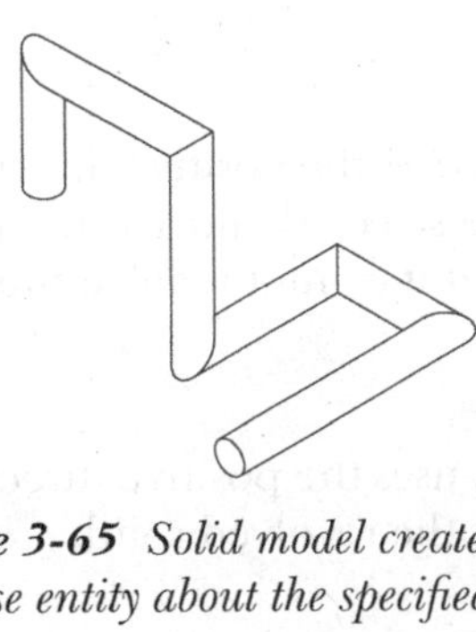

Figure 3-65 Solid model created on extruding the base entity about the specified path

Extruding using Expressions
This option is used to specify the extrusion depth in terms of formula or equations as you have created parametric drawings.

CREATING REVOLVED SOLIDS

Ribbon: Home > Modeling > Solid Creation drop-down > Revolve
Menu Bar: Draw > Modeling > Revolve **Toolbar:** Modeling > Revolve
Command: REV(REVOLVE)

The **Revolve** tool is used to create a complex model by revolving 2D entities or regions about a specified revolution axis. The entire 2D entity should be on one side of the revolution axis. Self-intersecting and crossed entities cannot be revolved using this tool. Remember that the direction of revolution is determined using the right-hand thumb rule. The axis of rotation is defined by specifying two points using the *X* or *Y* axis of the current UCS, or using an existing object. Similar to the **Extrude** tool, you can create a solid/surface model by specifying the mode after invoking the **Revolve** tool. On specifying the mode and selecting the object, the **Specify axis start point or define axis by [Object/X/Y/Z]** prompt will be displayed. Specify the axis of revolution. After setting the revolution axis option, you will be prompted to specify the angle of revolution. The default value is 360°. You can enter the required value at this prompt.

The options that are used to specify the axis are discussed next.

Start Point for the Axis of Revolution
This option is used to define the axis of revolution using two points: the start point and the endpoint of the axis of revolution. The positive direction of the axis will be from the start point to the endpoint and the direction of revolution will be defined using the right-hand thumb rule. Before revolving, make sure the complete 2D entity is on one side of the axis of revolution.

Object
This option is used to create a revolved model by revolving a selected 2D entity or a region about a specified object. The valid entities that can be used as an object for defining the axis of revolution can be a line or a single segment of a polyline. If the polyline selected as the object consists of more than one entity, then AutoCAD draws an imaginary line from the start point of the first segment to the endpoint of the last segment. This imaginary line is then taken as the object for revolution.

X
This option uses the positive direction of the *X* axis of the current UCS for revolving the selected entity. If the selected entity is not completely on one side of the *X* axis, it will give you an error message that it cannot revolve the selected object.

Y
This option uses the positive direction of the *Y* axis of the current UCS as the axis of revolution for creating the revolved solid.

Z

This option uses the positive direction of the *Z* axis of the current UCS as the axis of revolution for creating the revolved solid.

Figure 3-66 shows the entity to be revolved and the revolution axis along with the revolved solid. Figure 3-67 shows the same solid revolved through an angle of 270°.

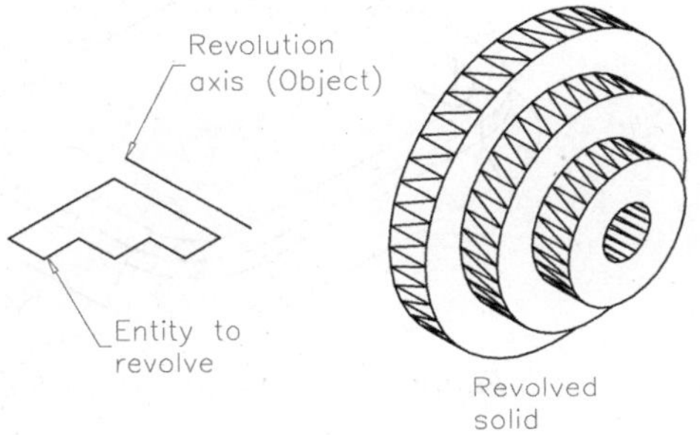

Figure 3-66 Creating a revolved solid

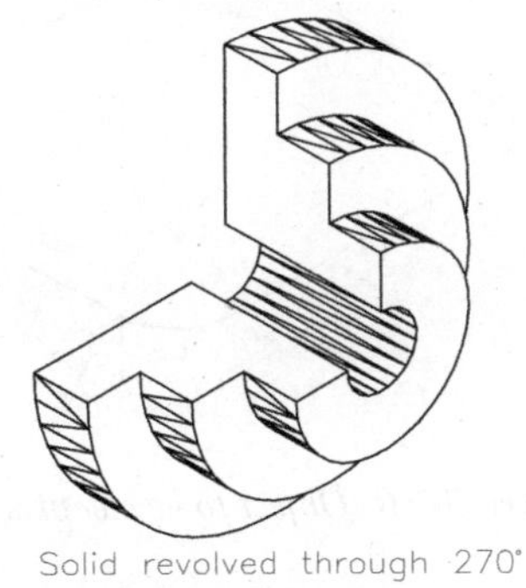

Figure 3-67 Solid revolved to an angle

CREATING SWEPT SOLIDS

Ribbon: Home > Modeling > Solid Creation drop-down > Sweep
Menu Bar: Draw > Modeling > Sweep **Toolbar:** Modeling > Sweep
Command: SWEEP

The **Sweep** tool is used to sweep an open or a closed profile along a path. This tool is also available in the **Solid** panel of the **Solid** tab. To create this model by using this tool, you need an object and a path. The object is a cross-section for the sweep feature and the path is the course taken by the object while creating the swept solid. Figure 3-68 shows the object to be swept and the path to be followed and Figure 3-69 shows the resulting sweep feature.

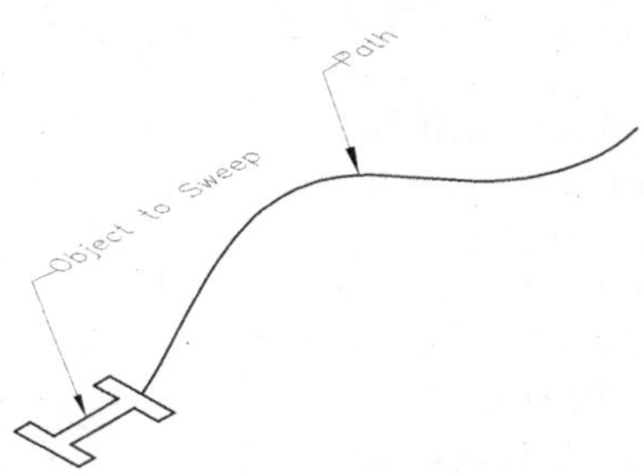

Figure 3-68 Object to be swept and the path

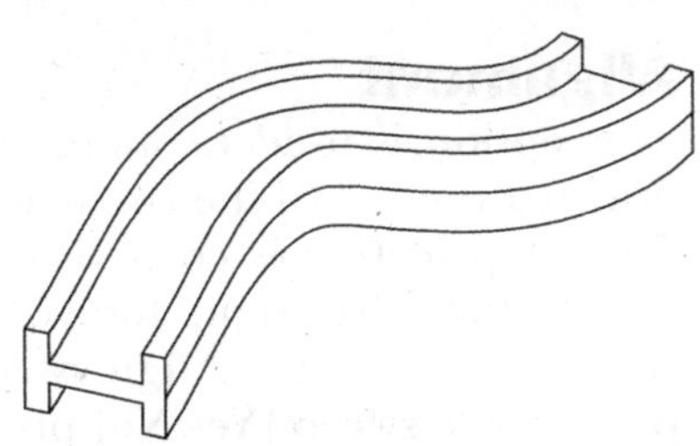

Figure 3-69 Resulting sweep feature

The path specified for the profile and the object for the cross-section of the swept model can be open or closed. If the object for the cross-section is open, or closed but not forming a single region, the generated feature will result in a surface sweep. If the object for the section is closed and it forms a single region, the generated feature will be a solid. Figure 3-70 shows the object and the closed path and Figure 3-71 shows the resulting sweep feature.

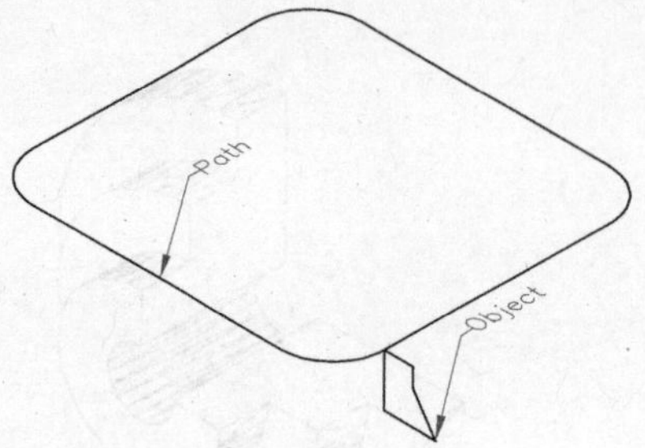

Figure 3-70 *Object to be swept with a closed path*

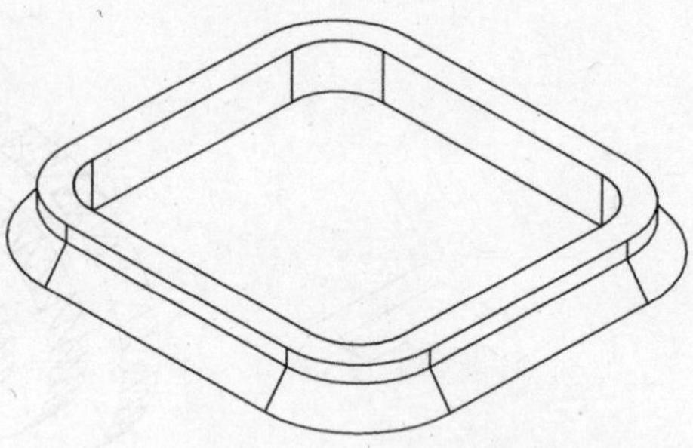

Figure 3-71 *Resulting sweep feature*

Note
The path selected for the ***Sweep*** *tool should not form a self-intersecting loop.*

You can select more than one section at a time to be swept along a path, but all these sections should be drawn on the same plane. To create a sweep, draw the cross section profile, path, and select the **Sweep** tool. Then, follow the prompt sequence given next.

Select objects to sweep or [MOde]: *Select the object to be swept.*
Select objects to sweep or [MOde]: *Select more objects to be swept or press ENTER.*
Select sweep path or [Alignment/Base point/Scale/Twist]: *Select the path to be followed by the object or enter an option.*

Depending on your requirement, you can invoke the following options at the **Select sweep path or [Alignment/ Base point/Scale/Twist]** prompt:

Alignment

This option is used to specify whether the object will be oriented normal to the curve at the start point. By default, the sweep feature is created with a section normal to the path at the start point. To avoid this, choose **No** from the shortcut menu at the **Align sweep object perpendicular to path before sweep [Yes/No]** prompt. Figure 3-72 shows the object and the path for the sweep tool. Figure 3-73 shows the resulting sweep feature on choosing the aligned option **Yes** and Figure 3-74 shows the resulting sweep feature on choosing the aligned option **No**.

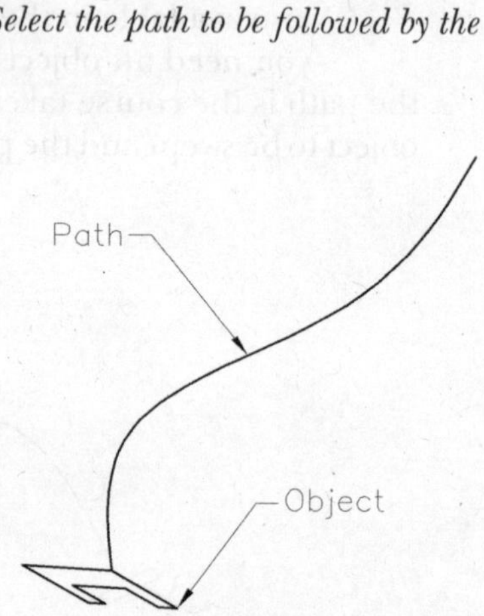

Figure 3-72 *Object and path for* ***sweep*** *command*

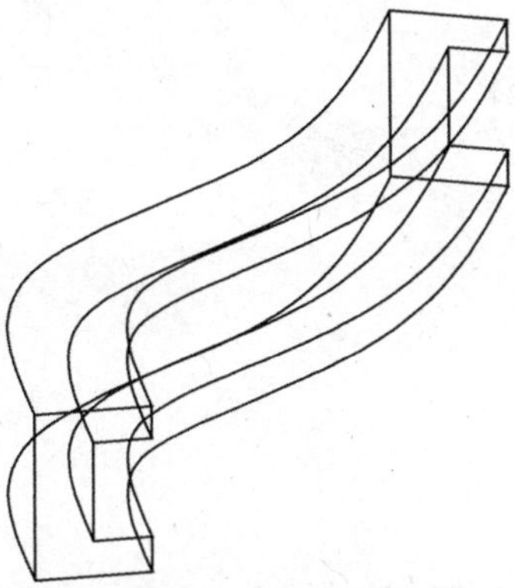

Figure 3-73 Swept solid with the aligned option ***Yes***

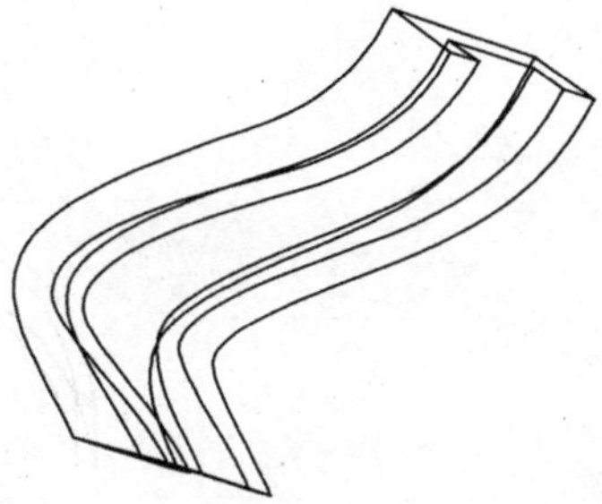

Figure 3-74 Swept solid with the aligned option ***No***

Base Point

This option is used to specify a point on the object that will be attached to the path while sweeping it. You can specify the location of the cross-section while sweeping it when prompted to specify the base point. Figure 3-75 shows the path and the cross-section with base points P1 and P2. Figure 3-76 shows the resulting sweep feature with P1 as the base point and Figure 3-77 shows the resulting sweep feature with P2 as the base point.

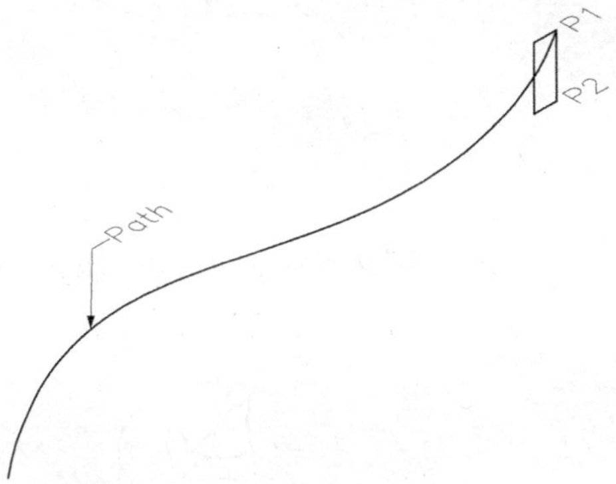

Figure 3-75 Path with object and P1 and P2 as base points

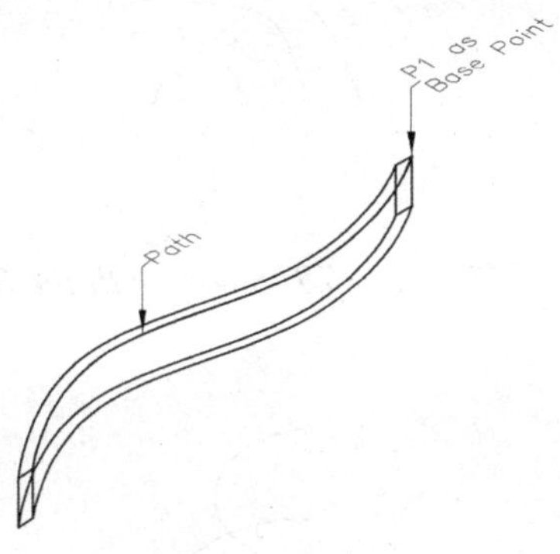

Figure 3-76 Sweep with P1 as base point

Scale

This option is used to scale an object uniformly from the start of the path to the end of the path while sweeping it. Note that the size of the start section will remain the same and then end section will be scaled by the specified value. Also, the transition from the beginning to the end is smooth. Figure 3-78 shows a pentagon swept along a path with a scale factor of 0.25.

Twist

You can rotate an object about a path uniformly from the start to the end with a specified angle. The value of the twist should be less than 360 degrees. Figure 3-79 shows a sweep feature with 300 degrees of twist.

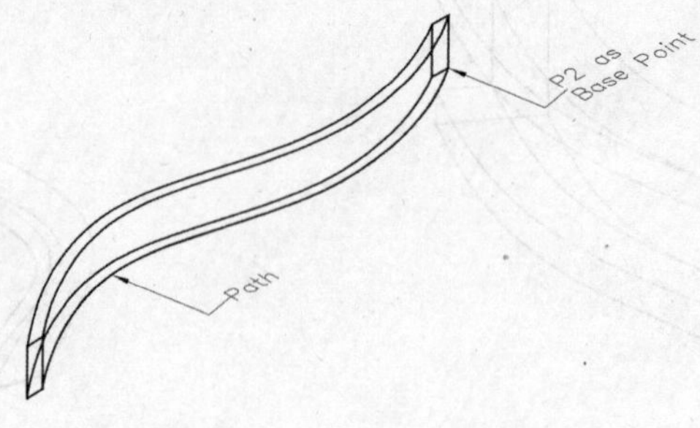

Figure 3-77 Sweep with P2 as the base point

Note

*A helix can also be used as the path for the **Sweep** tool. Figure 3-80 shows the object and a helical path generated using the **Helix** tool and Figure 3-81 shows the resulting swept solid.*

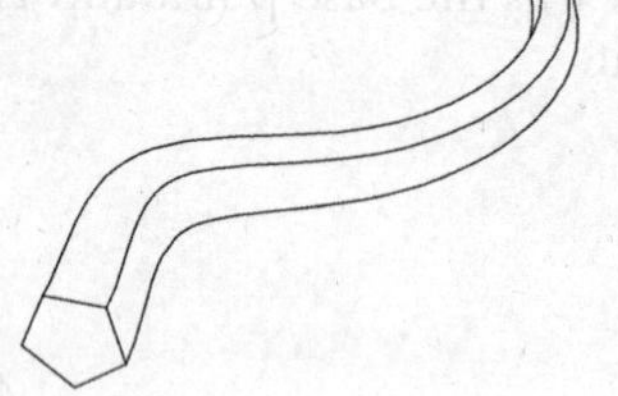

*Figure 3-78 Sweep with the **Scale** option*

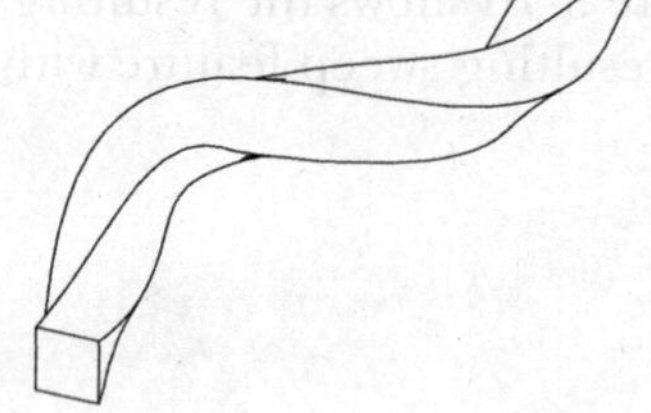

*Figure 3-79 Sweep with the **Twist** option*

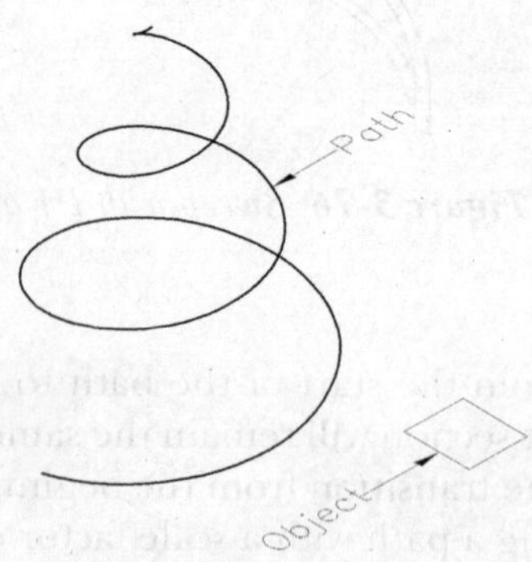

Figure 3-80 Helical path and object to be swept

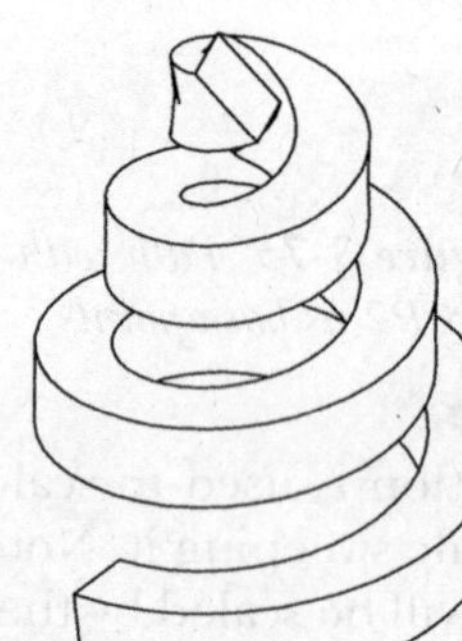

Figure 3-81 Sweep feature with the helical path

CREATING LOFTED SOLIDS

Ribbon: Home > Modeling > Solid Creation drop-down > Loft
Menu Bar: Draw > Modeling > Loft **Toolbar:** Modeling > Loft
Command: LOFT

The **Loft** tool is used to create a feature by blending two or more similar or dissimilar cross-sections together to get a free form shape. These similar or dissimilar cross-sections may or may not be parallel to each other. To create a loft feature, choose the **Loft** tool from the **Solid** panel, refer to Figure 3-82; the following prompt sequence will be displayed:

Select cross sections in lofting order or [POint/Join multiple edges/MOde]: _MO
Closed profiles creation mode [SOlid/SUrface] <Solid>: _SO
Select cross sections in lofting order or [POint/Join multiple edges/MOde]

Figure 3-82 Selecting the ***Loft*** *tool from the* ***Sweep*** *drop-down in the* ***Solid*** *panel*

Next, select at least two sections in a sequence in which you want to blend them. The prompt sequence that will be followed after choosing the **Loft** tool is given next.

Select cross sections in lofting order or [POint/Join multiple edges/MOde]: 1 found
Select cross sections in lofting order or [POint/Join multiple edges/MOde]: 1 found, 2 total
Enter
Select cross sections in lofting order or [POint/Join multiple edges/MOde]: 2 cross sections selected
Enter an option [Guides/Path/Cross sections only/Settings] <Cross sections only>: Enter

Note

As you are prompted to select cross-sections while creating a loft, you can select open or closed sections. Note that if you select an open section first, all subsequent sections should be open. The model thus created will be a surface. Similarly, if you select a closed section, all subsequent sections should be closed. The model created using these sections can be solid/surface. By default, a loft model is solid. Therefore, if cross sections selected are closed profiles and you need a surface model, then first you need to change the mode by entering ***MO*** *at the* ***Select cross sections in lofting order or [POint/Join multiple edges/MOde]*** *prompt.*

After specifying the mode, you can select the cross sections, an imaginary point as the start point of the loft, or multiple edges on a solid model.

These options are discussed next.

POint

In AutoCAD, you can start a loft such that it begins from an imaginary point and passes through different sections. To do so, enter **PO** at the **Select cross sections in lofting order or [POint/Join multiple edges/MOde]** prompt and specify the start point of the loft, as shown in Figure 3-83. Next, select the cross sections in succession and press ENTER after selecting all cross sections; the preview of the loft feature will be displayed. Also, a Look up grip near the last cross section and the **Enter an option [Guides/Path/Cross sections only/Settings/COntinuity/Bulge magnitude] <Cross sections only>** prompt will be displayed. Select the **Cross sections only** option and press ENTER; the loft will be created, as shown in Figure 3-84.

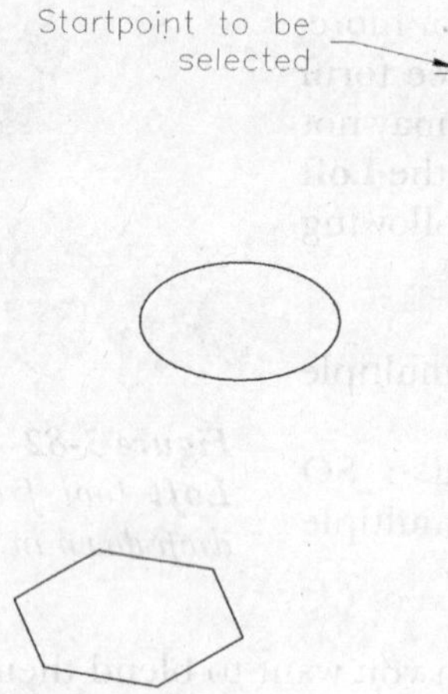

***Figure 3-83** Sections and the imaginary start point to be selected*

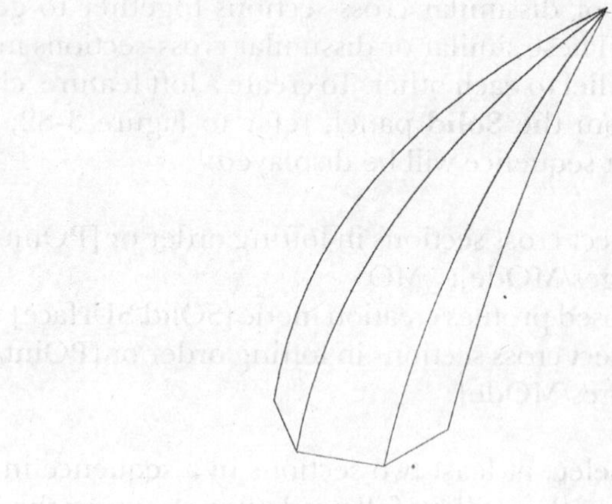

***Figure 3-84** Loft feature created by using the **PO** option*

Join multiple edges

In AutoCAD, you can create a loft feature between the edges of a solid model and a profile. To do so, enter **J** at the **Select cross sections in lofting order or [POint/Join multiple edges/MOde]** prompt; the cursor will have the symbol of solid and you will be prompted to select edges that are to be joined to a single cross section. Select the edges in succession, and press ENTER, refer to Figure 3-85. Then, select the cross sections and press ENTER; the preview of the loft will be displayed. One look up grip at the start of the loft surface and other look up grip near the base of the model will be displayed. The Look up grip at the start of the loft will have the surface continuity symbol, and the other Look up grip will have the Loft symbol, refer to Figure 3-86. Click on the Look up grip that has the surface continuity symbol and select the required option from the flyout displayed. The options in the other look up grip will be discussed later.

Given below is the prompt sequence to select the edges on the top face of the cuboid and a circle as the cross section.

Select cross sections in lofting order or [POint/Join multiple edges/MOde]: **J** Enter
Select edges that are to be joined into a single cross section: (*Select the first edge*)1 found
Select edges that are to be joined into a single cross section: (*Select the second edge*) 1 found, 2 total
Select edges that are to be joined into a single cross section: (*Select the third edge*) 1 found, 3 total
Select edges that are to be joined into a single cross section: (*Select the fourth edge*) 1 found, 4 total
Select edges that are to be joined into a single cross section: Enter

Select cross sections in lofting order or [POint/Join multiple edges/MOde]: 1 found
Select cross sections in lofting order or [POint/Join multiple edges/MOde]: Enter
2 cross sections selected Enter
Enter an option [Guides/Path/Cross sections only/Settings/COntinuity/Bulge magnitude] <Cross sections only>: Enter *(Preview of the loft will be displayed with grips, refer to Figure 3-86. Press ENTER; the loft surface will be created, refer to Figure 3-87.*

After selecting all cross sections and on pressing ENTER, the **Enter an option [Guides/Path/Cross sections only/Settings/COntinuity/Bulge magnitude] <Cross sections only>** prompt will be displayed. The **COntinuity** and **Bulge magnitude** options will be displayed in the Command prompt only if you have selected the edges of a model as one of the cross sections. Depending on requirement, you can invoke any one of those options. These options are discussed next.

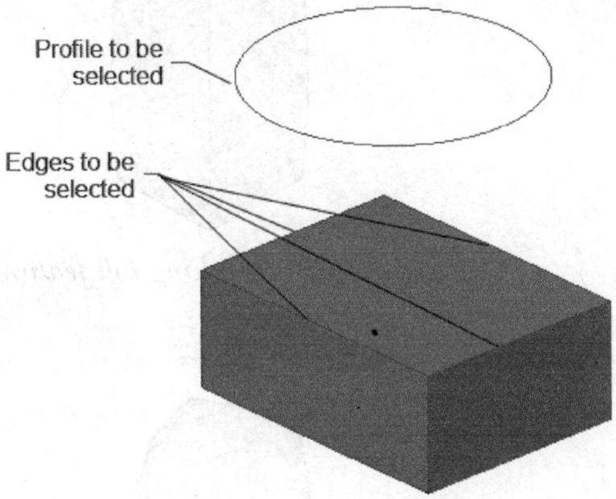

Figure 3-85 *Edges and the profile to be selected*

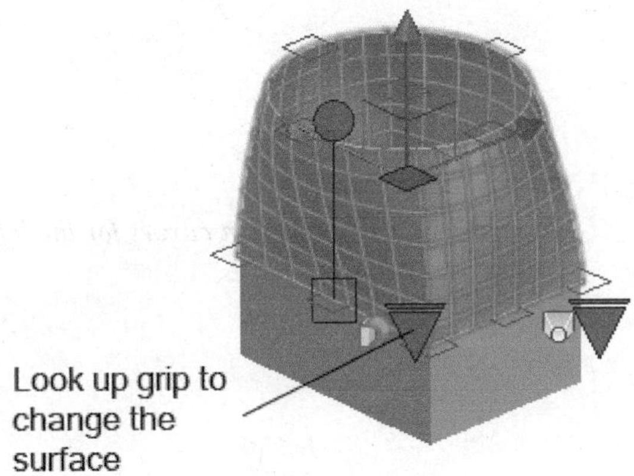

Figure 3-86 *Look up grips displayed*

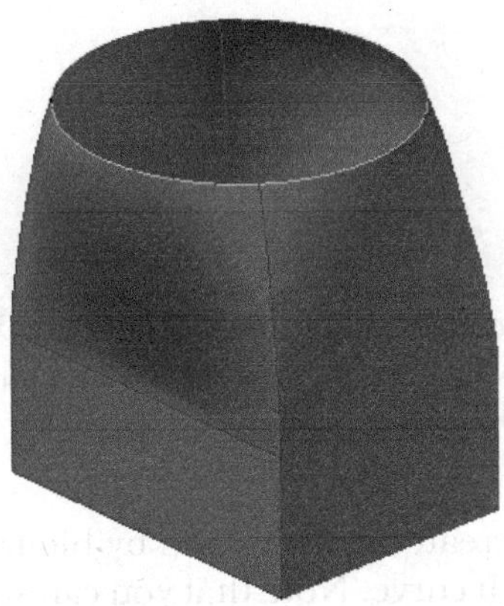

Figure 3-87 *Loft surface created*

Guide

AutoCAD enables you to select guide curves between the sections of the loft feature. These guide curves define the shape of the material addition between the selected sections for the loft feature. Guide curves also specify the points of different sections to be joined while adding material between them. This reduces the possibility of an unnecessary twist in the resulting feature. You can select as many guide curves as you require. But these guide curves should pass through or should touch each section that you selected for loft feature. Also the guides should start from the first section and terminate at the last section. Figure 3-88 shows three sections for the loft feature. Figure 3-89 shows the resulting loft feature. Figure 3-90 shows the sections to be lofted and the guide curves and Figure 3-91 shows the resulting model.

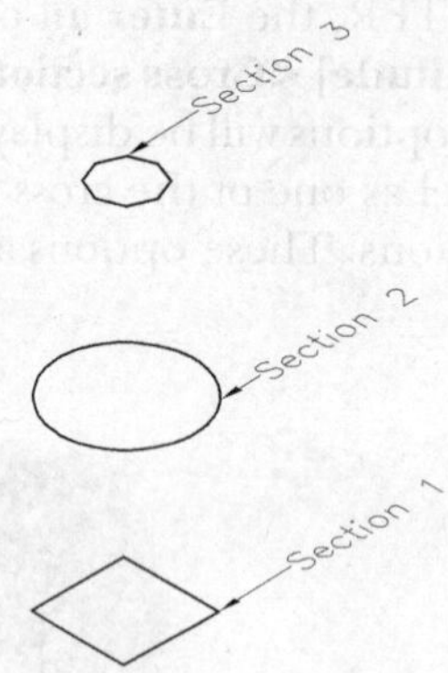

Figure 3-88 Three section curves for the loft feature

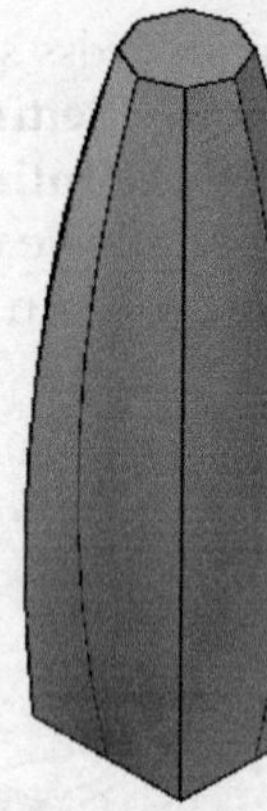

Figure 3-89 Resulting loft feature

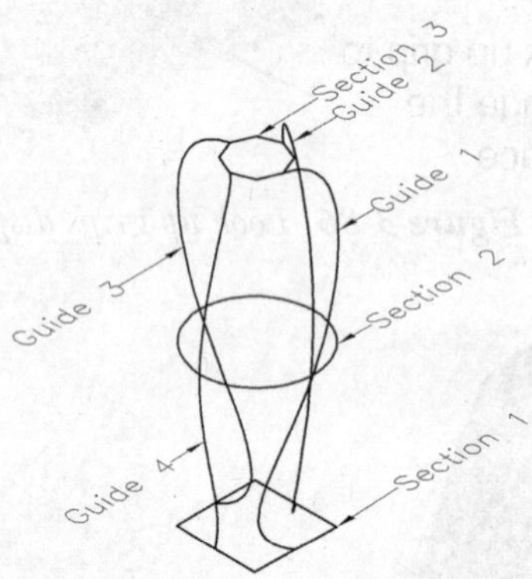

Figure 3-90 Sections and guide curves for the loft feature

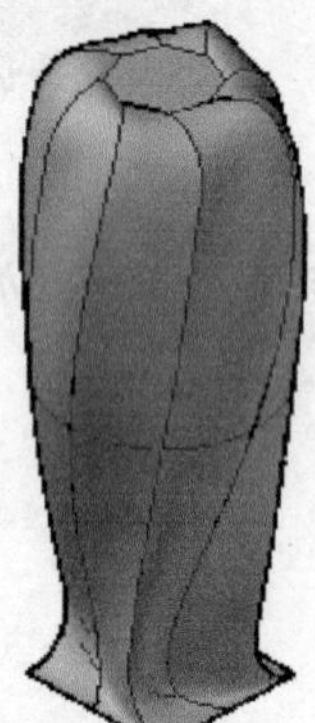

Figure 3-91 The loft feature created by using the guide curve

Path

The path option is used to create a loft feature by blending more than one section along the direction specified by the path curve. Note that you can select only one path curve. The selected path curve may or may not touch all sections, but it should pass through all sketching planes of the sections. Figure 3-92 shows the sections and the path along which the blending of material will propagate and Figure 3-93 shows the resulting loft feature.

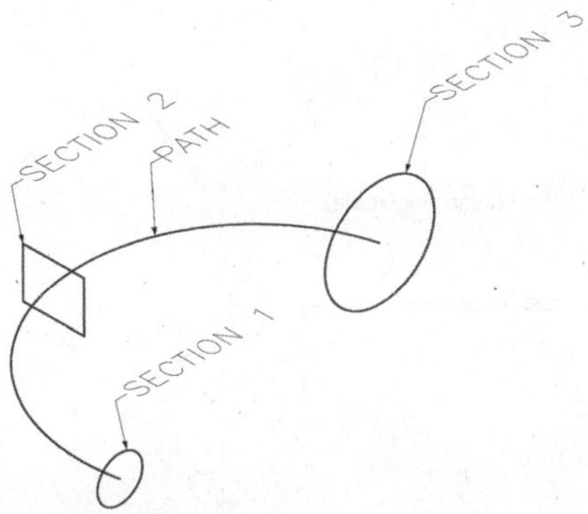

Figure 3-92 *Sections and path to be used for the **Loft** option*

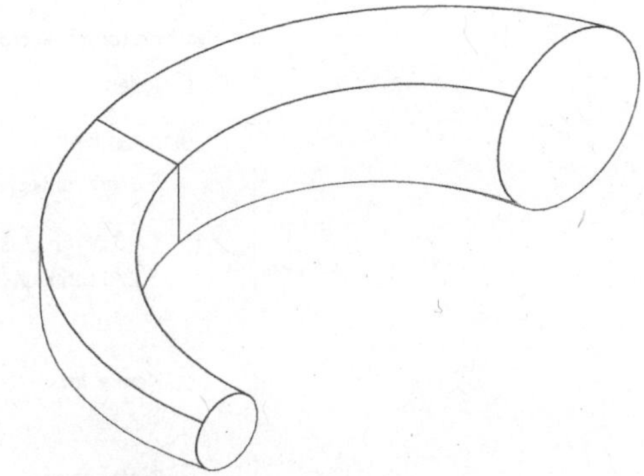

Figure 3-93 *Resulting loft feature after using the **Path** option*

Cross sections only

This is the default option displayed at the **Enter an option [Guides/Path/Cross sections only/ Settings/COntinuity/Bulge magnitude] <Cross sections only>** prompt. If you need to create a loft without a guide or path, press ENTER; the loft feature will be created by using the cross sections only.

Settings

When you select **Settings**, the **Loft Settings** dialog box will be displayed, as shown in Figure 3-94. This dialog box is used to control the shape of the material addition between sections without specifying any guide curve or path. You can also select these options from the Look up grip displayed along with the preview. Various options in the **Loft Settings** dialog box are discussed next.

Ruled

If you select the **Ruled** radio button, a straight blend will be created by connecting different sections with straight lines. The loft feature created by this option will have sharp edges at the sections. Figure 3-95 shows the loft feature when the **Ruled** radio button is selected.

Smooth Fit

If you select the **Smooth Fit** radio button, a smooth loft will be created between sections. The loft feature created by this option will have smooth edges at the intermediate section. Figure 3-96 shows the loft feature when the **Smooth Fit** radio button is selected.

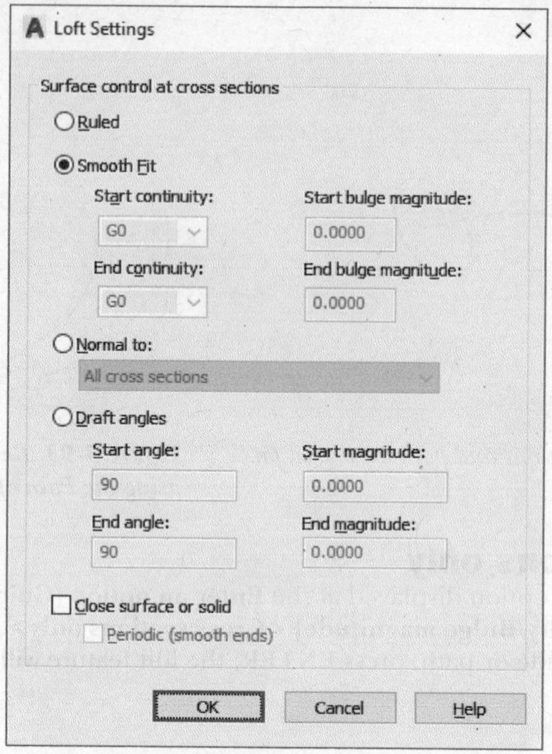

***Figure 3-94** The **Loft Settings** dialog box*

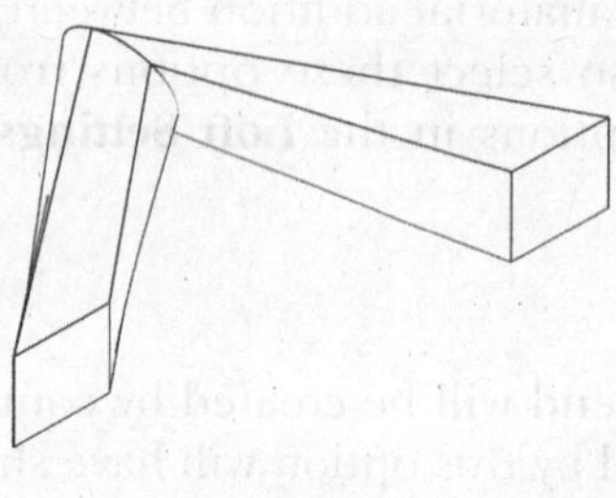

***Figure 3-95** Loft solid with the **Ruled** radio button selected*

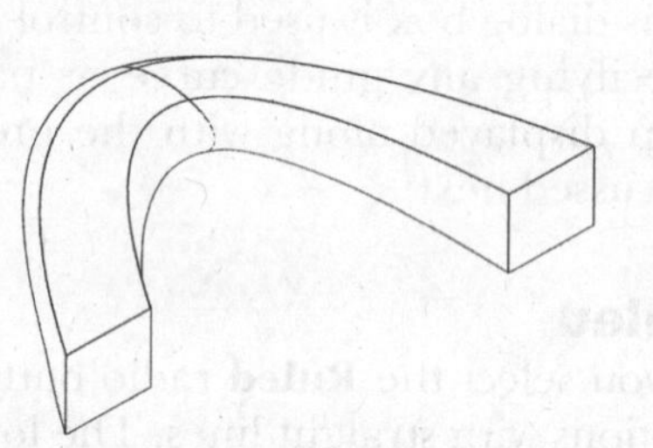

***Figure 3-96** Loft solid with the **Smooth Fit** radio button selected*

Normal to

This option controls the shape of the loft between the sections. When you select this radio button, the drop-down list will be enabled. The following options are available in this drop-down list:

Start cross section. In this option, the normal of the lofted feature is normal to the start section. The loft feature starts normal to the start section and follows a smooth polyline as it approaches the next section. Figure 3-97 shows the section selected to create the loft and Figure 3-98 shows the loft created by specifying the **Start cross section** option.

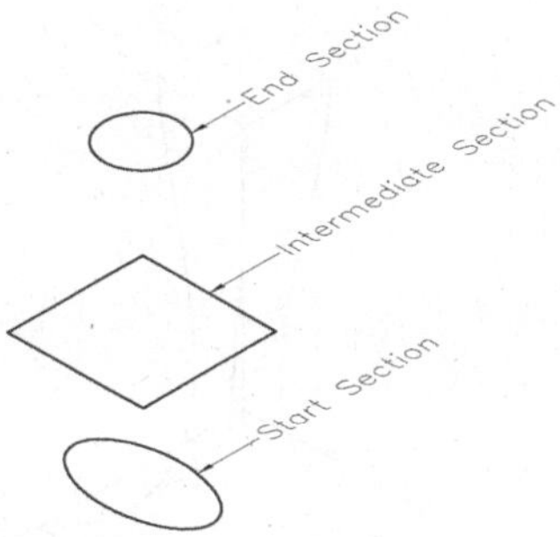

Figure 3-97 *Start and end sections to create loft*

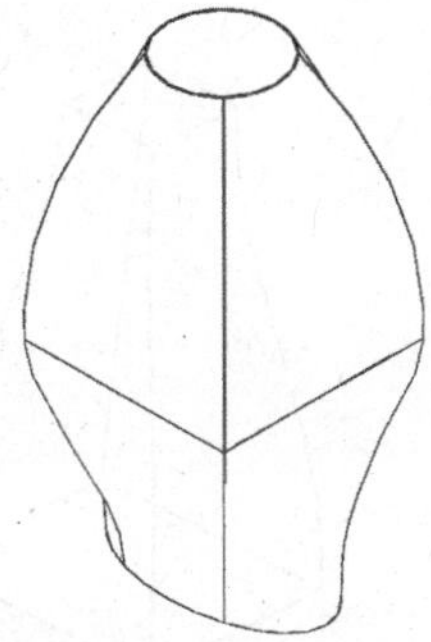

Figure 3-98 *Loft solid created by blending material normal to the start section*

End cross section. In this option, the normal to the blending material is normal to the end section. At the second last section, the blending material starts along a spline and while reaching up to end section, it becomes normal to it, as shown in Figure 3-99.

Start and End cross sections. In this option, the normal to the blending material is normal to both the start and end sections.

All cross sections. In this option, the normal to the blending material always remains normal to all cross-sections, as shown in Figure 3-100.

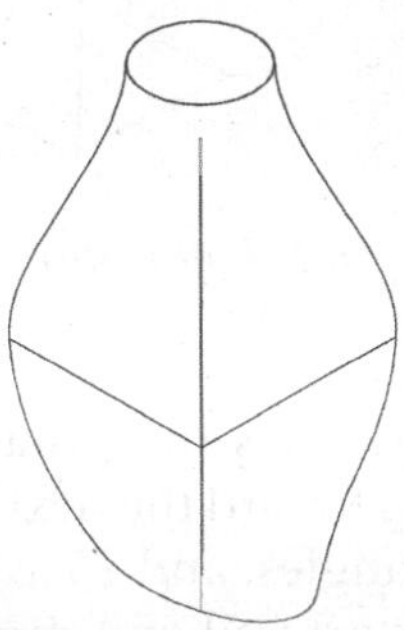

Figure 3-99 *Loft solid created by blending material normal to the end section*

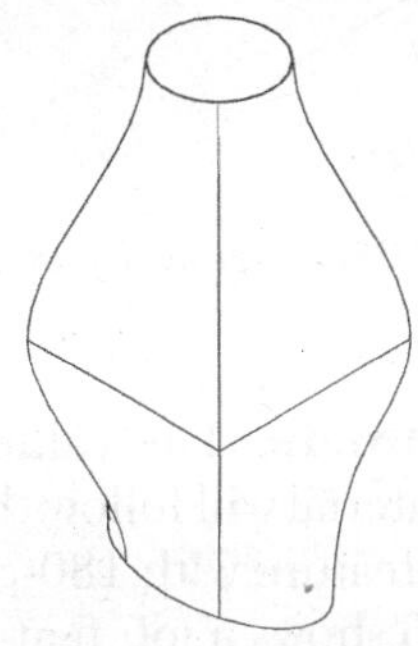

Figure 3-100 *Loft solid created by blending material normal to all sections*

Draft angles

In this option, you can define the angle at the start section and the end section of the loft. Remember that you cannot define an angle for the intermediate sketches. You can also specify the distance up to which the blending material will follow this draft angle before bending toward the intermediate sections. The various options for specifying the draft angle are discussed next.

Start angle. This edit box is used to specify the draft angle at the start section of the loft. Figure 3-101 shows the two sections to be blended and Figure 3-102 shows the loft with the start and end angles as 0-degree. Figures 3-103 and 3-104 show the loft feature with the start angle as 90-degree and 180-degree, respectively.

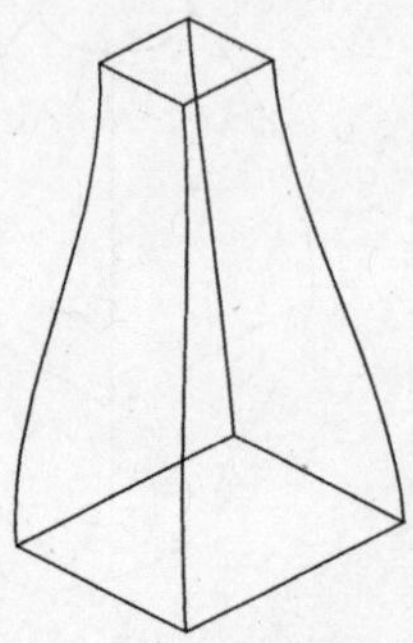

Figure 3-101 Loft feature with 90-degree start and end angles

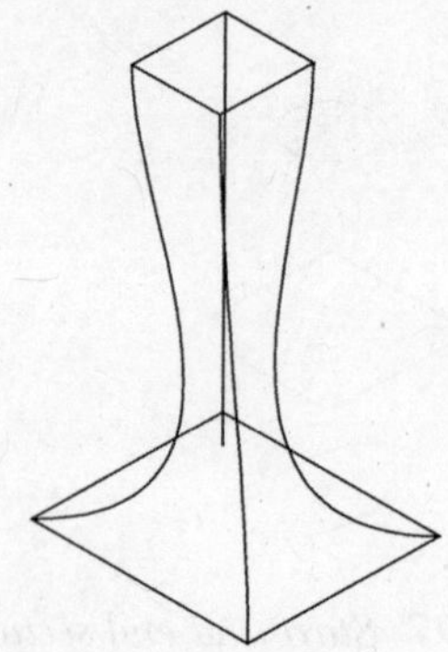

Figure 3-102 Loft feature with 180-degree start angle and 90-degree end angle

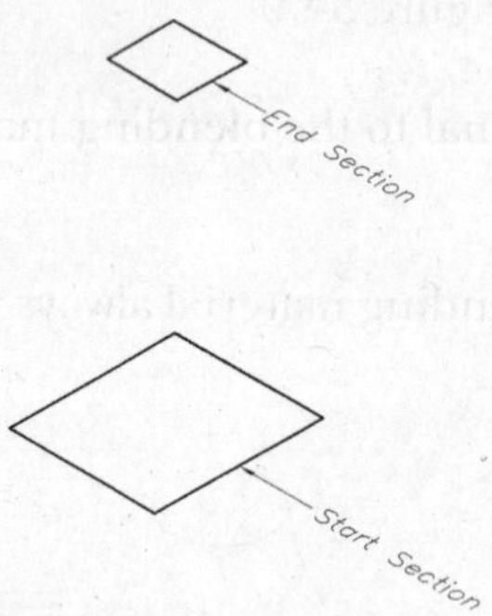

Figure 3-103 Start and end sections of the loft feature

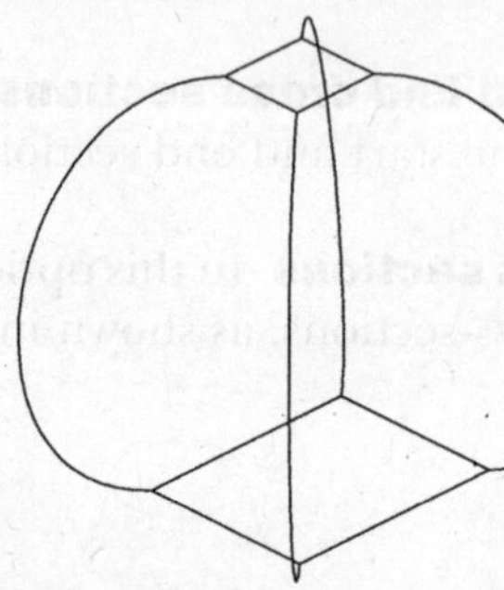

Figure 3-104 Loft feature with 0-degree start and end angles

Start magnitude. The value specified in this region signifies the distance up to which the blending material will follow the start angle before bending toward the next section. Figure 3-105 shows a loft feature with 180-degree as the start and end angles, and 15 as the start magnitude. Figure 3-106 shows a loft feature with 180-degree as the start and end angles and 2 as the start magnitude. Notice the difference in the extent up to which the blended material follows the start angle in the two figures.

End angle. This edit box is used to specify the draft angle at the end section of the loft. Figure 3-101 shows two sections to be blended and Figure 3-102 shows the loft with the start and end angle as 0-degree. Figure 3-103 and Figure 3-104 show the loft feature with the end angle as 90-degree.

End magnitude. The value specified in this region signifies the distance up to which the blending material will follow the end angle before approaching the last section. Figure 3-105 shows a loft feature with 180-degree as the start and end angle, and 2 as the end magnitude. Figure 3-106 shows a loft feature with 180-degree as the start and end angle, and 10 as the end magnitude. Notice the difference in the extent up to which the blended material follows the end angle in the two figures.

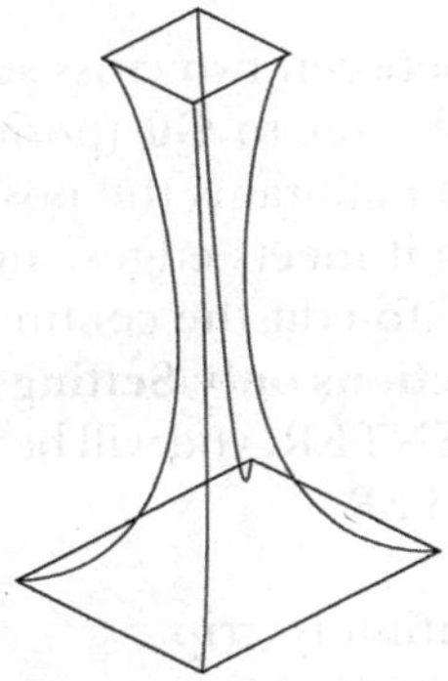

Figure 3-105 Loft feature with 180-degree as the start and end angle, 15 as the start magnitude, and 2 as the end magnitude

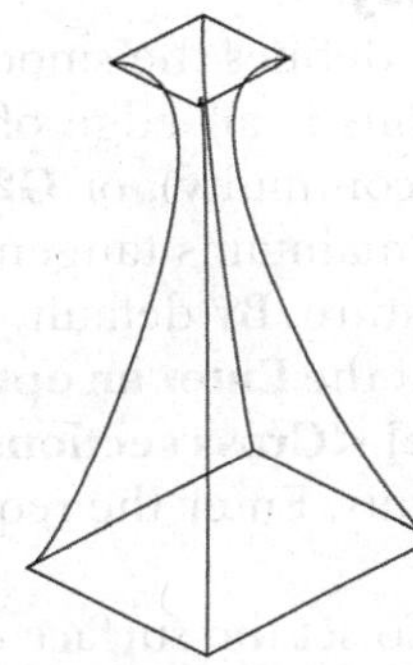

Figure 3-106 Loft feature with 180-degree as the start and end angle, 2 as the start magnitude, and 10 as the end magnitude

Close surface or solid

The **Close surface or solid** check box is selected to close a loft feature by joining the end section with the start section. Figure 3-107 shows a loft feature created with this check box cleared and Figure 3-108 shows the same sections lofted by this check box selected.

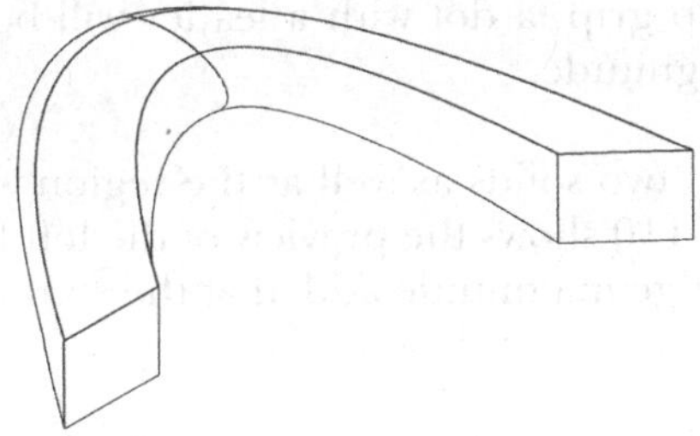

*Figure 3-107 Loft solid with the **Close surface or solid** check box cleared*

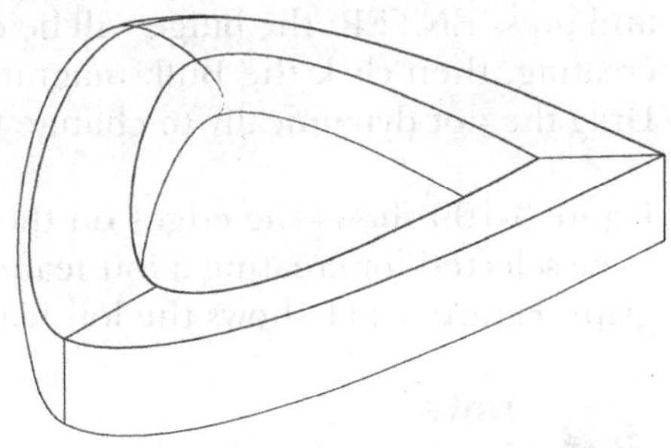

*Figure 3-108 Loft solid with the **Close surface or solid** check box selected*

Note

*To visualize the effect of the **Close surface or solid** option, the loft feature should contain at least three sections. If not so, the extra blending material will be added at the same location where the loft feature would have been created without selecting this check box, thereby resulting in no change.*

Periodic (smooth ends). If this check box is selected, the seam of the closed surface will not buckle, if you alter the shape of the surface.

Tip

You can also use a point as a section for the loft feature, but it should always be the start section or the end section of the loft feature.

Continuity

Continuity defines the smoothness of the loft surface between two cross sections, if one of the cross sections is an edge of a model. Continuity can be set to **G0** (position continuity), **G1** (tangency continuity), or **G2** (curvature continuity). **G0** maintains the position of the selected edges, **G1** maintains tangency of the loft surface where it meets edges, and **G2** maintains the same curvature. By default, the continuity is set to G0. To edit the continuity setting of a loft, enter **CO** at the **Enter an option [Guides/Path/Cross sections only/Settings/COntinuity/Bulge magnitude] <Cross sections only>** prompt and press ENTER; you will be prompted to specify the continuity. Enter the required option and press ENTER.

You can also set the surface continuity by using the Continuity grip.

Bulge magnitude

The bulge magnitude determines the roundness or the amount of bulge between two cross sections, if one of the cross sections is an edge of a model. By default, the bulge magnitude is set to 0.5. If you want to edit the bulge magnitude, enter **B** at the **Enter an option [Guides/Path/Cross sections only/Settings/COntinuity/Bulge magnitude] <Cross sections only>** prompt and press ENTER; you will be prompted to enter the loft bulge magnitude at the start. Enter a value and press ENTER. If there is only one solid edge as a cross section, then the bulge will be created. If there are two solid edges as cross sections (one at the start and the other at the end), then you will be prompted to enter the bulge magnitude at the start and end. Type a value and press ENTER; the bulge will be created. If you need to change the bulge magnitude while creating, then click the Bulk magnitude Look up grip; a dot with a leader will be displayed. Drag the dot dynamically to change the bulk magnitude.

Figure 3-109 shows the edges on the top faces of two solids as well as the region which needs to be selected for creating a loft feature. Figure 3-110 shows the preview of the loft feature with grips. Figure 3-111 shows the loft feature with bulge magnitude added at the start and end.

Note

You can also set the surface continuity and the bulge continuity in the ***Loft Settings*** *dialog box.*

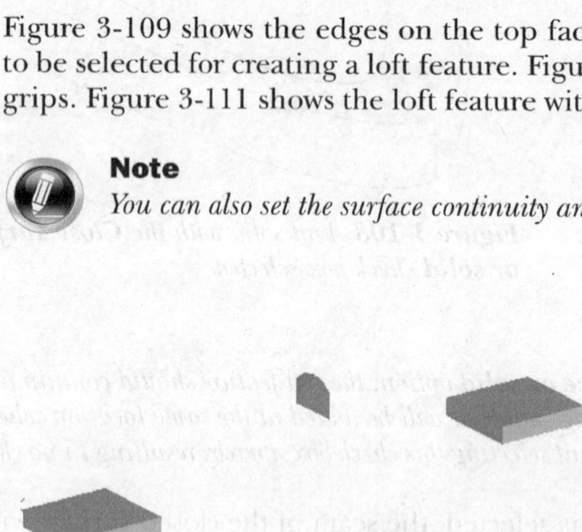

Figure 3-109 Two solids and a region to create a loft

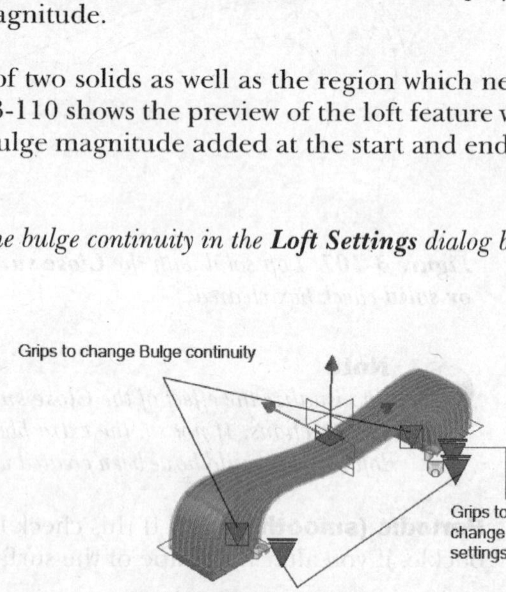

Figure 3-110 Preview of the loft and the grips displayed

Figure 3-111 Loft surface created

CREATING PRESSPULL SOLIDS

Ribbon: Home > Modeling > Presspull **Toolbar:** Modeling > Presspull
Command: PRESSPULL

The **Presspull** tool is used to remove or add material of any desired shape in a model. As the name presspull indicates, if you press a closed boundary inside an existing model, it will remove the material of the shape of the closed boundary. However, if you pull a closed boundary outside an existing model, it will add material to the model. To perform this operation, choose the **Presspull** tool from the **Modeling** panel. Next, click inside a closed boundary that you want to press or pull and then move the mouse in the desired direction. You can specify the desired height by entering a value or by clicking the mouse. Figure 3-112 shows the solid model with the closed area to be presspulled. Figure 3-113 shows the model created by pressing the closed region and Figure 3-114 shows the model created by pulling the closed area.

Given below is the prompt sequence displayed while creating the presspull feature.

Select object or bounded area : *Select any closed bounded area that you want to presspull*
Specify extrusion height or [Multiple] : *Click anywhere to specify the height of extrusion*
Select object or bounded area : Enter

If the sketch that you select to press or pull has nested loops, as shown in Figure 3-115, the inner closed loops will be deleted from the outer loop, as shown in Figure 3-116. The closed area you select for the presspull should consist of lines, polylines, 3D face, edges, regions, and faces of a 3D solid. But all these entities should form a coplanar closed area.

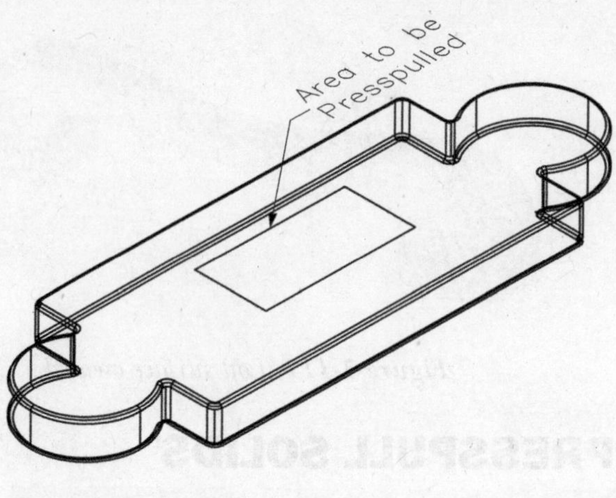

***Figure 3-112** Model with closed area to be presspulled*

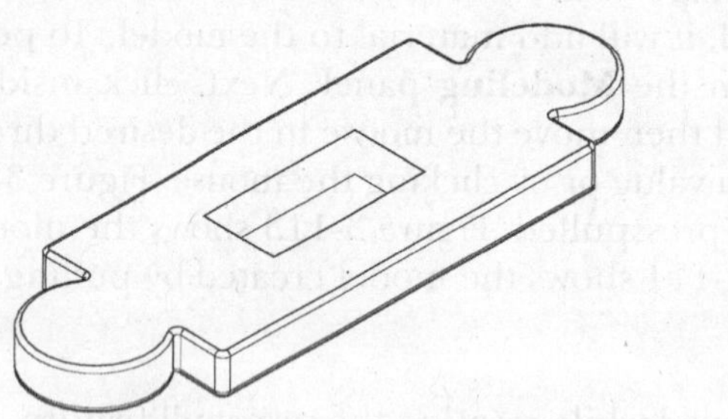

***Figure 3-113** Model with the closed area pressed*

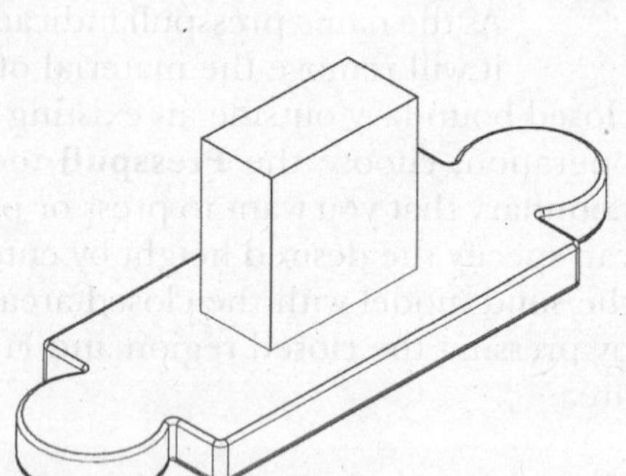

***Figure 3-114** Model with closed area pulled*

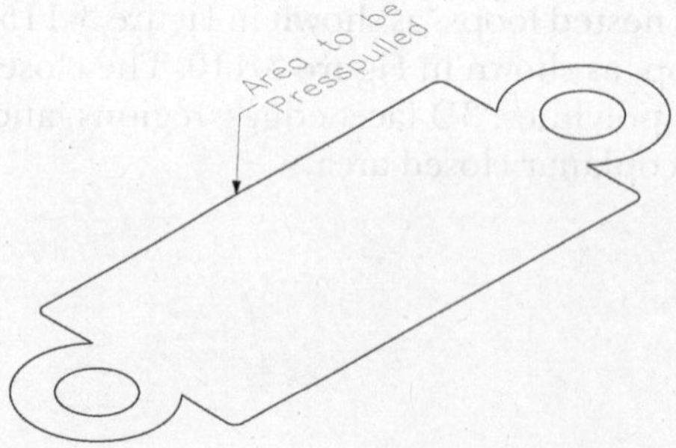

***Figure 3-115** Area to be presspulled with closed boundary inside it*

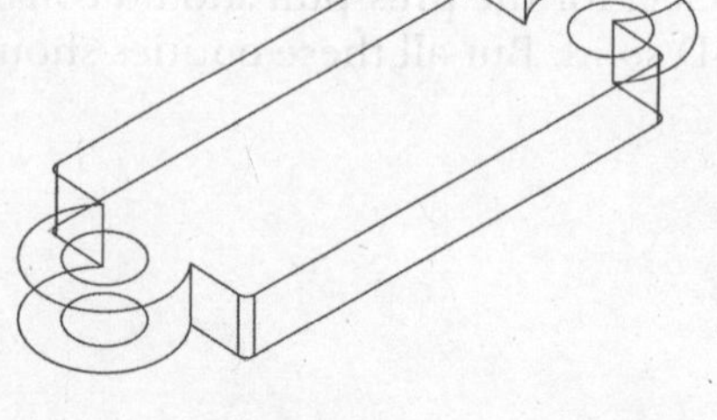

***Figure 3-116** The model after the presspull operation is performed*

Example 2

In this example, you will create the solid model shown in Figure 3-117.

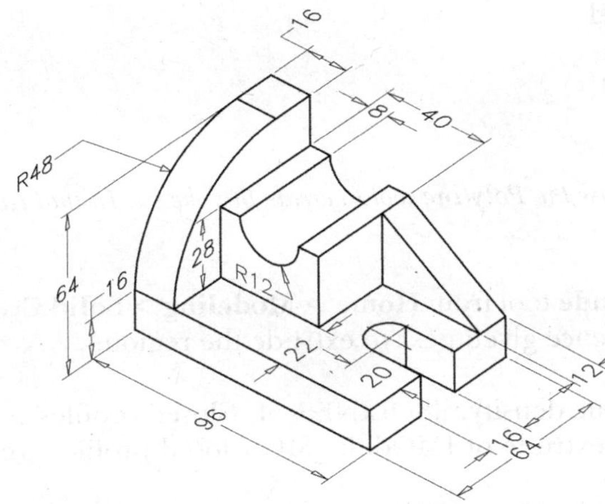

Figure 3-117 Solid model for Example 2

1. Start a new file using the *acad3D.dwt* template.

2. Set the drawing limits of the workspace to 120,120. Next, type ZOOM or Z at the command prompt and select **All** option from the options displayed.

3. Set the view to SE Isometric by using the ViewCube. Then, right-click on the ViewCube and choose the **Parallel** option.

4. Switch on the ortho mode. Using lines and arc, create the base of the model with the dimensions shown in Figure 3-118.

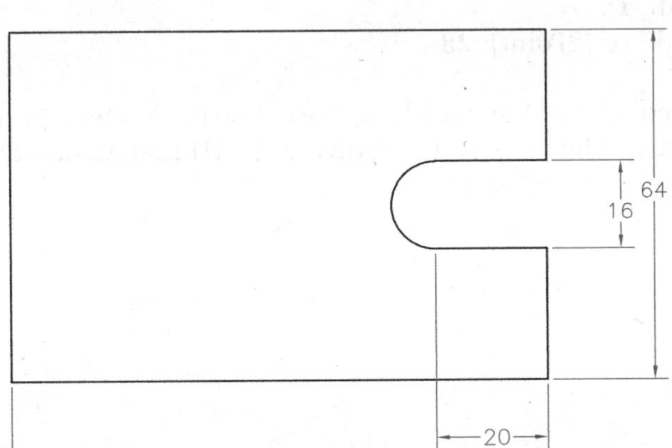

Figure 3-118 Base for the solid model

5. Choose the **Region** tool from the **Draw** panel in the **Home** tab and follow the prompt sequence given next to convert the sketch drawn into a region.

   Select objects: *Select the complete base.*
   Select objects: Enter
   1 loop extracted.
   1 Region created.

Note

You can also use the ***Polyline*** *tool to create this sketch. In that case, you do not need to convert it into a region.*

6. Choose the **Extrude** tool from **Home > Modeling > Solid Creation** drop-down and follow the prompt sequence given next to extrude the region.

   Current wire frame density: ISOLINES=4, Closed profiles creation mode = Solid
   Select objects to extrude or [MOde]: _MO Closed profiles creation mode [SOlid/SUrface] <Solid>: _SO
   Select objects to extrude or [MOde]: *Select the region* Enter
   1 found
   Select objects to extrude or [MOde]: Enter
   Specify height of extrusion or [Direction/Path/Taper angle/Expression]: **16**

7. Change the visual style to Wireframe by choosing the **Wireframe** option from the **Visual Style Controls** drop-down list in the **In-canvas Viewport control**.

8. Choose the **Wedge** tool from **Home > Modeling > Solid Primitives** drop-down and follow the prompt sequence given next to create the next feature.

   Specify first corner or [Center]: *Pick a point on the screen.*
   Specify other corner or [Cube/Length]: **L**
   Specify length: **40**
   Specify width: **12**
   Specify height or [2Point]: **28**

9. Move this wedge and align it with the base. Use the **Vertex** option of the **3D Object Snap** to snap the vertex. The model after applying the **Hidden** visual style is shown in Figure 3-119.

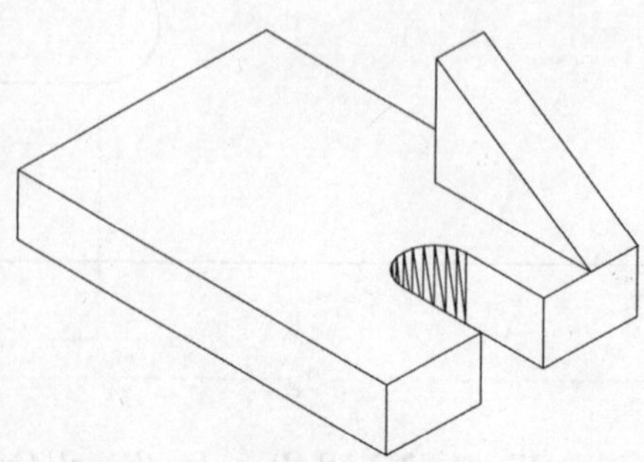

Figure 3-119 *Wedge aligned with the base*

10. Orient the view to **Front** by clicking on **Front** in the ViewCube and choose **WCS > New UCS** from the drop-down list below it; you are prompted to specify the origin.

11. Enter **V** at the **Specify origin of UCS or [Face/NAmed/OBject/Previous/View/World/X/Y/Z/ ZAxis] <World>** prompt and press ENTER.

12. Draw the profile shown in Figure 3-120 at any place in the drawing area and then convert it into a region.

13. Choose the **Extrude** tool from **Home > Modeling > Solid Creation** drop-down and extrude the region to a depth of 42 units.

14. Move this extrude feature and align it with the wedge feature. Use the **Vertex** option of the **3D Object Snap** to snap the vertex of the wedge feature.

The isometric view of the model after aligning the extrude feature is shown in Figure 3-121.

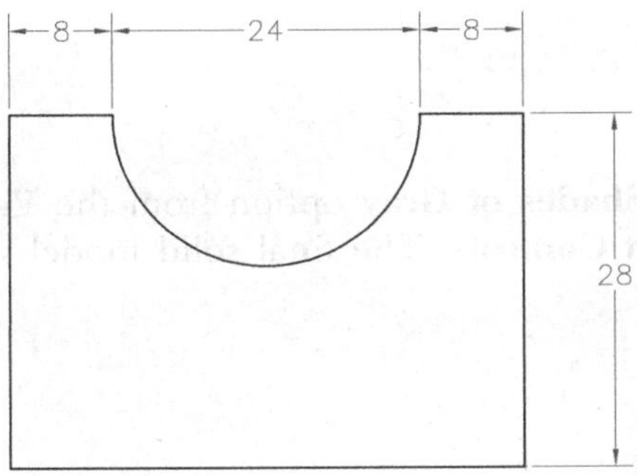

Figure 3-120 *The region to be extruded*

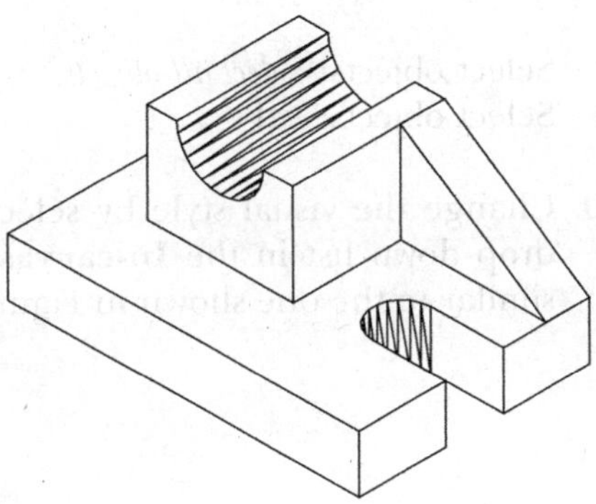

Figure 3-121 *Solid aligned with the base*

15. Orient the view to Right by clicking **Right** in the ViewCube and choose **WCS > New UCS** from the drop-down list below it; you are prompted to specify the origin.

16. Enter **V** at the **Specify origin of UCS or [Face/NAmed/OBject/Previous/View/World/X/Y/Z/ ZAxis] <World>** prompt and press ENTER.

17. Draw the profile shown in Figure 3-122 at any place in the drawing area and then convert it into a region.

18. Extrude the region to a depth of 16 units and then move it so that it is properly aligned with the base, refer to Figure 3-123.

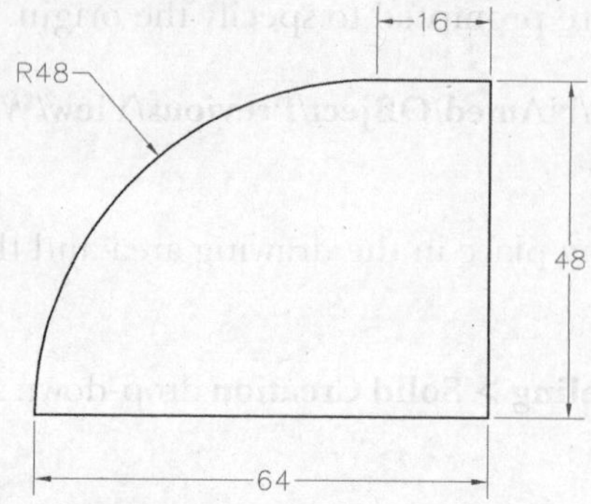

Figure 3-122 *The region before extrusion*

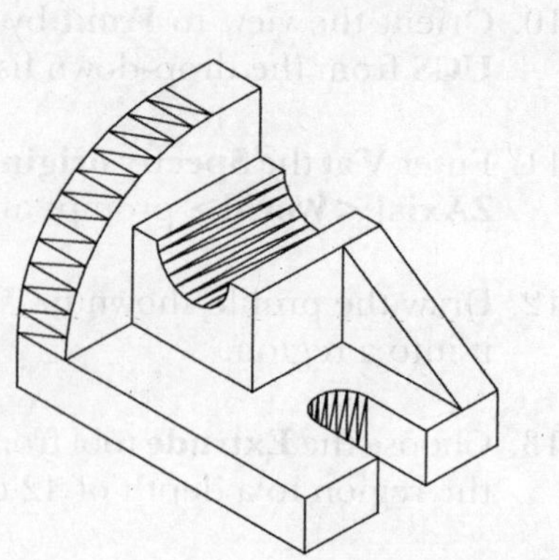

Figure 3-123 *Solid aligned with the base*

19. Choose the **Solid, Union** tool from the **Solid Editing** panel and follow the prompt sequence given next:

Select objects: *Select all objects.*
Select objects: Enter

20. Change the visual style by selecting the **Shades of Gray** option from the **Visual Styles** drop-down list in the **In-canvas Viewport Controls**. The final solid model should look similar to the one shown in Figure 3-124.

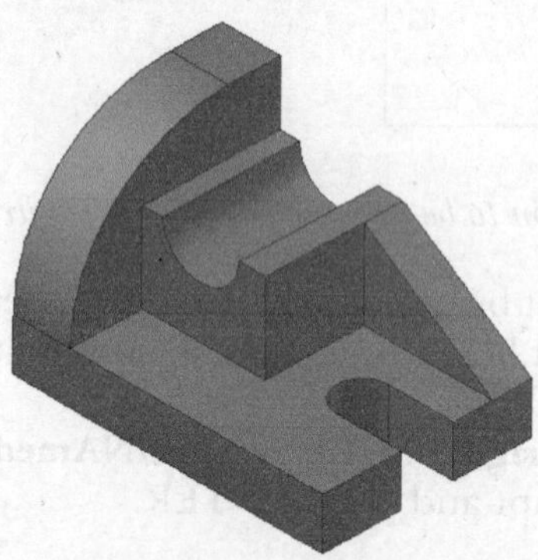

Figure 3-124 *Solid model for Example 2*

Example 3

In this example, you will create the solid model shown in Figure 3-125.

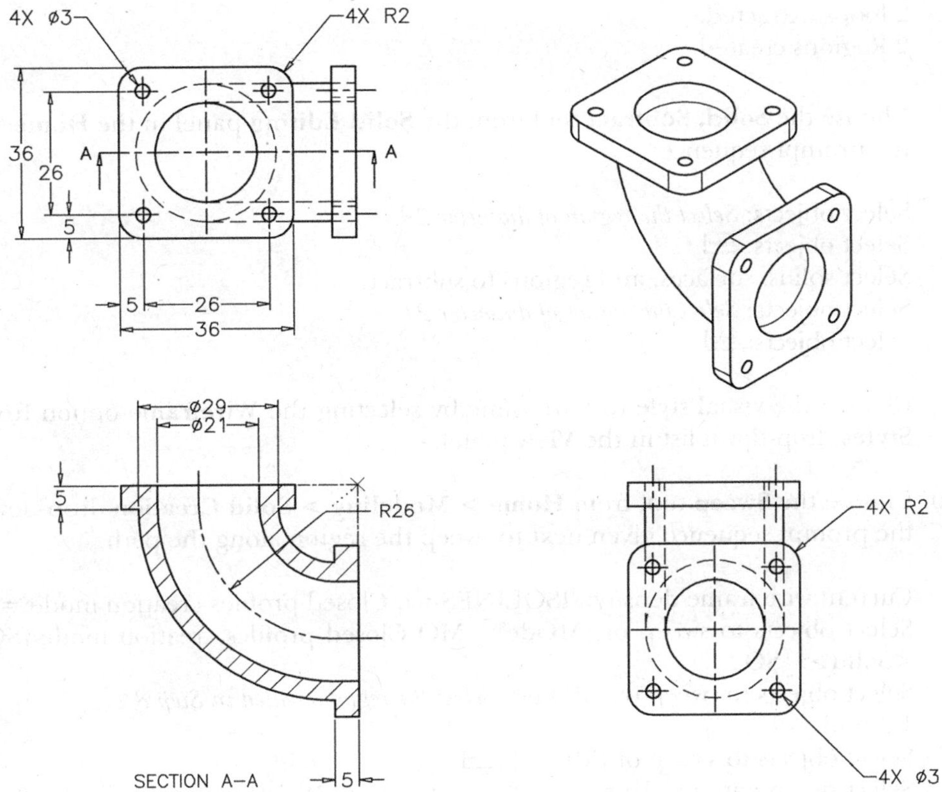

Figure 3-125 Solid model for Example 3

1. Start a new file using the *acad3D.dwt* template.

2. Set the drawing limits of the workspace to 75,75. Next, type ZOOM or Z at the command prompt and select the **All** option from the options displayed.

3. Orient the view to Left by choosing **Left** in the ViewCube and choose **WCS > New UCS** from the drop-down list below it; you are prompted to specify the origin.

4. Enter **V** at the **Specify origin of UCS or [Face/NAmed/OBject/Previous/View/World/X/Y/Z/ZAxis] <World>** prompt and press ENTER.

5. Right-click on the ViewCube and choose the **Parallel** option.

6. Draw the cross section and path of the sweep feature, as shown in Figure 3-126.

7. Choose the **Region** tool from the **Draw** panel in the **Home** tab and follow the prompt sequence given next to convert the sketch into a region.

Select objects: *Select both the circles.*
Select objects: Enter
2 loops extracted.
2 Regions created.

8. Choose the **Solid, Subtract** tool from the **Solid Editing** panel in the **Home** tab and follow the prompt sequence:

Select objects: *Select the region of diameter 29.*
Select objects: Enter
Select solids, surfaces, and regions to subtract.
Select objects: *Select the region of diameter 21.*
Select objects: Enter

9. Change the visual style to Wireframe by selecting the **Wireframe** option from the **Visual Styles** drop-down list in the **View** panel.

10. Choose the **Sweep** tool from **Home > Modeling > Solid Creation** drop-down and follow the prompt sequence given next to sweep the region along the path.

Current wire frame density: ISOLINES=4, Closed profiles creation mode = Solid
Select objects to sweep or [MOde]: _MO Closed profiles creation mode [SOlid/SUrface] <Solid>: _SO
Select objects to sweep or [MOde]: *Select the region created in Step 8*
1 found
Select objects to sweep or [MOde]: Enter
Select sweep path or [Alignment/Base point/Scale/Twist]: *Select the arc created in Step 6.*

11. Set the view to **SW Isometric** by choosing the appropriate hotspot in the ViewCube. Also, select the **Realistic** option in the **Visual Styles** drop-down list in the **View** panel. The resulting model should look similar to the one shown in Figure 3-127.

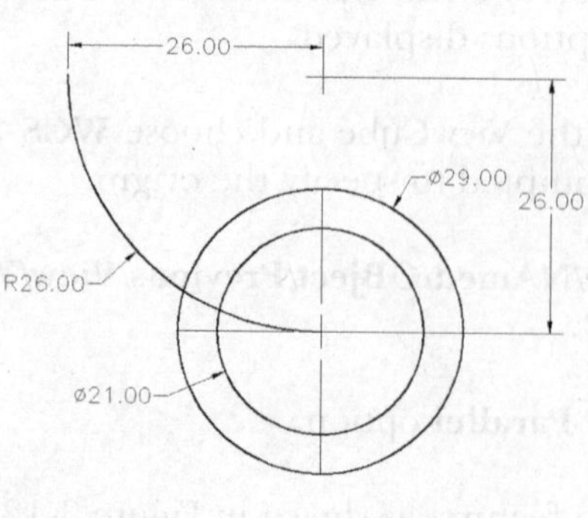

Figure 3-126 *Sketch for base pipe feature*

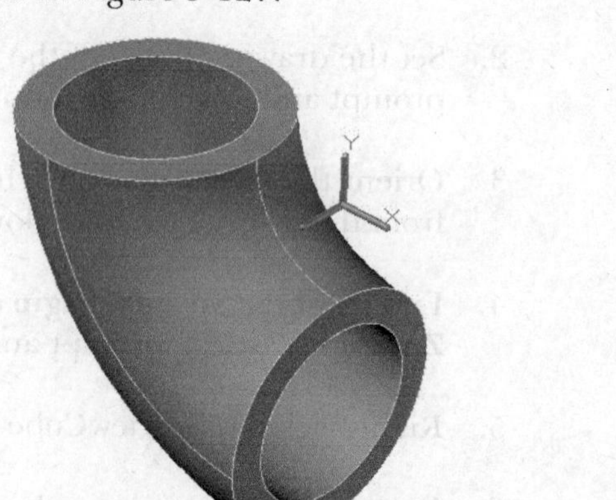

Figure 3-127 *Resulting sweep feature*

12. Choose the **Top** option from the **3D Navigation** drop-down in the **View** panel and draw the sketch with the dimensions shown in Figure 3-128.

13. Change the view to **SW Isometric**. The model after drawing the sketch and turning off the dimension is shown in Figure 3-129.

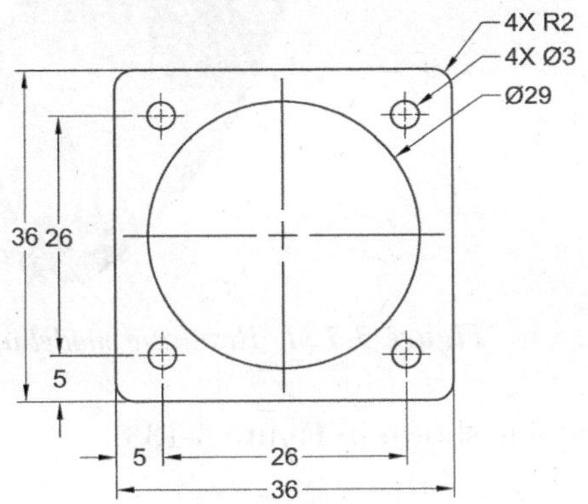

Figure 3-128 Sketch for the area to Press/Pull

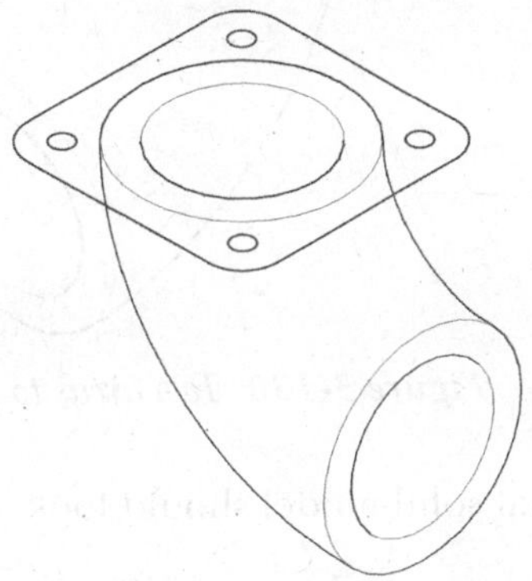

Figure 3-129 Location of the sketch

14. Using the **Region** and **Solid, Subtract** tools, create a region Area A, as shown in Figure 3-130.

15. Choose the **Extrude** tool from **Home > Modeling > Solid Creation** drop-down and select the region created in previous step and press ENTER. Next, move the mouse in the upward direction, enter the value **5** at the Command prompt, and press ENTER.

16. Choose the **Presspull** tool and pull the area shown as Area B in Figure 3-130 by the same value as specified in Step 15. The resulting model should look similar to the one shown in Figure 3-131.

17. Similarly, create the flange for the other face of the pipe. The resulting model should be similar to the one shown in Figure 3-132.

18. Choose the **Solid Union** tool from the **Solid Editing** panel in the **Home** tab and follow the prompt sequence given next.

Select objects: *Select all objects.*
Select objects: Enter

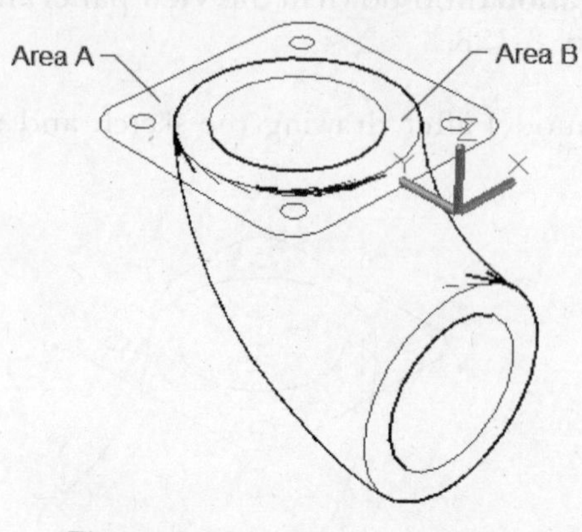

Figure 3-130 *Two areas to presspull*

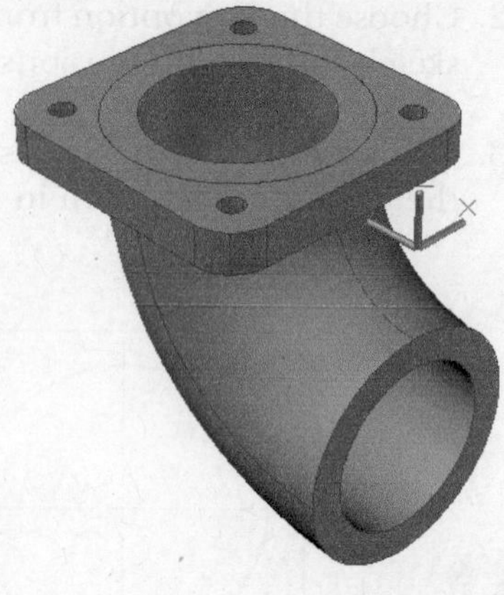

Figure 3-131 *Resulting model after Step 16*

The final solid model should look similar to the one shown in Figure 3-133.

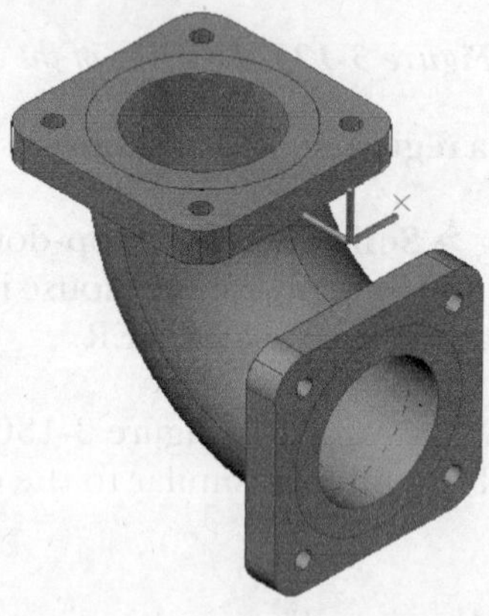

Figure 3-132 *Resulting model after Step 17*

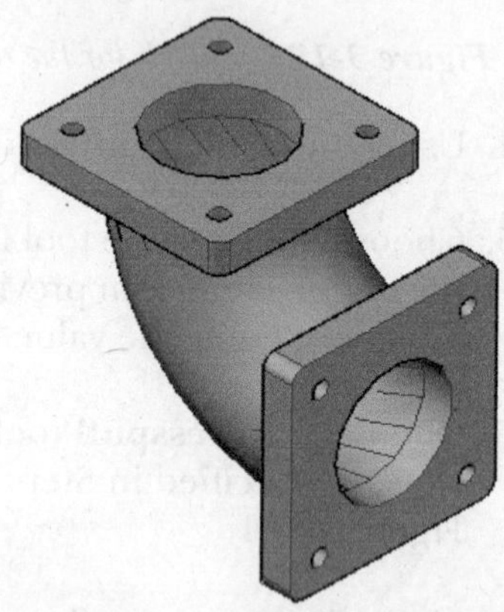

Figure 3-133 *Final model after Union*

Self-Evaluation Test

Answer the following questions and then compare them to those given at the end of this chapter:

1. The __________ tool can be used to add as well as remove material from a model.

2. The __________ tool is used to generate a helical curve.

3. The number of paths for a loft feature cannot be more than __________ .

4. At least __________ cross-sections are required to create a loft feature.

5. You can extrude the selected region about a path using the __________ option of the **Extrude** tool.

6. Open entities can be converted into regions. (T/F)

7. An ellipse can be converted into a polysolid. (T/F)

8. You can twist a cross-section while sweeping it. (T/F)

9. In AutoCAD, you can create a pyramid of maximum 42 sides. (T/F)

10. The **Cone** tool can be used to create a solid cone with a circular and an elliptical base. (T/F)

Review Questions

Answer the following questions:

1. Which of the following values for the taper angle is used to taper the extruded model from the base?

   (a) Positive (b) Negative
   (c) Zero (d) None of these

2. Which of the following tools is used to create a cube?

   (a) **Box** (b) **Cuboid**
   (c) **Polygon** (d) **Cylinder**

3. Which of the following commands is used to check the interference between selected solid models?

   (a) **INTERFERE** (b) **INTERSECT**
   (c) **INTERFERENCE** (d) **CHECK**

4. For which of the following functions is the **Presspull** tool used?

   (a) Add material (b) Remove material
   (c) Both add and remove material (d) Neither add nor remove material

5. The __________ direction is known as the extrusion direction.

6. The __________ tool is used to create an apple-like structure.

7. The __________ tool is used to create a revolved solid.

8. Guides for the **Loft** tool should always __________ the cross-section.

9. The __________ option of the **Revolve** tool is used to select a 2D entity as the revolution axis.

10. You can revolve an open entity. (T/F)

11. You cannot apply Boolean operations on regions. (T/F)

12. The entity to be revolved should lie completely on one side of the revolution axis. (T/F)

13. You cannot apply the **Presspull** tool on an open object. (T/F)

14. There cannot be more than one guide for the loft feature. (T/F)

15. A curve generated by the **Helix** tool can be used as a path for the swept solids. (T/F)

Exercise 1

In this exercise, you will create the solid model shown in Figure 3-134. Assume the missing dimensions.

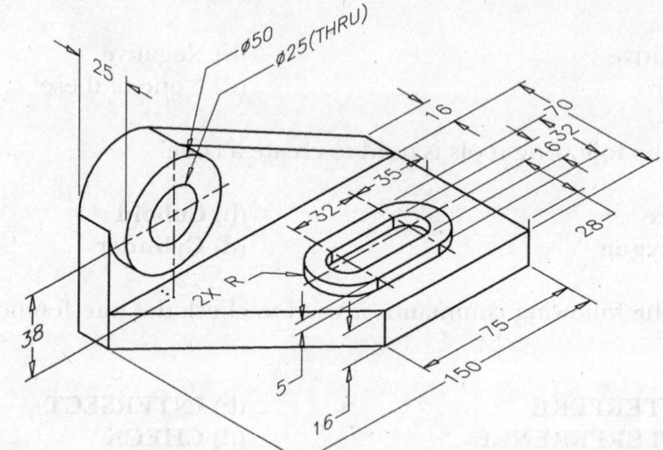

Figure 3-134 Model for Exercise 1

Problem-Solving Exercise 1

In this exercise, you will create the solid model with dimensions shown in Figure 3-135.

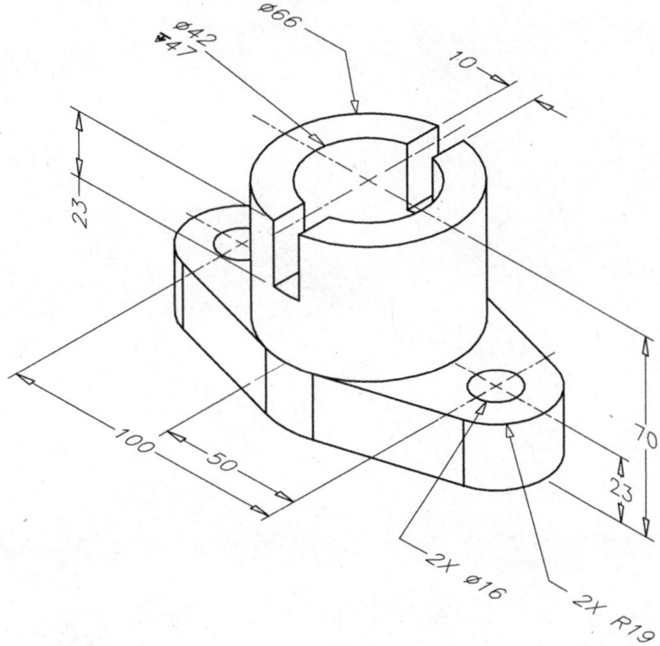

Figure 3-135 Solid model for Problem-Solving Exercise 1

Answers to Self-Evaluation Test

1. **Presspull**, 2. **Helix**, 3. one, 4. two, 5. **Path**, 6. F, 7. T, 8. T, 9. F, 10. T

Chapter 4

Editing 3D Objects-I

Learning Objectives

After completing this chapter, you will be able to:

- *Create fillets and chamfers in the solid models*
- *Rotate and mirror solid models in 3D space*
- *Create an array in 3D space*
- *Align the solid models*
- *Extract the edges of a solid model*
- *Slice the solid models and create cross-sections*
- *Convert objects to surfaces and solids*
- *Convert surfaces to solids*
- *Attaching the Point Cloud*

Key Terms

- *Fillet Edges*
- *Chamfer Edges*
- *Rotate 3D*
- *3D Mirror*
- *3D Move*
- *3DARRAY*
- *Align*
- *3D Align*
- *Extract Edges*
- *Convert to Surface*
- *Convert to Solid*
- *Thicken*
- *Slice*
- *SECTION*

FILLETING SOLID MODELS

Ribbon: Solid > Solid Editing > Fillet Edge drop-down > Fillet Edge
Menu Bar: Modify > Solid Editing > Fillet edges **Command:** FILLETEDGE

As the **Fillet** tool in the **Modify** panel is used to fillet the sharp corners in a sketch, the **Fillet Edge** tool in the **Fillet Edge** drop-down is used to round the edges of a model, refer to Figure 4-1. On invoking this tool, following prompt sequence will be displayed:

Select an edge or [Chain/Loop/Radius]:

Select an edge; the preview of the fillet with default radius will be displayed and you will be prompted to select another edge. If you need to fillet multiple edges, select the edges in succession, refer to Figure 4-2. After selecting the edge or edges, press ENTER to end the selection.

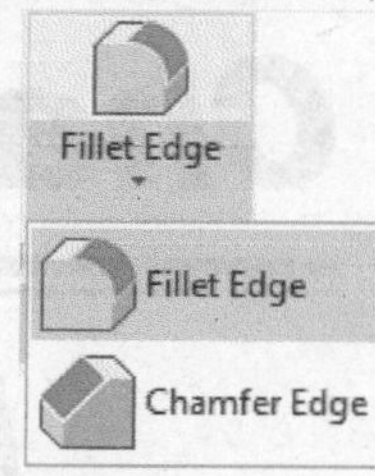

Figure 4-1 *Tools in the* ***Fillet Edge*** *drop-down*

On doing so, you will be prompted to press ENTER again to accept the default radius or enter a new radius. Also, a grip will be displayed on the fillet. Enter **R** for a new radius; specify radius value and press ENTER, or drag the grip to edit the fillet radius and press ENTER; the fillet will be created, as shown in Figure 4-3.

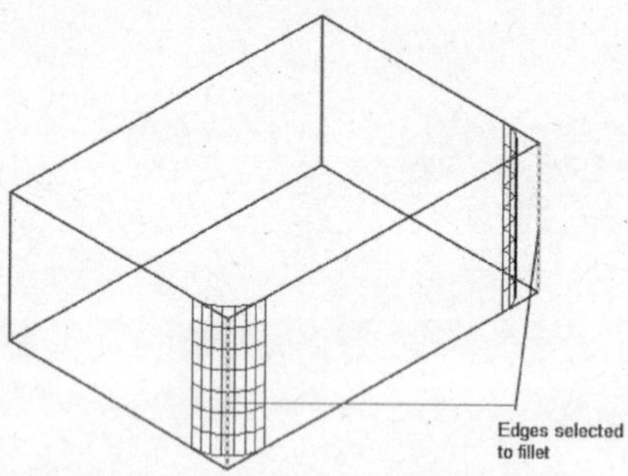

Figure 4-2 *The edges to be filleted*

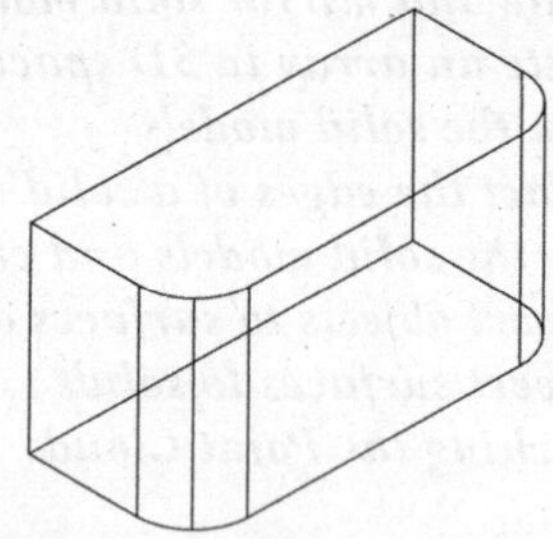

Figure 4-3 *Model after filleting the edges*

Other options in the Command prompt are discussed next.

Chain

On choosing this option, you can select all tangential edges on the face of a solid model in a single attempt, refer to Figure 4-4. Figure 4-5 shows the resulting fillet.

Loop

With this option, you can select any of the loops attached to the selected edge. On choosing this option, preview of the selected loop will be displayed and a contextual menu will open. In this menu, you can accept the loop displayed or select next to check the next possible loop.

Radius

This option is used to redefine the fillet radius. You can also define the radius using an expression.

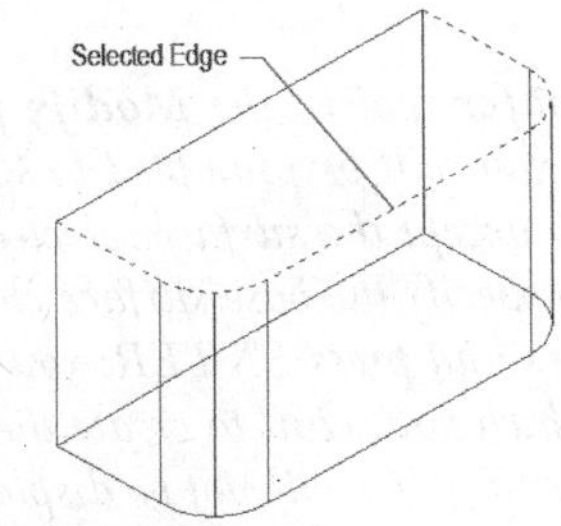

*Figure 4-4 Edge that will be selected using the **Chain** option*

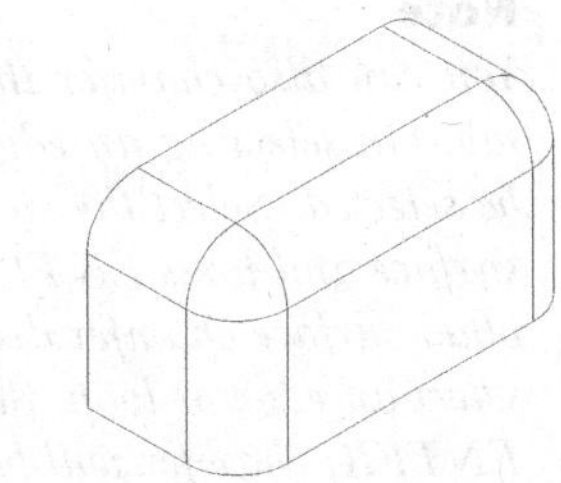

Figure 4-5 The resulting fillet

CHAMFERING SOLID MODELS

Ribbon: Solid > Solid Editing > Fillet Edge drop-down > Chamfer Edge
Menu Bar: Modify > Solid Editing > Chamfer edges **Command:** CHAMFEREDGE

The **Chamfer Edge** tool is used to bevel the edges of solid models. The working of this tool is similar to that of the **Fillet Edge** tool. To create a chamfer, invoke the **Chamfer Edge** tool from the **Solid Editing** panel, refer to Figure 4-1, and then select the edges of the same face in succession; the preview of the chamfer will be displayed. Press ENTER to complete the selection; you will be prompted to specify a value for the new chamfer distance or press ENTER to accept the default value. Also, two grips will be displayed at the edge selected to chamfer. You can enter the chamfer distances or drag the grips on each surface to change the chamfer distance. Then, press ENTER to create the chamfer.

Figures 4-6 and 4-7 show the solid model before and after chamfering, respectively.

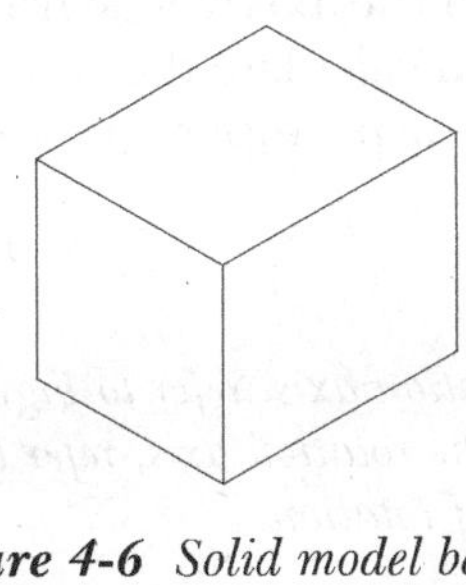

Figure 4-6 Solid model before chamfering

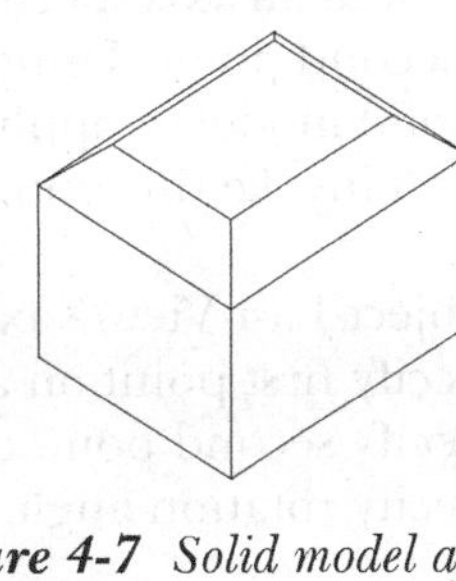

Figure 4-7 Solid model after chamfering

Loop

This option is used to select all edges that make a closed loop on the selected face of the solid model. To select edges using the loop option, enter **L** at the **Select an edge or [Loop/Distance]** prompt and select any one of the edges that forms the loop; all edges will be selected.

Distance

This option is used to define the chamfer distances. When the preview is displayed, you can also drag the grips displayed on the edge to be chamfered and change the chamfer distance.

Note

*You can also chamfer the edges by using the **Chamfer** tool in the **Modify** panel of the **Home** tab. On selecting an edge after invoking this tool, you will be prompted to specify the surface to be selected. Select the surface and press ENTER to accept the surface selected, or select the next surface and press ENTER; you will be prompted to specify the base surface chamfer distance and other surface chamfer distance. Enter suitable values and press ENTER; you will be prompted to select an edge or loop. Select the edge or loop on which you want to create the chamfer and press ENTER; chamfer will be created. In this case, the edit grips will not be displayed.*

ROTATING SOLID MODELS IN 3D SPACE

Command: ROTATE3D

The **ROTATE3D** command is used to rotate the selected solid model in the 3D space about a specified axis. The right-hand thumb rule will be used to determine the direction of rotation of the solid model in 3D space. The prompt sequence that will follow when you invoke this command is given next.

Current positive angle: ANGDIR=counterclockwise ANGBASE=0
Select objects: *Select the solid model.*
Select objects: Enter
Specify first point on axis or define axis by
[Object/Last/View/Xaxis/Yaxis/Zaxis/2Points]: *Specify a point on the axis of rotation or select an option.*

2points

This is the default option for rotating solid models. This option allows you to rotate the solid model about an axis specified by two points. The direction of the axis will be from the first point to the second point. Using the direction of the axis, you can calculate the direction of rotation of the solid model by applying the right-hand thumb rule. The prompt sequence that will follow when you invoke this option is given next.

[Object/Last/View/Xaxis/Yaxis/Zaxis/2points]:2 Enter
Specify first point on axis: *Specify the first point of the rotation axis, refer to Figure 4-8.*
Specify second point on axis: *Specify the second point of the rotation axis, refer to Figure 4-8.*
Specify rotation angle or [Reference]: *Specify the angle of rotation.*

Object

This option is used to rotate the solid model in the 3D space using a 2D entity. The 2D entities that can be used are line, circle, arc, or 2D polyline segment. If the selected entity is a line or a straight polyline segment, then it will be directly taken as the rotation axis. However, if the selected entity is an arc or a circle, then an imaginary axis will be drawn starting from the center and normal to the plane in which the arc or circle is drawn. The object will then be rotated about this imaginary axis. The prompt sequence that will follow when you invoke this option is given next.

[Object/Last/View/Xaxis/Yaxis/Zaxis/2points]: **O** Enter
Select a line, circle, arc, or 2D-polyline segment: *Select the 2D entity, as shown in Figure 4-9.*
Specify rotation angle or [Reference]: *Specify the angle of rotation.*

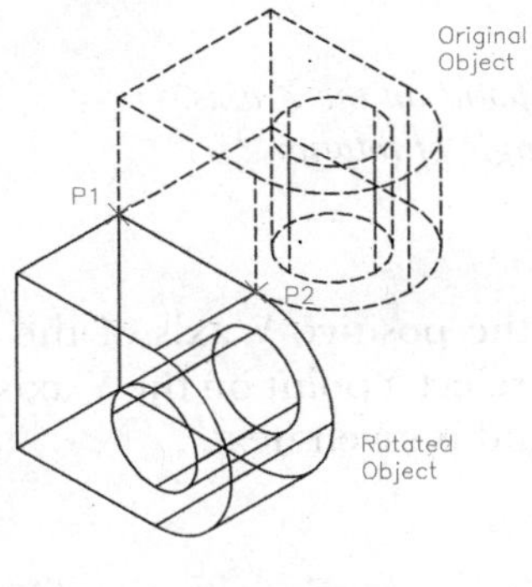

Figure 4-8 *Rotating the solid model using the* ***2points*** *option*

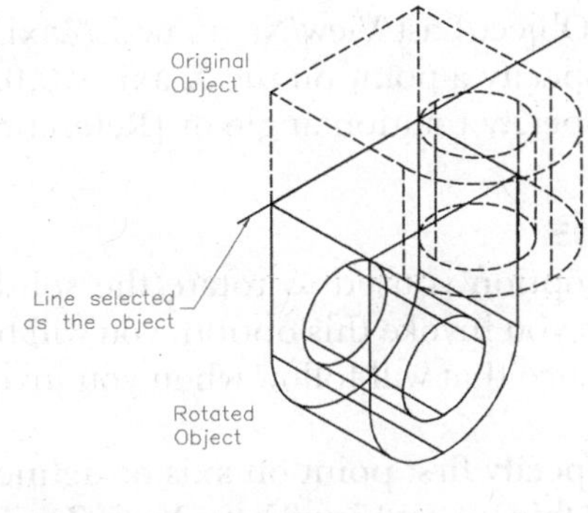

Figure 4-9 *Rotating the solid model using the* ***Object*** *option*

Last

This option uses the same axis that was last selected to rotate the solid model.

View

This option is used to rotate the solid model about the viewing plane. In this case, the viewing plane is the screen of the computer. This option draws an imaginary axis starting from the specified point which continues normal to the viewing plane. The model is then rotated about this axis. The prompt sequence that will follow when you invoke this option is given next.

Specify first point on axis or define axis by
[Object/Last/View/Xaxis/Yaxis/Zaxis/2points]: **V**
Specify a point on the view direction axis <0,0,0>: *Specify the point on the view plane, as shown in Figure 4-10.*
Specify rotation angle or [Reference]: *Specify the angle of rotation.*

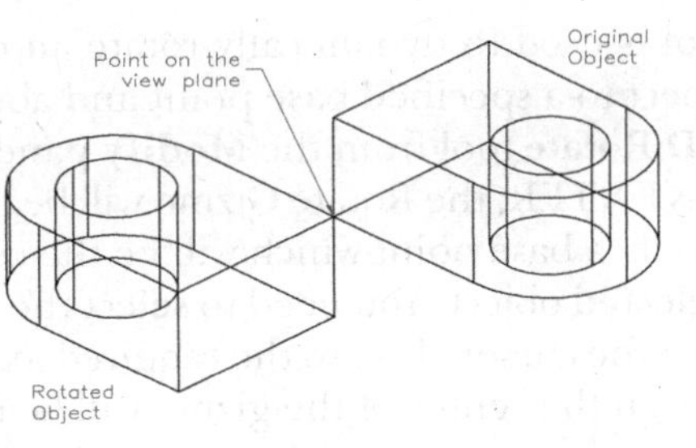

Figure 4-10 *Rotating the solid model using the* ***View*** *option through an angle of 180°*

Xaxis

This option is used to rotate the solid model about the positive X axis of the current UCS. On invoking this option, you will be prompted to select a point on the X axis. The prompt sequence that will follow when you invoke this command is given next.

Specify first point on axis or define axis by
[Object/Last/View/Xaxis/Yaxis/Zaxis/2points]: **X**
Specify a point on the X axis <0,0,0>: *Specify the point on the X axis.*
Specify rotation angle or [Reference]: *Specify the angle of rotation.*

Yaxis

This option is used to rotate the solid model about the positive Y axis of the current UCS. When you invoke this option, you will be prompted to select a point on the Y axis. The prompt sequence that will follow when you invoke this command is given next.

Specify first point on axis or define axis by
[Object/Last/View/Xaxis/Yaxis/Zaxis/2points]: **Y**
Specify a point on the Y axis <0,0,0>: *Specify the point on the Y axis.*
Specify rotation angle or [Reference]: *Specify the angle of rotation.*

Zaxis

This option is used to rotate the solid model about the positive Z axis of the current UCS. When you invoke this option, you will be prompted to select a point on the Z axis. The prompt sequence that will follow when you invoke this command is given next.

Specify first point on axis or define axis by
[Object/Last/View/Xaxis/Yaxis/Zaxis/2points]: **Z**
Specify a point on the Z axis <0,0,0>: *Specify the point on the Z axis.*
Specify rotation angle or [Reference]: *Specify the angle of rotation.*

ROTATING SOLID MODELS ABOUT AN AXIS

Ribbon: Home > Modify > 3D Rotate
Menu Bar: Modify > 3D Operations > 3D Rotate
Toolbar: Modeling > 3D Rotate **Command:** 3DROTATE

The **3D Rotate** tool is used to dynamically rotate an object or sub-objects such as edges and faces with respect to a specified base point and about a selected axis. To perform this operation, choose the **3D Rotate** tool from the **Modify** panel and select the object or subobject to be rotated. Then, press ENTER; the Rotate Gizmo will be displayed at the center of the object, refer to Figure 4-11. Specify a base point which will be the center point of rotation about which you need to rotate the selected object. You need to select the axis about which you want to rotate the object. To do so, move the cursor close to the required axis handle; the axis gets highlighted and an axis passing through the center of the gizmo will be displayed, as shown in Figure 4-12. Click once and drag the cursor or enter a value at the Command prompt.

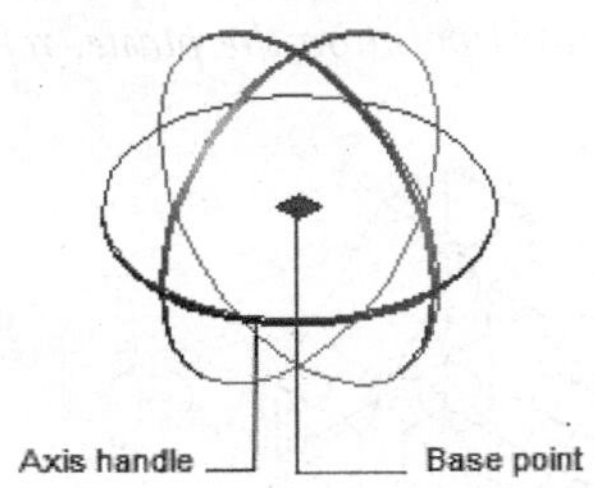

Figure 4-11 The ***Rotate Gizmo***

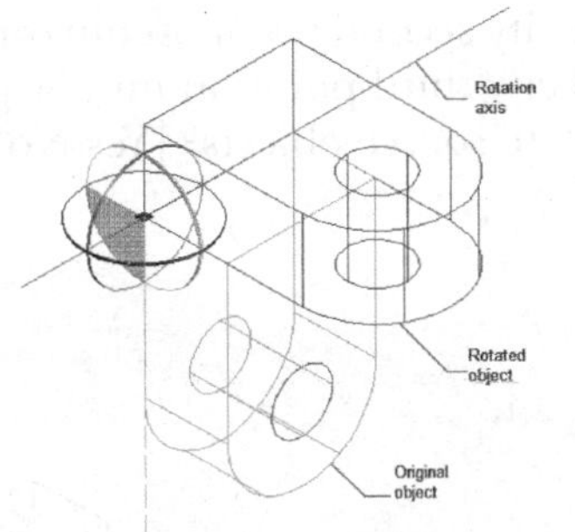

Figure 4-12 Model rotated by 90 degrees about the X axis

Tip

If you select a model in ***3D Modeling*** *workspace with 3D visual style, the Move Gizmo will be displayed on it. This is because the default gizmo displayed in the* ***Selection*** *panel of the* ***Home*** *tab is the Move Gizmo. If you choose the* ***Rotate Gizmo*** *tool from the* ***Gizmo*** *drop-down and select a model, the* ***Rotate Gizmo*** *will be displayed. Using this gizmo, you can directly rotate the model in 3D space.*

MIRRORING SOLID MODELS IN 3D SPACE

Ribbon: Home > Modify > 3D Mirror
Menu Bar: Modify > 3D Operations > 3D Mirror **Command:** MIRROR3D

The **3D Mirror** tool is used to mirror the solid models about a specified plane in the space. To mirror a solid model, choose the **3D Mirror** tool from the **Modify** panel and follow the prompt sequence given next.

Select objects: *Select the solid model to be mirrored.*
Select objects: Enter
Specify first point of mirror plane (3 points) or
[Object/Last/Zaxis/View/XY/YZ/ZX/3points] <3points>: *Specify the first point on the mirror plane or select an option.*

The options in this prompt are discussed next.

3points

This is the default selected option for mirroring the solid models. As discussed earlier, a line can be defined by specifying two points through which the line will pass. Similarly, a plane can be defined by specifying three points through which it passes. This option allows you to specify the three points through which the mirroring plane passes. The prompt sequence that follows when you invoke this tool is given next.

Specify first point of mirror plane (3 points) or
[Object/Last/Zaxis/View/XY/YZ/ZX/3points] <3points>: Enter
Specify first point on mirror plane: *Specify the first point on the plane, refer to Figure 4-13.*

Specify second point on mirror plane: *Specify the second point on the plane, refer to Figure 4-13.*
Specify third point on mirror plane: *Specify the third point on the plane, refer to Figure 4-13.*
Delete source objects? [Yes/No] <N>: Enter

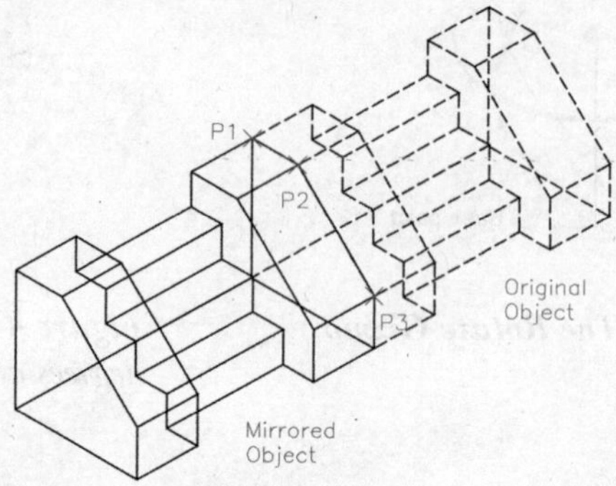

***Figure 4-13** Mirroring the solid model using the **3points** option*

Object

This option is used to mirror the solid model using a 2D entity, refer to Figure 4-14. The 2D entities that can be used to mirror the solids are circles, arcs, and 2D polyline segments. The prompt sequence that follows when you invoke this option is given next.

Specify first point of mirror plane (3 points) or
[Object/Last/Zaxis/View/XY/YZ/ZX/3points] <3points>: **O**
Select a circle, arc, or 2D-polyline segment: *Select the 2D entity, as shown in Figure 4-14.*
Delete source objects? [Yes/No] <N>: Enter

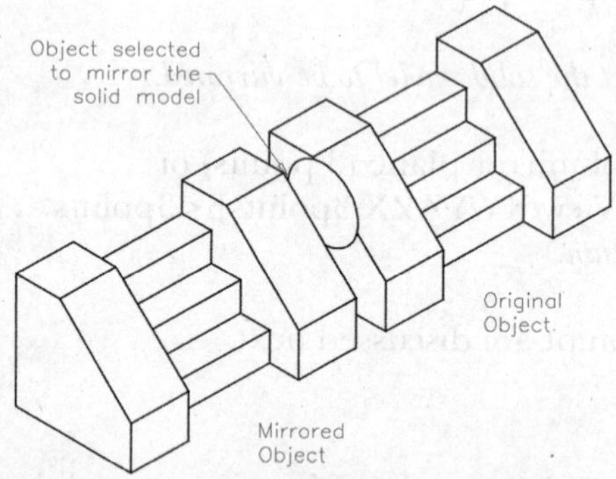

***Figure 4-14** Mirroring the solid model using the **Object** option*

Zaxis

This option allows you to define a mirroring plane using two points. The first point is the point on the mirroring plane and the second point is a point on the positive direction of the Z axis of that plane or normal to that plane. The prompt sequence that follows when you invoke this option is given next.

Specify first point of mirror plane (3 points) or
[Object/Last/Zaxis/View/XY/YZ/ZX/3points] <3points>: **Z**
Specify point on mirror plane: *Specify the point on the plane, as shown in Figure 4-15.*
Specify point on Z-axis (normal) of mirror plane: *Specify the point on the Z direction of the plane, refer to Figure 4-15.*
Delete source objects? [Yes/No] <N>: Enter

View

This is one of the interesting options provided for mirroring solid models. This option is used to mirror the selected solid model about the viewing plane. The viewing plane, in this case, is the screen of the monitor, refer to Figure 4-16. The prompt sequence that follows when you invoke this tool is given next.

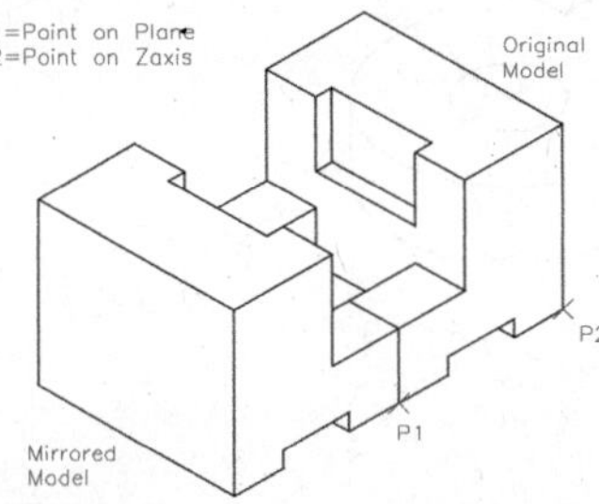

Figure 4-15 *Mirroring the solid model using the* ***Zaxis*** *option*

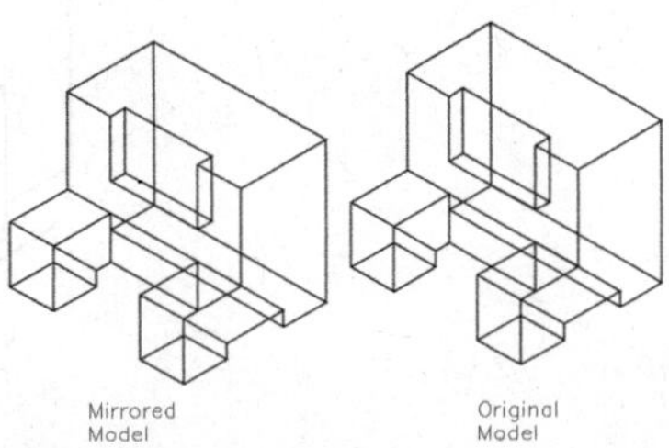

Figure 4-16 *A solid model mirrored using the* ***View*** *option and then moved*

Specify first point of mirror plane (3 points) or
[Object/Last/Zaxis/View/XY/YZ/ZX/3points] <3points>: **V**
Specify point on view plane <0,0,0>: *Specify the point on the view plane.*
Delete source objects? [Yes/No] <N>: Enter

> **Tip**
> *As the model is mirrored about the view plane, the new model will be placed over the original model when you view it from the current viewpoint. The best option to view the mirrored model is to hide the hidden lines using the* ***Hide*** *tool. You can also move the new model away from the last model using the* ***Move*** *tool or change the viewpoint for viewing both the models simultaneously.*

XY/YZ/ZX

These options are used to mirror the solid model about the XY, YZ, or ZX plane of the current UCS.

> **Tip**
> *All these planes will be considered with reference to the current orientation of the UCS and not with its world position. This means that when you select the* ***XY*** *option to mirror the solid model, then the XY plane of the current UCS will be considered to mirror the model and not the XY plane of the world UCS.*

Example 1

In this example, you will create the solid model shown in Figure 4-17. Assume the missing dimensions.

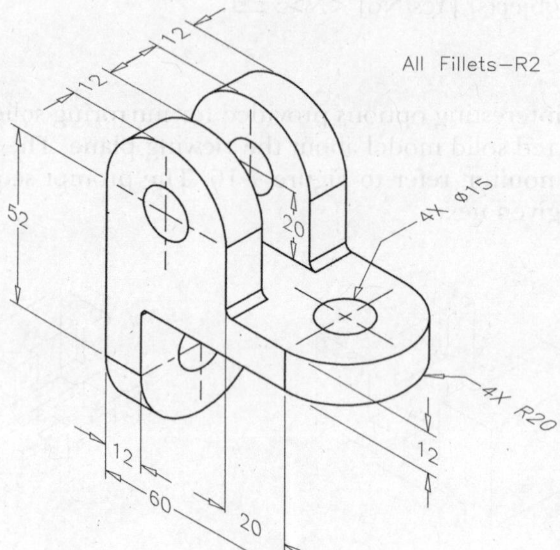

Figure 4-17 Solid model for Example 1

1. Start a new 3D template drawing file in **3D Modeling** workspace. Set the drawing limits of the workspace to 100,100.

2. Orient the view to top by choosing **Top** in the ViewCube. Next, choose **WCS > New UCS** from the **WCS** drop-down list below the ViewCube; you will be prompted to specify the origin. Enter **V** at the **Specify origin of UCS or [Face/NAmed/OBject/Previous/View/World/X/Y/Z/ZAxis] <World>** prompt and press ENTER.

3. Create the base of the model and then change the view to the **SE Isometric** using the ViewCube, refer to Figure 4-18.

4. Next, orient the view to front by choosing **Front** in the ViewCube. Next, choose **WCS > New UCS** from the **WCS** drop-down list below the ViewCube; you will be prompted to specify the origin. Enter **V** at the **Specify origin of UCS or [Face/NAmed/OBject/Previous/View/World/X/Y/Z/ZAxis] <World>** prompt and press ENTER.

5. Draw the sketch for the next object using the **Rectangle** tool. Convert one side of the rectangle to an arc by using the shortcut menu that is displayed when you hover the cursor on the middle grip. Then, create the object by using the **Region**, **Extrude**, and **Subtract** tools. The resulting object is shown in Figure 4-19.

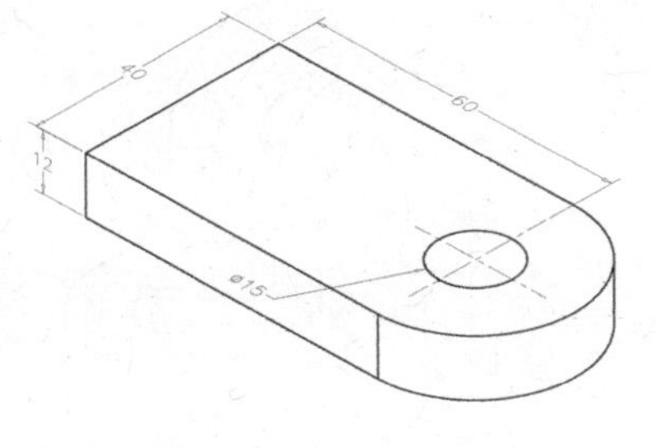

Figure 4-18 *Base of the model*

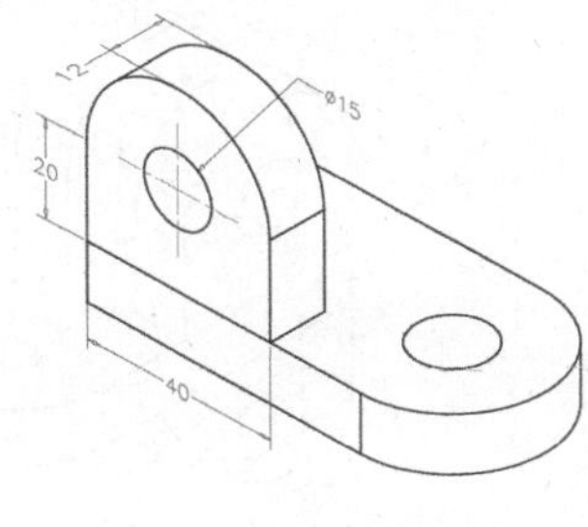

Figure 4-19 *Model after creating the next object*

6. Invoke the **3D Mirror** tool from the **Modify** panel and follow the prompt sequence given next.

Select objects: *Select the last object.*
Select objects: Enter
Specify first point of mirror plane (3 points) or
[Object/Last/Zaxis/View/XY/YZ/ZX/3points] <3points>: **Z**
Specify point on mirror plane: *Select P1, as shown in Figure 4-20.*

Specify point on Z-axis (normal) of mirror plane: *Select P2, as shown in Figure 4-20.*
Delete source objects? [Yes/No] <N>: Enter

7. The object after mirroring and hiding the hidden lines should look similar to the model shown in Figure 4-21.

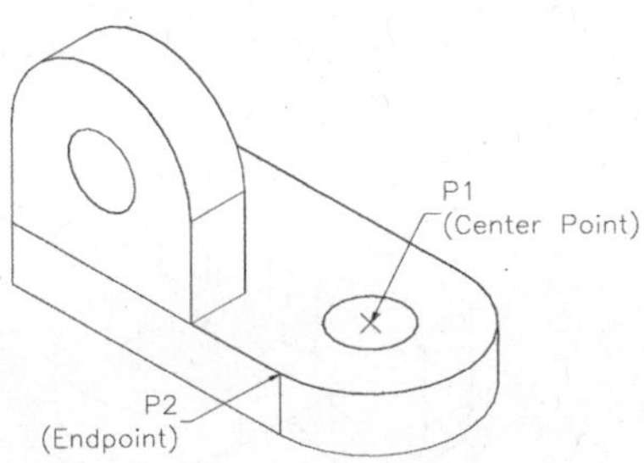

Figure 4-20 *Selecting the points to be mirrored*

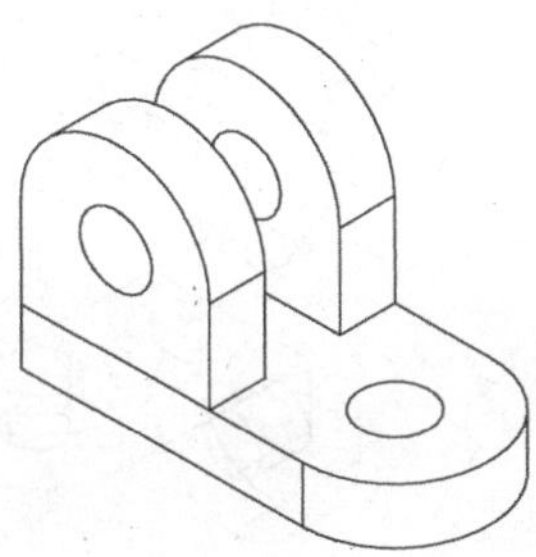

Figure 4-21 *Model after mirroring*

8. Set the UCS in the **Left** view and create the feature at the bottom, as shown in Figure 4-22.

9. Choose the **Solid, Union** tool from the **Solid Editing** panel and then unite all objects, refer to Figure 4-23.

Figure 4-22 Model after creating the next object at the bottom

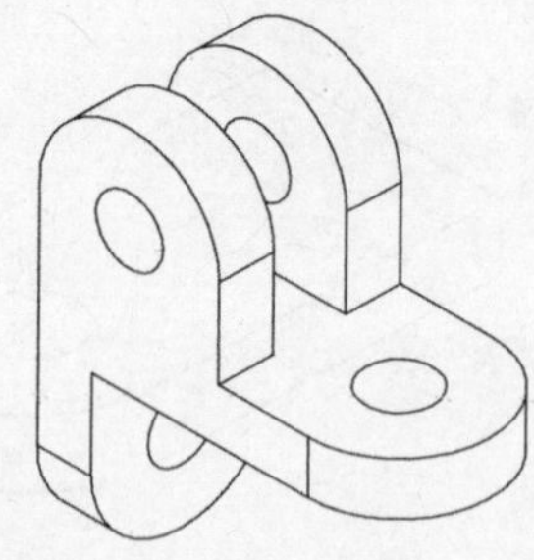

Figure 4-23 Model after creating the union

10. Choose the **Fillet Edge** tool from **Solid > Solid Editing > Fillet Edge** drop-down and follow the prompt sequence given below.

    Select an edge or [Chain/Loop/Radius]: *Select first edge, as shown in Figure 4-24.*
    Select an edge or [Chain/Loop/Radius]: *Select the second edge, as shown in Figure 4-24.*
    Select an edge or [Chain/Loop/Radius]: *Select the third edge, as shown in Figure 4-24.*
    Select an edge or [Chain/Loop/Radius]: Enter
    3 edge(s) selected for fillet
    Press Enter to accept the fillet or [Radius]: **R**
    Specify Radius or [Expression]<1.0000>: **2** Enter
    Press Enter to accept the fillet or [Radius]: Enter

11. The final model for Example 1 should look similar to the model shown in Figure 4-25.

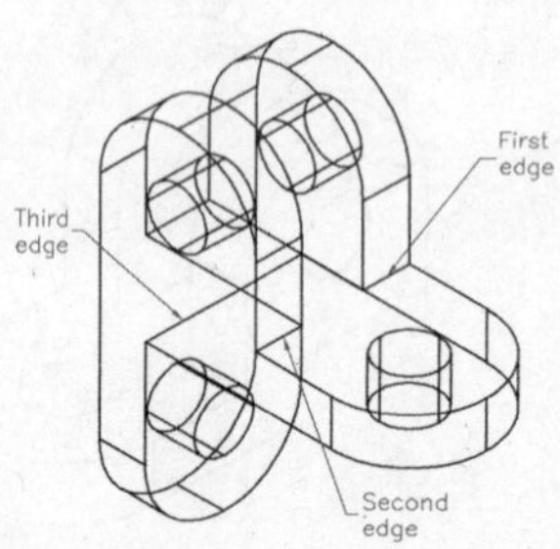

Figure 4-24 Selecting the edges for filleting

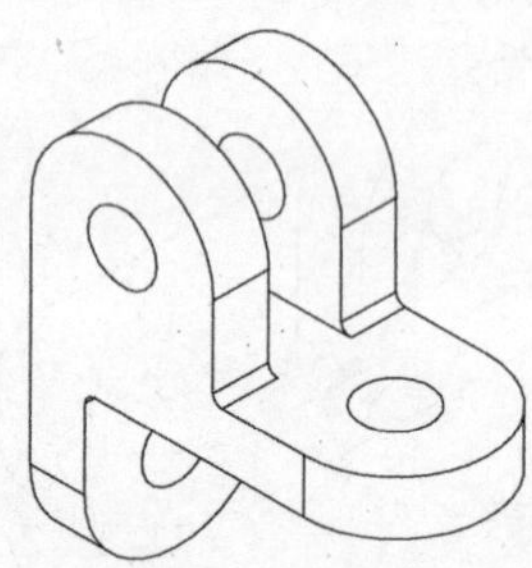

Figure 4-25 The final model for Example 1

MOVING MODELS IN 3D SPACE

Ribbon: Home > Modify > 3D Move
Menu Bar: Modify > 3D Operations > 3D Move **Toolbar:** Modeling > 3D Move
Command: 3DMOVE

Sometimes, you need to move objects such as edges or faces of a solid model or the entire solid in 3D space. In such cases, you can use the **3D Move** tool to translate them to the desired location. You can move the selected object or subobject at an orientation parallel to a plane or along an axial direction. To perform this operation choose the **3D Move** tool from the **Modify** panel and select the object or subobject to be moved and press ENTER; the **Move Gizmo** will be displayed on the selected object, refer to Figure 4-26. To move the object in 3D space with respect to a base point other than the default one, click in the drawing area; the new base point will be specified. Then, specify the displacement or drag the cursor and place the component.

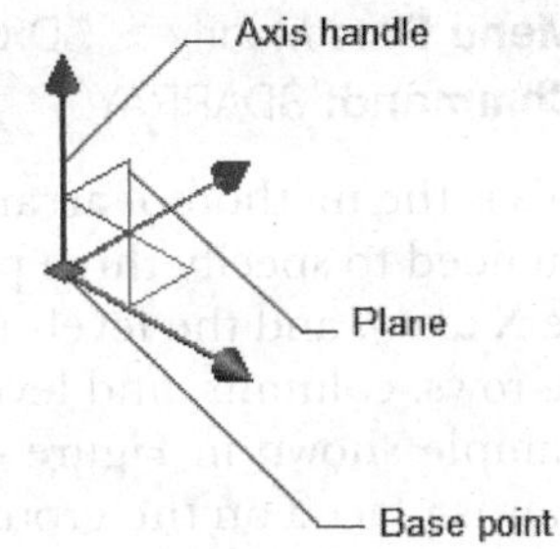

*Figure 4-26 The **Move Gizmo***

To move an object along a particular direction, move the cursor near the axis handle corresponding to that direction; a line of the same color as the selected axis will be displayed. Click when the axis is highlighted and drag the cursor to move the object along that direction. To move a face or an edge of a solid model in a particular plane, invoke the **3D Move** tool, press the CTRL key, select a face or an edge, and press ENTER; the move gizmo will be displayed on the selected object. Next, move the cursor near the desired plane in the **Move Gizmo**; the plane, including the corresponding axis handle, will turn golden in color. Press and hold the left mouse button when the plane is highlighted and then drag; the selected object will move only parallel to the selected plane.

Tip

*By default, the **Move Gizmo** option is selected in the **Default Gizmo** drop-down available in the **Selection** panel. Therefore, on selecting an object, the **Move Gizmo** will be displayed on the object and you can translate the selected object. Also, by default, the **No Filter** option is selected in the **Filter** drop-down list. As a result, you can select a face, an edge, or a vertex of a model. However, if any other option is selected in the **Filter** drop-down list, then only the corresponding entity can be selected.*

CREATING ARRAYS IN 3D SPACE

Menu Bar: Modify > 3D Operations > 3D Array **Toolbar:** Modeling > 3D Array
Command: 3DARRAY

As mentioned earlier, the arrays are defined as the method of creating multiple copies of the selected object in a rectangular or a polar fashion. The 3D arrays can also be created similar to the 2D arrays. The only difference is that in a 3D array, another factor called the Z axis is also taken into consideration. There are two types of 3D arrays and these are discussed next.

3D Rectangular Array

Menu Bar: Modify > 3D Operations > 3D Array
Command: 3DARRAY

This is the method of arranging the solid model along the edges of a box. In this type of array, you need to specify three parameters. They are the rows (along the Y axis), the columns (along the X axis), and the levels (along the Z axis). You will also have to specify the distances between the rows, columns, and levels. The 3D rectangular array can be easily understood by taking an example shown in Figure 4-27. This figure shows two floors of a building. Initially, only one chair is placed on the ground floor. Now, if you create a 2D rectangular array, the chairs will be arranged only on the ground floor. However, when you create the 3D rectangular array, then the chairs will be arranged on the first floor (along the Z axis) as well as the ground floor, refer to Figure 4-28. In this example, the number of rows is three, columns is four, and levels is two.

The prompt sequence that will follow when you choose this tool is given next.

Select objects: *Select the object to array.*
Select objects: Enter
Enter the type of array [Rectangular/Polar] <R>: Enter
Enter the number of rows (---) <1>: *Specify the number of rows along the Y axis.*
Enter the number of columns (|||) <1>: *Specify the number of columns along the X axis.*
Enter the number of levels (...) <1>: *Specify the number of levels along the Z axis.*
Specify the distance between rows (---): *Specify the distance between the rows.*
Specify the distance between columns (|||): *Specify the distance between the columns.*
Specify the distance between levels (...): *Specify the distance between the levels.*

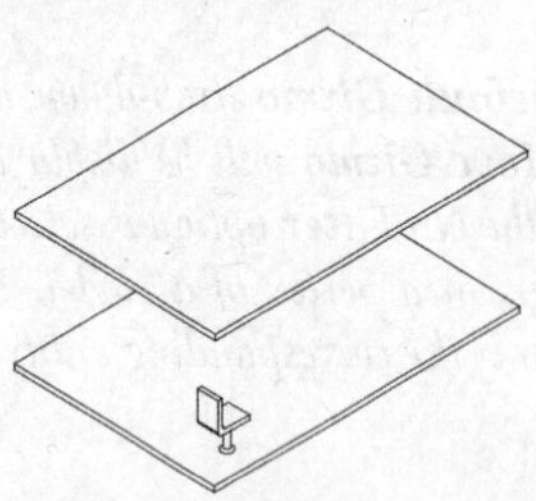

***Figure 4-27** The model before creating the rectangular array*

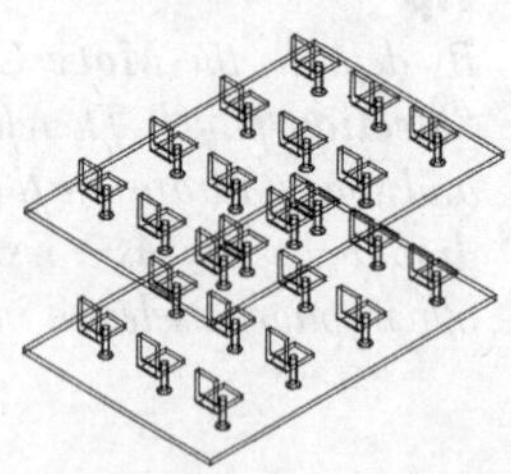

***Figure 4-28** The model after creating the array in 3D space*

3D Polar Array

Menu Bar: Modify > 3D Operations > 3D Array
Command: 3DARRAY

The 3D polar arrays are similar to the 2D polar arrays. The only difference between them is that in 3D, you will have to specify an axis about which the solid models will be arranged. For example, consider the solid models shown in Figure 4-29. This figure shows a circular plate that has four holes. Now, to place the bolts in this plate, you can use the 3D polar array, as shown in Figure 4-30. The axis for an array is defined using the centers at the top and the bottom faces of the circular plate. The prompt sequence that will follow is given next.

Select objects: *Select the object to array.*
Select objects: Enter
Enter the type of array [Rectangular/Polar] <R>: **P**
Enter the number of items in the array: *Specify the number of items.*
Specify the angle to fill (+=ccw, -=cw) <360>: Enter
Rotate arrayed objects? [Yes/No] <Y>: Enter
Specify center point of array: *Specify the first point on the axis.*
Specify second point on axis of rotation: *Specify the second point on the axis.*

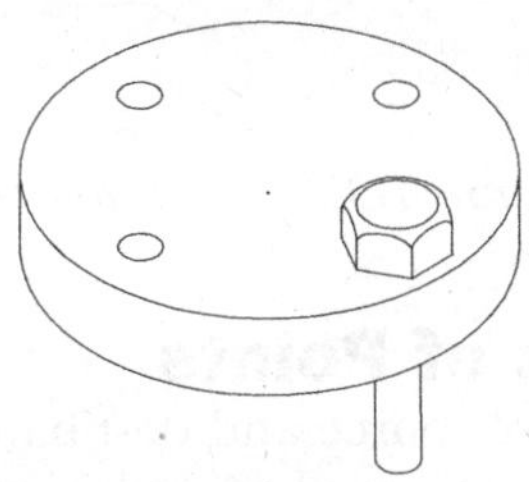

Figure 4-29 *Model before creating an array*

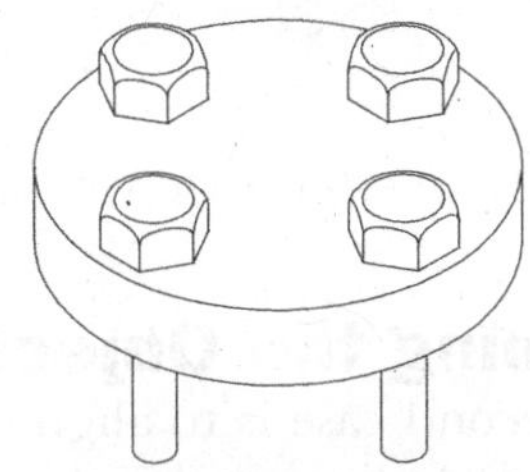

Figure 4-30 *Model after creating an array*

ALIGNING SOLID MODELS

Ribbon: Home > Modify > Align
Menu Bar: Modify > 3D Operations > Align **Command:** ALIGN

The **Align** tool is extensively used in solid modeling. As the name suggests, this tool is used to align the selected solid model with another solid model. It can also be used to translate, rotate, and scale the selected solid model. This tool uses pairs of source and destination points to align the solid model. The source point is a point with which you want to align the object. The destination point is a point on the destination object at which you want to place the source object. You can specify one, two, or three pairs of points to align the objects. However, the working of this tool will be different in all the three cases. All these three cases are discussed next.

Aligning the Objects Using One Pair of Points

When you align the object using just one pair of points, the working of this tool will be similar to the **Move** tool. This means that the source object will be moved as it is from its original location and will be placed on the destination object. Here, the source point will work as the first point of displacement and the destination point will work as the second point of displacement. Also, a reference line will be drawn between the source and the destination points. This line will disappear once you exit the tool. The prompt sequence is as follows:

Select objects: *Select the object to align.*
Select objects: Enter
Specify first source point: *Select S1, as shown in Figure 4-31.*
Specify first destination point: *Select D1, as shown in Figure 4-31.*
Specify second source point: Enter

Figure 4-32 shows the models after aligning.

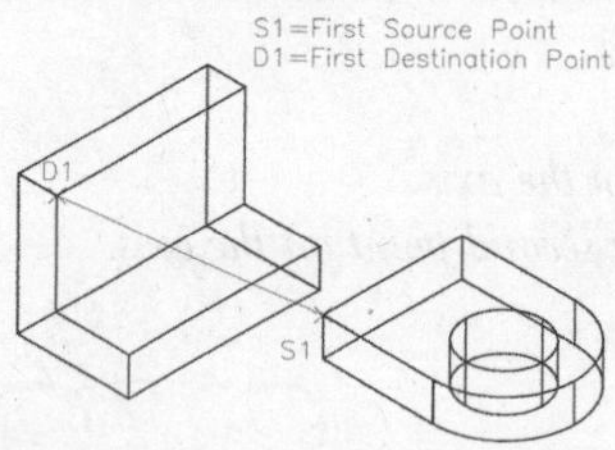

***Figure 4-31** Models before aligning*

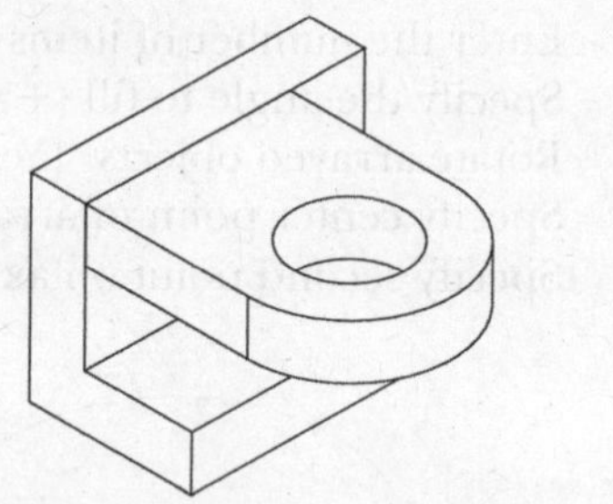

***Figure 4-32** Models after aligning*

Aligning the Objects Using Two Pairs of Points

The second case is to align the objects using two pairs of source and destination points. This method of aligning the objects forces the selected object to translate and rotate once. You are also provided with an option of scaling the source object to align with the destination object. The prompt sequence that follows is given next.

Select objects: *Select the object to align.*
Select objects: Enter
Specify first source point: *Select S1, as shown in Figure 4-33.*
Specify first destination point: *Select D1, as shown in Figure 4-33.*
Specify second source point: *Select S2, as shown in Figure 4-33.*
Specify second destination point: *Select D2, as shown in Figure 4-33.*
Specify third source point or <continue>: Enter
Scale objects based on alignment points? [Yes/No] <N>: **Y** *(You can also enter **N** at this prompt, if you do not want to scale the object).*

Figure 4-34 shows the objects after aligning and scaling.

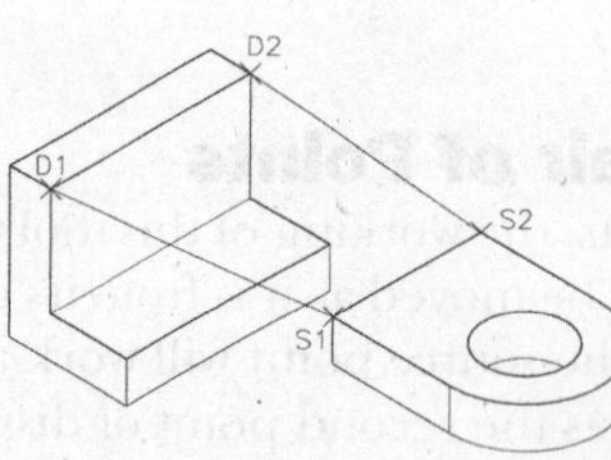

***Figure 4-33** Objects before aligning*

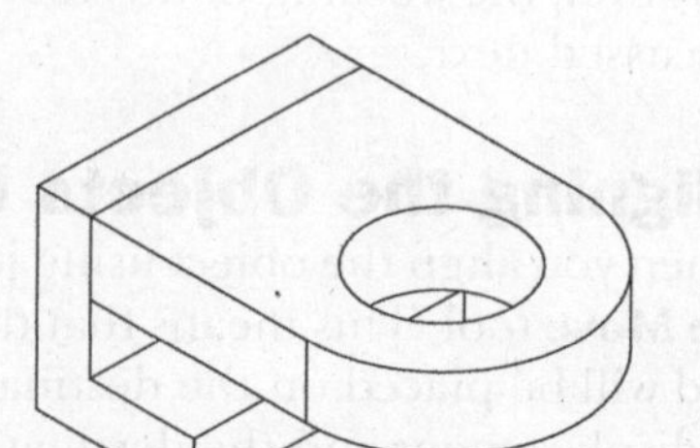

***Figure 4-34** Objects after aligning and scaling*

Aligning the Objects Using Three Pairs of Points

The third case is to align the objects using three pairs of points. This option forces the selected object to rotate and then translate, refer to Figures 4-35 and 4-36. The first pair of source and destination points is used to specify the base point of alignment, the second pair of source and destination points is used to specify the first rotation angle, and the third pair of source and destination points is used to specify the second rotation angle. In this case, you will not be allowed to scale the object. The prompt sequence that follows is given next.

Select objects: *Select the object to align.*
Select objects: Enter
Specify first source point: *Select S1, as shown in Figure 4-35.*
Specify first destination point: *Select D1, as shown in Figure 4-35.*
Specify second source point: *Select S2, as shown in Figure 4-35.*
Specify second destination point: *Select D2, as shown in Figure 4-35.*
Specify third source point or <continue>: *Select S3, as shown in Figure 4-35.*
Specify third destination point: *Select D3, as shown in Figure 4-35.*

Figure 4-36 shows the objects after aligning and rotating.

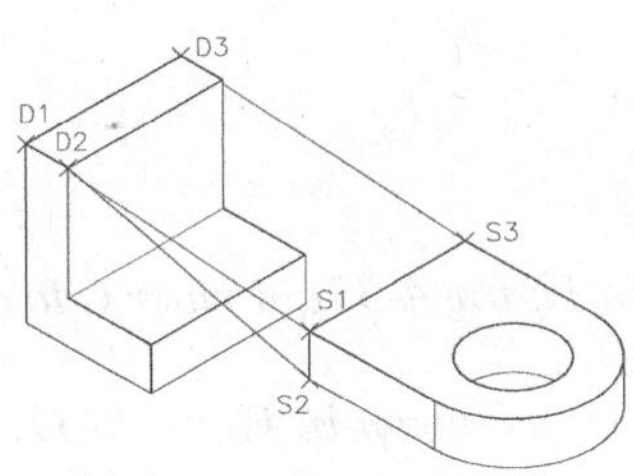

Figure 4-35 *Objects before aligning*

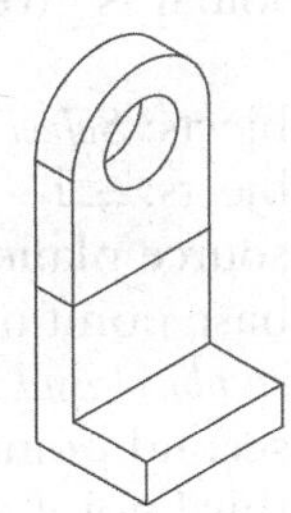

Figure 4-36 *Objects after aligning and rotating*

ALIGNING SOLIDS BY DEFINING AN ALIGNMENT PLANE

Ribbon: Home > Modify > 3D Align
Menu Bar: Modify > 3D Operations > 3D Align
Toolbar: Modeling > 3D Align
Command: 3DALIGN

The **3D Align** tool is used to align the selected solids or the copy of those solids with another solid object. To do so, define a plane for the source and destination objects that are to be aligned to each other. In this tool, you are prompted to specify the first, second, and third points continuously on the source to define a plane for the source. Then, you will be prompted to specify the first, second, and third points on the destination object to define a plane for the destination. As a result, these planes will be automatically aligned to each other. While specifying the points on the destination object, you get a dynamic preview for the placement of the source object. The following is the significance of each point that you specify on the source and destination objects.

First point on source. This is the base point on the source object that later coincides with the first point of the destination object.

Second point on source. This point defines the direction of the X axis on the new XY plane that will be created on the source object.

Third point on source. This point is specified on the new XY plane to define the direction of the Y axis. This completely defines the new XY plane of the source. After specifying this point, the source object is rotated to make this new XY plane parallel to the XY plane of the current UCS.

First point on destination. This is the base point of the destination. The base point of the source will coincide with this point.

Second point on destination. This point defines the direction of the X axis on the new XY plane of the destination object. The X axis of the source will get aligned to the X axis of the destination object.

Third point on destination. This point is specified on the new XY plane to define the direction of the Y axis. This completely defines the new XY plane of the destination.

The prompt sequence that will be followed when you choose the **3D Align** tool from the **Modeling** toolbar is given next.

Select objects: *Select the object to align.*
Select objects: Enter
Specify source plane and orientation ...
Specify base point or [Copy]: *Select S1, as shown in Figure 4-37, or enter C to align the copy of the selected object and leave the original one as it is.*
Specify second point or [Continue] <C>: *Select S2, as shown in Figure 4-37.*
Specify third point or [Continue] <C>: *Select S3, as shown in Figure 4-37.*
Specify destination plane and orientation ...
Specify first destination point: *Select D1, as shown in Figure 4-37.*
Specify second destination point or [eXit] <X>: *Select D2, as shown in Figure 4-37.*
Specify third destination point or [eXit] <X>: *Select D3, as shown in Figure 4-37.*

Figure 4-38 shows the model after aligning.

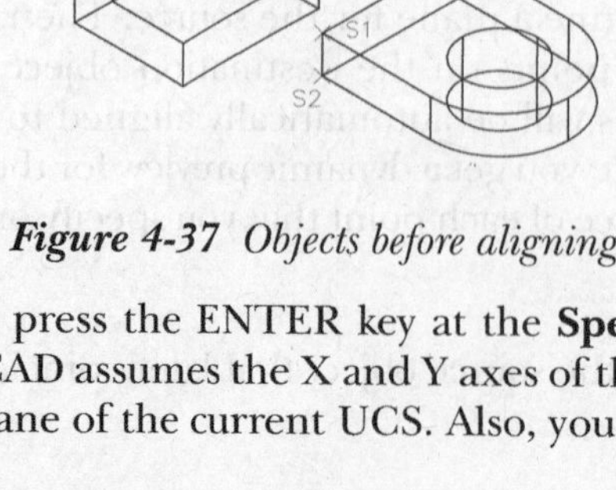

***Figure 4-37** Objects before aligning*

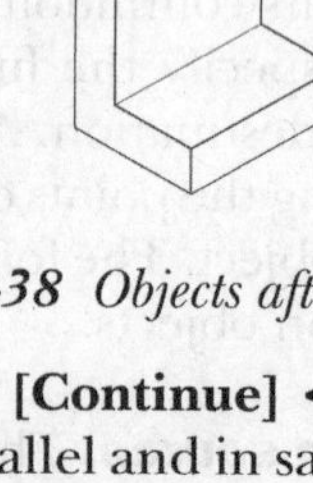

***Figure 4-38** Objects after aligning*

If you press the ENTER key at the **Specify second point or [Continue] <C>** prompt, then AutoCAD assumes the X and Y axes of the new plane to be parallel and in same direction of the XY plane of the current UCS. Also, you will be prompted to select the first destination point.

If you press the ENTER key at the **Specify second destination point or [eXit] <X>** prompt, then AutoCAD assumes the X and Y axes of the new plane for the destination to be parallel and in the same direction as the XY plane of the current UCS. Also, the XY plane of the source object will get aligned to this plane.

EXTRACTING EDGES OF A SOLID MODEL

Ribbon: Home > Solid Editing > Edge Editing drop-down > Extract Edges
Menu Bar: Modify > 3D Operations > Extract Edges **Command:** XEDGES

The **Extract Edges** tool is used to automatically generate the wireframe from a previously created solid model. The wireframe will be generated at the same location and with the same orientation where the parent model was located. The prompt sequence that will follow when you choose the **Extract Edges** tool from the **Solid Editing** panel is given next, refer to Figure 4-39 .

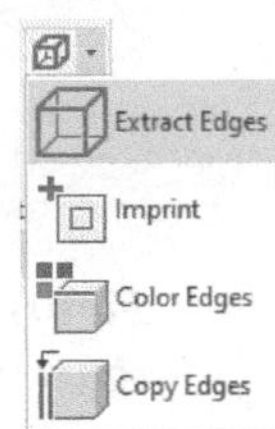

*Figure 4-39 The **Extract Edges** tool in the **Edge Editing** drop-down*

Select objects: *Select object from which you want to extract the edges.*
Select objects: *Select more objects or press* Enter

Figure 4-40 shows a model from which the edges are to be extracted and the wireframe extracted from that model after moving it to another location.

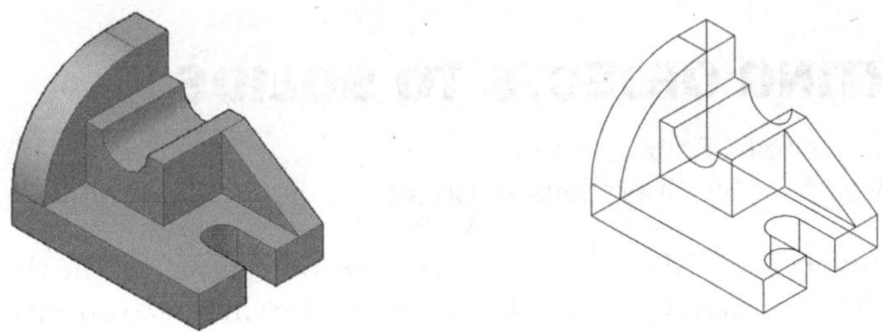

Figure 4-40 Model and the resulting edges after extraction

Note
*The **Extract Edges** tool can only be applied to regions, surfaces, and solids.*

Tip
To extract edges from a particular edge or face of the model, press and hold the CTRL key during the selection of the objects.

CONVERTING OBJECTS TO SURFACES

Ribbon: Home > Solid Editing > Convert to Surface
Menu Bar: Modify > 3D Operations > Convert to Surface **Command:** CONVTOSURFACE

The **Convert to Surface** tool is used to convert objects into surfaces. The objects that can be converted to surfaces are arcs and lines with nonzero thickness, open zero width polyline having a nonzero thickness, 2D solids, donuts, boundary, regions, and 3D faces created on a plane.

To convert objects to surfaces, choose the **Convert to Surface** tool from the **Solid Editing** panel and then select the objects to be converted into a surface. Figure 4-41 shows a boundary to be converted into a surface and Figure 4-42 shows the resulting surface.

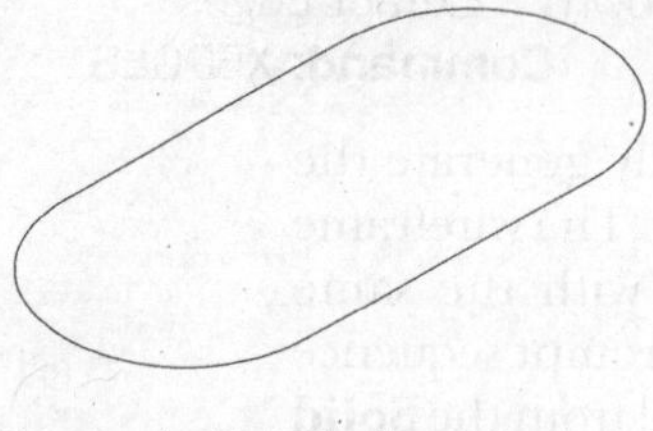

Figure 4-41 *The boundary to be converted into a surface*

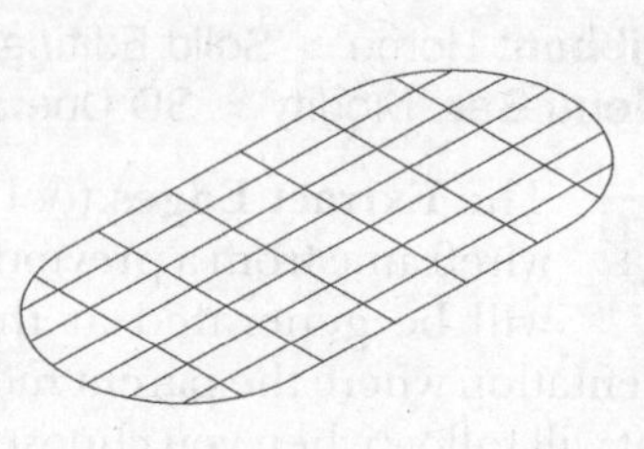

Figure 4-42 *The resulting surface*

Tip

*You can convert 3D solids with curved faces to surfaces by using the **Explode** tool. On invoking this tool, the curved faces of the solid will be converted into surfaces and the planar faces will be converted into regions.*

CONVERTING OBJECTS TO SOLIDS

Ribbon: Home > Solid Editing > Convert to Solid
Menu Bar: Modify > 3D Operations > Convert to Solid **Command:** CONVTOSOLID

The **Convert to Solid** tool is used to convert objects with some thickness into solid models. The solid generated by using this option will be similar to an extruded solid having height equal to the thickness of the object. The objects that can be converted into solids are open polylines with nonzero uniform width and thickness, closed polylines with thickness, and circles with thickness.

To convert objects into solids, choose the **Convert to Solid** tool from the **Solid Editing** panel and then select the objects to be converted into solids. Figure 4-43 shows a closed zero width polyline having a nonzero thickness and Figure 4-44 shows the resulting solid.

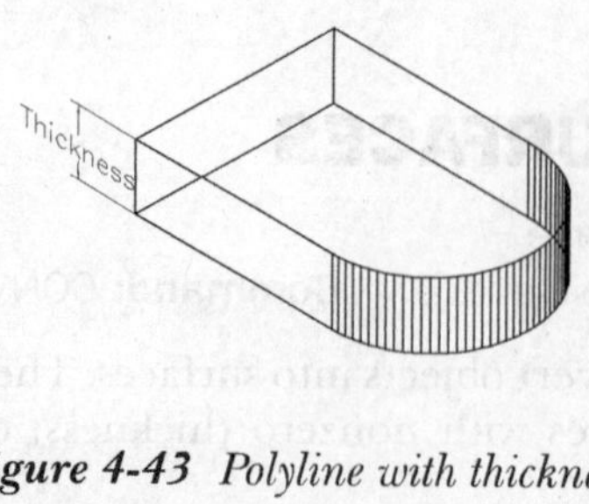

Figure 4-43 *Polyline with thickness*

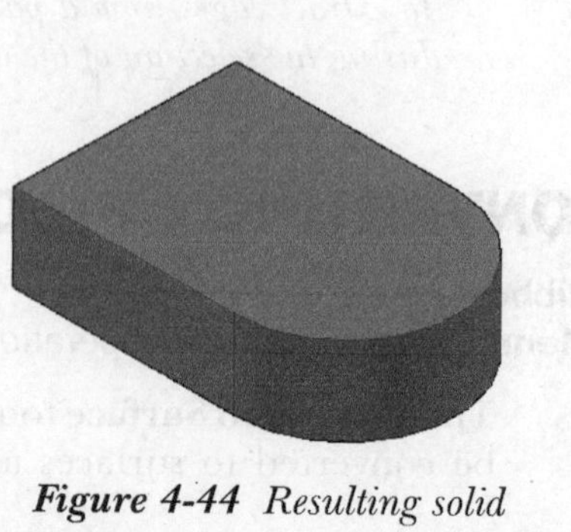

Figure 4-44 *Resulting solid*

CONVERTING SURFACES TO SOLIDS

Ribbon: Home > Solid Editing > Thicken
Menu Bar: Modify > 3D Operations > Thicken **Command:** THICKEN

The **Thicken** tool is used to convert any surface into a solid by adding material of a specified thickness to the surface. The material addition takes place in the direction normal to the surface. To convert surfaces into solids, choose the **Thicken** tool from the **Solid Editing** panel. Next, select the surface to thicken and then specify the thickness of the material to be added to the surface. Figure 4-45 shows the surface to be thickened and Figure 4-46 shows the resulting solid after thickening.

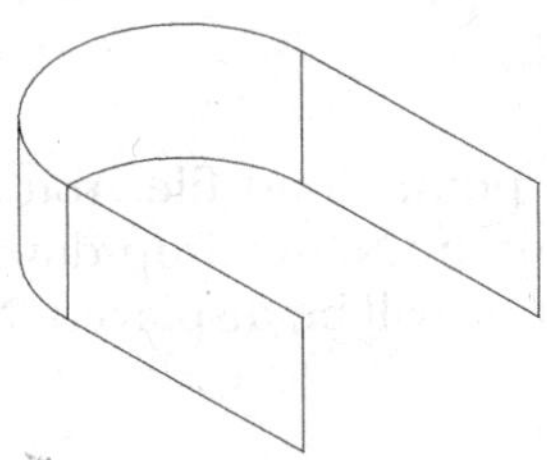

Figure 4-45 *Surface to be thickened*

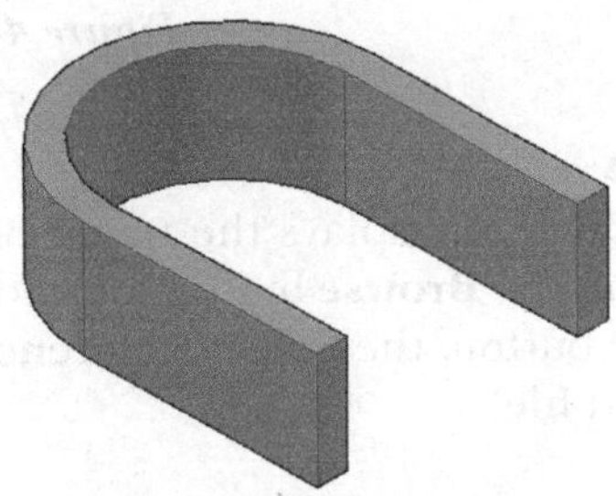

Figure 4-46 *The solid after thickening*

POINT CLOUD

The point cloud is a 3D scanned image consisting of a number of points having different x, y, and z coordinates. This image depicts the shape of the model. It is usually used as a guideline for drawing a model. After inserting point cloud in working environment, you can modify its properties like density, rotation, scale, color mapping, clipping boundaries, and so on. You can create or attach the point cloud file to the drawing file.

Attaching the Point Cloud

Ribbon: Insert > Reference > Attach **Command:** POINTCLOUDATTACH

To attach a point cloud to drawing, choose the **Attach** tool from the **Reference** panel of the **Insert** tab; the **Select Reference File** dialog box will be displayed. Now, browse to the location where the point cloud file is saved and then select it. Note that you can select the files having the *.rcp* and *.rcs* file formats only. After selecting the required file, choose the **Open** button; the **Attach Point Cloud** dialog box will be displayed, as shown in Figure 4-47. Some of the options available in the dialog box are discussed next.

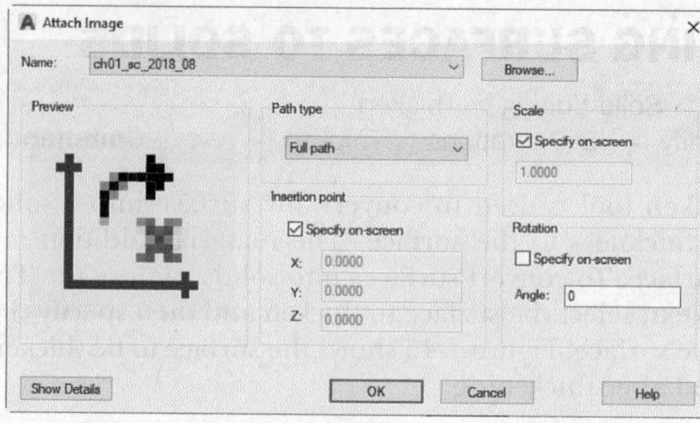

***Figure 4-47** The **Attach Image** dialog box*

Name

This edit box displays the name of the selected point cloud file. You can browse the file by choosing the **Browse** button located on the right of the **Name** drop-down list. On choosing the **Browse** button, the **Select Reference File** dialog box will be displayed. Now, you can select the required file.

Preview Area

This area is used to show the preview of the point cloud file that is to be attached in the drawing file.

Insertion Point

In this area, you can specify the position of the point cloud in the drawing area. You can specify the position by entering values in the **X, Y,** and **Z** edit boxes. If you select the **Specify on-screen** check box, you need to specify the insertion point on the screen.

Scale Area

In this area, you can specify the scaling value of the point cloud. If you select the **Specify on-screen** check box, you need to specify the scale in the drawing area.

Rotation Area

In this area, you can specify the rotation value of the point cloud.

After specifying all the parameters in the **Attach Image** dialog box, choose the **OK** button; you will be prompted to specify the insertion point. Specify the insertion point; the point cloud will be inserted, refer to Figure 4-48.

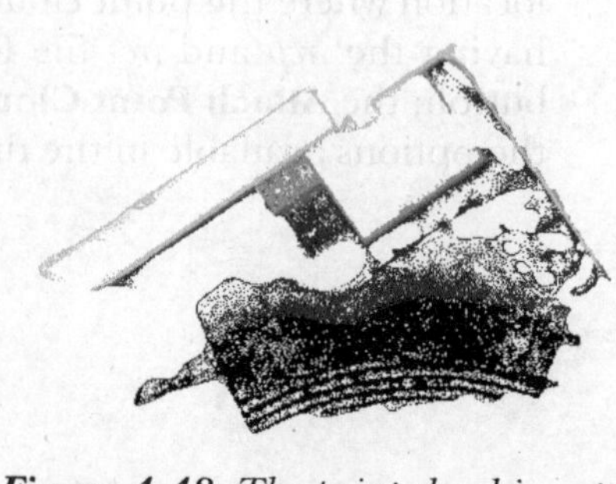

***Figure 4-48** The point cloud inserted*

You can also change the properties of point cloud such as density and clipping boundary by selecting the suitable options from the **Point Cloud** contextual tab, which is displayed after selecting the point cloud in the drawing area, as shown in Figure 4-49.

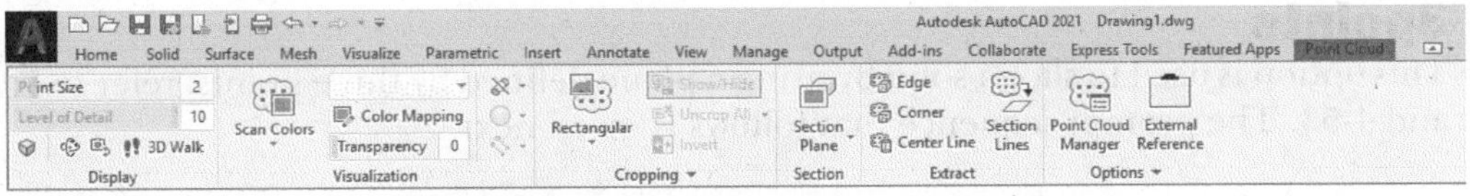

Figure 4-49 The ***Point Cloud*** *contextual tab*

In AutoCAD, you can change the color style of the point cloud by using the options in the **Visualization** panel. In this panel, the **Scan Colors** option is used to assign the original colors of the scanned file to the point cloud. The **Object Color** option is used to assign the current object color to the point cloud. The **Normal** option is used to assign the colors based on the normal direction of the points in a point cloud. The **Intensity** option is used to assign colors based on the intensity of the point cloud. Moreover, there are additional options available in the **Cropping** panel to specify the clipping boundary of the point cloud. You can specify the rectangular, polygonal, or circular boundary using the **Rectangular**, **Polygonal**, and **Circular** tools available in the **Crop** drop-down of the **Cropping** panel to specify the clipping boundary.

Figures 4-50 and 4-51 show the point cloud after decreasing the density and changing the clipping boundary, respectively.

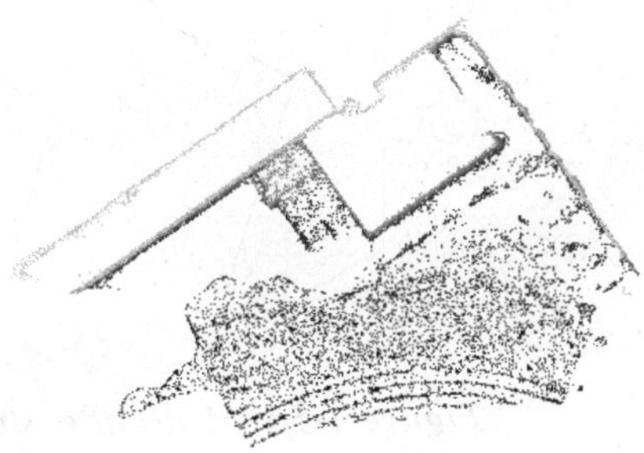

Figure 4-50 *The point cloud after decreasing density*

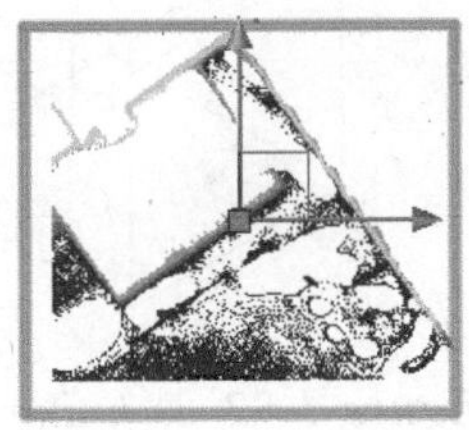

Figure 4-51 *The point cloud after clipping the boundary*

SLICING SOLID MODELS

Ribbon: Home > Solid Editing > Slice
Menu Bar: Modify > 3D Operations > Slice
Command: SLICE

As the name suggests, the **Slice** tool is used to slice the selected solid with the help of a specified plane. You will be given an option to select the portion of the sliced solid that has to be retained. You can also retain both the portions of the sliced solids.

The prompt sequence that follows is given next.

Select objects to slice: *Select the object to slice.*
Select objects to slice: ENTER
Specify start point of slicing plane or [planar Object/Surface/Zaxis/View/XY/YZ/ZX/3points] <3points>: *Specify a point on the slicing plane or select an option.*

3points

This option is used to slice a solid by using a plane defined by three points, refer to Figures 4-52 and 4-53. The prompt sequence that follows is given next.

Select objects to slice: *Select the object to be sliced.*
Select objects to slice: Enter
Specify start point of slicing plane or [planar Object/Surface/Zaxis/View/XY/YZ/ZX/3points] <3points>: Enter
Specify first point on plane: *Specify the point P1 on the slicing plane, as shown in Figure 4-52.*
Specify second point on plane: *Specify the point P2 on the slicing plane, as shown in Figure 4-52.*
Specify third point on plane: *Specify the point P3 on the slicing plane, as shown in Figure 4-52.*
Specify a point on desired side or [keep Both sides] <Both>: *Select the portion of the solid to retain or enter B to retain both the portions of the sliced solid.*

The model after slicing is shown in Figure 4-53.

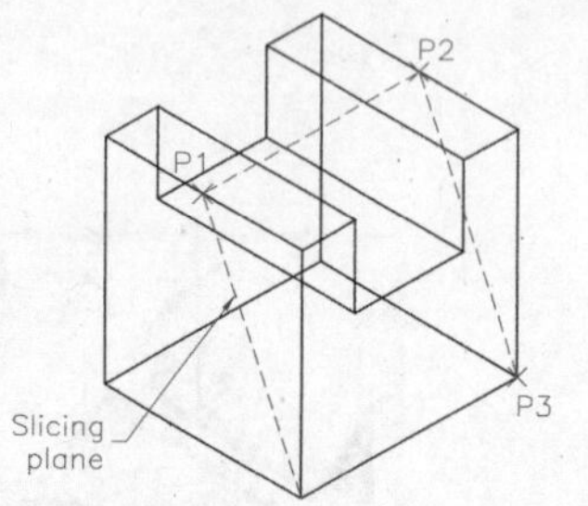

Figure 4-52 *Defining the slicing plane*

Figure 4-53 *Model after slicing*

planar Object

This option is used to slice the solid model using an object. The objects that can be used to slice the solid model include arcs, circles, ellipses, 2D polylines, and splines. The prompt sequence that will follow is given next.

Select objects to slice: *Select the object to slice.*
Select objects to slice: Enter
Specify start point of slicing plane or [planar Object/ Surface/Zaxis/View/XY/YZ/ZX/3points] <3points>: **O**

Select a circle, ellipse, arc, 2D-spline, 2D-polyline to define the slicing plane: *Select the object to slice the solid.*
Specify a point on desired side or [keep Both sides]: *Specify the portion of the solid to retain.*

Surface

This option is used to slice the solid model using a surface. Note that the ruled, tabulated, revolved, or edge surfaces cannot be used for slicing the solids. Figure 4-54 shows the object to be sliced and the slicing surface and Figure 4-55 shows the model after slicing. The prompt sequence that will follow is given next.

Select objects to slice: *Select the object to slice.*
Select objects to slice: Enter
Specify start point of slicing plane or [planar Object/Surface/Zaxis/View/XY/YZ/ZX/3points] <3points>: **S**
Select a surface: *Select the surface to slice the solid.*
Select sliced object to keep or [keep Both sides] <Both>: *Specify the portion of the solid to retain.*

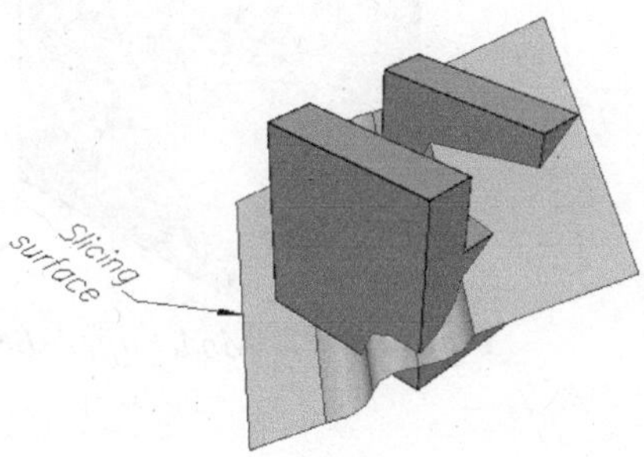

Figure 4-54 *Model with slicing surface*

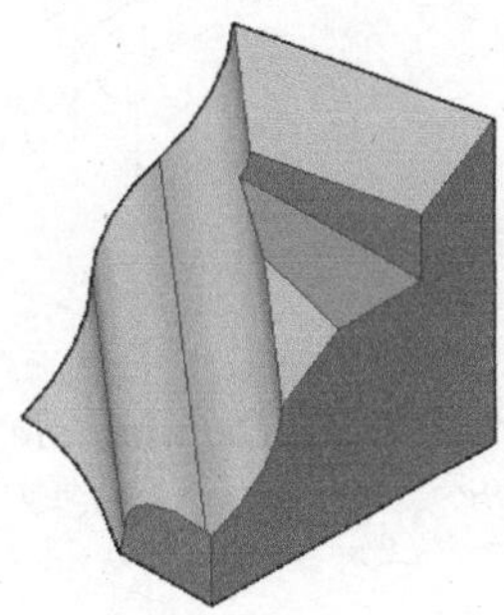

Figure 4-55 *Model after slicing*

Zaxis

This option is used to slice the solid using a plane defined by two points. The first point is the point on the section plane and the second point is the point in the direction of the Z axis of the plane. The prompt sequence that follows is given next.

Select objects to slice: *Select the object to slice.*
Select objects to slice: Enter
Specify start point of slicing plane or [planar Object/Surface/Zaxis/View/XY/YZ/ZX/3points] <3points>: **Z**
Specify a point on the section plane: *Specify the point on the section plane.*
Specify a point on the Z-axis (normal) of the plane: *Specify the point in the direction of the Z axis of the section plane.*
Specify a point on desired side or [keep Both sides] <Both>: *Select the portion to retain.*

View

This option is used to slice the selected solid about the viewing plane, refer to Figures 4-56 and 4-57. The viewing plane in this case will be the screen of the monitor. On selecting this option, you will be prompted to specify a point on the solid model through which the viewing plane will pass. The prompt sequence that will follow is given next.

Select objects to slice: *Select the object to slice.*
Select objects to slice: Enter
Specify start point of slicing plane or [planar Object/Surface/Zaxis/View/XY/YZ/ZX/3points] <3points>: **V**
Specify a point on the current view plane <0,0,0>: *Specify the point P1, as shown in Figure 4-56.*
Specify a point on the desired side or [keep Both sides] <Both>: *Specify the portion of the solid to retain.*

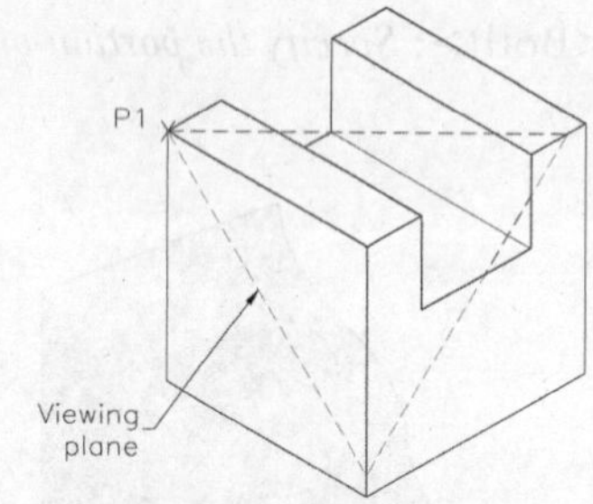

Figure 4-56 *Defining the slicing plane*

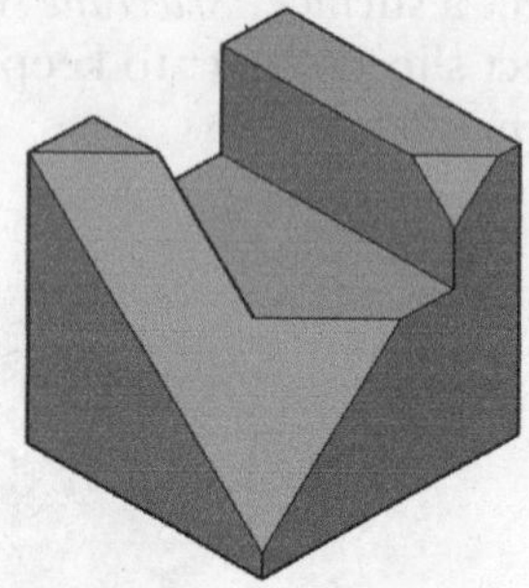

Figure 4-57 *Model after slicing*

XY/YZ/ZX

These options are used to slice the selected solid about the XY, YZ, or the ZX plane respectively. When you invoke this option, you will be prompted to select the point on the plane. The prompt sequence that will follow is given next.

Select objects to slice: *Select the object to slice.*
Select objects to slice: Enter
Specify start point of slicing plane or [planar Object/ Surface/Zaxis/View/XY/YZ/ZX/3points] <3points>: *Select the XY, YZ, or the ZX plane.*
Specify a point on the XY-plane <0,0,0>: *Specify the point on the slicing plane.*
Specify a point on desired side or [keep Both sides] <Both>: *Specify the portion to retain.*

CREATING THE CROSS-SECTIONS OF SOLIDS

Command: SEC(SECTION)

The **SECTION** command works similar to the **Slice** tool. The only difference between these two is that this command does not chop the solid. Instead, it creates a cross-section along the selected section plane. The cross-section thus created is a region. You need to move the region created to view the cross section. If needed, you can hatch the region. Note that the regions are created in the current layer and not in the layer in which the sectioned solid is stored. The prompt sequence that follows when you enter the **SECTION** command is given next.

Select objects: *Select the object to section.*
Select objects: Enter
Specify first point on section plane by [Object/Zaxis/View/XY/YZ/ZX/3points] <3points>:

3points
This option is used to define the section plane using three points.

Object
This option is used to specify the section plane using a planar object. The objects that can be used to create the sections are arcs, circles, ellipses, splines, or 2D polylines.

View
This option uses the current viewing plane to define the section plane. You will be prompted to specify the point on the current view plane. It will then automatically create a cross-section parallel to the current viewing plane and passing through the specified point.

XY/YZ/ZX
These options are used to define the section planes that are parallel to the XY, YZ, or the ZX planes, respectively. On invoking this option, you will be prompted to specify the points through which the selected plane will pass. Figure 4-58 displays the YZ plane which is being used to create the cross-section and Figure 4-59 displays the created section along the YZ plane, which is first isolated and then hatched for clarity purposes.

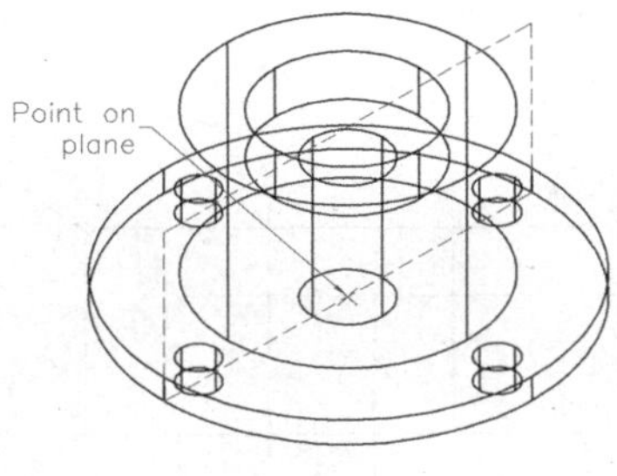

Figure 4-58 *Creating the cross-section along the YZ plane*

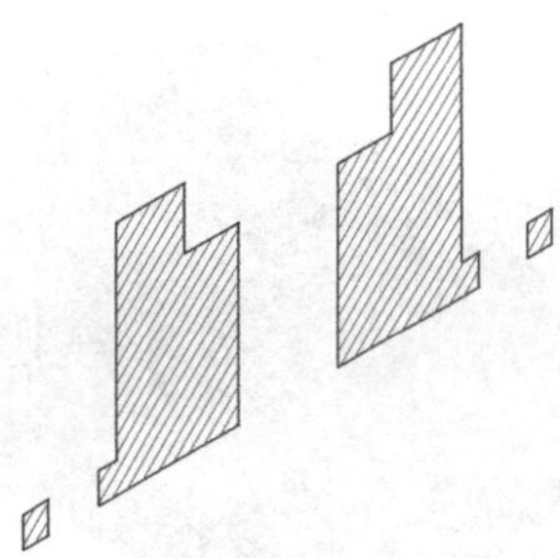

Figure 4-59 *Cross-section created, isolated, and hatched for clarity*

Tip

1. The number of regions created as cross-sections will be equal to the number of solids selected to create the cross-section.

2. You can also hatch the cross-section created using the ***SECTION*** *command. To do so, you need to select the entire region as the object for hatching. You may also have to define a new UCS based on the section to hatch it.*

Example 2

In this example, you will draw the solid model shown in Figure 4-60. The dimensions of the model are shown in Figure 4-61. After creating it, slice it as shown in Figure 4-62.

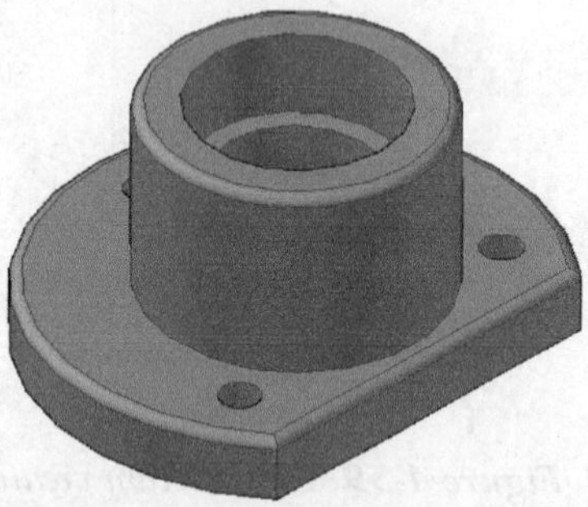

Figure 4-60 *Model for Example 2*

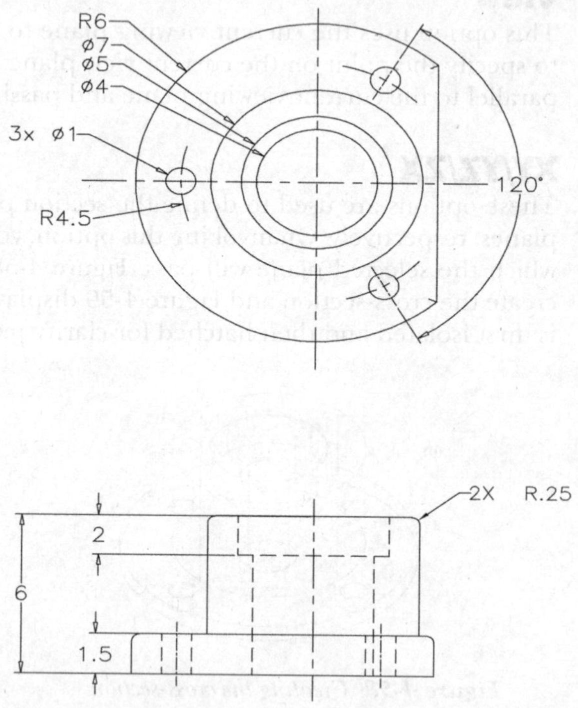

Figure 4-61 *Orthographic views of the solid model*

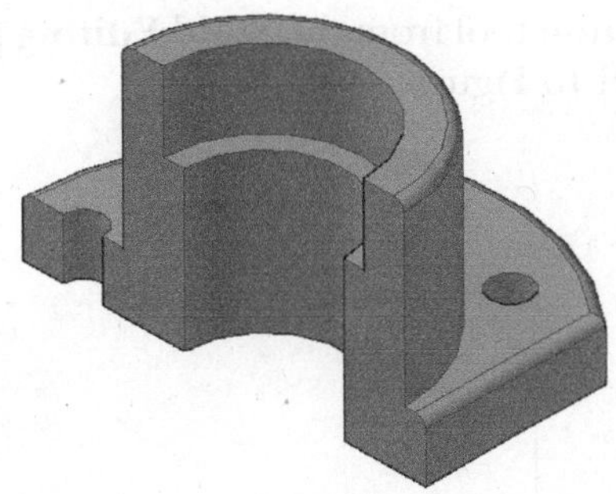

Figure 4-62 The sliced solid

1. Start a new 3D template drawing file and then draw the sketch for the base of the model in the Top view, as shown in Figure 4-63. Choose the **Region** tool from the **Draw** panel in the **Home** tab and convert the sketch to a region.

2. Choose the **Extrude** tool from **Home > Modeling > Solid Creation** drop-down and extrude the region to a distance of 1.5.

3. Set the view to **SW Isometric** by using the ViewCube. The model will look similar to the model shown in Figure 4-64.

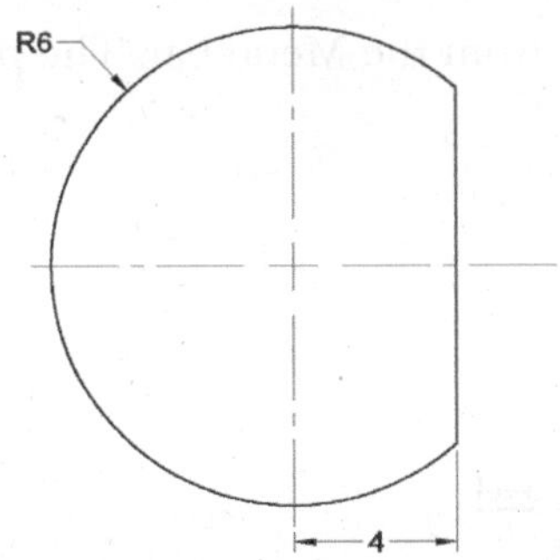

Figure 4-63 Sketch for the base of the model

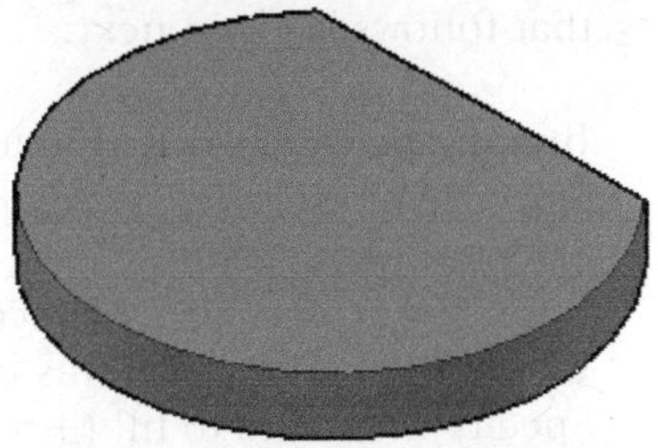

Figure 4-64 Base of the model

4. Set the view to **Front** and set the **UCS** aligned to this view. Draw the sketch for the next feature anywhere in the drawing area and convert it into a region, refer to Figure 4-65.

5. Choose the **Revolve** tool from **Home > Modeling > Solid Creation** drop-down and then revolve the sketch to an angle of 360 degrees.

6. Right-click on the **3D Object Snap** button in the Status Bar and select the **Center of face** option. Also, clear the other snap options.

7. Ensure that the **3D Object Snap** is on and **Object Snap** is off. Move the revolved feature by snapping the center point of the lower face and place it at the center of the upper face of the base of the model.

8. Choose the **Solid, Union** tool from the **Solid Editing** panel in the **Home** tab and then unite both the objects, refer to Figure 4-66.

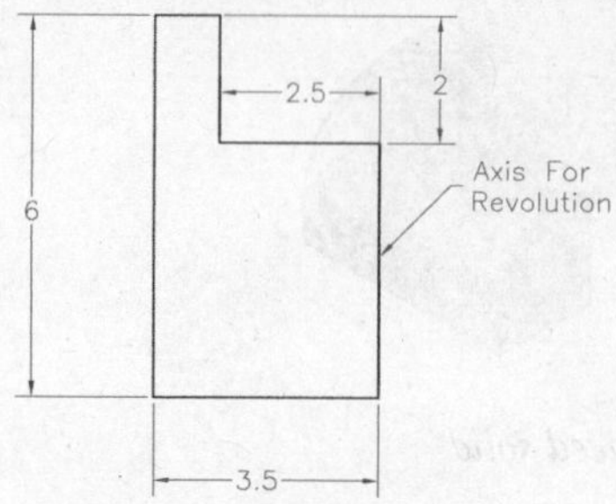

***Figure 4-65** Sketch for the next feature*

***Figure 4-66** Model after union*

9. Create a new cylinder of diameter 1 unit of the same height as that of the base.

10. Draw a circle of radius 4.5 units on the top face of the base.

11. Move the cylinder by snapping the center of the top face and place it on the quadrant point along the X-axis of the circle.

12. Choose **Modify > 3D Operations > 3D Array** from the Menu bar. The prompt sequence that follows is given next:

Initializing... 3DARRAY loaded.
Select objects: *Select the cylinder.*
Select objects: Enter
Enter the type of array [Rectangular/Polar] <R>: **P**
Enter the number of items in the array: **3**
Specify the angle to fill (+=ccw, -=cw) <360>: Enter
Rotate arrayed objects? [Yes/No] <Y>: Enter
Specify center point of array: *Select the center of the base of the model.*
Specify second point on axis of rotation: *Select the center of the top face of the model.*

13. Subtract all three cylinders from the model by choosing the **Solid, Subtract** tool from the **Solid Editing** panel.

14. Create a cylinder of diameter 4 units and height 6 units and subtract it from the model to create the central hole.

15. Choose the **Fillet Edge** tool from **Solid > Solid Editing > Fillet Edge** drop-down; you are prompted to select the edges to be filleted.

16. Select the edges to fillet and press ENTER; you are prompted to enter the radius. Specify the fillet radius as 0.25 units. The model after making the changes will look similar to the model shown in Figure 4-67, when you set the view to **SE Isometric** by using the ViewCube.

17. Relocate the UCS at the WCS.

18. Choose the **Slice** tool from the **Solid Editing** panel to cut the solid model to half. The prompt sequence is as follows:

    Select objects to slice: *Select the model.*
    Select objects to slice: Enter
    Specify start point of slicing plane or [planar Object/Surface/Zaxis/View/XY/YZ/ZX/3points] <3points>: **ZX**
    Specify a point on the ZX-plane <0,0,0>: *Select the center of the top face of the model.*
    Specify a point on desired side or [keep Both sides]: *Specify a point on the back side of the model to retain it.*

The final model for Example 2 will look similar to the model shown in Figure 4-68.

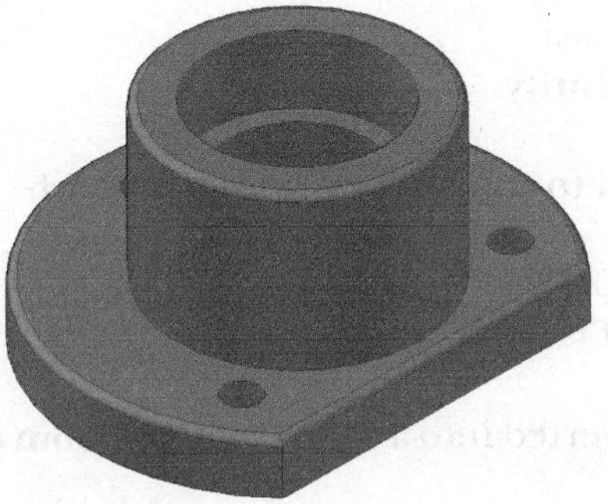

***Figure 4-67** Model after creating the fillet*

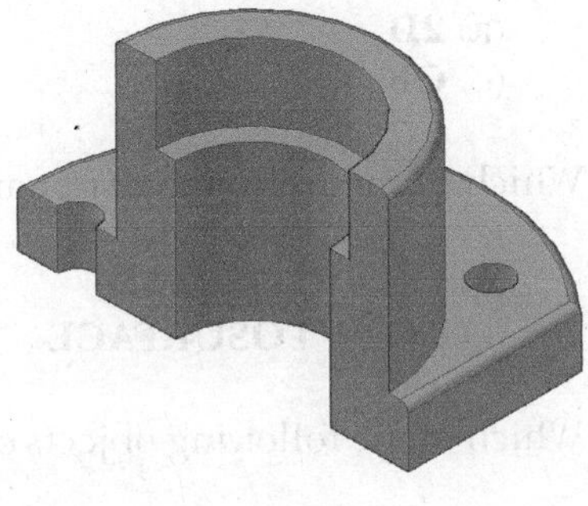

***Figure 4-68** Final model after slicing*

Self-Evaluation Test

Answer the following questions and then compare them to those given at the end of this chapter:

1. The __________ rule is used to determine the direction of rotation of the solid model in 3D space.

2. The __________ tool is used to extract edges from a solid model.

3. The __________ tool is used to move, rotate, and scale the solid model in a single attempt.

4. The **SECTION** command is used to create a __________ along the plane of a section.

5. The __________ tool is used to align solids by defining an alignment plane.

6. A model can be dynamically moved using the **3D Move** tool. (T/F)

7. The edges of a solid model can be filleted using the **3D Fillet** tool. (T/F)

8. You can select an ellipse as an object to rotate the solid model using the **Rotate 3D** tool. (T/F)

9. The **Convert to Surface** tool can be used to convert an open zero-width polyline having a nonzero thickness into a surface. (T/F)

10. The **SECTION** command is used to create a cross-section and also slice a model. (T/F)

Review Questions

Answer the following questions:

1. Which of the following options of the **ROTATE3D** command is used to select a 2D entity as an object for rotating the solid models?

   (a) **2D** (b) **Last**
   (c) **Object** (d) **Entity**

2. Which of the following commands is used to convert a surface to a solid?

   (a) **CONVTOSOLID** (b) **CONVQUILT**
   (c) **CONVTOSURFACE** (d) **THICKEN**

3. Which of the following objects can be converted into a solid using the **Convert to Solid** tool?

   (a) Rectangle (b) Circle
   (c) Ellipse (d) None of these

4. Which of the following options of the **3D Mirror** tool is used to mirror the object about the view plane?

   (a) **Object** (b) **Last**
   (c) **View** (d) **Zaxis**

5. What is the least number of points that you have to define on the source object to align it using the **3D Align** tool?

   (a) One (b) Two
   (c) Three (d) Four

6. The __________ command gives a dynamic preview while aligning the solid model.

7. The __________ option of the **3D Rotate** tool is used to select the same axis that was last selected to rotate the solid model.

8. While creating a 3D array using the **3D Array** tool, the levels are arranged along the __________ axis.

9. The object having some __________ can be converted into a solid using the **Convert to Solid** tool.

10. The __________ option is used to slice a model by using a sketched entity.

11. A surface can be used to slice a model using the **Slice** tool. (T/F)

12. The **Convert to Solid** tool is used to convert objects with a zero thickness into a solid. (T/F)

13. You can also extract an individual edge of a solid model using the **Extract Edges** tool. (T/F)

14. You can select all tangential edges of the selected solid model for filleting using the **Chain** option of the **Fillet Edges** tool. (T/F)

15. Regions can be converted to surfaces by using the **Convert to Surface** tool. (T/F)

Exercise 1

In this exercise, you will create a solid model shown in Figure 4-69. The dimensions of the model are shown in Figures 4-70. After creating it, slice it to get the model shown in Figure 4-71.

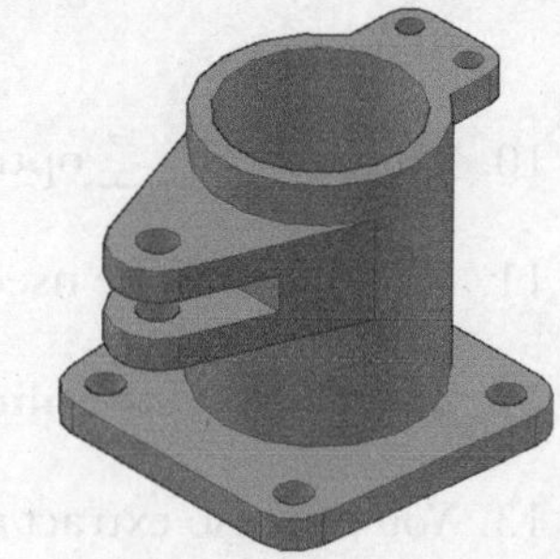

Figure 4-69 Model for Exercise 1

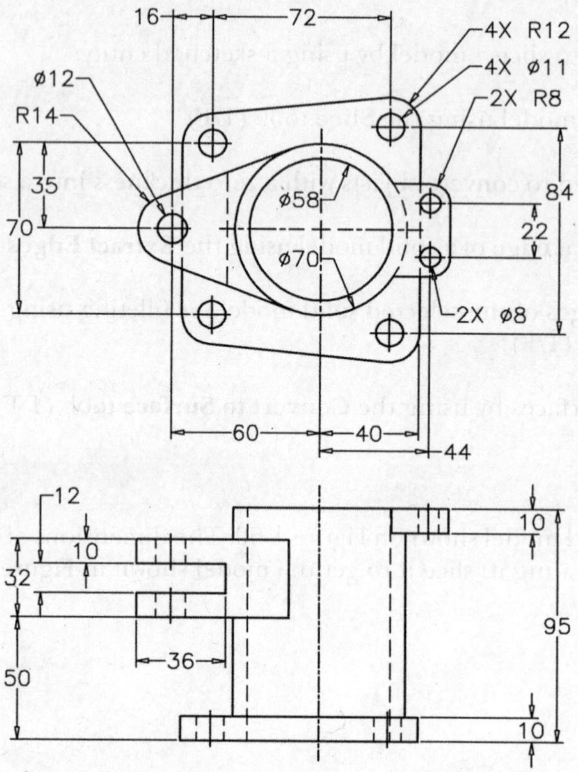

Figure 4-70 Orthographic views of the model

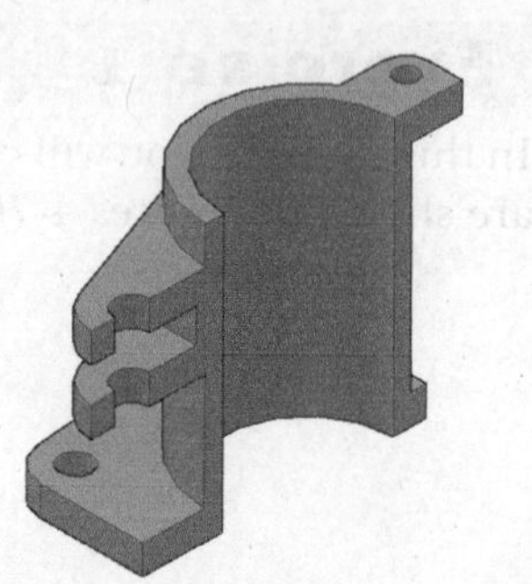

Figure 4-71 Model after slicing

Exercise 2

In this exercise, you will create the solid model shown in Figure 4-72. The dimensions of the model are given in the drawing shown in the same figure.

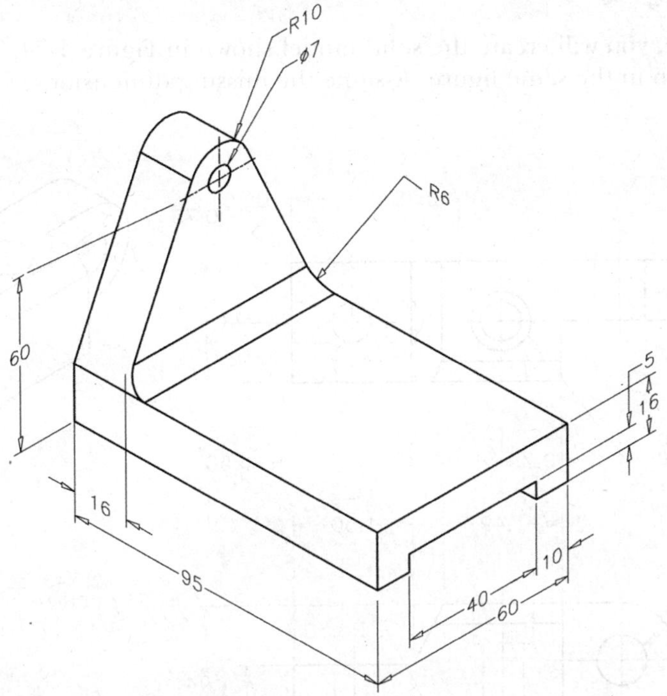

Figure 4-72 Solid model for Exercise 2

Exercise 3

In this exercise, you will create the solid model shown in Figure 4-73. The dimensions for the model are given in the same figure. The fillet radius is 0.13 units.

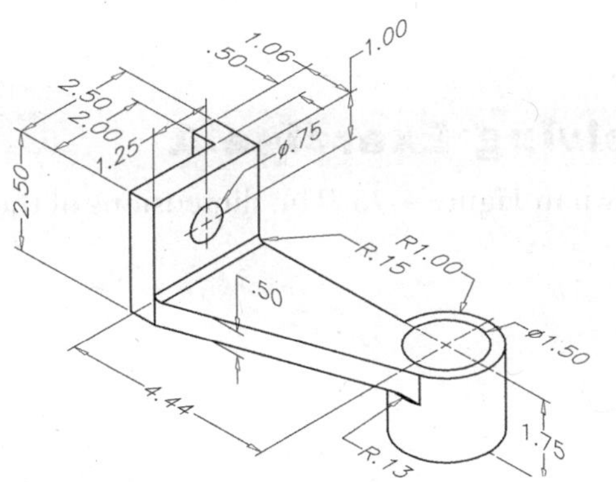

Figure 4-73 Solid model for Exercise 3

Exercise 4

In this exercise, you will create the solid model shown in Figure 4-74. The dimensions for the model are given in the same figure. Assume the missing dimensions.

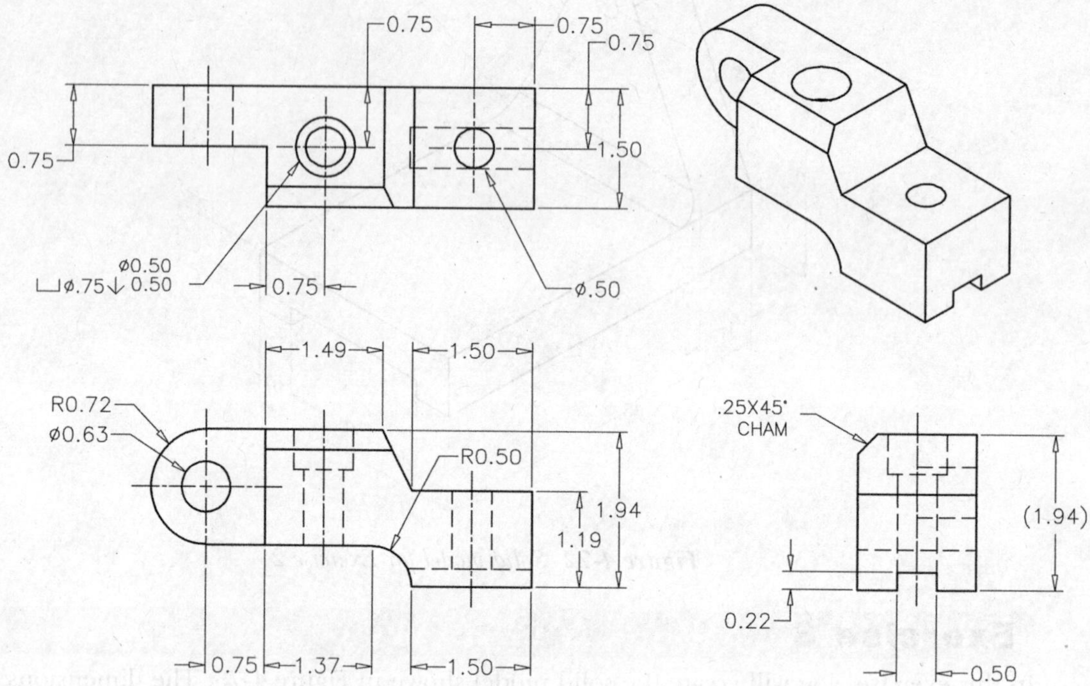

Figure 4-74 Solid model and its orthographic views

Problem-Solving Exercise 1

Create the model shown in Figure 4-75. The dimensions of the model are given in same figure.

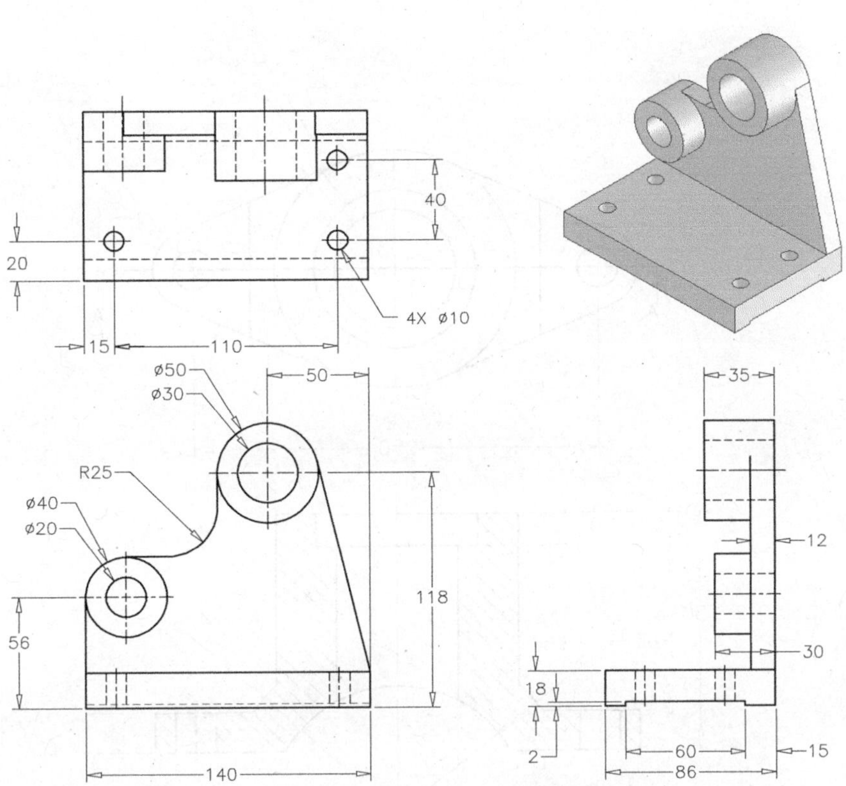

Figure 4-75 Solid model for Problem-Solving Exercise 1

Problem-Solving Exercise 2

Create the model shown in Figure 4-76. The dimensions of the model are given in Figure 4-77.

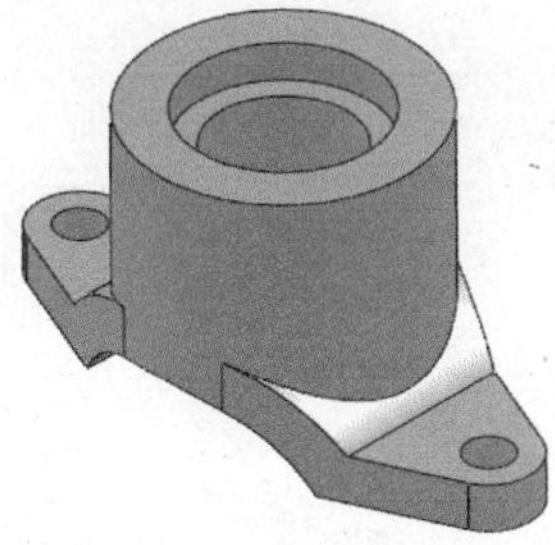

Figure 4-76 Solid model for Problem-Solving Exercise 2

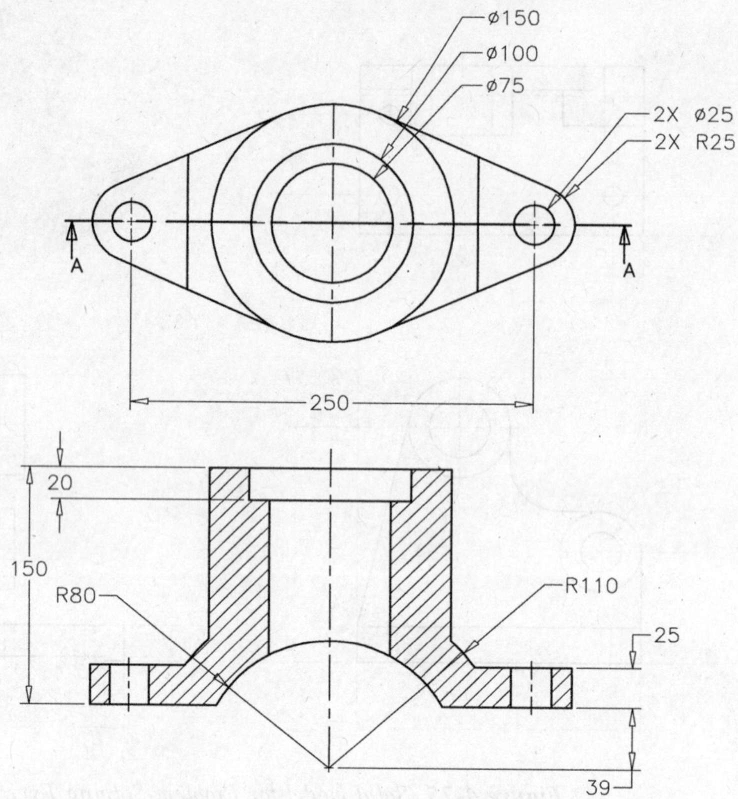

Figure 4-77 Dimensions for the solid model

Problem-Solving Exercise 3

Create the model shown in Figure 4-78. The sectioned view and dimensions of the model are given in Figure 4-79.

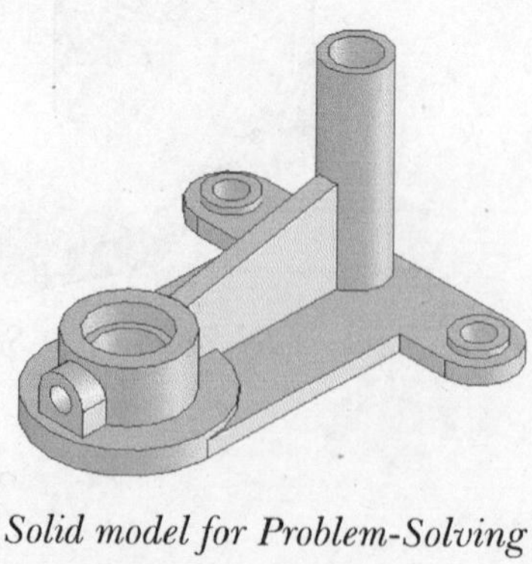

Figure 4-78 Solid model for Problem-Solving Exercise 3

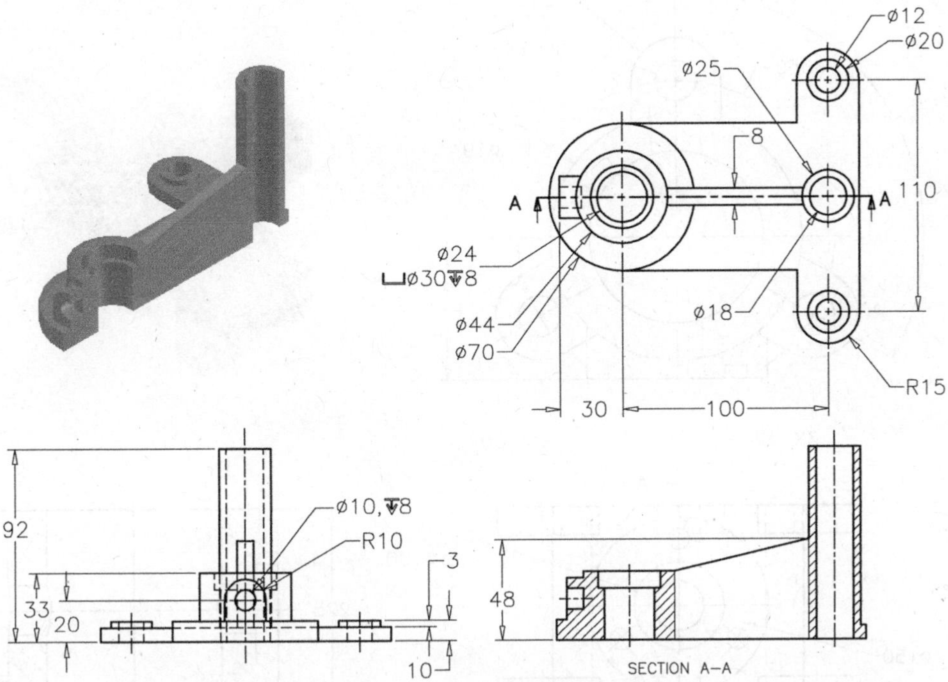

Figure 4-79 Sectioned view and dimensions for the solid model

Problem-Solving Exercise 4

Create the model shown in Figure 4-80. The sectioned view and dimensions of the model are given in Figure 4-81.

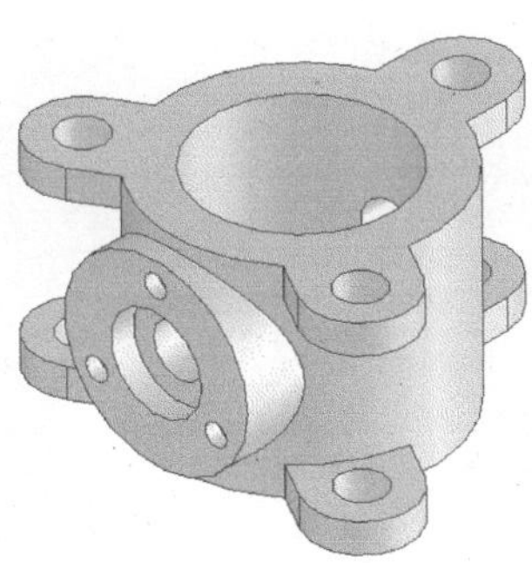

Figure 4-80 Solid model for Problem-Solving Exercise 4

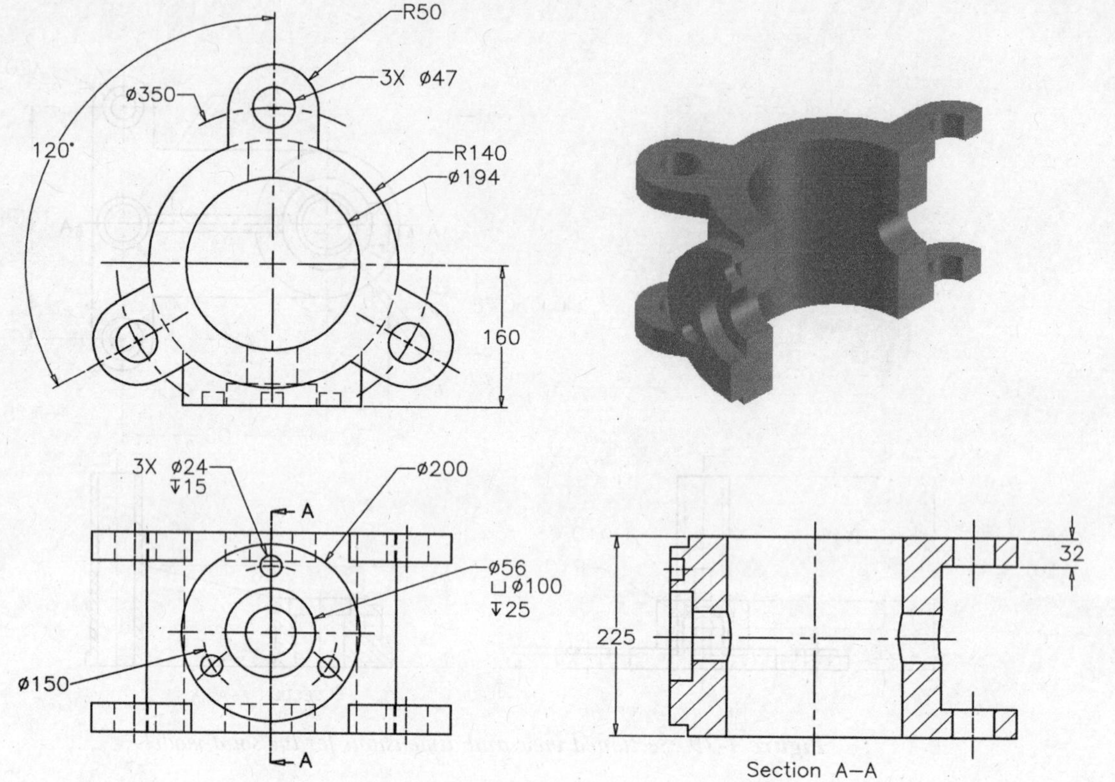

Figure 4-81 Sectioned view and dimensions of the solid model

Answers to Self-Evaluation Test

1. right-hand thumb, **2. Extract Edges**, **3. Align**, **4.** Cross-section, **5. 3D Align**, **6.** T, **7.** F, **8.** F, **9.** T, **10.** F

Chapter 5

Editing 3D Objects-II

Learning Objectives

After completing this chapter, you will be able to:

- *Edit solid models using the SOLIDEDIT command*
- *Generate sections of a model*
- *Modify a composite solid using the Solid History tool*
- *Generate drawing views of a solid model using the SOLVIEW command*
- *Generate profiles and sections in drawing views using the SOLDRAW command*
- *Create the profile images of a solid model using the SOLPROF command*
- *Calculate the mass properties of the solid models using the MASSPROP command*
- *Use the Action Recorder*
- *Use the ShowMotion tool for presentation*
- *Generate drawing views*

Key Terms

- *Extrude Faces*
- *Taper Faces*
- *Move Faces*
- *Copy Faces*
- *Offset Faces*
- *Delete Faces*
- *Rotate Faces*
- *Color Faces*
- *Extract Edges*
- *Color Edges*
- *Imprint*
- *Copy Edges*
- *Offset Edge*
- *Section Plane*
- *Live Section*
- *Solid History*
- *SOLVIEW*
- *SOLPROF*
- *Drawing Views*
- *Mass Properties*
- *Record*
- *ShowMotion*
- *Section Views*

EDITING SOLID MODELS

Ribbon: Home > Solid Editing	**Menu Bar:** Modify > Solid Editing
Toolbar: Solid Editing	**Command:** SOLIDEDIT

One of the major enhancements in the recent releases of AutoCAD is the editing of the solid models. The editing of the solid models has made solid modeling very user-friendly. It is done using the tools available in the **Solid Editing** panel. These tools can be used to edit selected faces, selected edges, or entire body of a solid model. Various editing processes and the tools used to perform them are discussed next.

Editing Faces of a Solid Model

You can edit the faces of the solid models by using the tools in the **Face Editing** drop-down of the **Solid Editing** panel, refer to Figure 5-1. The tools available in this drop-down are **Extrude Faces**, **Taper Faces**, **Move Faces**, **Copy Faces**, **Offset Faces**, **Delete Faces**, **Rotate Faces**, and **Color Faces**. These editing tools are discussed next.

Extrude Faces

The **Extrude Faces** tool is used to extrude the selected faces of a solid model to a specific height or along a selected path, refer to Figure 5-2. To extrude faces, choose the **Extrude Faces** tool from the **Face Editing** drop-down of the **Solid Editing** panel in the **Home** tab. The prompt sequence that will follow when you invoke this tool is given next.

Select faces or [Undo/Remove]: *Select faces to extrude or enter an option.*
Select faces or [Undo/Remove/ALL]: *Select another face, an option, or* Enter.

***Figure 5-1** The **Face Editing** drop-down*

The **Undo** option cancels the selection of the most recently selected face. The **Remove** option allows you to remove a previously selected face from the selection set for extrusion. The **ALL** option selects all the faces of the specified solid. After you have selected a face for extrusion, the next prompt is given below:

Specify height of extrusion or [Path]: *Enter a height value or enter **P** to select a path.*

The **Path** option allows you to select a path for extrusion based on a specified line or curve. At the **Select extrusion path** prompt, select the line, circle, arc, ellipse, elliptical arc, polyline, or spline to be specified as the extrusion path. Note that this path should not lie on the same plane as the selected face and should not have areas of high curvature.

A positive value for the height of extrusion extrudes the selected face outwards, whereas a negative value extrudes the selected face inwards. After specifying the height of extrusion, the prompt sequence followed is given next.

Specify angle of taper for extrusion <0>: *Specify a value between -90 and +90 degree or press ENTER to accept the default value.*

A positive angle value tapers the selected face inwards, refer to Figure 5-2 and a negative value tapers the selected face outwards.

Move Faces

The **Move Faces** tool is used to move the selected faces from one location to the other without changing the orientation of the solid, refer to Figure 5-3. For example, you can move holes from one location to the other without actually modifying the solid model. To move faces, choose the **Move Faces** tool from the **Face Editing** drop-down of the **Solid Editing** panel. The prompt sequence that will follow when you invoke this tool is given next.

Select faces or [Undo/Remove]: *Select one or more faces or enter an option.*
Select faces or [Undo/Remove/ALL]: *Select one or more faces, enter an option, or* Enter.
Specify a base point or displacement: *Specify a base point.*
Specify a second point of displacement: *Specify a point or* Enter.

The face moves to the specified location.

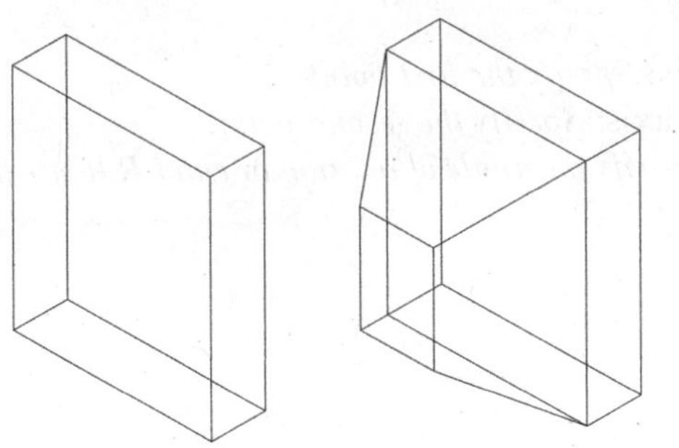

*Figure 5-2 Using the **Extrude Faces** tool to extrude a solid face with a positive taper angle*

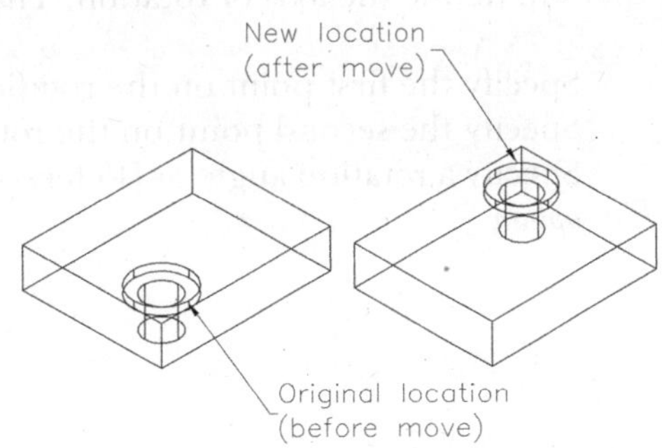

*Figure 5-3 Using the **Move Faces** tool to move the hole from the original position*

Tip
If the feature you want to move consists of more than one face, then you must select all the faces to move the entire feature.

Offset Faces

The **Offset Faces** tool is used to offset the selected faces of a solid model uniformly through a specified distance on the model. Offsetting takes place in the direction of the positive side of the face. For example, you can offset holes to a larger or smaller size in a 3D solid through a specified distance. In Figure 5-4, the hole on the solid has been offset to a larger size. To offset faces, choose the **Offset Faces** tool from the **Face Editing** drop-down of the **Solid Editing** panel. The prompt sequence that will follow when you choose this tool is given next.

Select faces or [Undo/Remove]: *Select one or more faces or enter an option.*
Select faces or [Undo/Remove/ALL]: *Select one or more faces, enter an option, or* Enter.
Specify the offset distance: *Specify the offset distance.*

The direction of offset can be controlled by entering positive or negative values of offset distance.

Rotate Faces

The **Rotate Faces** tool is used to rotate the selected faces of a solid model through a specified angle. For example, you can rotate cuts or slots around a base point through an absolute or relative angle, refer to Figure 5-5. The direction in which the rotation takes place is determined by the right-hand thumb rule. To rotate faces, choose the **Rotate Faces** tool from the **Face Editing** drop-down of the **Solid Editing** panel. The prompt sequence that will follow when you choose this tool is given next.

Select faces or [Undo/Remove]: *Select face(s) or enter an option.*
Select faces or [Undo/Remove/ALL]: *Select face(s), or enter an option, or* Enter.
Specify an axis point or [Axis by object/View/Xaxis/Yaxis/Zaxis] <2points>: *Select a point, enter an option, or* Enter.

If you press ENTER to use the **2points** option, you will be prompted to select the two points that will define the axis of rotation. The prompt sequence is given next.

Specify the first point on the rotation axis: *Specify the first point.*
Specify the second point on the rotation axis: *Specify the second point.*
Specify a rotation angle or [Reference]: *Specify the angle of rotation or enter **R** to use the reference option.*

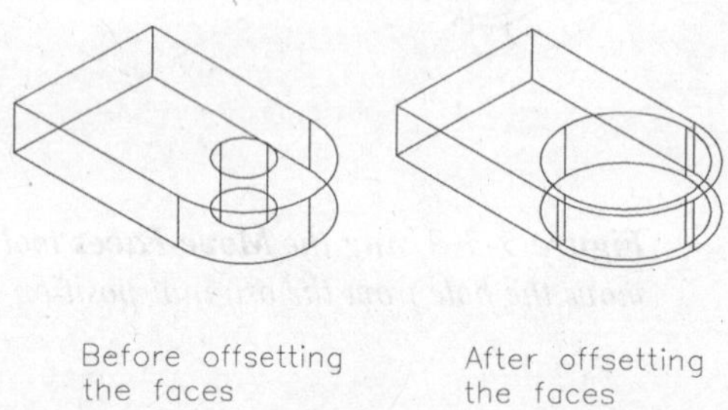

***Figure 5-4** Using the **Offset Faces** tool to offset a solid face with a positive taper angle*

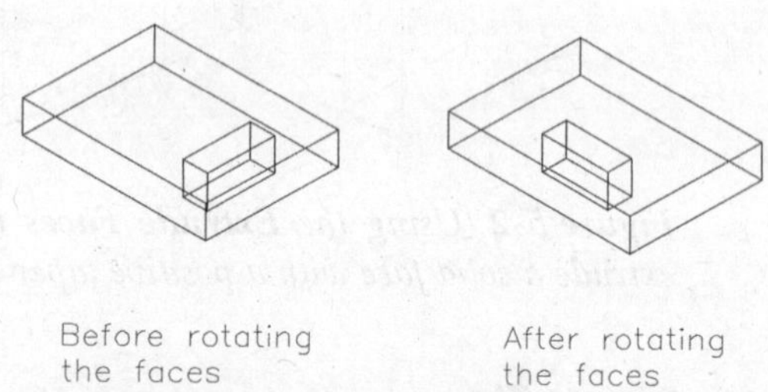

***Figure 5-5** Using the **Rotate Faces** tool to rotate the faces from the original position*

The **Axis by object** option is used to select an object to define the axis of rotation. The axis of rotation is aligned with the selected object; for example, if you select a circle, the axis of rotation will be aligned along the axis that passes through the center of the circle and will be normal to the plane of the circle. The selected object can also be a line, ellipse, arc, 2D polyline, 3D polyline, or even a spline. The prompt sequence is given next.

Select a curve to be used for the axis: *Select the object to be used to define the axis of rotation.*
Specify a rotation angle or [Reference]: *Specify rotation angle or use the reference angle option.*

The **Xaxis**, **Yaxis**, and **Zaxis** options align the axis of rotation with the axis that passes through the specified point. The prompt sequence is given next:

Specify the origin of rotation <0,0,0>: *Select a point through which the axis of rotation will pass.*
Specify a rotation angle or [Reference]: *Specify the rotation angle or use the reference angle option.*

Taper Faces

The **Taper Faces** tool is used to taper the selected face(s) through a specified angle, refer to Figure 5-6. Tapering takes place depending on the selection sequence of the base point and the second point along the selected face. It also depends on whether the taper angle is positive or negative. A positive value tapers the face inwards and a negative value tapers the face outwards. You can enter any value between -90-degree and +90-degree. The default value 0-degree extrudes the face along the axis that is perpendicular to the selected face. If you have selected more than one face, they will be tapered through the same angle. To create taper faces, choose the **Taper Faces** tool from the **Face Editing** drop-down of the **Solid Editing** panel. The prompt sequence that will follow when you choose this tool is given next.

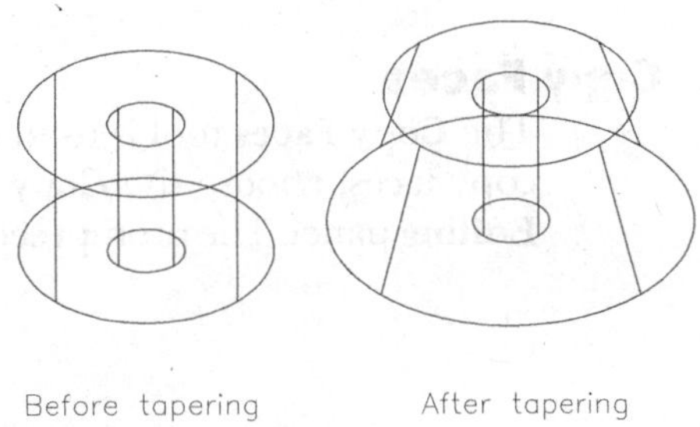

Figure 5-6 *Tapering the faces using the* ***Taper Faces*** *tool*

Select faces or [Undo/Remove]: *Select face(s) or enter an option.*
Select faces or [Undo/Remove/ALL]: *Select one or more faces, enter an option, or* Enter.
Specify the base point: *Specify a base point.*
Specify another point along the axis of tapering: *Specify a point.*
Specify the taper angle: *Specify an angle between –90 and +90-degree.*

Delete Faces

The **Delete Faces** tool is used to remove the selected face(s) from the specific 3D solid. It also removes chamfers and fillets, refer to Figure 5-7. To remove faces, choose the **Delete Faces** tool from the **Face Editing** drop-down of the **Solid Editing** panel. The prompt sequence that will follow when you choose this tool is given next.

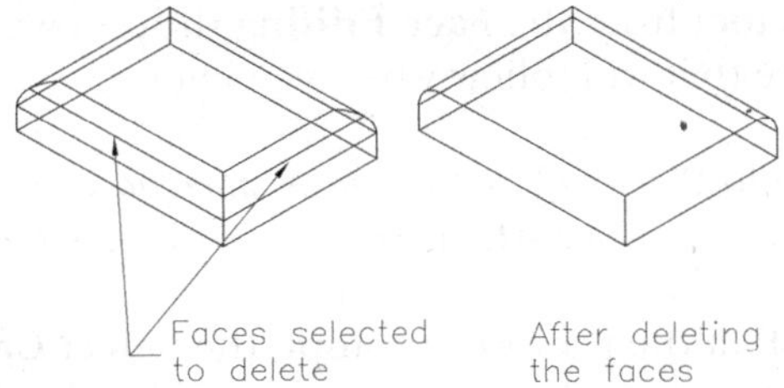

Figure 5-7 *Deleting the faces using the* ***Delete Faces*** *tool*

Enter a solids editing option [Face/Edge/Body/Undo/eXit] <eXit>: F
Enter a face editing option
[Extrude/Move/Rotate/Offset/Taper/Delete/Copy/coLor/mAterial/Undo/eXit] <eXit>: D
Select faces or [Undo/Remove]: *Select the face to remove.*
Select faces or [Undo/Remove/ALL]: *Select one or more faces, enter an option, or* Enter.
Solid validation started.
Solid validation completed.

Copy Faces

The **Copy Faces** tool is used to copy a face as a body or a region, refer to Figure 5-8. To copy faces, choose the **Copy Faces** tool from the **Face Editing** drop-down of the **Solid Editing** panel. The prompt sequence that will follow when you choose this tool is given next.

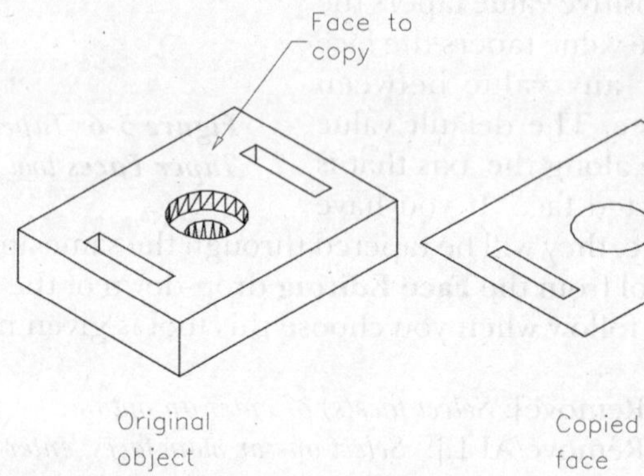

Figure 5-8 Copying the face using the ***Copy Faces*** *tool*

Select faces or [Undo/Remove]: *Select the faces to copy.*
Select faces or [Undo/Remove/ALL]: *Select one or more faces, enter an option, or* Enter.
Specify a base point or displacement: *Specify a base point.*
Specify a second point of displacement: *Specify the second point.*

Color Faces

The **Color Faces** tool is used to change the color of the selected face. To do so, choose the **Color Faces** tool from the **Face Editing** drop-down of the **Solid Editing** panel. The prompt sequence that will follow when you choose this tool is given next.

Select faces or [Undo/Remove]: *Select one or more faces, enter an option, or* Enter.
Select faces or [Undo/Remove/ALL]: *Select more faces, enter an option, or* Enter.

When you press ENTER at the previous prompt, the **Select Color** dialog box will be displayed. You can assign the color to the selected face using this dialog box.

The above-mentioned face editing tools can also be assessed using the **Face** option of the **SOLIDEDIT** command. The other options available through this command are **mAterial, Undo** and **eXit**. These options are discussed next.

mAterial

This option is used to apply material to a selected face and is invoked using the **SOLIDEDIT** command. The prompt sequence that will follow is given next.

Command: **SOLIDEDIT**
Solids editing automatic checking: SOLIDCHECK=1
Enter a solids editing option [Face/Edge/Body/Undo/eXit] <eXit>: *Enter F*
Enter a face editing option
[Extrude/Move/Rotate/Offset/Taper/Delete/Copy/coLor/mAterial/Undo/eXit] <eXit>:
Enter A
Select faces or [Undo/Remove]: *Select one or more faces to apply the material.*
Select faces or [Undo/Remove/ALL]: *Select one or more faces, enter an option, or* Enter
Enter new Material name <ByLayer>: *Enter the name of the material or* Enter

Undo

This option is used to cancel the changes made to the faces of a solid model. This option will be available only when you invoke the **SOLIDEDIT** command by using the Command prompt.

eXit

This option is used to exit the face editing operations. This option will be available only when you invoke the **SOLIDEDIT** command using the Command prompt.

Tip

*You can select a face, edge, or solid and perform the editing operation. To select an entity with ease, set the appropriate option from the **Filter** drop-down in the **Selection** panel.*

Editing Edges of a Solid Model

To modify the properties of the edges of a solid, you can use the tools available in the **Edge Editing** drop-down of the **Solid Editing** panel, refer to Figure 5-9. The edge editing tools available in this drop-down are: **Extract Edges**, **Imprint**, **Color Edges**, and **Copy Edges**. Also you can use the **Offset Edge** tool to offset the edges of the model. These editing tools are discussed next.

Extract Edges

The **Extract Edges** tool is used to extract all the edges of a solid, a surface, or a mesh. The edges are copied as lines, polylines, arcs, circles, ellipses, or splines depending upon the model selected. To extract the edges, choose the **Extract Edges** tool from the **Edge Editing** drop-down of the **Solid Editing** panel. The prompt sequence that will follow when you choose this tool is given next.

Select objects: *Select the solid from which edges are to be extracted*
Select objects: 1 found
Select objects: Enter

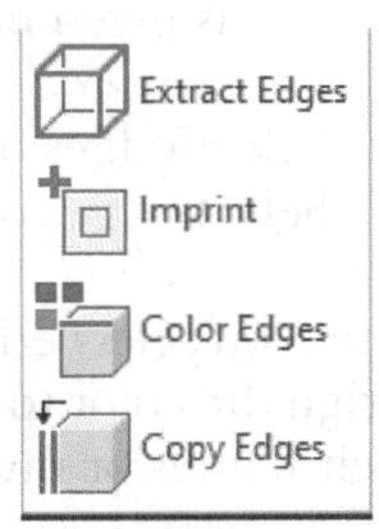

***Figure 5-9** The **Edge Editing** drop-down*

All the edges of the solid will be extracted and you can select these edges individually.

Imprint

The **Imprint** tool is used to imprint an object on a 3D solid object. Remember that the object to be imprinted should intersect one or more faces of a solid object. The objects that can be imprinted are arcs, circles, lines, 2D and 3D polylines, ellipses, splines, regions, bodies, and 3D solids. To invoke this tool, choose the **Imprint** tool from the **Edge Editing** drop-down of the **Solid Editing** panel. The prompt sequence that will follow when you choose this tool is given next.

Select a 3D solid or surface: *Select an object.*
Select an object to imprint: *Select an object to be imprinted.*
Delete the source object [Yes/No] <N>: *Select an option or* Enter.
Select an object to imprint: *Select a new object or* Enter.

The above-mentioned body editing tools can also be accessed using the **Body** option of the **SOLIDEDIT** command. Other body editing options available for this command are **Undo** and **eXit**. The **Undo** option cancels the modifications made during the **Body** option of the **SOLIDEDIT** command, and **eXit** option is used to exit the **Body** option of this command.

Copy Edges

The **Copy Edges** tool is used to copy the individual edges of a solid model. The edges are copied as lines, arcs, circles, ellipses, or splines. To invoke this tool, choose the **Copy Edges** tool from the **Edge Editing** drop-down of the **Solid Editing** panel. The prompt sequence that will follow when you choose this tool is given next.

Select edges or [Undo/Remove]: *Select the edges to be copied.*
Select edges or [Undo/Remove]: Enter
Specify a base point or displacement: *Specify the first point of displacement.*
Specify a second point of displacement: *Specify the second point of displacement.*

Color Edges

The **Color Edges** tool is used to change the color of a selected edge of a 3D solid. To invoke this tool, choose the **Color Edges** tool from the **Edge Editing** drop-down of the **Solid Editing** panel. The prompt sequence that will follow when you choose this tool is given next.

Select edges or [Undo/Remove]: *Select one or more edges or enter an option.*
Select edges or [Undo/Remove]: Enter

After you select edges and press ENTER, the **Select Color** dialog box will be displayed. You can assign the color to the selected edges using this dialog box. You can also assign color by entering their names or numbers. Individual edges can be assigned individual colors.

The discussed edge editing tools can also be assessed using the **Edge** option of the **SOLIDEDIT** command. The other edge editing options available for this command are **Undo** and **eXit**.

The **Undo** option cancels the modifications made during the **Edge** editing of the **SOLIDEDIT** command, and the **eXit** option is used to exit the **Edge** editing of this command.

Offset Edge

The **Offset Edge** tool is used to offset the boundary edges of a planar solid face or a surface. You can offset the edges either dynamically or by setting the offset distance. Note that all the edges should lie on the same plane. Depending upon the position of the cursor, the selected edges will offset inwards or outwards. During the operation, you can choose the **Corner** option to make the corners of the offset edges sharp or rounded. To offset the boundary edges, choose the **Offset Edge** tool from the **Solid Editing** panel of the **Solid** tab. The prompt sequence for the **Offset Edge** tool is given next.

Corner = Sharp
Select face: *Select the face whose edges are to be offset.*
Specify through point or [Distance/Corner]: *Specify the point or [distance].*
Select face: Enter

If you enter **Corner** at the **Specify through point or [Distance/Corner]** prompt, then the resulting offset profile will have filleted corners.

If you enter **Distance** at the **Specify through point or [Distance/Corner]** prompt, then you can specify the distance at which the offset edges will be created.

Editing Entire Body of a Solid Model

To edit the entire body of a solid model, you can use the tools available in the **Body Editing** drop-down of the **Solid Editing** panel, refer to Figure 5-10. The tools available in this drop-down are: **Separate**, **Clean**, **Shell**, and **Check**. Besides these tools, the **Imprint** tool available in the **Edge Editing** drop-down of the **Solid Editing** panel can also be used for editing a solid body, refer to Figure 5-9. The body editing tools are discussed next.

Separate

The **Separate** tool is used to separate 3D solids with disjointed volumes into separate 3D solids. Solids with disjointed volumes are created by the union of two solids that are not in contact with each other. Note that the composite solids created by performing the Boolean operations and share the same volume cannot be separated using this option. To invoke this tool, choose the **Separate** tool from the **Body Editing** drop-down of the **Solid Editing** panel. The prompt sequence that will follow when you choose this tool is given next.

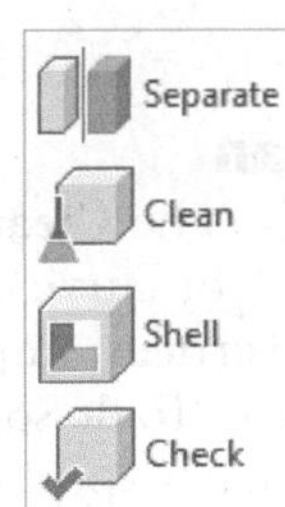

*Figure 5-10 The **Body Editing** drop-down*

Select a 3D solid: *Select a solid object with multiple lumps.*

Shell

The **Shell** tool is one of the most extensively used tools for body editing. This tool is used to create a shell of a specified 3D solid model. Shelling is defined as a process of scooping out material from a solid model in such a manner that the walls with some thickness are left. One 3D object can have only one shell. You can exclude certain faces before scooping out the material. This means the selected face will not be included during the shelling, refer to Figure 5-11. To invoke this tool, choose the **Shell** tool from the **Body Editing** drop-down of the **Solid Editing** panel. The prompt sequence that will follow when you choose this tool is given next.

Select a 3D solid: *Select an object.*
Remove faces or [Undo/Add/ALL]: *Select one or more faces or enter an option.*
Remove faces or [Undo/Add/ALL]: *Select a face, enter an option, or* Enter
Enter the shell offset distance: *Specify the wall thickness.*

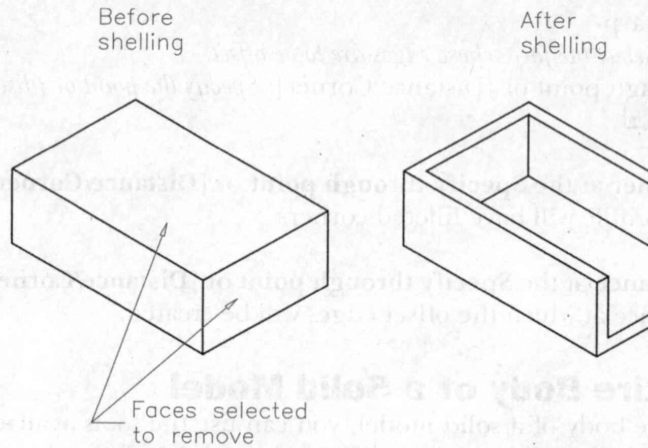

Figure 5-11 *Creating a shell in the solid model*

Tip

If you have specified a positive distance, the shell will be created on the inside perimeter of a solid and if it is negative, the shell will be created on the outside perimeter of the 3D solid.

Clean

The **Clean** tool is used to remove the shared edges or vertices sharing the same surface or curve definition on either side of the edge or vertex. It removes all redundant edges and vertices, imprinted as well as unused geometry. It also merges faces that share the same surface. To do so, choose the **Clean** tool from the **Body Editing** drop-down of the **Solid Editing** panel. The prompt sequence that will follow when you choose this tool is given next.

Select a 3D solid: *Select the solid model to clean.*

Check

The **Check** tool can be used to check if a solid object created is a valid 3D solid object. This option is independent of the settings of the **SOLIDCHECK** variable. The **SOLIDCHECK** variable turns on or off the solid validation for the current drawing session. The solid validation is turned on when the value of the **SOLIDCHECK** variable is set to 1, which is the default value. If a solid object is a valid 3D solid object, you can use solid editing options to modify it without AutoCAD displaying ACIS error messages. Solid editing can take place only on valid 3D solids. To invoke this tool, choose the **Check** tool from the **Body Editing** drop-down of the **Solid Editing** panel. The prompt sequence that will follow when you choose this tool is given next.

Select a 3D solid: *Select the solid you want to check.*
This object is a valid ShapeManager solid.

Example 1 *Solid Editing*

In this example, you will create the solid model shown in Figure 5-12. After creating the model, modify it, as shown in Figure 5-13, using the tools in the **Solid Editing** panel.

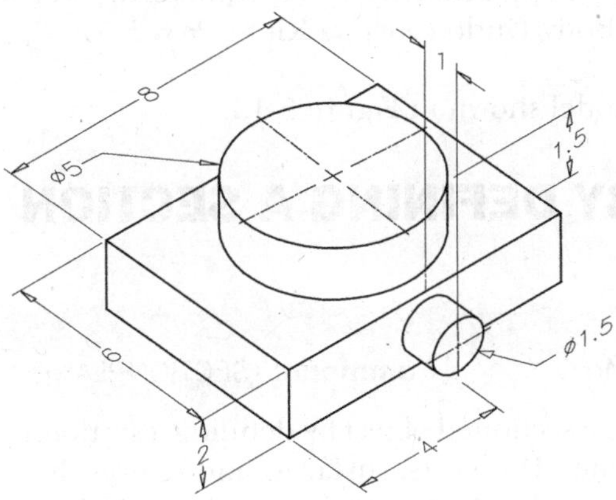

Figure 5-12 *Model for Example 1*

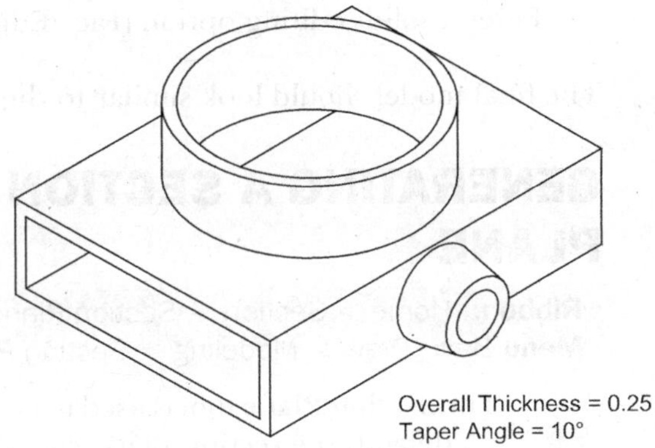

Figure 5-13 *Model after modification*

1. Create a box and two cylinders at appropriate position, refer to Figure 5-12.
2. Combine all the objects to make them a solid model.
3. Choose the **Shell** tool from **Home > Solid Editing > Body Editing** drop-down and follow the prompt sequence given below:

Select a 3D solid: *Select the solid.*
Remove faces or [Undo/Add/ALL]: *Click on the top face of the bigger cylinder.*
Remove faces or [Undo/Add/ALL]: *Click on the front face of the smaller cylinder.*
Remove faces or [Undo/Add/ALL]: *Click on the left face of the box.*
Remove faces or [Undo/Add/ALL]: Enter
Enter the shell offset distance: **0.25** Enter
Solid validation started
Solid validation completed
Enter a body editing option

[Imprint/sePar ate solids/Shell/cLean/Check/Undo/eXit] <eXit>: Enter
Enter a solids editing option [Face/Edge/Body/Undo/eXit] <eXit>: *Press ESC.*

4. Choose the **Taper Faces** tool from **Home > Solid Editing > Face Editing** drop-down and follow the prompt sequence given below:

   Select faces or [Undo/Remove]: *Click on the cylindrical face of the smaller cylinder*
   Select faces or [Undo/Remove/ALL]: Enter
   Specify the base point: *Select the center of the front face of the smaller cylinder*
   Specify another point along the axis of tapering: *Select the center at the back face of the smaller cylinder*
   Specify the taper angle: **-10** Enter
   Solid validation started.
   Solid validation completed.
   Enter a face editing option
   [Extrude/Move/Rotate/Offset/Taper/Delete/Copy/coLor/mAterial/Undo/eXit] <eXit>: Enter
   Enter a solids editing option [Face/Edge/Body/Undo/eXit] <eXit>: *Press ESC*

The final model should look similar to the model shown in Figure 5-13.

GENERATING A SECTION BY DEFINING A SECTION PLANE

Ribbon: Home > Section > Section Plane
Menu Bar: Draw > Modeling > Section Plane **Command:** SECTIONPLANE

Section Plane

The **Section Plane** tool is used to create a sectioned object by defining a sectioning plane. By default, the section plane cuts all the 3D objects, surfaces, and regions lying in the line of this plane even if the section plane does not actually pass through them. Various methods of defining the section plane are discussed next.

Defining a Section Plane by Selecting a Face

In this method, the section plane will be aligned to the plane of the selected face of the 3D solid. Choose the **Section Plane** tool from the **Section** panel and select the desired face on the solid object; a section plane aligned with the selected face will be displayed, as shown in Figure 5-14. The prompt sequence is given next.

Select face or any point to locate section line or [Draw section/Orthographic/Type]: *Select a face on the 3D solid where you want to align the section plane*

Now, you can move the section plane along normal direction to place it at the intended location. To do so, select a section line visible on that section plane, the **Move Gizmo** will be displayed at the center of the section line. Use the **Move Gizmo** to move the plane in any desired direction. Even if the display of gizmo is turned off, you can move the section plane along normal direction by using the triangular arrow grip displayed at the midpoint of the section line, refer to Figure 5-15. After moving the section plane at the desired location, click once to place the plane; the preview of the remaining section of the model will be displayed. Figure 5-16 shows the remaining section of the solid model after moving the section plane shown in Figure 5-14, to the center of the model.

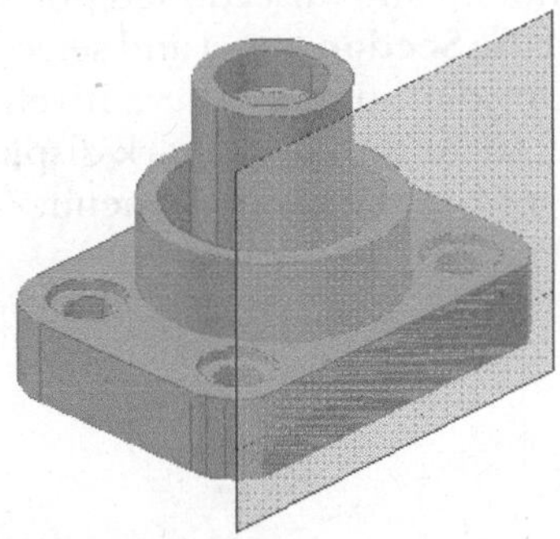

Figure 5-14 Model with a section plane

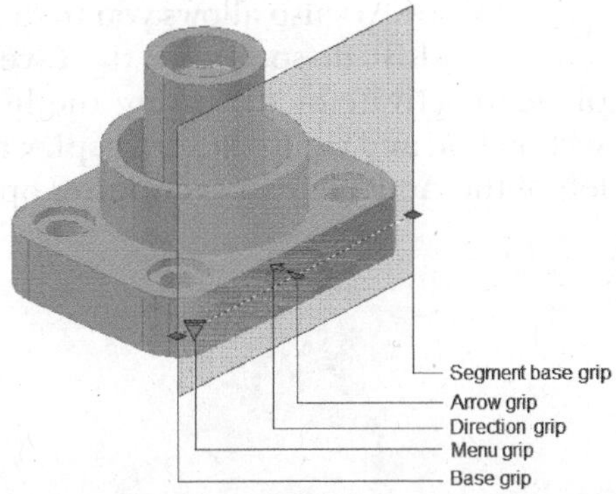

Figure 5-15 Various grip visible on the section line

You can also flip the direction of the sectioned portion of the model. To do this, click on the section line and then click on the direction grip, refer to Figure 5-17. To rotate the section plane, select the selection line and right click on it and then choose the **Rotate** option from the shortcut menu. Next, select the base point about which you want to rotate the section plane and specify the rotation angle. Figure 5-18 shows the remaining section of the model after rotating the section plane by -90-degree about the midpoint of the section line.

Instead of displaying only the section plane, you can show the section boundary with the section plane. The section boundary displays a two dimensional rectangular sketch. Only the object lying within this boundary will be displayed as the remaining section. To create a section boundary, click on the menu grip and choose the **Boundary** option. You can also show the section volume with the section boundary and the section plane. The section volume displays a three dimensional box and only the object lying within this boundary will be displayed as the remaining section. To create a section volume, choose the **Volume** option from the menu grip. Figure 5-19 shows a model with a section plane, section boundary, and section volume. The size of the section boundary and the section plane can also be edited with the help of grips.

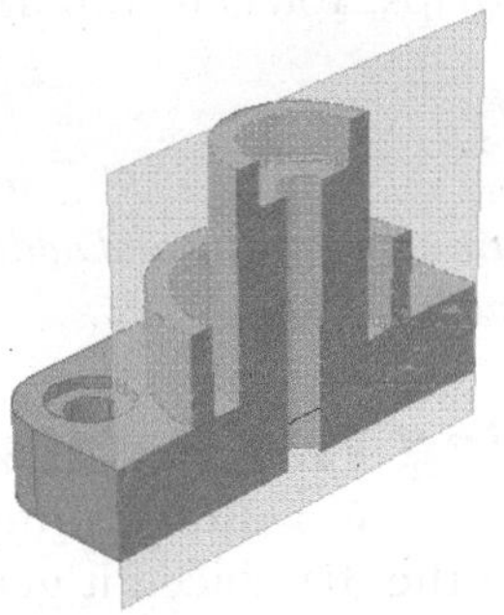

Figure 5-16 Remaining section of the model after moving the section plane

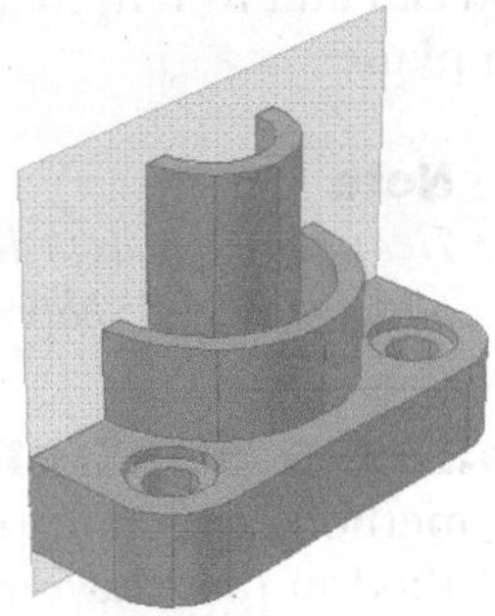

Figure 5-17 Resulting model after flipping the direction of the section plane

Generating a section by a section plane does not affect the original model. The original model is hidden and only the remaining section of the model is displayed. If you delete the section line from the drawing, the model will be redisplayed without any section.

AutoCAD also allows you to display both the sectioned and unsectioned portions of a 3D solid. To do so, choose the **Live Section** tool from the **Section** panel and select the section plane to activate or deactivate the live sectioning of the solid model. Alternatively, select the section line and right-click to display the shortcut menu. Clear the check mark displayed on the left of the **Activate live sectioning** option by choosing it from the shortcut menu.

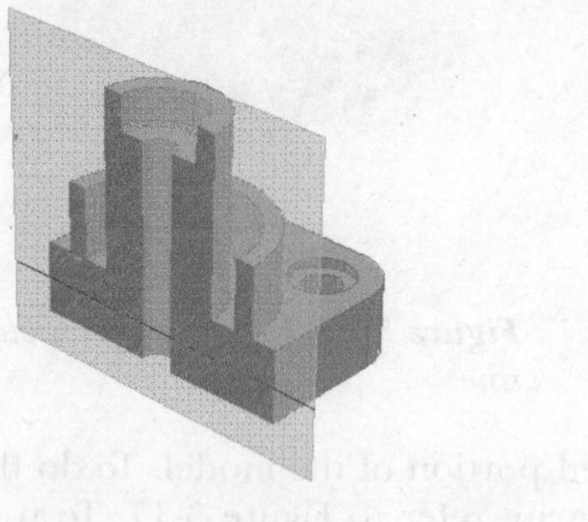

Figure 5-18 Resulting model after rotating the section plane by -90º

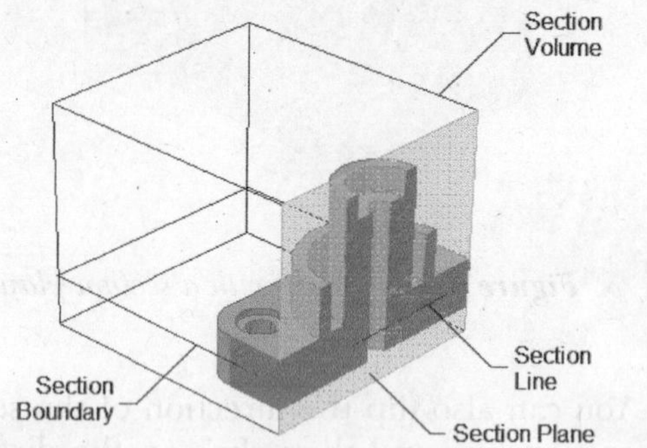

*Figure 5-19 Model after choosing the **Volume** option from the menu grip*

Even if the live sectioning is on, you can display the sectioned portion of the solid model. To do so, select the section line, invoke the shortcut menu, and choose the **Show cut-away geometry** option from it; a translucent and red colored sectioned model will be displayed.

You can add jogs to the section plane. A jog provides a 90-degree bend to the section plane for a certain distance and after that the section plane again continues in the original direction. To create a jog, choose the **Add Jog** tool from the **Section** panel; you will be prompted to select the section object. Select the section line from the drawing area. Next, you will be prompted to specify a point on the section line where you want to add the jog. Specify a location on the section line to create the jog. Alternatively, select the section line and choose **Add jog to section** from the shortcut menu to add a jog in the section line. After adding the jog, you can edit its length and location with the help of grips. You can add multiple jogs to the section plane.

Note

In all the methods to define a section plane, the procedure of modifying and adding jogs to a section plane, and of displaying the sectioned portion of the model is same.

Defining a Section Plane by Specifying Two Points

In this method, a section plane is generated such that it passes through the two points that are specified in the drawing area. If you select a face on the 3D object, it generates a section plane at the selected face, but if you specify the first point at any location in the drawing area or on the 3D object, this point acts as the base point about which the section plane can rotate. Specifying the second point will fix the through point of the section plane. A section plane will be generated passing through these two points, refer to Figure 5-20. The prompt sequence for this option is given next.

Select face or any point to locate section line or [Draw section/Orthographic/Type]: *Specify a point on the screen or on the 3D object.*
Specify through point: *Specify the other point through which the section line will pass.*

Once you generate the section plane, you will not get a preview of the sectioned object. This is because the **Activate live sectioning** option is not active by default when you generate a section plane by specifying two points. To activate the live sectioning, choose the **Live Section** tool from the **Section** panel and select the section plane. Figure 5-20 displays a model sectioned by specifying two points with the live sectioning turned on. The prompt sequence for this tool is given next.

Select section object: *Select the section line on the section plane.*

Defining a Section Plane by Drawing the Section Line

In this method, you can draw a section line and generate a section plane that passes along it. You can section a 3D object in many planes by picking points through which the section plane will pass. To do so, choose the **Section Plane** tool from the **Section** panel. Next, right-click in the drawing area and choose the **Draw section** option from the shortcut menu. Now, specify the point from which the section line will start and then specify the points through which it will pass. After specifying all the points, press the ENTER key and then specify the side of the object to be retained after sectioning. By default, the section plane in this case will be displayed as the section boundary with the live sectioning deactivated. Figure 5-21 shows the model sectioned by drawing a section line with the live sectioning activated.

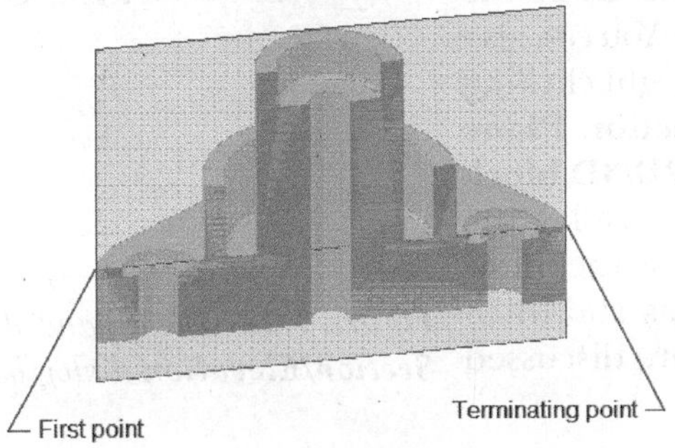

Figure 5-20 *Model sectioned by specifying two points*

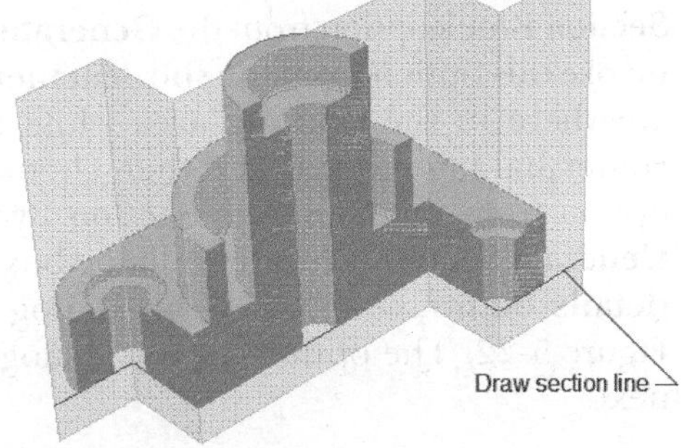

Figure 5-21 *Model sectioned by drawing the section line*

Note

A section line should be drawn only on one sketching plane. Otherwise, you will not be able to visualize the sectioned model after activating the live sectioning. Also, the drawn section line should not be self-intersecting.

Defining a Section Plane by Selecting a Preset Orthographic Plane

In this method, a section plane will be generated parallel to preset orthographic planes such as front, top, right so on, and passes through an imaginary center of a box. This box is calculated by enveloping all the solids, surfaces, and regions present in the drawing. Choose the **Section Plane** tool from the **Section** panel. Next, right-click in the drawing area and choose the **Orthographic** option from the shortcut menu; you will be prompted to select the predefined orthographic plane with which the generated section plane will be aligned. On selecting this, you get a sectioned solid whose material is chopped from the side you selected as the preset orthographic plane. In this option, you will instantaneously get the sectioned object because live sectioning is activated automatically.

Generating 2D and 3D Sections

As mentioned earlier, sectioning a model by generating a section plane does not affect the original model. The original model is hidden and only the remaining section of the sectioned model is displayed. On deleting the section plane, the sectioned object will get deleted. If you want to retain the generated section as a 2D or 3D section with the original model, you can use the **Generate Section** tool.

To generate a 2D or a 3D section, choose the **Generate Section** tool from the **Section** panel in the **Home** tab; the **Generate Section/Elevation** dialog box will be displayed. Alternatively, you can select a section plane to activate the **Section Plane** contextual tab and choose the **Generate Section Block** option from the **Generate** panel. You can also invoke this option from the shortcut menu by right clicking anywhere in the drawing area while the **Section Plane** contextual tab invoked and then choose the **2D/3D block** option from the **Generate Section** flyout to display the **Generate Section/Elevation** dialog box. Choose the **Show details** button to expand this dialog box, as shown in Figure 5-22. The options in this dialog box are discussed next.

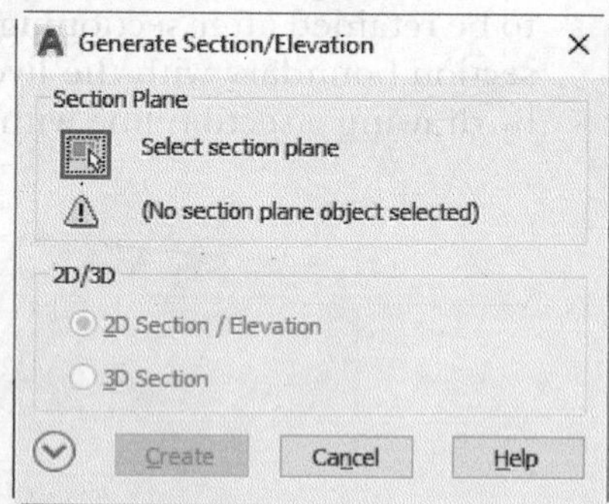

*Figure 5-22 The expanded **Generate Section/Elevation** dialog box*

Section Plane Area

Choose the **Select section plane** button from this area and select the section plane for which you need to create 2D/3D sections.

2D/3D Area

This area allows you to specify the type of section you want to generate. The **2D Section / Elevation** option is used to generate a two dimensional sketch of the sectioned object on the XY plane of the current UCS. The **3D Section** option generates a 3D sketch of the sectioned object on a plane parallel to the section plane. Figure 5-23 shows the model with its 2D section and Figure 5-24 shows the model with its 3D section.

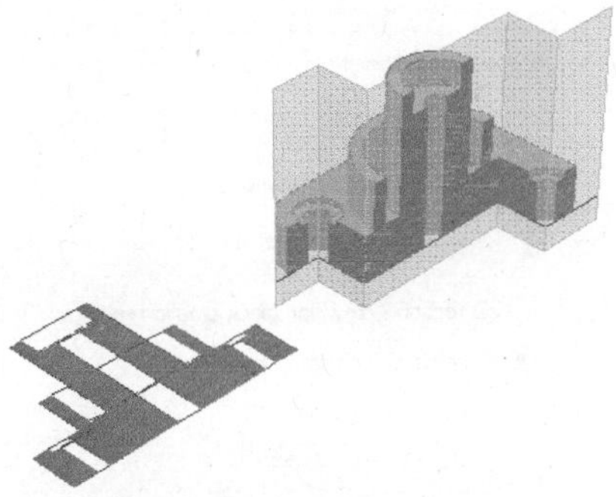

Figure 5-23 Model with its 2D section

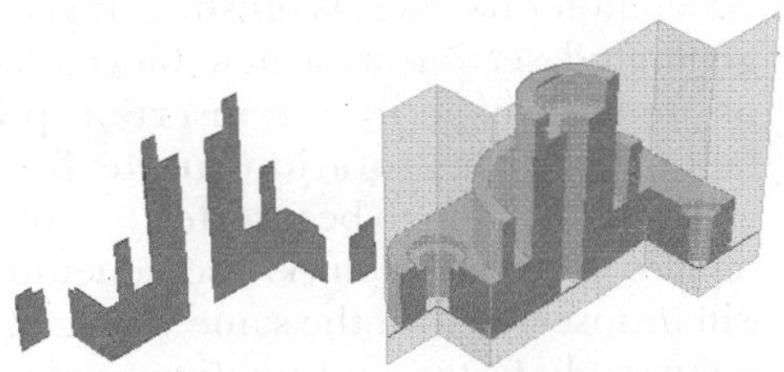

Figure 5-24 Model with its 3D section

Source Geometry Area

This area allows you to specify the objects of the drawing that you want to include while creating the 2D or 3D section. The **Include all objects** radio button, if selected, includes all the 3D objects, surfaces, and regions in the drawing. It also includes the external reference objects and blocks. The **Select objects to include** option allows you to select the objects to be included in the section generation. If you select the **Select objects to include** radio button and then choose the **Select objects** button, the **Generate Section/Elevation** dialog box will disappear allowing you to select the solids. After selecting the solids, surfaces, or regions, press the ENTER key; the **Generate Section/Elevation** dialog box will reappear, displaying the number of selected objects below the **Select objects** button.

Destination Area

This area provides the option to specify how you want to use the generated section. The **Insert as new block** option inserts the generated section in the same drawing file as a block. The **Replace existing block** option inserts the generated section by replacing an existing block. Choose the **Select block** button to select the block to be replaced by the newly generated section block. The **Export to a file** option allows you to create a new drawing file with the generated section. To save it as a new file, choose the **Browse [...]** button to specify the location where you want to save the new drawing file.

Section Settings

This button is used to invoke the **Section Settings** dialog box, refer to Figure 5-25. You can also invoke this dialog box by clicking on the inclined arrow in the title bar of the **Section** panel. If you select the **2D Section/Elevation** option in the 2D/3D area, the **Section Settings** dialog box will be displayed with the **2D section / elevation block creation settings** radio button selected by default. Similarly, if you select the **3D section block creation settings** option in the 2D/3D area, the **Section Settings** dialog box will be displayed with the **3D section block creation settings** option selected by default. The **Section Settings** dialog box is used to modify the properties of the sections generated. These properties are displayed depending on the radio button selected.

Create

When you choose this button from the **Generate Section/Elevation** dialog box, the section generation process gets finished. If you insert the generated section as a new block, you will be prompted to specify the insertion point, scale factor, and the rotation angle for the new generated section to be inserted as a block. If you replace an existing block, the generated section will be inserted with the same values of insertion point, scale factor, and rotation angle as for the block selected to be replaced. If you choose to export the generated section to a new file, a new file will be created and the section will be created at the same location with the same scale and orientation as the model in the previous file.

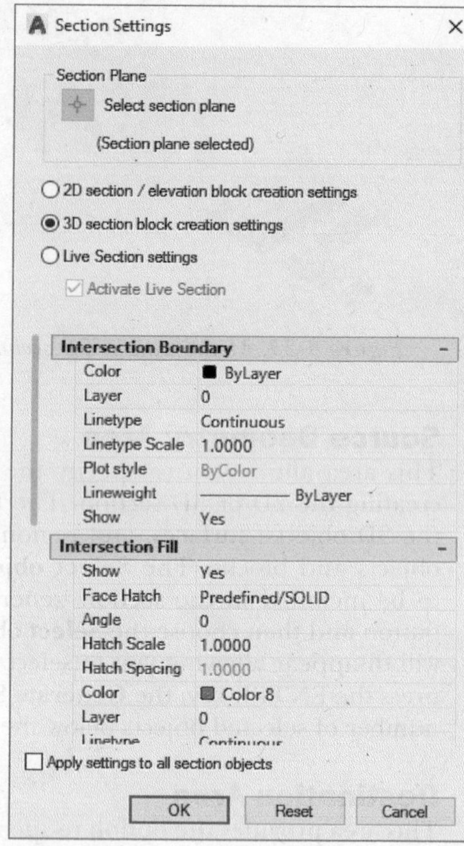

*Figure 5-25 The **Section Settings** dialog box*

Live Section settings

This option is used to control the dynamic display of a sectioned solid in the drawing. Select the section line and choose **Live Section settings** from the shortcut menu; the **Section Settings** dialog box will be displayed with the **Live Section settings** option selected by default. The options available to control the display of the live sectioning of the model are similar to the options discussed in the **Section Settings** dialog box. The **Face Transparency** and **Edge Transparency** options in the **Cut-away Geometry** area are only available for the live section settings. These two options control the transparency of the edge and the face of the cut-away solid for a better view of the section and the remaining portion of the model. The value of transparency signifies the amount of light that passes through the cut-away part.

SOLID HISTORY

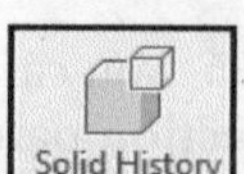

The **Solid History** button is available in the **Primitive** panel of the **Solid** tab. By default, this button is not chosen. As a result, you can directly edit faces, edges and vertices of a solid. If you choose the **Solid History** tool, the history of individual solid object is recorded. So, if a composite solid model is created by performing a Boolean operation, the features used to create solid will be saved with the composite solid. Therefore, you can modify the shape of the composite solid by modifying the original features.

Consider a case in which a composite solid is created by subtracting a wedge from the cylinder, as shown in Figures 5-26 and 5-27. To modify this composite solid, choose the **Solid History** option from **Solid > Selection > Subobject** drop-down; the solid history symbol will be attached to the cursor. Move the cursor near the composite solid and select the wedge when its preview is displayed, refer to Figure 5-28. You can also use the **Selection list** box to select the wedge. When the grips of the wedge are displayed, drag the grips and modify the shape of the wedge; the shape of the composite solid gets changed automatically, as shown in Figure 5-29.

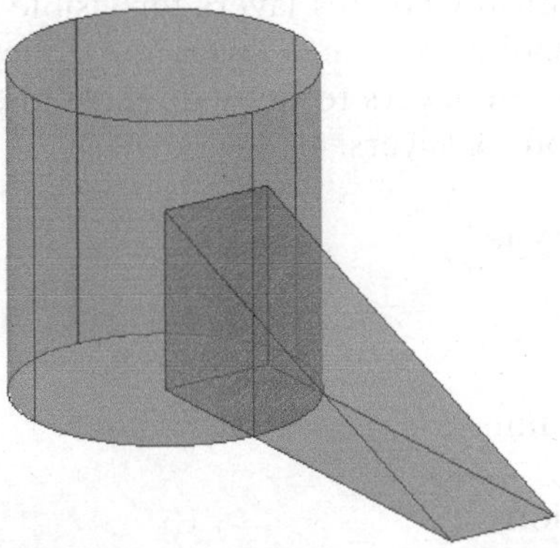

Figure 5-26 A cylinder and a wedge as two separate solid bodies

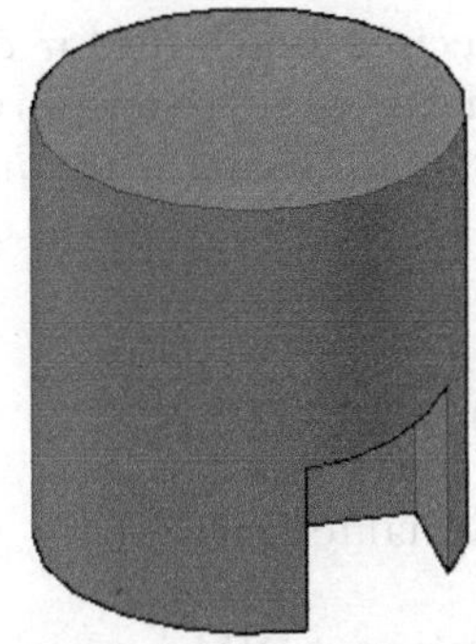

Figure 5-27 Resulting composite solid model after subtracting the wedge from the cylinder

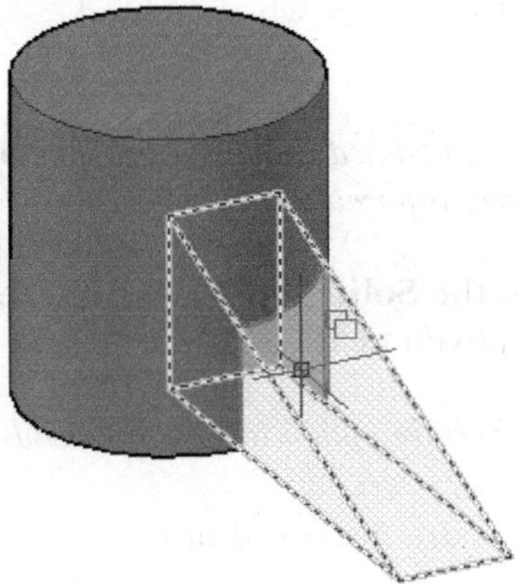

Figure 5-28 Wedge with the preview displayed

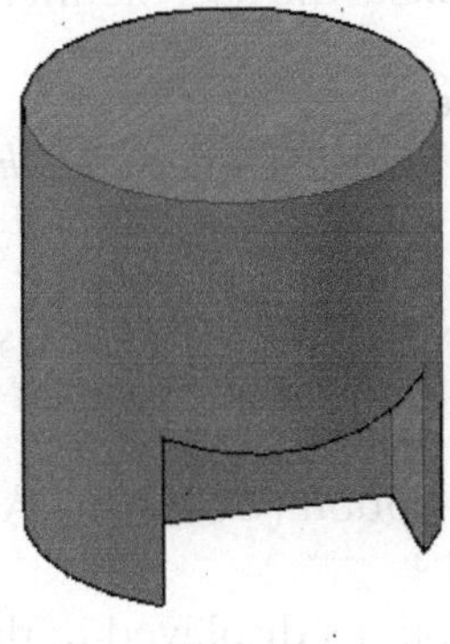

Figure 5-29 Composite solid model after editing

GENERATING DRAWING VIEWS OF A SOLID MODEL

As mentioned earlier, one of the major advantages of working with a solid model is that the drawing views of a solid model are automatically generated once you have the solid model with you. All you have to do is to specify the type of drawing view required. This is done using the **Solid View**, **Solid Drawing**, and **Solid Profile** tools. All these tools are discussed next.

Solid View

Ribbon: Home > Modeling > Solid View
Menu Bar: Draw > Modeling > Setup > View **Command:** SOLVIEW

The **Solid View** tool is an externally defined ARX application (*solids.arx*). This tool is used to create the documentation of the solid models in the form of the drawing views. This tool guides you through the process of creating orthographic or auxiliary views. The **Solid View** tool creates floating viewports using orthographic projections to layout sectional view and multiview drawings of solids, while you are in the **layout** tab.

For the ease of documentation, this tool automatically creates layers for visible lines, hidden lines, and section hatching for each view. This tool also creates layers for dimensioning that are visible in individual viewports. You can use these layers to draw dimensions in individual viewports. The following is the naming convention for layers.

Layer name	**Object type**
View name-VIS	Visible lines
View name-HID	Hidden lines
View name-DIM	Dimensions
View name-HAT	Hatch patterns (for sections)

The view name is the user-defined layer name given to the view when created.

Note

*The information stored on these layers is deleted and updated when you use the **Solid Drawing** tool. Therefore, do not place any permanent drawing information on these layers.*

To create the drawing views of a solid model, choose the **Solid View** tool from the **Modeling** panel. The prompt sequence that will be displayed is given next.

Enter an option [Ucs/Ortho/Auxiliary/Section]: *Select an option to generate the drawing view.*

These four options displayed in the Command prompt are discussed next.

Ucs Option

This option is used to create a profile view relative to a UCS. This is the first view that has to be generated. The reason for this is that the other options require existing viewports. The UCS can either be the current UCS or any other named UCS. The view generated using this option will be parallel to the *XY* plane of the current UCS. After selecting the **Ucs** option, the next prompt sequence is:

Enter an option [Named/World/?/Current] <Current>: *Enter an option or* Enter *to accept the current UCS.*

The **Named** option uses a named UCS to create the profile view. The prompt sequence is as follows:

Enter name of UCS to restore: *Enter the name of the UCS you want to use.*
Enter view scale <1.0>: *Enter a positive scale factor.*

This view scale value you enter is equivalent to zooming into your viewport by a factor relative to the paper space. The default ratio is 1:1. The next prompt sequence is as follows:

Specify view center: *Specify the location of the view.*
Specify view center <specify viewport>: Enter

This point is based on the Model space extents. The next prompt sequence is as follows.

Specify the first corner of viewport: *Specify a point.*
Specify opposite corner of viewport: *Specify a point.*
Enter view name: *Enter a name for the view.*

The **World** option uses the *XY* plane of the WCS to create a profile view. The prompt sequences are the same as the **Named** option.

The ? option lists all the named UCSs. The prompt sequence is given next.

Enter UCS names to list<*>: *Enter a name or press ENTER to list all the named UCSs.*

The **Current** option uses the *XY* plane of the current UCS to generate the profile view. This is also the default option.

Ortho Option

An orthographic view is generated by projecting the lines on to a plane normal to an existing view. The **Ortho** option generates an orthographic view from the existing view. Keep in mind that the orthographic views created in AutoCAD are folded views and not the unfolded views. AutoCAD prompts you to specify the side of the viewport from where you want to project the view. The resultant view will depend on the side of the viewport selected. The prompt sequence is given next.

Specify side of viewport to project: *Select the edge of a viewport.*
Specify view center: *Specify the location of the orthographic view.*
Specify view center <specify viewport>: Enter
Specify first corner of viewport: *Select the first point.*
Specify opposite corner of viewport: *Select the second point.*
Enter view name: *Specify the view name.*

Auxiliary Option

This option is used to create an auxiliary view from an existing view. An auxiliary view is the one that is generated by projecting the lines from an existing view on to a plane that is inclined at a certain angle. AutoCAD prompts you to define the inclined plane used for the auxiliary projection. The prompt sequence is as follows.

Specify first point of inclined plane: *Specify the first point on the inclined plane.*
Specify second point of inclined plane: *Specify the second point on the inclined plane.*
Specify side to view from: *Specify a point.*
Specify view center: *Specify the location of the view.*
Specify view center <specify viewport>: Enter
Specify first corner of viewport: *Specify the first corner of the viewport.*
Specify opposite corner of viewport: *Specify the second corner of the viewport.*
Enter view name: *Enter the view name.*

Section Option

This option is used to create the section views of the solid model. The type of the section view depends on the alignment of the section plane and the side from which you view the model. Initially, the crosshatching is not displayed in the section view. To display the crosshatching, invoke the **Solid Drawing** tool. AutoCAD prompts you to define the cutting plane and the prompt sequence is as follows.

Specify first point of cutting plane: *Specify the first point on the cutting plane.*
Specify second point of cutting plane: *Specify the second point on the cutting plane.*

Once you have defined the cutting plane, you can specify the side to view from and the view scale relative to paper space. The prompt sequence is given next.

Specify side to view from: *Specify the point in the direction from which the section is viewed.*
Enter view scale <current>: *Enter a positive number.*
Specify view center: *Specify the location for the view.*
Specify view center <specify viewport>: Enter
Specify first corner of viewport: *Specify the first corner of the viewport.*
Specify opposite corner of viewport: *Specify the second corner of the viewport.*
Enter view name: *Enter the view name.*

Solid Drawing

Ribbon: Home > Modeling > Solid Drawing
Menu Bar: Draw > Modeling > Setup > Drawing **Command:** SOLDRAW

The **Solid Drawing** tool generates profiles and sections in the viewports that were created with the **Solid View** tool. The basic function of this tool is to clean up the viewports created by the **Solid View** tool. It displays the visible and hidden lines that represent the silhouettes and edges of the solids in a viewport, and then projects them in a plane that is perpendicular to the viewing direction. When you use the **Solid Drawing** tool with the sectional view, a temporary copy of the solid is created.

This temporary copy is then chopped at the section plane defined by you. Then the **Solid Drawing** tool creates the visible half as the section and discards the copy of the solid model. The crosshatching is automatically created using the current hatch pattern (HPNAME), hatch angle (HPANG), and hatch scale (HPSCALE). In this case, the layer **View name- HID** is frozen. If there are any existing profiles and sections in the selected viewports, they are deleted and replaced with new ones. The prompt sequence is as follows.

Select viewports to draw...
Select objects: *Select viewports to be drawn.*

Solid Profile

Ribbon: Home > Modeling > Solid Profile
Menu Bar: Draw > Modeling > Setup > Profile **Command:** SOLPROF

The **Solid Profile** tool creates profile images of 3D solids by displaying only the edges and silhouettes of the curved surfaces of the solids in the current view. Note that before you invoke this tool, you must be in the temporary model space of the layout. This means that the value of the **TILEMODE** variable should be set to 0, but you should switch to the model space using the **MSPACE** command. The prompt sequence that follows when you invoke the **Solid Profile** tool is given next.

Select objects: *Select the object in the viewport.*
Select objects: Enter
Display hidden profile lines on separate layer? [Yes/No] <Y>: *Specify an option.*
Project profile lines onto a plane? [Yes/No] <Y>: *Specify an option.*
Delete tangential edges? [Yes/No] <Y>: *Specify an option.*
One solid selected.

DRAWING VIEWS

In AutoCAD, drafting has become easier due to the introduction of a new tab called **Layout** tab in the **Ribbon**. Most of the tools available in this tab can be used only in the drafting space (Layouts). With the help of these tools, you can generate a base view, projected view, section view, and detail view of the solid or surface present in the model space. You can also generate views of a model created in **Autodesk Inventor**. The options available in the **Layout** tab are discussed next.

Base

The tools available in the **Base** drop-down are used to create the base view of a model opened in the Model Space or created in Autodesk Inventor. The tools available in this drop-down are discussed next.

From Model Space

Ribbon: Layout > Create View > Base > From Model Space **Command:** VIEWBASE

The **From Model Space** tool is used to create the base view of the model opened in the Model Space of the current session of AutoCAD. To use this tool, you need a solid model created or opened in AutoCAD. Note that only the visible entities can be imported in this process. If the model space is empty and you invoke this tool, then the **Select File** window will be displayed and you will be prompted to select an Autodesk Inventor model. Figure 5-30 shows a solid model and its drawing views. To create the base view of this model, you need to follow the procedure given next.

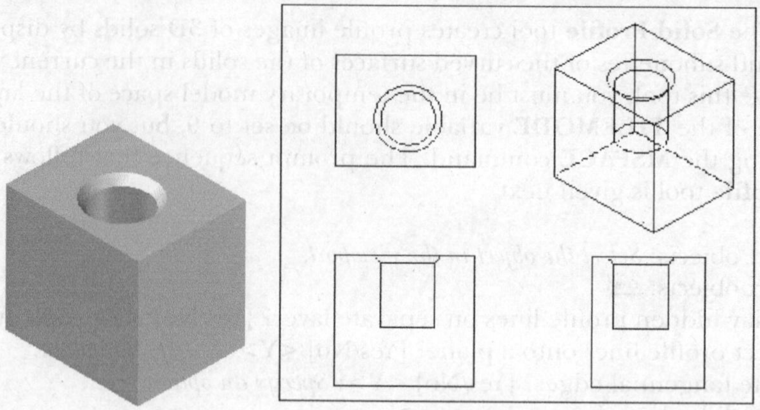

Figure 5-30 *Model and its drawing views*

Choose the Layout workspace and then delete the default viewport. Next, choose the **Base** tool from the **Create View** panel of the **Layout** tab; a flyout with the **From Model Space** and **From Inventor** tools will be displayed. Choose the **From Model Space** option from the flyout; a **Drawing View Creation** contextual tab will be displayed in the **Ribbon**, as shown in Figure 5-31. Select the desired orientation of the model for the drawing view from the **Orientation** list box. You can also choose the visual style of the base view from the **View Style** drop-down in the **Appearance** panel. You can specify the absolute scale of the object using the **Scale** drop-down list. You can control the visibility of the objects by selecting the check boxes provided in the **Edge Visibility** drop-down list. The check boxes available in the **Edge Visibility** drop-down list are discussed next.

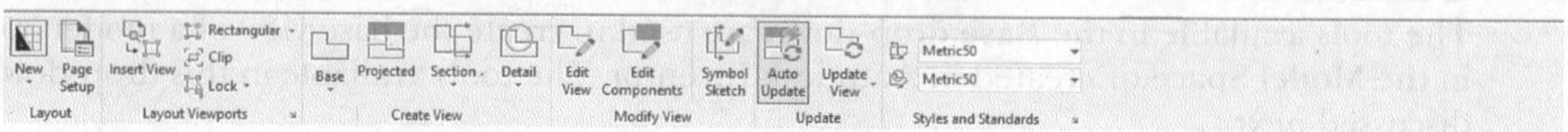

Figure 5-31 *The **Drawing View Creation contextual** tab*

Interference edges. This check box is used to toggle the visibility of both hidden and visible edges which are not displayed due to an intersection condition.

Tangent edges. This check box is used to toggle the visibility of the edges formed by tangential intersection of surfaces.

Tangent edges foreshortened. This check box is used to shorten the length of tangential edges to differentiate them from the visible edges.

Bend extents. This check box is used to toggle the display of the sheet metal extent lines. If there is a bend in the sheet metal part, then the **Bend extents** tool will be used to display the extent line of the sheet metal.

Thread features. This check box is used to toggle the display of thread lines on screws or tapped holes.

Presentation trails. This check box is used to display the lines that indicate the directions along which the components will move when assembled.

You can also specify the justification of a view by using the **View Options** in the **Appearance** panel. This dialog box can be invoked by clicking on the inclined arrow in the title bar of the **Appearance** panel. When you specify the scale of the view, the drawing view stretches or shrinks. If you select **Fixed** from the **View Justification** drop-down list, the alignment will remain unchanged. But if you select **Centered**, then the drawing view will be adjusted to the center position.

You can move the view to the required position by choosing the **Move** button in the **Modify** panel of the **Drawing View Creation** tab. This tab will become active only after placing the base view.

After specifying all the properties, click on the screen at the desired location; the base view will be created. Choose the **OK** button to place the base view; the **Drawing View Creation** tab will disappear and you will be prompted to specify the location of the projected view. The orientation of the projected view depends upon its location. Specify the location of projected view and exit by pressing ENTER.

From Inventor

Ribbon: Layout > Create View > Base > From Inventor **Command:** VIEWBASE

The **From Inventor** tool is used to create the base view of the model created in Autodesk Inventor. On invoking this tool, the **Select File** window will be displayed and you will be prompted to select the **Autodesk Inventor** file to create the base view.

Projected View

Ribbon: Layout > Create View > Projected View **Command:** VIEWPROJ

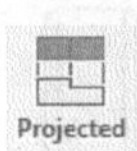

The **Projected View** tool is used to create a projected view from the base view present in the layout workspace. By default, there are eight projected views, four orthogonal, and four isometric. You can create a projected view by using the procedure discussed next.

Choose the **Projected View** tool from the **Create View** panel of the **Layout** tab; you will be prompted to select the parent view. Select the existing view in the layout; the projected view will be attached to the cursor and you will be prompted to specify the location of the projected view. Specify the location; you will be prompted to specify the location of the projected view again. You can specify the location or you can exit by pressing ENTER.

Edit View

Ribbon: Layout > Modify View > Edit View **Command:** VIEWEDIT

The **Edit View** tool is used to change the settings of a view such as representation, visibility, view style scale, and so on. After invoking this tool, you need to click on the drawing view; the **Drawing View Editor** contextual tab will be added to the **Ribbon**. Now, you can change the

settings by selecting the required option from the **Drawing View Editor** tab. You can also move the view using the **Edit View** tool, but you cannot reorient it. Alternatively, you can invoke this tool by simply double-clicking on the drawing view.

Update View

Ribbon: Layout > Update > Update View **Command:** VIEWUPDATE

The **Update View** tool is used to update the layout. If you change the viewport, the drawing view will not be updated automatically. Therefore, you need to invoke the **Update View** tool to update the views. If you make changes to the model from which the views are derived, then the views in the layout will be displayed with a red mark on each corner. This red mark indicates that the model has been modified or removed. Also, a pop-up window is displayed at the bottom notifying that the model has been changed. You can update the views by choosing the **Update View** tool from the **Update** panel in the **Layout** tab. However, note that the **Update View** tool updates only the selected view. If you want to update all thé views in the layout, then you have to choose the **Update all Views** tool from the **Update view** drop-down in the **Update** panel.

Auto Update

Ribbon: Layout > Update > Auto Update

The **Auto Update** tool is used to update the layout automatically when the source model is changed. By default, the **Auto Update** tool is activated in the **Update** panel. As a result, the layout views updates automatically, if any modification is made in the source model.

Drafting Standard

The **Drafting Standard** tool is used to set the default settings for drafting. These settings will be applied to the newly generated views. To invoke this tool, click on the inclined arrow located on the right of the **Styles and Standards** panel of the **Layout** tab; the **Drafting Standard** dialog box will be displayed, as shown in Figure 5-32. The three areas in this dialog box, **Projection type**, **Thread style**, and **Shading/Preview**, are discussed next.

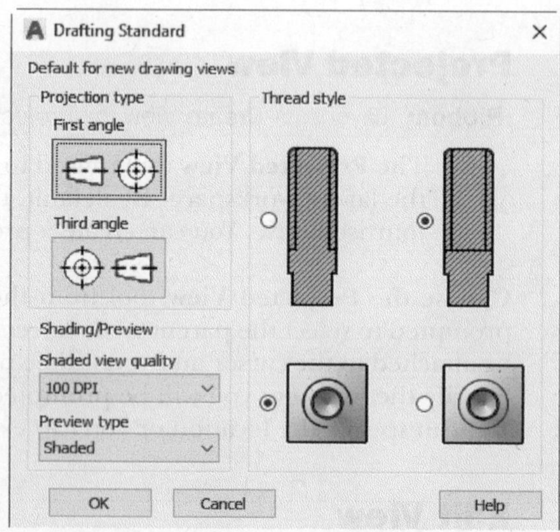

***Figure 5-32** The **Drafting Standard** dialog box*

Projection type. In this area, there are two buttons: **First angle** and **Third angle**. These buttons represent the first angle projection and the third angle projection, respectively. By default, **Third angle** is chosen.

Thread style. In this area, there are four radio buttons: **Partial section thread end, Full section thread end, Partial circular thread edge,** and **Full circular thread edge**. You can select the desired radio button to represent the threads.

Shading/Preview. In this area, there are two drop-down lists: **Shaded view quality** and **Preview type**. You can set the dot per inch quality of the shaded view in the drawing view by selecting the desired option from the **Shaded view quality** drop-down list. From the **Preview type** drop-down list, you can either select the **Shaded** preview or the **Bounding box** preview. If you select **Shaded**, the model is displayed shaded. If you select **Bounding box**, only the bounding box will be displayed in the preview, not the model.

Generating Section Views

In AutoCAD, you can generate the section views of the drawing view which are generated from a 3D model. The section views are generated by taking a portion of the existing view by using a cutting plane defined by the sketched line. The tools used for creating the section views are discussed next.

Full Section View

Ribbon: Layout > Create View > Section drop-down > Full **Command:** VIEWSECTION

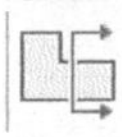

The **Full** tool is used to create the full section view of a model. This section view is created by cutting the model through its entire length. To do so, choose the **Full** tool from the **Section** drop-down in the **Create View** panel of the **Layout** tab and select the view of the model to be sectioned. Next, you will be prompted to specify the first point of the cutting section plane. Figure 5-33 shows the full section view created by using the **Full** tool. The prompt sequence for creating the full section view is given next.

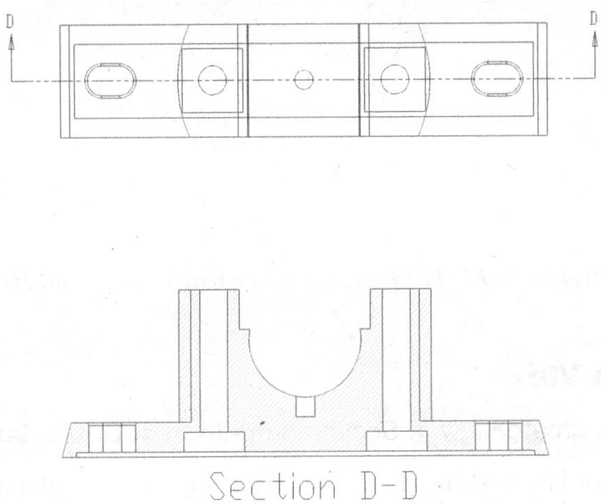

Figure 5-33 *Full section view created using the **Full** tool*

Select parent view: *Select a view*
Specify start point: *Specify the start point to create the section plane defined by sketched line*
Specify end point or undo : *Specify the end point which cuts the view through out the length*
Specify location of the section view: *Specify the location of the view*
Select option [Hidden lines/Scale/Visibility/Projection/Depth/Annotation/hatCh/Move/eXit] <eXit> : Enter

Half Section View

Ribbon: Layout > Create View > Section drop-down > Half **Command:** VIEWSECTION

The **Half** tool is used to create the half section view of a model. The half section view is created by cutting the model through a portion of its length. To do so, choose the **Half** tool from the **Section** drop-down in the **Create View** panel of the **Layout** tab and select the view of the model to be sectioned. Create the cutting section plane which cuts the model through half of its length. Figure 5-34 shows the half section view created by using the **Half** tool. The prompt sequence for creating the half section view is given next.

Select parent view: *Select a view*
Specify start point: *Specify the start point to create the section plane defined by sketched line*
Specify next point or [Undo] : *Specify the next point*
Specify end point or [Undo] : *Specify the end point*
Specify location of the Section view or: *Specify the location of the view*
Select option [Hidden lines/Scale/Visibility/Projection/Depth/Annotation/hatCh/Move/eXit] <eXit> : Enter

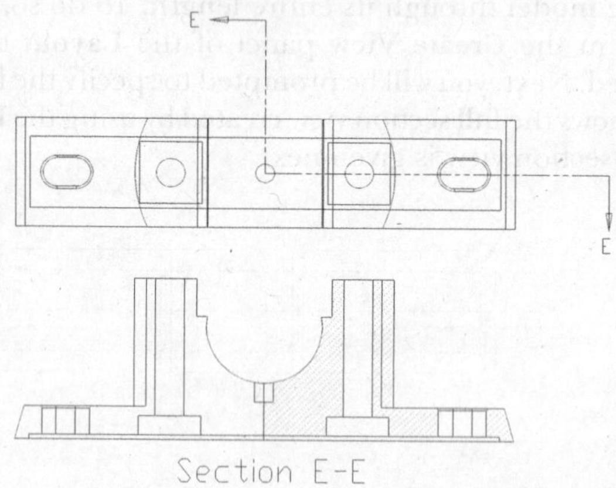

***Figure 5-34** Half section view created using the **Half** tool*

Offset Section View

Ribbon: Layout > Create View > Section drop-down > Offset **Command:** VIEWSECTION

The **Offset** tool is used to create the offset section view of a model. The offset section view is created by cutting the model at offset positions of the cutting plane. To create the offset section view, choose the **Offset** tool from the **Section** drop-down of the **Create View** panel in the **Layout** tab; you will be prompted to select the parent view. Select the model view and create the cutting section plane. Figure 5-35 shows the offset section view created by using the **Offset** tool. The prompt sequence for creating the offset section view is explained next.

Select parent view: *Select a view*
Specify start point: *Specify the start point to create the section plane defined by sketched line*
Specify next point or [Undo] : *Specify the next point*
Specify next point or [Undo] : *Specify the next point and continue to specify the points*

Specify next point or [Undo Done] <Done> : Enter
Specify location of the Section view or: *Specify the location of the view*
Select option [Hidden lines/Scale/Visibility/Projection/Depth/Annotation/hatCh/Move/eXit] <eXit> : Enter

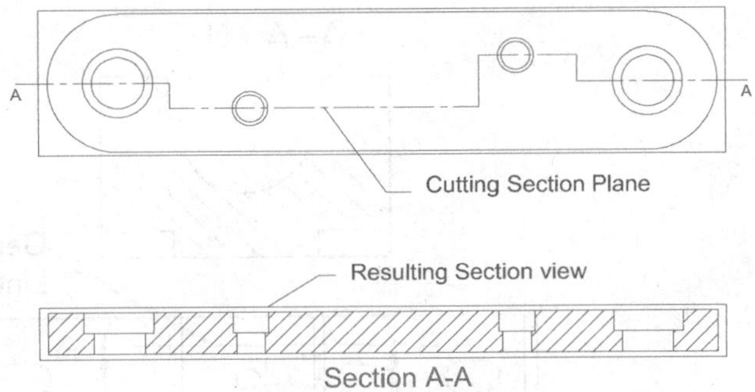

Figure 5-35 *Offset section view created using the **Offset** tool*

Aligned Section View

Ribbon: Layout > Create View > Section drop-down > Aligned **Command:** VIEWSECTION

The **Aligned** tool is used to create the aligned section view of a model. The aligned section view is created by cutting the model at different angles and lengths. To create the aligned section view, choose the **Aligned** tool from the **Section** drop-down of the **Create view** panel in the **Layout** tab; you will be prompted to select the section view. Next, create the cutting section axis which cuts the model at different angles and lengths. Figure 5-36 shows the aligned section view created using the **Aligned** tool. The prompt sequence for creating the aligned section view is given next.

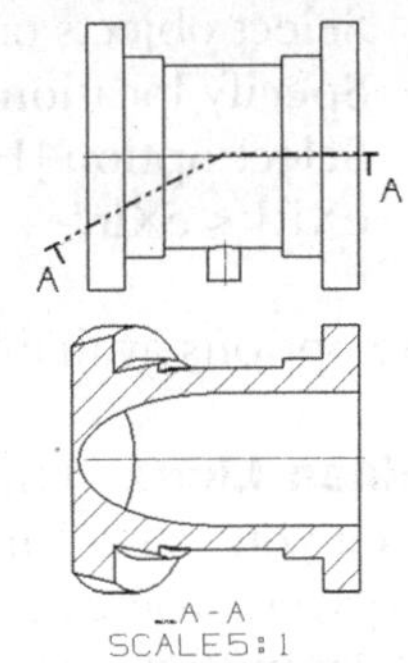

Figure 5-36 *Aligned Section view created using **Aligned** tool*

Select parent view: *Select a view*
Specify start point: *Specify the start point to create the section plane defined by sketched line*
Specify next point or [Undo] : *Specify the next point*
Specify next point or [Undo Done] <Done> : Enter
Specify location of the Section view: *Specify the location of the view*
Select option [Hidden lines/Scale/Visibility/Projection/Depth/Annotation/hatCh/Move/eXit] <eXit> : Enter

From Object Section View

Ribbon: Layout > Create View > Section drop-down > From Object **Command:** VIEWSECTION

The **From Object** tool is used to create the object section view of a model. This object section view is created by cutting the model with an existing geometry line. To create object section view, draw a geometric line on the parent view through which you want to create the section view. Choose the **From Object** tool from the **Section** drop-down of the **Create View** panel in the **Layout** tab and select the parent view of the model. Figure 5-37 shows the section view created by using the **From Object** tool. The following prompt sequence for creating the object section view is explained next.

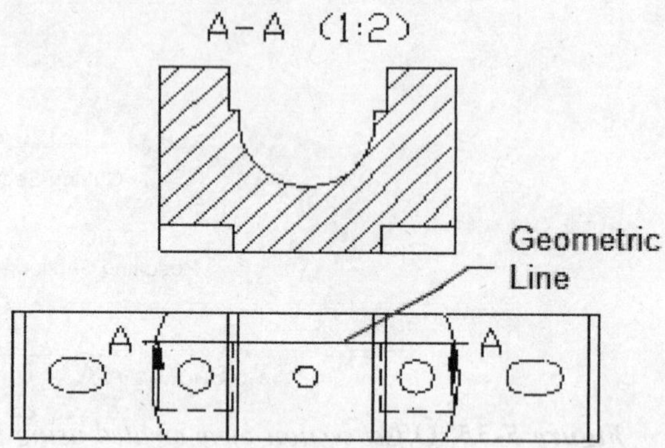

***Figure 5-37** Section view created using the **From Object** tool*

Select parent view: *Select a view*
Select objects or [Done] : *Section the geometry to specify as a section line,* Enter
Specify location of the Section view: *Specify the location of the view*
Select option [Hidden lines/Scale/Visibility/Projection/Depth/Annotation/hatCh/Move/eXit] <eXit> : Enter

The options available in the command prompt are discussed next.

Hidden Lines. This option is used to specify the line types displayed for the section view. When you select this option, you will be prompted to select the style of the hidden lines to be displayed. You can select any desired style to display the hidden lines by using the options in the command prompt.

Scale. This option is used to specify the scale of the section view. By default, the scale of the new section view is chosen from the base view. You can also specify the required scale for the section view.

Visibility. This option allows you to specify the type of visibility of the edges, features, and so on for the section view.

Projection. This option is used to specify the type of projection for the section view.

Depth. This option is used to specify the depth of the cut for the section view.

Annotation. This option is used to specify the type of annotations like the label and identifier of the section view.

Hatch. This option is used to turn on or off the display of the hatching for the section view.

CREATING FLATSHOT

Ribbon: Home > Section > Flatshot OR Solid > Section > Flatshot **Command:** FLATSHOT

The **Flatshot** tool creates a 2D sketch of a model by projecting the model in the current view on the XY plane of the current UCS. The created sketch is inserted in the drawing as a block. A flatshot can be created in any preset orthographic view or a view created in the parallel projection. If you create a flatshot in the perspective view, a 3D wireframe of the entire model will be created by projecting the model in the current view on the XY plane of the current UCS. Choose the **Flatshot** tool from the **Section** panel; the **Flatshot** dialog box will be displayed, refer to Figure 5-38. The options in this dialog box are discussed next.

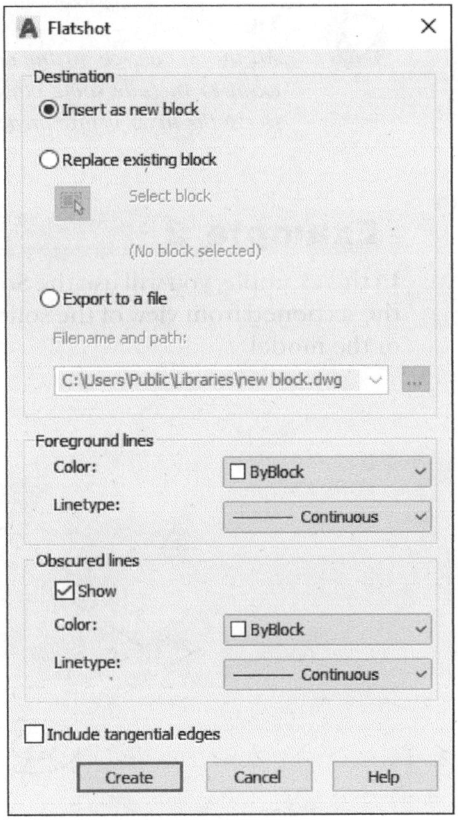

*Figure 5-38 The **Flatshot** dialog box*

Destination Area

By using the options in this area, you can specify how you want to use the generated flatshot. The **Insert as new block** radio button inserts the generated flatshot in the same drawing file as a block. The **Replace existing block** button inserts the generated flatshot by replacing an existing block. Choose the **Select block** button to select the block to be replaced by the newly generated block. The **Export to a file** radio button allows you to create a new drawing file with the generated flatshot. To save it as a new file, choose the **Browse [...]** button to specify the location where you want to save the new drawing file.

Foreground lines Area

The options in this area control the color and line type of the edges in the front at the time of the flatshot creation.

Obscured lines Area

The options in this area control the display, color, and line type of the hidden edges at the time of the flatshot creation.

Create

Choosing this button finishes the flatshot creation process.

Include tangential edges

Select this check box to include the tangential edges of the curved surface into the flatshot.

Note

The 3D objects that are sectioned by the section plane will be flatshot as if they are not sectioned.

Tip

All the 3D objects in the current drawing are included in the flatshot creation. If you do not want to include some objects in the flatshot creation, transfer them to a separate layer and freeze the layer before creating the flatshot.

Example 2 — *Solid View & Solid Drawing*

In this example, you will use the **Solid View** and **Solid Drawing** tools to generate the top view and the sectioned front view of the solid model shown in Figure 5-39. Assume the missing dimensions of the model.

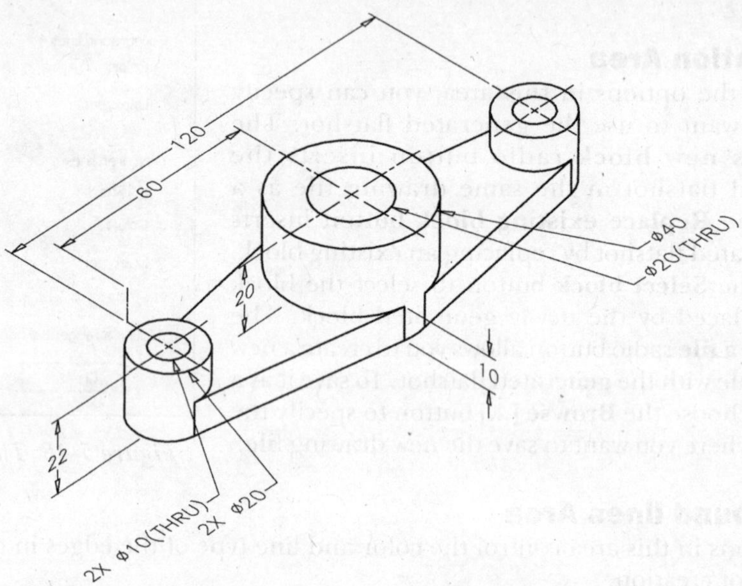

***Figure 5-39** Solid model to generate drawing views*

1. Create the solid model by assuming the dimensions.

2. Switch to **Layout1**; the default viewport is displayed.

3. Delete the default viewport. To do so, invoke the **Erase** tool, select the Viewport, and press ENTER.

4. Choose the **Solid View** tool from the **Modeling** panel and follow the prompt sequence given below:

Enter an option [Ucs/Ortho/Auxiliary/Section]: **U**
Enter an option [Named/World/?/Current] <Current>: **W**
Enter view scale <1.0000>: Enter
Specify view center: *Specify the view location close to the top left corner of the drawing window.*
Specify view center <specify viewport>: Enter
Specify first corner of viewport: *Specify the point of the viewport, P1, refer to Figure 5-40.*
Specify opposite corner of viewport: *Specify the second point, P2, refer to Figure 5-40.*
Enter view name: **Top**
Enter an option [Ucs/Ortho/Auxiliary/Section]: Enter

5. Double-click in the viewport to switch to the temporary model space. Zoom the drawing to the extents using the **Extents** option of the **ZOOM** command. Now, switch back to the paper space by choosing the **MODEL** button displayed in the Status Bar. The layout after generating the top view should look similar to the layout shown in Figure 5-41.

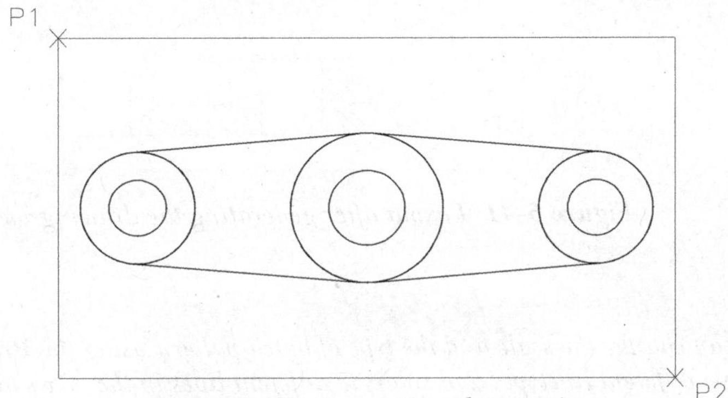

Figure 5-40 *Generating the top view*

6. Again, choose the **Solid View** tool from the **Modeling** panel and follow the prompt sequence given below:

Enter an option [Ucs/Ortho/Auxiliary/Section]: **S**
Specify first point of cutting plane: *Select the left quadrant of the left cylindrical portion in the top view.*
Specify second point of cutting plane: *Select the right quadrant of the right cylindrical portion in the top view.*
Specify side to view from: *Select a point below the top view in the viewport.*
Enter view scale <current>: Enter
Specify view center: *Specify the location of the view below the top view.*
Specify view center <specify viewport>: Enter
Specify first corner of viewport: *Select first corner of the viewport.*
Specify opposite corner of viewport: *Select the second corner of the viewport.*
Enter view name: **FRONT**
Enter an option [Ucs/Ortho/Auxiliary/Section]: Enter

7. Choose the **Solid Drawing** tool from the **Modeling** panel and follow the prompt sequence given next.
Select viewports to draw.

Select objects: *Select the first viewport.*
Select objects: *Select the second viewport.*
Select objects: Enter

8. The drawing view should look similar to the layout shown in Figure 5-41.

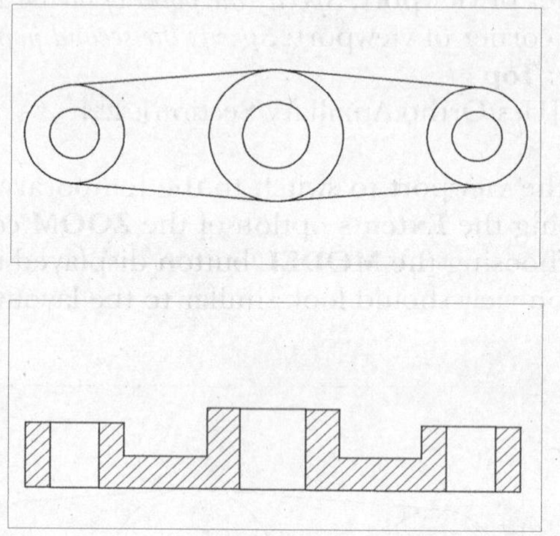

***Figure 5-41** Layout after generating the drawing views*

Tip
*You can change the scale and the type of hatch pattern using the **Properties** palette. You can also set different linetypes and colors to different lines in the views by selecting their respective layers using the **Layer Properties** tool.*

CALCULATING THE MASS PROPERTIES OF SOLID MODELS

Menu Bar: Tools > Inquiry > Region/Mass Properties
Toolbar: Inquiry > Region/Mass Properties **Command:** MASSPROP

The mass properties of the solids or the regions can be automatically calculated using the **Region/Mass Properties** tool. Various mass properties are displayed in the AutoCAD Text Window. You can also write these properties to a file. This file will be in the *.mpr* format. The properties thus calculated can be used in analyzing the solid models. Note that the mass properties are calculated by taking the density of the material of the solid model as one unit.

It is very important for you to first understand the various properties that will be calculated using this tool. The properties are:

Mass. This property provides the measure of mass of a solid. This property will not be available for the regions.

Area. This property provides the measure of area of the region. This property will be available only for the regions.

Volume. This property tells you the measure of the space occupied by the solid. Since AutoCAD assigns a density of 1 to solids, the mass and volume of a solid are equal. This property will be available only for the solids.

Perimeter. This property, providing the measure of the perimeter of the region, will be available only for the regions.

Bounding Box. If the solid were to be enclosed in a 3D box, the coordinates of the diagonally opposite corners would be provided by this property. Similarly, for regions, the *X* and the *Y* coordinates of the bounding box are displayed.

Centroid. This property provides the coordinates of the center of mass for the selected solid. The density of a solid is assumed to be unvarying.

Moments of Inertia. This property provides the mass moments of inertia of a solid about the three axes. The equation used to calculate this value is given next.

mass_moments_of_inertia = object_mass * (radius of axis)^2

The radius of axis is nothing but the radius of gyration. The values obtained are used to calculate the force required to rotate an object about the three axes.

Products of Inertia. The value obtained with this property helps you to determine the force resulting in the motion of the object. The equation used to calculate this value is:

product _of_inertia YX, XZ = mass * dist centroid_to_YZ * dist centroid_to_XZ

Radii of Gyration. The equation used to calculate this value is given next.

gyration_radii = (moments_of_inertia/body_mass)$^{1/2}$

Principal moments and X-Y-Z directions about centroid. This property provides you with the highest, lowest, and middle value for the moment of inertia about an axis passing through the centroid of the object.

The prompt sequence that follows when you invoke the **Region/Mass Properties** tool is given next.

Select objects: *Select the solid model.*
Select objects: Enter

```
---------------- SOLIDS ----------------

Mass:                    67278.5917
Volume:                  67278.5917
Bounding box:            X: 1.4012 -- 151.4012
                         Y: 118.6406   -- 158.6406
                         Z: 0.0000     -- 25.0000
Centroid:                X: 76.4012
                         Y: 138.6406
                         Z: 9.2026

Moments of inertia:      X: 1308864825.5181
                         Y: 507244127.3062
                         Z: 1799135898.4724
Products of inertia:     XY: 712635884.7490
                         YZ: 85837337.1138
                         ZX: 47302745.3493
Radii of gyration:       X: 139.4790
                         Y: 86.8301
                         Z: 163.5285
Principal moments and X-Y-Z directions about centroid:
Press ENTER to continue: Enter
                         I: 9991363.2928 along [1.0000 0.0000 0.0000]
                         J: 108831209.8607 along [0.0000 1.0000 0.0000]
                         K: 113244795.9294 along [0.0000 0.0000 1.0000]

Write analysis to a file? [Yes/No] <N>: Specify an option.
```

If you enter **Y** at the last prompt, the **Create Mass and Area Properties File** dialog box will be displayed. This dialog box is used to specify the name of the *.mpr* file. The mass properties will then be written in this file.

RECORDING THE DRAWING STEPS BY USING THE ACTION RECORDER

Ribbon: Manage > Action Recorder > Record
Menu Bar: Tools > Action Recorder > Record **Command:** ACTRECORD

The **Record** tool helps you to record the drawing steps quickly and easily. These steps are called actions. These actions are saved to a named macro for repeated use. To record an action, choose the **Record** tool from the **Action Recorder** panel of the **Manage** tab. On invoking this tool, a red circle appears near the cursor, indicating that the actions are recorded. Now, if you perform any action, it will be recorded. Also, the **Action Tree** will be expanded and the actions you perform will get updated simultaneously, as shown in Figure 5-42. If you need any message to be displayed during playback, choose the **Insert Message** tool from the **Action Recorder** panel; the **Insert User Message** dialog box will be displayed. Enter the message and choose the **OK** button; the message will be added to the **Action Tree**. This message will be displayed during playback. Similarly, if you want the user to input any values while playback, you can choose the **Pause for User Input** tool from the **Action Recorder** panel and continue recording the action. After recording the actions, choose the **Stop** button in the **Action Recorder** panel to stop the recording; the **Action Macro** dialog box will be displayed, as shown in Figure 5-43. Specify a name for the action macro in the **Action Macro Command Name** edit box. If you want to give any description of the action, enter it in the **Description** edit box. The check boxes in the **Restore pre-playback view** area are used to invoke the playback message box when you play the action macro. If you select the **Check for inconsistencies when playback begins** check box and if there is inconsistency in the workspace, template, or any other while you playback the action macro, then a warning box will be displayed. Remember that if you invoke any dialog boxes such as **Hatch and Gradient** or **OSnap** and change any settings during recording, then those settings will not be recorded. As a result, during the playback, the corresponding dialog box will be displayed again and you need to set the parameters again in it.

The **Folder Path** display box in the **Action Macro** dialog box displays the default path where the action macro is saved.

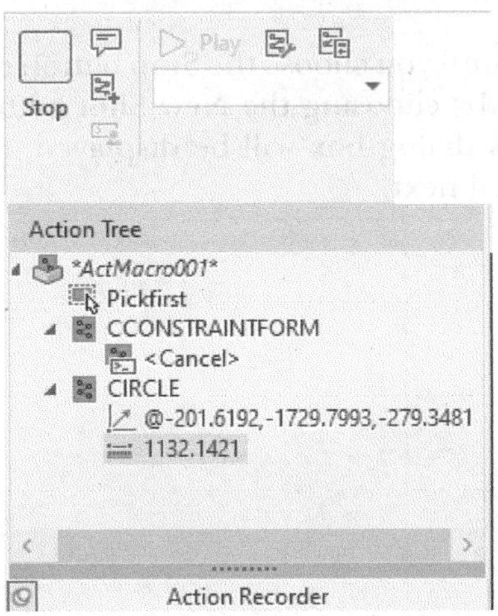

***Figure 5-42** The **Action Recorder** panel recording the actions performed*

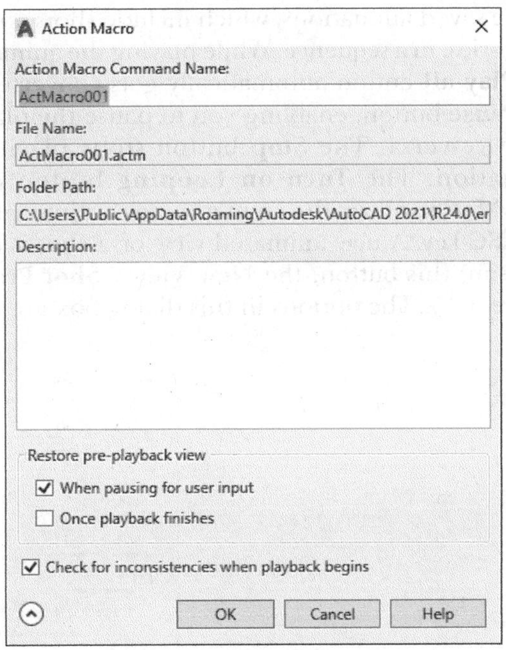

***Figure 5-43** The **Action Macro** dialog box*

The **ACTRECPATH** command is used to change the path where the action macro is stored, by default. On entering this command, the following prompt sequence will be displayed:

Command: **ACTRECPATH**
Enter new value for ACTRECPATH, or . for none <"C:\Documents and Settings\User\Application Data\Autodesk\A...">: *Enter the new location within the quotes (" ")*

To playback the recorded action macro, select the action macro from the **Available Action Macro** drop-down list in the **Action Recorder** panel and choose the **Play** button; the action macro will start playing. You can use an existing action macro in a new drawing. To do so, open a new drawing file in the same template as used for the action macro. Next, choose the **Play** button from the **Action Recorder** panel.

USING SHOWMOTION FOR PRESENTATION

Menu Bar: View > ShowMotion **Navigation Bar:** ShowMotion **Command:** NAVSMOTION

The **ShowMotion** tool is used to create the animated views of the current drawing. This can be used to quickly step through different named views in the drawing, enabling you to play the animated views for presentations or to review the drawings.

On invoking this tool, a control panel for **ShowMotion** with six buttons will be displayed above the **Status Bar**, refer to Figure 5-44. The **Play all** button is used to play all the saved animations, which include shots and view categories, in a sequence. While playing the animations, the **Play all** button automatically gets converted into the **Pause** button, enabling you to pause the playback and vice-versa. The **Stop** button stops playing the animation. The **Turn on Looping** button of the **ShowMotion** allows the animation to continue playing until you choose the **Stop** button or press the ESC key. A new animated view or a shot is created by choosing the **New Shot** button. On choosing this button, the **New View / Shot Properties** dialog box will be displayed, refer to Figure 5-45. The options in this dialog box are discussed next.

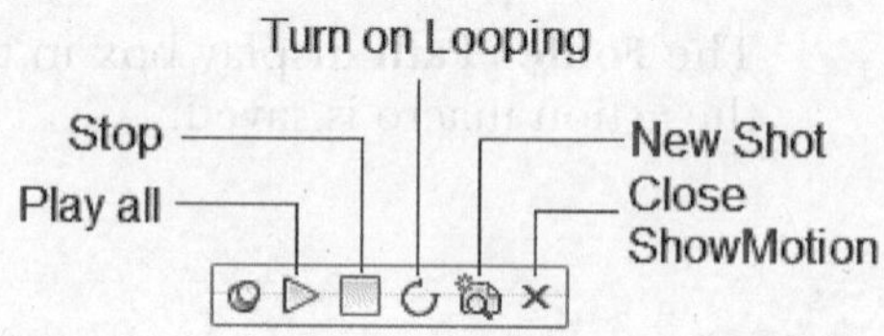

***Figure 5-44** The **ShowMotion** control panel*

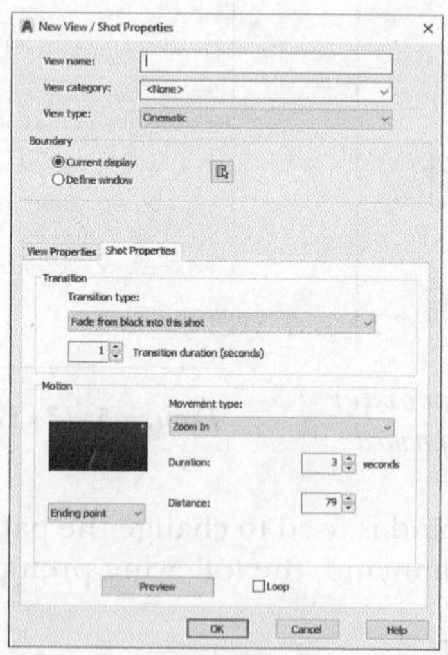

***Figure 5-45** The **New View/Shot Properties** dialog box*

View name. You can specify the name for the shot in the **View name** edit box. These names will be displayed below the respective shot thumbnails.

View category. You can enter the name of the category in this edit box. You can also group a sequence of shots of the same view categories. The different view categories are displayed as a series of thumbnails at the bottom of the drawing area.

View type. You can take three different types of shots using this drop-down list. These are **Still, Cinematic** and **Recorded Walk**. You can give transition effects between two shots, and the length or duration of the effects can be specified in the **Transition** area. Select an option in the **Transition type** drop-down list to specify the transition effects between two shots. You can see the preview of any view type in the preview box available in the **Motion** area of the **Shot Properties** tab of the dialog box.

If you select the **Still** option from the **View type** drop-down list, the position of camera will be fixed and you can set the duration of the shot in the **Motion** area of the dialog box.

If you select the **Cinematic** option from the **View type** drop-down list, you can move the camera position and set the duration of the recording. Select the type of movement in the **Movement type** drop-down list and specify the duration and distance in the respective spinners. On selecting the **Crane up** or **Crane down** option in the **Movement type** drop-down list, the **Shift left** check box becomes available. Consequently, you can specify the amount by which the camera shifts to left or right during the movement. On selecting the **Always look at camera pivot point** check box, the view is always focused at the camera.

If you select the **Recorded Walk** option from the **View type** drop-down list, you can create an animated view. To do so, choose the **Start Recording** button available in the **Motion** area of the **Shot Properties** tab. The dialog box disappears and a navigation tool is attached to the cursor. Next, press and hold the left mouse button and move the cursor. Once you release the left mouse button, the dialog box reappears. Choose the **OK** button to exit the dialog box.

Playing the Animation

Each **View Category** and its shots are displayed as thumbnails at the bottom of the drawing area. Each **View Category** thumbnail contains its corresponding name at its bottom. The series of shots under each category are displayed as smaller thumbnails above the **View Category** thumbnails, as shown in Figure 5-46. However, the thumbnails are enlarged when the cursor moves over them. Each thumbnail contains two buttons, **Play** and **Go**. Choosing the **Play** button on the shot thumbnail plays that particular animated shot whereas choosing the **Play** button on the **View Category** thumbnail plays the sequence of shots under that particular category. On choosing the **Go** button available on the right side of the thumbnails, you can move the camera to the camera position of the first shot. To play all the shots, choose the **Play all** button from the control panel.

You can rename, delete, recapture, or update a shot using the shortcut menu displayed on right-clicking on a thumbnail. You can also re-order the sequence of shots by moving them to the left or right using the options in the shortcut menu. To create a new shot, choose the **New View / Shot** option from the shortcut menu. To modify the shots, choose the **Properties** option from the shortcut menu; you will be prompted to enter the name of the view you want to edit. Type the name of the view and press ENTER; the **New View / Shot Properties** dialog box will be displayed. Now, you can change the required properties in this dialog box.

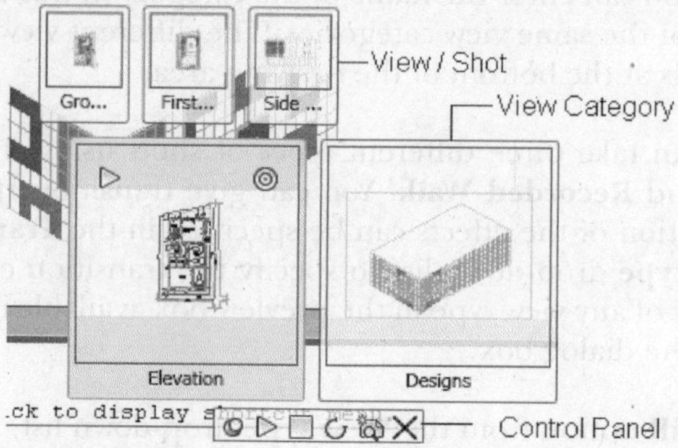

*Figure 5-46 The **ShowMotion** control panel and the **View Category** thumbnails*

Self-Evaluation Test

Answer the following questions and then compare them to those given at the end of this chapter:

1. The __________ tool is used to generate the drawing views of a solid model.

2. The mass properties of a selected solid model can be written into a file of __________ format.

3. The __________ tool creates a 2D sketch of a model by projecting the model in the current view on the XY plane of the current UCS.

4. Choose the __________ tool to separate 3D solids from the 3D solids with disjointed volumes.

5. The impression on a solid model can be removed using the __________ tool.

6. Solid models can be edited using the **EDITSOLID** command. (T/F)

7. You can create a shell in a solid model using the **Shell** tool. (T/F)

8. A section plane cuts all 3D objects, surfaces, and regions only if the section plane actually passes through them. (T/F)

9. The **Record** tool in the **Action Recorder** panel is used to create the animated views of the current drawing. (T/F)

10. The history of a composite solid created by performing the Boolean operation is saved along with the composite solid. (T/F)

Review Questions

Answer the following questions:

1. Which of the following tools is used to generate the profiles and sections in the viewports created using the **Solid View** tool?

   (a) **Solid Draw** (b) **Solid Profile**
   (c) **Solid Edit** (d) None of these

2. Which of the following methods is used to create a section plane?

   (a) by Specifying Two Points (b) by Selecting a Preset Orthographic Plane
   (c) by Drawing the Section Line (d) All of the above

3. Which option of the **SOLIDEDIT** command is used to edit the faces of a solid model?

   (a) **Body** (b) **Face**
   (c) **Solid** (d) None of these

4. Which of the following options of the **Solid View** tool is used to generate the drawing view relative to the current UCS?

   (a) **New** (b) **Section**
   (c) **UCS** (d) **Ortho**

5. Which of the following commands is used to calculate mass properties of the solid model?

   (a) **PROPERTIES** (b) **MASSPROP**
   (c) **CALCULATE** (d) **MASSPROPERTIES**

6. You can edit a wireframe model by using the **SOLIDEDIT** command. (T/F)

7. You can move a selected face of a solid model from one location to the other. (T/F)

8. You can assign different colors to different faces of a solid model. (T/F)

9. After adding a jog, you can edit its length and location with the help of grips. (T/F)

10. The sketch created using the **Flatshot** tool is inserted into a drawing as a block. (T/F)

Exercise 1

In this exercise, you will create the solid model shown in Figure 5-47. After creating the model, generate its top and sectioned front views and then shade the model by using the Shaded with Visible Lines option.

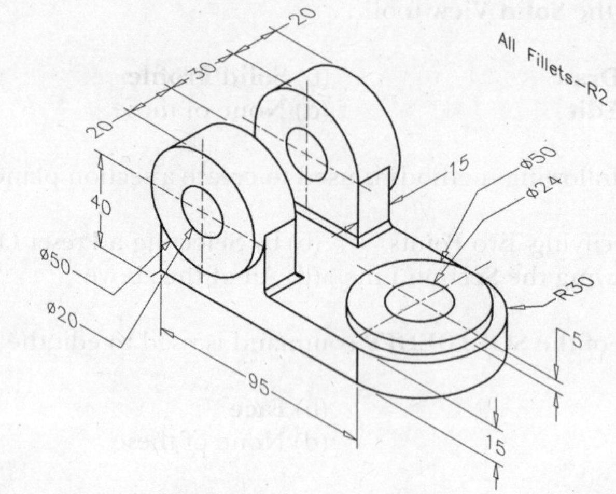

***Figure 5-47** Solid model for Exercise 1*

Exercise 2

In this exercise, you will create the solid model shown in Figure 5-48. After creating the model, shade and rotate it in the 3D space using the **Orbit** tool. Assume the missing dimensions.

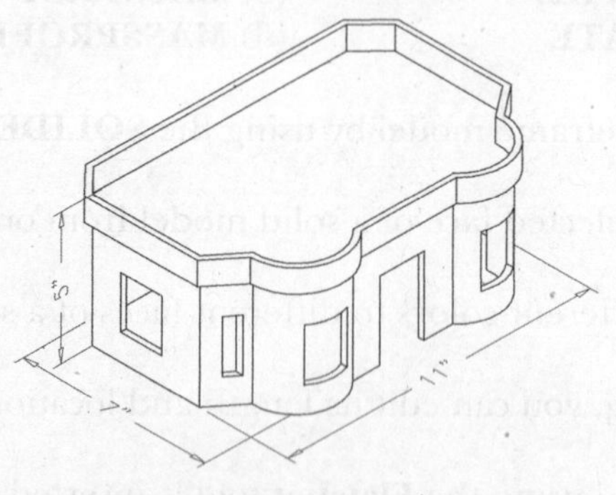

***Figure 5-48** Solid model for Exercise 2*

Problem-Solving Exercise 1

Draw the Piece part drawings shown in Figure 5-49. Then assemble them and create the Bill of Materials, as shown in Figure 5-50. The solid model of the assembled Tool Organizer is shown in Figure 5-51.

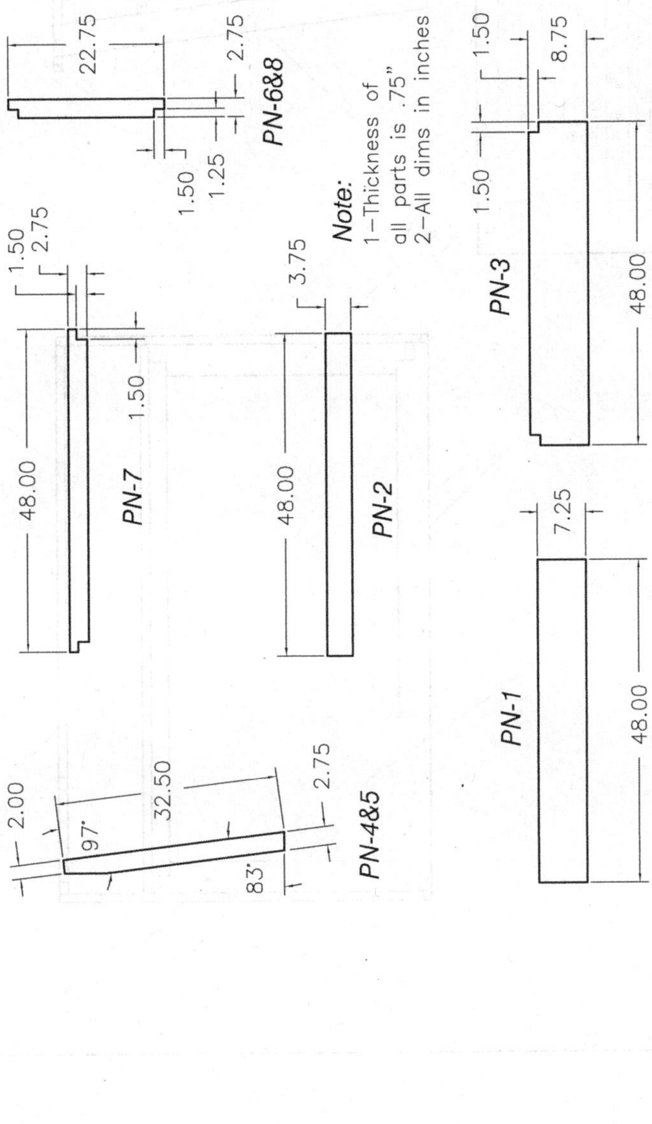

***Figure 5-49** Piece part drawing of the Tool Organizer*

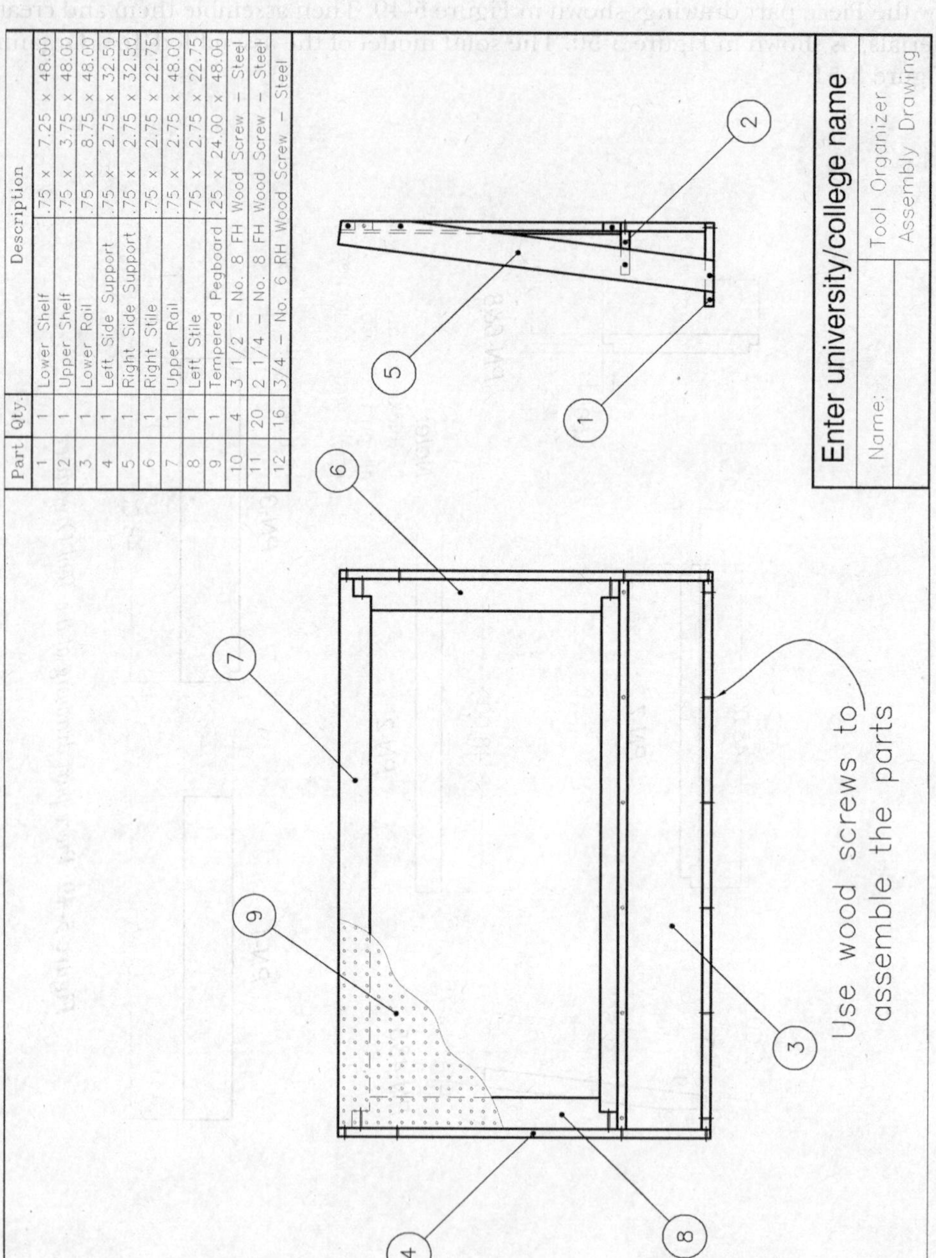

Part	Qty.	Description	
1	1	Lower Shelf	.75 x 7.25 x 48.00
2	1	Upper Shelf	.75 x 3.75 x 48.00
3	1	Lower Rail	.75 x 8.75 x 48.00
4	1	Left Side Support	.75 x 2.75 x 32.50
5	1	Right Side Support	.75 x 2.75 x 32.50
6	1	Right Stile	.75 x 2.75 x 22.75
7	1	Upper Rail	.75 x 2.75 x 48.00
8	1	Left Stile	.75 x 2.75 x 22.75
9	1	Tempered Pegboard	.25 x 24.00 x 48.00
10	4	3 1/2 – No. 8 FH Wood Screw – Steel	
11	20	2 1/4 – No. 8 FH Wood Screw – Steel	
12	16	3/4 – No. 6 RH Wood Screw – Steel	

***Figure 5-50** Assembly drawing and BOM of the Tool Organizer*

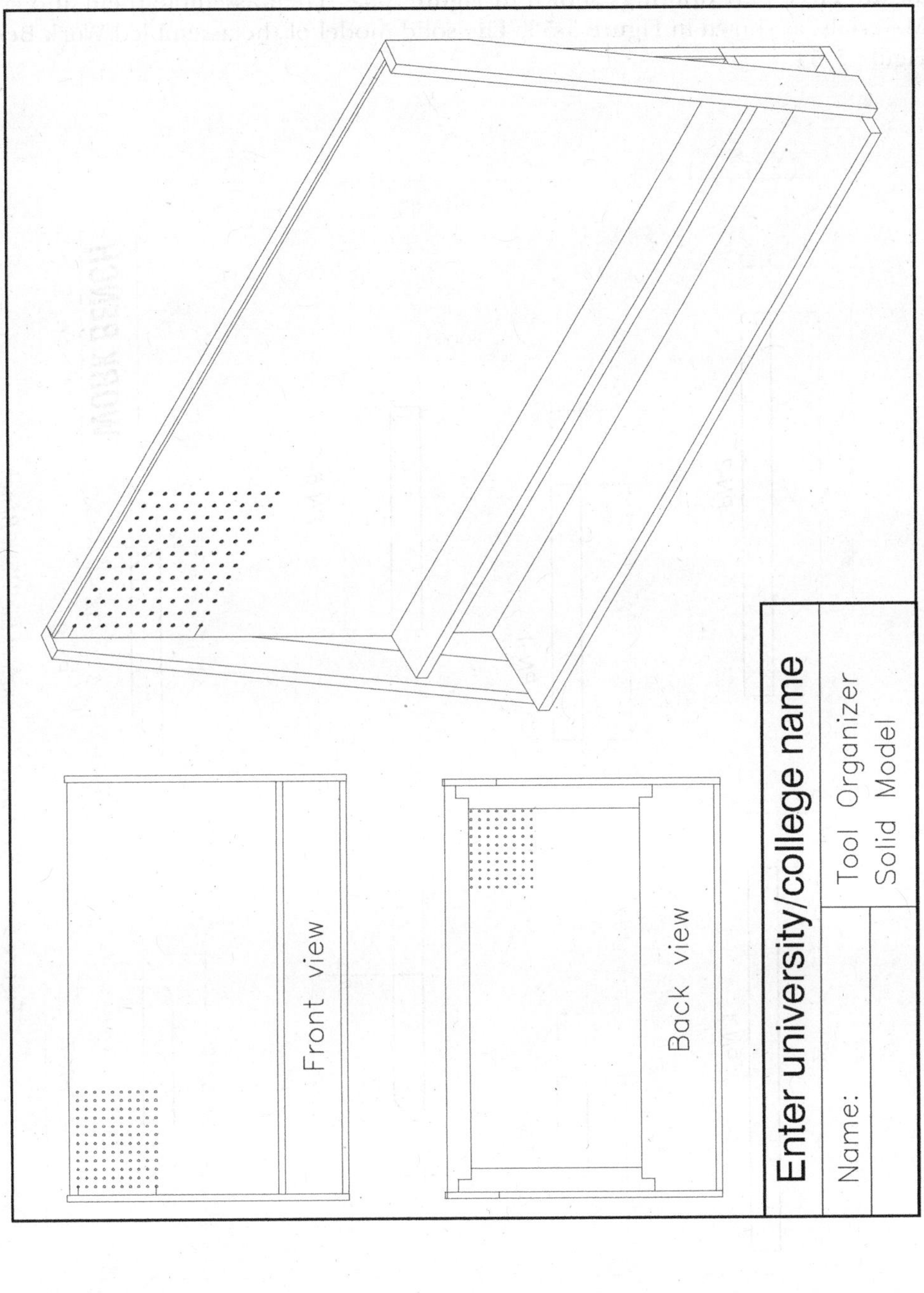

***Figure 5-51** Solid model of the Tool Organizer*

Problem-Solving Exercise 2

Draw the Piece part drawings shown in Figure 5-52. Then assemble them and create the Bill of Materials, as shown in Figure 5-53. The solid model of the assembled Work Bench is shown in Figure 5-54.

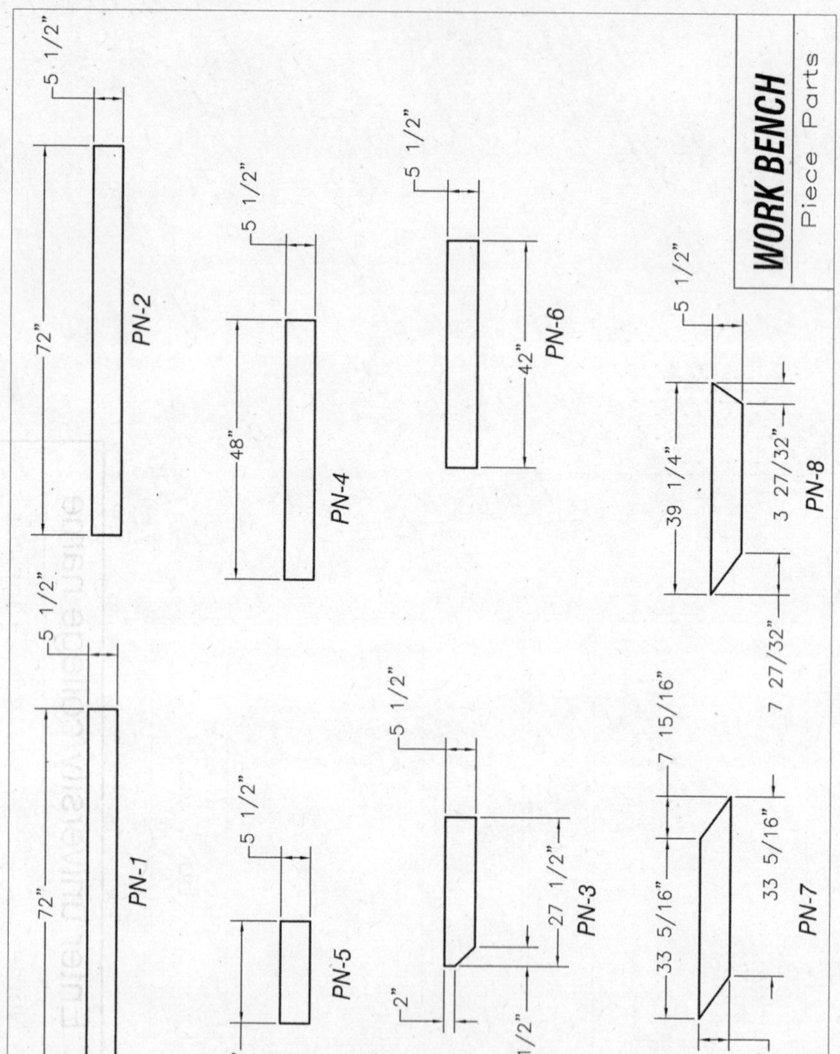

Figure 5-52 Piece part drawings of the Work Bench

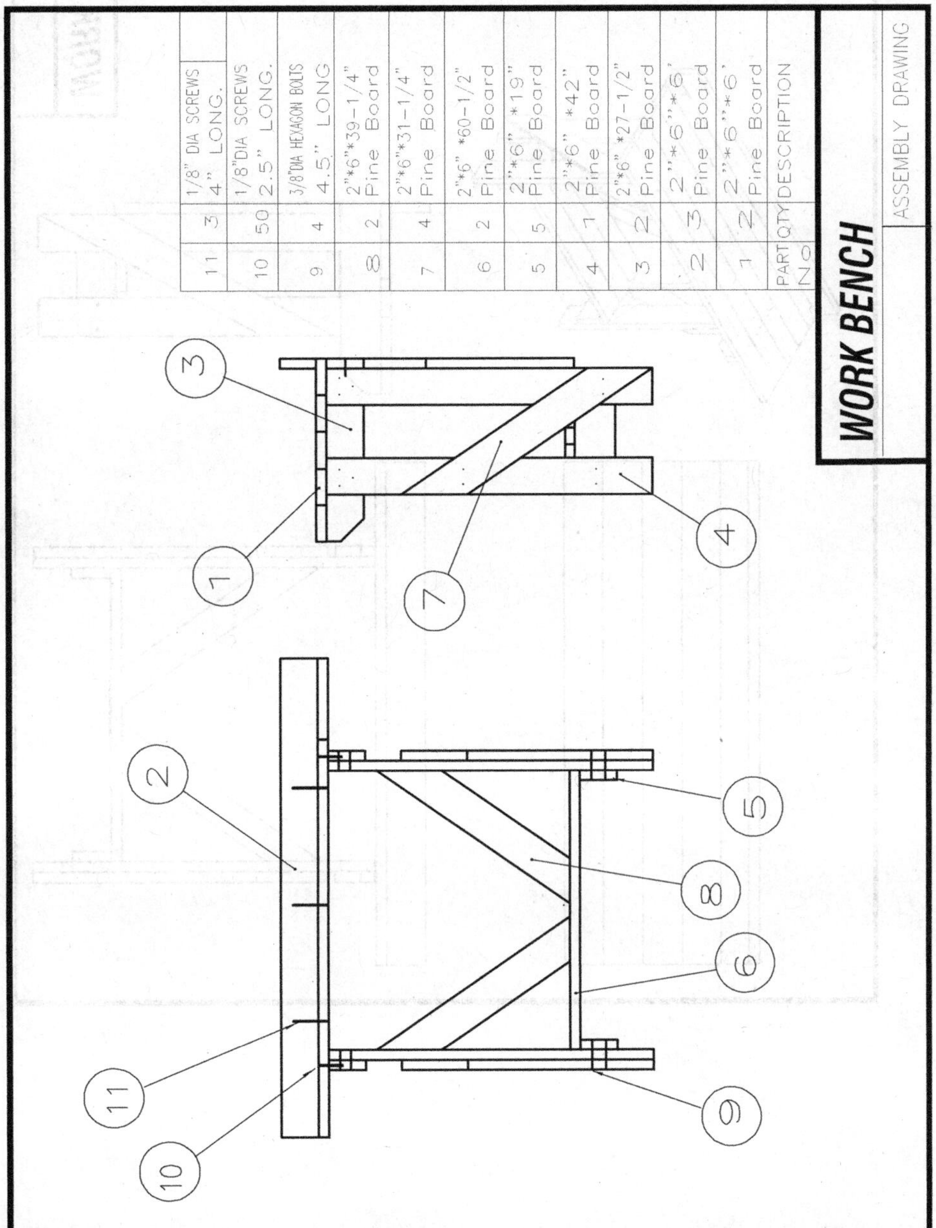

PART No	QTY	DESCRIPTION
11	3	1/8" DIA SCREWS 4" LONG.
10	50	1/8"DIA SCREWS 2.5" LONG.
9	4	3/8"DIA HEXAGON BOLTS 4.5" LONG
8	2	2"*6"*39-1/4" Pine Board
7	4	2"*6"*31-1/4" Pine Board
6	2	2"*6" *60-1/2" Pine Board
5	5	2"*6" *19" Pine Board
4	1	2"*6" *42" Pine Board
3	2	2"*6" *27-1/2" Pine Board
2	3	2"*6"*6' Pine Board
1	2	2"*6"*6' Pine Board

Figure 5-53 *Assembly drawing and BOM of the Work Bench*

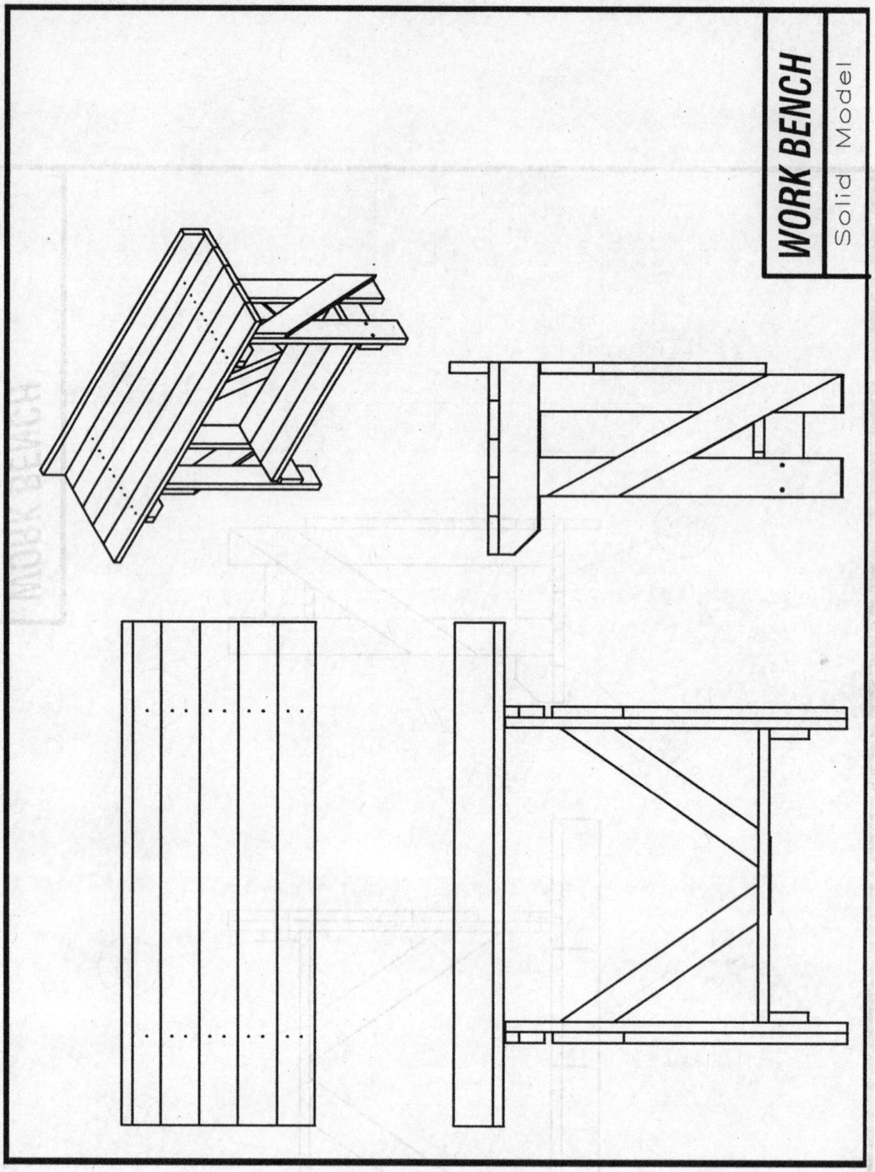

***Figure 5-54** Solid model of the Work Bench*

Problem-Solving Exercise 3

Create the model shown in Figure 5-55. Also, create the section view of the model as shown in Figure 5-56. The dimensions of the model are given in Figure 5-57.

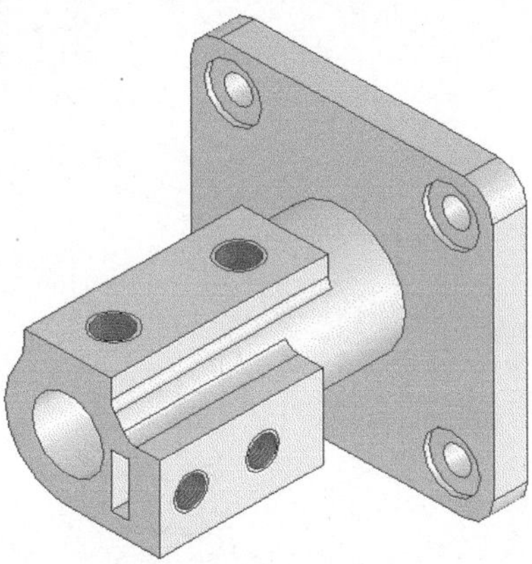

Figure 5-55 *Solid model*

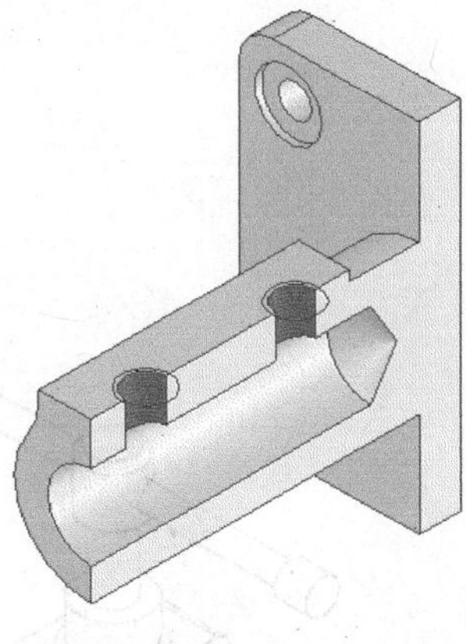

Figure 5-56 *Section view of the model*

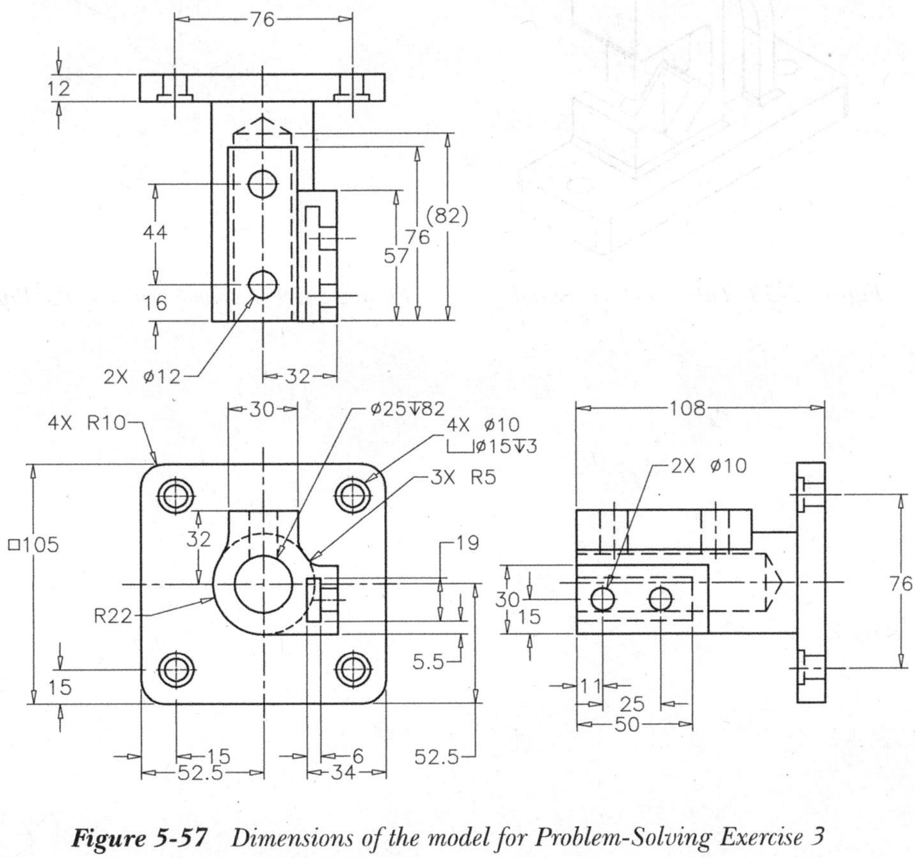

Figure 5-57 *Dimensions of the model for Problem-Solving Exercise 3*

Problem-Solving Exercise 4

Create various components of the Pipe Vice assembly and then assemble them by moving, rotating, and aligning. The Pipe Vice assembly is shown in Figure 5-58. For your reference, the exploded view of the assembly is shown in Figure 5-59. The dimensions of the individual components are shown in Figures 5-60 and 5-61.

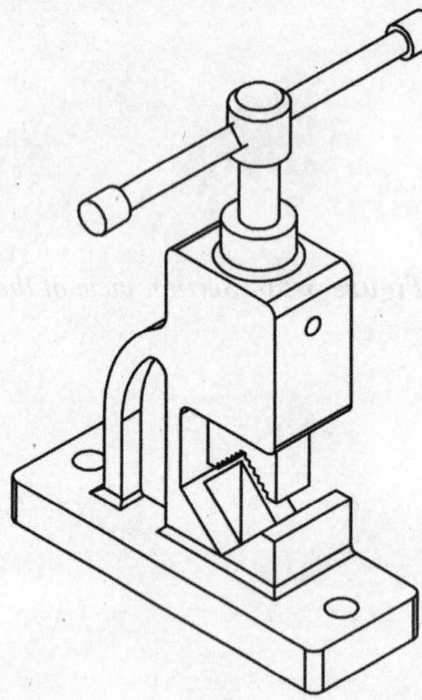

Figure 5-58 *The Pipe Vice assembly*

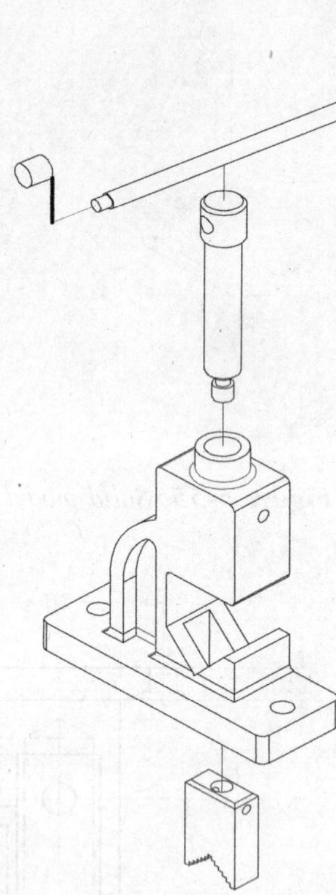

Figure 5-59 *Exploded view of the Pipe Vice assembly*

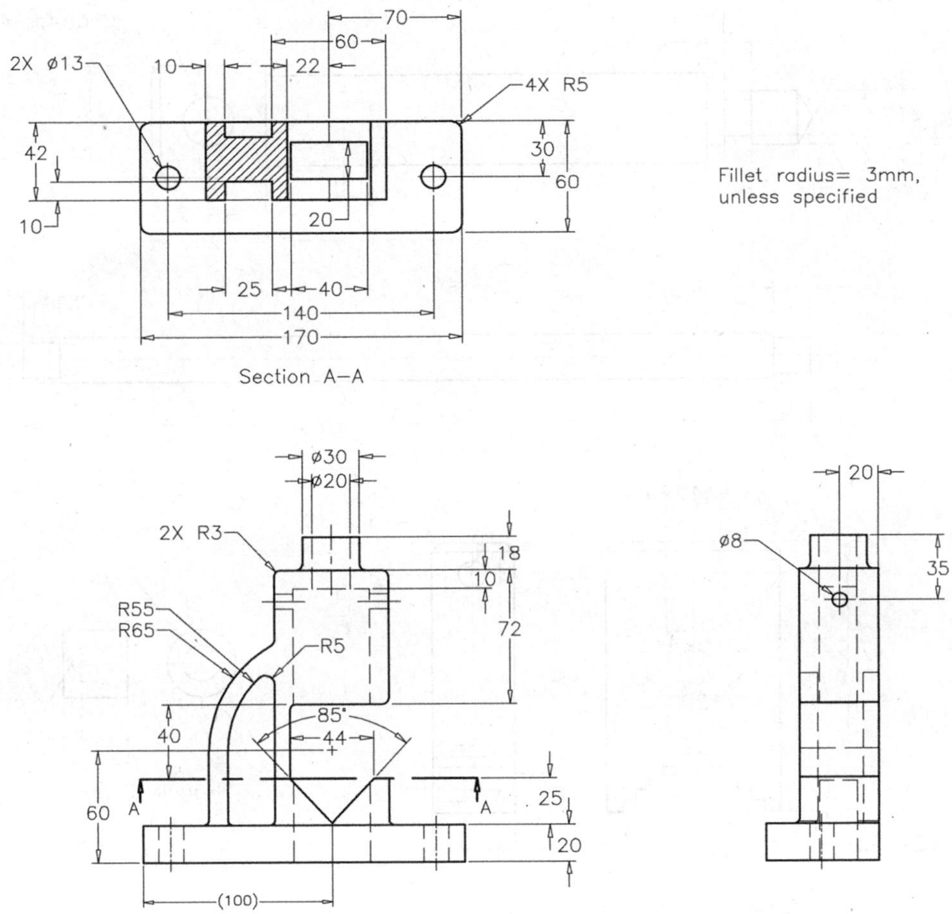

Figure 5-60 Dimensions of the Base

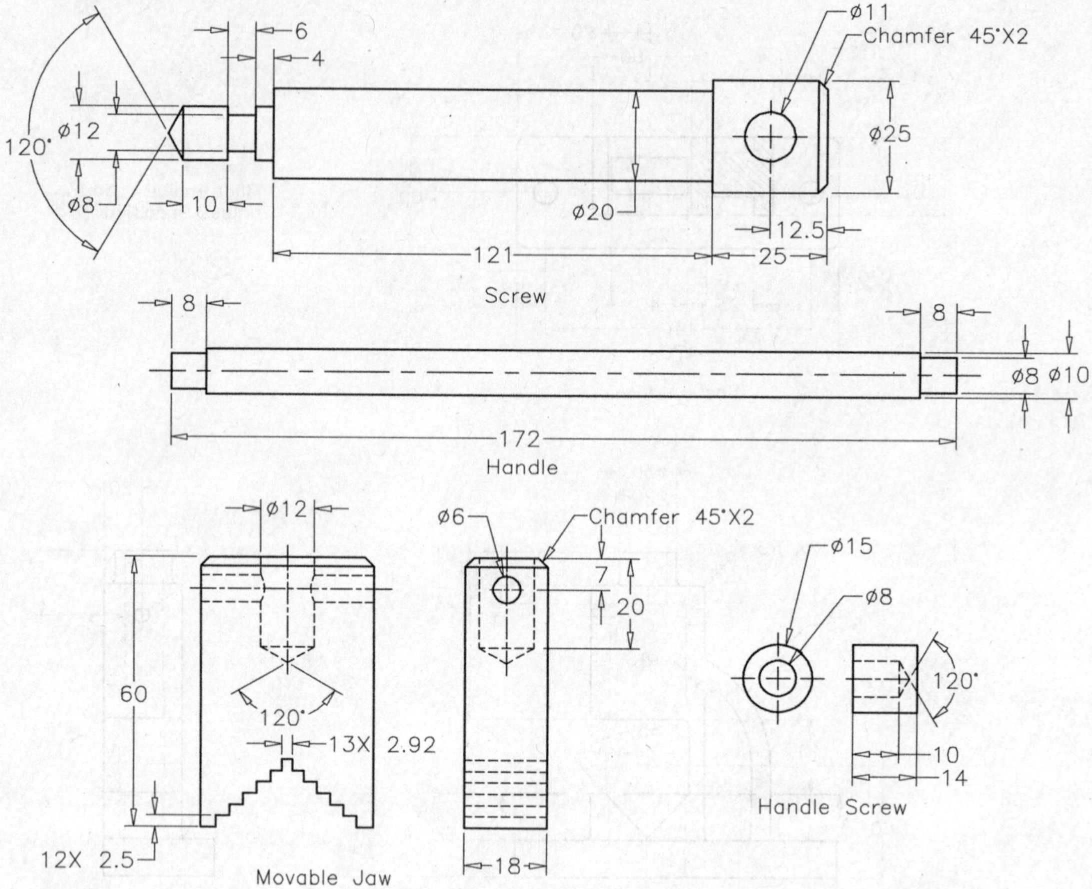

***Figure 5-61** Dimensions of the Screw, Handle, Movable Jaw, and Handle Stop*

Answers to Self-Evaluation Test

1. Solid View, **2.** *.mpr*, **3. Flatshot**, **4. Separate**, **5. Clean** **6.** F, **7.** T, **8.** F, **9.** F, **10.** T

Chapter 6

Surface Modeling

Learning Objectives

After completing this chapter, you will be able to:

- *Create wireframe elements*
- *Create extruded, revolved, and loft surfaces*
- *Create planar and network surfaces*
- *Create blend, patch, and offset surfaces*
- *Fillet, trim, untrim, extend, and sculpt surfaces*
- *Edit, add, remove, and rebuild the CVs of a NURBS surface*
- *Project geometries onto a surface*
- *Perform the zebra, curvature, and draft angle analysis on the surfaces*

Key Terms

- *SPLINE*
- *Spline Freehand*
- *PLANESURF*
- *SURFNETWORK*
- *Surface Associativity*
- *NURBS Creation*
- *Continuity*
- *Bulge magnitude*
- *SURFPATCH*
- *Constraining Geometry*
- *Solid*
- *Connect*
- *Surffillet*
- *Extend*
- *Projection Direction*
- *Untrim*
- *Sculpt*
- *Convert to NURBS*
- *CV Edit Bar*
- *Insert Knots*
- *Rebuild*
- *AutoTRIM*
- *Project to UCS*
- *Project to View*
- *Project to 2 Points*
- *Zebra Analysis*
- *Curvature Analysis*
- *Draft Analysis*
- *Isolines curves*

SURFACE MODELING

Surface models are three-dimensional (3D) models of zero thickness. Surface modeling is a technique that is used for creating planar or non-planar geometries of zero thickness.

Most of the real world models are solid models. However, some models are complex, therefore, first you need to create surfaces to get the desired complex shapes. After creating the required shape of a model using surfaces, you can convert it into a solid model. The technique of creating a surface using the surface modeling tools is discussed in this chapter. If you are familiar with the concept of solid modeling, it will be easier for you to learn surface modeling.

Surface modeling is used to create procedural as well as NURBS surfaces. These surfaces are discussed later in this chapter. In AutoCAD, the **Surface** tab contains all tools for creating and editing surfaces. In this chapter, you will learn to use all these tools.

CREATING WIREFRAME ELEMENTS

Wireframe elements help in creating surfaces. These elements can be used as profiles, guide curves, paths, and so on. The tools for constructing these wireframe elements are available in the **Curves** panel of the **Surface** tab. These tools include **Spline CV**, **Spline Fit**, **3D/2D Polyline**, **Line**, and so on. The **Spline** tools are grouped in the **Spline** drop-down. These tools have the compatible options for creating NURBS surfaces. The tools in the **Spline** drop-down are discussed next.

Spline CV

Ribbon: Surface > Curves > Spline drop-down > Spline CV **Command:** SPLINE

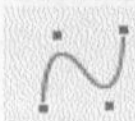

The **Spline CV** tool is used to draw a 3D spline by defining specific points that do not lie on that curve. These points act as control vertices for the curve, refer to Figure 6-1. You can modify the position of any control vertex. When you do so, only the part of the curve that is corresponding to CV point will be affected. You can also add, remove, or refine control points. These processes are discussed later in this chapter. To create a spline CV, choose the **Spline CV** tool from the **Spline** drop-down, refer to Figure 6-2; the **Specify first point or [Method/Degree/Object]:** prompt will be displayed. Now, you can specify the location of CV in a sequence for creation of curve. You can also specify the method of spline creation, set the degree of curve, or select a polyline object to convert it into a CV spline.

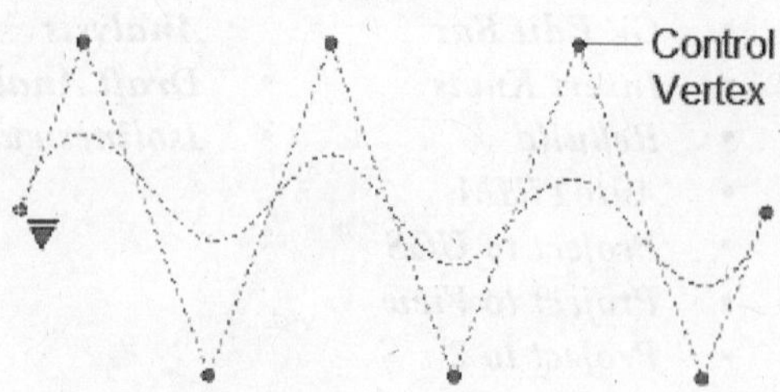

Figure 6-1 The Spline CV curve

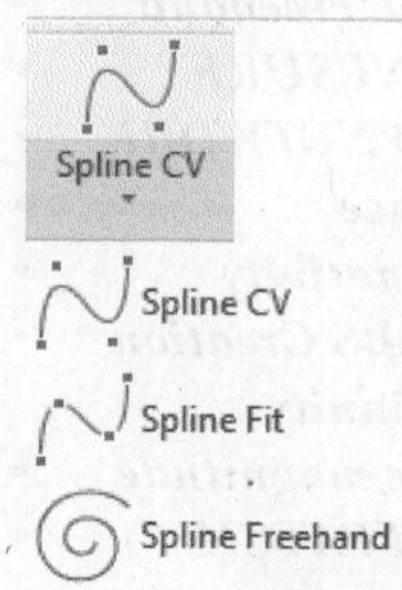

Figure 6-2 *The* ***Spline*** *drop-down*

Spline Fit

Ribbon: Surface > Curves > Spline drop-down > Spline Fit **Command:** SPLINE

The **Spline Fit** tool is used to draw a 3D spline by defining specific points that lie on that curve. These points are called knots or fit points. You can edit a curve directly by using these points, refer to Figure 6-3.

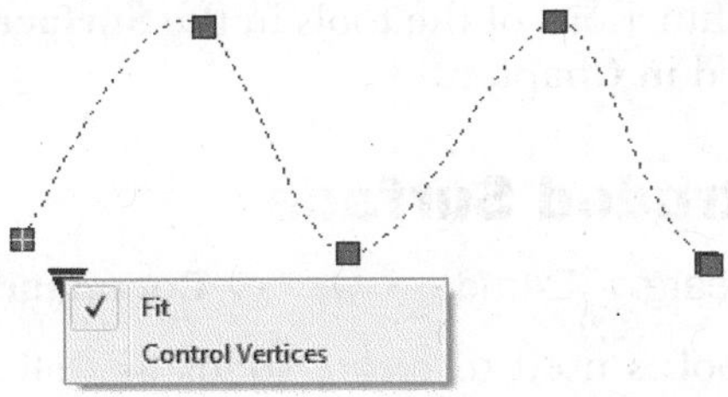

Figure 6-3 *Spline with fit points*

Spline Freehand

Ribbon: Surface > Curves > Spline drop-down > Spline Freehand **Command:** SKETCH

The **Spline Freehand** tool is used to create a spline by dragging the mouse in the drawing area. After the desired shape of curve is displayed on the screen, release the mouse button and press ENTER; a spline will be created and also the CV or fit points will be created automatically on it. You can switch between CV's and fit points as per your requirement.

Note

After drawing a spline, if you select it, a menu grip will be displayed, refer to Figure 6-3. You can click on the grip and switch between control vertices and fit points. When you switch from ***Control Vertices*** *to* ***Fit****, the curve shown in Figure 6-3 will be displayed.*

Extract Isoline Curves

Ribbon: Surface > Curves > Extract Isolines **Toolbar:** Surface Editing
Menu Bar: Modify > 3D Operations > Extract Isolines **Command:** SURFEXTRACTCURVE

You can create isoline curves from the existing curves oredges of the surfaces or faces of 3D model, refer to Figure 6-4. To create an isoline curve, invoke the **Extract Isolines** tool from the **Curves** panel of the **Surface** tab; you will be prompted to select the surface, solid model or face of the solid model. Select the surface of the model; an isoline will be displayed on the selected surface. This isoline will move as you move the cursor on the selected surface. Move the cursor till the point where you want to specify the isoline curve and then left-click; the curve will be created. Similarly, you can specify the directions and splines on the surfaces.

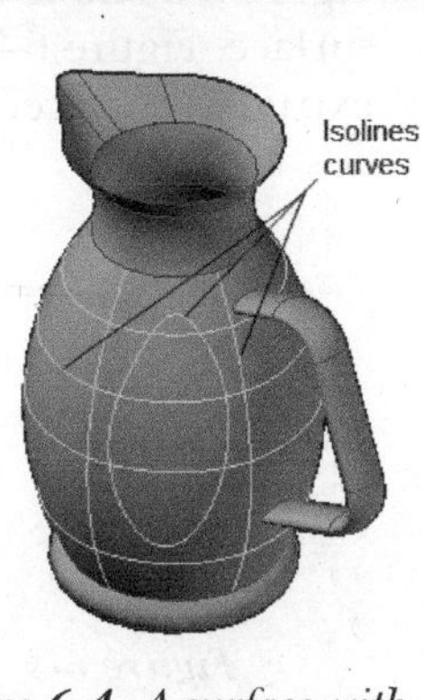

Figure 6-4 *A surface with isolines*

CREATING SURFACES BY USING PROFILES

The profile used to create surfaces can be open/close geometries, planar/non-planar geometries, or edges of an existing solid or surface. Open geometries always result in a surface, whereas closed geometries result in a solid or a surface, depending on the tool selected in the **Solid** or **Surface** tab. You can also create a surface when the **Solid** tab is active by changing the mode of creation. The profile surfaces include extruded surface, revolved surface, lofted surface, and swept surface. The functions of the tools in the **Surface** tab are similar to that of the **Solid Modeling** tools discussed in Chapter 3.

Creating an Extruded Surface

Ribbon: Surface > Create > Extrude **Command:** EXTRUDE

The **Extrude** tool is used to create solids as well as surfaces. Extruded surfaces are similar to extruded solids and are created by extending a profile in 3D space. As discussed earlier, if the profile drawn is an open curve, the resultant extruded model will be a surface only. But if the profile is a closed curve, the resultant model will be a surface, if this tool is selected from the **Surface** tab. To create an extruded surface, choose the **Extrude** tool from the **Create** panel. The command sequence that will follow when you choose this tool is given next.

Select objects to extrude or [MOde]: *Select an object to extrude*
Select objects to extrude or [MOde]: *Select other object to extrude or* Enter
Specify height of extrusion or [Direction/Path/Taper angle/Expression] <Current>:

Specify the height of extrusion and then, press ENTER. You can also specify the direction, path, or taper angle of extrusion. These options have already been discussed in Chapter 3.

Note

*If you want to create a surface model by using the **Extrude** tool in the **Solid** tab, enter **MO** at the **Select objects to extrude or [MODE]** prompt; two options, **Solid** and **Surface**, will be displayed. Choose **Surface** to create the surface model. Next, select the required entities and press ENTER; you will be prompted to define the height of extrusion.*

Figure 6-5 shows the open profile to be extruded and Figure 6-6 shows the resulting extruded surface. Figure 6-7 shows the closed profile to be extruded and Figure 6-8 shows the resulting extruded surface.

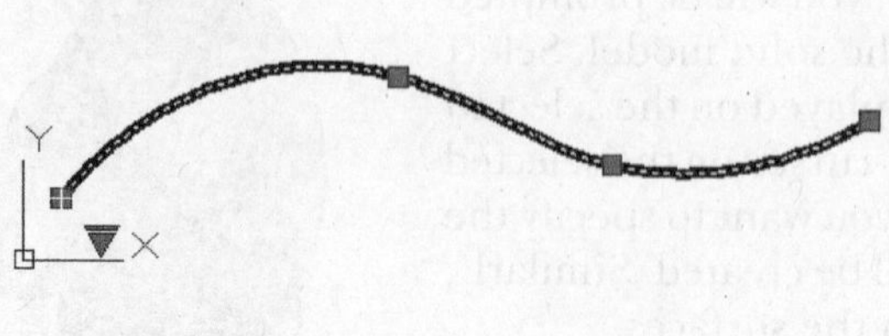

Figure 6-5 *Open profile to be extruded*

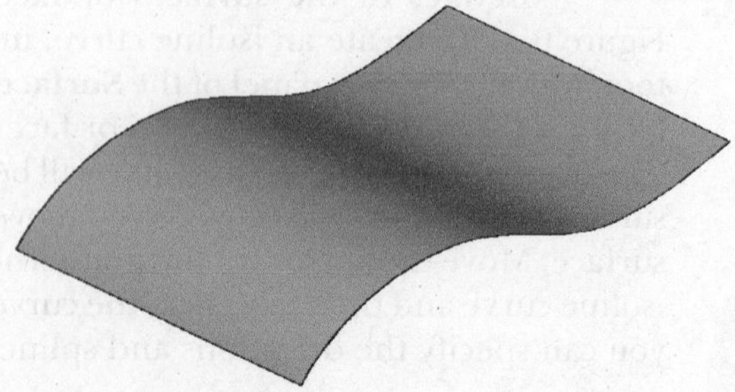

Figure 6-6 *The resulting extruded surface*

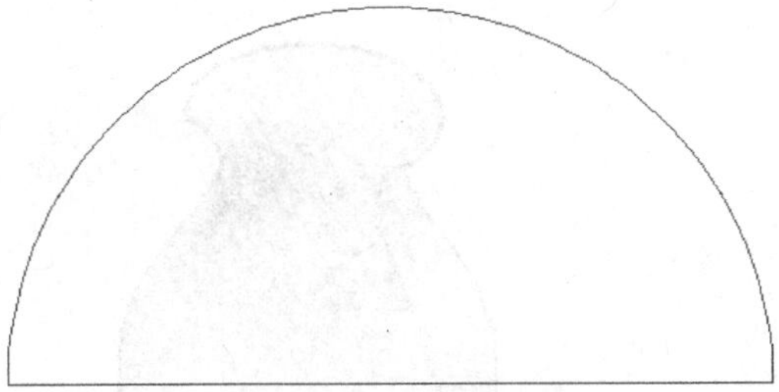

Figure 6-7 *Closed profile to be extruded*

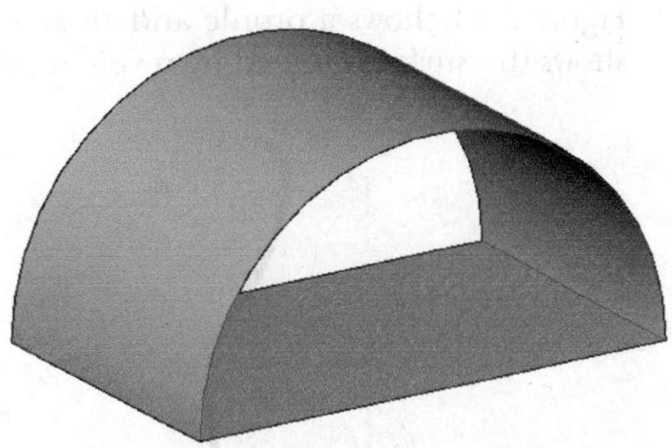

Figure 6-8 *The resulting extruded surface*

Select the extruded surface created; the grips will be displayed on it. You can drag the grip that is along the direction of extrusion to increase the extrusion depth. And, you can drag the grip that is normal to the direction of extrusion to provide a draft to the extruded surface. Figure 6-9 shows how to change distance by dragging one of the grips and Figure 6-10 shows how to change the angle by dragging another grip. Apart from these two grips, other grips will be displayed at the base and they are used to change the shape of the surface.

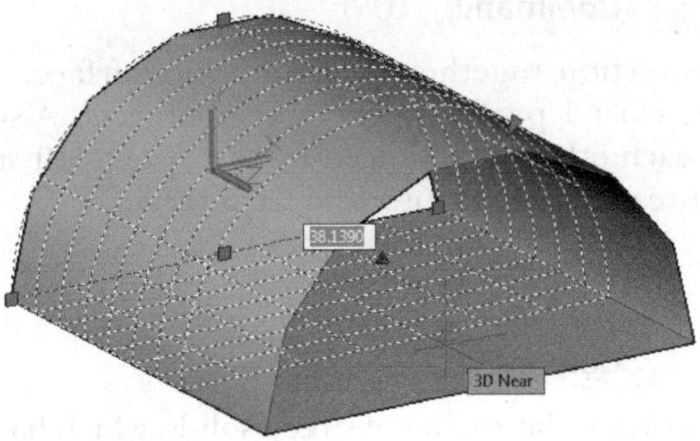

Figure 6-9 *Changing the distance*

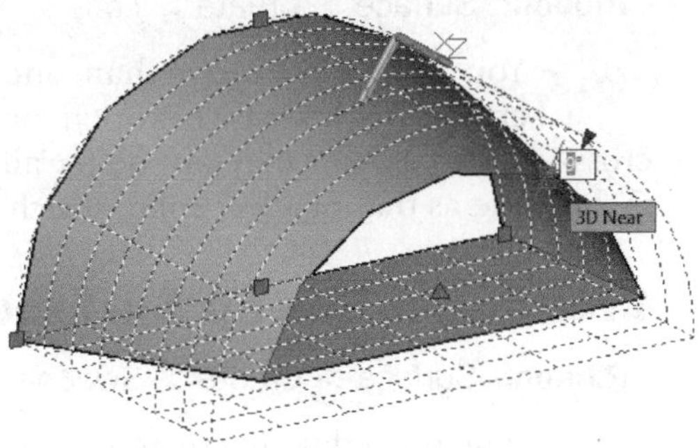

Figure 6-10 *Changing the angle*

Creating a Revolved Surface

Ribbon: Surface > Create > Revolve **Command:** REVOLVE / REV

You can create revolved surfaces by revolving a profile curve around an axis. To create a revolved surface, first draw the profile and then choose the **Revolve** tool from the **Create** panel. Next, select the objects to be revolved and then press ENTER; the **Specify axis start point or define axis by [Object X Y Z] <Object> :** prompt will be displayed. Specify the axis start and end points or the object about which you want to revolve your object; the **Specify angle of revolution or [STart angle Reverse EXpression] <360> :** prompt will be displayed. Now, using the options available in this prompt, you can specify the angle of revolution, specify the start angle of the revolution, and reverse the direction of revolution.

Figure 6-11 shows a profile and an axis of revolution to create a revolved surface. Figure 6-12 shows the surface created by revolving the profile through an angle of 180 degrees.

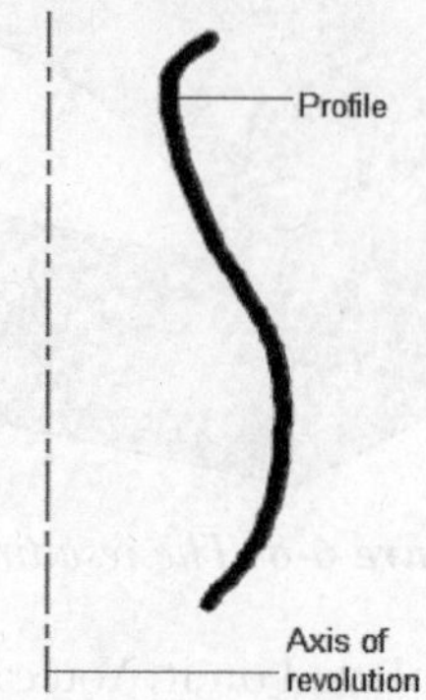

Figure 6-11 *The profile and the axis of revolution*

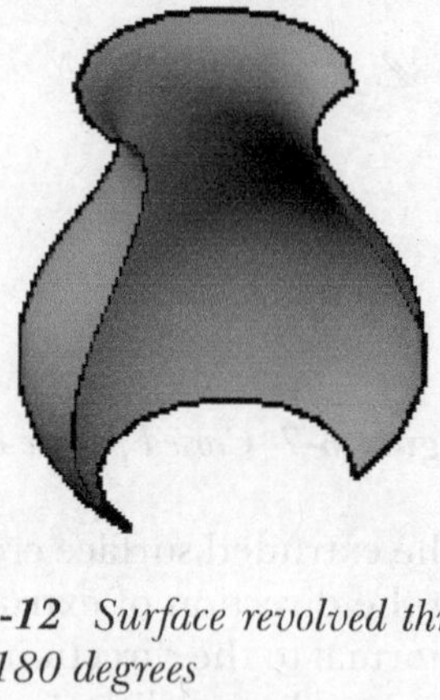

Figure 6-12 *Surface revolved through an angle of 180 degrees*

Creating a Loft Surface

Ribbon: Surface > Create > Loft	**Command:** LOFT

You can blend more than one cross-section together to form a loft surface. These cross-sections can be open profiles, closed profiles, or edge subobjects. Also, the cross-sections may or may not be parallel to each other. The procedure to create a loft surface is the same as that of a loft solid, which has already been discussed in Chapter 3.

Creating a Sweep Surface

Ribbon: Surface > Create > Sweep	**Command:** SWEEP

The procedure to create sweep surfaces is similar to that of sweep solids, which has been discussed in Chapter 3.

Creating a Planar Surface

Ribbon: Surface > Create > Planar	**Toolbar:** Modeling > Planar Surface
Menu Bar: Draw > Modeling > Surfaces > Planar	**Command:** PLANESURF

The **Planar** tool is used to generate 2D surfaces by specifying two diagonally opposite points. These two points specify the rectangular area to be covered by this planar surface, refer to Figure 6-13. The prompt sequence for this tool is discussed next.

Specify first corner or [Object] <Object>: *Specify the first corner point of the planar surface.*
Specify other corner: *Specify the diagonally opposite point of the planar surface.*

You can also convert an existing object into a surface by entering **O** at the **Specify first corner or [Object] <Object>** prompt. While selecting the object, you can directly select a region or a number of individual objects that result in a closed boundary, refer to Figure 6-14. The number of lines displayed on the surface is controlled by the **SURFU** and **SURFV** system variables.

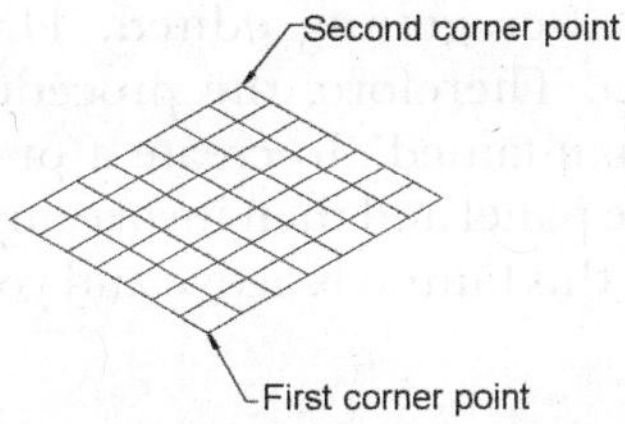

Figure 6-13 Planar surface created by specifying corner points

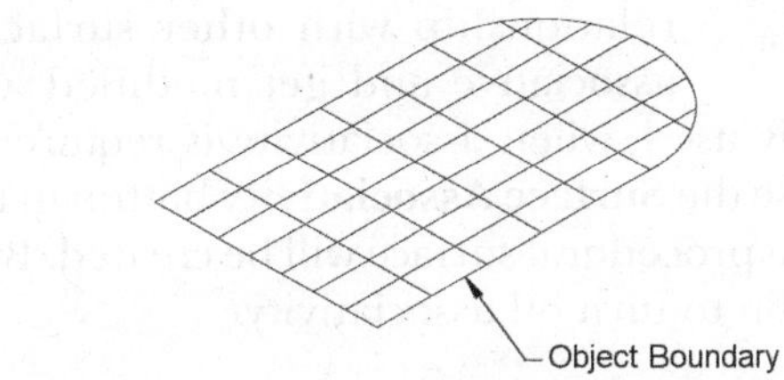

Figure 6-14 Planar surface created by selecting an object

Creating a Network Surface

Ribbon: Surface > Create > Network
Menu Bar: Draw > Modeling > Surfaces > Network **Command:** SURFNETWORK

The **Network** tool is used to create a surface between a number of boundary elements. These boundary elements can be 2D curves or existing edges of surfaces, solids, or regions. However, while creating a surface, there should not be any gap between the consecutive elements. Before creating a Network surface, you need to draw the boundary elements. After drawing them, choose the **Network** tool from the **Create** panel; you will be prompted to select curves or surface edges in the first direction. Select objects in the U or V direction and then press ENTER; you will be prompted to select curves or surface edges in the second direction. Select objects in the other direction and press ENTER again, network surface will be created. Figure 6-15 shows the elements to be selected. Here, Curve 1 and Curve 2 are selected in the first direction and Curve 3 and Curve 4 are selected in the second direction. Figure 6-16 shows the resulting network surface.

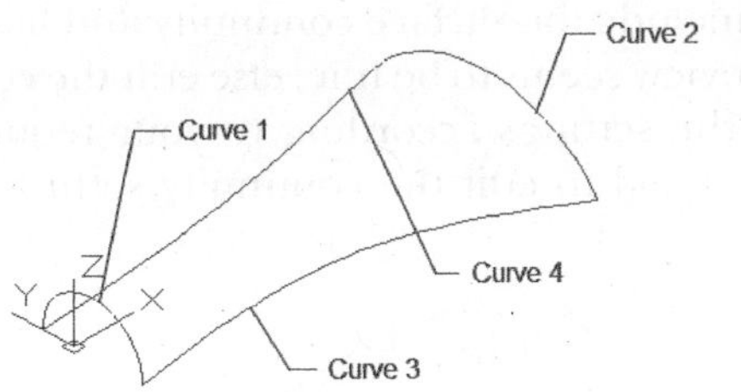

Figure 6-15 Curves to be selected

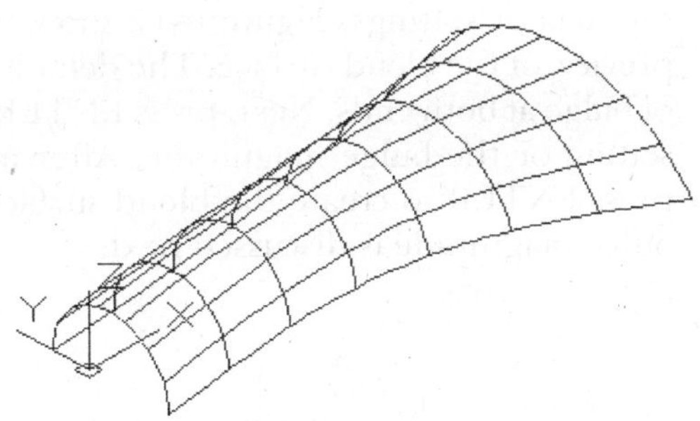

Figure 6-16 Network surface created

CREATING SURFACES FROM OTHER SURFACES

The tools discussed till now are used to create simple surfaces. But, most of the time, the product and industrial designers come up with some unique designs to make the products more attractive and presentable. In order to create such designs, you need some advanced tools. AutoCAD has some advanced tools like **Blend**, **Patch**, and **Offset** to create new surfaces by using the subobjects of other surfaces. These tools are discussed next.

Before you learn the usage of these tools, you need to learn about the procedural and NURBS surfaces in AutoCAD. The procedural surfaces are the surfaces that maintain relationship with other surfaces, even after getting edited. These surfaces are associative and get modified as a group. Therefore, the procedural surfaces are mostly used, when associativity is required to be maintained. To create a procedural surface, choose the **Surface Associativity** button in the **Create** panel and then invoke any surface creation tool; a procedural surface will be created. By default, this button is active and you need to choose it again to turn off associativity.

A NURBS surface is created when the shape of the surface needs to be modified. These surfaces are mostly used in ship building industries. These surfaces are parametric in nature and have multiple knots. These knots can be adjusted to modify the shape of the surface. To create a NURBS surface, choose the **NURBS Creation** button in the **Create** panel and then create a surface; the surface thus created will be a NURBS surface. You need to choose this button again to turn off the NURBS creation. Note that you can keep both the buttons, **Surface Associativity** and **NURBS Creation** on or off at the same time.

In the next section, you will learn about the tools that are used to create surfaces from other surfaces.

Creating a Blend Surface

Ribbon: Surface > Create > Blend **Command:** SURFBLEND

The **Blend** tool is used to create a new surface between two existing surfaces, solids, or regions. To create a blend surface, invoke the **Blend** tool from the **Create** panel; you will be prompted to select the first surface edge or edge chain to blend. Select the surface edge/s and press ENTER; you will be prompted to select the second surface edge or edge chain to blend. Select it and press ENTER again; preview of the blend surface will be displayed with the default settings. Figure 6-17 shows the entities selected to blend and Figure 6-18 shows preview of the blend surface. The default settings include the surface continuity and magnitude of bulge at both ends. Next, press ENTER if the preview seems to be fine, else edit the continuity setting or the bulge magnitude. After adjusting the settings according to your requirement, press ENTER to create the blend surface. The method to edit the continuity setting and the bulge magnitude is discussed next.

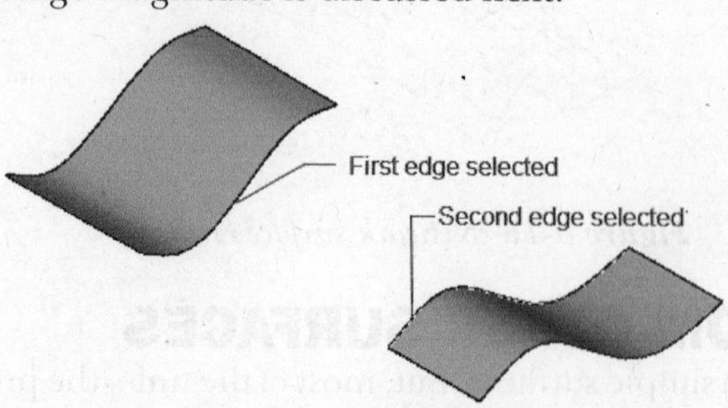

Figure 6-17 The edges selected

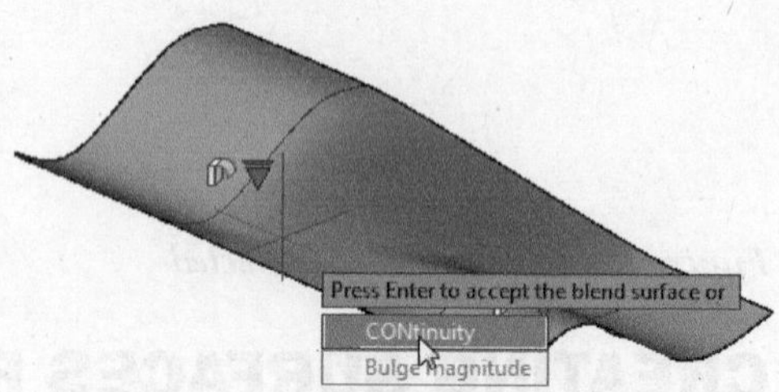

Figure 6-18 Preview of the resulting blend surface

Continuity

Continuity defines the smoothness of a blend surface at a point where it meets the other surface. Continuity can be set to **G0** (position), **G1** (Tangency), or **G2** (continuity). **G0** maintains the position of the selected edges, **G1** maintains the tangency of the blend surface where it meets the edges at both ends, and **G2** maintains the same curvature.

On selecting the **CONtinuity** option from the preview displayed in Figure 6-18, the continuity options for the first edge will be displayed. Choose the required option; you will be prompted to set the continuity of the second edge. Choose the required option; the preview of the blend surface will be updated. Also, you will be prompted to press ENTER to accept or edit the settings. Edit or accept the settings to create the blend surface.

You can also edit the continuity of a blend surface after it is created. To do so, select the blend surface; grips will be displayed on both the edges of the surface. Now, if you choose a grip displayed on the surface, a flyout with the continuity options will be displayed, refer to Figure 6-19. By default, **G1** is chosen in this flyout. You can select any other option from the flyout to set continuity as per your requirement. Similarly, you can set the continuity of the other edge by clicking on it.

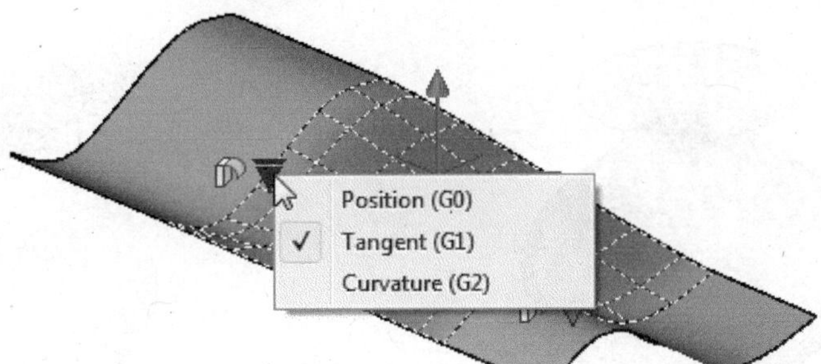

Figure 6-19 *Continuity options displayed on clicking a grip*

Bulge Magnitude

Bulge magnitude defines the roundness or the amount of bulge between the blend surface and the existing surface. In other words, it is the amount of curvature where two surfaces meet. This magnitude can only be applied to the surfaces that have the G1 or G2 continuity.

By default, the bulge magnitude is set to 0.5. If you want to edit the bulge magnitude, choose the respective option from the preview displayed or enter **B** at the **Press Enter to accept the blend surface or [CONtinuity/Bulge magnitude]:** Command prompt; you will be prompted to define the bulge magnitude for the first edge. Define the value of bulge for the first edge and then the value of bulge at the second edge. On entering 0 value, the surface will get flattened and on entering a value greater or equal to 1, the surface curvature will increase. The bulge magnitude has already been discussed in detail in Chapter 3.

You can modify a blend surface after it is created. To do so, select the blend surface and right-click; a shortcut menu will be displayed. Choose the **Properties** option from the shortcut menu; the **Properties** palette with the settings of the blend surface will be displayed. Using this palette, you can modify the continuity setting and the bulge magnitude of the surface at each edge, the appearance of the surface, and so on.

Creating a Patch Surface

Ribbon: Surface > Create > Patch **Command:** SURFPATCH

Using the **Patch** tool, you can close the open edges of an existing surface. To create a patch surface, invoke the **Patch** tool from the **Create** panel; you will be prompted to select the edges to create a patch. Select the edges one by one and then press ENTER; the preview of the patch with the default settings will be displayed. Also, you will be prompted to either accept the preview, or change the settings for continuity between the patch surface and the edges selected, define the bulge magnitude, or define the geometry to be constrained. Figure 6-20 shows the model with open edge and Figure 6-21 shows the patch created on the open edge.

By default, the continuity is set to G0 and the bulge magnitude is set to 0.5. Continuity and bulge magnitude have already been discussed in the previous topic, and the method to specify the geometry to be constrained is discussed next.

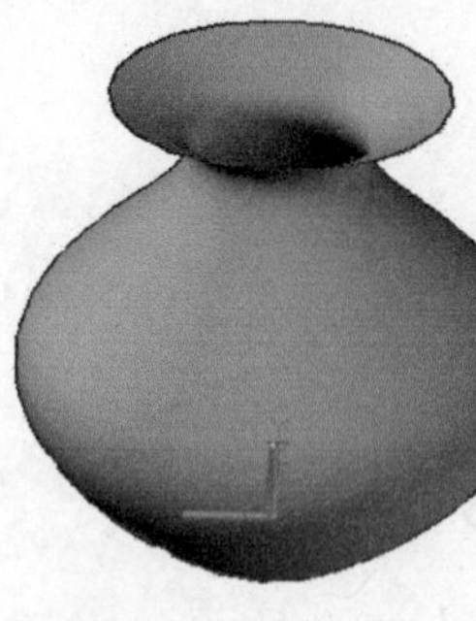

Figure 6-20 *Model before creating the patch*

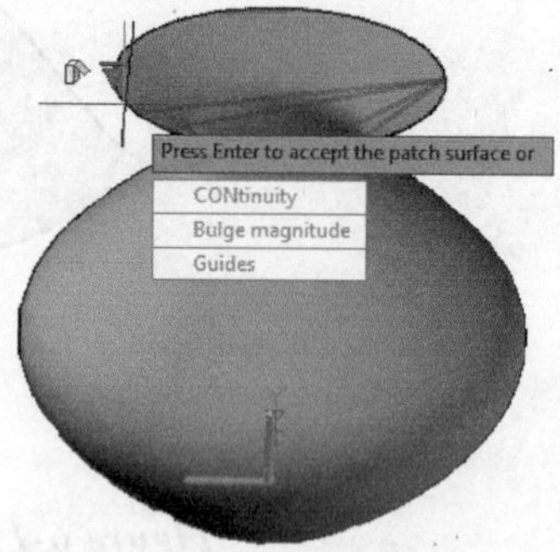

Figure 6-21 *Model after creating the patch*

Guides

You can use some additional curves as guide curves to create the patch. Guide curves are used to guide the shape of the patch as per the geometry of the guide curve. Note that you need to draw the guide curve first and then invoke the **Patch** tool. Choose this option when the **Press Enter to accept the patch surface or [CONtinuity/Bulge magnitude/Guides]:** prompt is displayed. Next, select the guide curve and press ENTER; a patch will be created. If you select the patch surface after it is created, a grip will be displayed. On clicking the grip, the options for continuity will be displayed. You can choose an option to specify the required continuity. Figure 6-22 shows the guide curve created for constraining the geometry and Figure 6-23 shows the patch created using the guide curve.

You can modify a patch surface by using the **Properties** palette. Invoke the **Properties** palette; the patch settings will be displayed in the **Geometry** area. You can modify the continuity option, the bulge magnitude, the number of isolines in the U and V directions, and so on using this palette.

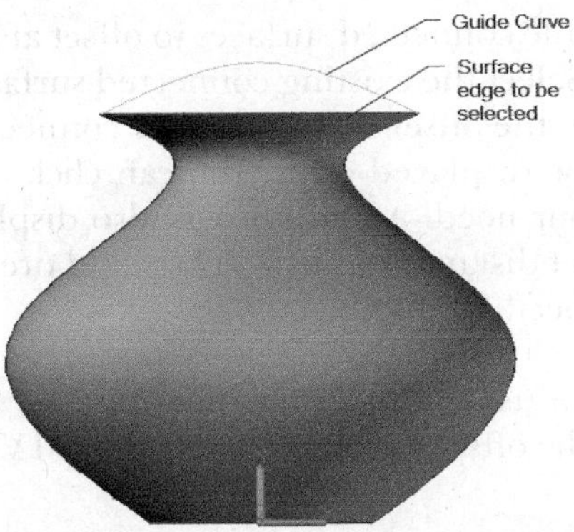

Figure 6-22 *Model before creating the patch*

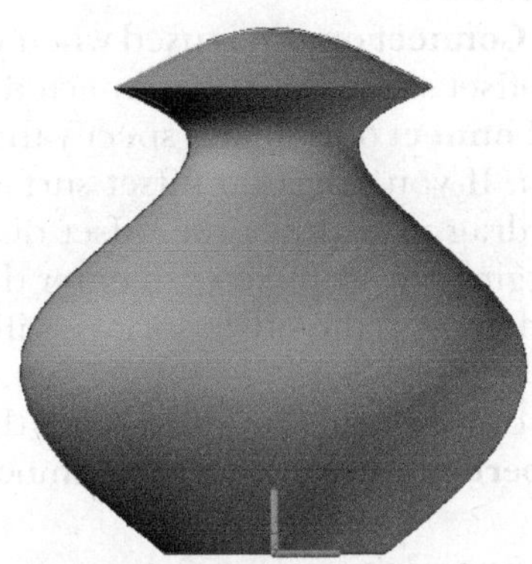

Figure 6-23 *Model after creating the patch*

Creating an Offset Surface

Ribbon: Surface > Create > Offset	Command: SURFOFFSET

Offset

The **Offset** tool is used to create a surface at an offset distance from an existing surface. To do so, choose the **Offset** tool from the **Create** panel; you will be prompted to select surfaces or regions to offset. Select a surface and press ENTER; the direction arrows will indicate the direction of the offset and the **Specify offset distance or [Flip direction/Both sides/Solid/Connect/Expression] <Current>:** prompt will be displayed. The options displayed in this prompt are discussed next.

Specify offset distance

If the direction of offset is as you want, then specify the required offset distance and press ENTER; an offset surface will be created. Figure 6-24 shows the original surface and the offset surface.

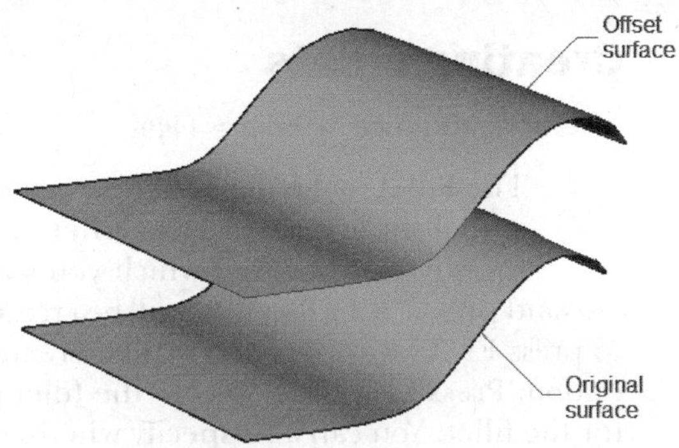

Figure 6-24 The original and offset surfaces

Flip direction

If you want to change the direction of offset surface creation, choose the **Flip direction** option in the prompt; the direction will be changed. Next, you can specify the offset distance.

Both sides

To create offset surfaces on both sides of the selected surface, choose the **Both sides** option. On doing so, you will notice that the direction arrows are displayed on both sides of the selected surface. Specify the offset distance.

Solid

The **Solid** option is used to create a solid by offsetting an existing surface. After selecting the surface, choose the **Solid** option; you will be prompted to specify the offset distance. Specify the value of the offset distance and press ENTER; the resulting entity will be a solid.

Connect

The **Connect** option is used when you select multiple connected surfaces to offset and you need the offset surfaces to be connected to each other. Select the existing connected surfaces, choose the **Connect** option and specify the offset distance; the offset surfaces will be connected to each other. If you select an offset surface, a grip will be displayed on it. You can click on the grip and drag it to adjust the offset distance as per your need. An edit box is also displayed while dragging the grip. You can enter the required offset distance in this edit box and press ENTER. On doing so, the offset surface will move to the specified distance.

You can control the display of the offset surface using the **Properties** palette. Invoke the **Properties** palette to set the number of isolines of the offset surface along the U and V directions.

Expression

The **Expression** option is used to relate the dimensional constraint applied in the drawing to the offset value. Also, you can setup an equation for calculating the offset value using different dimensional constraints.

EDITING SURFACES

After creating the surfaces, you may need to modify them. AutoCAD provides you with the surface operation tools to modify surfaces. The surface operation tools are used regularly while creating surface models. These tools are used to enhance the surfaces and help in creating complex geometries. They save a lot of modeling time as well. Various surface editing operations are discussed next.

Creating Fillets

Ribbon: Surface > Edit > Fillet **Command:** SURFFILLET

The **Fillet** tool is used to create a rounded surface between two existing surfaces. To create a fillet surface, invoke the **Fillet** tool from the **Edit** panel; you will be prompted to select the surfaces between which you want the fillet to be created. Select the surfaces one by one and press ENTER; a fillet will be created with the default settings. Also, you will be prompted to press ENTER to accept the fillet created, or set the new fillet radius, or set the trim surface option. Press ENTER to accept the fillet or choose the **Radius** option to enter the new radius for the fillet. You can also specify whether or not to trim the surfaces after creating the fillet by choosing the **Trim surface** option. If you select the fillet surface after creating it, a grip will be displayed. Click on the grip and drag it to modify the fillet radius dynamically. Figure 6-25 shows the model before creating the fillet and Figure 6-26 shows the model after creating the fillet.

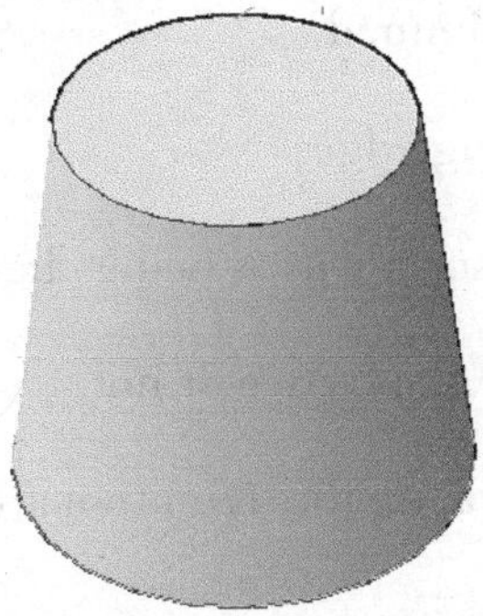

Figure 6-25 *Model before creating the fillet*

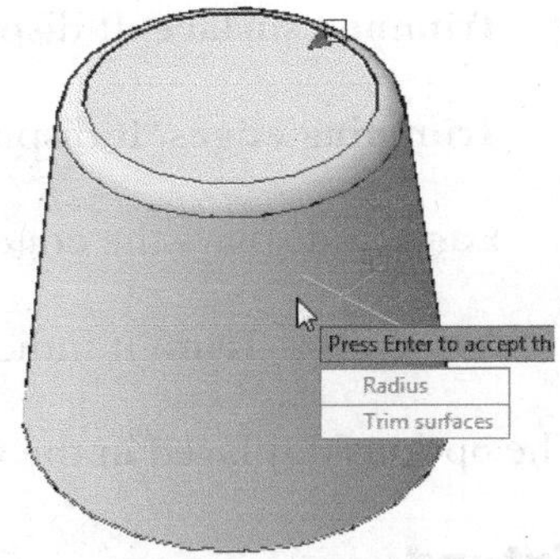

Figure 6-26 *Model after creating the fillet*

Trimming Surfaces

Ribbon: Surface > Edit > Trim
Toolbar: Surface Editing > Surface Trim
Menu Bar: Modify > Surface Editing > Trim
Command: SURFTRIM

The **Trim** tool is used to trim a portion of a surface or a region by using an intersecting object. The lines, arcs, ellipses, polylines, splines, curves, 3D polylines, 3D splines, helix, regions, and surfaces can be used as intersecting objects. You can invoke the **Trim** tool from the **Edit** panel. But before invoking this tool, you need to have the object to be trimmed and the object to be used as the cutting element. On invoking this tool, you will be prompted to select the objects to be trimmed. Select the object/s to be trimmed and press ENTER; you will be prompted to select the cutting element to be used for trimming. Select the cutting element/s; you will be prompted to click on the portion to be removed. Click on the portion/s of the object to be trimmed; the selected object will be trimmed with the default settings. You can also specify the extension type and the projection direction. Figure 6-27 shows the surface before trimming and Figure 6-28 shows the surface after trimming.

Figure 6-27 *The untrimmed surface*

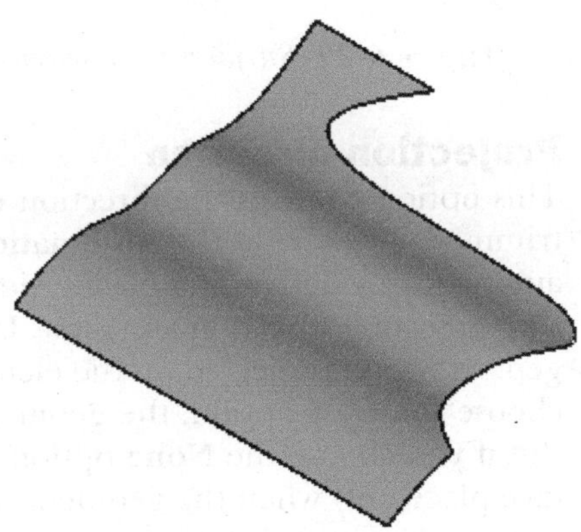

Figure 6-28 *The trimmed surface*

Select a trimmed surface and then right-click on it; a shortcut menu will be displayed. Choose the **Properties** option from this shortcut menu; the **Properties** palette will be displayed. Expand the **Trims** rollout in this window; various parameters in this rollout will be displayed. These parameters are discussed next.

- **Trimmed surface**. It displays **Yes** if the surface is trimmed.
- **Trimming edges**. It displays the number of trimming edges.
- **Edge**. It displays the edge number for which the associativity is being checked.
- **Associative Trim**. It indicates if the current edge is Associative or not.

The options displayed in the Command prompt on invoking the **Trim** tool are discussed next.

Extend

This option is used when the cutting element is a surface and it does not intersect the surface to be trimmed. If you set the **Extend** option to **Yes** at the Command prompt displayed on invoking the **Trim** tool, the selected surface gets trimmed at the imaginary intersection of the cutting element. But if it is set to **No,** the selected surface does not get trimmed as the surface does not intersect the cutting element. Figure 6-29 shows the surface to be trimmed and the cutting surface that is not intersecting the surface to be trimmed. Figure 6-30 shows the surface trimmed with the **Extend** option set to **Yes**.

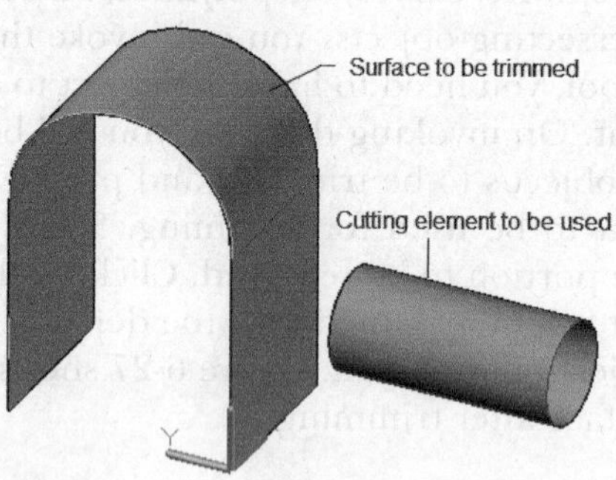

Figure 6-29 Surfaces to be selected

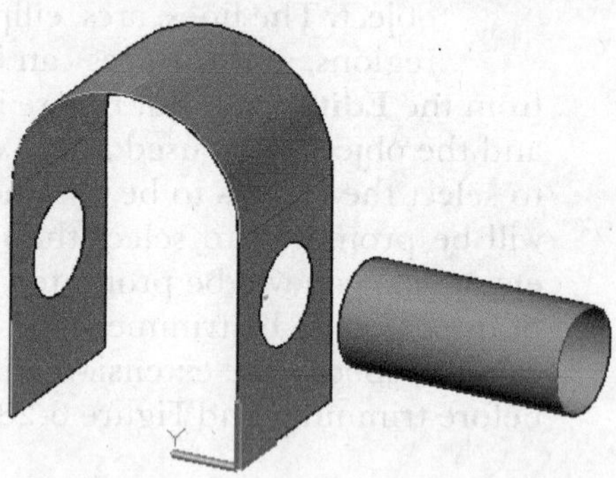

Figure 6-30 Surface after trimming

Projection direction

This option controls the direction of projection of the cutting element on the element to be trimmed. By default, the **Automatic** option is set. As a result, the direction of projection is set automatically depending on the view at which the trimming takes place. The other options in the projection direction are **View**, **UCS**, and **None**. If you choose the **View** option, the cutting geometry gets projected on the element to be trimmed along the current view direction. If you choose the **UCS** option, the geometry is projected in the +/- Z direction of the current UCS. But if you choose the **None** option, the geometry will not be projected and the trimming will take place only when the geometry will lie on the surface.

Note

If you select the objects after performing the trimming operation, grips will be displayed on both the trimmed object and as well as the trimming object. Click on the grip and drag; the trimmed object will move and the trim location will be updated automatically. Similarly, you can drag the grip of the cutting element to resize it. Figure 6-31 shows the model after moving the cutting element to its bottom and Figure 6-32 shows the model after resizing the cutting element.

Figure 6-31 *Model after moving the cutting element*

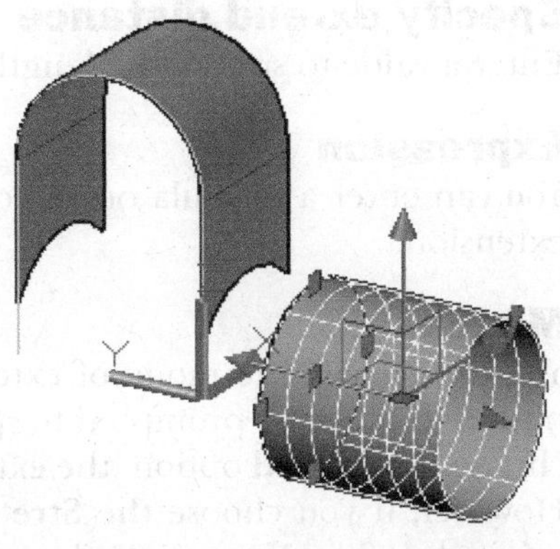

Figure 6-32 *Model after resizing the cutting element*

Untrimming Surfaces

Ribbon: Surface > Edit > Untrim	**Toolbar:** Surface Editing > Surface Untrim
Menu Bar: Modify > Surface Editing > Untrim	**Command:** SURFUNTRIM

The **Untrim** tool is used to untrim the trimmed edges or surfaces. To untrim a trimmed object, invoke the **Untrim** tool from the **Edit** panel; you will be prompted to select the trimmed edges or the trimmed surface. If you select the trimmed edges, only the portion removed at the selected edges will be regained. However, if you choose the **SURface** option from the Command prompt, then the portions removed from the selected surface will be regained. Figure 6-33 shows the edge selected from the surface to be untrimmed and Figure 6-34 shows the resultant untrimmed surface.

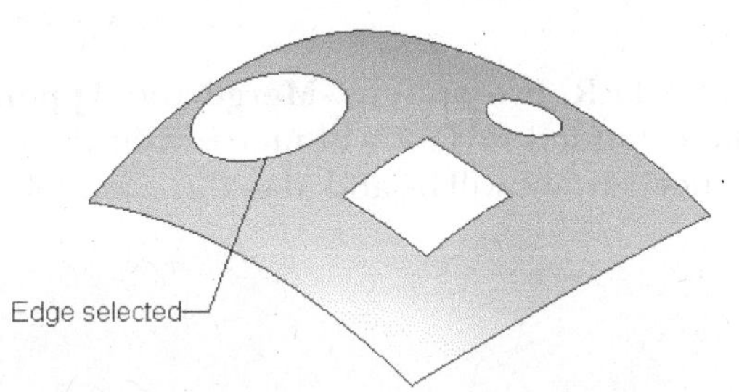

Figure 6-33 *Edge selected to be untrimmed*

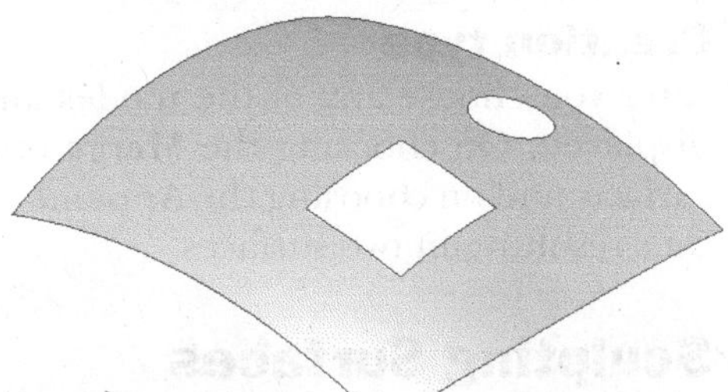

Figure 6-34 *Resultant untrimmed surface*

Extending Surfaces

Ribbon: Surface > Edit > Extend	**Toolbar:** Surface Editing > Surface Extend
Menu Bar: Modify > Surface Editing > Extend	**Command:** SURFEXTEND

You can extend or lengthen the edge/s of one or more surfaces to a certain distance. To extend a surface, invoke the **Extend** tool from the **Edit** panel; you will be prompted to select the edges of the surfaces to extend. Select the edges to extend and press ENTER; you will be prompted to enter a distance value or specify the mode of extension. The options displayed in the prompt on invoking the **Extend** tool are discussed next.

Specify extend distance

Enter a value to specify the length of extension and press ENTER; the surface will extend.

Expression

You can enter a formula or an equation at the Command prompt to control the geometry of extension.

Modes

You can specify the mode of extension by using the **Modes** option. On choosing the **Modes** option, you will be prompted to specify either the **Extend** or the **Stretch** extension type. If you choose the **Extend** option, the extended surface will resemble the shape of the original surface. However, if you choose the **Stretch** option, then the extended surface will not resemble the original surface. Figure 6-35 shows the surface extended using the **Extend** option and Figure 6-36 shows the surface extended using the **Stretch** option.

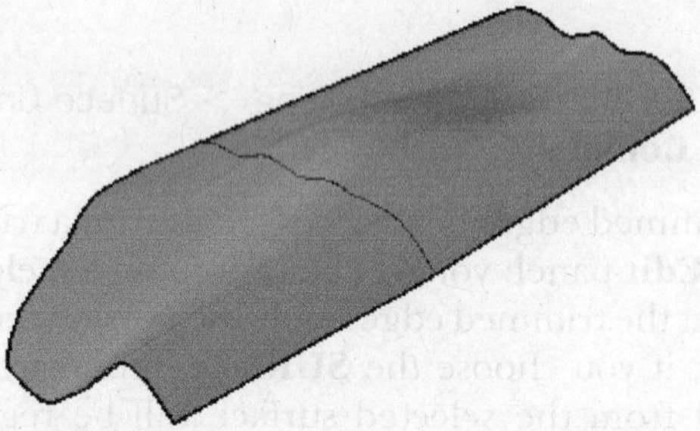

***Figure 6-35** Surface extended using the **Extend** option*

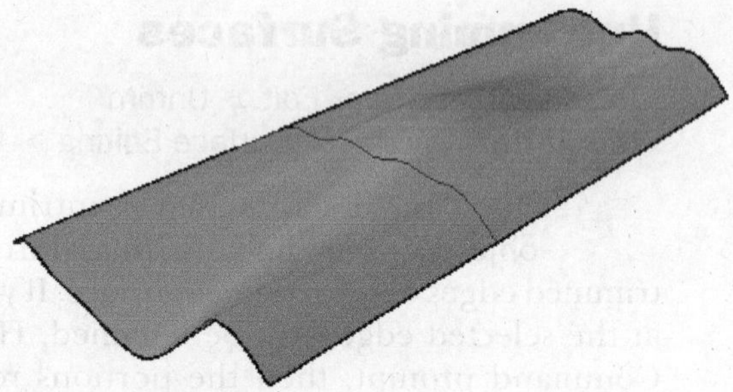

***Figure 6-36** Surface extended using the **Stretch** option*

Creation type

After you choose any of the modes and press ENTER, two options, **Merge** and **Append**, are displayed. On choosing the **Merge** option, the extended surface will merge with the existing surface, and on choosing the **Append** option, a new surface will be added to the existing surface, thus resulting in two surfaces.

Sculpting Surfaces

Ribbon: Surface > Edit > Sculpt	**Toolbar:** Surface Editing > Surface Sculpt
Menu Bar: Modify > Surface Editing > Sculpt	**Command:** SURFSCULPT

The **Sculpt** tool is used to create a 3D solid by combining and trimming the surfaces that form a closed volume. To sculpt surfaces, invoke the **Sculpt** tool from the **Edit** panel; you will be prompted to select the continuous surfaces. Select the surfaces forming a sealed area and press ENTER; the surfaces will get trimmed and a 3D solid will be formed. Figure 6-37 shows the surfaces enclosing a volume and Figure 6-38 shows the 3D solid created after sculpting the surfaces.

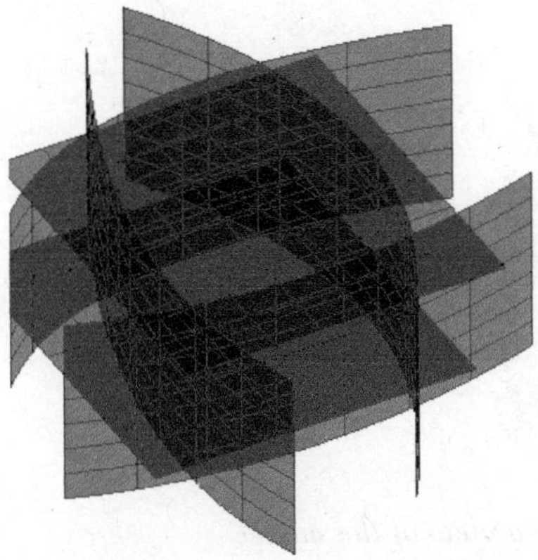

Figure 6-37 Surfaces enclosing a volume

Figure 6-38 3D solid created after sculpting

Extracting Intersections

Ribbon: Surface > Edit > Extract Intersections
Menu Bar: Modify > 3D Oprerations > Interference Checking **Command:** INTERFERE

The **Extract Intersections** tool is used to create a solid, surface, or spline by extracting the intersections of two solids, a solid and a surface, or two surfaces, respectively. To extract intersection of two surfaces, invoke the **Extract Intersections** tool from the **Edit** panel of the **Surface** tab. You will be prompted to select two objects. Select two intersecting surfaces and press ENTER; you will be asked if you want to create an intersecting object or not. Select **Yes** or type **Y** and press ENTER; the spline will be created. Figure 6-39 shows two intersecting surfaces and Figure 6-40 shows the spline generated.

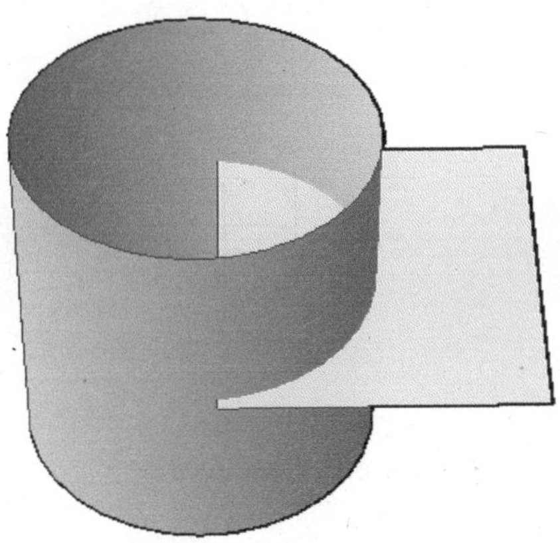

Figure 6-39 Two intersecting surfaces

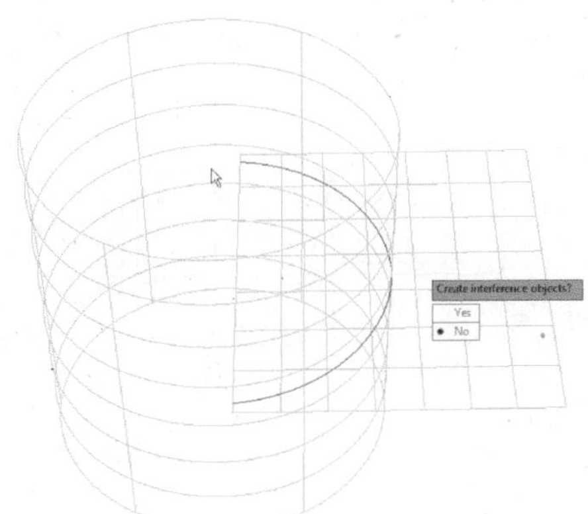

Figure 6-40 Interference spline

Example 1 — Surface Creation

In this example, you will create the model shown in Figure 6-41. Its views and dimensions are shown in Figure 6-42. The dimensions are given for your reference only. You can use your own dimensions.

Figure 6-41 The isometric view of the model

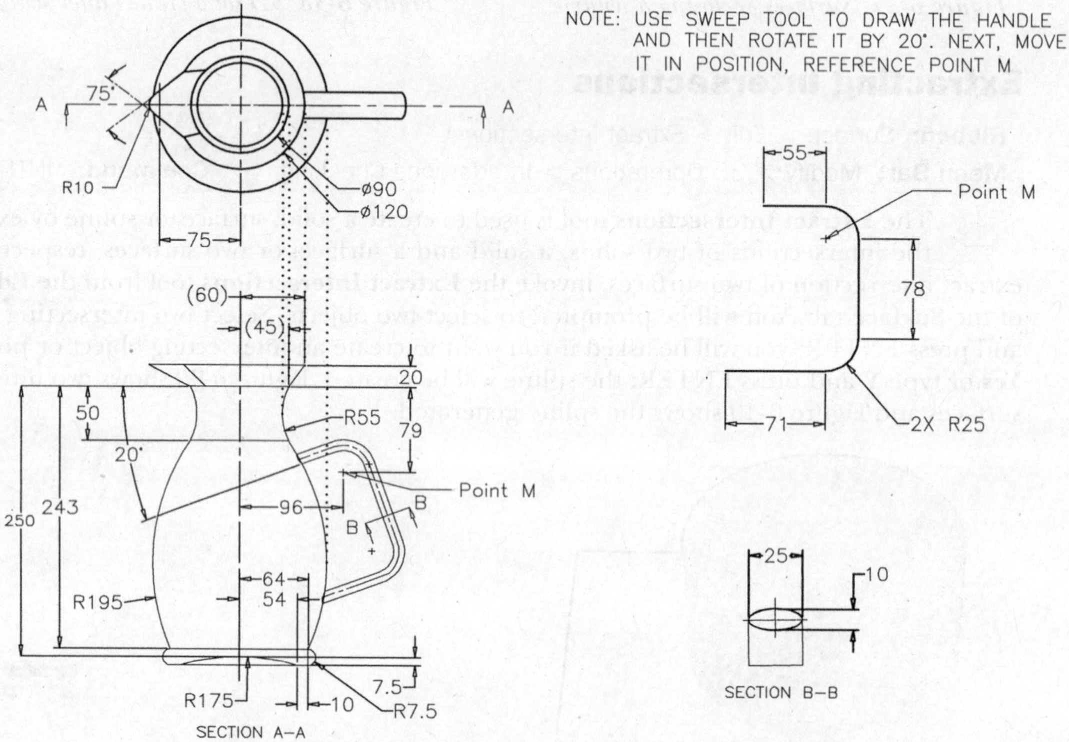

Figure 6-42 Orthographic views and dimensions of the model

1. Start a new drawing with **acad3D.dwt** template and draw the sketch of a circle with its center at the origin and diameter 90. This sketch is the first cross-section for the loft.

2. Draw another sketch for the second cross-section, as shown in Figure 6-43. Then, convert the sketch to a polyline by using the **Edit Polyline** tool.

3. Move the second sketch to a distance of 20 units along the Z axis.

4. Choose the **Loft** tool from the **Create** panel in the **Surface** tab; you are prompted to select the cross-sections that you want to loft. Select the two sketches one by one and press ENTER; the preview of the loft surface is displayed.

5. Press ENTER to create the loft surface, as shown in Figure 6-44.

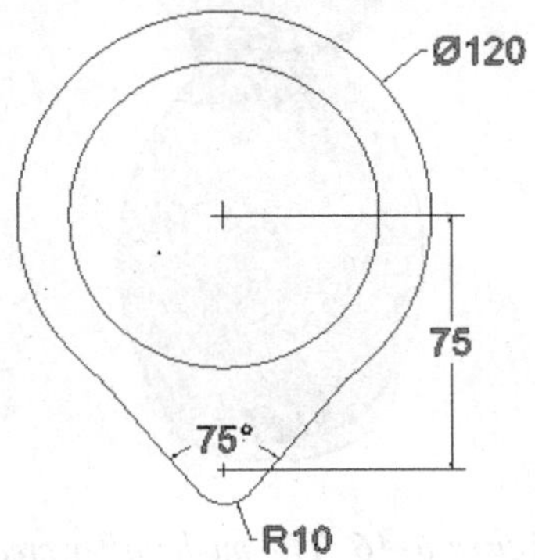

Figure 6-43 The sketch for the second cross-section

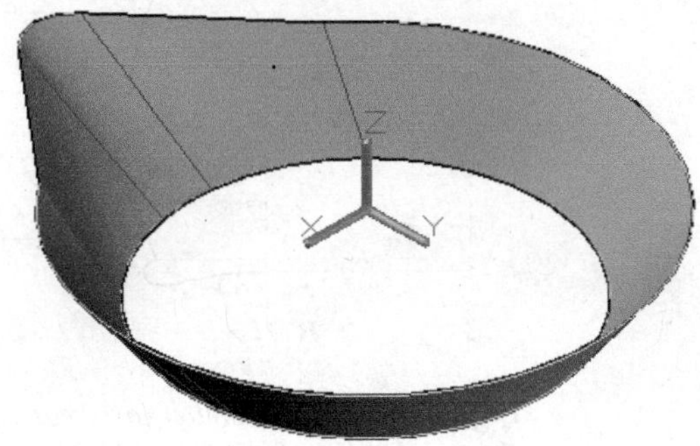

Figure 6-44 The resulting loft surface

Next, you need to create the revolved surface.

6. Switch to **Front** view.

7. Draw the sketch for the revolved feature, as shown in Figure 6-45, using the lines and arcs in the front view. Refer to Figure 6-42 for the missing dimensions. However, the profile may not be of exact dimensions.

8. Convert the profile into a polyline by using the **Join** tool.

9. Choose the **Revolve** tool from the **Create** panel in the **Surface** tab; you are prompted to select the profile to be revolved.

10. Select the sketch and press ENTER; you are prompted to select the axis of revolution. You can select the axis of co-ordinate system in this case or draw a vertical line at the center for axis of revolution. Select the axis of revolution and press ENTER; the revolved surface is created, as shown in Figure 6-46.

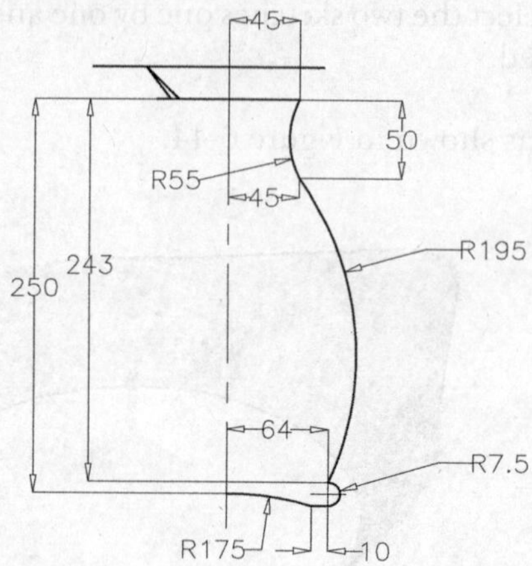

Figure 6-45 *The sketch for creating the revolved surface*

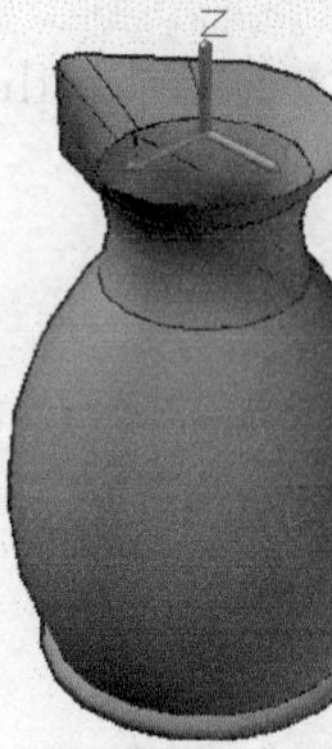

Figure 6-46 *The model after creating the revolved surface*

Next, you need to create the handle of the jug by sweeping a profile along a guide curve.

11. Draw the path for the sweep surface in the front view by using the **Polyline** tool, as shown in Figure 6-47. Note that the profile is rotated by 20 degrees.

12. Draw the profile of an ellipse, as shown in Figure 6-48, for creating the sweep surface. This profile can be drawn anywhere in the drawing area.

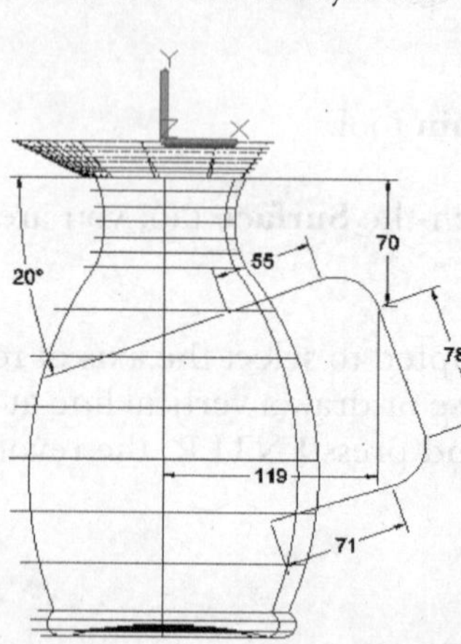

Figure 6-47 *The path for the sweep surface*

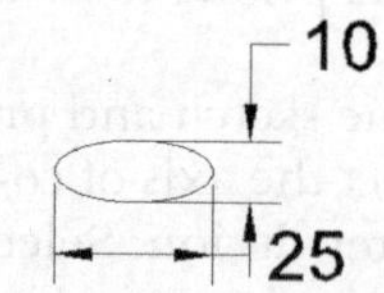

Figure 6-48 *The profile for the sweep surface*

13. Choose the **Sweep** tool from the **Create** panel in the **Surface** tab; you are prompted to select the profile to be swept.

14. Select the ellipse and press ENTER; you are prompted to select the sweep path.

15. Select the sweep path created in Step 11 and press ENTER; the sweep surface is created.

16. Create a new layer for profiles, move profiles to the new layer, and then freeze the layer so that the profiles are not displayed on the model. Next, the handle of the jug needs to be trimmed so that it does not penetrate the model.

17. Choose the **Trim** tool from the **Edit** panel in the **Surface** tab; you are prompted to select the surfaces to trim.

18. Select the sweep surface of the handle and press ENTER; you are prompted to select the cutting elements.

19. Select the revolved surface of the jug and press ENTER; you are prompted to select the area to be trimmed.

20. Rotate the model, select the inner portion of the sweep surface, and press ENTER; the sweep surface penetrating the revolved surface is trimmed and the final model of the jug is created.

Exercise 1 — *Surface Creation*

In this exercise, you will create the model shown in Figure 6-49. Its drawing views and dimensions are shown in Figure 6-50.

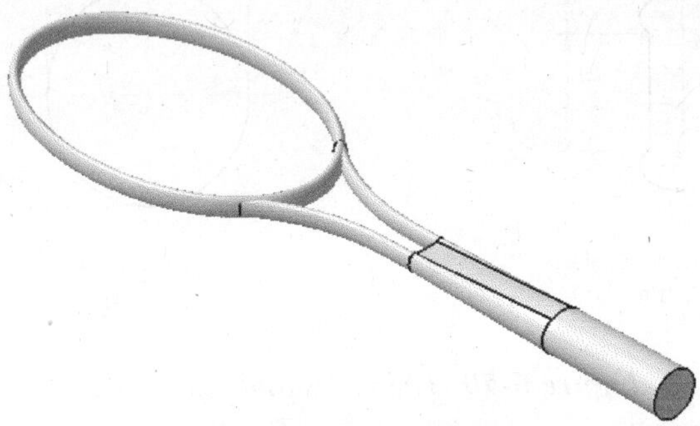

Figure 6-49 *The isometric view of the model*

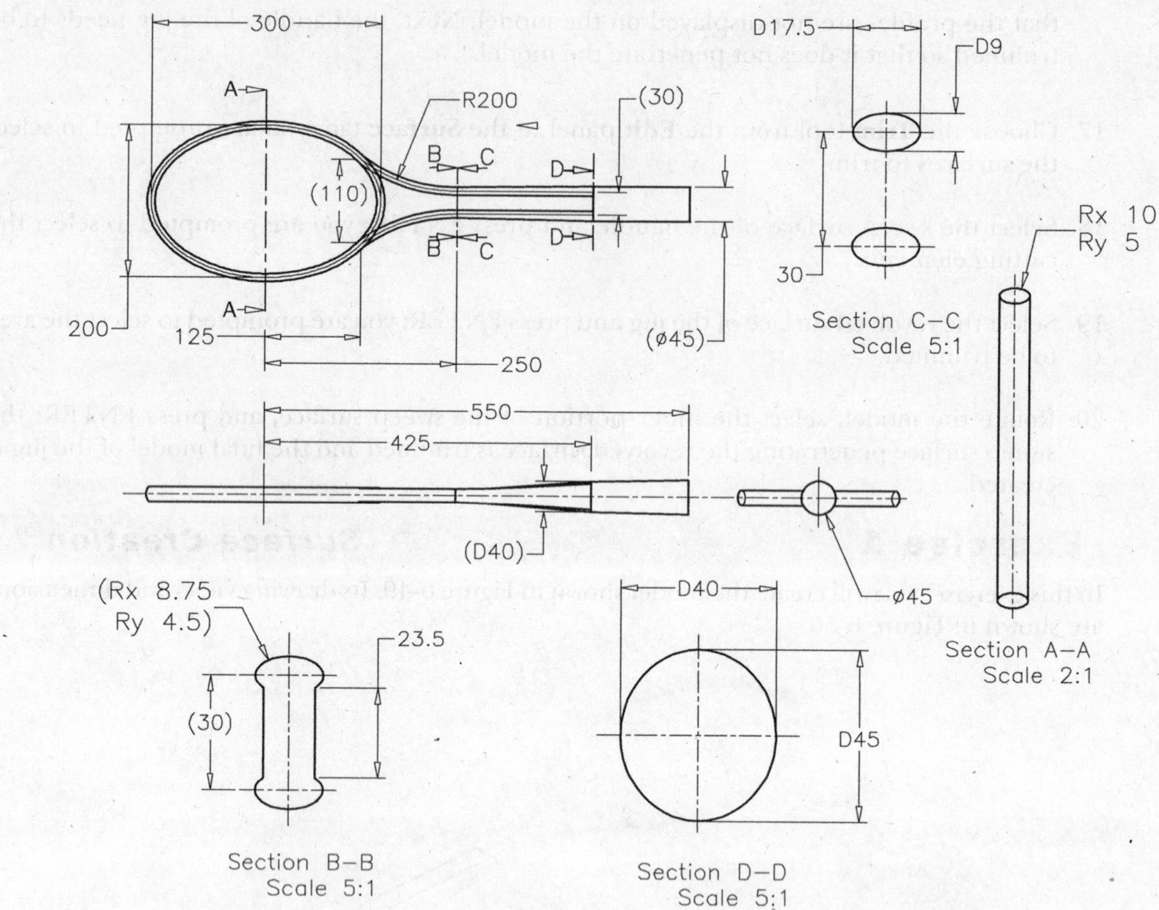

Figure 6-50 The views and dimensions of the model

Example 2 — Surface Editing

In this example, you will create the model of the back cover of a toy monitor, as shown in Figure 6-51. You will create this model using the editing tools. After creating the surface model, you need to convert it into a solid body. The orthographic views and dimensions of the model are shown in Figure 6-52.

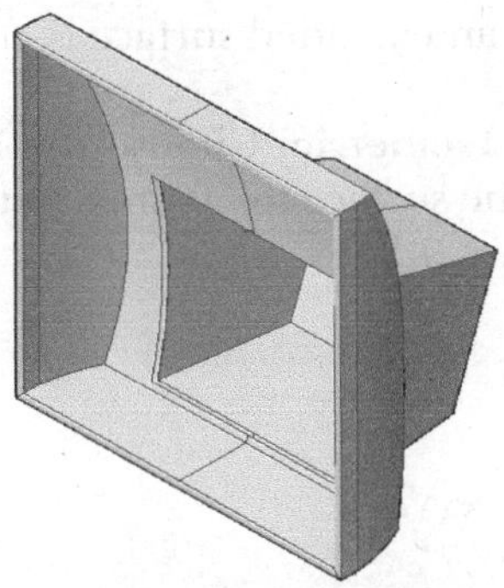

Figure 6-51 Back cover of the toy monitor

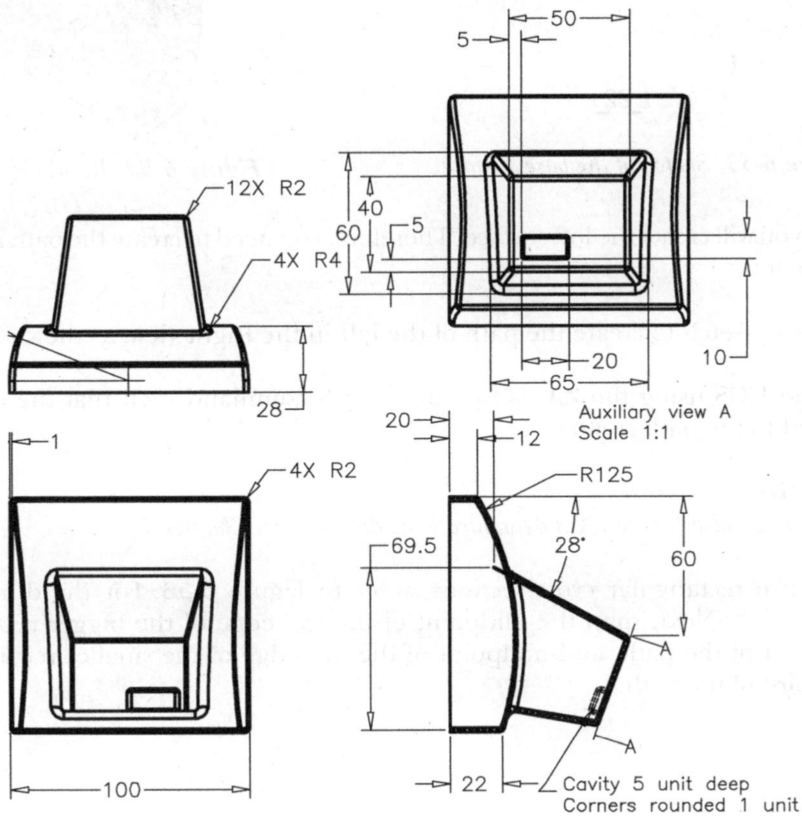

Figure 6-52 *Orthographic views and dimensions of the model for Example 2*

1. Start a new drawing file with **acad3D.dwt** template and switch to **Right** view.

2. Draw the sketch of the monitor, as shown in Figure 6-53, using the **Line** and **Arc** tools. Next, convert it into a polyline by using the **Join** tool.

3. Choose the **Extrude** tool from the **Create** panel of the **Surface** tab and extrude the sketch to a distance of 50 units; an extruded surface is created.

4. Change the view to **SW Isometric**. Choose the **Extend** tool from the **Edit** panel of the **Surface** tab and extend the surface to 50 units in the opposite direction; the base surface is created, as shown in Figure 6-54.

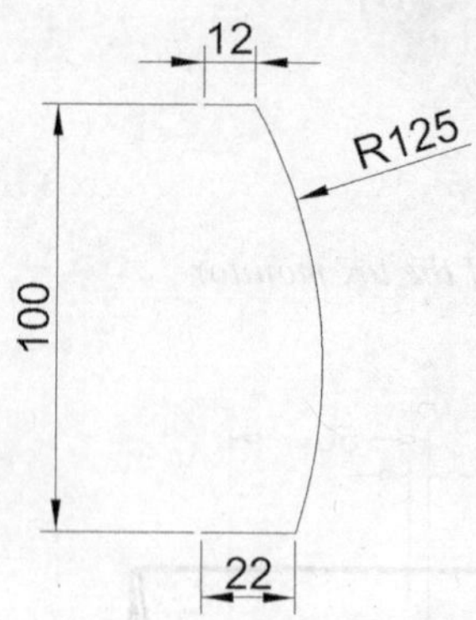

Figure 6-53 *Sketch of the base surface*

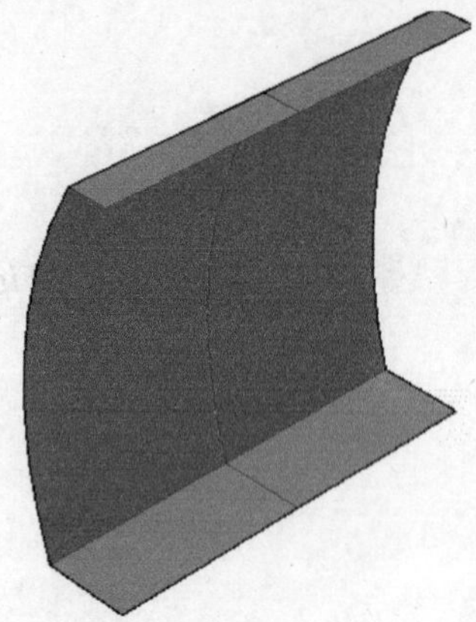

Figure 6-54 *Resulting base surface*

Next, you will create the loft surface. Therefore, you need to create the path and cross-sections for the loft.

5. Draw the sketch to create the path of the loft in the Right view, as shown in Figure 6-55.

6. Tilt the UCS using the **ZAxis** option of UCS command such that the cross-sections are aligned to the path created.

Note

You can also tilt the UCS dynamically as discussed in Chapter 1.

7. Draw two rectangular cross-sections, refer to Figure 6-56. For the dimensions refer to Figure 6-52. Next, snap the midpoint of the top edge of the bigger rectangle to the left endpoint of the path, and midpoint of the top edge of the smaller rectangle to the right endpoint of the path.

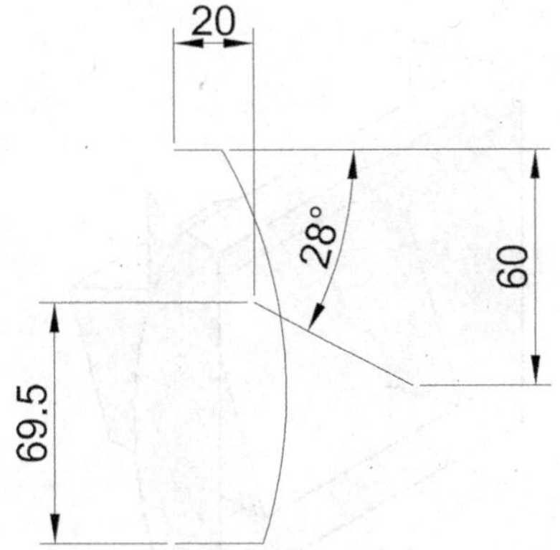

Figure 6-55 Path of the loft

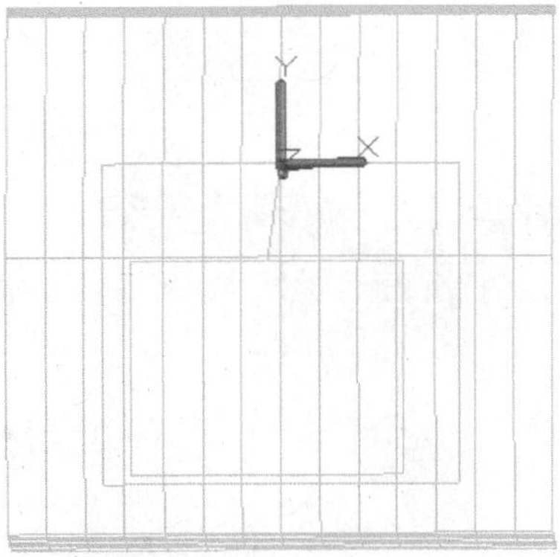

Figure 6-56 Cross-sections for the loft

8. Choose the **Loft** tool from the **Create** panel in the **Surface** tab; you are prompted to select the cross-sections.

9. Select the cross-sections one by one and press ENTER; the preview of the loft is displayed and you are prompted to press ENTER to accept or select a guide curve or a path.

10. Choose the **Path** option and select the line segment; the loft is created, as shown in Figure 6-57. Next, press ENTER.

11. Draw the sketch on both sides on the top face of the base surface, as shown in Figure 6-58.

12. Choose the **Extrude** tool and extrude the sketch to coincide it with the bottom part of the first surface, refer to Figure 6-59. Use the 3D object snap to snap the extrusion height.

Next, you need to trim the unwanted portions of the surfaces.

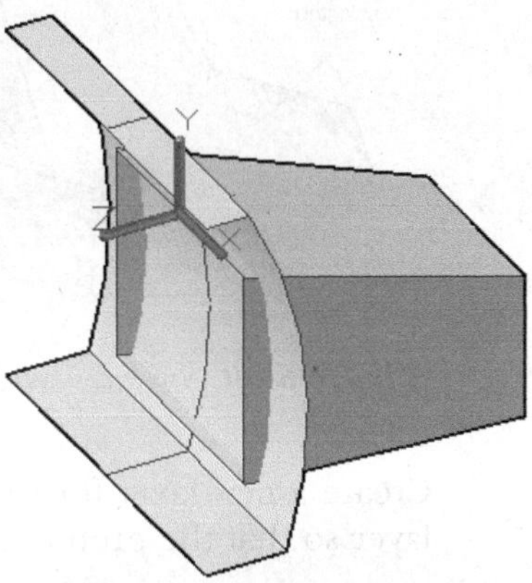

Figure 6-57 Resulting loft surface

13. Choose the **Trim** tool from the **Edit** panel of the **Surface** tab; you are prompted to select the surfaces to be trimmed.

14. Select the back face of the base surface and press ENTER; you are prompted to select the surfaces used to trim. Select the left and right extruded surfaces, refer to Figure 6-60, and press ENTER; you are prompted to select the portions to trim.

15. Select the part of the base surface that is projecting outward; the base surface gets trimmed.

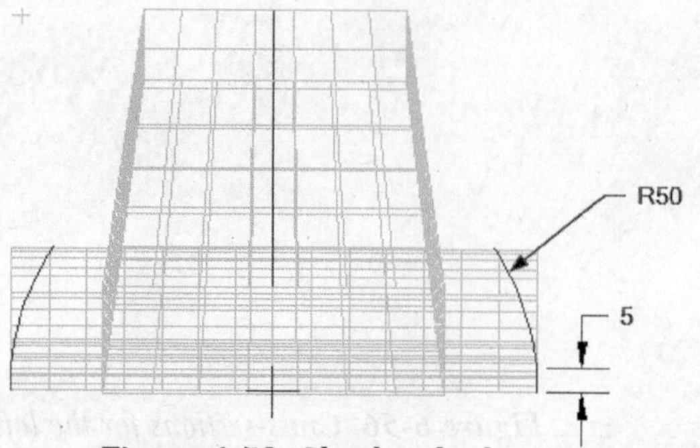

Figure 6-58 Sketch to be drawn

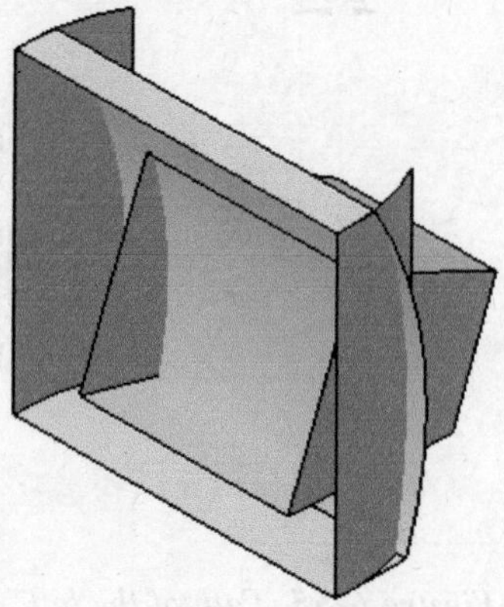

Figure 6-59 Resulting extruded surface

16. Similarly, trim all unwanted portions of the surfaces, as shown in Figure 6-61.

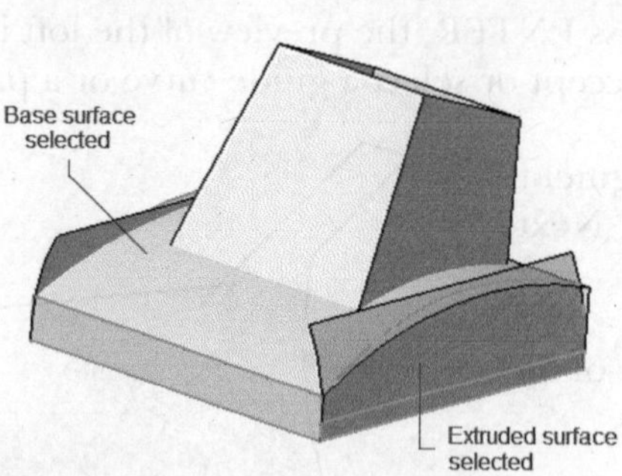

Figure 6-60 Surfaces selected for trimming

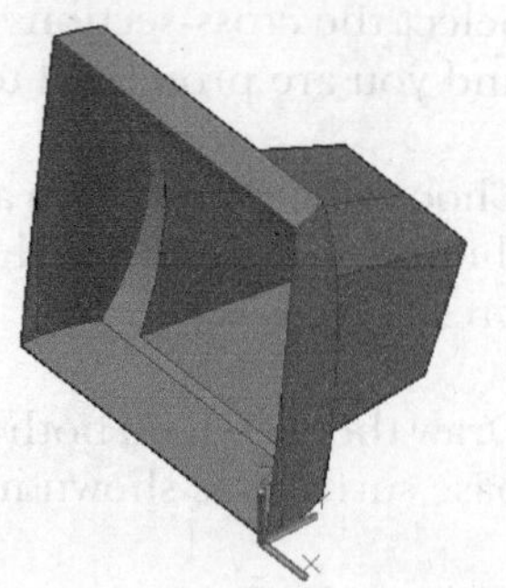

Figure 6-61 The model after trimming the surfaces

17. Create a new layer for the profiles, move all profiles to the new layer, and then freeze the layer so that the profiles are not displayed on the model.

Next, you need to close the back face of the loft.

18. Invoke the **Patch** tool from the **Create** panel of the **Surface** tab; you are prompted to select the edges of the surfaces to patch.

19. Choose the **CHain** option and select all the four edges of the back face of the lofted surface and press ENTER; the preview of the patch surface is displayed. Press ENTER to accept it.

Next, you need to create the frame of the monitor.

20. Now, create the cavity on the back face of the lofted surface, refer to Figure 6-52 for dimensions.

21. Choose the **Offset Surface** tool from the **Create** panel of the **Surface** tab. Select the extruded and extended surface and press ENTER; the direction arrows are displayed. If

the direction arrows are pointing outward, flip them. When the arrows point inward, set the offset value to 1.

22. Similarly, offset the other two sides inward to a distance of 1 units, refer to Figure 6-62.
23. Trim the four surfaces to form corners, refer to Figure 6-62.

Next, you need to create a panel by closing the offset faces and the original faces.

24. Invoke the **Blend** tool from the **Create** panel in the **Surface** tab; you are prompted to select the first surface edge to blend.
25. Select the top edge of the extruded and extended surface, and then press ENTER; you are prompted to select the second surface edge to blend.
26. Select the offset surface below the top edges and press ENTER; the preview of the blend surface is created.
27. Press ENTER to accept the settings of the blend surface. Similarly, blend all surfaces. The final model of the toy monitor after blending all surfaces is shown in Figure 6-63.

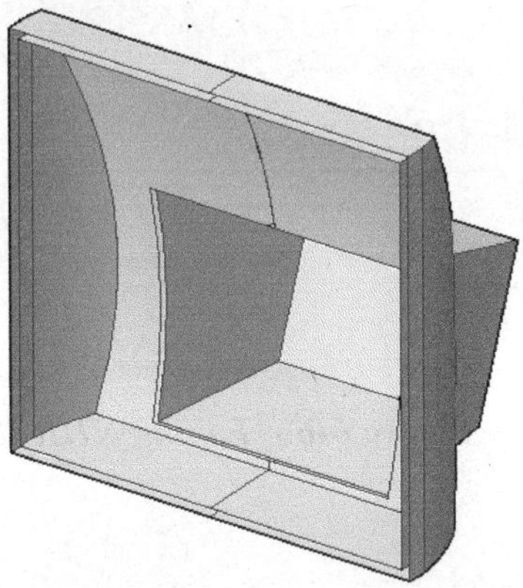

Figure 6-62 Model after offsetting and trimming surfaces

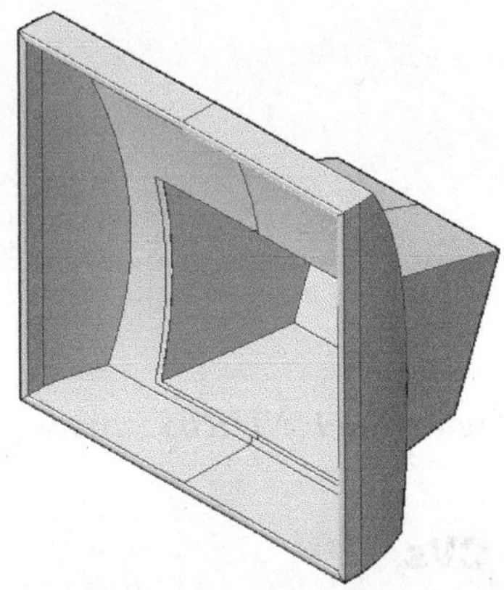

Figure 6-63 Back cover of the toy monitor

NURBS Surfaces

Ribbon: Surface > Control Vertices > Convert to NURBS
Menu Bar: Modify > Surface Editing > Convert to NURBS
Command: CONVTONURBS

NURBS is an acronym for 'Non-Uniform Rational B-Splines' and encompasses all characteristics of bezier curves or splines. However, in AutoCAD, splines are optimized to create NURBS. You can adjust the control points, fit points, and degree of a spline to control its shape, thereby controlling the NURBS surface. NURBS surface consists of control vertices and fit points, which can be used to modify the overall shape of a surface. While creating any surface, if you choose the **NURBS Creation** button, the NURBS surface will be created.

You can also convert an existing surface into a NURBS surface. To do so, choose the **Convert to NURBS** tool from the **Control Vertices** panel; you will be prompted to select the object to be converted into a NURBS surface. Select the surface and press ENTER; the selected surface will be converted into a NURBS surface. Figure 6-64 shows a NURBS surface with its control vertices. If the CVs are not displayed on the NURBS surface, you need to invoke the **Show CV** tool. This tool is discussed next.

Displaying CVs

Ribbon: Surface > Control Vertices > Show CV/Hide CV
Menu Bar: Modify > Surface Editing > NURBS Surface Editing > Show CV/Hide CV
Command: CVSHOW/CVHIDE

You can edit the shape of a NURBS surface by dragging its control vertices or fit points. By default, control vertices are not displayed on the NURBS surface. To view the control vertices on the surface, choose the **Show CV** tool from the **Control Vertices** panel; the CVs will be displayed on the surface. You can drag these control vertices to new locations to edit the surface, refer to Figure 6-65. After editing the surface, if you want to hide the CVs from the NURBS surface, choose the **Hide CV** tool.

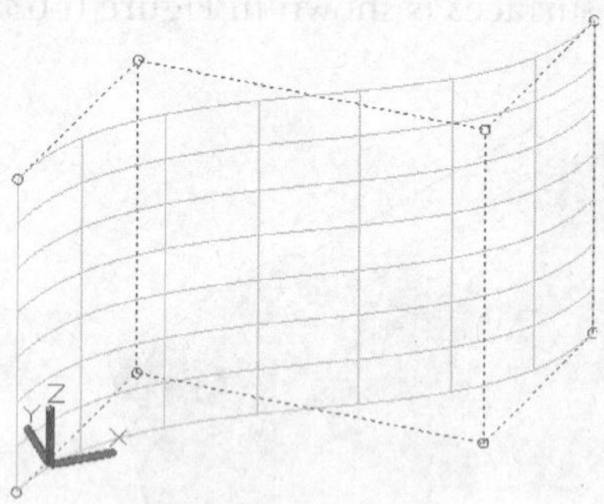

Figure 6-64 NURBS surface

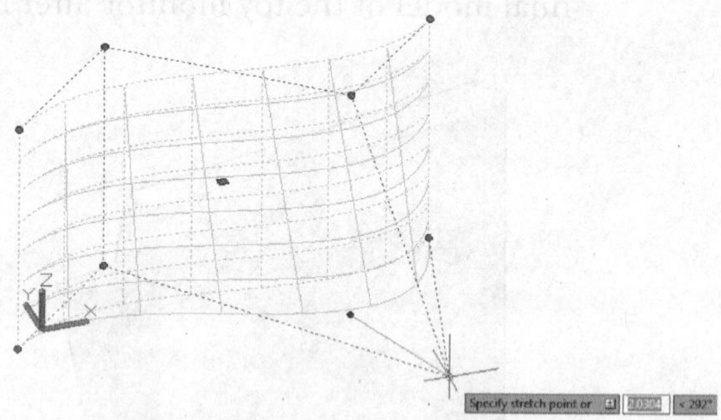

Figure 6-65 Editing NURBS surface

Editing CVs

Ribbon: Surface > Control Vertices > CV Edit Bar **Command:** 3DEDITBAR

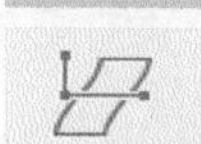

While converting an existing surface into a NURBS surface, the CVs are formed at the corners of the NURBS surface. However, you can specify a point on the NURBS surface to create a CV at that particular point. To do so, choose the **CV Edit Bar** tool from the **Control Vertices** panel; you will be prompted to select a surface. Select the NURBS surface; the cursor will turn red. Now, you can specify the direction of creation of the CV on the surface. After specifying a point, a move gizmo along with two handles will be displayed on the specified point, refer to Figure 6-66. Using these handles, you can edit the shape of the NURBS surface. The horizontal triangular handle is used to specify the magnitude of drag and the square handle is used to move the selected point to a new place.

You can set the tangency conditions and position of a control vertex using the triangular grip displayed on the gizmo, refer to Figure 6-66. Right-click on the triangular grip; a shortcut menu will be displayed, as shown in Figure 6-67. The options in the shortcut menu are discussed next.

By default, the **Move Point Location** option is chosen in this shortcut menu. As a result, the NURBS surface will be modified with respect to the point but the tangency will not be modified. If you select the **Move Tangent Direction** option, the tangency of the curve will be modified. If you select the **U Tangent Direction** or **V Tangent Direction** option, the tangency will be modified only in the U-direction or V-direction, respectively. The **Normal Tangent Direction** option is used to edit the tangency of the curve normal to the current UCS. You can also constrain the change in tangency or point location to a particular axis using the **Set Constraint** option. You can also relocate the base point or realign the gizmo using the **Relocate Base Point** and **Align Gizmo With** options, respectively in this shortcut menu.

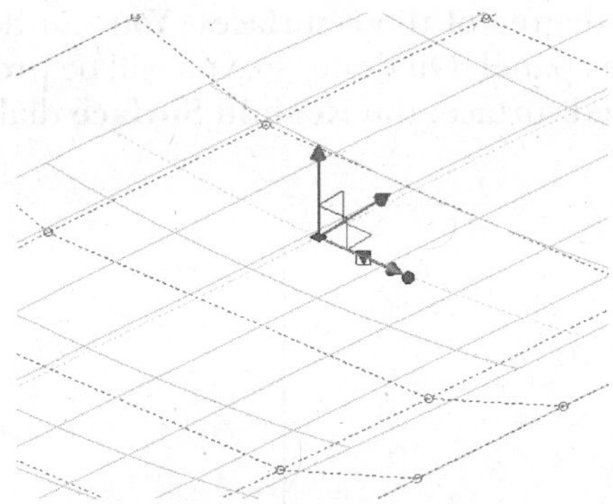

Figure 6-66 *Editing CVs*

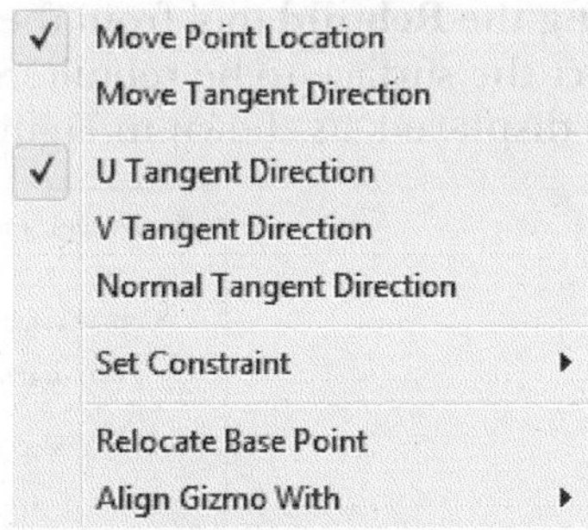

Figure 6-67 *Shortcut menu displayed at the triangular grip*

Adding CVs

Ribbon: Surface > Control Vertices > Add
Menu Bar: Modify > Surface Editing > NURBS Surface Editing > Add CV
Command: CVADD

When you create a NURBS surface, some CVs are displayed on it by default. However, you can add more CVs to it if you need. To add CVs, choose the **Add** tool from the **Control Vertices** panel; you will be prompted to select a NURBS surface or curve where you want to add CVs. Select the NURBS surface; preview of the CVs will be attached to the cursor, refer to Figure 6-68. By default, the CVs get added in the U-direction. If you want to add CVs in the V-direction, choose the **Direction** option from the Command prompt; the CVs will be added in the V-direction.

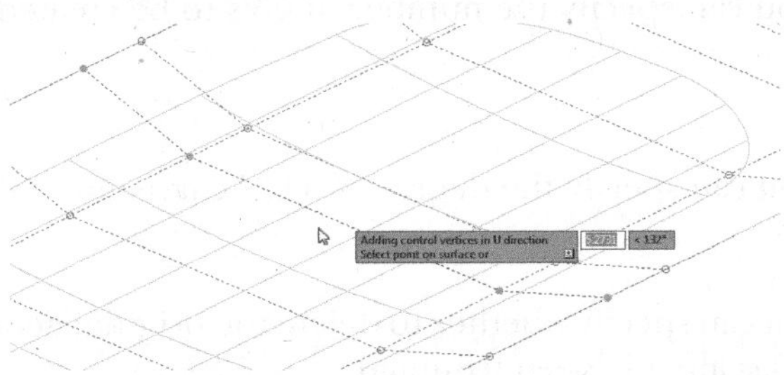

Figure 6-68 *Preview of CVs*

If you want to create knots on the surface, choose the **insert Knots** option from the Command prompt; knots or fit points will be created on the surface instead of CVs.

Rebuilding a NURBS Surface

Ribbon: Surface > Control Vertices > Rebuild **Command:** CVREBUILD
Menu Bar: Modify > Surface Editing > NURBS Surface Editing > Rebuild

You can reconstruct a NURBS surface by defining the number of CVs created on it and the degree of the CV curve. For example, the surfaces created by line, arc, or circle are of less than 3 degrees. You may need to change the degree of these surfaces. You can do so by invoking the **Rebuild** tool from the **Control Vertices** panel. On doing so, you will be prompted to select the surface to be rebuilt. Select the required surface; the **Rebuild Surface** dialog box will be displayed, as shown in Figure 6-69.

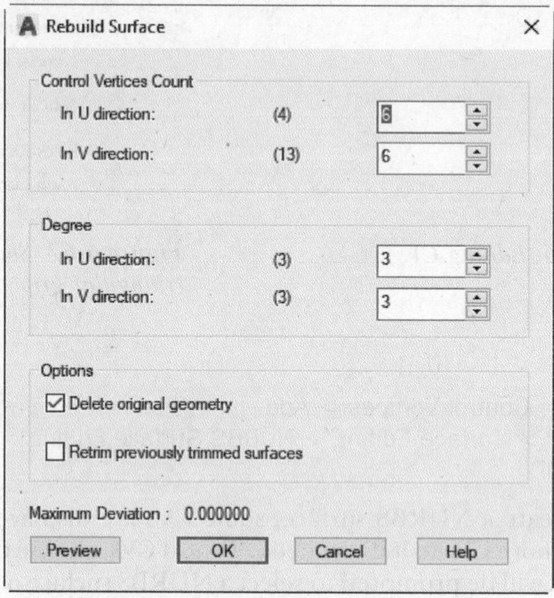

*Figure 6-69 The **Rebuild Surface** dialog box*

The areas in the dialog box are discussed next.

Control Vertices Count

In this area, you can specify the number of CVs to be created on the surface in the U and V directions.

Degree

In this area, you can specify the degree of a CV curve along the U and V directions.

Options

In this area, you can specify whether to delete the original geometry of a CV curve or retrim a surface that has already been trimmed.

Preview Button

You can preview the CVs created on a surface. To do so, first set the required values in the **Rebuild Surface** dialog box and then choose the **Preview** button; the preview of the CVs created will be displayed. If the preview of the CVs created is satisfactory, press ENTER. If you want to change the values, press the ESC key.

Removing CVs

Ribbon: Surface > Control Vertices > Remove
Menu Bar: Modify > Surface Editing > NURBS Surface Editing > Remove CV
Command: CVREMOVE

You can remove the unwanted CVs from a NURBS surface. To do so, choose the **Remove** tool from the **Control Vertices** panel; you will be prompted to select a NURBS surface to remove the CVs. Select a NURBS surface and press ENTER; you will be prompted to select a point on the surface to remove vertices in the U-direction. Select a point on the surface near the CV that you want to remove. If you want to change the direction of removal of CVs, use the **Direction** option; the CVs will be set to remove from the V-direction. Remember that the minimum number of CVs in each direction is 2.

Projecting Geometries

The Projection tools are used to project one or more elements on a surface. These tools are available in the **Project Geometry** panel of the **Surface** tab. You can project curves, lines, points, 2D polyline, 3D polyline, or helix onto a solid or a surface. When you project a curve, a duplicate of that curve is created. You can move, modify, change, delete this curve without affecting the original curve. You can also trim the surface onto which the curve has been projected. This can be done by using the **Auto Trim** button. When this button is active, the surface will be trimmed automatically on projecting the curve onto the surface. The projection of curves can be normal to the surface along a specified direction, normal to the current view, or along a specified path. These projection tools are discussed next.

Project to UCS

Using this tool, you can project a curve on a surface along the +z or -z axis of the current UCS.

Project to View

This tool enables you to project a curve on a surface based on the current view.

Project to 2 Points

Using this tool, you can project a curve along a path defined by two points.

Figure 6-70 shows a surface and the curve to be projected. Figure 6-71 shows the curve projected using the **Project to UCS** tool with the **Auto Trim** button chosen and Figure 6-72 shows the curve projected using the **Project to View** tool with the **Auto Trim** button chosen. Figure 6-73 shows the curve projected on the surface by specifying the 2 endpoints of the line segment as the direction of projection with the **Auto Trim** button deactivated.

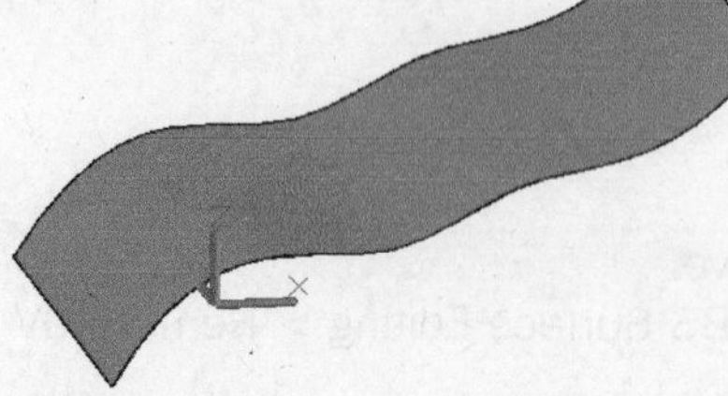

Figure 6-70 Surface and curve to be projected

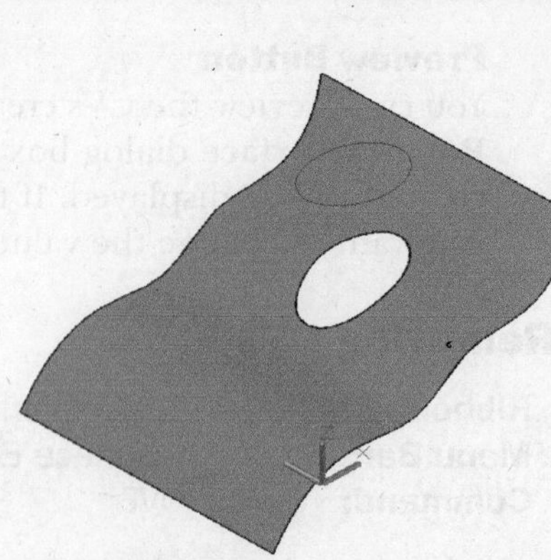

*Figure 6-71 Curve projected using the **Project to UCS** tool*

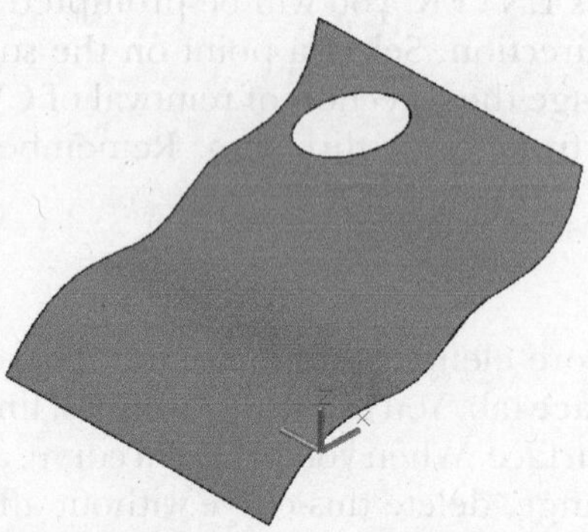

*Figure 6-72 Curve projected using the **Project to View** tool*

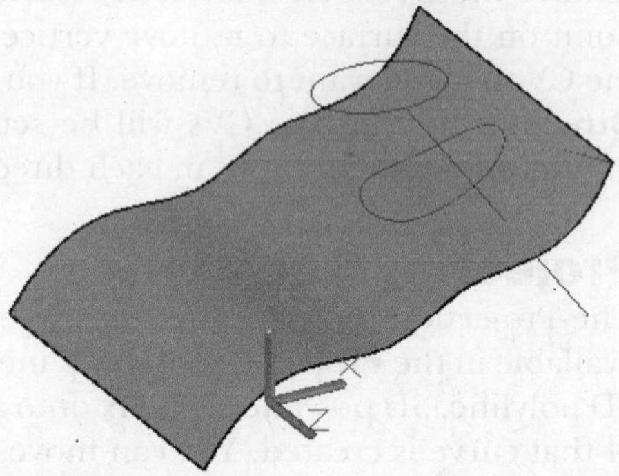

*Figure 6-73 Curve projected using the **Project to 2 Points** tool*

Example 3 — Editing Tools

In this example, you will create the model of eyeglasses, as shown in Figure 6-74. The dimensions of the model are shown in Figures 6-74(a) through 6-74(g). Assume the missing dimensions.

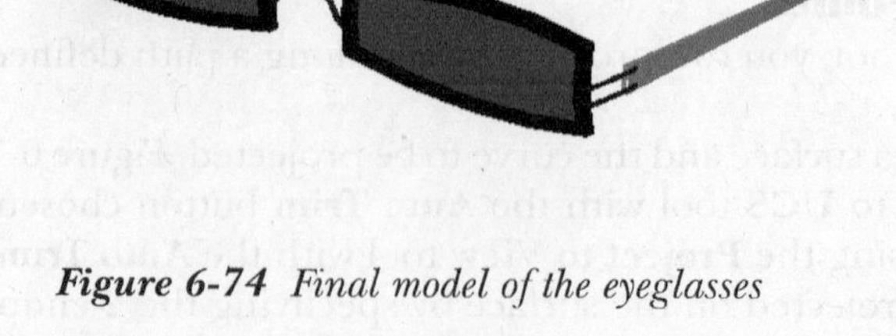

Figure 6-74 Final model of the eyeglasses

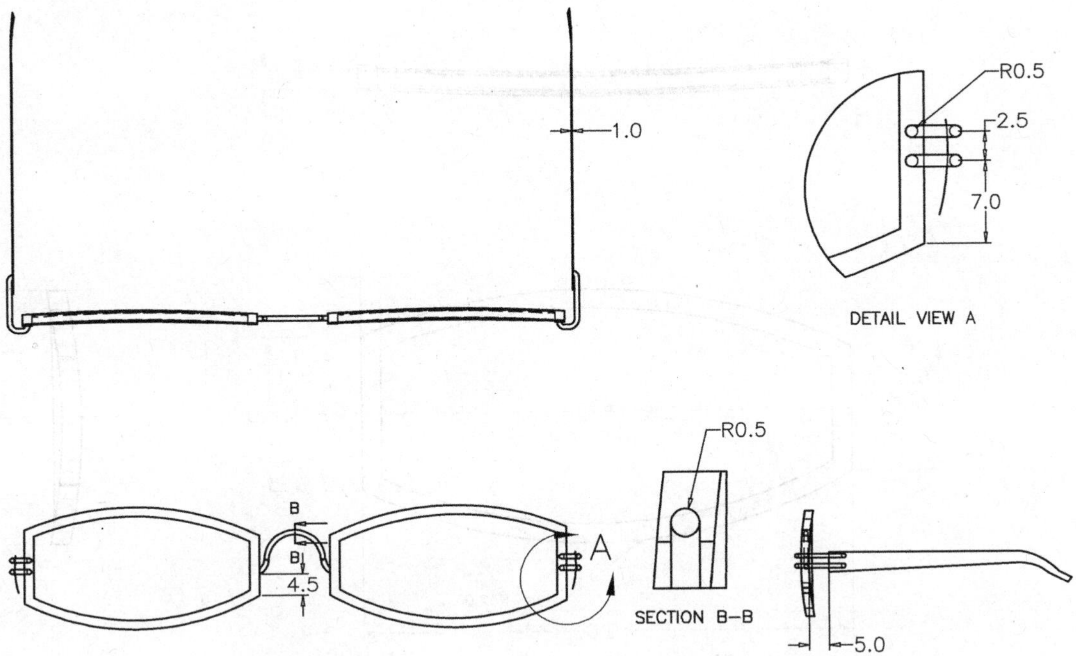

Figure 6-74(a) Orthographic views of the model for Example 3

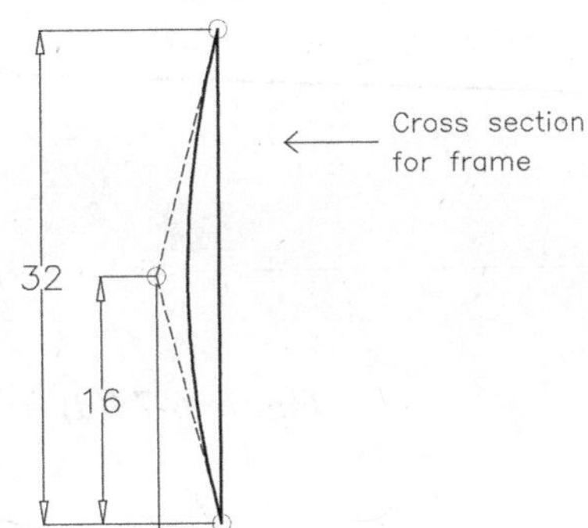

Figure 6-74(b) Cross section for frame

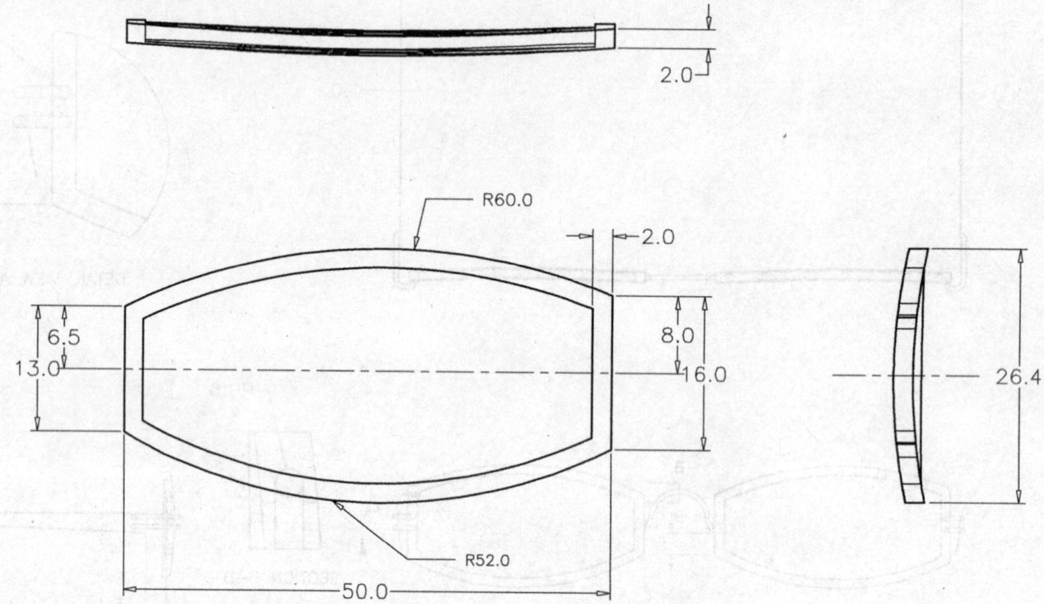

Figure 6-74(c) Orthographic views of the lenses

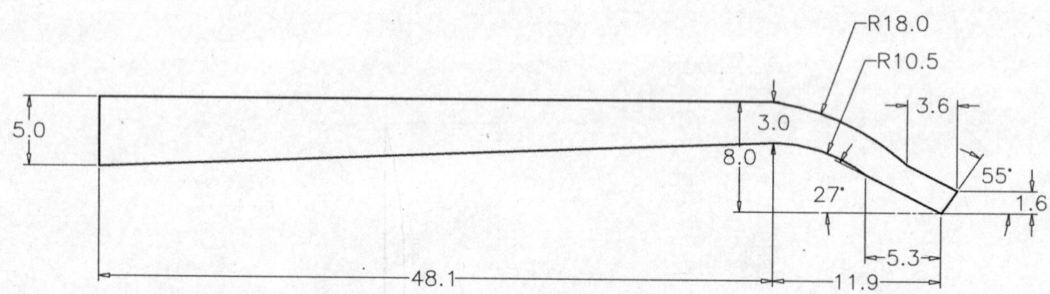

Figure 6-74(d) Profile for the Temples

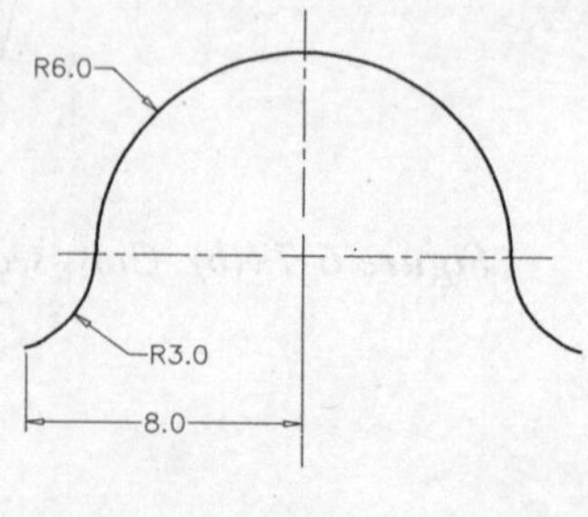

Figure 6-74(e) Profile for the Bridge

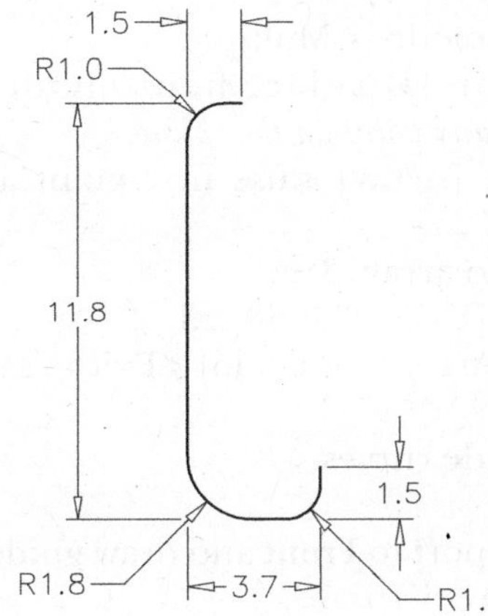

Figure 6-74(f) *Profile for the End Piece*

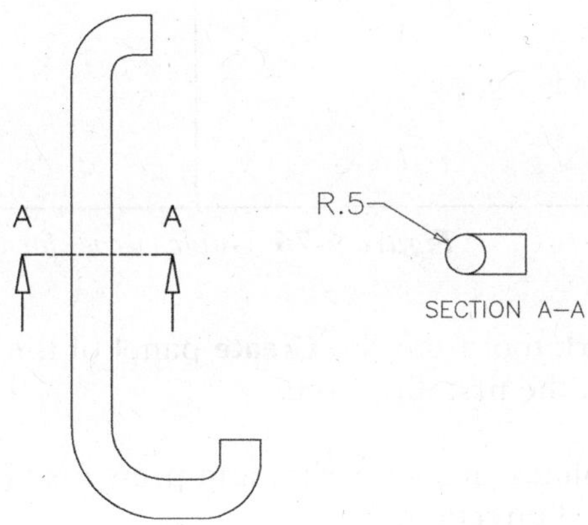

Figure 6-74(g) *Sectioned view of the End Piece*

1. Start a new drawing file using the **acad3D.dwt** template.
2. Switch to **Right** view.
3. Select the **Parallel** projection option from the **In-canvas Viewport Controls**.
4. Draw the spline using the **Spline CV** tool, as shown in Figure 6-75.
5. You need to array this spline along the Z-axis. To do so, invoke the **Copy** tool and create two more instances of spline by using the prompt sequence given next.

Select objects: *Select the spline.*
Select objects: Enter
Current settings: Copy mode = Multiple
Specify base point or [Displacement/mOde] <Displacement>:*Select any point on the spline.*
Specify second point or [Array] <use first point as displacement>: **ARRAY** Enter
Enter number of items to array: **3** Enter
Specify second point or [Fit]: **@0,0,60** Enter
Specify second point or [Array/Exit/Undo] <Exit>: Enter

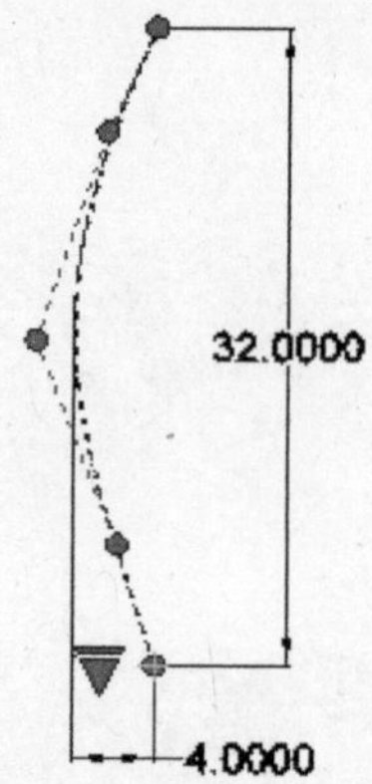

Figure 6-75 *Cross-section for frame*

Next, you need to create guide curves.

6. Change the current viewport to **Front** and draw guide curves, as shown in Figure 6-76.

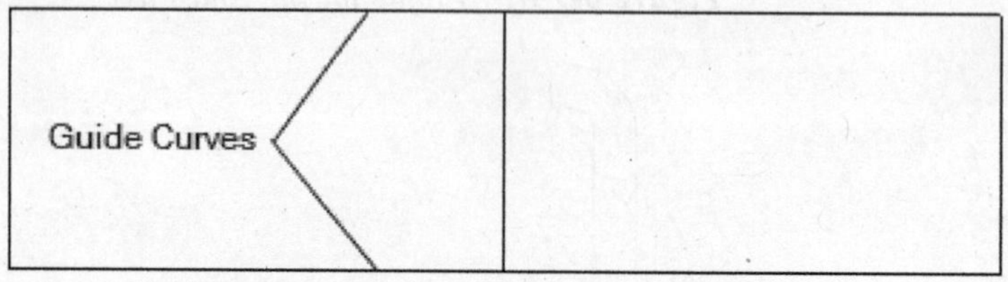

Figure 6-76 *Guide curves for frame*

7. Invoke the **Network** tool from the **Create** panel of the **Surface** tab; you are prompted to select the curves in the first direction.

8. Select the three splines created earlier and press ENTER; you are prompted to select the curves in the second direction.

9. Select the two joining guide curves drawn previously and press ENTER; the network surface is created. Change the current viewport to **SE Isometric** and then change the visual style; the surface will be displayed, as shown in Figure 6-77.

   Next, you need to draw the shape of the frame and then trim the unwanted portion.

Figure 6-77 *Network surface created*

10. Align the UCS on the network surface and draw the sketch using the **Line** and **Arc** tools in the **Front** view, as shown in Figure 6-78. Refer to Figure 6-79 for dimensions.

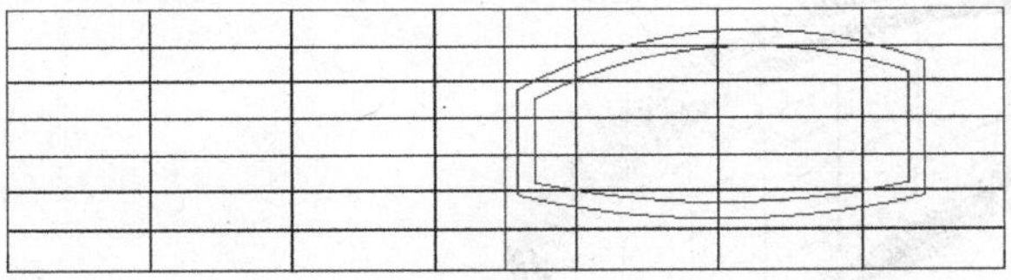

Figure 6-78 *Sketch to be drawn*

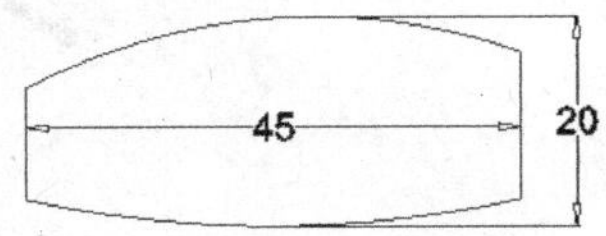

Figure 6-79 *Dimensions for sketch*

Note

The sketch created should be joined using the ***Join*** *tool.*

11. Invoke the **Trim** tool from the **Edit** panel in the **Surface** tab; you are prompted to select the objects to trim.
12. Select the network surface and press ENTER; you are prompted to select the cutting curves.
13. Select the two joined curves and press ENTER; you are prompted to select the area to be trimmed.
14. Select the innermost and outermost areas of the curves and press ENTER; the surface is created and displayed, as shown in Figure 6-80.

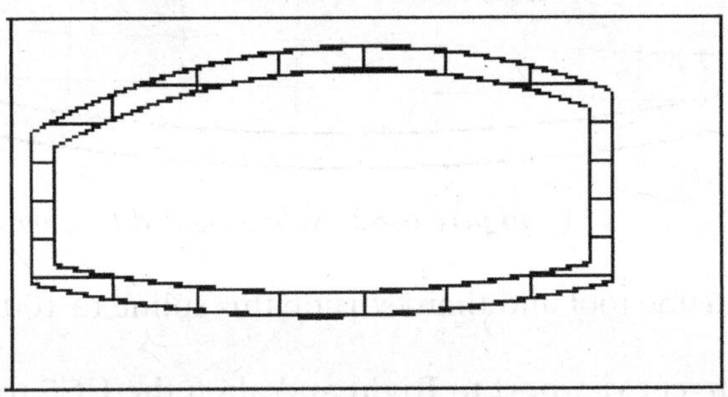

Figure 6-80 *Partial view of glass frame*

15. Create a new layer, move all profiles to the new layer, and then freeze the layer so that the profiles are not displayed on the model.
16. Change the current viewport to **SE Isometric**.
17. Invoke the **Extrude** tool, select the surface, and then extrude it by 2 units.

    Next, you need to create a surface for glasses.

18. Invoke the **Patch** tool from the **Create** panel of the **Surface** tab; you are prompted to select the surface edges. Select the innermost edge of the frame and press ENTER twice; the surface will be created, as shown in Figure 6-81.

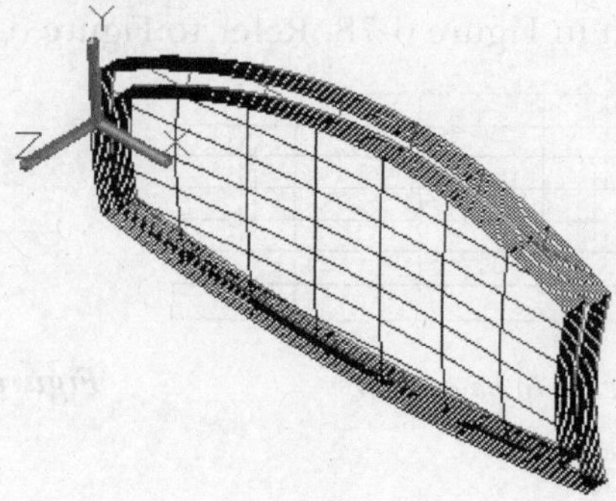

Figure 6-81 The patch surface created

Next, you need to create the side arm.

19. Change the current view to **Front** using the **In-canvas Viewport Controls** and then create a spline by using the **CV** method, refer to Figure 6-82.

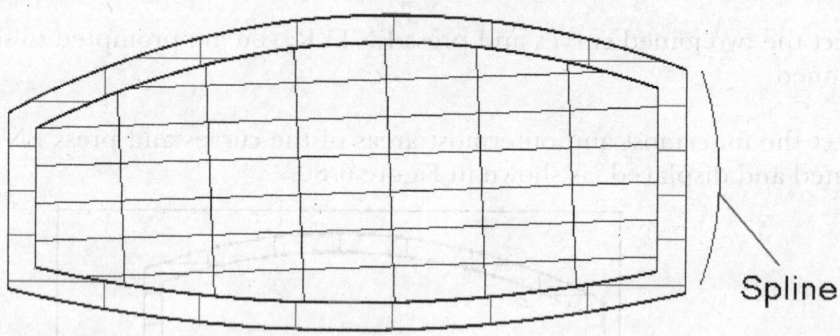

Figure 6-82 Spline created for arm

20. Invoke the **Extrude** tool and then extrude this spline to 100 units along negative Z-axis.

21. Change the current viewport to **Right** and align the UCS to the extruded surface created in Step 19.

22. Create a profile for side arm and join it using the **Join** tool, as shown in Figure 6-83.

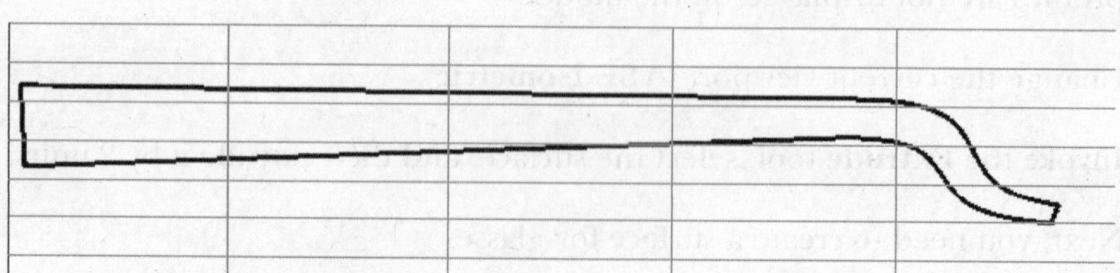

Figure 6-83 Profile for arm

23. Invoke the **Trim** tool from the **Edit** panel in the **Surface** tab; you are prompted to select the objects to trim.

24. Select the extruded surface and press ENTER; you are prompted to select the curves for trimming the object.

25. Select the profile created for the arm and press ENTER; you are prompted to select the area to be trimmed.

26. Select the outer area of the profile and press ENTER; the surface is created.

27. Move the profiles to the frozen layer.

28. Select the newly created surface and extrude it to 1 unit along negative Z-axis.

29. Change the current viewport to **Front** and align the UCS to the front face of the frame.

30. Create two circles of radius 0.45 each and a spline, as shown in the Figure 6-84.

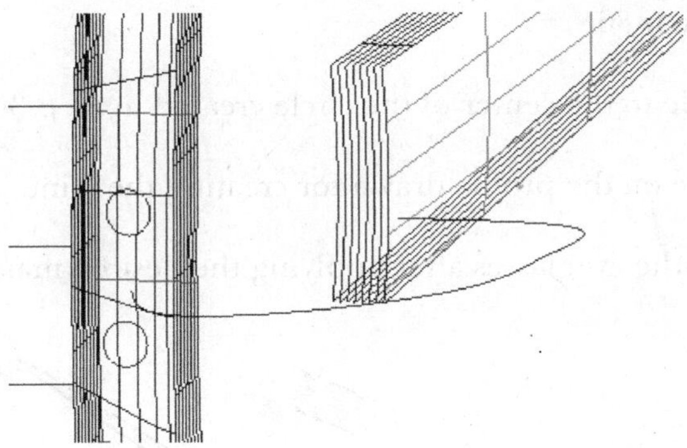

Figure 6-84 *Section and path for sweep feature*

31. Invoke the **Sweep** tool, select the two circles, and press ENTER; you are prompted to select the sweep path.

32. Select the spline curve; the sweep feature is created. Move the profiles to the frozen layer.

33. Change the current viewport to **Front** and mirror all the features using the **Mirror** tool about a line drawn at a distance of 7.5 units from the edge opposite to the edge joined with the arm.

    Next, you need to link the mirrored feature with the original feature.

34. Align the UCS to the side face of the frame, as shown in the Figure 6-85, and create a circle of radius 0.5 at **0,0** co-ordinate.

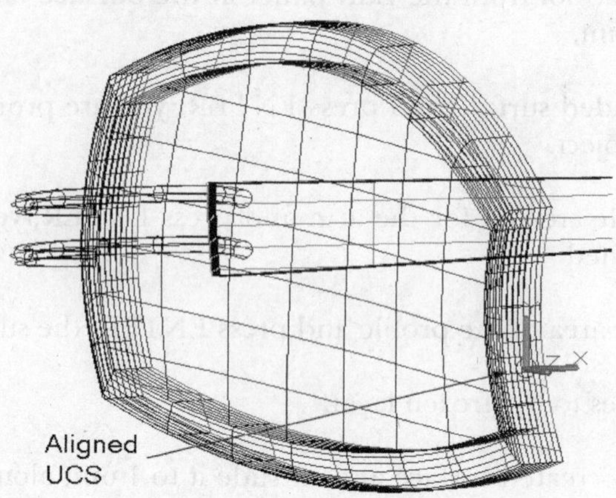

Figure 6-85 Aligning the UCS and creating the circle

35. Set the UCS to WCS, change the viewport to **Front**, and create a profile for the joint, as shown in Figure 6-86.

36. Move the profile to the center of the circle created in Step 34.

37. Sweep the circle on the profile drawn for creating the joint.

The final model of the eyeglasses after applying the desired materials is shown in shaded view in Figure 6-87.

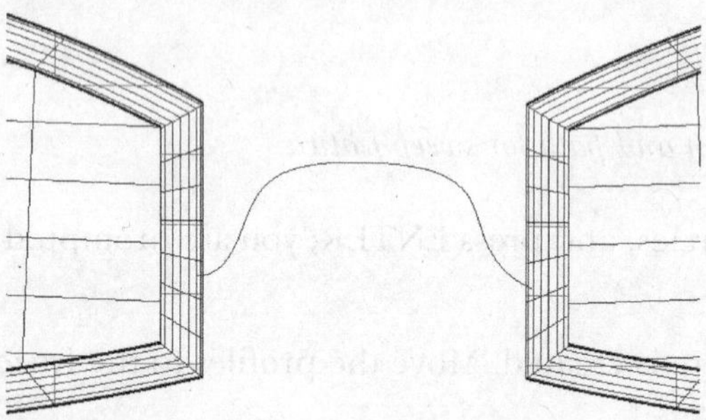

Figure 6-86 Profile for joint

Figure 6-87 Final model of the eyeglasses

Note
You will learn about applying materials in Chapter 8.

PERFORMING SURFACE ANALYSIS

AutoCAD allows you to analyze the surface continuity, curvature, and draft angles of surfaces using the surface analysis tools. You can also validate surfaces and curves before manufacturing using these tools. There are three types of surface analysis tools: **Zebra**, **Curvature**, and **Draft**.

Note that these tools work only in 3D visual styles. These tools are discussed in detail in the next section.

Zebra

Ribbon: Surface > Analysis > Analysis Zebra **Command:** ANALYSISZEBRA

The **Zebra** tool projects the zebra stripes on the selected model. This tool is used to visualize the curvature of surfaces and to determine if there are any surface discontinuities and inflections. To perform the **Zebra** analysis, invoke the **Zebra** tool from the **Analysis** panel of the **Surface** tab; you will be prompted to select the solid or surface on which you want to perform the analysis. Select the required surface and press ENTER; zebra strips will be displayed on the selected model. Figure 6-88 shows the zebra analysis performed on a binocular. The way these strips are aligned or curved on the model allows you to interpret the smoothness of the surfaces. This type of analysis is mostly used where one surface joins with the other surface.

You can also change the settings of zebra stripes as per your requirements. To do so, choose the **Analysis Options** button from the **Analysis** panel; the **Analysis Options** dialog box will be displayed, as shown in Figure 6-89. By default, the **Zebra** tab is chosen in the dialog box.

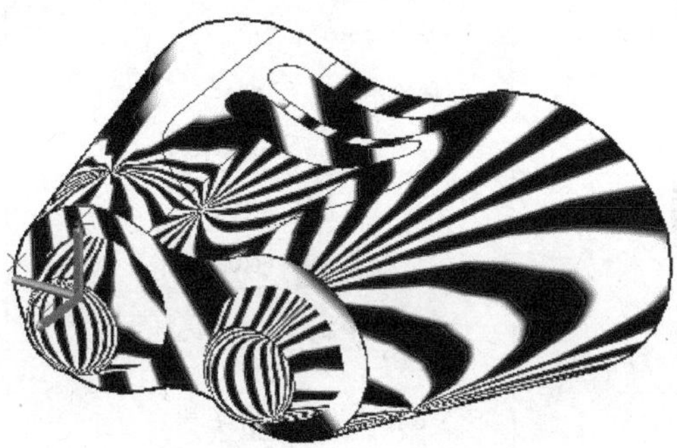

Figure 6-88 Zebra analysis performed

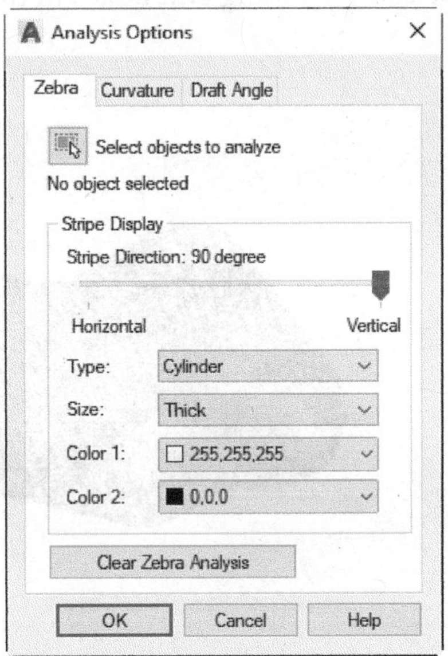

Figure 6-89 The ***Analysis Options*** *dialog box*

You can set the angle of stripes by using the slider available in the **Stripe Display** area of this dialog box. The value in the slider varies from 0 to 90. On setting 0, horizontal stripes are displayed on the model, whereas on setting 90, vertical stripes are displayed on the model. As you change the value on the slider bar, the zebra stripes will also change dynamically on screen. You can also set the type, color, and thickness of zebra strips in the **Stripe Display** area. Choose the **Clear Zebra Analysis** button in this dialog box to clear the zebra analysis. If you want to select objects for analysis, choose the **Select objects to analyze** button; the dialog box will disappear for a while, allowing you to select the objects from the screen.

Analysis Curvature

Ribbon: Surface > Analysis > Analysis Curvature **Command:** ANALYSISCURVATURE

The **Analysis Curvature** tool is used to display a color gradient or contours on the selected model. This color contour allows you to graphically visualize the radius of curvature of a model and evaluate the high and low areas of curvature. The contour also allows you to ensure that the model is within a certain range. The areas of high curvature or positive Gaussian value are displayed in red and the areas of low curvature or negative Gaussian value are displayed in blue. The mean curvature or a zero Gaussian value is displayed in red, which indicates a flat surface.

To perform the curvature analysis, choose the **Curvature** tool from the **Analysis** panel; you will be prompted to select the solid or surface on which you want to perform the analysis. Select the required objects and press ENTER; the color gradient will be displayed on the model. Figure 6-90 shows the curvature analysis performed on the binocular. You can change the settings for the curvature analysis by choosing the **Curvature** tab in the **Analysis Options** dialog box. Figure 6-91 shows the **Analysis Options** dialog box with the **Curvature** tab chosen. You can set the display style of curvature to **Gaussian**, **Mean**, **Max radius**, or **Min radius** using the **Display style** drop-down list in this dialog box. You can also set the minimum and maximum range in the corresponding edit boxes in the **Color Mapping** area of the dialog box.

Figure 6-90 Curvature analysis performed

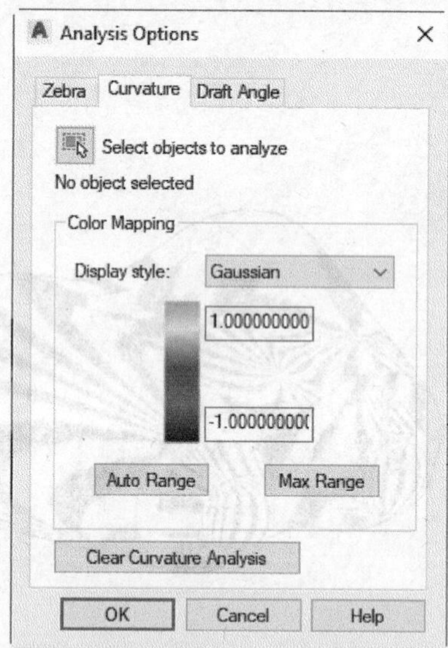

***Figure 6-91** The **Analysis Options** dialog box with the **Curvature** tab chosen*

To clear the curvature analysis, choose the **Clear Curvature Analysis** button in the **Analysis Options** dialog box.

Analysis Draft

Ribbon: Surface > Analysis > Analysis Draft **Command:** ANALYSISDRAFT

The **Analysis Draft** tool is used to visualize the draft applied on the selected model. If you are designing a model that can be cast, then this tool is used to check whether a part can be removed from a mold or die. Then, it calculates whether there is sufficient draft between the part and the mold, based on the pull direction. To perform the draft analysis, choose the **Draft** tool from the **Analysis** panel; you will be prompted to select the object on which you want to perform the analysis. Select the object and press ENTER; the draft analysis will be performed on the object. Figure 6-92 shows the draft analysis performed on the binocular.

Surface angles are defined with respect to the draft plane. The colors displayed on the model after performing the draft analysis will depend on the angles defined. You can set these colors by using the **Draft Angle** tab of the **Analysis Options** dialog box, refer to Figure 6-93. Choose the **Clear Draft Angle Analysis** button to clear the draft angle analysis.

Figure 6-92 Draft analysis performed

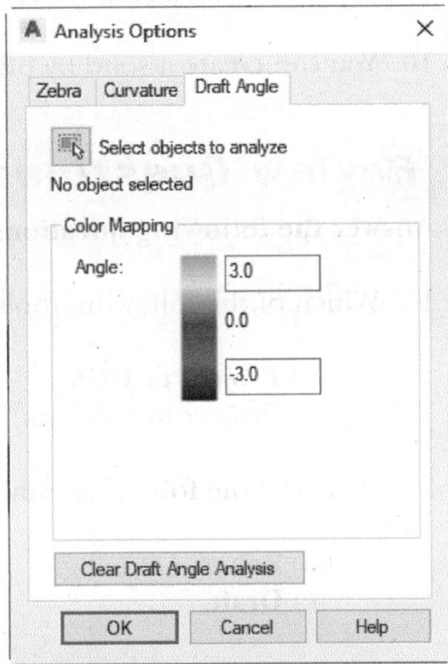

*Figure 6-93 The **Analysis Options** dialog box with the **Draft Angle** tab chosen*

Self-Evaluation Test

Answer the following questions and then compare them to those given at the end of this chapter:

1. Which of the following tools can be used to edit a surface?

(a) **Fillet** (b) **Trim**
(c) **Extend** (d) All of these

2. You can control the number of lines displayed in a Planar surface by using the ________ and ________ system variables.

3. To create procedural surfaces, the ________ button must be turned on.

4. Continuity can be set to ________, ________, or ________.

5. The ________ tool is used to fill the area formed between the open edges of a surface.

6. The ________ tool is used to create a 3D solid from a closed volume.

7. The ________ button is used to trim a surface when a geometry is projected on that surface.

8. You can create CVs and knots in curves using the **Spline** tool. (T/F)

9. You can create solids as well as surfaces using the **Extrude** tool. (T/F)

10. You can create a solid by offsetting a surface. (T/F)

Review Questions

Answer the following questions:

1. Which of the following tools can be used to project geometries on a surface?

   (a) **Project to UCS** (b) **Project to View**
   (c) **Project to 2 Points** (d) All of these

2. Which of the following analyses can be performed on a surface?

   (a) **Zebra** (b) **Curvature**
   (c) **Draft** (d) All of these

3. The ________ tool is used to create a surface between the elements forming a closed boundary.

4. To create a NURBS surface, the ________ button must be turned on.

5. The ________ defines the smoothness of the blend surface where it meets the other surfaces.

6. The bulge magnitude varies between ________ and ________.

7. In the **Extend** tool, the ________ and ________ options are available.

8. You can convert an existing surface into a NURBS surface using the ________ tool.

9. The ________ dialog box can be used to reconstruct the shape of a NURBS surface.

10. You can add, remove, or rebuild the CVs of the surfaces. (T/F)

Exercise 2 — Web Camera

In this exercise, you will create the model of a web camera, as shown in Figure 6-94. The reference dimensions for the model are given in Figure 6-95. Assume the missing dimensions.

Figure 6-94 Model of a web camera

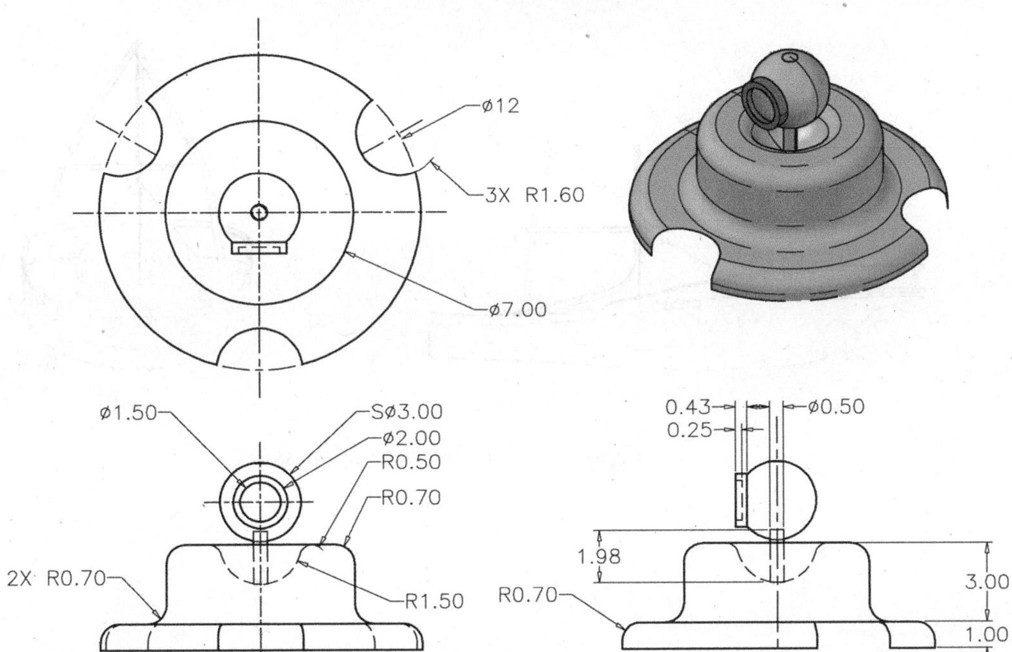

Figure 6-95 Orthographic views of the model for Exercise 2

Exercise 3 — Surface Tools

In this exercise, you will create the model of a ship, as shown in Figure 6-96. The other views of the ship are shown in Figure 6-97. Assume the dimensions.

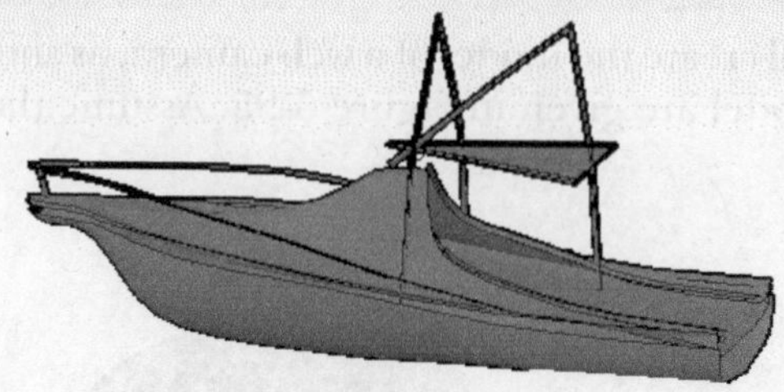

Figure 6-96 Model of a ship

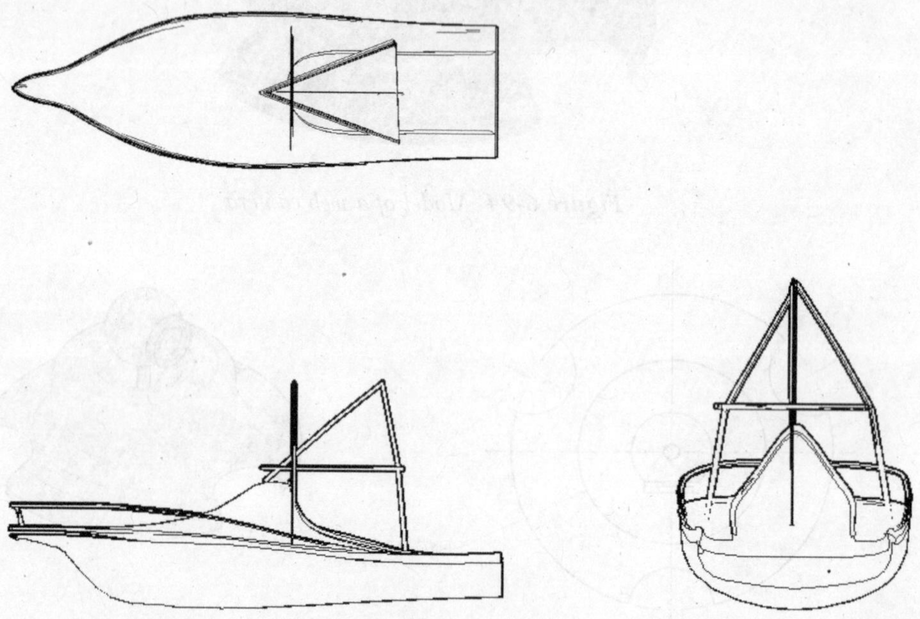

Figure 6-97 Other views of the ship

Answers to Self-Evaluation Test

1. d, **2. SURFU**, **SURFV**, **3. Surface Associativity**, **4.** G0, G1, G2, **5. Patch**, **6. Sculpt**, **7. Auto Trim**, **8.** T, **9.** T, **10.** T

Chapter 7

Mesh Modeling

Learning Objectives

After completing this chapter, you will be able to:

- *Create standard mesh primitives*
- *Create mesh surfaces*
- *Smoothen, refine, and crease mesh objects*
- *Edit mesh faces*
- *Convert mesh objects to solids and surfaces*
- *Work with gizmos*

Key Terms

- *MESH*
- *REVSURF*
- *EDGESURF*
- *RULESURF*
- *TABSURF*
- *Smooth Object*
- *Refine Mesh*
- *MESHCREASE*
- *Split Face*
- *MESHEXTRUDE*
- *Merge Face tool*
- *MESHCAP tool`*
- *MESHCOLLAPSE*
- *Spin Triangle Face*
- *CONVTOSOLID*
- *CONVTOSURFACE*
- *Move Gizmo*
- *Rotate Gizmo*
- *Scale Gizmo*

INTRODUCTION

A mesh model is similar to a solid model without mass and volume properties. The mesh modeling tools are available in the **3D Modeling** workspace. You can create mesh primitives as you create solid primitives and then create freeform designs from these mesh primitives. The mesh models are easily editable and can be smoothened to give a rounded effect. You can refine the meshes at required areas for precision. You can perform editing operations such as gizmo editing, extrusion on the mesh model, and so on to create freeform designs. Some of the important features of mesh modeling are that you can deform a mesh model using gizmos, add creases to sharpen the mesh model, split mesh faces to segment the meshes as required, and extrude mesh faces. You will learn all these techniques later in this chapter.

CREATING MESH PRIMITIVES

Mesh primitives are standard shapes that help you create complex models. These standard shapes include box, cone, cylinder, pyramid, sphere, wedge, and torus. You can create mesh primitives as you create solid models. By default, mesh primitives are not smooth. However, you can make these primitives smooth by adding smoothness to them. Note that as you smoothen the mesh, the model becomes complex and the system performance gets low. Therefore, you must perform the editing operations first and then smoothen the mesh to reduce the complexity of the model. The procedure for creating mesh primitives is given next.

Creating a Mesh Box

Ribbon: Mesh > Primitives > Mesh Primitives drop-down > Mesh Box
Command: Mesh

You can create a 3D mesh box similar to a solid or surface box. To do so, invoke the **Mesh Box** tool from the **Primitives** panel and follow the command sequence given next.

Specify first corner or [Center]: *Specify the first corner*
Specify other corner or [Cube/Length]: *Specify the diagonally opposite corner*
Specify height or [2Point] : *Specify the height of the mesh box*

After you specify the height of the mesh box, it will be created in the drawing area. Figure 7-1 shows the mesh box created.

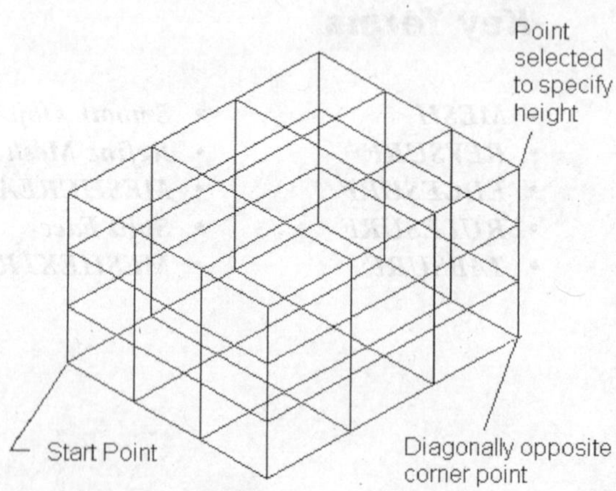

***Figure 7-1** The mesh box created*

You can create a mesh box in five ways using the above prompt. These ways are listed below:

1. Dynamically.
2. By first specifying the two corners of the rectangular base and then, the height of the box.
3. By first specifying the center, a corner of the box and then, the height of the box.
4. By specifying a corner and the length of the edge of cube.
5. By specifying the length, width, and height of the box.

The number of faces/divisions in a mesh box depend upon the values specified in the **Mesh Primitive Options** dialog box, refer to Figure 7-2. This dialog box can be invoked by clicking on the inclined arrow available in the **Primitives** panel of the **Mesh** tab. Specify the required values in the **Tessellation Divisions** rollout of this dialog box. Next, if you invoke the **Mesh Box** tool to create a new mesh, the model will be created based on the newly specified values. You can also change the appearance of the mesh by changing the level of smoothness of the model. Various areas of the **Mesh Primitive Options** dialog box are discussed next.

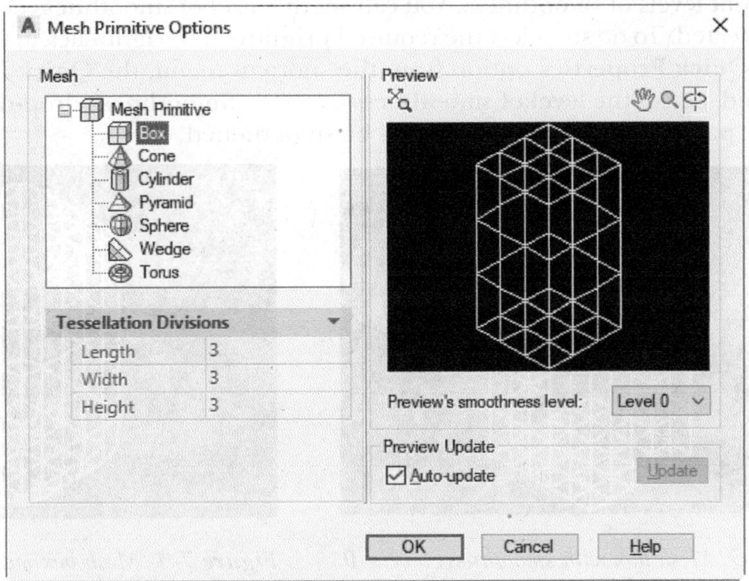

***Figure 7-2** The **Mesh Primitive Options** dialog box*

The Mesh Area

The **Mesh** area displays a list of mesh primitives and its corresponding parameters. You can select the required primitive from the **Mesh Primitive** list to control its appearance. The **Tessellation Divisions** rollout in this area displays the parameters of the selected primitive. You can edit the corresponding parameters to set the number of divisions on it. For example, if you choose **Cylinder** from the **Mesh Primitive** node in the **Mesh** area, the **Axis**, **Height**, and **Base** parameters will be available in the **Tessellation Divisions** rollout. Now, you can edit the number of faces along the axis, height, and base. Note that to create a mesh primitive with desired settings, first you need to set the values of the parameters and then create the mesh primitive.

The Preview Area

The **Preview** area displays the preview of the selected meshed primitive. The buttons in the **Preview** area are used to pan, zoom, or rotate the mesh primitive. To perform any of these operations, choose the respective button from the **Preview** area and then click on the preview screen. If you want the preview to be automatically updated according to the settings specified in the **Tessellation Divisions** rollout, select the **Auto-update** check box in the **Preview Update** area. Otherwise, choose the **Update** button to update the preview manually.

Note

*To change the visual style of the model in the **Preview** area, right-click and choose the required option from the **Visual Styles** menu.*

The **Preview's smoothness level** drop-down list in the **Preview** area is used to specify the level of smoothness of the mesh primitive. By default, **Level 0** is set in the drop-down list, which means, the mesh primitives created will not be smooth by default. Figures 7-3 to 7-5 show a mesh box with different levels of smoothness. You can set the level of smoothness even after the primitive has been created. To do so, select the required primitive and right-click in the display area. Next, select the **Quick Properties** option from the shortcut menu, the **Quick Properties** panel will be displayed. Select the level of smoothness from the **Smoothness** drop-down list in the **Quick Properties** panel; the mesh primitive will be smoothened.

Figure 7-3 *Mesh box with smoothness level=0*

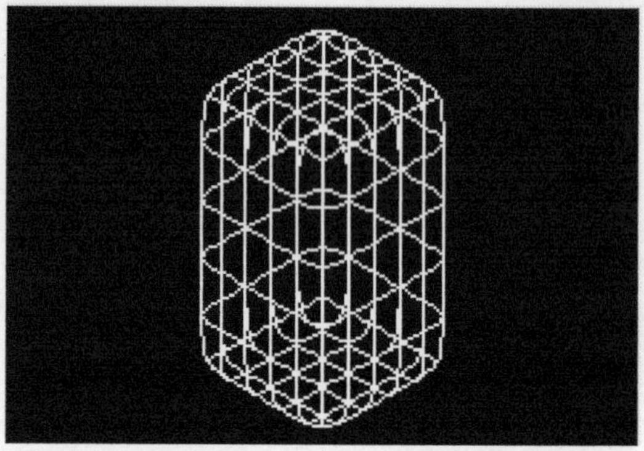

Figure 7-4 *Mesh box with smoothness level=2*

Like mesh box, the **MESH** command can also be used to create pointed or frustum mesh cones with circular or elliptical base, mesh cylinders with circular or elliptical base, mesh pyramids, mesh spheres, mesh wedges, and mesh torus. You can set the corresponding parameters of the mesh primitive in the **Mesh Primitive Options** dialog box. The procedure to create primitives is the same as that of solids.

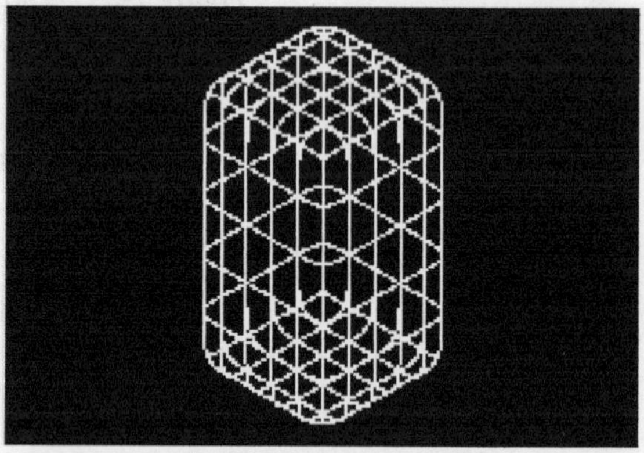

Figure 7-5 *Mesh box with smoothness level=4*

Note

*By default, the **Realistic** visual style is selected in the **Visual Styles** drop-down list of the **Visual Styles** panel in the Visualize tab. For clarity of printing, the visual style is set to **Wireframe**.*

CREATING SURFACE MESHES

Apart from creating basic mesh primitives, you can create various types of surface meshes. Surface meshes are created by filling the space between objects consisting of straight or curved edges. There are various types of surface meshes such as revolved surface, edge surface, ruled surface, and tabulated surface mesh. These surface meshes as well as the tools used to create them are discussed next.

Creating Revolved Surface Meshes

Ribbon: Mesh > Primitives > Modeling, Meshes, Revolved Surface
Command: REVSURF

In AutoCAD, you can create a revolved surface by choosing the **Modeling, Meshes, Revolved Surface** tool from the **Primitives** panel. A revolved surface is formed by revolving a path curve about the axis of rotation. You can select an open or a closed entity as the path curve. The direction of the revolution depends upon the side from which you select the revolution axis. Since it is not possible to define the clockwise and counterclockwise directions in 3D space, therefore, AutoCAD uses the right-hand thumb rule (refer to Chapter 2, Getting Started with 3D) to determine the direction of revolution. To create a revolved surface mesh, choose the **Modeling, Meshes, Revolved Surface** tool from the **Primitives** panel and follow the prompt sequence given next:

Select object to revolve: *Select the object to revolve around the axis*
Select object that defines the axis of revolution: *Select the axis of revolution*
Specify start angle <0>: *Specify the start angle to start the mesh at an offset from the profile curve*
Specify included angle (+=ccw, -=cw) <360>: *Specify the included angle that indicates the distance through which the profile curve will be swept*

Figure 7-6 shows a path curve and a revolution axis and Figure 7-7 shows the resultant revolved surface. You can specify the start angle and the included angle for the revolved surface as per your requirement, refer to Figures 7-8 and 7-9.

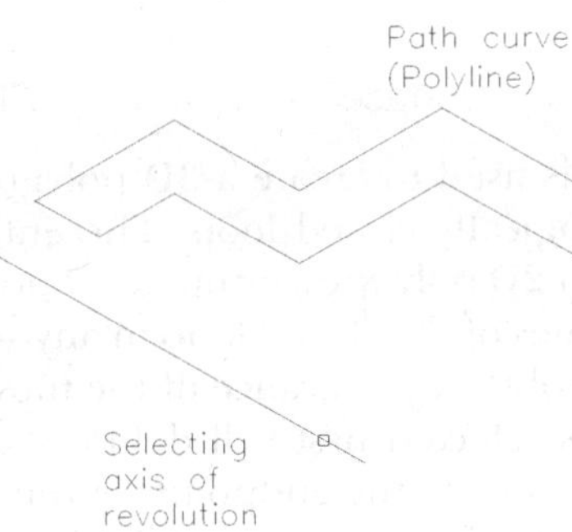

Figure 7-6 *The path curve and revolution axis*

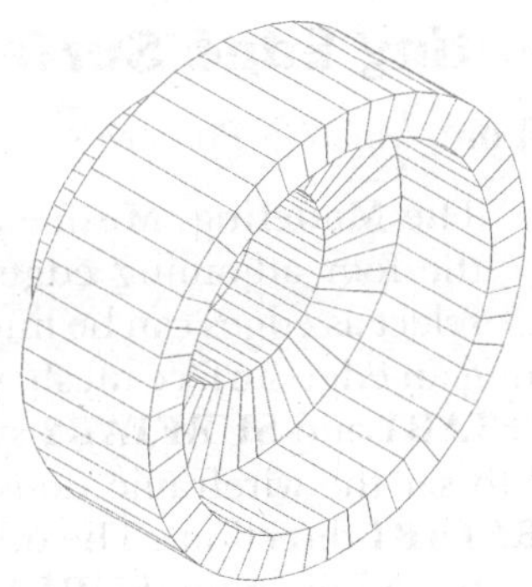

Figure 7-7 *The resultant revolved surface*

The smoothness of the revolved surface and the total number of lines that AutoCAD window will draw depend upon the value of the **SURFTAB1** system variable. AutoCAD draws tabulated lines in the direction of revolution. The number of tabulated lines is defined by the value of the **SURFTAB2** system variable, refer to Figure 7-10.

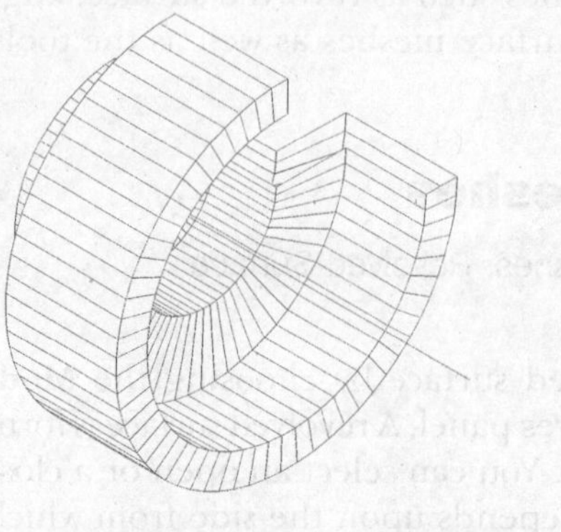

*Figure 7-8 Revolved surface created with the start angle **0** and included angle **270***

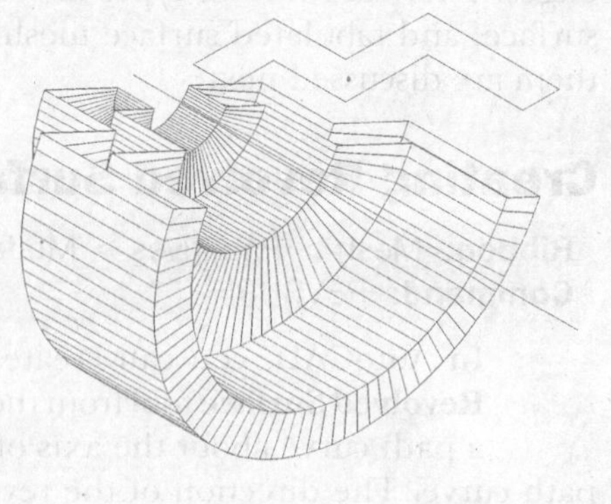

*Figure 7-9 Revolved surface created with the start angle **25** and included angle **180***

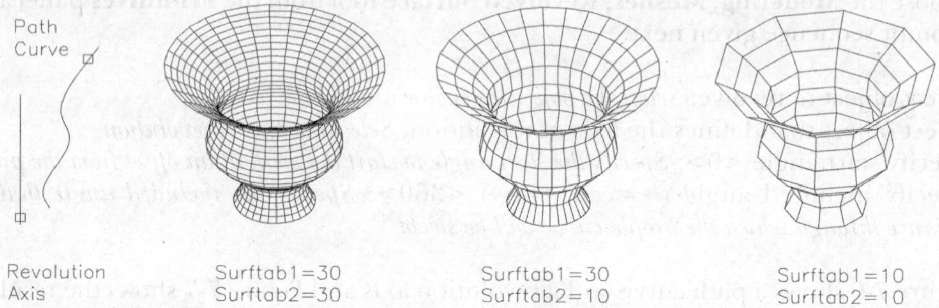

*Figure 7-10 Revolved surface created with different values of the **SURFTAB1** and **SURFTAB2** system variables*

Creating Edge Surface Meshes

Ribbon: Mesh > Primitives > Modeling, Meshes, Edge Surface **Command:** EDGESURF

The **Modeling, Meshes, Edge Surface** tool is used to create a 3D polygon mesh from the four adjoining edges that form a topologically closed loop. The entities that you select as edges can be lines, arcs, splines, open 2D polylines, or open 3D polylines. While creating an edge surface mesh, you can select the edges of the closed loop in any sequence. The **SURFTAB1** and **SURFTAB2** system variables control the appearance of the mesh and can be used to set the wireframe density. The edge that is selected first will define the M-direction (**SURFTAB1** direction). The other two edges that start from the endpoints of the first edge will define the N-direction (**SURFTAB2** direction), refer to Figures 7-11 and 7-12.

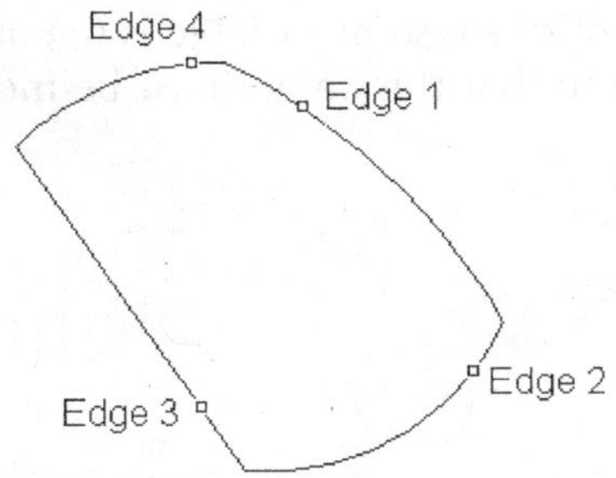

Figure 7-11 *Edges to be selected*

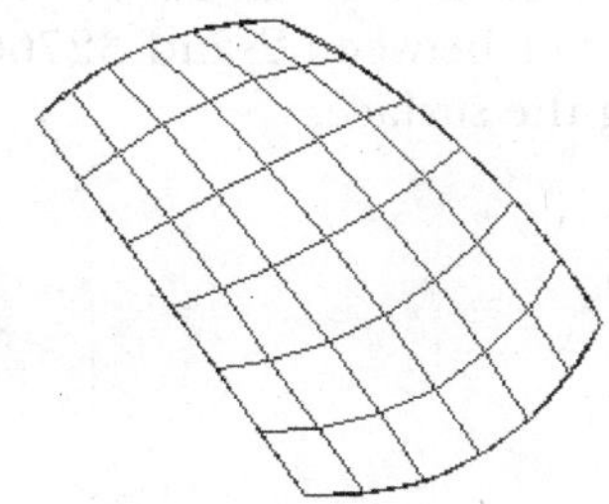

Figure 7-12 *An edge surface mesh created*

Creating Ruled Surface Meshes

Ribbon: Mesh > Primitives > Modeling, Meshes, Ruled Surface **Command:** RULESURF

You can create a ruled surface between two defined entities by choosing the **Modeling, Meshes, Ruled Surface** tool from the **Primitives** panel. The defined entities can be lines, circles, ellipses, arcs, polylines, curves, or splines. You can create a ruled surface mesh between two closed entities, two open entities, a point and a closed entity, and a point and an open entity. However, you cannot create a ruled surface between a closed and an open entity. Also, two points do not define a surface and therefore, a ruled surface cannot be created between them.

If the two defining entities are closed, the selection point does not make any difference in the resultant surface. In case of circles, the start point of the surface is determined by the combination of direction of the *X* axis and the current value of the **SNAPANG** system variable. In case of closed polylines, the ruled surface starts from the last vertex of the polyline and proceeds backward along the polyline segment.

If the two defined entities are open, the selection points do make a difference in the resultant surface. If you select open entities at the same end, a straight polygon mesh is created. If you select open entities at opposite ends, a self-intersecting polygon mesh is created, refer to Figures 7-13 and 7-14.

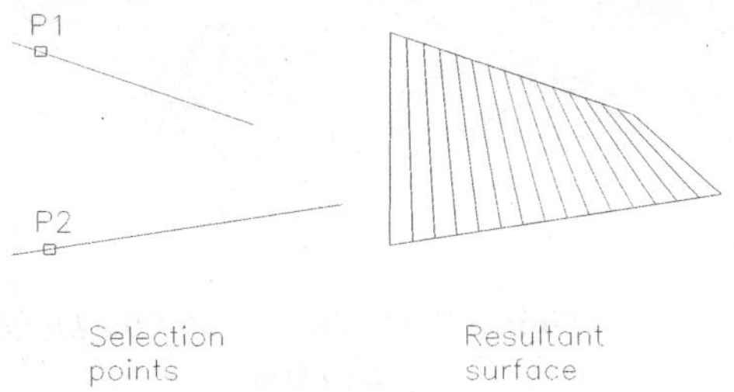

Figure 7-13 *Selecting objects at same ends and the resultant surface*

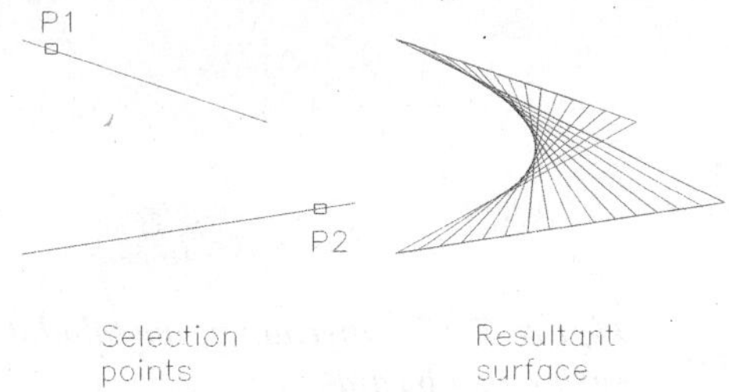

Figure 7-14 *Selecting objects at opposite ends and the resultant surface*

The smoothness of the ruled surface can be increased using the **SURFTAB1** system variable, refer to Figures 7-15 and 7-16. The default value of this system variable is 6, but it can accept any integer between 2 and 32766 as its value. Note that this value must be increased before creating the surface.

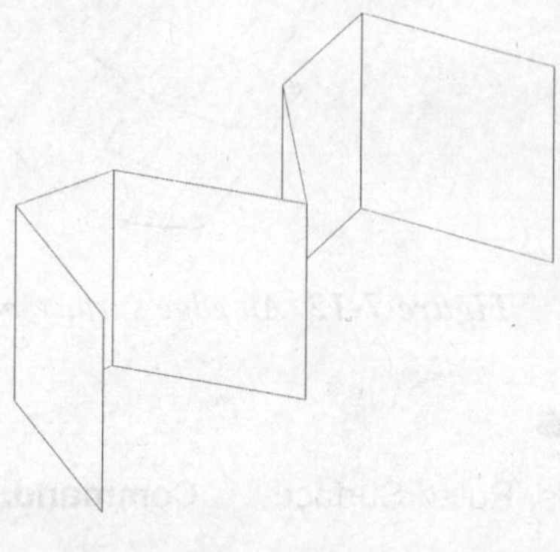

***Figure 7-15** The ruled surface created with 6 as the value of the **SURFTAB1** system variable*

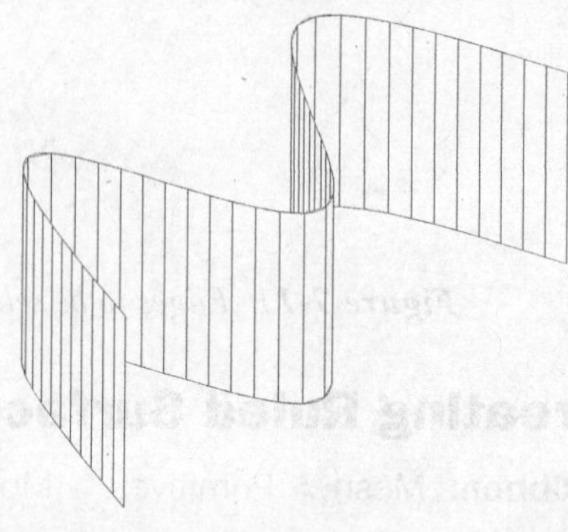

***Figure 7-16** The ruled surface created with 50 as the value of the **SURFTAB1** system variable*

Creating Tabulated Surface Meshes

Ribbon: Mesh > Primitives > Modeling, Meshes, Tabulated Surface **Command:** TABSURF

You can create a tabulated surface mesh by choosing **Modeling, Meshes, Tabulated Surface** from the **Primitives** panel. The tabulated surface mesh is formed when a profile is swept along the direction defined by the direction vector. The profile curves can be lines, circles, arcs, splines, 2D polylines, 3D polylines, or ellipses. The length of the tabulated surface will be equal to the length of the direction vector which in turn will be determined by the point selected for the direction vector, refer to Figures 7-17 and 7-18.

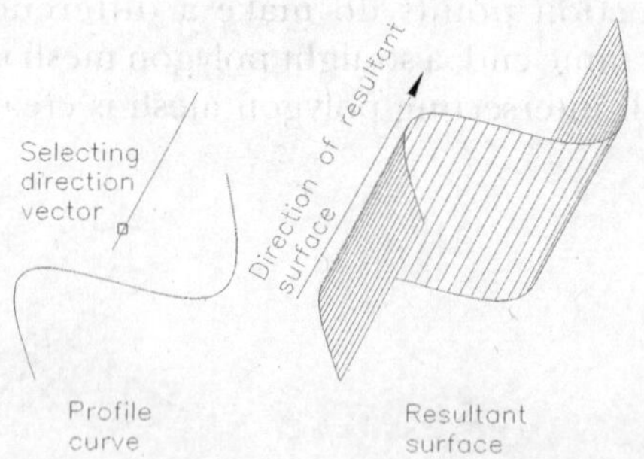

***Figure 7-17** Direction of the tabulated surface is upward*

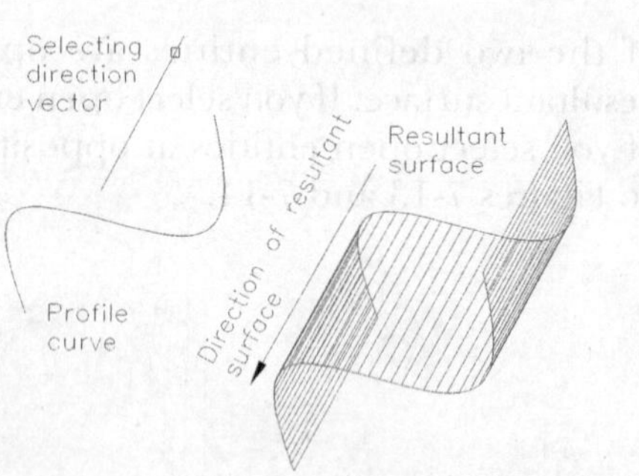

***Figure 7-18** Direction of the tabulated surface is downward*

If there are more than one direction vectors, all intermediate points will be ignored and an imaginary vector will be drawn between the first and last points on the polyline. The imaginary vector will be considered as the direction vector and the tabulated surface will be created along it, as shown in Figure 7-19.

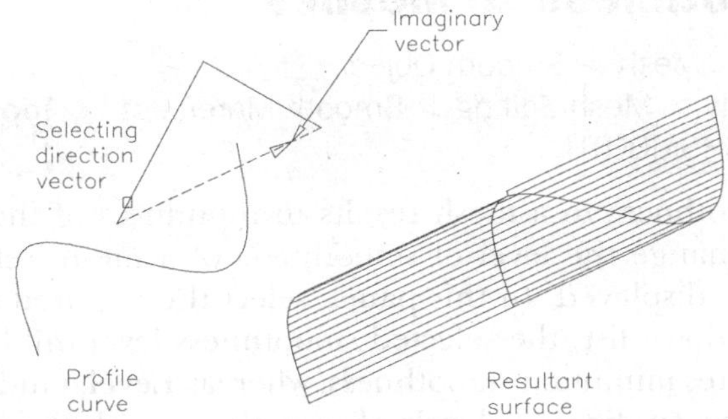

Figure 7-19 Tabulated surface created along the imaginary vector

Note

1. You cannot select a curved entity as the direction vector for defining the direction of the tabulated surface.

*2. You can increase the smoothness of the tabulated surface by increasing the value of the **SURFTAB1** system variable.*

*3. Apart from surface meshes, the **Modeling, Meshes, Revolved Surface, Edge Surface, Ruled Surface,** and **Tabulated Surface** commands can also be used to create surface models.*

Exercise 1 — Surfaces

In this exercise, you will create the model of a table, as shown in Figure 7-20, by using different types of surfaces. Assume the dimensions of the table.

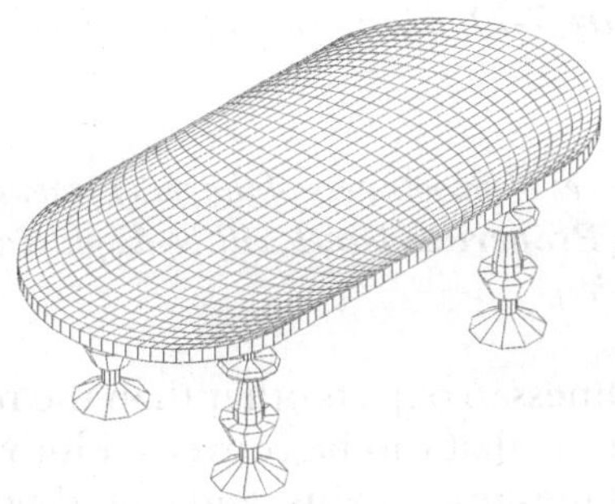

Figure 7-20 Model for Exercise 1

MODIFYING MESH OBJECTS

Mesh models can be modified to create freeform designs. This can be done by changing their smoothing levels, refining specific areas, adding creases to sharpen the edges, and so on. Various types of modifications that can be applied on meshes are discussed next.

Adding Smoothness to Meshes

Ribbon: Mesh > Mesh > Smooth Object
Menu Bar: Modify > Mesh Editing > Smooth More/Less **Toolbar:** Smooth Mesh
Command: MESHSMOOTH

Adding smoothness to a mesh results in roundness of the sharp edges of the meshed model. To change the level of smoothness of a mesh, select it; the **Quick Properties** panel will be displayed. In this panel, select the required level of smoothness from the **Smoothness** drop-down list; the selected smoothness level will be applied to the mesh. Note that **Level 0** indicates minimum smoothness, whereas **Level 4** indicates maximum smoothness. You can switch between different levels of smoothness with the help of the **Quick Properties** panel. Remember that the higher level of smoothness makes the mesh complex and thus, decreases the system performance. Figure 7-21 shows a mesh with different levels of smoothness applied to it. It is recommended that you first perform the required editing of the mesh and then apply smoothness to it.

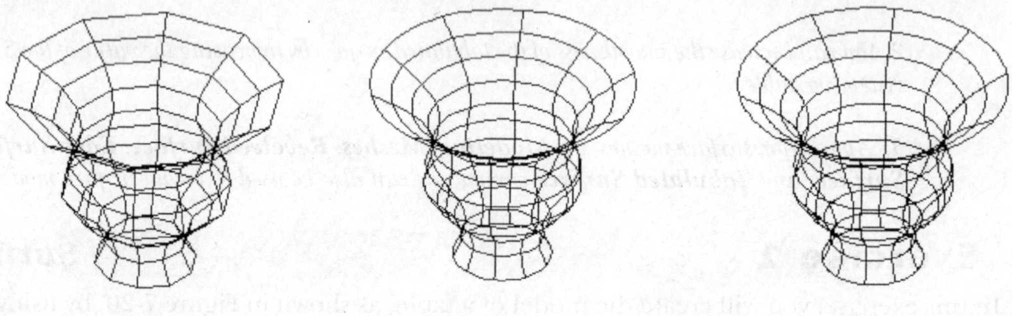

Figure 7-21 Mesh with different levels of smoothness

Note

You can also set the level of smoothness of the mesh from the ***Properties*** *palette. Also, on selecting an object, the* ***Quick Properties*** *panel will be displayed only if the* ***Quick Properties*** *button is enabled in the status bar.*

If you need to apply smoothness to objects other than the mesh objects, first convert the objects into mesh models. The objects that can be converted into mesh models include 3D solids, 3D surfaces, 3D faces, polygon meshes, regions, and closed polylines.

To convert an object into a mesh object, choose the **Smooth Object** tool from the **Mesh** panel; you will be prompted to select the object to convert. Select an object and press ENTER; the 3D object will be converted into a mesh object. Now, you can perform the editing operations such as smoothening, refining, splitting, and so on. Note that the smoothening operation works best for primitive solids. But if you select objects other than the primitive solids, a message box will be displayed, as shown in Figure 7-22. Choose **Create mesh** from the message box; the selected objects will be converted into mesh models with default parameters.

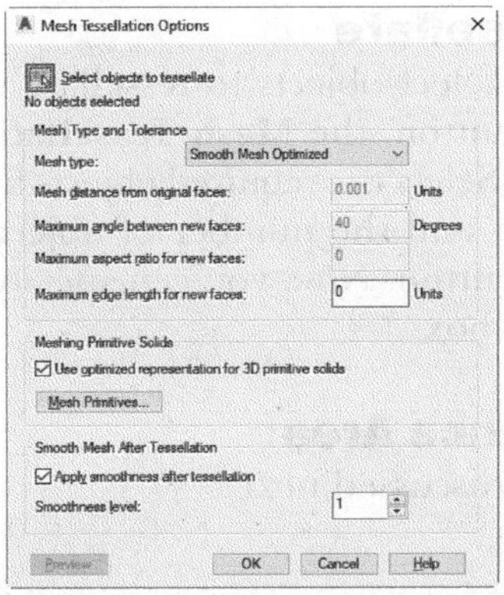

*Figure 7-22 The **Smooth Mesh - Non-primitive Objects Selected** message box*

However, you can modify the default parameters as per your requirement by invoking the **Mesh Tessellation Options** dialog box. To invoke this dialog box, click on the inclined arrow in the **Mesh** panel; the **Mesh Tessellation Options** dialog box will be displayed, as shown in Figure 7-23.

The options in this dialog box are discussed next.

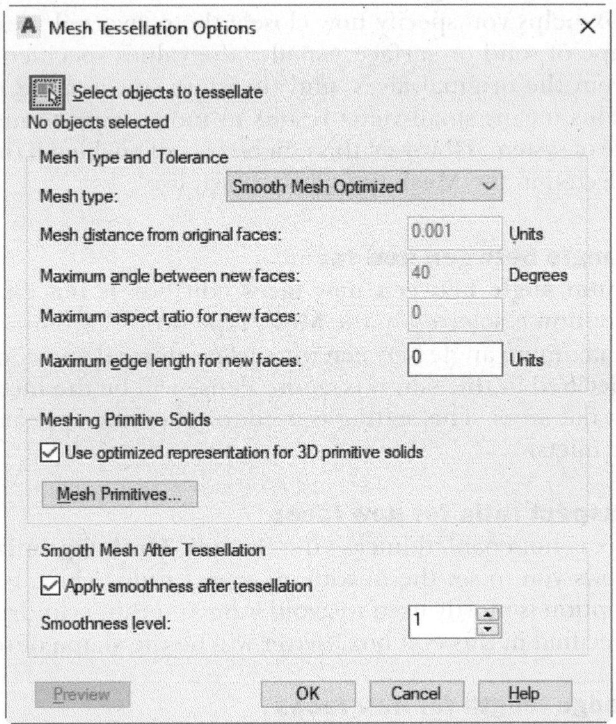

*Figure 7-23 The **Mesh Tessellation Options** dialog box*

Select objects to tessellate

This button enables you to select objects to tessellate while the **MESHOPTIONS** command is active. On choosing this button, the **Mesh Tessellation Options** dialog box will disappear allowing you to select objects. Select the required objects from the drawing area and press ENTER; the dialog box will reappear and the number of objects selected will be displayed below the **Select objects to tessellate** button. Now, you can specify the required parameters in the **Mesh Tessellation Options** dialog box.

Mesh Type and Tolerance Area

The options in this area are discussed next.

Mesh type

This drop-down list is used to specify the mesh type that you want to create. This drop-down list has three options: **Smooth Mesh Optimized**, **Mostly Quads**, and **Triangle**. By default, the **Smooth Mesh Optimized** option is selected and therefore, the shape of the mesh face will be the optimized mesh shape that can adapt to the shape of the mesh object. If you select the **Mostly Quads** option, the shape of the mesh face will be quadrilateral to its maximum possible, and if you select the **Triangle** option, the shape of the mesh face will be triangular to its maximum possible.

Mesh distance from original faces

This edit box helps you specify how closely the converted mesh object will adhere to the original shape of solid or surface. Smaller the values specified in this edit box, lesser the deviation from the original faces, and therefore, greater the number of faces created in the mesh. This means small value results in more accurate mesh objects but with slower performance of system. However, this edit box is not enabled if the **Smooth Mesh Optimized** option is selected in the **Mesh type** drop-down list

Maximum angle between new faces

The **Maximum angle between new faces** edit box is not enabled if the **Smooth Mesh Optimized** option is selected in the **Mesh type** drop-down list. This edit box allows you to specify the maximum angle between the surface normal and continuous mesh faces. Larger the value specified in this edit box, more dense will be the mesh at higher curvatures and less dense at flat areas. This setting is used to refine the appearance of the curved features like holes or fillets.

Maximum aspect ratio for new faces

This edit box is not enabled in case the **Smooth Mesh Optimized** option is selected. This edit box allows you to set the maximum aspect ratio, which is, height/width ratio of new faces. This option is mostly used to avoid long and thin cylindrical faces. Note that smaller the value specified in this edit box, better will be the shape of the mesh.

Maximum edge length for new faces

This edit box is used to set the maximum length of the edges of the mesh objects that are created by converting solids and surfaces. Smaller the value specified in this edit box, better will be the shape/appearance of the mesh.

Meshing Primitive Solids

The options in this area are discussed next.

Use optimized representation for 3D primitive solids

Select this check box to apply the mesh settings specified in the **Mesh Primitive Options** dialog box and clear this check box to apply the settings specified in the **Mesh Tessellation Options** dialog box.

Mesh Primitives

The **Mesh Primitives** button will be enabled only when the **Use optimized representation for 3D primitive solids** check box is selected. On choosing the **Mesh Primitives** button, the **Mesh Primitive Options** dialog box will be displayed where you can specify the required settings for the mesh object.

Smooth Mesh After Tessellation

This area will be active only when the **Smooth Mesh Optimized** option is selected in the **Mesh type** drop-down list. This is because the mesh objects converted on selecting any of the other two options from the drop-down list do not have any smoothness. The options in this area are discussed next.

Apply smoothness after tessellation

Select this check box to apply smoothness to newly created mesh objects.

Smoothness level

This spinner will be available only when the **Apply smoothness after tessellation** check box is selected and you can set the level of smoothness of the mesh object in it.

Preview

This button is available when the objects required to be converted into meshes are selected. You can choose this button to preview the effect of the current settings in the drawing area. To go back to the dialog box, press ESC or press ENTER to accept the mesh tessellation options.

Note

To increase the smoothness of mesh by one level, choose the ***Smooth More*** *button from the* ***Mesh*** *panel; the mesh will become more smooth (rounded). Similarly, if you choose the* ***Smooth Less*** *button, the smoothness of the mesh will be decreased by one level.*

Refining the Meshes

Ribbon: Mesh > Mesh > Refine Mesh
Menu Bar: Modify > Mesh Editing > Refine Mesh **Toolbar:** Smooth Mesh
Command: MESHREFINE

Refining the mesh means increasing the number of divisions in the mesh of an object, resulting in a dense mesh. You can refine the complete mesh object or a particular face of an object. Refining is mostly used for finer and detailed models, in which modification of small or refined divisions of the mesh is required. But remember that, denser the mesh, slower will be the performance of the system. To refine the mesh, choose the **Refine Mesh** tool from the **Mesh** panel; you will be prompted to select the mesh object or faces of the mesh object to refine. Select the entity and press ENTER; the selected entity will get refined. Note that the **Refine Mesh** tool works only when the smoothness option of the selected mesh object is set to Level 1 or higher. Also note that, as you refine the object, its level of smoothness becomes zero. To refine it again, you need to set the smoothness level to 1 or higher, and then follow the same procedure of refining. Figure 7-24 shows the mesh object before and after refinement.

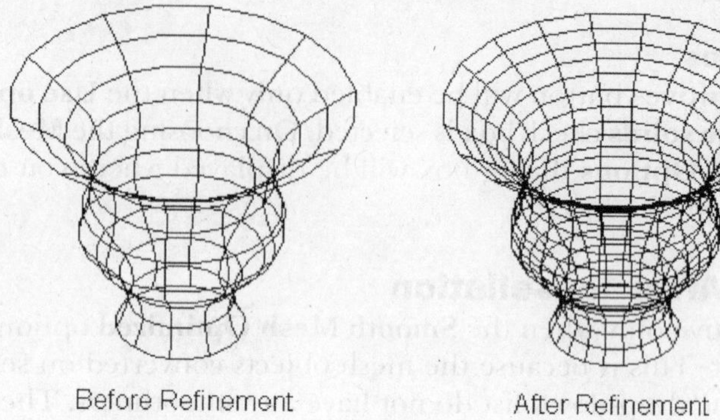

***Figure 7-24** Object before and after refinement*

To refine the faces of the selected mesh object, first you need to set the criteria for selecting faces. To do so, right-click anywhere on the screen, and then choose **Subobject Selection Filter > Face** from the menu displayed. Alternatively, choose **Face** from the **Subobject Selection filter** drop-down in the **Selection** panel of the **Solid** tab. After the selection criteria have been set, invoke the **Refine Mesh** tool. Next, you need to select a face of the mesh object. To do so, press CTRL and click on the required mesh face, and then press ENTER; the specified face will be subdivided into four faces, as shown in Figure 7-25.

Note that refining an object resets the smoothness level to 0, whereas refining face/s does not affect the smoothness level.

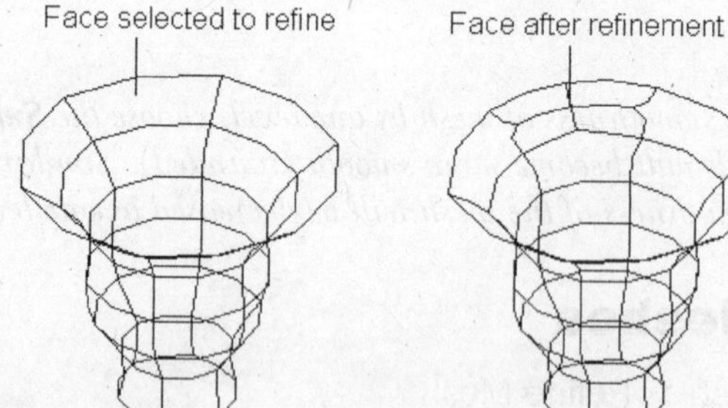

***Figure 7-25** Face before and after refinement*

Adding Crease to Meshes

Ribbon:	Mesh > Mesh > Add Crease	**Menu Bar:**	Modify > Mesh Editing > Crease
Toolbar:	Smooth Mesh	**Command:**	MESHCREASE

You can also modify a mesh object by adding creases to it. Creases are added to an object in order to sharpen the mesh sub-objects, thereby deforming the mesh object. You can sharpen the faces, edges, or vertices of a mesh object. To add crease to the selected mesh object, choose the **Add Crease** tool from the **Mesh** panel; you will be prompted to select the required mesh sub-objects. Select the mesh sub-objects and press ENTER; the **Specify crease value [Always] <Always>:** prompt will be displayed. By default, the crease is set to **Always** which means the crease will retain its sharpness even if you smoothen or refine the mesh object. You can also specify a crease value at which the crease will start losing its sharpness. The crease value set to **-1** is the same as the crease value set to **Always**. If you specify **0** as the crease value, the existing crease will be removed. On sharpening a sub-object, the edges adjoining the selected sub-object are updated according to the modified model. Figures 7-26 through 7-31 show the effect of adding crease on various sub-objects.

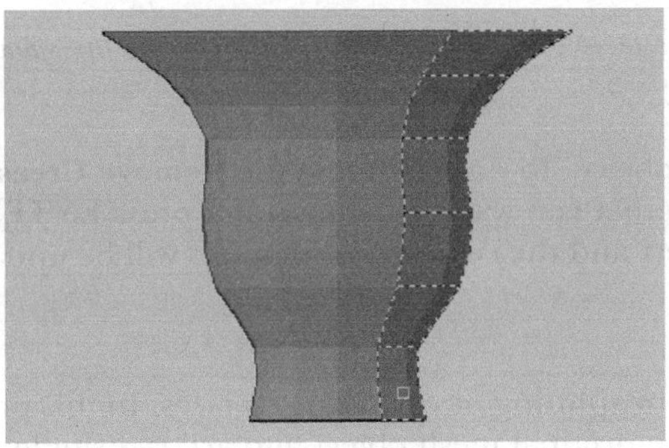

Figure 7-26 *Faces selected to be creased*

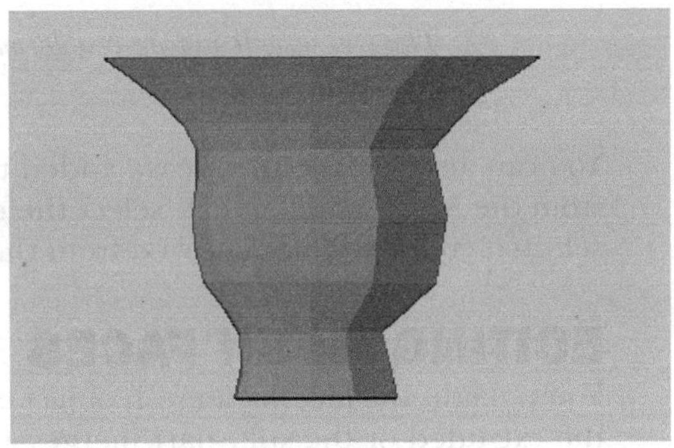

Figure 7-27 *Faces after adding crease*

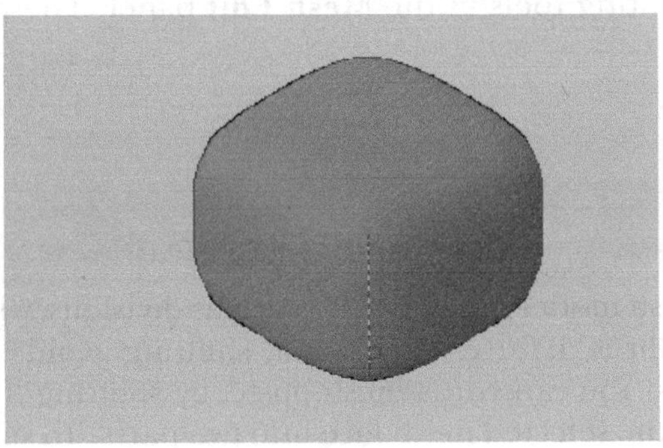

Figure 7-28 *Edge selected to be creased*

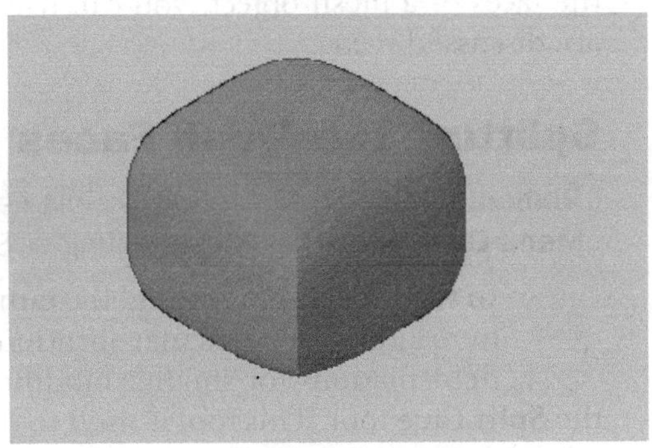

Figure 7-29 *Edge after adding crease*

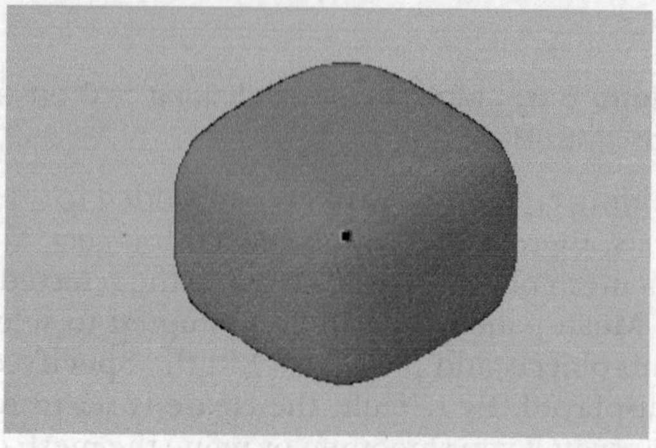

Figure 7-30 Vertex selected to be creased

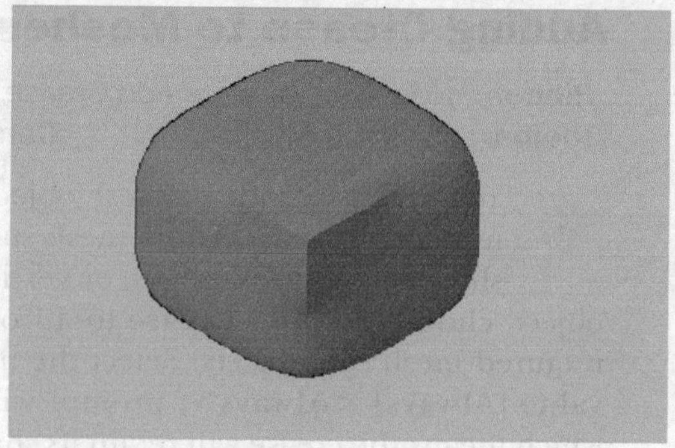

Figure 7-31 Vertex after adding crease

Note

*1. To select specific entities, right-click in the drawing area; a shortcut menu is displayed. Choose the desired sub-option of the **Subobject Selection Filter** option from this shortcut menu.*

2. The crease will not be visible when the level of smoothness is 0. So, increase the smoothness level to make it visible.

You can also remove the crease added to an object. To do so, choose the **Remove Crease** tool from the **Mesh** panel. Next, select the crease that you want to remove and press ENTER; the selected crease will be removed from the object and the corresponding faces will be updated.

EDITING MESH FACES

You can edit the faces of a mesh object either by splitting or extruding its faces. In this process, the extruded or the split part merges with the original mesh object and act as a single entity. The splitting and extruding operations are useful for detailed and advanced modeling. To edit the faces of a mesh object, you can use the editing tools in the **Mesh Edit** panel. These tools are discussed next.

Splitting the Mesh Faces

Ribbon: Mesh > Mesh Edit > Split Face
Menu Bar: Modify > Mesh Editing > Split Face **Command:** MESHSPLIT

In the process of refining, the entire mesh model gets split into various divisions, whereas in Splitting, a particular location of split is defined. As a result, splitting avoids larger deformations for smaller modifications. You can edit a mesh object by splitting it using the **Split Face** tool. This tool is used to divide the selected mesh face into two parts. To split the mesh, choose the **Split Face** tool from the **Mesh Edit** panel; you will be prompted to select the face of mesh to split. Select the face to split; a knife symbol will be displayed with the cursor and you will be prompted to specify the cut in the mesh. Now, specify the start and end points of the split line; the mesh will split along the line joining the specified points, and the adjoining faces will separate accordingly. Figure 7-32 shows the points selected for splitting the mesh face.

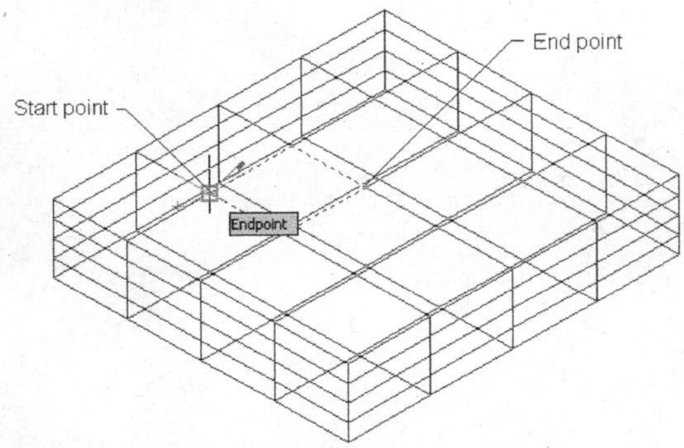

Figure 7-32 Points selected for splitting the mesh

Tip
In case of detailed modeling, it is advisable to first split the mesh faces and then refine the mesh model.

Extruding the Mesh Faces

Ribbon: Mesh > Mesh Edit > Extrude Face
Menu Bar: Modify > Mesh Editing > Extrude Face **Command:** MESHEXTRUDE

Extruding the mesh models is similar to extruding the 3D models. The only difference between the two processes is that in 3D modeling, the extruded part is created as a separate entity, whereas in mesh modeling, the extruded part merges with the mesh object and acts as a single entity. To extrude the mesh faces, choose the **Extrude Face** tool from the **Mesh Edit** panel; the Command sequence that will be displayed is given next.

Command: **MESHEXTRUDE**
Adjacent extruded faces set to: Join
Select mesh face(s) to extrude or [Setting]: *Select one or more faces to extrude*
Specify height of extrusion or [Direction/Path/Taper angle] <100>: *Specify the height of extrusion.*

You can control the extrusion style of multiple adjacent mesh faces. To do so, set the adjacent mesh faces to be extruded as a single unit or select each face separately. By default, the setting is **Join**. As a result, the adjacent faces are extruded as a single unit. If you want to change the setting to **Unjoin**, then press **S** when **Select mesh face(s) to extrude or [Setting]** prompt is displayed; you will be prompted to specify whether to join the adjacent mesh faces or not. Choose **No**; the extrusion style is set to **Unjoin**.

You can extrude the mesh faces dynamically. Alternatively you can do so by specifying height, by specifying the direction of extrusion, by specifying the path of extrusion, or by specifying an angle of taper for extrusion. All these options work in the same way as in the 3D modeling. Figure 7-33 shows a mesh model after splitting and Figure 7-34 shows a mesh box with extruded split faces. The splitting and extruding operations on mesh models result in creation of new designs.

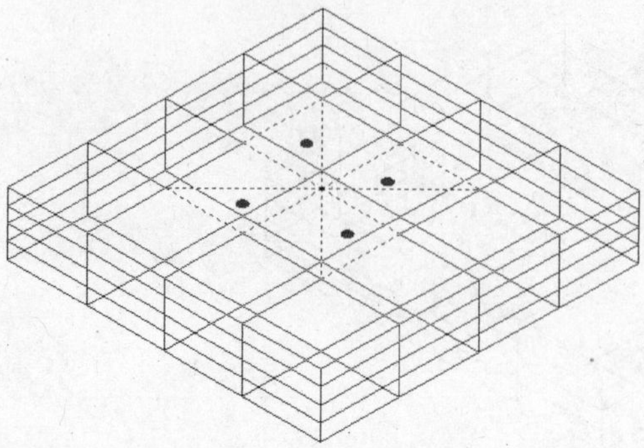

Figure 7-33 Mesh model after splitting

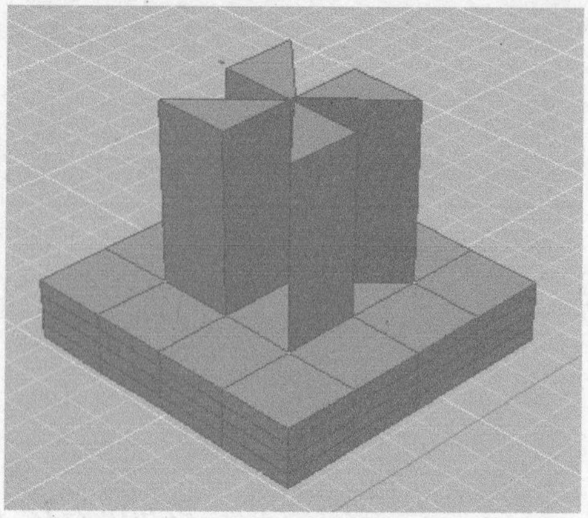

Figure 7-34 Mesh model with extruded split faces

> **Tip**
> *To select the faces that you want to extrude, click on the required faces of the mesh object. Continue till the selection is completed. To remove a face from the selection, press SHIFT + CTRL and click on the face to be deselected.*

Merging the Mesh Faces

Ribbon: Mesh > Mesh Edit > Merge Face
Menu Bar: Modify > Mesh Editing > Merge Face **Command:** MESHMERGE

Using the **Merge Face** tool, you can merge one or more faces adjacent to a face into a single face. To merge the faces, invoke the **Merge Face** tool from the **Mesh Edit** panel; you will be prompted to select the adjacent faces of the specified face. Select the required number of faces and press ENTER; the selected faces will be merged.

Closing the Gaps

Ribbon: Mesh > Mesh Edit > Close Hole
Menu Bar: Modify > Mesh Editing > Close Hole **Command:** MESHCAP

Sometimes, some gaps or holes are created due to open edges on the mesh object. You can fill these holes or gaps by selecting the edges surrounding the hole by using the **Close Hole** tool. To do so, invoke the **Close Hole** tool from the **Mesh Edit** panel; you will be prompted to select the connecting edges to form a mesh face. Select the edges and press ENTER; a new mesh face will be formed between the connecting edges. Figure 7-35 shows the edges connecting the hole and Figure 7-36 shows a cap created on the hole.

You can also form gaps in the mesh objects. To do so, you can remove the faces, edges, or vertices of the mesh object by pressing the DELETE key from the keyboard. You can also use the **Erase** tool to delete faces and form gaps. Note that on removing a face, only the selected face will be removed. However, on removing an edge, the adjacent face will also be removed and on removing a vertex, all the faces shared by the vertex will also be removed.

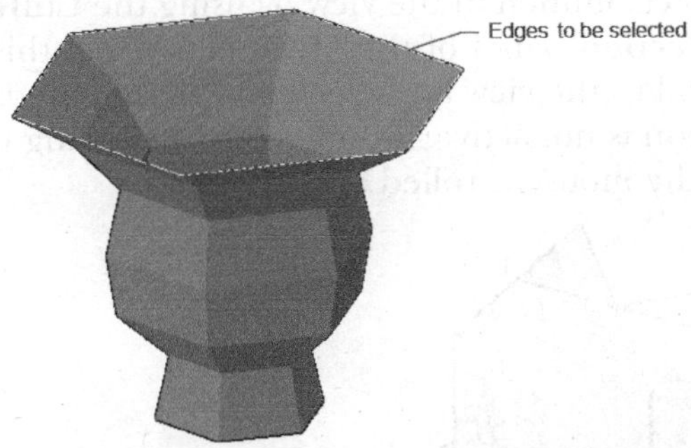

Figure 7-35 Edges connecting the hole

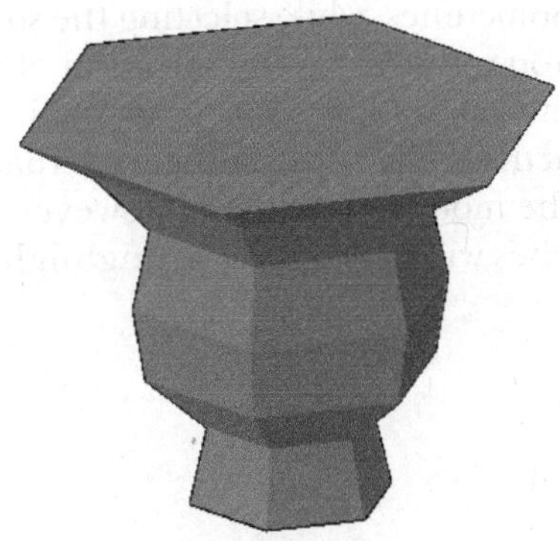

Figure 7-36 Cap created

Collapsing the Mesh Vertices

Ribbon: Mesh > Mesh Edit > Collapse Face or Edge
Menu Bar: Modify > Mesh Editing > Collapse Face or Edge **Command:** MESHCOLLAPSE

The **Collapse Face or Edge** tool is used to converge the vertices of surrounding mesh faces to the center of the selected edge or face. To do so, invoke this tool from the **Mesh Edit** panel; you will be prompted to select the mesh face or edge to collapse. Select a mesh face or an edge; the vertices of the selected mesh face will be merged. Also, the adjacent faces will be updated based on the removed vertices. Figure 7-37 shows the model after collapsing the top face of the model shown in Figure 7-36.

Figure 7-37 The top face collapsed

Spinning the Edges of Triangular Faces

Ribbon: Mesh > Mesh Edit > Spin Triangle Face
Menu Bar: Modify > Mesh Editing > Spin Triangle Face **Command:** MESHSPIN

You can rotate the edge that is shared by two triangular mesh faces. To do so, invoke the Spin Triangle Face tool from the Mesh Edit panel; you will be prompted to select the triangular mesh faces adjacent to each other. Select the mesh faces; the edge shared by the two triangular mesh faces spins to connect the opposite vertices. For example, Figure 7-38 shows the model after spinning the triangular faces of the model.

Sometimes, while selecting the subobjects of a meshmodel, the hidden subobjects also get selected. You can control the selection of the subobjects hidden in the view by using the **Culling Object** button. This button is available in the **Selection** panel of the **Mesh** tab. When this button is active, only those subobjects that are normal to the view are selected or highlighted on rolling the mouse over them. However, if this button is not active, all subobjects including the hidden ones will be selected or highlighted when the mouse is rolled over them.

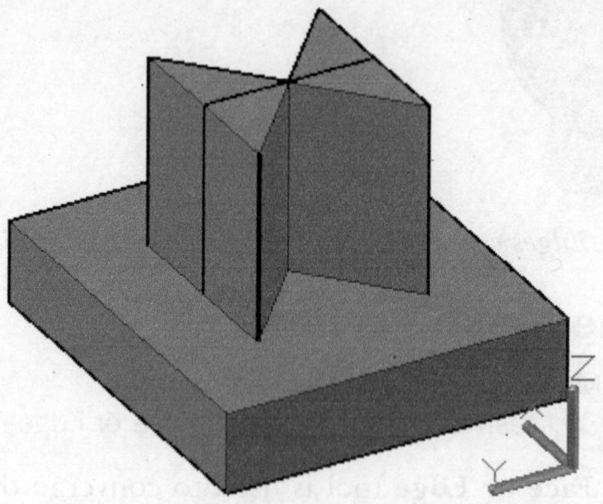

***Figure 7-38** Model after spinning*

Example 1 — *Mesh Edit Tools*

In this example, you will create a flash drive having dimensions = 50 X 18 X 8, as shown in Figure 7-39. The dimensions of the model are shown in Figure 7-39(a).

***Figure 7-39** Flash drive*

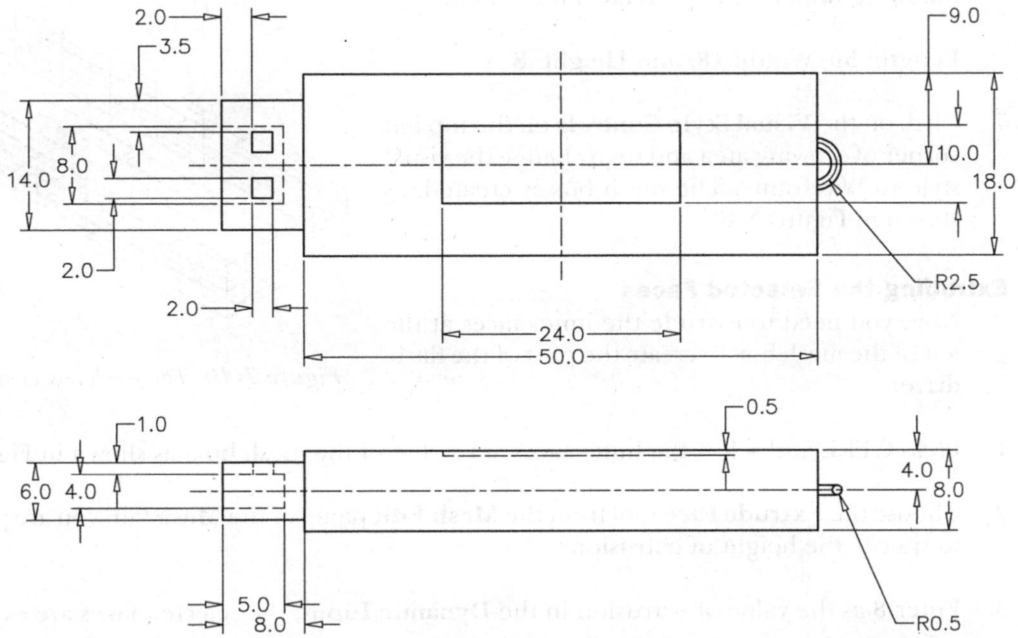

Figure 7-39(a) Orthographic views and dimensions of the Flash drive

Creating a Mesh Box

To create a mesh box, first you need to specify the parameters of the tessellation divisions on the mesh box.

1. Start a new *acad3D.dwt* file in the **3D Modeling** workspace.

2. Invoke the **Mesh Primitive Options** dialog box by clicking on the inclined arrow displayed at the lower right corner of the **Primitives** panel in the **Mesh** tab.

3. Select the **Box** option from the **Mesh Primitive** list box and set the following tessellation divisions: Length: **7**, Width: **7**, and Height: **7**. Choose the **OK** button from the **Mesh Primitive Options** dialog box to accept the settings and close the dialog box.

4. Choose the **Mesh Box** tool from **Mesh > Primitives > Mesh Primitives** drop-down; you are prompted to specify the first corner point.

5. Turn on the Ortho mode and specify the start point of the mesh box by clicking at the desired location in the drawing area; the **Specify other corner or [Cube/Length]** prompt is displayed.

6. Enter **L** at the Command prompt and specify the following dimensions to create a mesh box:

   Length: **50**, Width: **18**, and Height: **8**

7. Click on the **Visual Style Controls** on the top left corner of drawing area and then change the visual style to Wireframe. The mesh box is created, as shown in Figure 7-40.

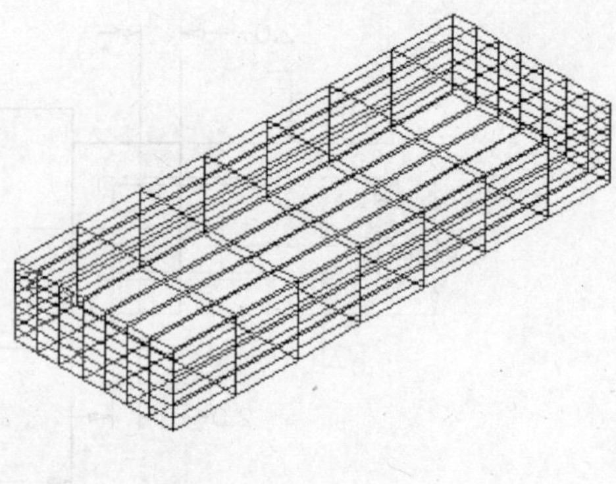

***Figure 7-40** The mesh box created*

Extruding the Selected Faces

Now, you need to extrude the inner faces at the left of the mesh box to create the port of the flash drive.

1. Press CTRL and select the inner faces at the left of the mesh box, as shown in Figure 7-41.

2. Choose the **Extrude Face** tool from the **Mesh Edit** panel of the **Mesh** tab; you are prompted to specify the height of extrusion.

3. Enter **8** as the value of extrusion in the **Dynamic Input**; the selected faces are extruded.

   The final extruded model after changing the visual style is shown in Figure 7-42.

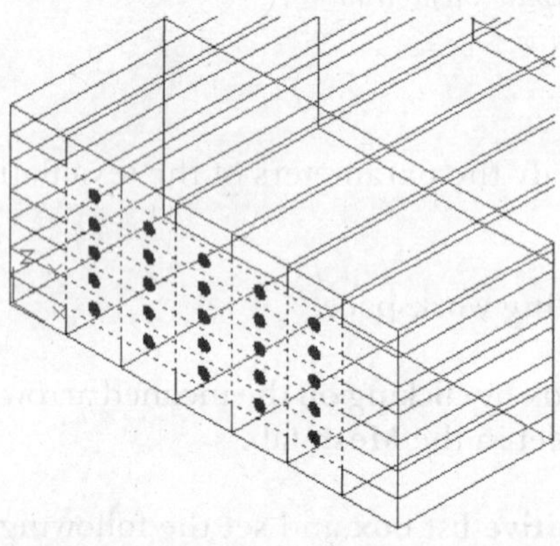

***Figure 7-41** Faces selected to extrude*

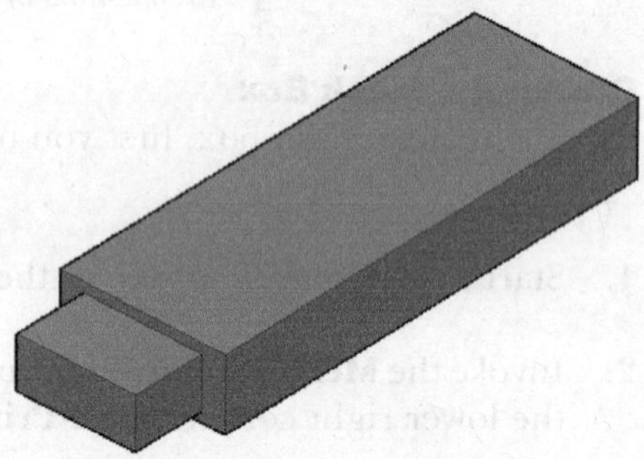

***Figure 7-42** The model after extruding*

Creating a Cut in the Port

To create a cut in the port, you need to extrude the inner faces of the port in negative direction.

1. Choose the **Extrude Face** tool from the **Mesh Edit** panel and then select the inner faces on the left of the port to create a cut, as shown in Figure 7-43.

2. Enter **-5** in the edit box displayed in the drawing area to specify the height of extrusion. Note that the negative value will extrude the inner faces inward, thereby creating a cut.

Next, you need to create a cut on the top of the port. But before creating the cut, you need to split the top mesh faces to the size of the cut.

3. Choose the **Split Face** tool from the **Mesh Edit** panel and select the second mesh face on the top of the port; you are prompted to select the first split point on the selected face.

4. Specify the first split point on the mesh face at a distance of 2 units from the outer end by using the **From** snap. Then, specify the second split point using the **Perpendicular** snap; one split line is created on it.

5. Create the other split line at a distance of 2 units from the first split line, refer to Figure 7-44.

6. Create another split on the fourth face at the top of the port, refer to Figure 7-44.

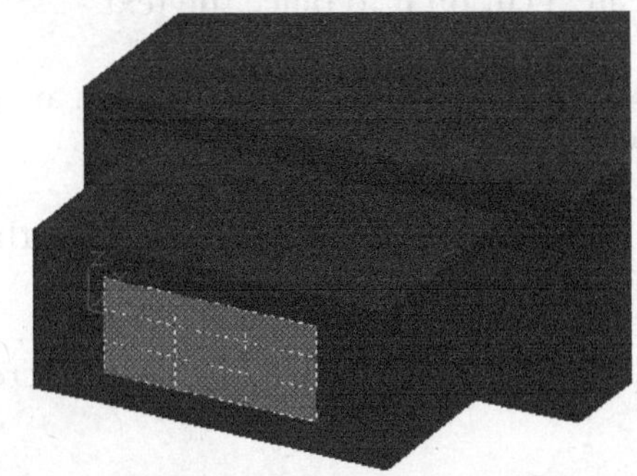

Figure 7-43 *Mesh faces selected to create a cut*

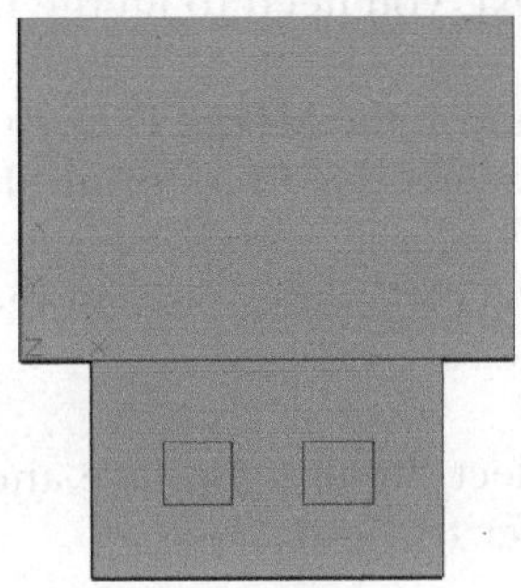

Figure 7-44 *Model after splitting faces*

7. Next, you need to create a cut at the top. Select the new mesh faces created by splitting and extrude them downward upto the inner face so that the model looks like Figure 7-45.

Creating a Loop

Next, you need to create a loop of torus shape which can be used for hanging the flash drive.

1. Invoke the **Mesh Primitive Options** dialog box and change the tessellation division of torus as follows:

   Radius: **30** Sweep path: **30**

2. To create a loop, you need to create a torus of radius 2.50 and tube radius 0.5.

3. Place the torus at the end of the flash drive, as shown in Figure 7-46.

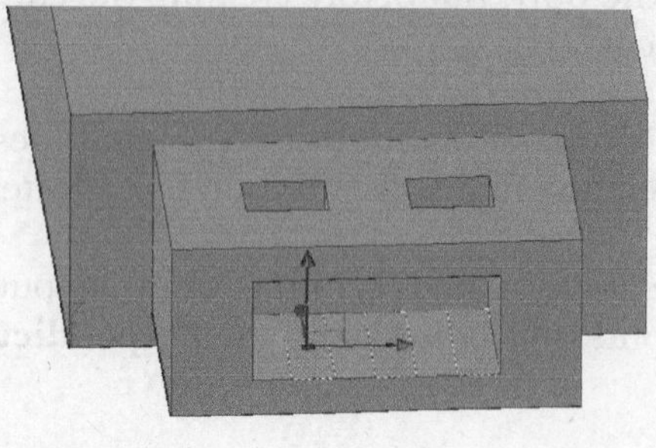

Figure 7-45 *Mesh faces selected to create a cut*

Figure 7-46 *Model after adding a loop*

Merging Faces

Next, you need to merge faces and then create a cut on it to place the text.

1. Choose the **Merge Face** tool from the **Mesh Edit** panel of the **Mesh** tab; you are prompted to select the adjacent mesh faces on the model.

2. Select the inner faces of the mesh, as shown in Figure 7-47, and press ENTER; the selected faces are merged.

3. Select the merged face and extrude it to 0.5 unit along negative direction to create a cut, refer to Figure 7-48.

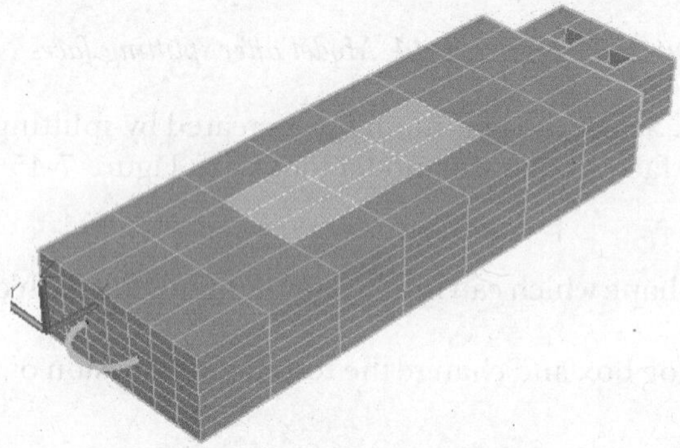

Figure 7-47 *Faces selected to be merged*

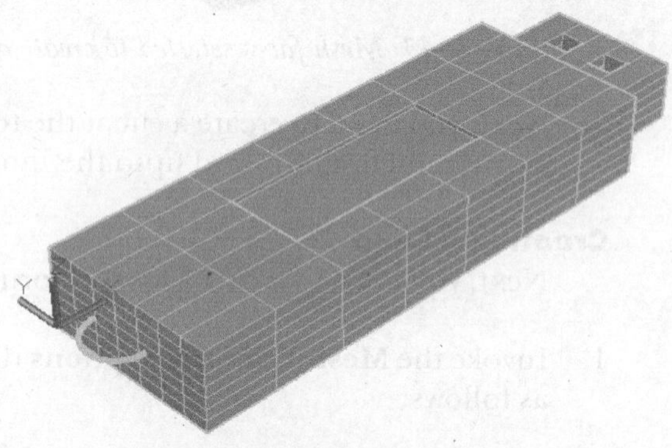

Figure 7-48 *Model after extruding the merged face*

4. Choose **Smooth More** from the **Mesh** panel of the **Mesh** tab; you are prompted to select the objects to be smoothened.

5. Select the mesh object and press ENTER; the entire model gets smoothened.

   As the port and the cut created cannot be smoothened, therefore, you need to sharpen them.

6. Choose the **Add Crease** tool from the **Mesh** panel; you are prompted to select the mesh subobjects to add crease.

7. Select the mesh objects, as shown in Figure 7-49, and press ENTER; you are prompted to specify the crease value. Press ENTER to retain the sharpness of the selected mesh object; the crease is applied to the selected edges, refer to Figure 7-50.

8. Similarly, select the subobjects to be sharpened such that the final model created looks similar to Figure 7-50.

Figure 7-49 *Mesh faces selected to add crease*

Figure 7-50 *The final model after adding crease to the required entities*

CONVERTING MESH OBJECTS

You have already learned that 3D solids and surfaces can be converted into mesh objects using the **Smooth Object** tool so that they can be smoothened, refined, creased, and so on. Now, you will learn how to convert mesh objects into 3D solids or surfaces so that you can perform the solid modeling techniques such as union, subtraction, intersection, on them. Also, you can specify the settings such that the mesh objects converted into 3D solids or surfaces are smooth or faceted, or have merged faces.

Converting Mesh Objects into Solids

Ribbon: Mesh > Convert Mesh > Convert to Solid
Menu Bar: Modify > 3D Operations > Convert to Solid **Command:** CONVTOSOLID

To convert a mesh object into solid, choose the **Convert to Solid** tool from the **Convert Mesh** panel; you will be prompted to select a mesh object. Select the required mesh object and press ENTER; the selected mesh object will be converted into a solid with default settings. To convert a mesh object into a solid with the user-defined settings, you need to specify the new settings before the conversion. You can also specify whether the converted solid will be smooth or faceted, or have merged faces.

Note

Other than the meshes, the closed polygons and circles with thickness, as well as the 3D surfaces can also be converted into solids. However, the objects like exploded solids, separate and continuous edges forming a surface, separate and continuous surfaces forming volumes, meshewith gaps between faces, and meshes with intersecting boundaries cannot be converted into solids.

To specify pre-defined settings for the solids that will be created from meshes, choose **Smooth, optimized** from the **Smooth Mesh Convert** drop-down, refer to Figure 7-51. The different tools in this drop-down are discussed next.

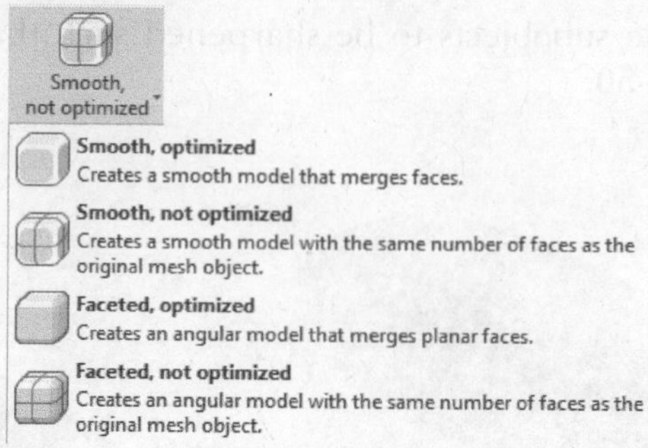

***Figure 7-51** The **Smooth Mesh Convert** drop-down*

Smooth, optimized

On choosing this tool, all tessellations of the mesh in the same plane will be merged into a single face in the solid. Also, the edges of the solid model will be rounded. Figure 7-52 shows a mesh box and Figure 7-53 shows the solid created from the mesh box on choosing the **Smooth, optimized** option.

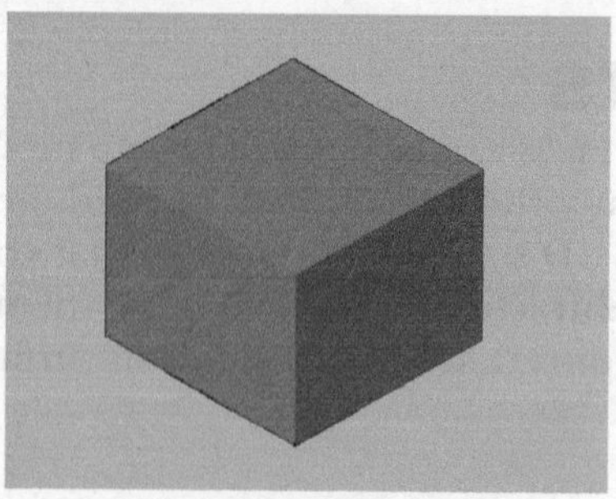

***Figure 7-52** A mesh box*

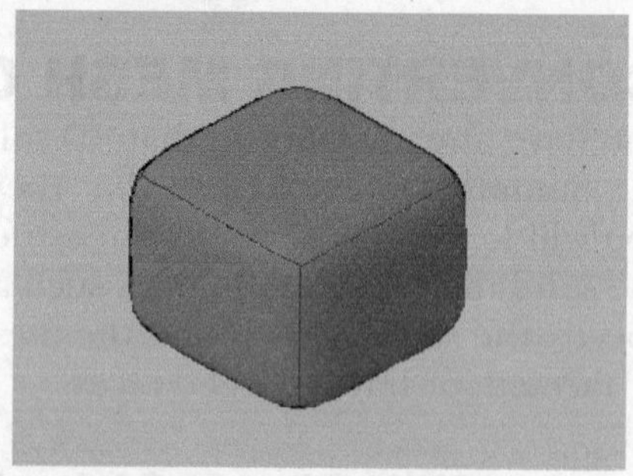

***Figure 7-53** The solid created on choosing the **Smooth, optimized** option*

Smooth, not optimized

On choosing this tool, the edges of the mesh will be rounded when the mesh is converted to solid, but the resulting faces will not be merged, and will remain the same as in the mesh object, as shown in Figure 7-54.

Faceted, optimized

On choosing this tool, all tessellations of the mesh in the same plane will be merged into a single face in the solid. Also, the edges in the resulting solid will not be rounded, but creased, as shown in Figure 7-55.

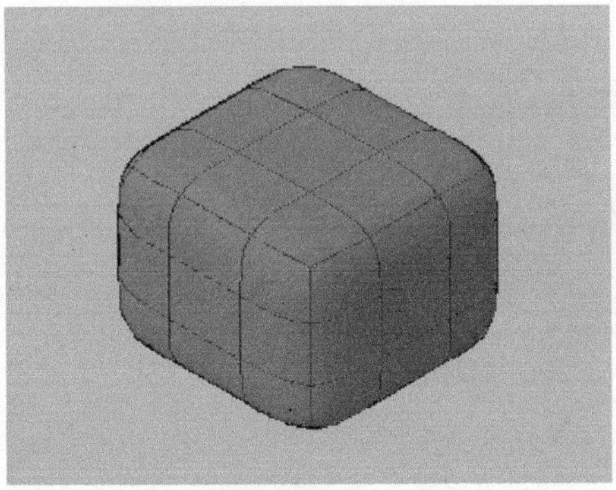

*Figure 7-54 The solid created on choosing the **Smooth, not optimized** tool*

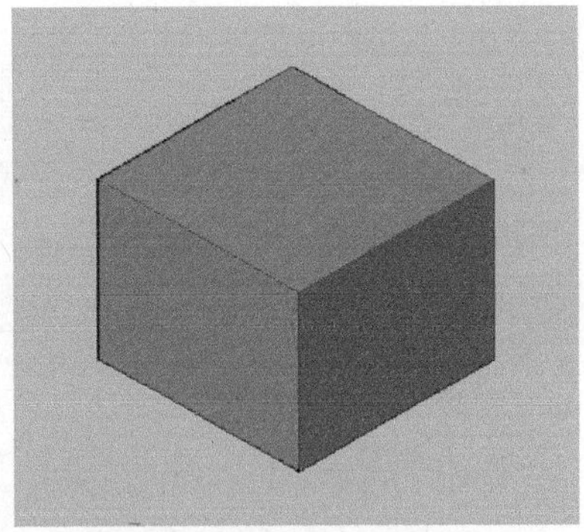

*Figure 7-55 The solid created on choosing the **Faceted, optimized** tool*

Faceted, not optimized

On choosing this tool, the faces of the converted solid will not be merged and the edges will not be rounded, as shown in Figure 7-56.

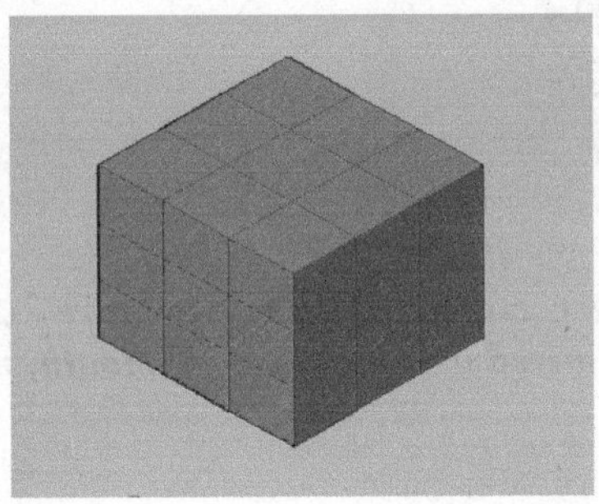

*Figure 7-56 The solid created on choosing the **Faceted, not optimized** tool*

Converting Mesh Objects into Surfaces

Ribbon: Mesh > Convert Mesh > Convert to Surface
Menu Bar: Modify > 3D Operations > Convert to Surface **Command:** CONVTOSURFACE

Like converting a mesh object into solid, you can also convert a mesh object into a surface. To do so, choose the **Convert to Surface** tool from the **Convert Mesh** panel; you will be prompted to select a mesh object. Select the required mesh object; the mesh object will be converted into a surface with default settings. You can change the default settings of the surface created as you did with solids. Figure 7-57 shows a mesh object and Figures 7-58 through Figure 7-61 show the surfaces created on applying different settings on this object.

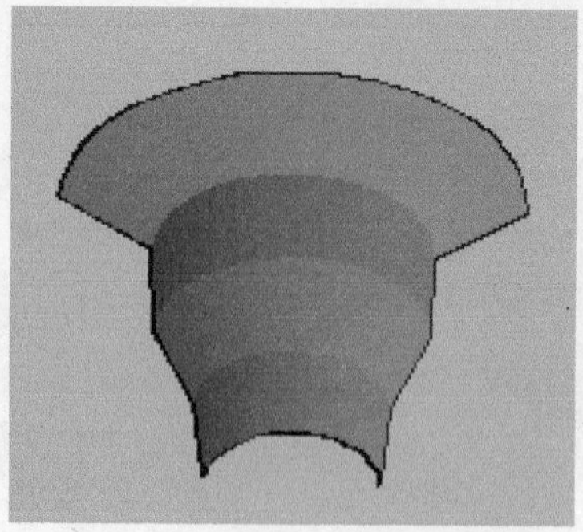

Figure 7-57 *A mesh object*

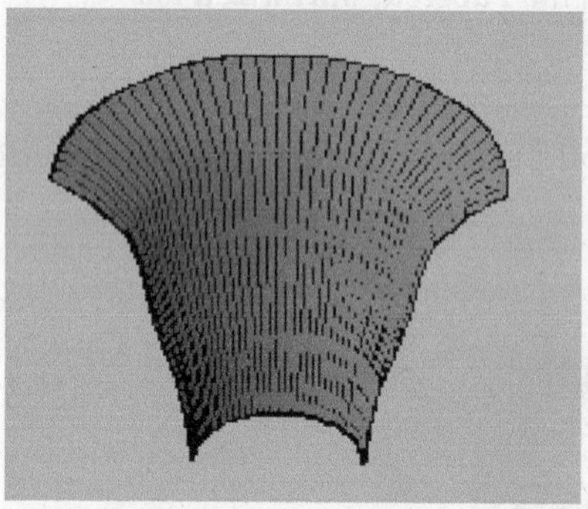

Figure 7-58 *The surface created on choosing the* ***Smooth, optimized*** *tool*

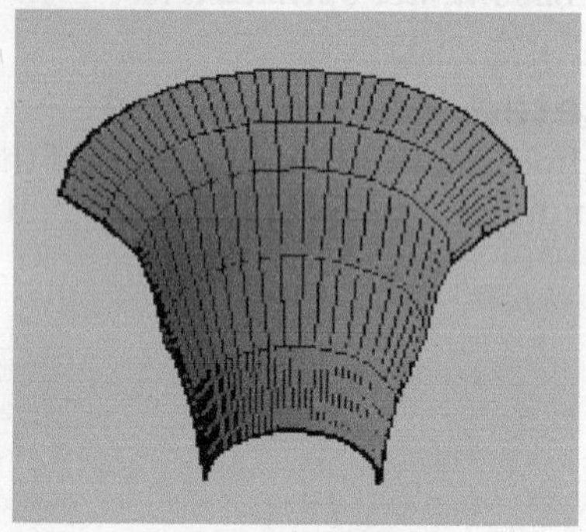

Figure 7-59 *The surface created on choosing the* ***Smooth, not optimized*** *tool*

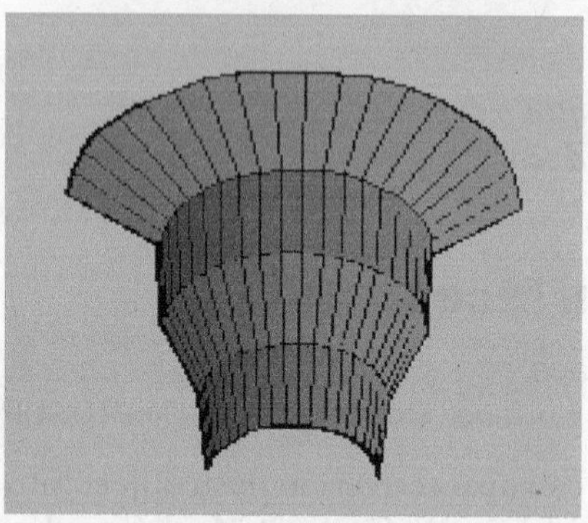

Figure 7-60 *The surface created on choosing the* ***Faceted, optimized*** *tool*

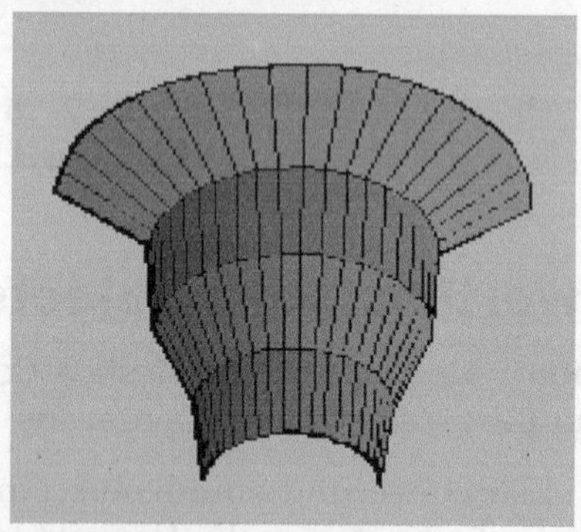

Figure 7-61 *The surface created on choosing the* ***Faceted, not optimized*** *tool*

Note

Other than meshes, regions, lines and arcs with some thickness, the planar 3D faces and 2D closed regions can also be converted into surfaces. Refer to Chapter 4 for details.

Tip

*You can create section views of the meshed models as you did for solid models in Chapter 3. The tools for creating section views are available in the **Section** panel of the **Home** tab or the **Mesh** tab.*

WORKING WITH GIZMOS

Ribbon: Mesh > Selection > Gizmo drop-down

Gizmo is a tool that helps you move, rotate, or scale 3D objects or their sub-objects along a specified axis or plane. When you select objects or subobjects in any 3D visual style, a gizmo is displayed. A gizmo is of three types: move, rotate, and scale, as shown in Figure 7-62. To set the gizmo that you want to be displayed by default, choose the required gizmo from the **Selection** panel. Also, if you do not want any gizmo to be displayed, specify it in the **Selection** panel. Various types of gizmos are discussed next.

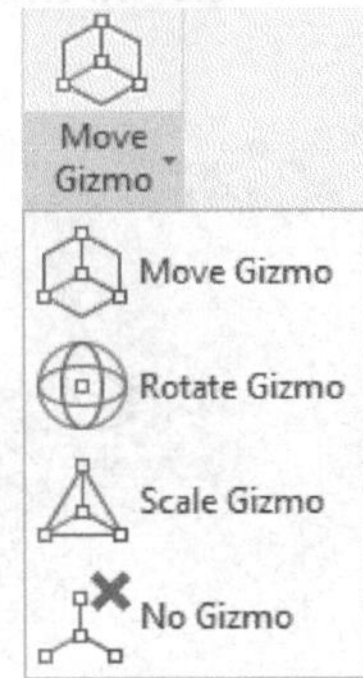

***Figure 7-62** The **Gizmo** drop-down*

Move Gizmo

When **Move Gizmo** is chosen from the **Selection** panel, the move gizmo is displayed on the first selected object or sub-object, refer to Figure 7-63. Move gizmo tool has three axis handles, three planes, and a base point. Using this gizmo, you can move the selected faces or edges of objects along any axis or plane, and thus, create freeform designs as per your requirement.

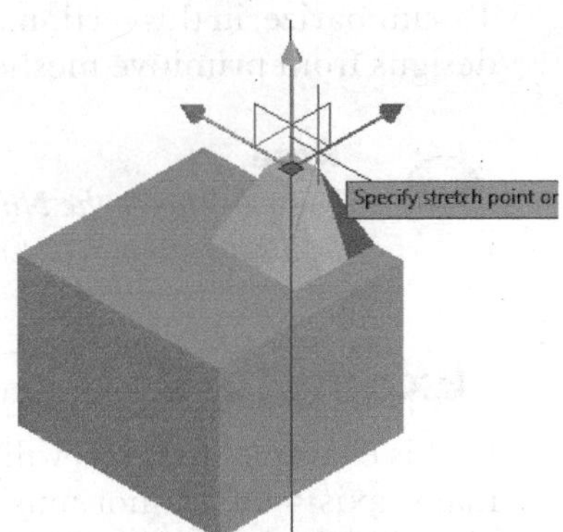

***Figure 7-63** **Move Gizmo** on the mesh object*

To move the selected object along any particular axis, click on the axis handle of the gizmo and drag along the axis; the selected object will move accordingly. To move the selected object anywhere along a plane, click on the rectangle formed in between the axes handles; the object will move along the specified plane. To relocate the base point of the gizmo, right-click on the gizmo, and then choose **Relocate Gizmo** from the shortcut menu displayed. You can also switch between various gizmos using this shortcut menu.

Rotate Gizmo

The rotate gizmo is displayed on the mesh object when **Rotate Gizmo** is chosen from the **Selection** panel. The rotate gizmo is displayed as a sphere with three axes and a base point on it. Figure 7-64 shows the rotate gizmo on the mesh model. The **Rotate Gizmo** tool is used to rotate the selected objects about a particular axis. By default, the gizmo is displayed at the center of the selected object. As you move the cursor over the rotate gizmo, the nearest axis of the gizmo will be highlighted. Click when the required axis gets highlighted and specify the rotation angle. You can relocate the gizmo as well as switch between various gizmos using the shortcut menu that is displayed on right-clicking on the gizmo.

Scale Gizmo

The scale gizmo is displayed when **Scale Gizmo** is chosen from the **Selection** panel. This tool is used to scale the selected objects uniformly along an axis or a plane. As you move the cursor toward the gizmo, the axis of scale will be displayed. Click and drag the axis to scale the object in that direction. To scale the object uniformly, click on the triangle that is formed between the axes. Figure 7-65 shows the scale gizmo on the mesh model.

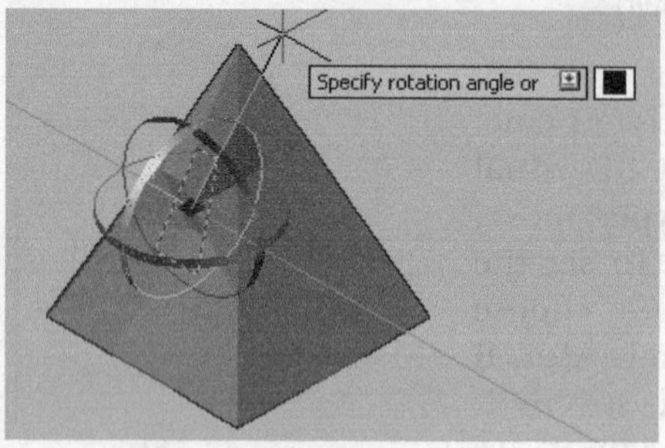

Figure 7-64 *The rotate gizmo on the mesh object*

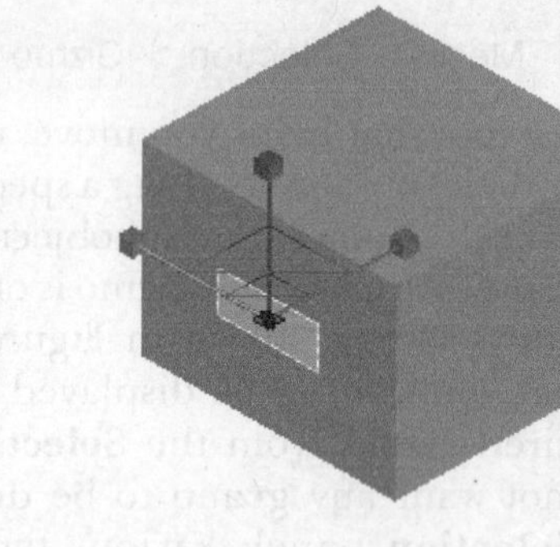

Figure 7-65 *The scale gizmo on the mesh object*

To summarize, in this section, you learned that all the three gizmos can be used to create freeform designs from primitive meshes. The next example illustrates the use of these gizmos.

Note

*You can choose the **No Gizmo** option from the **Selection** panel, if you do not want any gizmo to be displayed on selecting the objects in the 3D visual style.*

Example 2 — Gizmos

In this example, first you will create an elliptical mesh cylinder with the following dimensions: major axis = 55, minor axis = 15, and height = 100. Then, you will modify it using various gizmos. The final model should look similar to Figure 7-66.

Figure 7-66 *The final model of an elliptical mesh cylinder*

Creating an Elliptical Cylinder

First, you need to start a new drawing file, specify the settings for the number of faces in the cylinder, and then create the cylinder.

1. Start a new *acad3D.dwt* file in the **3D Modeling** workspace.
2. Choose the inclined down-arrow displayed at the lower right corner of the **Primitives** panel of the **Mesh** tab; the **Mesh Primitive Options** dialog box is displayed.
3. In this dialog box, select **Cylinder** from the **Mesh Primitive** area and set the following parameters in the **Tessellation Divisions** rollout:

   Axis: **10** Height: **5** Base: **3**

4. Choose **OK** to accept the settings specified in the rollout and exit the dialog box.
5. Turn on the **Ortho Mode** and invoke the **Mesh Cylinder** tool from **Mesh > Primitives > Primitives** drop-down. Then, follow the Command sequence given next to create the mesh cylinder.

   Specify center point of base or [3P/2P/Ttr/Elliptical]: *Enter* ***E*** *to create elliptical base*
   Specify endpoint of first axis or [Center]: *Enter* ***C*** *to specify the center of base*
   Specify center point: *Specify the center point for the base of the cylinder*
   Specify distance to first axis: *Drag the cursor along X axis and enter* ***55*** *in the Dynamic Input to specify a point on the first axis*
   Specify endpoint of second axis: *Drag the cursor along Y axis and enter* ***15*** *in the Dynamic Input to specify a point on the second axis*
   Specify height or [2Point/Axis endpoint]: *Enter* ***100*** *to specify the height of the cylinder*

6. Change the view to **SW Isometric** and the visual style to **Wireframe**. Figure 7-67 shows the mesh model.

Moving the Edges

To move the edges, you first need to select the Edge selection filter and then move them.

1. To filter the selection, choose the **Edge** tool from **Mesh > Selection > Subobject Selection Filter** drop-down.
2. Change the visual style to **Realistic** from the **In-Canvas Visual Style Controls** at the top-left of the drawing area.
3. Press CTRL and then select the required edge, as shown in Figure 7-68; the move gizmo is displayed by default.

Note
If move gizmo is not displayed by default, choose the ***Move Gizmo*** *tool from the* ***Default Gizmo*** *drop-down list in the* ***Selection*** *panel.*

4. Click on the X handle of the move gizmo such that the base of the cylinder is elongated; the preview of the moved edge is displayed. Next, click on the screen at the required distance (here, it is **20**). Similarly, move the edge on the other side to the same distance.

5. Now, you need to smoothen the mesh model. To do so, select it; the **Quick Properties** panel is displayed (if it does not appear, choose the **Quick Properties** button from the Status Bar). In this panel, select **Level 1** from the **Smoothness** drop-down list.

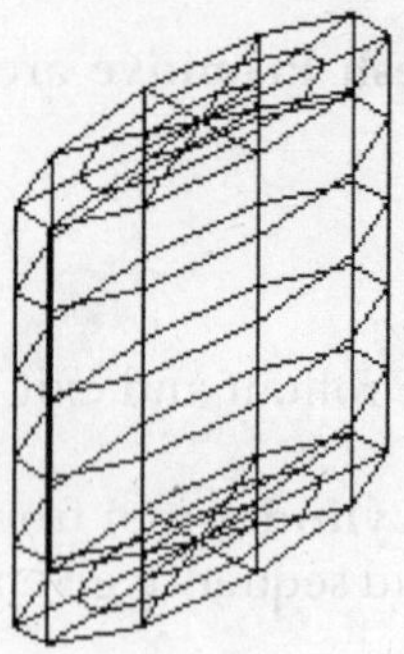

Figure 7-67 *The mesh model created*

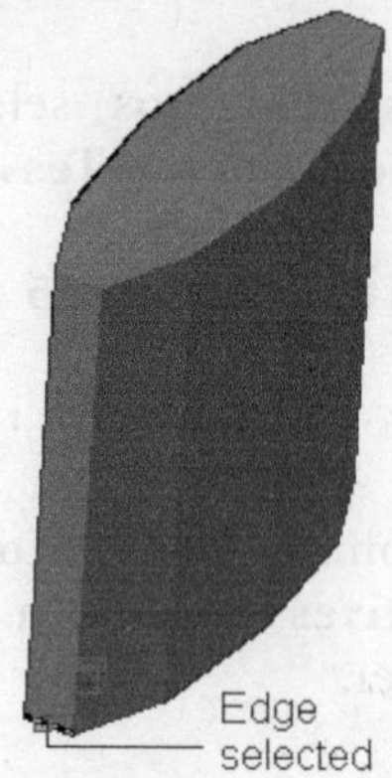

Figure 7-68 *Edge selected to be moved*

Rotating the Edges

You need to rotate the edges. Make sure the **Edge** option is selected in the **Subobject Selection Filter** drop-down list.

1. To invoke the rotate gizmo, choose the **Rotate Gizmo** tool (if the tool is not displayed then use 3DROTATE) from **Mesh > Selection > Gizmo** drop-down.

2. Select the required edges from the mesh model, as shown in Figure 7-69; the rotate gizmo is displayed on the first selected edge.

3. Click on the red handle of the rotate gizmo such that the adjoining faces are rotated inward; the preview of rotation is displayed. Click when the desired rotation is achieved (here, it is 60 degrees).

   Similarly, select the third set of edges in the same face and rotate the face. The final model, after rotating the edges, is shown in Figure 7-70.

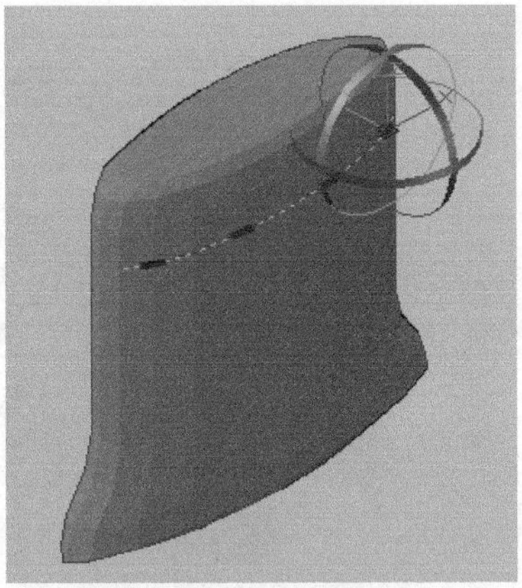

Figure 7-69 Edges selected to be rotated

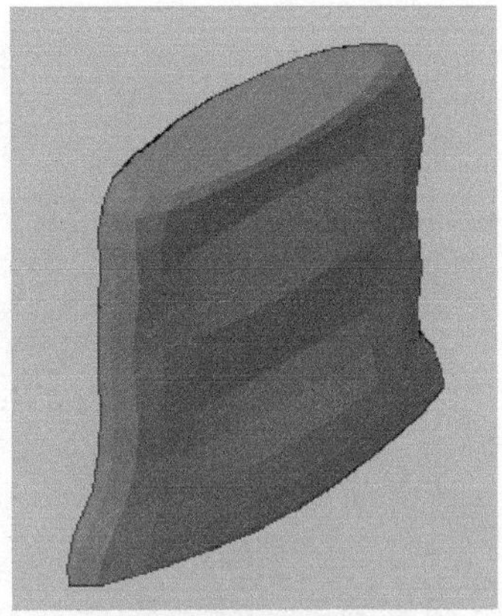

Figure 7-70 Final model after rotating the edges

Moving the Inner Faces of the Model

Now, you need to change the selection filter from edges to faces and then move faces.

1. To select faces, choose **Face** from **Mesh > Selection > Subobject Selection Filter** drop-down.
2. Choose the **Move Gizmo** tool (if the tool is not active then use **3DMove**) from **Mesh > Selection > Gizmo** drop-down.
3. Select the faces in the inner circular region at the top of the mesh model; the move gizmo is displayed on the selected faces.
4. Click on the Z handle of the gizmo and drag it; the selected faces are elongated. Click when the desired height is achieved.

Scaling the Entire Model

Now, you can elongate the model using the scale gizmo.

1. Choose the **Scale Gizmo** tool (if the tool is not active then use **3DSCALE**) from **Mesh > Selection > Gizmo** drop-down.
2. Select the model; the scale gizmo is displayed, as shown in Figure 7-71.
3. Click on the Z handle; the model is elongated in the Z-direction. Click in the drawing area at the required distance. The final model is created, as shown in Figure 7-72.

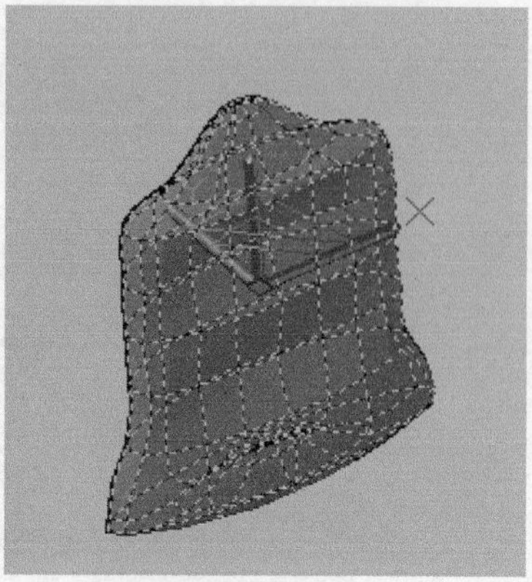

Figure 7-71 The scale gizmo displayed

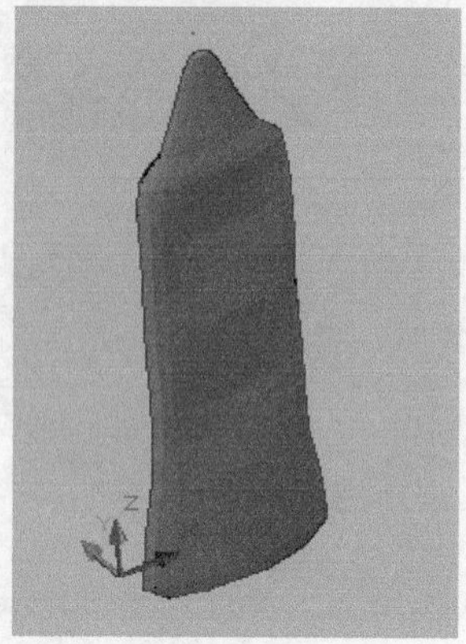

Figure 7-72 The final model

Example 3 Mesh Tools

In this example, you will create a toy plane, refer to Figure 7-73 using various mesh tools.

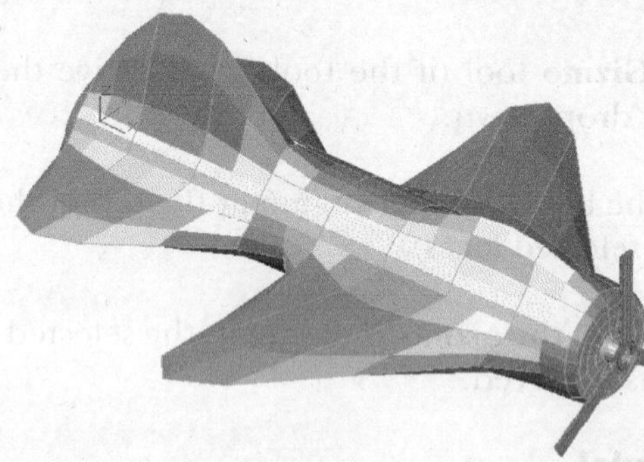

Figure 7-73 Final model of the toy plane

Creating the Cylinder

First, you need to create a cylinder facing the right view.

1. Start a new *acad3D.dwt* file in the **3D Modeling** workspace.

2. Set UCS to WCS and switch to the **Right** viewport. Rotate the WCS around the Y-axis by -90 degrees.

3. Select the **Wireframe** view style from the **In-Canvas View Controls**.

4. Invoke the **Mesh Primitive Options** dialog box and then choose **Cylinder** from the **Mesh Primitive** list.

5. Enter the following data in the **Tessellation Divisions** rollout:

   Axis = **16** Height = **8** Base = **5**

6. Choose **OK** to exit the dialog box.

7. Choose the **Mesh Cylinder** tool from **Mesh > Primitives > Mesh Primitives** drop-down; you are prompted to specify a centerpoint for the base of the cylinder.

8. Enter **0**; you are prompted to specify the base radius.

9. Enter **4** as radius; you are prompted to specify the height of the cylinder.

10. Enter **40** as the height; the cylinder is created.

    Now, you need to change the **UCS** to **WCS** and change the view to **SE Isometric**.

11. Choose the **WCS** option from the **WCS** drop-down below the ViewCube in the drawing area and click on the **SE-Isometric** hotspot in the ViewCube. The mesh cylinder will look similar to the model shown in Figure 7-74.

Extruding the Faces of the Cylinder

Now, you need to extrude the faces of the cylinder.

1. Select the inner faces on the right side of the cylinder, as shown in Figure 7-75.

2. Click on the red handle of the move gizmo to extrude; an edit box is displayed.

3. Enter **2** in the edit box; the faces are extruded.

Figure 7-74. *Mesh cylinder created*

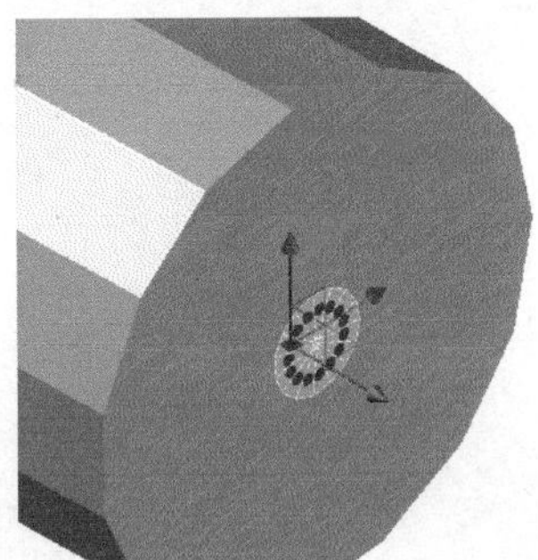

Figure 7-75 *Faces selected to be extruded*

Creating the Blades

To create blades, you need to create a thin and long mesh box. Before creating the mesh box, you need to change the UCS to Right.

1. Set UCS to WCS and switch to the **Right** viewport. Rotate the WCS around the Y-axis by -90°.

2. Choose the **Mesh Box** tool from **Mesh > Primitives > Mesh Primitives** drop-down; you are prompted to specify the first point of the mesh box.

3. Specify the point anywhere in the drawing, but not on the mesh model and create a mesh box of dimensions = 1 x 7 x 0.1.

4. Move the blade to the point on the circumference of extruded face of the cylinder, refer to Figure 7-76.

5. Now, you need to create a polar array of the blade. To do so, select the blade and invoke the **Array** tool; you are prompted to select the array type.

6. Choose the **POlar** option from the dynamic input box and specify the center point of the cylinder as the center point of the array. You can also enter **0,0** as the coordinates of the centerpoint.

7. Enter **3** in the number of items to fill; you are now prompted to specify the angle to fill.

8. Press **ENTER** to accept the default angle which is 360 degrees; the preview of the array is displayed and you are prompted to accept or modify the settings.

The model after creating the blades is shown in Figure 7-76.

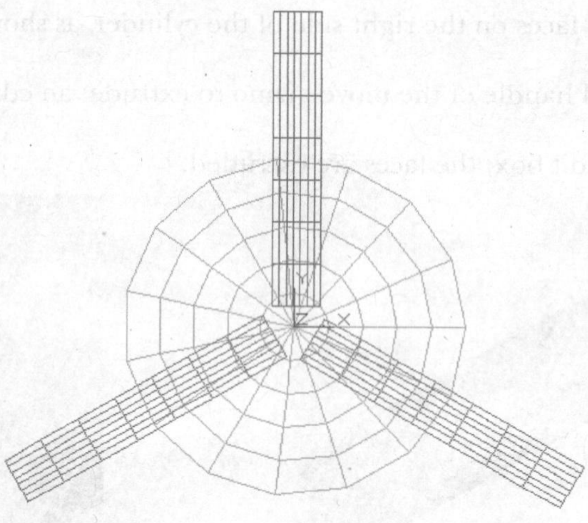

***Figure 7-76** Model created by combining various features*

Creating a Torus

You need to create a torus around the blades.

1. Choose the **Mesh Torus** tool from **Mesh > Primitives > Mesh Primitives** drop-down; you are prompted to specify a center point for the torus.

2. Specify the center point of the cylinder as thecenter point of torus and create the torus covering the start points of the blades.

The model after creating the torus is shown in Figure 7-77.

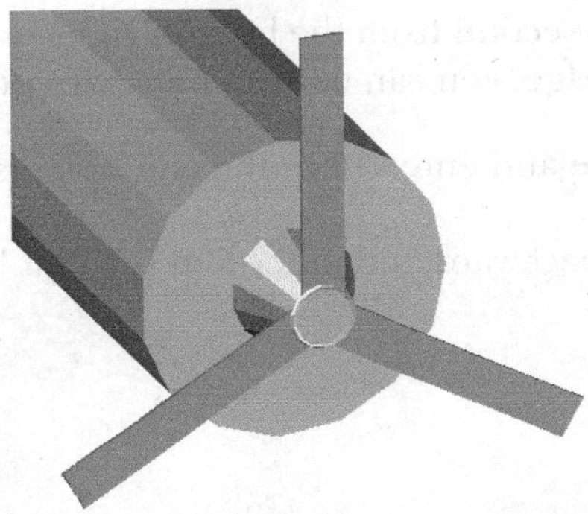

Figure 7-77 Model after creating the torus

Using Transform Gizmos and Stretching the Edge to Create a Plane

Now, you need to use various gizmos to get the shape of the plane. Before doing so, you need to set UCS to WCS and then switch to the **NE Isometric** view from the ViewCube.

1. Select the **Edge** option from the **Subobject Selection Filter** drop-down list and the **Move Gizmo** from the **Default Gizmo** drop-down list in the **Selection** panel.

2. Select the edge that is fourth on the right and third from the starting point of the mesh cylinder, as shown in Figure 7-78, to transform.

3. Now, click on the green handle; an edit box is displayed. Enter **20** in it.

4. Next, click on the red handle, move the handle backward, and enter **10** in the edit box displayed.

   The model after stretching the edge on the right is shown in Figure 7-79.

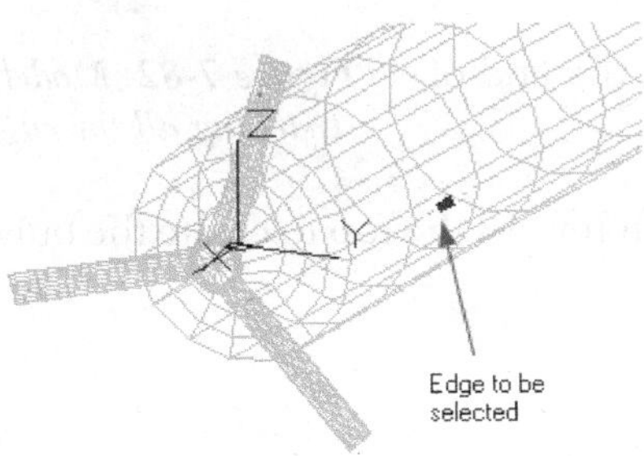

Figure 7-78 Model created by combining various features

Figure 7-79 Model after stretching the edge

5. Similarly, stretch the edge on the other side of the model. The top view of the model after stretching edges at both sides is shown in Figure 7-80.

   Now, you need to stretch the edges on the bottom right side of the model.

6. Select the edge that is second from the bottom right end, as shown in Figure 7-81. For easy identification of the edge, you can use the **Back** viewport.

7. Drag the green handle and enter **10** in the edit box displayed.

8. Drag the red handle backward and enter **5** in the edit box displayed.

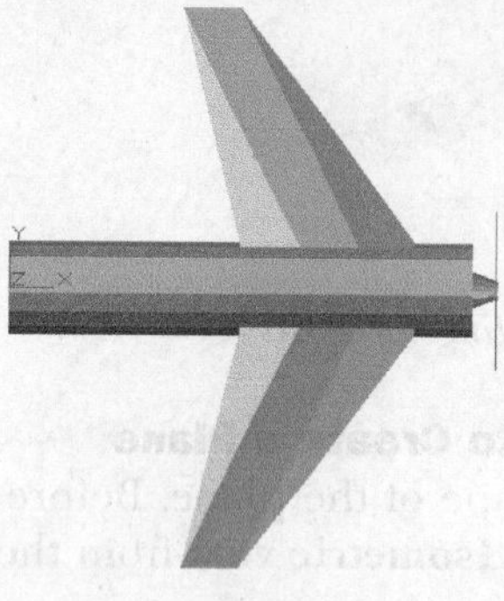

Figure 7-80 *Model after stretching the edge on the other side*

Figure 7-81 *Edge selected*

9. Similarly, modify the edge on the other side. The model after stretching the edges on both sides is shown in Figure 7-82.

Now, you will create a bulge at the top of the toy plane.

10. Select the second edge on the top of the plane, as shown in Figure 7-83.

11. Drag the blue handle and specify **2** as the distance of bulge.

Now, you need to create a bulge on the top at the end of the model.

Figure 7-82 *Model after stretching all the edges*

12. Select the edge second from the end and drag it toward the top to create the bulge, as shown in Figure 7-84.

Figure 7-83 Selecting an edge to create the bulge

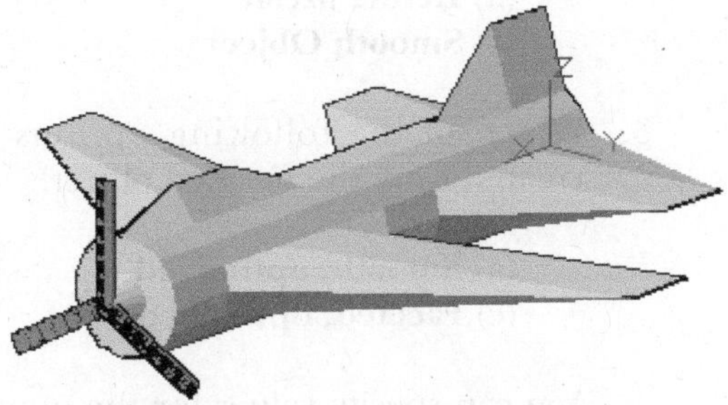

Figure 7-84 Model after creating both bulges

Smoothening the Mesh

1. Select the mesh model and choose the **Smooth More** tool from the **Mesh** panel of the **Mesh** tab.

   The final model of the toy plane after smoothening is shown in Figure 7-85.

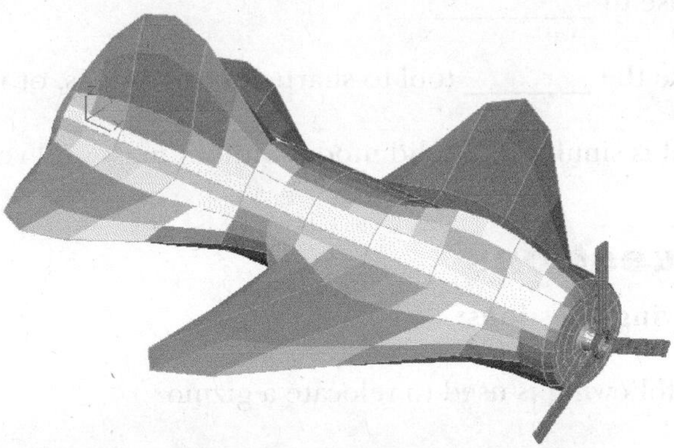

Figure 7-85 Final model of the toy plane

Self-Evaluation Test

Answer the following questions and then compare them to those given at the end of this chapter:

1. Which of the following objects can be converted into mesh objects?

   (a) 3D objects (b) Closed Polygons
   (c) Regions (d) All the above

2. Which of the following options is used to convert 3D objects into meshed objects?

   (a) **Refine Mesh** (b) **Smooth More**
   (c) **Smooth Object** (d) None of these

3. Which of the following options is used to specify the default settings for the solid created from the meshed object?

   (a) **Smooth, optimized** (b) **Smooth, not optimized**
   (c) **Faceted, optimized** (d) All the above

4. You can specify values for the number of faces in the primitive mesh in the __________ dialog box.

5. The __________ command is used to create mesh primitives.

6. The __________ tool is used to create a mesh by adjoining four continuous edges or curves.

7. The mesh editing tools are available in the __________ panel of the **Mesh** tab of the **Ribbon**.

8. To retain the sharpness of the crease even when you smoothen or refine the mesh, you need to set the crease to __________.

9. You can invoke the ________ tool to sharpen faces, edges, or vertices of mesh objects.

10. A mesh model is similar to a solid model without mass and volume properties. (T/F)

Review Questions

Answer the following questions:

1. Which of the following is used to relocate a gizmo?

   (a) Mouse (b) shortcut menu
   (c) **Ribbon** (d) All the above

2. The __________ and __________ commands are used to set the wireframe density of primitives.

3. To create mesh cones with frustum, you need to choose the ________ option of the **Mesh Cone** tool.

4. The **Mesh Tessellation Options** dialog box will be displayed on entering __________ at the Command prompt.

5. To remove creases from the model, you need to enter _________ at the Command prompt.

6. In smoothening, the complexity of a model is decreased. (T/F)

7. You can set the level of smoothness of mesh objects using the **Properties** palette. (T/F)

8. The curves used to create ruled surfaces can be lines, arcs, polylines, curves, and splines. (T/F)

9. The **Refine Mesh** tool works only when the smoothening of the mesh object is set to **Level 1** or higher. (T/F)

10. Refining an object resets the smoothening level to 0, whereas refining a face does not reset the smoothing level. (T/F)

Exercise 2 *Mesh Surface*

Create the 3D model of a globe shown in Figure 7-86 arbitrarily using the mesh modeling tools. The dimensions of the model are shown in Figure 7-86(a).

Figure 7-86 *Model of a globe*

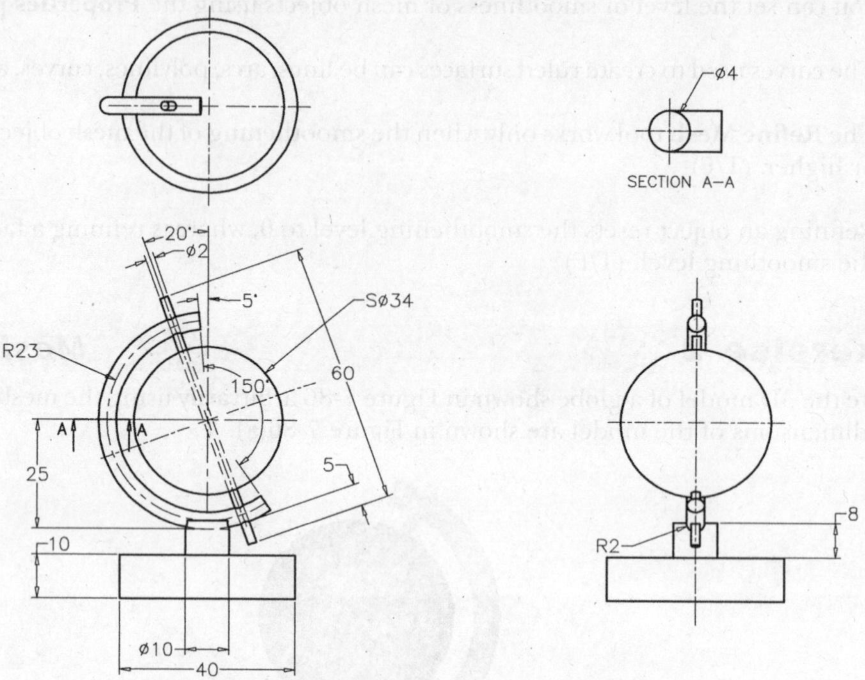

Figure 7-86(a) Orthographic views and dimensions of the Model

Exercise 3 — Mesh Surface

Create the drawing shown in Figure 7-87. First, create the base unit (transition) and then the dish and cone.

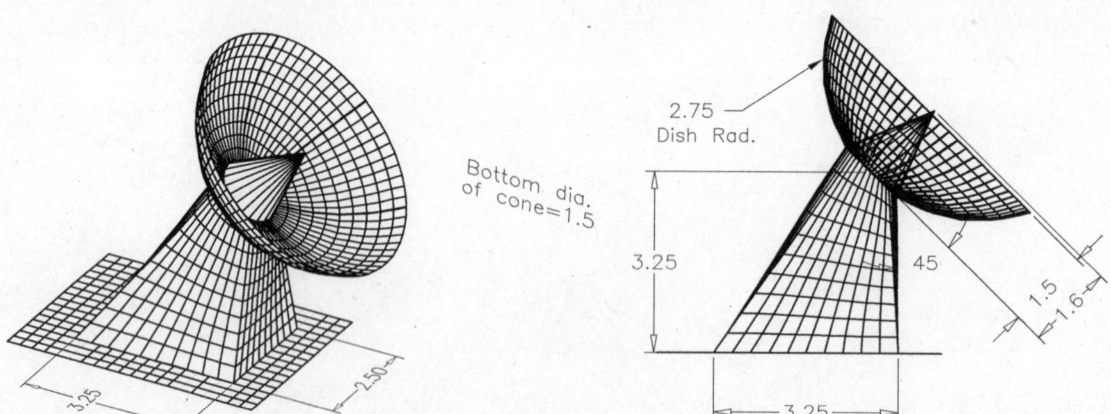

Figure 7-87 Dimensions for the mesh model

Exercise 4 Mesh Surface

Create the drawing shown in Figure 7-88. First, create one of the segments of the base and then use the **Rectangular Array** tool to complete it.

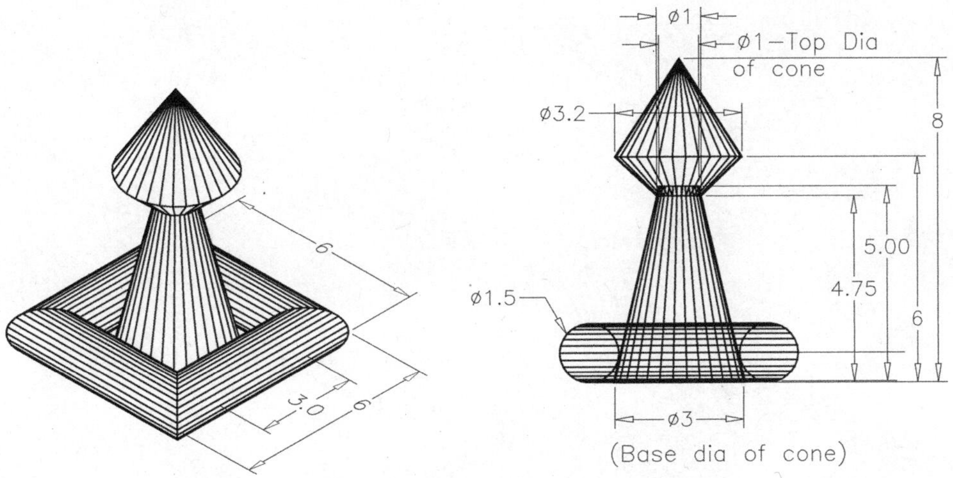

Figure 7-88 *Dimensions for the mesh model*

Answers to Self-Evaluation Test

1. d, **2.** c, **3.** d, **4. Mesh Primitive Options**, **5. MESH**, **6. Edge Surface**, **7. Mesh Edit**, **8.** Always, **9. Add Crease**, **10.** T

Chapter 8

Rendering and Animating Designs

Learning Objectives

After completing this chapter, you will be able to:

- *Render objects*
- *Browse and manage material libraries*
- *Assign materials to the drawing objects*
- *Create new materials as well as edit existing materials*
- *Map materials on objects*
- *Convert old materials into new materials*
- *Insert and modify light sources*
- *Convert old lights into new lights*
- *Select rendering types and render objects*
- *Define and modify rendering settings*
- *Replay and print renderings*
- *Define and apply background*
- *Save the rendering objects*
- *Configure, load, and unload AutoCAD Render*
- *Work with cameras*
- *Create animations*

Key Terms

- *Materials Browser*
- *Libraries*
- *Attach By Layer*
- *Materials Editor*
- *RENDER*
- *Material types*
- *Material properties*
- *Material Mapping*
- *Texture Editor*
- *Default Light*
- *Point Light*
- *Spot Light*
- *Distant Light*
- *Web Light*
- *Sun Light*
- *Set Location*
- *Render Presets*
- *History pane*
- *Shade plot*
- *CAMERA*
- *Set Camera View*
- *Animation Settings*
- *Motion Path*

UNDERSTANDING THE CONCEPT OF RENDERING

A rendered image makes it easier to visualize the shape and size of a 3D object as compared to a wireframe image or a shaded image. A rendered object also makes it easier to express your design ideas to other people. For example, to make a presentation of your project or design, you do not need to build a prototype. You can use a rendered image to explain your design more clearly because you have a complete control over the shape, size, color, surface material, and lighting of the rendered image.

Additionally, any required changes can be incorporated into the object, and it can be rendered to check or demonstrate the effect of these changes. Thus, rendering is a very effective tool for communicating ideas and demonstrating the shape of an object.

Generally, the process of adding a realistic effect to models (rendering) can be divided into the following four steps:

1. Selecting the material to be assigned to the design.
2. Assigning materials and textures to the design.
3. Applying additional effects to the model by assigning lights at different locations.
4. Using the **Render** tool to render the objects.

ASSIGNING MATERIALS

After creating a model, you need to assign various types of materials to the objects in it to give it a realistic appearance. These materials create three types of effects. These effects are discussed next.

In the first type of material effect, the object is rendered without actually displaying the effect of the material applied. A global material is assigned to all objects. On rendering, the color of the rendered image depends on the color of the object. Rendering by using this type of material effect does not give a realistic effect to the model, refer to Figure 8-1.

In the second type of material effect, a material is assigned to the object. AutoCAD provides you with a number of predefined materials and material libraries from which you can select a material and apply to the model. The material libraries contain thousands of materials and you can browse them using the **Materials Browser**. The **Materials Browser** is discussed next. Once you have selected the material, you can assign it directly to the object, individual faces, blocks, or layers, and render the model. Figure 8-2 shows a model to which a material has been applied and then rendered.

The third type of material effect is photorealistic. In this type, additional parameters such as the mirror effect, reflection, and refraction can be defined for the material, refer to Figure 8-3. You can set these parameters in the **MATERIALS EDITOR**.

Figure 8-1 *Model rendered after applying the default global material*

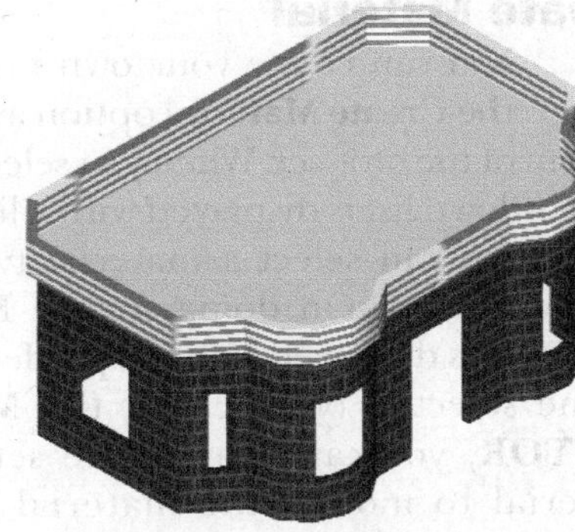

Figure 8-2 *Model rendered after applying the material*

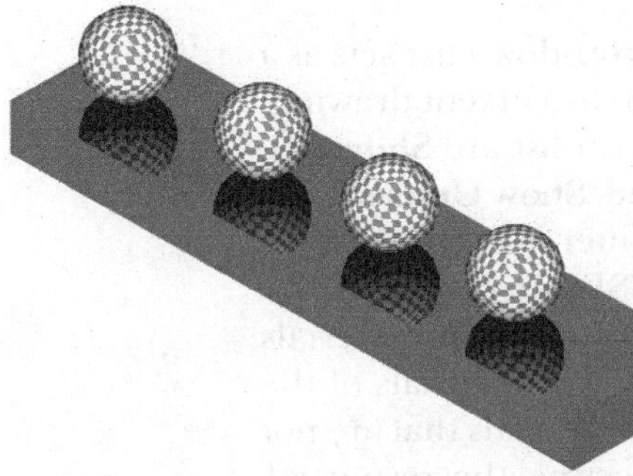

Figure 8-3 *Model rendered by adding effects such as the mirror effect*

Materials Browser

Ribbon: Visualize > Materials > Materials Browser
Menu Bar: View > Render > Materials Browser
Toolbar: Render **Command:** MAT or MATBROWSEROPEN

You can browse materials, manage material libraries, and apply the selected material to the drawing objects using the **Materials Browser** tool. You can download the Autodesk materials library available on the internet and install it, whenever required. When you choose the library to install, the library automatically gets installed in *Program Files (x86)\Common Files\Autodesk Shared\Materials\2021* folder. Also, the materials get automatically arranged into sub-folders. To apply material, choose the **Materials Browser** tool from the **Materials** panel of the **Visualize** tab. The **MATERIALS BROWSER** window will be displayed, as shown in Figure 8-4. For better utilization of the materials library, materials are arranged in nested categories. The different options of the **MATERIALS BROWSER** are discussed next.

Search

You can search a material from all the available material libraries by entering its name or keyword in the **Search** edit box.

Create Material

You can create your own materials using the **Create Material** option available at the bottom of the browser. When you select this option, a drop-down list is displayed with a list of material types. You can select a material type from the drop-down list. On doing so, the **MATERIALS EDITOR** is displayed with the predefined settings of the selected type. Using the **MATERIALS EDITOR**, you can change the settings of the material to modify the material as per your requirement. The **MATERIALS EDITOR** is discussed later in this chapter.

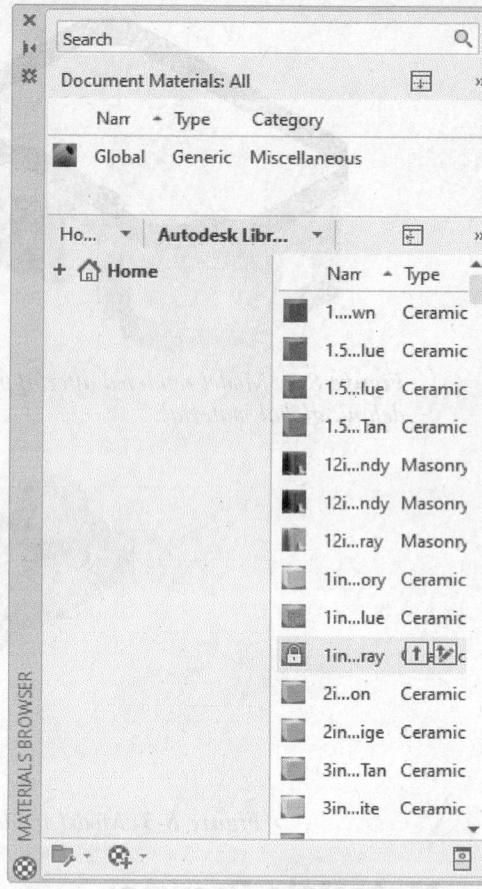

Figure 8-4 The MATERIALS BROWSER

Document Materials

The **Document Materials** drop-down list acts as a filter to the materials used in the current drawing. The options in this drop-down list are **Show All**, **Show Applied**, **Show Selected**, **Show Unused**, and **Purge All Unused**. You can filter materials display in the **MATERIALS BROWSER** to display either all materials in the browser, only the materials applied to the drawing, only the materials of the selected entities, or only the materials that are not used in the drawing by selecting the respective option from the **Document Materials** drop-down list. You can also purge or delete the unused materials in the drawing.

Autodesk Library

In this area, the Autodesk library with its pre-defined materials as well as other libraries with their user-defined materials are displayed. You can sort these materials by name, category, type, or material color using the drop-down list available on the extreme right of the Autodesk library drop-down above the **Preview** area. In this area, the preview swatches of the materials for the selected category/library are displayed. You can set the size of the preview swatches using the **Thumbnail Size** options available at the bottom of the drop-down list. You can set the display of swatches to icons, list, or text. After browsing to the required material, select the required material by clicking on it; the selected material will be added to the **Document Materials** list area. This material can now be applied to the drawing objects.

Manage

You can add, remove, or edit a library, or create or delete a category using the **Manage** drop-down list. The options in the **Manage** drop-down list are discussed next.

Open Existing Library

On selecting this option, the **Add Library** dialog box will be displayed. Using this dialog box, you can open an existing library.

Create New Library
On selecting this option, the **Create Library** dialog box will be displayed. Using this dialog box, you can save the newly created library.

Remove Library
You can remove the selected library using this option.

Create Category
You can create a new category of materials in the library by using the **Create Category** option. You can add materials under a new category by dragging and dropping.

Delete Category
You can delete the selected category by using the **Delete Category** option.

Rename
You can rename the selected category by using the **Rename** option.

Assigning Selected Materials to Objects
Once you have selected the materials to be applied to the object, you need to assign them to the objects in the current drawing. To do so, first invoke the **MATERIALS BROWSER** by choosing the **Materials Browser** button from the **Materials** panel of the **Visualize** tab and then browse to the required material from the library. After selecting the required material, drag and drop it on the drawing object on which you want to apply the selected material. If the visual style is set to Realistic, the material will be displayed instantaneously on the objects you select. Note that if a material is already applied to an object and you apply a new material on it again, then the new material will be updated on the object automatically.

Apart from dragging and dropping, you can also assign materials to the selected entities. To do so, select the object and then hover the cursor over the desired material in the **MATERIALS BROWSER**; the **Adds material to document** button will be displayed in the category column. Choose the button; the material will be applied to the selected object. Also, the material will be added to the **Document Materials** list automatically. Alternatively, select the entities, right-click on the selected material in the Browser, and then choose **Assign to Selection** from the shortcut menu displayed.

If you need to reuse certain materials again and again, then you can add those materials to the **My Materials** list, to the current drawing list, or to the active **Tool Palette**. To do so, right-click on the desired material; a shortcut menu will be displayed. Choose **Add to** from the shortcut menu; the **Document Materials**, **Favorites**, and **Active Tool Palette** sub-options are displayed. Using these sub-options, you can add the selected material to the required place.

Removing Materials from Selected Objects
To detach a material that has been applied to an object, invoke the **Remove Materials** tool from the **Materials** panel; the cursor will change into a paintbrush and you will be prompted to select the object from which you want to detach the material. Select the object; the material will be removed from it. By default, the global material will again be assigned to the object from which you have detached the material.

Attaching Material by Layers

Ribbon: Visualize > Materials > Attach By Layer **Command:** MATERIALATTACH

You can assign a particular material to a layer by choosing the **Attach By Layer** tool from the **Materials** panel. This means that you can apply a specified material to all the objects that are placed on a layer. When you choose this tool, the **Material Attachment Options** dialog box will be displayed. In this dialog box, all materials in the current drawing are placed under the **Material Name** column, the layers are placed in the **Layer** column, and the material attached to this layer is placed under the **Material** column, refer to Figure 8-5. To assign a material to a layer, select the material from the **Material Name** column and drag it to the desired layer in the **Layer** column. All objects placed in the selected layer will now be assigned with the specified material. After attaching the material to a layer, the **Detach** button is automatically added on the right of the **Material** column. You can detach the material from the selected layer by choosing the **Detach** button.

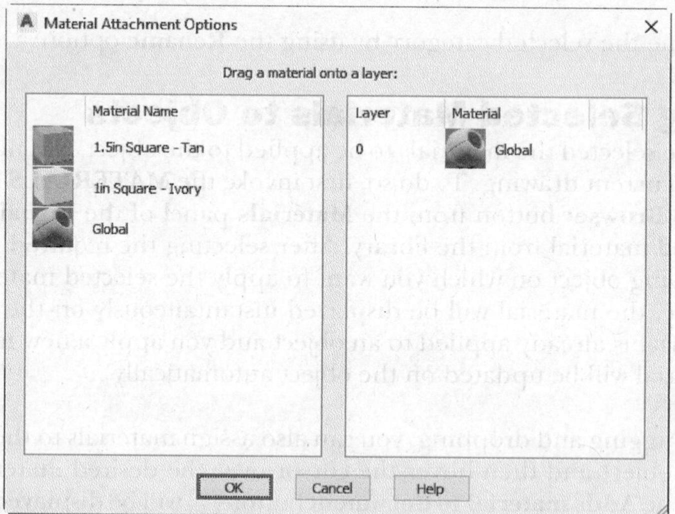

*Figure 8-5 The **Material Attachment Options** dialog box*

Creating and Editing Materials

Ribbon: Visualize > Materials > Materials Editor (Inclined arrow)
Menu Bar: View > Render > Materials Editor **Toolbar:** Render

In AutoCAD, you can create a new material or edit an existing material according to your requirements. This is done using the **MATERIALS EDITOR**. To edit an existing material, double-click on it in the **MATERIALS BROWSER**; the **MATERIALS EDITOR** will be displayed, as shown in Figure 8-6. Using the **MATERIALS EDITOR**, you can change the color, adjust material properties, and add textures to the selected material. The **MATERIALS EDITOR** has 2 tabs: **Appearance** and **Information** and these tabs are discussed next.

Note

*The **MATERIALS EDITOR** is also used to create new materials. In this case, you need not double-click on any material to invoke it. You can invoke it directly by choosing the inclined*

arrow on the title bar of the ***Materials*** *panel of the* ***Visualize*** *tab. The procedure to create new materials is discussed later.*

Appearance Tab

In the **Appearance** tab, all the properties of a material are defined. These properties include glossiness, reflectivity, transparency, luminosity and so on. You can also add textures to the material, if required. Various areas in this tab are discussed next.

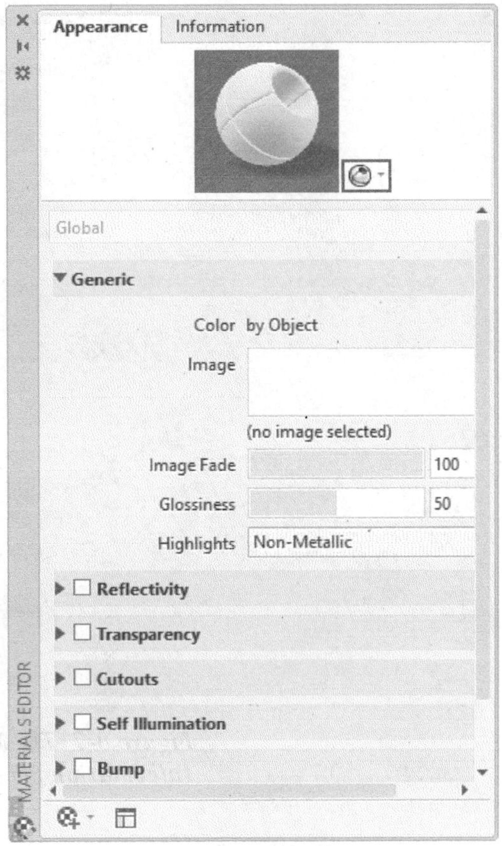

Figure 8-6 The ***MATERIALS EDITOR***

Preview

The preview area at the top of the **Appearance** tab displays the preview of the material. When you modify the material properties, the preview of the material also gets updated automatically. This helps you preview the materials with desired properties before you finally set the properties of the material and apply them to the model.

You can also select the shape of the thumbnail and render quality of the preview for better visualization of the material. To do so, choose the down arrow available in the lower right corner of the preview area; a list containing **Scene**, **Environment** and **Render Settings** is displayed. The Scene types include **Sphere**, **Cube**, **Cylinder**, **Canvas**, **Plane**, **Object**, **Vase**, **Draped Fabric**, **Glass Curtain Wall**, **Walls**, **Pool of liquid**, **Utility** and **Torus**. Select the required scene thumbnail. **The Render Settings** include **Quick**, **Draft**, and **Production** Qualities. Select the required render quality of the preview of the material. Note that higher the quality, slower the process of updating the materials.

Information Tab

In this tab, you can view the file properties as well as specify the description and keywords for the material created. The **MATERIALS EDITOR** with the **Information** tab chosen is shown in Figure 8-7.

Information

You can specify a name for the existing/new material by entering a new name in the **Name** edit box in the **Information** area of the **Information** tab. On entering a new name, the name will be updated in the **MATERIALS BROWSER** also. In the **Description** edit box, enter the material category. For easy indexing in the **Search** option, enter the keywords in the **Keywords** edit box.

About

This area displays the type and version of material.

Texture Paths
This area displays the path of the edited material in the selected storage media.

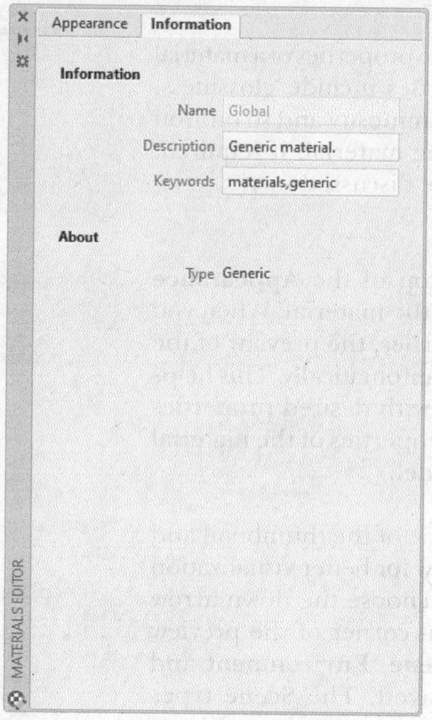

*Figure 8-7 The **MATERIALS EDITOR** with the **Information** tab chosen*

Note
*You cannot rename the **Global** material.*

Displays the MATERIALS BROWSER
This button is available at bottom left of the **MATERIALS EDITOR**. This is a toggle button and is used to display and hide the **MATERIALS BROWSER**.

The process of creating materials and adding texture maps is discussed later in this chapter.

BASIC RENDERING

Ribbon: Visualize > Render > Render to size drop-down **Toolbar:** Render
Menu Bar: View > Render **Command:** RENDER

In this section, you will learn about elementary or basic rendering. When you invoke the **Render** tool, the **Render** window will be displayed and the rendering process will be carried out. After the rendering has been completed, the rendered image will be displayed in the **Render** window, refer to Figure 8-8.

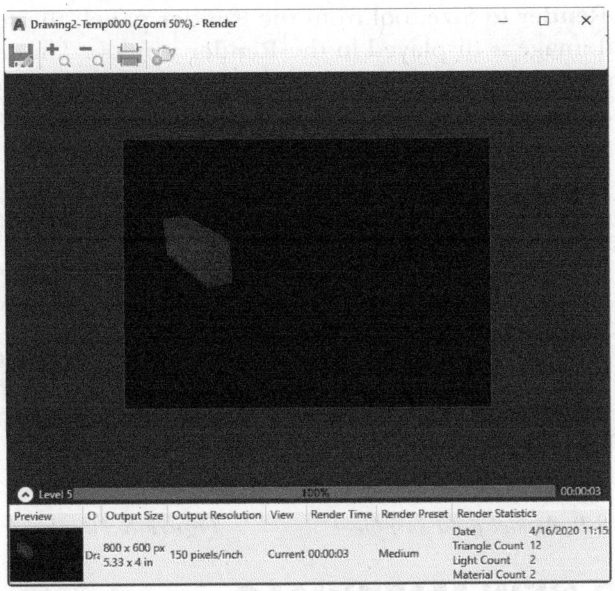

***Figure 8-8** The **Render** window*

Example 1

In this example, you will download the drawing file of the staircase shown in Figure 8-9 from *https://www.cadcim.com*. The path of the file is as follows: *Textbooks > CAD/CAM > AutoCAD Advanced > Advanced AutoCAD 2021: A Problem-Solving Approach (3D and Advanced) > Input Files*. Next, you will assign materials to the model and then render it. The materials that you need to assign to the model are given next.

Stairs	Flooring - Wood - Parquet - Brown
Balusters and Handrail	Metal Fabricated - Handrails and Railings - Painted White

1. Download the drawing file of the staircase shown in Figure 8-9 using the path mentioned above.

2. Invoke **MATERIALS BROWSER** from the **Materials** panel of the **Visualize** tab.

3. Select the **Flooring - Wood** category from the **Autodesk Library** list; all materials in the category are displayed in the preview list. Browse to the **Parquet - Brown**, select it, and then drag and drop it on stairs; the material is applied to the stairs.

4. As explained in Step 3, select the **Metal - Fabricated** category from the **Autodesk Library** list. Next, select **Handrails and Railings - Painted White** from the materials displayed and apply it to the balusters and handrails.

Note

*You will notice that the materials selected in Step 3 and Step 4 are automatically attached to the current drawing and displayed in the **Document Materials** list in the **MATERIALS BROWSER**.*

5. Choose the **Render to Size** tool from the **Render** panel; the rendering process starts and the rendered image is displayed in the **Render** window. The rendered image should look similar to the one shown in Figure 8-10. The background of the image is black by default. However, in this figure, the background has been changed to white for the clarity in print.

Figure 8-9 Model for Example 1

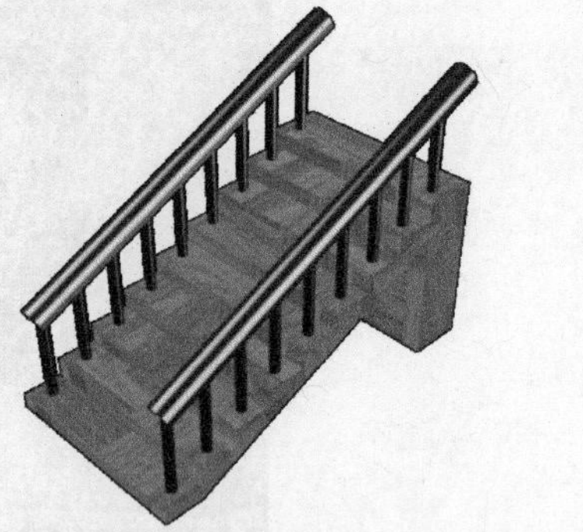

Figure 8-10 Rendered image of staircase

CREATING NEW MATERIALS

In AutoCAD, you can create new materials according to your requirement. To create a new material, click on the **Create Material** drop-down at the bottom of the **MATERIALS BROWSER**; a drop-down list with various material types will be displayed. Select the required material type; the **MATERIALS EDITOR** with the properties of the sample material type will be displayed, refer to Figure 8-6.

You can also create a new material directly from the **MATERIALS EDITOR**. To do so, choose the **Create Material** button in the **MATERIALS EDITOR**; a drop-down list will be displayed, refer to Figure 8-11. Select the required material type from the drop-down list; all material properties based on the selected material type will be grouped together. For example, if you select metal, then the properties such as relief pattern, cutouts, and so on will be displayed. Whereas, if you select the **Wood** material, the properties displayed will be different. The preview of the selected material is displayed in the preview area. In the **Information** tab, you can rename the new material in the **Name** edit box. Also, you can give its description as well as specify the keywords to be used for searching it. This material will be automatically added in the **MATERIALS BROWSER**. Now, you can define the properties of the new material in the **MATERIALS EDITOR** by modifying the properties of the old material.

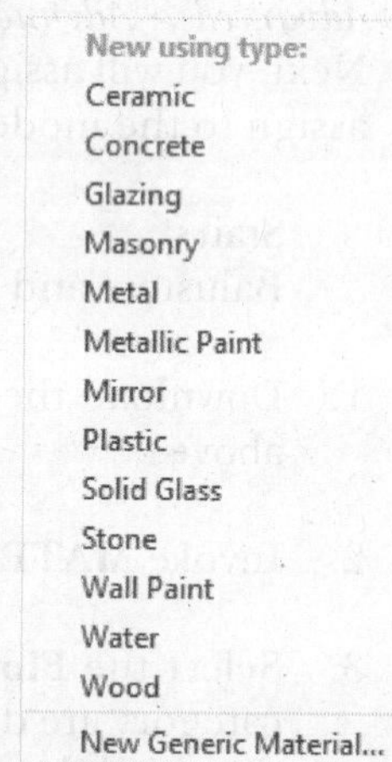

Figure 8-11 The create material drop-down list

Generic

In the **Generic** material type, almost all material properties are displayed. These properties are discussed next.

Color

By default, the **Color** option is selected in this area and therefore, the color of the object is assigned to the material. To assign any other color to the material, click on the arrow displayed on the right of the **Color** option; a drop-down list will be displayed, as shown in Figure 8-12. Select the **Color** option from the drop-down list; a color swatch will be displayed. Click on the swatch; the **Select Color** dialog box will be displayed. Select the required color from the dialog box; the selected color will be assigned to the material.

Image

You can assign textures to the color of the material. To do so, choose the arrow on the right in the **Image** area; a drop-down list will be displayed with a list of texture maps, refer to Figure 8-13. There are nine types of texture maps: **Image**, **Checker**, **Gradient**, **Marble**, **Noise**, **Speckle**, **Tiles**, **Waves**, and **Wood**.

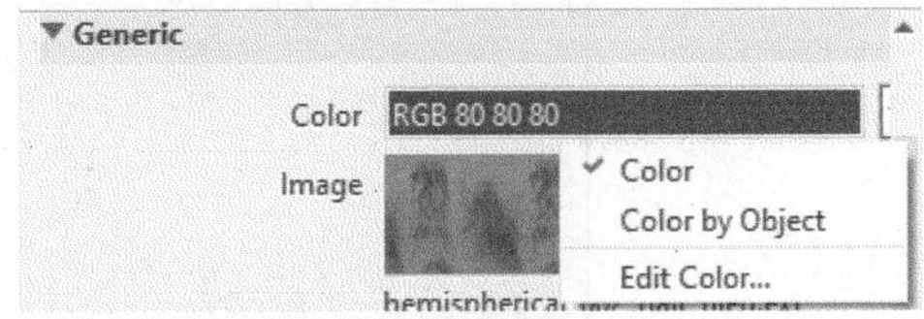

*Figure 8-12 The **Color** drop-down list*

If you select the **Image** option, the **Material Editor Open File** dialog box will be displayed, as shown in Figure 8-14. Browse to the required image and choose the **Open** button from the dialog box; the respective image will be displayed in the image area. Next, click on the displayed image; the **Texture Editor** window will be displayed. The **Texture Editor** displays the link for the texture image used, a slider to adjust the brightness of the image, a **Transforms** node that enables you to set the position, scale, and repetition of the image. Similarly, you can select other texture maps such as checker or gradient and then edit the appearance properties of the image and transform it according to your requirement.

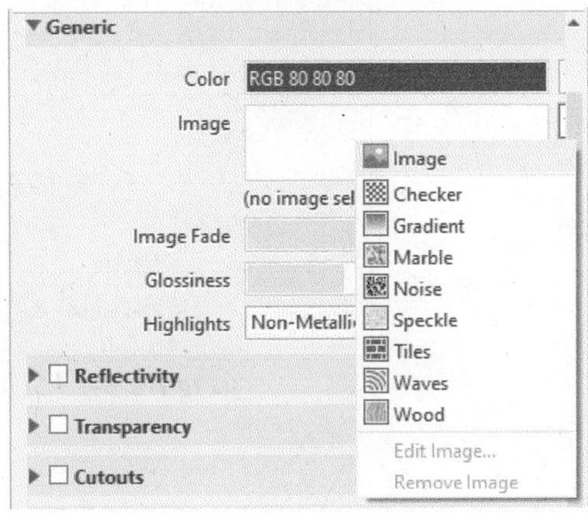

*Figure 8-13 The **Image** drop-down list*

If you select the **Marble** option from the drop-down list, the material will be mapped to the image of the marble and the properties of the marble will be displayed in the **Texture Editor**, refer to Figure 8-15. Click on the **Stone Color** swatch to change the color of the base stone and the **Vein Color** swatch to change the color of the veins displayed on the base stone. To interchange the color of the stone and vein, click on the down arrow next to the **Stone Color** swatch and choose the **Swap Colors** option. The **Vein Spacing** and **Vein Width** edit boxes are used to control the relative spacing between the veins and the relative size of the width of the vein, respectively.

If you select the **Wood** option from the drop-down list, the material will be mapped to the image of the wood. Also, the **Texture Editor** will be displayed. You can edit the image of an existing wood structure applied on the material. To do so, click in the preview swatch; the **Texture Editor** will be displayed with the properties of **Wood**, refer to Figure 8-16. Click on the required color buttons to change the color of the wood base and the pattern. Choose the **Swap Colors** option that is displayed on right-clicking on the color swatch to interchange the wood base and pattern colors. The **Radial Noise** and the **Axial Noise** options are used to decide the relative occurrence of patches of the wood in the radial and axial directions, respectively. The **Grain Thickness** option is used to specify the relative size of the grain patches in the material. All the values specified in this edit box are relative to the size of the object on which it will be applied.

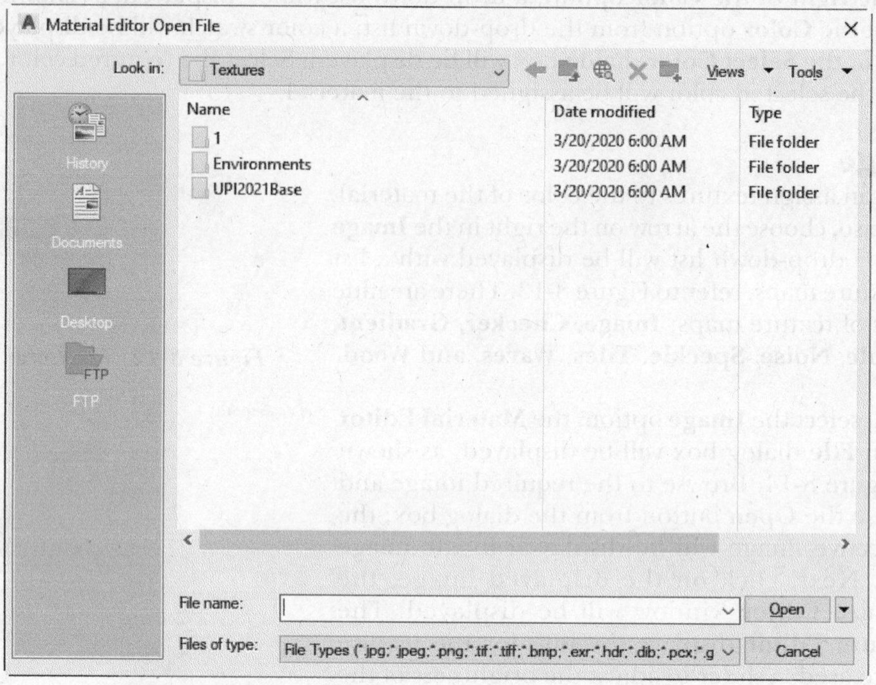

***Figure 8-14** The **Material Editor Open File** dialog box*

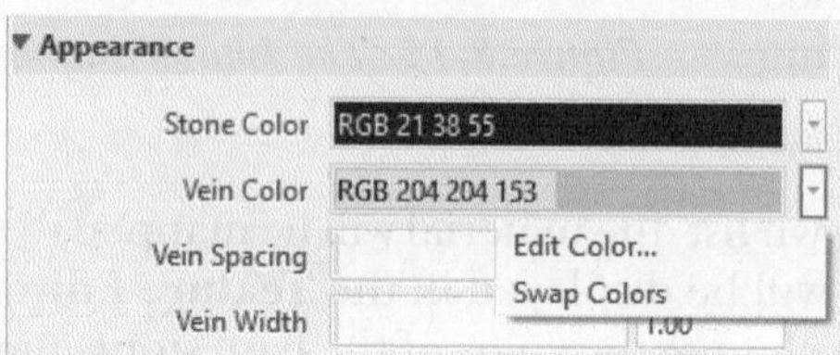

Figure 8-15** Material properties for **Marble

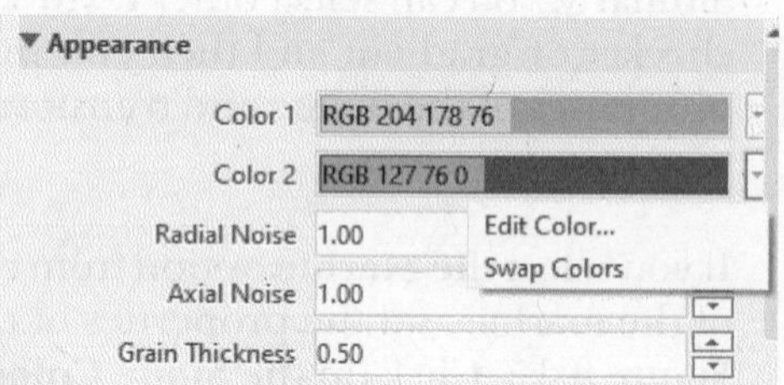

Figure 8-16** Material properties for **Wood

Image Fade

Use this slider bar to specify the extents of the effect of the texture map on the material. Figure 8-17 shows the **Image Fade** slider. At 0 value, there will be no effect of the texture map and only the material will be displayed. Also, as this value increases, the effect of the texture map becomes more dominant on the material and at the value of 100, only the texture map will be displayed on the object.

***Figure 8-17** The **Image Fade** slider*

Glossiness

This property is used to set the shininess of the texture. It is actually the ability of a surface to reflect the light. If the material is more glossy, it will reflect more light and the color of the portion of the object hit by the light will become whitish because white is the default color assigned to glossiness. However, you can assign any other color to it. You can set the shininess value as well as apply an image or texture to the gloss.

Highlights

This property is used to disperse light non-uniformly from the material. You can set metallic or non-metallic highlight for the texture. The **Metallic** option is used to highlight the color of the material and the **Non-Metallic** option is used to highlight the color of the light hitting the material.

Apart from the general properties discussed above, there are some other properties that are used to add extra effects to the material. These properties are discussed next.

Reflectivity

Reflectivity is the reflective property of the material. A hundred percent reflective material displays the surrounding objects on its surface. The **Reflectivity** area is used to specify the environment reflecting qualities of a material. Select the **Reflectivity** check box on the left of the node to apply the reflection effect. By default, sliders are displayed for both the **Direct** and **Oblique** options. To apply a reflection map to an object, click on the black arrow at the right of the **Direct/Oblique** slider; a list of options will be displayed, refer to Figure 8-18.

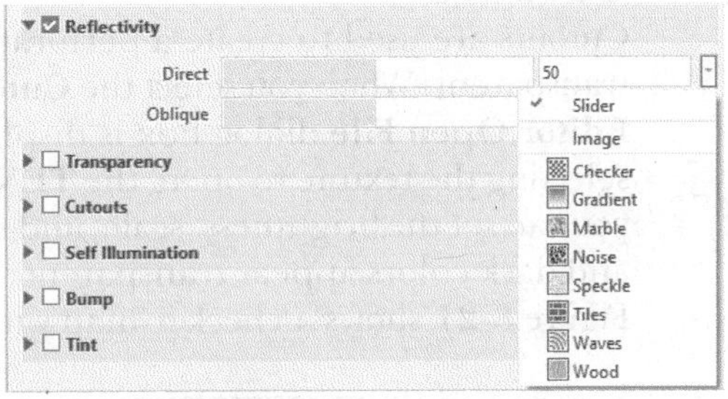

*Figure 8-18 Options available in the **Reflectivity** node*

Choose the required option from it. You can set an image file or some predefined textures to be reflected from the object as if the surrounding of the material is composed of this image/texture file. If you choose the **Image** option, the **Material Editor Open File** dialog box will be displayed. In this dialog box, you can select an image file to be reflected from the object. Similarly, you can select some predefined reflection maps from the drop-down list such as **Checker**, **Marble**, **Noise**, and so on. After selecting the map type, the **Texture Editor** will be displayed. Use the slider bar to set the brightness of the reflection map. The name of the texture file is displayed below the preview swatch and you can click on it to change the attached texture file. You can select or clear the **Reflectivity** check box to turn its effect on or off.

Transparency

Transparency controls the opaqueness of the material. The material with no transparency is opaque. The **Transparency** area is used to define an imaginary transparency or opacity effect of the material. Select the **Transparency** check box to apply the transparency settings on the object. You can specify the extent of transparency on the material by using the **Amount** slider. At 0 value, the material appears to be totally opaque and as this value increases, the transparency of the object also increases. You can set the image or texture for the transparency and adjust its color as discussed earlier. You can turn on or off the transparency effect by selecting or clearing this check box.

Translucency controls the amount of light transmittedand scattered within an object. At 0 translucency, all the light will be transmitted through the material without scattering. As the value of translucency increases, the amount of light scattered within the material also increases. You can set the image or texture for the transparency, refer to Figure 8-19 and adjust its color as discussed earlier. Refractive index defines the extent by which the view of an object will distort if it is placed behind a translucent object. For a refractive index of 1 (Air), the view of the object will not distort at all. If this value is increased (1.5 for glass, 2.3 for diamond, and so on), the extent of distortion will also increase. The maximum value of refractive index is 5.

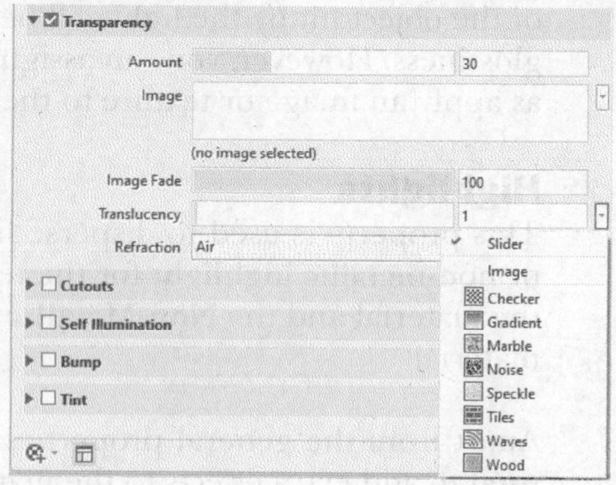

*Figure 8-19 The opacity map settings available for the **Translucency** option in the **Transparency** node*

Cutouts

Cutouts are used to create a perforation effect on the material and make the material partially transparent. When you select the **Cutouts** check box in the **MATERIALS EDITOR**, the **Material Editor Open File** dialog box is displayed. In this dialog box, you can select cutout maps. After selecting the texture to open, the **TEXTURE EDITOR** is displayed. In the **TEXTURE EDITOR**, you can set the brightness, scale, and size of the cutout map. Note that light colors appear opaque and dark colors appear transparent. Figure 8-20 shows a checker map without cutout effect and Figure 8-21 shows a checker map with cutout effect.

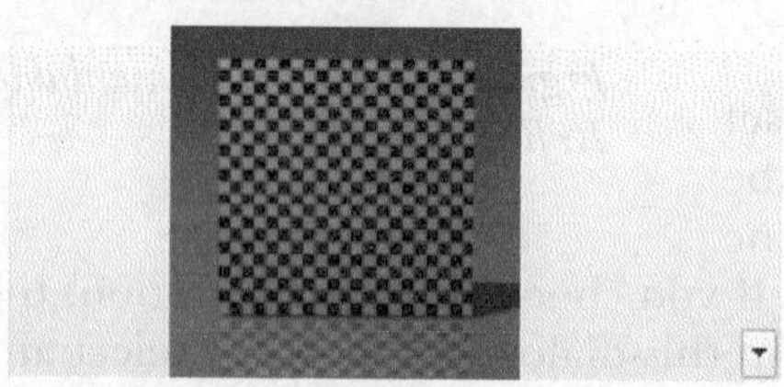

Figure 8-20 Checker map without cutout effect

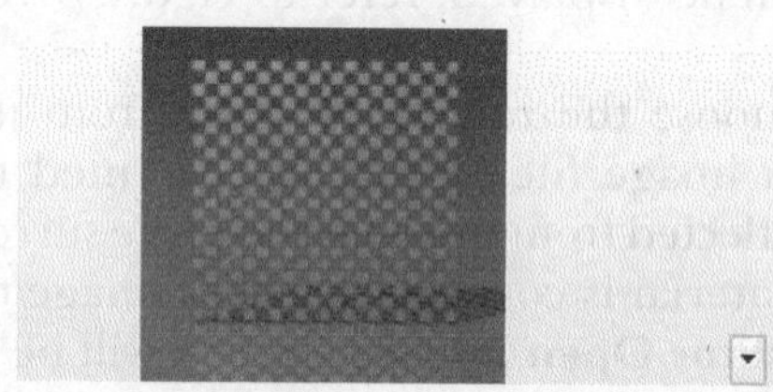

Figure 8-21 Checker map with cutout effect

Self-Illumination

Self-illumination makes the material appear as if the light is coming from the material itself. To apply this effect, select the **Self-Illumination** check box. You can control the **Filter Color**, **Luminance**, and **Color Temperature** by using the options activated upon selecting this check box. The **Filter Color** is used to define a color on the illuminated material. Luminance controls the amount of light reflected from a surface. It is a measure of how bright or dark a surface will appear. By default, the **Dim Glow** option is set in this option. The other options in the **Luminance** drop-down list are shown in Figure 8-22. You can specify the value of luminance in the edit box in terms of candelas/meter^2. You can also define the color of the illumination using the **Color Temperature** option. The options displayed in the **Color Temperature** drop-down list are shown in Figure 8-23.

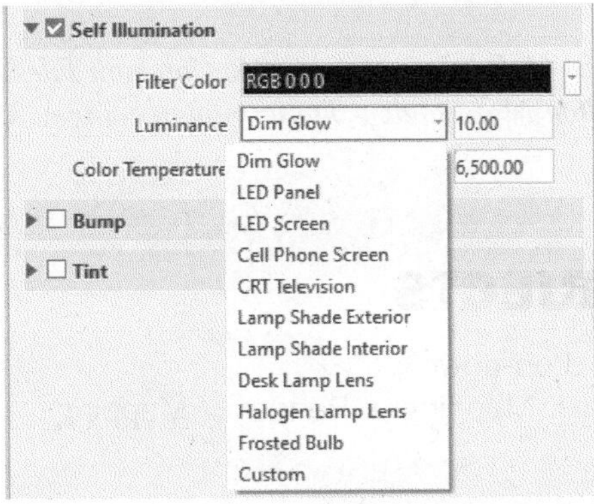

*Figure 8-22 The **Luminance** options*

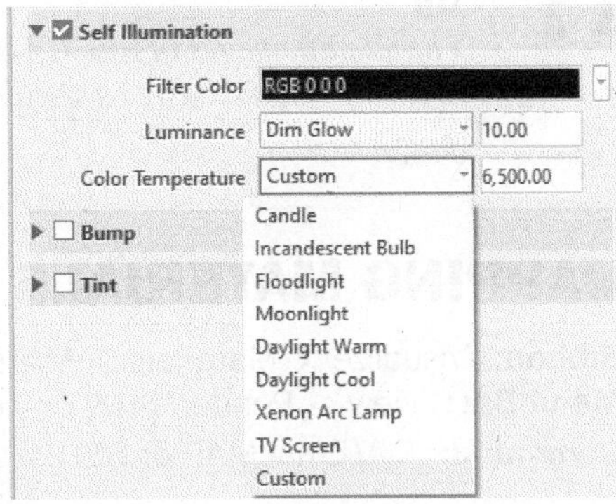

*Figure 8-23 The **Color Temperature** options*

Bump

The **Bump** area is used to add a bumpy or irregular effect to the surface of the material. Select the **Bump** check box to apply the reflection map settings on the object. On doing so, the **Material Editor Open File** dialog box will be displayed. You can use this dialog box to attach the required bump map. The attached map type in this area will appear to be engraved on the surface of the material. The light colors in this area will be projected outward or inward and the dark colors will remain as they are. Use the slider bar to adjust the extent of the bump. The value of the bump ranges from -1000 to 1000. For negative values, the brighter colors will appear to be projected inwards and for positive values, the brighter colors will appear to be projected outwards.

Note that the depth effect of a bump map is limited because it does not affect the profile of the object and cannot be self-shadowing. If you want extreme depth in a surface, you should use modeling techniques instead.

Note

1. The additional effects add realism to the object but at the same time increase the rendering time significantly.

*2. You can control the display of materials and textures from the **Materials/Textures** drop-down list in the **Materials** panel of the **Visualize** tab in the **Ribbon**. You can select the **Materials/Textures Off** or **Materials On/Textures Off**, or **Materials/Textures On** option from the **Material/Texture** drop-down list. On doing so, you can control the rendering time as well.*

*3. You can create a material similar to the original AutoCAD material. To do so, select the original material from the **MATERIALS BROWSER** and double-click to invoke the **MATERIALS EDITOR**. Next, click on the **Creates or duplicates a material** drop-down list and select the **Duplicate** option; the duplicate of the selected material will be created.*

4. The other options in the Materials window, the concept of mapping materials on an object, and the procedure of adjusting and modifying the maps will be discussed in later topics of this chapter.

Tip

The bitmap images in AutoCAD are stored in C:\Program Files (x86)\Common Files\Autodesk Shared\Materials\2021\assetlibrary_base.fbm\Mats folder. These bitmap images are in the .png format.

MAPPING MATERIALS ON OBJECTS

Ribbon: Visualize > Materials > MATERIALMAP drop-down
Menu Bar: View > Render > Mapping **Toolbar:** Mapping or Render > Mapping
Command: MATERIALMAP or SETUV

In AutoCAD, mapping is defined as the method used for adjusting the coordinates and the bitmap of the pattern of the material attached to a solid model. Mapping is required when the pattern of the material is not properly displayed on the object after rendering. Therefore, to display the material properly, you need to adjust the coordinates and the bitmap of the material properly.

To perform mapping on a model, choose the **Material Mapping** drop-down from the **Materials** panel; different types of mapping will be displayed, as shown in Figure 8-24. Choose the mapping type that you want to use on the object. The different types of tools available for mapping are: **Planar**, **Box**, **Cylindrical**, and **Spherical**. First, select an object; a material mapper grip tool will be displayed on the object. Use the grip tools on the object to adjust the display of the image on the model or on the face of the model. You can move or rotate the mapping about an axis by selecting the axis and right-clicking. Figure 8-25 shows a model with the **Planar** mapping and Figure 8-26 shows a model with the **Cylindrical** mapping.

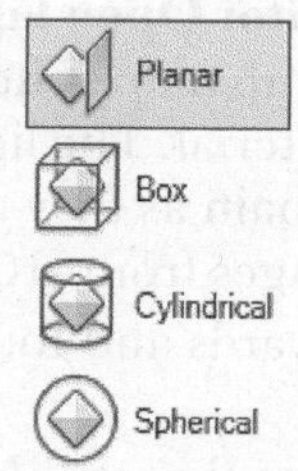

***Figure 8-24** The **Material Mapping** drop-down*

You can invoke the following options depending on your requirements.

Box

This tool is used to map an image on a box such that the image is repeated on each side of the object. The prompt sequence that will be followed on choosing the **Box** tool from the **Material Mapping** drop-down is given next.

Select an option [Box/Planar/Spherical/Cylindrical/copY mapping to/Reset mapping]<Box>: **_B**
Select faces or objects: *Select a face or object on which the image will be mapped by using the arrows .*
Select faces or objects: *Select more faces or objects on which the image will be mapped or* Enter.
Accept the mapping or [Move/Rotate/reseT/sWitch mapping mode]: *Accept the mapping as it is or select an option to modify it.*

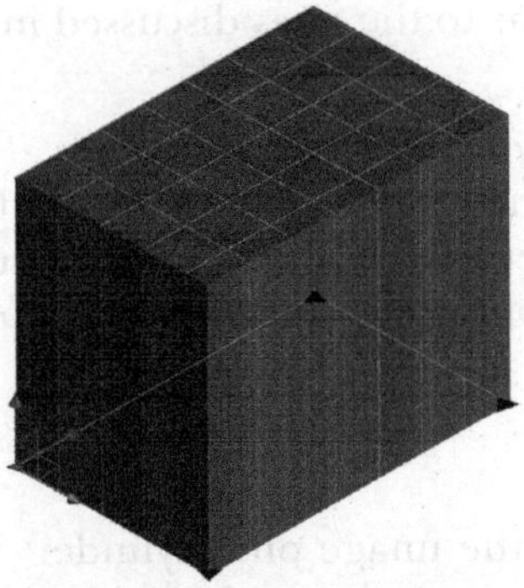

*Figure 8-25 Model with the **Planar** mapping*

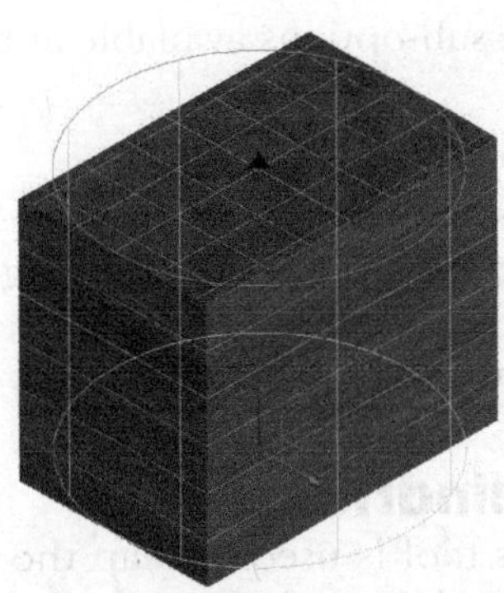

*Figure 8-26 Model with the **Cylindrical** mapping*

The sub-options that you can select at this prompt are given next.

Move
On selecting this sub-option, the move gizmo will be displayed on the object. You can move and adjust the mapped image along any selected axis handle. Dynamic grips are also displayed on the mapping box, which can be dragged to resize the map.

Rotate
On selecting this sub-option, the rotate gizmo will be displayed on the object. You can rotate and adjust the mapped image along any selected axis handle. Dynamic grips are also displayed on the mapping box, which can be dragged to resize the map.

reseT
This sub-option is used to reset all adjustments made in the mapping coordinate to the default one.

sWitch mapping mode
This sub-option is used to redisplay the main prompt sequence on the screen to change the type of mapping.

Planar
This tool is used to map the image on an object such that it seems to be projected on that object. The projected image is scaled automatically according to the size of the object. The prompt sequence that will follow on choosing the **Planar** tool from the **Material Mapping** drop-down is given next.

> Select an option [Box/Planar/Spherical/Cylindrical/copY mapping to/Reset mapping]<Box>: **P**
> Select faces or objects: *Select a face or object on which the image will be mapped*
> Select faces or objects: *Select more faces or objects on which the image will be mapped or* Enter
> Accept the mapping or [Move/Rotate/reseT/sWitch mapping mode]: *Accept the mapping as it is or select an option to modify it*

The sub-options available at this prompt are similar to the ones discussed in the **Box** tool.

Spherical

This tool is used to map the image by warping the image horizontally and vertically. In this type of mapping, the top edge of the image converges at the north pole of the object and the bottom edge converges at the south pole. The prompt sequence for this tool is similar to that discussed in the **Box** tool.

Cylindrical

This tool is used to map the image by wrapping the image on a cylinder. The height of the image is scaled along the cylinder axis. The prompt sequence for this tool is similar to that discussed in the **Box** tool.

copY mapping to

You can also acquire the mapping from an existing object and copy it on the selected object. You can do so by choosing the **Copy Mapping Coordinates** tool from the expanded options of the **Materials** panel in the **Visualize** tab. The prompt sequence for this option is given next.

Select an option [Box/Planar/Spherical/Cylindrical/copY mapping to/Reset mapping]<Box>: **Y**
Select faces or objects: *Select the source object to copy the mapping information*
Select the objects to copy the mapping to: *Select the object to apply the copied mapping information*
Select faces or objects: *Select more objects or* Enter

Reset mapping

This option is used to reset all the adjustments made in the mapping coordinates of the selected object to the default one produced by AutoCAD. To invoke this option, choose the **Reset Mapping Coordinates** tool from the expanded options of the **Materials** panel in the **Visualise** tab.

Adjusting the Bitmap Image on a Model

You can control the scale, tiling, and offset properties of a mapped image through the **Transforms** node of the **TEXTURE EDITOR**.

Figure 8-27 shows the **TEXTURE EDITOR** displayed on clicking on the **Checker** map applied to the color of the object in the **Generic** node.

In the **Appearance** area, you can modify the color of the selected texture map. The options displayed depend on the material selected. When you expand the **Transforms** node in the **Texture Editor**, the **Position, Scale**, and **Repeat** sub-nodes are displayed to enable you to transform the map, refer to Figure 8-28. Note that these sub-nodes are available only for the **Image**, **Checker**, **Gradient**, and **Tiles** map types.

In the **Position** sub-nodes, you can set the offset properties of the texture map. You can specify the start point of the map along the X and Y coordinates as well as rotate the map in this area. In the **Scale** area, you can specify the scale factor of the texture map in horizontal and vertical directions. You can also specify the method to be followed to create a pattern of the image. The options available in the **Repeat** area are used to set whether to tile the map in the Horizontal/ Vertical directions or not.

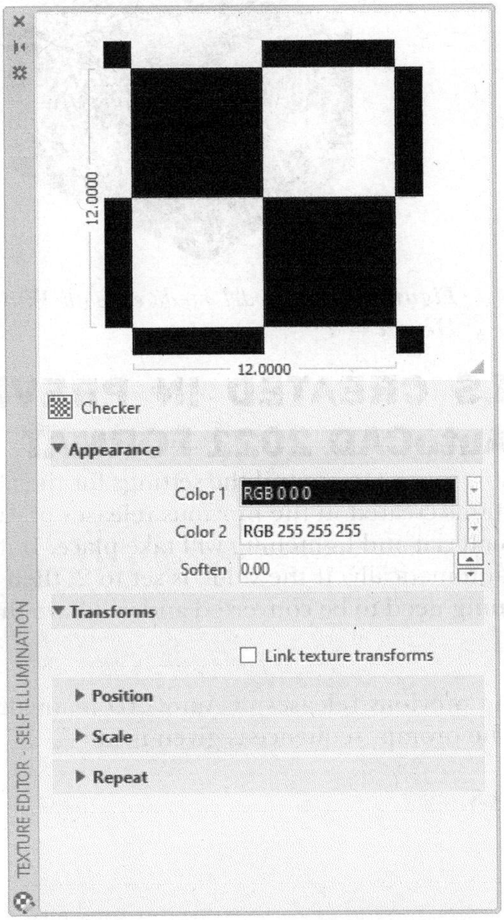

Figure 8-27** The **TEXTURE EDITOR

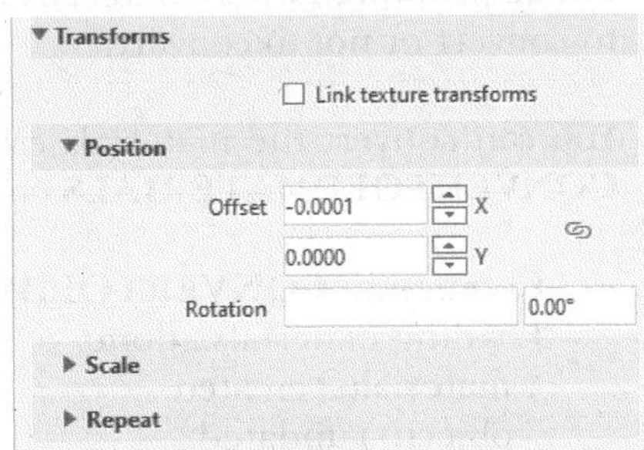

Figure 8-28** The **Transforms** area of the **TEXTURE EDITOR

Figures 8-29 and 8-30 show the models rendered with different width and height specified in the respective edit boxes in the **Scale** area of the **TEXTURE EDITOR**.

*Figure 8-29 Model rendered with **Width** = 8, **Height** = 2*

*Figure 8-30 Model rendered with **Width** = 4, **Height** = 1*

CONVERTING MATERIALS CREATED IN PREVIOUS AutoCAD RELEASE INTO AutoCAD 2021 FORMAT

The **3DCONVERSIONMODE** system variable is used to control the settings for the automatic conversion of the materials and light definitions created in the previous releases of AutoCAD. If the variable is set to 0, no conversion of material and lightening will take place. If it is set to a value of 1, the conversion will take place automatically. If the value is set to 2, then the user will be prompted when materials and lightening need to be converted and will have the option to convert or not to convert.

You can convert the materials created in the previous releases of AutoCAD manually by the **CONVERTOLDMATERIALS** command. The prompt sequence is given next.

Command: **CONVERTOLDMATERIALS**
Loading materials...done.
4 material(s) created.
7 object(s) updated.

The prompt sequence indicates that the four materials applied to seven objects have been converted to the AutoCAD 2021 format. This prompt sequence also indicates the materials which are not converted to AutoCAD 2021 format, if there are any.

ADDING LIGHTS TO THE DESIGN

Ribbon: Visualize > Lights > Create Light drop-down
Menu Bar: View > Render > Light **Toolbar:** Lights or Render > New Point Light
Command: LIGHT

Lights are vital to rendering a realistic image of an object. Without proper lighting, the rendered image may not show the features the way you expect. The lights can be added to the design using the **Lights** tool.

AutoCAD supports two types of lighting arrangements: Standard workflow and photometric workflow. The Photometric workflow is the default workflow in AutoCAD. The photometric workflow provides more accurate control over lighting through the photometric properties. The photometric workflow supports two types of lighting units: International (for example lux), and American (for example foot-candles). You can select the lighting workflow and its unit from the **Units for specifying the intensity of lighting** drop-down list in the **Lighting** area of the **Drawing Units** dialog box. To invoke this dialog box, choose **Drawing Utilities > Units** from the **Application Menu**. Alternatively, expand the **Lights** panel in the **Visualize** tab and specify the units from the **Lighting Units** drop-down.

Note

*The Standard workflow is enabled if **Generic lighting units** is selected as a unit in the **Lights** panel. Similarly, the Photometric workflow is enabled if **American lighting units** or **International lighting units** is selected as a unit in the **Lights** panel.*

All types of light sources supported by AutoCAD are discussed next.

Default Light

The default light is the natural light source that equally illuminates all surfaces of the objects, refer to Figure 8-31. The default light consists of two distance lights that do not have a source, and therefore, no location or direction. It is the default light that is automatically applied to the design. However, you can modify the brightness, contrast, and mid tone settings of the environment light by using the respective slider from the **Lights** panel in the **Visualize** tab, refer to Figure 8-32.

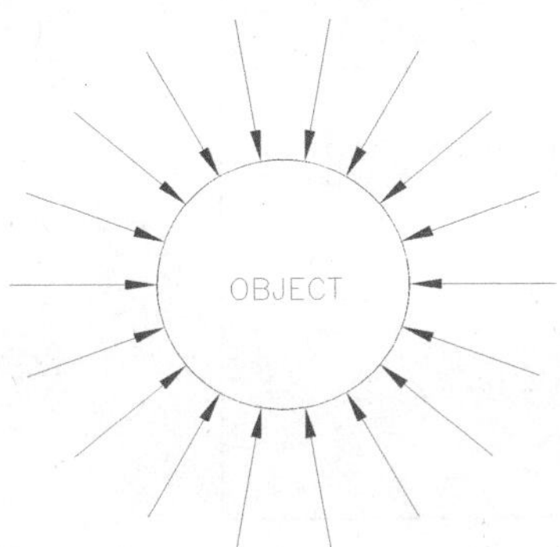

Figure 8-31 Default light emitting constant illumination

***Figure 8-32** The expanded **Lights** panel of the **Visualize** tab*

The **Exposure** and **White Balance** slider bars can be used to increase or decrease the exposure and white balance of the default light. By default, the color of the **Default lighting** is white. Figures 8-33 and 8-34 show the same model rendered using different values of exposure and white balance of the default light.

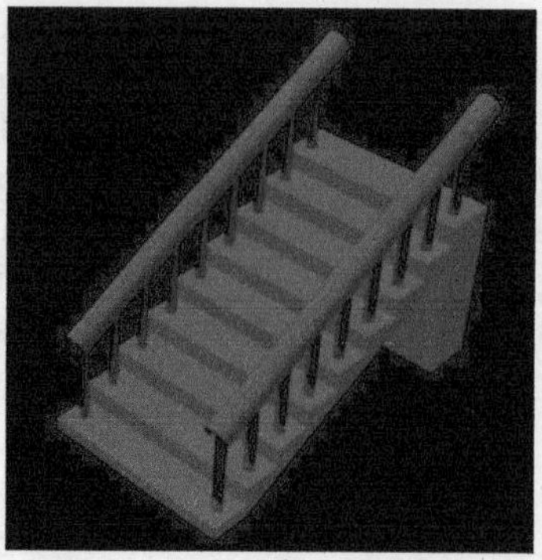

Figure 8-33 *Model rendered with high exposure and white balance value of ambient light*

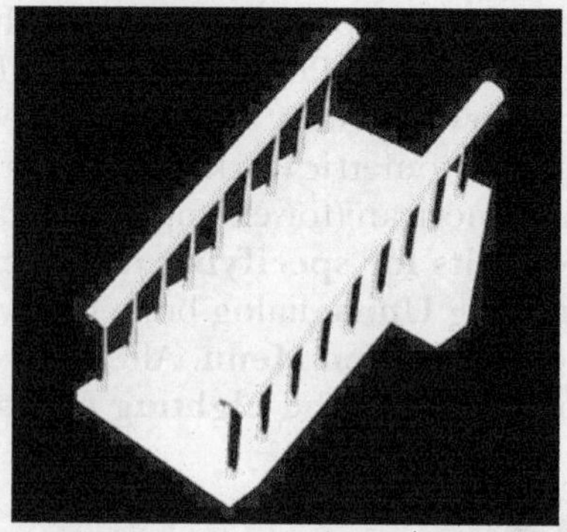

Figure 8-34 *Model rendered with less exposure and white balance value of ambient light*

The **Exposure** option is used to set the value of light in the scene. You can move the exposure slider to make a scene light or dark. While the **White balance** option gives a cool or warm effect to the rendered image. When you invoke any new light to create user-defined lights, the **Lighting - Viewport Lighting Mode** message will be displayed on the screen, refer to Figure 8-35. If you want to render the model using the user-defined lights only, then choose the **Turn off the default lighting (recommended)** option. But if you want to render the model using both the default and user defined lights, then choose the **Keep the default lighting turned on** option. However, if you will keep the default lights turned on, the effects of the user-defined lights will not be displayed properly, so you need to turn off the default lighting manually. If you invoke the **Lights** tool again after turning off the default light, the **Lighting - Viewport Lighting Mode** message will not be displayed on the screen.

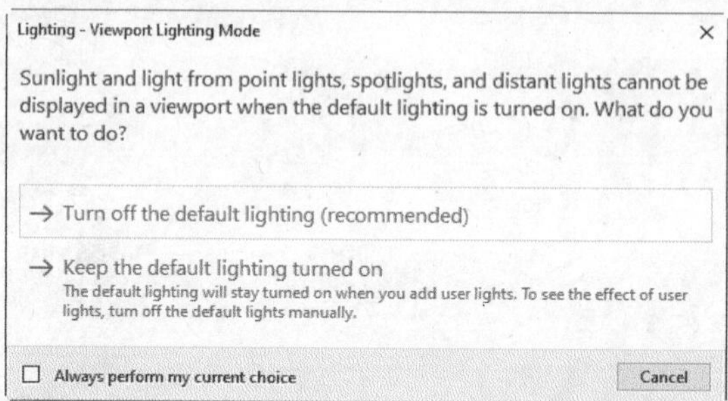

Figure 8-35 *The **Lighting - Viewport Lighting Mode** message box*

Point Light

Ribbon: Visualize > Lights > Create Light drop-down > Point
Menu Bar: View > Render > Light > New Point Light **Command:** POINTLIGHT

A point light source emits light in all directions and the intensity of the emitted light is uniform. You can visualize an electric bulb as a point light source. In AutoCAD render, if you select to add a point light, you can set the options of casting the shadow of the objects in the design. Figure 8-36 shows a point light source that radiates light uniformly in all directions.

As this is not the default light source, therefore, you will have to add it manually. This light source can be added by choosing the **Point** tool from the **Create Light** drop-down. The prompt sequence for the **Point** tool is given next.

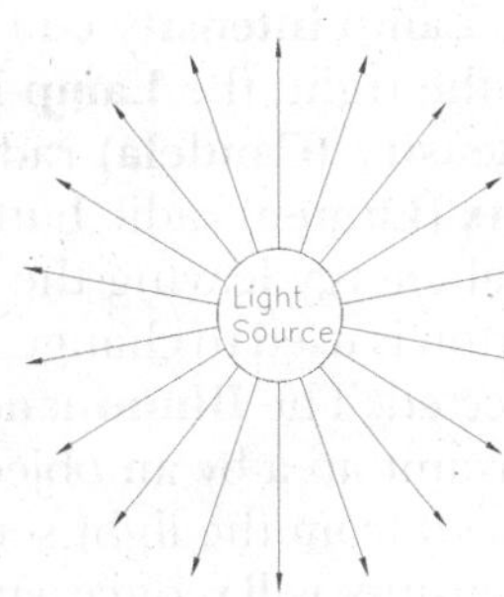

Figure 8-36 Point light source emitting light uniformly in all directions

Specify source location <0,0,0>: *Specify the location where you want to place the point light*
Enter an option to change [Name/Intensity factor/Status/Photometry/shadoW/Attenuation/filterColor/eXit] <eXit>: *Specify an option or press* Enter

The following options can be selected from this prompt:

Name

This option is used to specify the name of the point light. AutoCAD, by default, specifies a name to the newly created light. You can change the name by using this option.

Intensity factor

This option is used to specify the intensity of the point light. The prompt sequence that will be followed is given next.

Enter an option to change [Name/Intensity factor/Status/Photometry/shadoW/Attenuation/filterColor/eXit] <eXit>: **I** Enter
Enter intensity (0.00 - max float) <1.0000>: *Enter a value for the intensity of the light or press the* Enter *key to accept the default value.*

Status

This option is used to turn the point light on and off.

Photometry

This property will be available only when you work in the photometric environment, which means the **American lighting units** or **International lighting units** is selected as a unit in the **Lights** panel. The **Photometry** option is used to control the intensity, unit of intensity, color, and type of point lights, so that you can define the lights accurately according to the real world requirement. Instead of specifying the photometric properties of the point light in the tool itself, you can also specify or modify all the photometric properties later in the **PROPERTIES** palette of the point light, refer to Figure 8-37. The options in the **Photometric properties** rollout are discussed next.

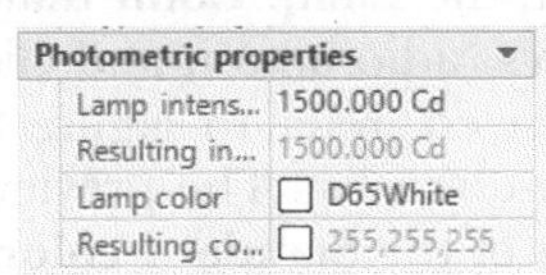

*Figure 8-37 The **Photometric properties** rollout of the **PROPERTIES** palette in the point light*

Lamp intensity. This property is used to specify the intensity, flux, or illuminance of the lamp. By default, the intensity of the light is specified in Candela. To change the properties, select the **Lamp intensity** edit box from the **PROPERTIES** palette and choose the swatch displayed on the right; the **Lamp Intensity** dialog box will be displayed, refer to Figure 8-38. Select the **Intensity (Candela)** radio button to specify the intensity of the point light in Candela. The **Flux (Lumen)** radio button is used to specify the flux of light in Lumen. The flux is the rate of total energy leaving the light source. The spinner on the right of the above mentioned radio button is used to change the value for both the intensity and flux depending on the radio button selected. The **Illuminance (Lux)** radio button is used to specify the amount of energy received per unit area by an object. In this case, you have to specify the distance at which the object is placed from the light source because the photometric lights are divergent by nature and their intensities will reduce with the increase of distance between the light source and the object. You can also increase or decrease the resulting intensity, flux, or illuminance of the light source by specifying a multiplying factor in the **Intensity factor** spinner of the **Resulting intensity** area. The resulting intensity will be the product of intensity input and the intensity factor.

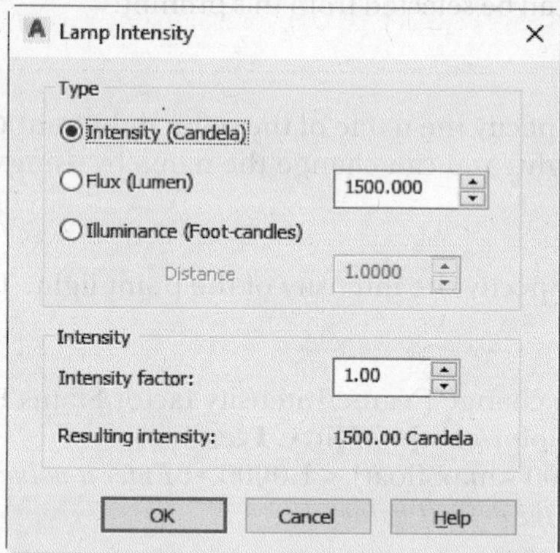

*Figure 8-38 The **Lamp Intensity** dialog box*

Resulting intensity. The **Resulting intensity** property displays the final intensity of the light source. This information is read-only.

Lamp color. This property is used to specify the lamp color of the light source. To specify or modify the lamp color, select the **Lamp color** edit box and choose the swatch displayed on the right; the **Lamp Color** dialog box will be displayed, refer to Figure 8-39. Select the **Standard colors** radio button and click on the down arrow; the **Standard colors** drop-down list will be displayed, refer to Figure 8-40. Select the standard predefined colored lights listed in this drop-down list. The preview of the selected light will be displayed in the color swatch on the right of the **Standard colors** drop-down list. An ideal black body emits a particular color at a particular temperature. To specify the lamp color with respect to temperature, select the **Kelvin colors** radio button. You can specify the temperature in Kelvin in the spinner just below the **Kelvin colors** radio button. The **Filter color** drop-down list in the **Resulting color** area is used to mix some colors with the lamp color. The final resulting color of the lamp will be a mixture of the lamp color and filter color. The preview of the resulting lamp color will be displayed in the color swatch in the **Resulting color** area.

Resulting color. The **Resulting color** property displays the resulting final color of the light source. This information is read-only.

shadoW

The sub-options provided under this option are used to control the display of the shadows of the objects after rendering. The sub-options are given next.

Off. This option is used to turn off the display of the shadow in rendering.

Sharp. This option is used to display the shadow of the objects with sharp edges.

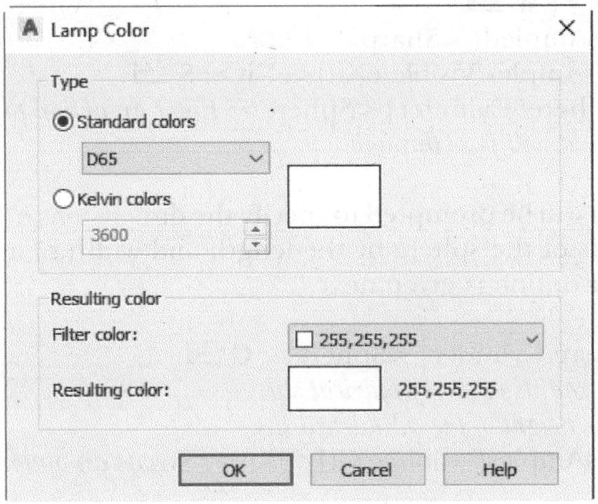

*Figure 8-39 The **Lamp Color** dialog box*

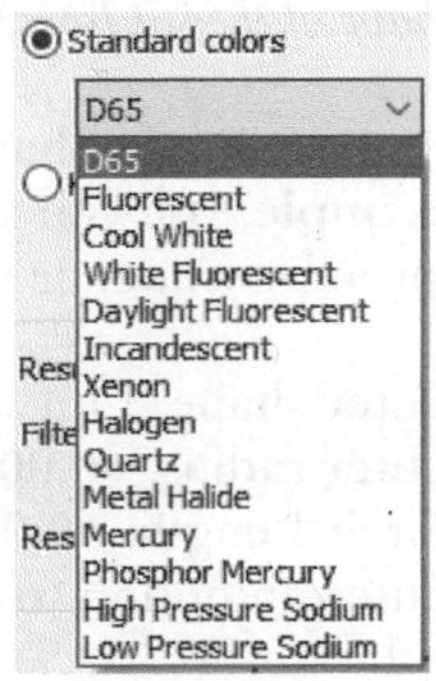

*Figure 8-40 The **Standard colors** drop-down list*

soFtmapped. This option is used to display the shadow with blurred edges. This gives a more realistic effect to the rendered image. If this sub-option is selected, you will have to specify the map size and softness of the shadow. The map size is calculated in terms of pixels. The greater the number of pixels, the better is the shadow. However, if the map size is large, the time taken to render the model will also increase. The shadow softness is used to specify the softness for the shadow. If the value of this option is increased, the shadow will be blurred. Figure 8-41 shows a model with a shadow map size=128 and softness=5, and Figure 8-42 shows a model with a shadow map size=1024 and softness=2.

*Figure 8-41 Shadow map size =**128** and softness = **5***

*Figure 8-42 Shadow map size =**1024** and softness = **2***

Tip

You can view the best shadow effect by keeping the value of the shadow map size 512 or 1024 and the shadow softness between 3 and 4.

softsAmpled. This option is used to specify the shape of the point light lamp. The shadow of the object will be displayed depending upon the shape of the point light lamp. The prompt sequence for this option is given next.

Enter an option to change [Name/Intensity factor/Status/Photometry/shadoW/ Attenuation/filterColor/eXit] <eXit>: **W** Enter
Enter [Off/Sharp/soFtmapped/softsAmpled] <Sharp>: **A** Enter
Enter an option to change [Shape/sAmples/Visible/eXit]<eXit>: **S** Enter
Enter shape [Linear/ Disk/ Rect/ Sphere/ Cylinder] <Sphere>: *Enter an option to specify the shape of the slit from which the point light will pass through.*

After specifying the shape of the slit, you will be prompted to specify the dimensions of the shape. For example, you can specify the radius of the sphere or the length and width of a rectangle. The prompt sequence for the **Cylinder** option is given next.

Enter shape [Linear/Disk/Rect/Sphere/Cylinder] <Sphere>: **C** Enter
Enter radius <0.0000>: *Specify the radius of the cylindrical slit.*
Enter Length <0.0000>: *Specify the height of the cylindrical slit.*
Enter an option to change [Shape/sAmples/Visible/eXit]<eXit>: *Specify an option or press* Enter

The **sAmples** option in the above prompt is used to specify the size of the shadow samples for light. The default value of the shadow sample is 16. The **Visible** option is used to specify whether to display the shape of the lamp in rendering or not. Figure 8-43 displays the rendered image of a cylindrical shape point light without the visibility of the point light shape. Figure 8-44 displays the same rendered image with the point light shape visible.

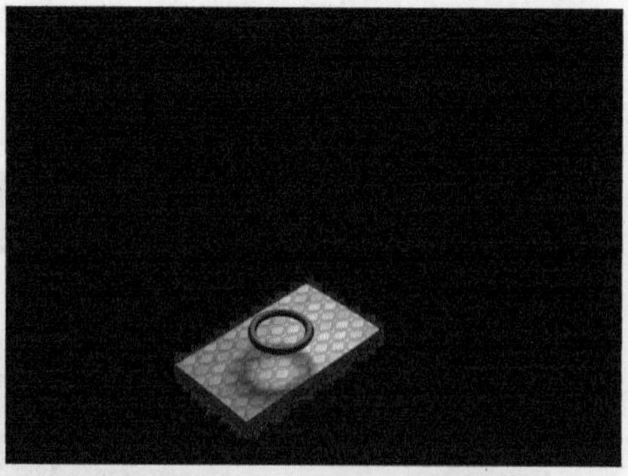

Figure 8-43 *Rendered image with the shape of cylindrical point light not visible*

Figure 8-44 *Rendered image with the shape of point light visible*

Note

The shape of the point light is also displayed in the drawing area close to the point light. When you move the cursor over the point light, the shape of the point light is highlighted in default color.

Attenuation

The light intensity is defined as the amount of light falling per unit of area. The intensity of light is inversely proportional to the distance between the light source and the object. Therefore, the intensity decreases as the distance increases. This phenomenon is called Attenuation. In AutoCAD, it occurs only with spotlights and a point light.

In Figure 8-45, light is emitted by a point source. Assume the amount of light incident on Area1 is I. Therefore, the intensity of light on Area1 = I/Area. As light travels farther from the source, it covers a larger area. The amount of light falling on Area2 is the same as on Area1 but the area is larger. Therefore, the intensity of light for Area2 is smaller (Intensity of light for Area2 = I/Area). Area1 will be brighter than Area2 because of a higher light intensity. The prompt sequence that will follow after selecting this option is given next.

Enter an option to change [attenuation Type/Use limits/attenuation start Limit/attenuation End limit/eXit] <eXit>:
Select a sub-option or press the Enter *key.*

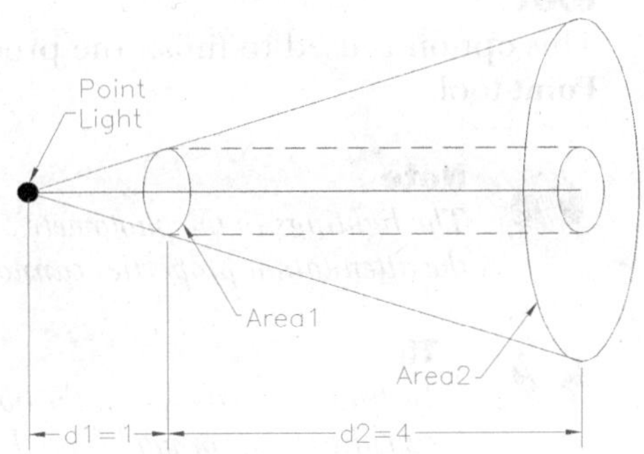

***Figure 8-45** Example of attenuation*

The sub-options that you can select at the above prompt are:

attenuation Type. AutoCAD render provides you with the following three types of attenuation.

None. If you select the **None** sub-option for the light falloff, the brightness of the objects will be independent of the distance. This means that the objects that are far away from the point light source will be as bright that are close to it.

Inverse linear. In this sub-option, the light falling on the object (brightness) is inversely proportional to the distance of the object from the light source (Brightness = 1/Distance). As the distance increases, the brightness decreases. For example, assume that the intensity of the light source is I and the object is located at a distance of 2 units from the light source. Now, the brightness or intensity = I/2. If the distance is 8 units, the intensity (light falling on the object per unit area) = I/8. The brightness is a linear function of the distance of the object from the light source.

inverse Squared. In this sub-option, the light falling on the object (brightness) is inversely proportional to the square of the distance between the object and the light source (Brightness = 1/Distance^2). For example, assume that the intensity of the light source is I and the object is located at a distance of 2 units from the light source. Now, the brightness or intensity = $I/(2)^2$ = I/4. If the distance is 8 units, the intensity (light falling on the object per unit area) = $I/(8)^2$ = I/64.

Use limits. This option is used to specify whether you want to use the sub-options of **attenuation start Limit and attenuation End limit**. The effect of these limits can only be visualized in rendering, if the sub-option of **Use limits** is turned on.

attenuation start Limit. This option is used to specify the distance from the centre of the light to the point where the light will start.

attenuation End limit. This option is used to specify the distance from the center of the light at which the light will finish. The objects beyond this limit will not be illuminated by this point light.

filterColor

This option is used to specify the color for the point light. You can define a custom color by using the RGB combination. You can select a color by choosing the **Index color** sub-option. Select the sub-option **Hsl** to define the color by Hue, Saturation, and Luminance. You can also specify the color of the point light from the color book by choosing the **colorBook** sub-option. Next, enter the name of the color book from which you want to choose the color.

eXit

This option is used to finish the process of defining the point light properties and to exit the **Point** tool.

Note

The lightings in the photometric workflow always follow the inverse squared attenuation type and the attenuation properties cannot be modified later on for photometric lights.

Tip

Instead of specifying all the above-mentioned properties of the point light in the tool itself, you can also specify or modify all the properties later on from the ***Properties*** *palette of the point light.*

Example 2

In this example, you will download the drawing file of the model shown in Figure 8-46 from *https://www.cadcim.com*. The path of the file is as follows: *Textbooks > CAD/CAM > AutoCAD Advanced > Advanced AutoCAD 2021: A Problem-Solving Approach(3D and Advanced) > Input Files*. Next, you will apply the point light at the lintel of the window and at the lintel of the door of the model, as shown in Figure 8-47. Choose your own materials to make the model look realistic and then render it.

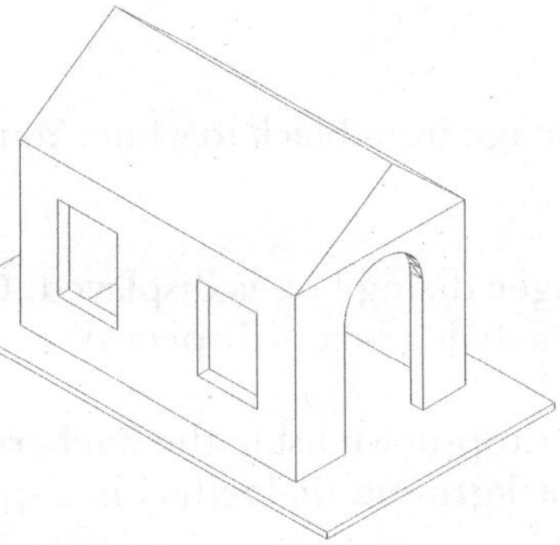

Figure 8-46 Model for Example 2

Figure 8-47 Model after rendering

1. Download the model shown in Figure 8-46 using the path mentioned above.
2. Choose materials from **Material Browser** and then attach them to the model as described in Example 1. (Recommended: Use **Masonry - Stone > Limestone - Ashlar Coursed** for Walls, **Ceramic - Tile > Mosaic Blue** for flooring, and **Flooring - Vinyl - Diamonds 1** for roof.)
3. Choose the **Point** tool from **Visualize > Lights > Create Light** drop-down to add a point light.
4. Choose the **Turn off the default lighting (recommended)** option from the **Lighting - Viewport Lighting Mode** message box. (This message box will be displayed when you create the light for the first time).
5. The prompt sequence of the **Point** light tool is given next.

Specify source location <0,0,0>: *Specify the location of the point light at the lintel of the first window*
Enter an option to change [Name/Intensity factor/Status/Photometry/shadoW/Attenuation/filterColor/eXit] <eXit>: **N** Enter
Enter light name <Pointlight>: **1** Enter
Enter an option to change [Name/Intensity factor/Status/Photometry/shadoW/Attenuation/filterColor/eXit] <eXit>: **C** Enter
Enter true color (R,G,B) or enter an option [Index color/Hsl/colorBook]<255,255,255>: **I** Enter
Enter color name or number (1-255): **Yellow** Enter
Enter an option to change [Name/Intensity factor/Status/Photometry/shadoW/Attenuation/filterColor/eXit] <eXit>: **I** Enter
Enter intensity (0.00 - max float) <1.0000>: *Specify the intensity based on the size of the objects in the drawing and press the* Enter key
Enter an option to change [Name/Intensity factor/Status/Photometry/shadoW/Attenuation/filterColor/eXit] <eXit>: **S** Enter
Enter status [oN/oFf] <On>: Enter

6. Similarly, you can set the second light at the lintel of the door. Set the color of the light to green.

   Now, you need to set the background of the image from black to white. You can also set any image as the background image.

7. Invoke the **VIEW** command; the **View Manager** dialog box is displayed. Choose the **New** button from it; the **New View/Shot Properties** dialog box is displayed.

8. Select the **Solid** option from the **Background** drop-down list in the **Background** area in the **View Properties** tab of the dialog box; the **Background** dialog box is displayed.

9. Click on the **Color** swatch and select the white color as the background color and exit the dialog box.

10. Assign a name to the view in the **New View/ Shot Properties** dialog box and then exit it.
11. Select the view from the **Views** list and choose the **Apply** button.
12. Choose the **Render to size** tool in the **Render** panel; the **Render** window is displayed and the rendering process starts. The rendered image is displayed in the **Render** window. The rendered image looks similar to the image shown in Figure 8-48.

***Figure 8-48** Rendered model of a house*

Tip

*You can increase the smoothness of the rendered curved object by increasing the value of the **FACETRES** system variable. The default value of this variable is 0.5. Set this value close to **6**.*

Spotlight

Ribbon: Visualize > Lights > Create Light drop-down > Spot
Menu Bar: View > Render > Light > New Spotlight **Command:** SPOTLIGHT

A spotlight emits light in the defined direction with a cone-shaped light beam. This light has a focused beam that starts from a point and is targeted at another point. This type of light is generally used to illuminate a specific point, such as illuminating a person on a stage. The phenomenon of attenuation also applies to spotlights. This light source can be added by choosing the **Spot** light tool from the **Create Light** drop-down. When you choose this tool, you will be prompted to enter two values. As already mentioned, this type of light source has a start point and a target point. Therefore, you will first be prompted to specify the light location and then the light target. The prompt sequence displayed when the **Spot** light tool is invoked is given next.

Specify source location <0,0,0>: *Specify the point where you want to place the spotlight*
Specify target location <0,0,-10>: *Specify the location on the object where you want to focus the spotlight*
Enter an option to change [Name/Intensity factor/Status/Photometry/Hotspot/Falloff/ shadoW/Attenuation/filterColor/eXit] <eXit>: *Specify an option or press* Enter

Most of the options in the **Spot** light tool are similar to those in the **Point** tool. The options that are different are discussed next.

Hotspot/Falloff

As mentioned earlier, the spotlight has a focused beam of light that is targeted at a particular point. Therefore, there are two cones that comprise the spotlight.

The hotspot is the same as the cone that carries the highest intensity light beam. In this cone, the light beam is the most focused and is defined in terms of an angle, refer to Figures 8-49(a) and 8-49(b).

The prompt sequence for the **Hotspot** option is given next.

Enter an option to change [Name/Intensityfactor/Status/Photometry/Hotspot/Falloff/ shadoW/Attenuation/filterColor/eXit]<eXit>: **H** Enter
Enter hotspot angle (0.00-160.00) <45.0000>: *Specify the interior angle of the cone in which the intensity of light will be high or press the* Enter *key to accept the default value*

The other cone is called a falloff and it specifies the full cone of light. It is the area around the hotspot where the intensity of the beam of light is not very high, as shown in Figures 8-49(a) and 8-49(b). It is defined in terms of an angle. The value of the hotspot and the falloff can vary from 0 to 160. The prompt sequence for the **Falloff** option is given next.

Enter an option to change [Name/Intensity factor/Status/Photometry/Hotspot/Falloff/ shadoW/Attenuation/filterColor/eXit]<eXit>: **F** Enter
Enter falloff angle (0.00-160.00) <current>: *Specify the interior angle of the cone in which the intensity of the light will be high or press the* Enter *key to accept the default value*

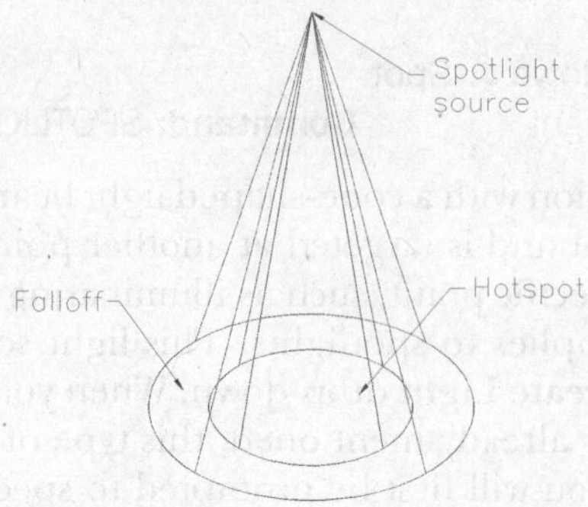

Figure 8-49(a) The hotspot and falloff cones

Figure 8-49(b) The hotspot and falloff after rendering

Tip

The value of hotspot should always be less than the value of falloff. If you set the value of the hotspot more than the value of the falloff, then the value of the falloff will automatically change to one degree greater than the value of the hotspot.

Distant Light

Ribbon: Visualize > Lights > Create Light drop-down > Distant
Toolbar: Lights > New Distant Light
Menu Bar: View > Render > Light > New Distant Light **Command:** DISTANTLIGHT

A distant light source emits a uniform parallel beam of light in a single direction only, refer to Figure 8-50. The intensity of the light beam does not decrease with the distance. It remains constant. For example, the sunrays can be assumed to be a distant light source because the light rays are parallel. When you use a distant light source in a drawing, the location of the light source does not matter; only the direction is critical. Distant light is mostly used to light objects or a backdrop uniformly and for getting the effect of the sunlight.

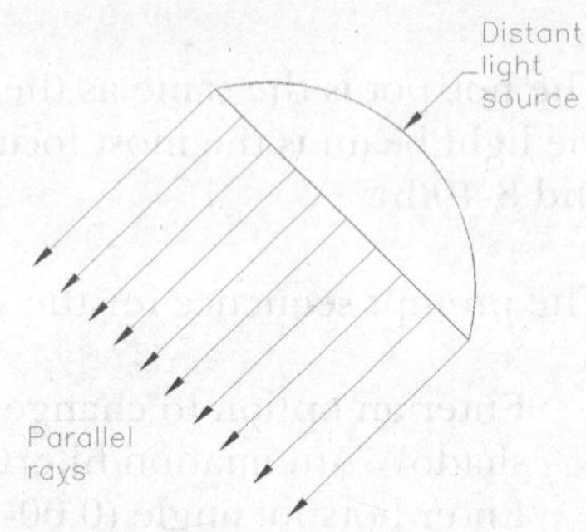

Figure 8-50 Distant light source

The distant lights are inaccurate and their use in photometric workflow is not preferred. Therefore, the **Distant** light tool is not available for the use in the photometric workflow. However, to use the distant light in photometric workflow, choose the **Distant** tool from the **Create Light** drop-down of the **Lights** panel in the **Visualise** tab; the **Lighting - Viewport Lighting Mode** message box will be displayed on the screen. Choose the **Turn off the default lighting (recommended)** option so that the effect of the distant lights can be seen. On doing so, the **Lighting - Photometric Distant Lights** message box is displayed, refer to Figure 8-51. Choose the **Allow distant lights** button from this message box to invoke the **Distant** light tool. The prompt sequence displayed when the **Distant** light tool is invoked is given next.

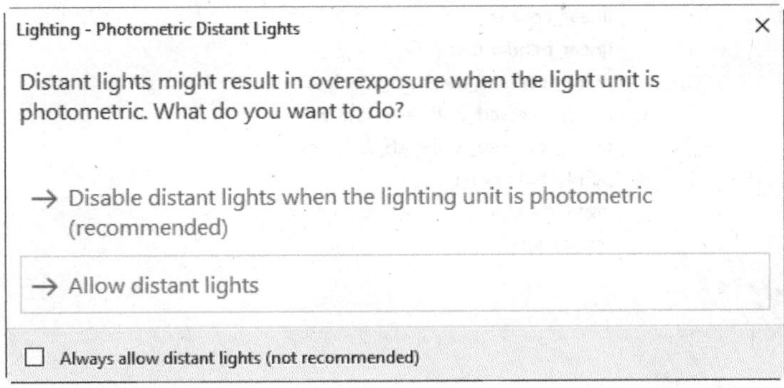

*Figure 8-51 The **Lighting - Photometric Distant Lights** message box*

Specify light direction FROM <0,0,0> or [Vector]: *Specify the start point to represent the viewing direction of the distant light or type **V** and press the ENTER key.*
Specify light direction TO <1,1,1>: *Specify the endpoint to represent the viewing direction of the distant light.*
Enter an option to change [Name/Intensity factor/Status/Photometry/shadoW/filterColor/eXit] <eXit>: *Specify an option.*

If you select the **Vector** option at the **Specify light direction FROM <0,0,0> or [Vector]** prompt, then you will have to specify the vector direction in which the distant light will focus. The options in the **Distant** light tool are similar to those in the **Point** tool.

Web Light

Ribbon: Visualize > Lights > Create Light drop-down > Weblight
Command: WEBLIGHT

Web lights are used to create illuminated scenes that look more realistic than those created by using the spot or point lights. You can create a web light by invoking the **Weblight** tool from the **Lights** panel. On invoking this tool, you are prompted to specify the source and then the target point. Specify the source and then the target point. Next, specify the name, intensity, status, photometry, web file, shadows, etc to create the web light. The web lights offer a detailed 3D distribution of the intensity of a light in all directions. The distribution can be isotropic or anisotropic. The isotropic distribution represents a sphere-shaped web, and its effect will be the same as that of point light. However, the web light is generally used for anisotropic or non-uniform light distribution. The anisotropic distribution gives a unique washed effect on the surface it hits. The information regarding this light distribution is saved in an AutoCAD program file having extension *.ies*. These files are generally provided by manufacturers of lights and fixtures. You can load the manufacturers' *.ies* files in the **Photometric Web** panel of the **Properties** palette.To load the .ies files, go to the **PROPERTIES** palette; choose the swatch displayed on the right in the web file box; the **Select Web File** dialog box will be displayed, refer to Figure 8-52. In this palette, you can set the other properties such as intensity, as well.

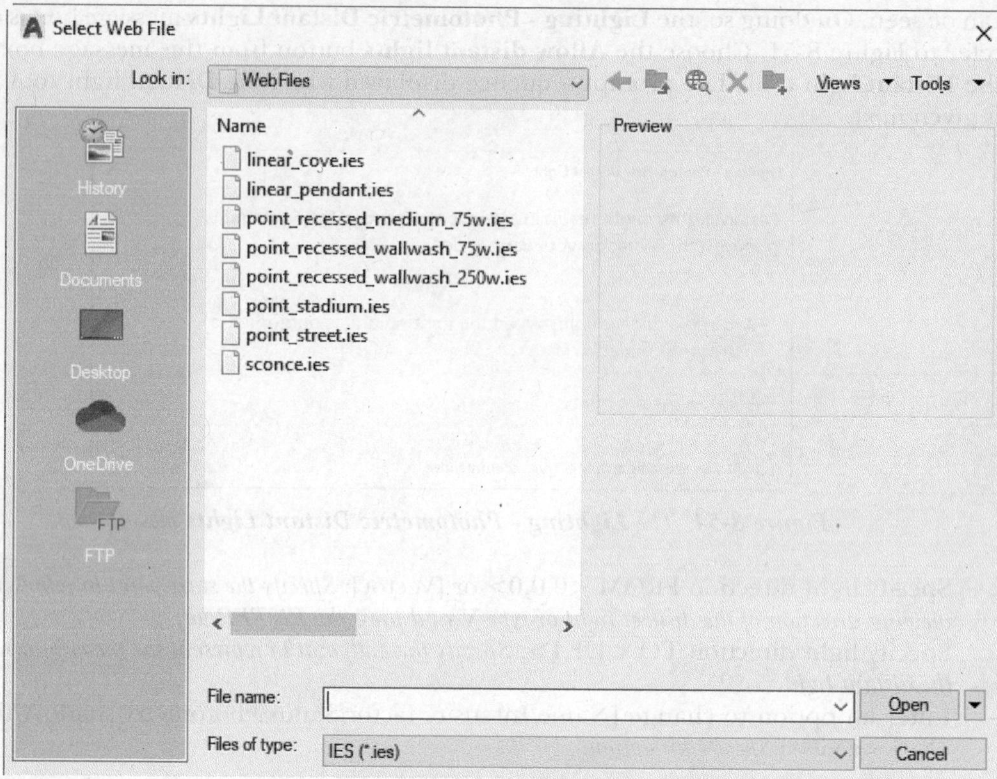

*Figure 8-52 The **Select Web File** dialog box*

Sun Light

Ribbon: Visualize > Sun & Location (Inclined Arrow)
Menu Bar: View > Render > Light > Sun Properties **Toolbar:** Lights > Sun Properties
Command: SUNPROPERTIES

This light is similar to the actual sun light in which the rays are parallel and have the same intensity at any distance. The angle subtended by rays on an object depends on the location, date, and time specified. You can also change the intensity and color of the sunlight. Unlike distant light, sunlight can only be one in number. In the photometric workflow, you can also control the illumination effect when the sky comes between the sunlight and the object. This helps in adding more realistic lighting caused by the interaction between the sun and the sky.

To use sunlight, click on the inclined arrow in the **Sun & Location** panel of the **Visualize** tab; the **SUN PROPERTIES** palette will be displayed, as shown in Figure 8-53. The options in this palette are discussed next.

General

In this area, you can switch on or off the sunlight and change its intensity and color.

Sky Properties

These properties are only available while working in the photometric workflow. You can use the sky in between the model and the sun for the illumination of the model. The options available in the **Status** drop-down list are **Sky Off**, **Sky Background**, and **Sky Background and Illumination**. These options are also available in the **Sky Status** drop-down list under **Sun & Location** panel of the **Visualize** tab. Note that these options are available in the Perspective view only.

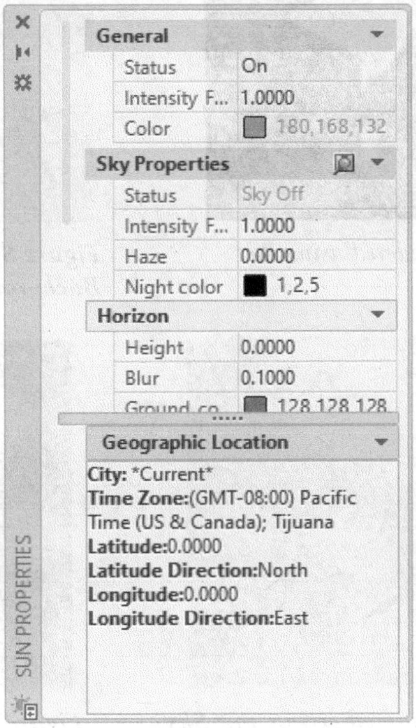

Figure 8-53 *The* ***SUN PROPERTIES*** *palette*

Figure 8-54 displays a model rendered by using the **Sky Off** option, Figure 8-55 displays a model rendered by using the **Sky Background** option, and Figure 8-56 displays the model rendered by using the **Sky Background and Illumination** option. The **Intensity Factor** edit box is used to magnify the brightness of the light reaching the object after passing through the sky. Figure 8-56 displays the rendered model by choosing the **Sky Background and Illumination** option and intensity factor set to **1** and Figure 8-57 displays the same model rendered by selecting the **Sky Background and Illumination** option and intensity factor set to **0.2**. The **Haze** edit box determines the amount of scattering in the atmosphere and the haze value can vary from 0 to 15. Figure 8-56 displays a rendered model with haze value set to **0** and Figure 8-58 displays the same model rendered with haze value set to **7**. The **Night Colour** edit box allows you to specify the colour of the night sky.

Figure 8-54 Model rendered using the ***Sky Off*** *option*

Figure 8-55 Model rendered using the ***Sky Background*** *option*

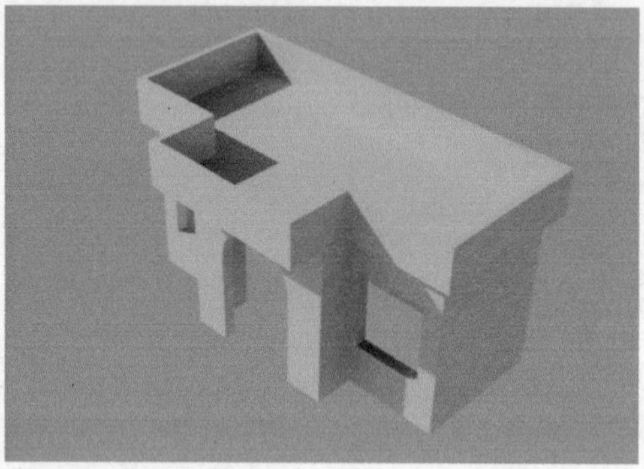

Figure 8-56 Model rendered using the ***Sky Background and Illumination*** *option with the intensity and haze values set to* ***1*** *and* ***0****, respectively*

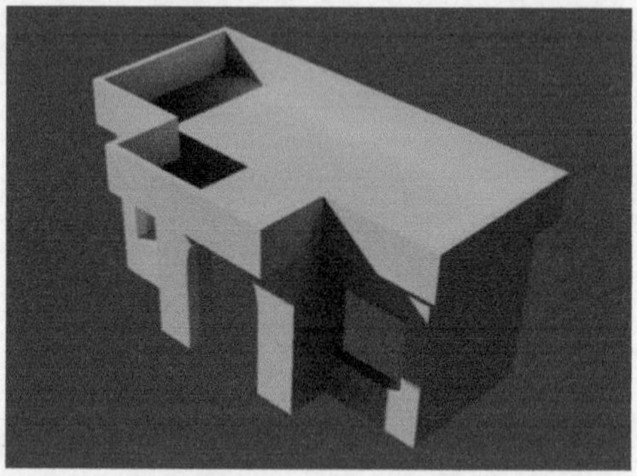

Figure 8-57 Model rendered using the ***Sky Background and Illumination*** *option with the intensity value set to* ***0.2***

Horizon. The options in this area are used to control the location and appearance of the ground. Figure 8-59 displays a rendered model created by selecting the **Sun & Sky Background** option and setting that view as current. The ground color for the rendered image is set to **Cyan**.

Sun disk appearance. The properties under this rollout are used to control the appearance of the sun disk such as its size, intensity, and so on, when a view is saved with the **Sun & Sky Background**.

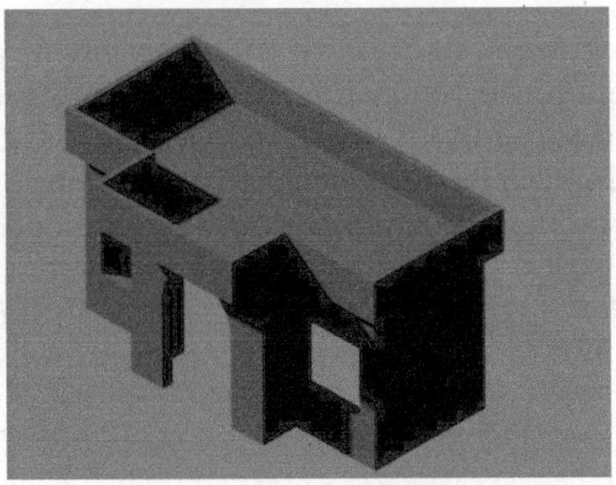

Figure 8-58 *Model rendered using the* ***Sky Background and Illumination*** *option with the intensity and haze values set to* ***1*** *and* ***7****, respectively*

Figure 8-59 *Model rendered with the view saved as* ***Sun & Sky Background*** *and ground color set to* ***Cyan***

Note

You can also specify or modify the ***Sky Properties*** *from the* ***Adjust Sun & Sky Background*** *dialog box which can be displayed by clicking on the swatch on the right side of the* ***Background*** *area in the* ***New View / Shot Properties*** *dialog box, refer to Figure 8-60.*

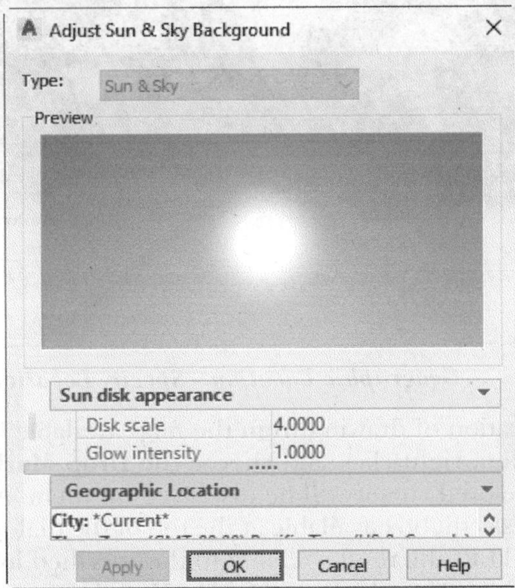

Figure 8-60 *The* ***Adjust Sun & Sky Background*** *dialog box*

Sun Angle Calculator

In this area, you can set the date and time in the **Date** and **Time** edit boxes, respectively. You can also switch on or off the effect of day light settings in the rendering. Apart from this, you can also view some read only information in this field such as the azimuth and altitude of the sun light direction. You can also view the default light source vector as the coordinates in the X, Y, and Z list boxes in the **Source Vector** area.

Geographic Location

This area displays information about the geographic location of the place where you want to view the light effect. You can edit this information by choosing the **From Map** tool from the **Set Location** drop-down of the **Sun & Location** panel of the **Visualize** tab; the **Geographic Location - Specify Location (Page 1 of 2)** window will be displayed with various options to define the location, refer to Figure 8-61. Note that you need to log into your Autodesk account to set the location from online maps. You can pick the location from this window. You can also define the location by importing the exact location data like longitude, latitude, and altitude from the *.kml* or *.kmz* files. To do so, choose the **From file** tool from the **Set Location** drop-down. The options in this dialog box are given next.

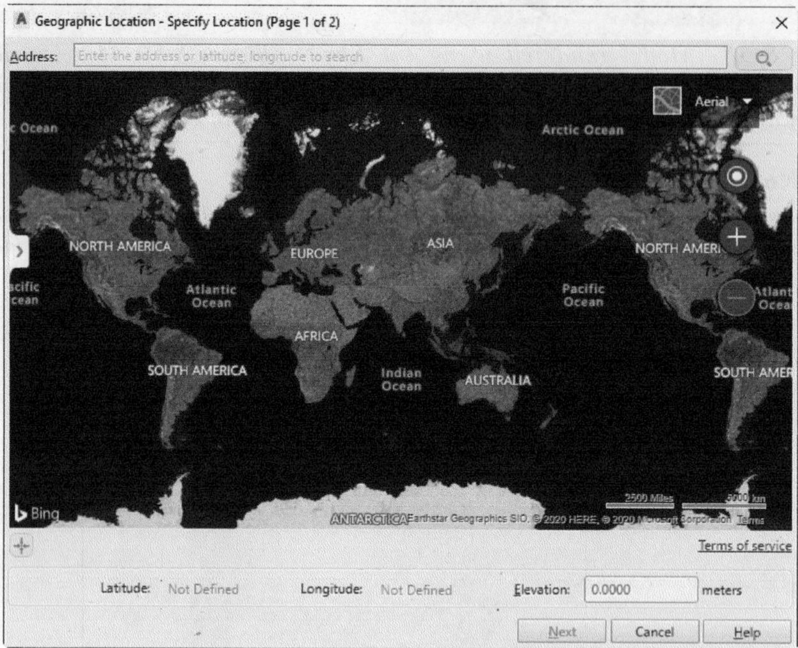

***Figure 8-61** The **Geographic Location - Specify Location (Page 1 of 2)** window*

You can select the location of drawing from the map available in this window. To do so, zoom to the required location, right-click and choose the **Drop Marker Here** option. On selecting the locations, a red colored cursor will be displayed on them. Alternatively, you can enter the location in the **Address** edit box available at the top of the dialog box. After entering the name of location, press ENTER; the results related to the specified location will be displayed on the left side of the dialog box. Also, the **Drop Marker Here** button will be displayed on the selected result. Choose the button; the marker will be placed at the specified location.

You can also specify the values for GIS Coordinate System. To do so, choose the **Next** button from the **Geographic Location - Specify Location (Page 1 of 2)**; the **Geographic Location - Set Coordinate System (Page 2 of 2)** will be displayed, as shown in Figure 8-62. Also, a list of different coordinate systems will be displayed. Select the required coordinate system from the list. You can also specify different time zones and drawing units by selecting required options from the **Time Zone** and **Drawing Unit** drop-down lists. Next, choose the **Next** button from the dialog box; you will be prompted to specify a point for the location. Specify the point; you will be prompted to specify the north direction angle. Specify the direction; the geographic map will be displayed in the drawing area. Also, the **Geolocation** contextual tab will be added in the **Ribbon**, as shown in Figure 8-63.

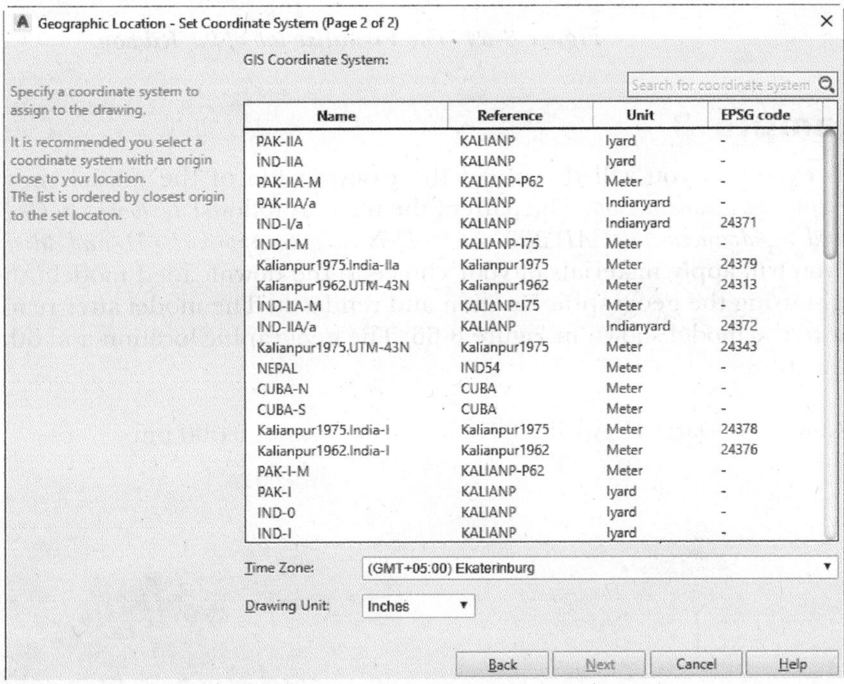

***Figure 8-62** The **Geographic Location - Specify Location (Page 2 of 2)** window*

You can use the options in this contextual tab to edit, reorient, remove, and map the locations. You can also capture area and viewport using the options in this tab.

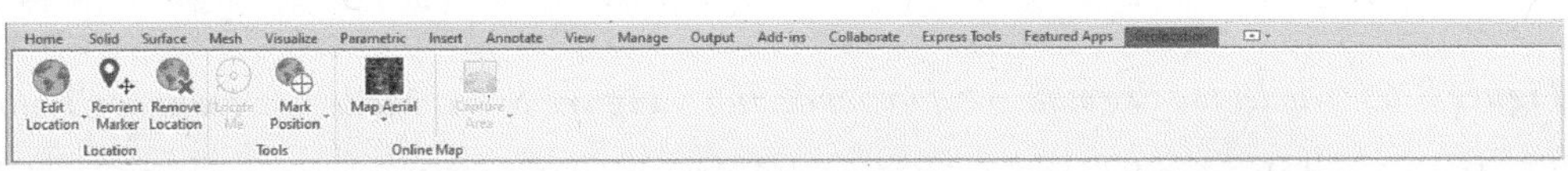

***Figure 8-63** The **Geolocation** contextual tab*

Note

*1. If the **Sun Status** button is chosen in the **Sun & Location** panel, sunlight is turned on.*

2. Except for the geographic location, the rest of the settings for the sun and the sky are saved for a particular viewport and not for the entire drawing.

You can also switch the sun light on and off, set the sky background illumination, change the date and time, open and close the **Sun Properties** palette and the **Geographic Location** window directly from the **Visualize** tab of the **Ribbon**, refer to Figure 8-64.

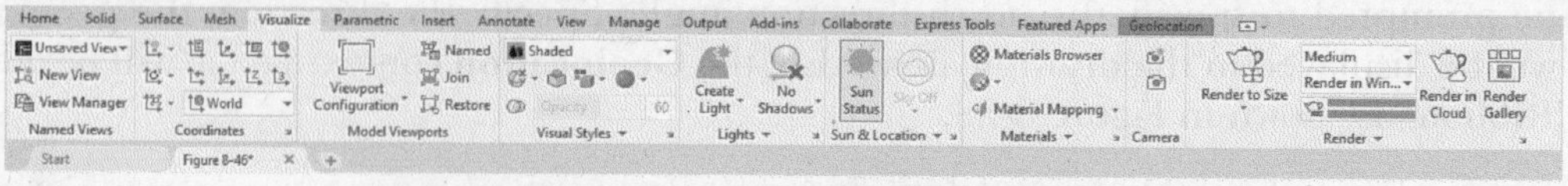

Figure 8-64 *The* ***Visualize*** *tab of the* ***Ribbon***

Example 3

In this example, you will download the drawing file of the model shown in Figure 8-65 from *https://www.cadcim.com*. The path of the file is as follows: *Textbooks > CAD/CAM > AutoCAD Advanced > Advanced AutoCAD 2021: A Problem-Solving Approach (3D and Advanced) > Input Files*. Next, you will apply materials of your choice to the downloaded model. Also, you will set the sun light using the geographic location and render it. The model after rendering should look similar to the model shown in Figure 8-66. The geographic location and other parameters are given next.

City: New York, Date: 15 April, 2021 Time: 04:00 pm

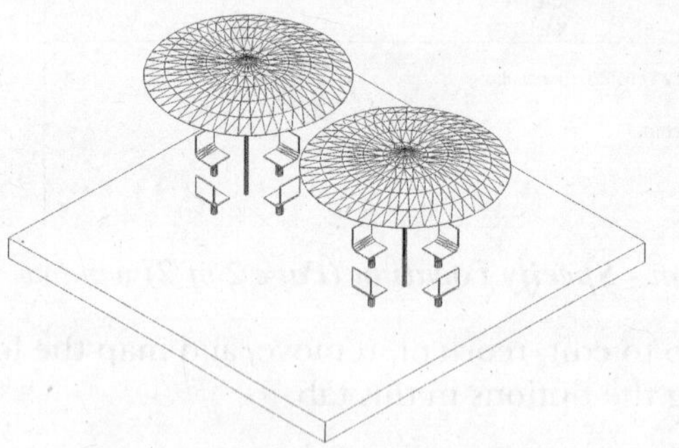

Figure 8-65 *Model for Example 3 before rendering*

Figure 8-66 *Model for Example 3 after rendering*

1. Download the model shown in Figure 8-65 using the path mentioned above.

2. Select the materials of your choice and apply them to the model, as explained earlier.

3. Choose the **Sky Background and Illumination** option from **Visualise > Sun & Location > Sky** drop-down.

4. Click on the inclined arrow in the **Sun & Location** panel of the **Visualize** tab to invoke the **SUN PROPERTIES** palette and set the **Intensity Factor** value to **2.0** under the **Sky Properties** rollout.

5. Specify a color of your choice for the ground in the **Ground color** edit box under the **Horizon** sub-rollout and then exit the **SUN PROPERTIES** palette.

6. Choose the **Set Location > From Map** tool from the **Sun & Location** panel of the **Visualize** tab; the **Geographic Location** window is displayed.

7. Enter **New York** in the search box located at the top of the **Geographic Location - Specify Location (Page 1 of 2)** window and choose the search button next to it; the search results are displayed on the left side of the window.

8. Place the cursor on **New York, NY** in the search results area and choose the **Drop Marker Here** button; a marker is placed in New York. Choose the **Next** Button; the **Geographic Location - Set Coordinate System (Page 2 of 2)** window will be displayed. The time zone is updated in the **Time Zone** drop-down list. Select any GIS coordinate system from the given list.

9. Choose the **Next** button from the dialog box; you are prompted to specify the location point in the drawing.

10. Select the point on the model, as shown in Figure 8-67; you are prompted to specify the north direction.

11. Move the cursor vertically and click to specify the north direction.

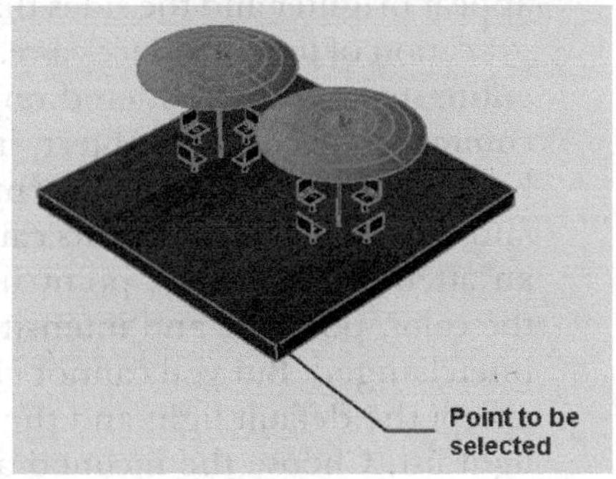

***Figure 8-67** Location point in the model*

12. Choose the **Sun Status** button from the **Sun & Location** panel of the **Visualize** tab; the **Lighting - Viewport Lighting Mode** message box is displayed. Choose the **Turn off the default lighting (recommended)** option.

13. Set the date and time as **4/15/2021** and **4:00 PM** in the **Date** and **Time** edit boxes, respectively in the **Sun & Location** panel of the **Visualize** tab.

14. Choose the **Render to size** tool from the **Visualize** tab to invoke the **Render** window. The rendering process will start and the rendered image will be displayed in the **Render** window.

CONVERTING LIGHTS CREATED IN AutoCAD'S PREVIOUS RELEASE INTO AUTOCAD 2021 FORMAT

For converting a model created in AutoCAD 2014 or earlier version of AutoCAD to AutoCAD 2021 format such that it supports both the standard workflow and the photometric workflow, set the value of **LIGHTINGUNITS** system variable to 1 or 2. The models and lights created prior to AutoCAD 2021 can be converted to the lights of AutoCAD 2021 by the **CONVERTOLDLIGHTS** command. The prompt sequence to do so is given next.

Command: **CONVERTOLDLIGHTS**
Loading materials...done.
2 light(s) converted

In the prompt sequence, only 2 lights have been converted for the current drawing. Therefore, the prompt sequence displays **2 light(s) converted**. The prompt sequence will display the number of lights converted and also the lights that are not converted. Note that after converting the lights, their effect is not always the same as in their original versions. Therefore, you have to modify some parameters such as intensity, color, and so on.

MODIFYING LIGHTS

As mentioned earlier, the lights and the lighting effects are important in rendering in order to create a realistic representation of an object. The sides of an object that face the light must appear brighter and the sides that are on the other side of the object must be darker. This smooth gradation of light produces a realistic image of the object. If the light intensity is uniform on the entire surface, the rendered object will not look realistic. For example, if you use the **SHADE** command to shade an object, it does not look realistic because the displayed model lacks any kind of gradation of light. Any number of lights can be added to the drawing. The color, location, and direction of all the lights can be specified individually. As mentioned earlier, you can specify an attenuation for the point lights and the spotlights. AutoCAD also allows you to change the color, position, and intensity of any light source. The point light and the spotlight can be interchanged. But you cannot change a distant light into a point light or a spotlight. All lights, except the default light and the sun light, attached to the current drawing are displayed in the light list. Choose the inclined arrow on the **Lights** panel of the **Visualize** tab of the **Ribbon**; the **LIGHTS IN MODEL** palette will be displayed, as shown in Figure 8-68. From this list box, select the light you want to modify, right-click, and then choose the **Properties** option from the shortcut menu displayed. Depending on the type of light selected, the **PROPERTIES** palette will be displayed. For example, if you select a distant light for modifications, the **PROPERTIES** palette with the distant light properties will be displayed. One such **PROPERTIES** palette is shown in Figure 8-69.

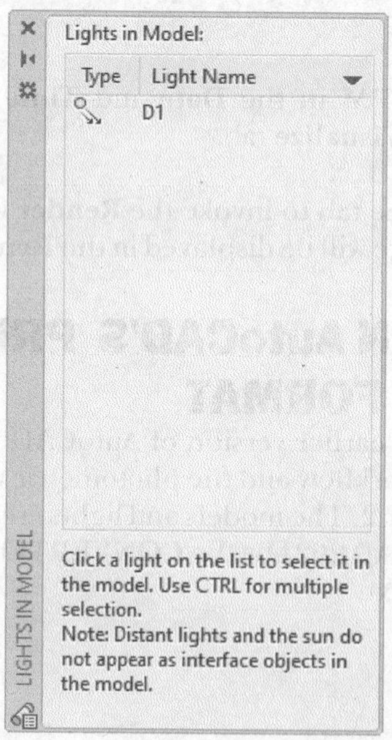

*Figure 8-68 The **LIGHTS IN MODEL** palette*

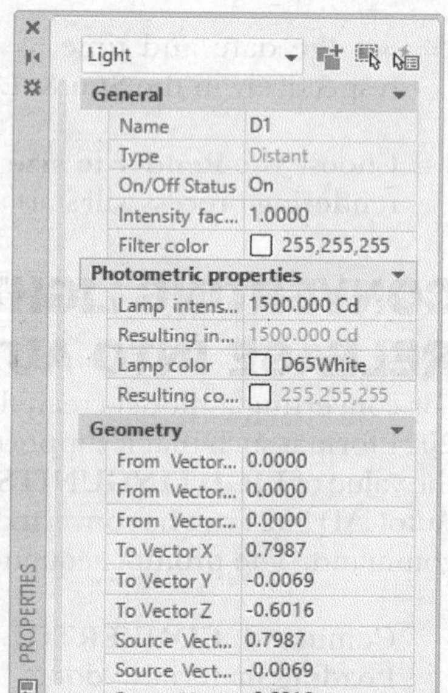

*Figure 8-69 The **PROPERTIES** palette for distant light*

All options in this window are similar to those under the **Point** tool. You can also modify the lights dynamically with the help of grips. This method provides a dynamic preview of the modifications made in lights. The symbols of the point light and the spot light can also be shown or hidden by choosing the **Light glyph display** button from the **Lights** panel of the **Visualize** tab.

UNDERSTANDING RENDERING PRESETS

As mentioned earlier, rendering allows you to control the appearance of the objects in the design. This is done by defining the surface material and the reflective quality of the surface and by adding lights to get the desired effects. The basic rendering has already been discussed earlier in this chapter.

You can also render the model using the **RENDER PRESETS MANAGER** window by choosing the **Render** button displayed at the upper right corner. To invoke the **RENDER PRESETS MANAGER** window, click on the inclined arrow in the **Render** panel of the **Visualize** tab. The options in this drop-down are discussed next.

Current Preset

The **current preset** drop-down list in the **RENDER PRESETS MANAGER** window contains six standard qualities of rendering as presets, refer to Figure 8-70. These are **Low, Medium, High, Coffee-Break Quality, Lunch Quality**, and **Overnight Quality**. The lowest quality of rendering is done in the **Low** preset. The quality of rendering goes on improving progressively on selecting different options, and it is the best when you select the **Overnight Quality** preset. However, you can also create your own render presets by creating copies of your current render settings, which will be explained in detail later in this chapter.

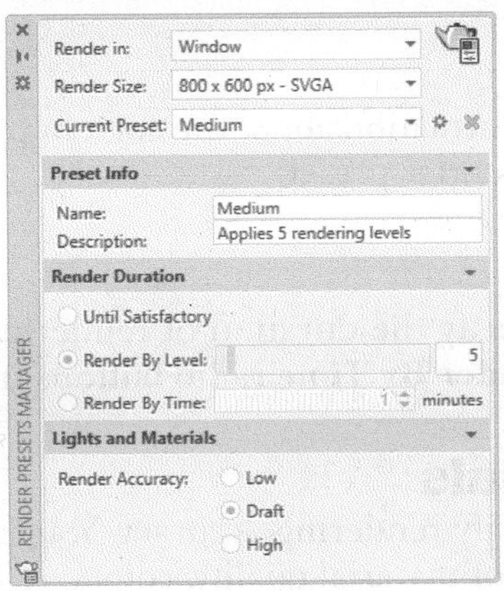

*Figure 8-70 The **RENDER PRESETS MANAGER** window*

Render Size

In this drop-down list, you can define custom output resolution of a rendered image. If you want to specify a user-defined resolution for output image, select **More Output Settings** from the drop-down list. On doing so, the **Render to Size Output Settings** window will be displayed. In this window, you can define settings for the custom resolution, as shown in Figure 8-71.

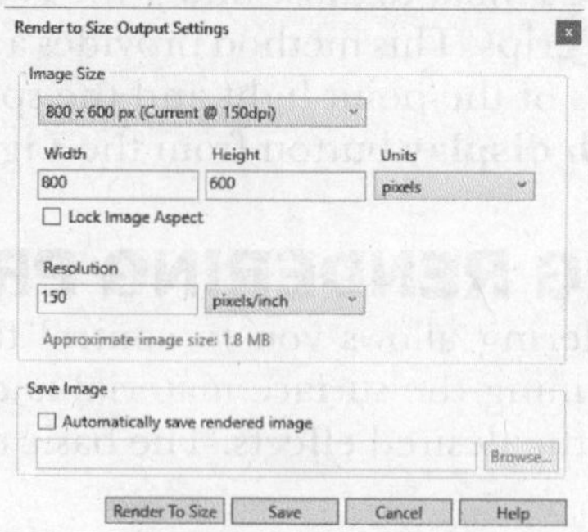

***Figure 8-71** The **Render to Size Output Settings** window*

Create Copy

This button is located on the right hand side of the **Current Preset** drop-down list and is used to create a copy of the selected render preset or a new render preset based on the selected render preset. Choose this button to create a copy of a render preset which will also be available in the custom section of the **Current Preset** drop-down list. Now, you can change the render properties of the newly created render preset according to your preferences.

Delete

This button is used to delete the selected custom render preset. You cannot delete the standard render preset.

Preset info

This rollout displays the information about the current preset. Here, you can edit the name and description of the custom render preset.

Render Duration

In this rollout, you can specify the duration of rendering. You can choose **Until Satisfactory, Render By Level**, and **Render By Time** radio buttons from this rollout.

Lights and Materials

In this rollout, you can specify rendering accuracy. You can choose **Low**, **Draft**, or **High** option to specify the desired level of material quality, colors, reflections, and shadows in the rendered image.

Note

*Some of the options in the **RENDER PRESETS MANAGER** window that are used for rendering a cropped region, selecting render presets, starting the rendering process, and specifying the resolution size of the rendered file can be directly changed from the **Render** panel in the **Visualize** tab, refer to Figure 8-72.*

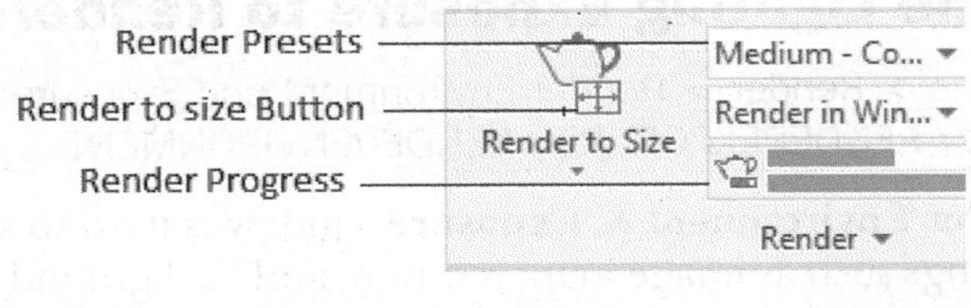

Figure 8-72 The **Render** panel of the **Visualize** tab

CONTROLLING THE RENDERING ENVIRONMENT

You can enhance the rendering by adding effects such as the surrounding environment of the model or by adding colors or images to the background of the model. The tools to do so are discussed next.

Rendering with a Background

You can render a model by changing its background. You can set a single color, combination of two colors, combination of three colors, an image, or sun and sky as the background of the model. To render the model with a background, you need to save a named view of the model with a background by using the **VIEW** command, as explained in the **View Manager** dialog box. Next, set the named view with a background as the current view and then render the model with the desired render settings. Figure 8-73 shows a rendered model with its named view saved with the gradient as the background, Figure 8-74 shows a rendered model with its named view saved with an image as the background, and Figure 8-75 shows a rendered model with its named view saved with the Sun and Sky as the background.

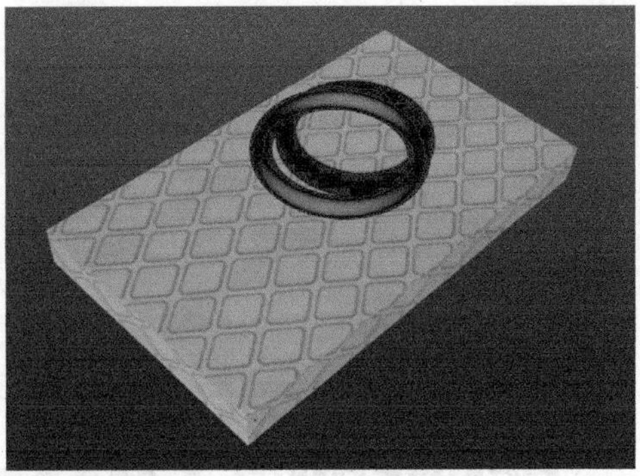

Figure 8-73 *The rendered model with the* ***Gradient*** *as the background*

Figure 8-74 *The rendered model with* ***Image*** *as the background*

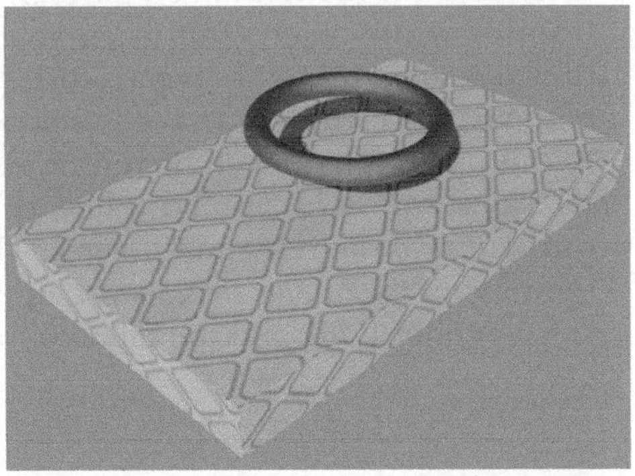

Figure 8-75 *The rendered model with the* ***Sun & Sky*** *as the background*

Adjusting the Lighting Exposure to Rendered Image

Ribbon: Visualize > Render > Render Environment and Exposure
Command: FOG / RENDEREXPOSURE / RENDERENVIRONMENT

The **Render Environment & Exposure** window is used to specify image-based lighting (IBL) settings such as image map, rotation, and background display, refer to Figure 8-76. You can use the toggle button in this dialog box to turn on and off the image based lighting when rendering. Using the **Image Based Lighting** drop-down list, you can specify different styles of image based lighting.

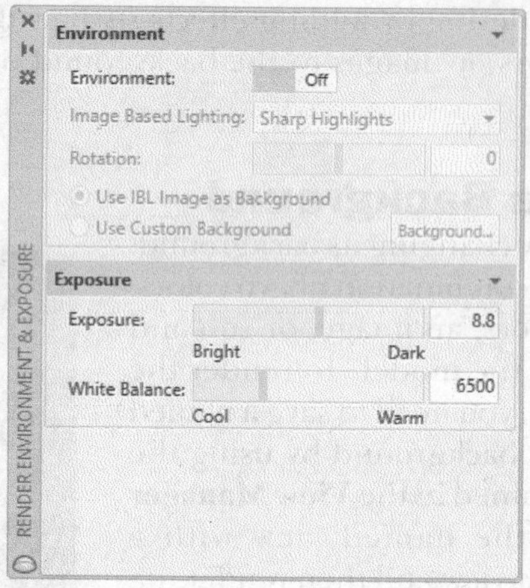

Figure 8-76 The ***RENDER ENVIRONMENT & EXPOSURE*** *dialog box*

RENDERING A MODEL WITH DIFFERENT RENDER SETTINGS

The rendering depends on the view that is current and the lights that are defined in the drawing. Sometimes, the current view or the lighting setup may not be enough to show all the features of an object. You might need different views with a certain light configuration to show different features of the object. But when you change the view or define the lights for rendering, the previous setup is lost. To bypass this, you can use the rendering information in the history pane of the **Render** window. In the lower portion of the **Render** window, the history pane is located. In this pane, you can get the recent history of the rendered images of the model in the drawing, refer to Figure 8-77. From this history pane, you can regain the previous rendering settings and can also save the rendered images. The data stored in the history pane includes: file name of the rendering, image size, view name (if no named view is used, the view is stored as current view), render time, and the name of the render preset used for the rendering.

Preview	Output File Name	Output Size	Output Resolution	View	Render Time	Render Preset	Render Statistics	
	C:\Users\Rajat Kamboj\Des	800 x 600 px 5.33 x 4 in	150 pixels/inch	Current	00:00:02	Medium - Copy 1	Date	3/21/2020 3:12:11 PM
							Triangle Count	13112
							Light Count	2
							Material Count	5

*Figure 8-77 The history pane in the **Render** window*

Right-clicking on a history entry displays a shortcut menu that contains the following options:

Render Again
This option restarts the renderer for the selected history entry with the same settings.

Save
This option displays the **Render Output File** dialog box where you can specify the name and format of the image file. After specifying the name and format of the image file, choose the **Save** button; the **BMP Image Options** dialog box will be displayed(if you choose BMP as the image format). You can choose the color quality of the image file from this dialog box, refer to Figure 8-78. Select the desired radio button and then choose the **OK** button to save the image file.

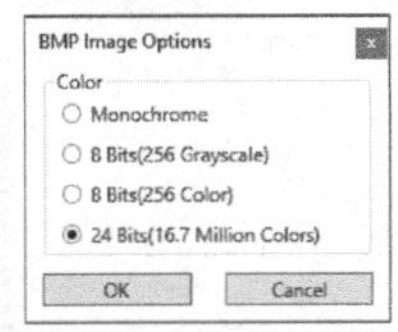

*Figure 8-78 The **BMP Image Options** dialog box*

Save Copy
This option saves the image to a new location without affecting the location stored in the entry.

Make Render Settings Current
This option loads the render settings associated with the selected history entry, if multiple history entries are present with different render presets.

Remove From The List
This option removes the entry from the history pane.

Delete Output File
This option removes the rendered image from the **Image** pane, but the entry remains in the history pane.

Note

Any entry that is not saved with the drawing exists only for the duration of the current drawing session. Once you close the file or exit the program, the unsaved history entries are lost.

Example 4

In this example, you will open the model used in Example 2 of this chapter and then create two rendered settings. Next, you will render the model with these settings and save the rendered image in a file. The first setting should display the effect of light 1 and the second setting should display the effect of light 2.

1. Open the drawing Example 2.

2. Choose the **Light glyph display** tool from the **Lights** panel of the **Visualize** tab.

3. Select light 2 from the **Lights in Model** palette and choose the **Properties** option from the shortcut menu; the **Properties** palette is displayed. In this palette, select the **Off** option from the **On/Off Status** drop-down list in the **General** rollout.

4. Choose the **Render to size** tool from the **Render** panel in the **Visualize** tab to perform rendering. The rendered model is displayed in the **Render** window with the effect of light 1 only, as shown in Figure 8-79.

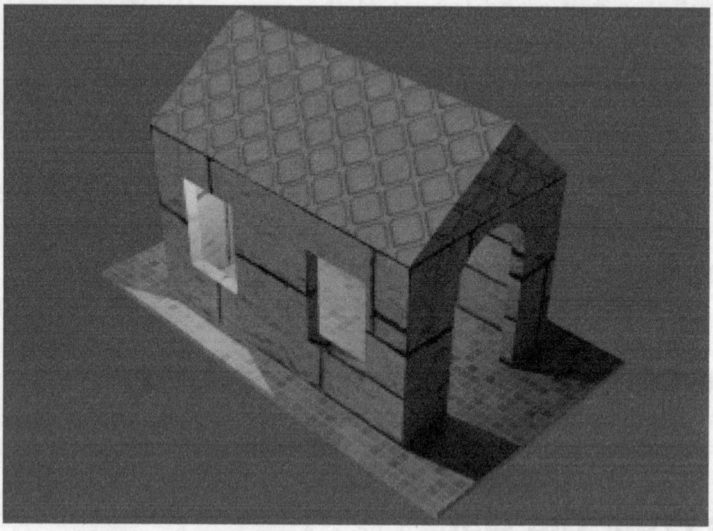

Figure 8-79 *Rendered model with the effect of light 1*

5. Next, switch off light 1 and switch on light 2, as explained in the previous steps, and then render the model. The rendered model is displayed in the **Render** window with the effect of light 2 only, as shown in Figure 8-80.

6. The history pane of the **Render** window displays both the render entries. Right click on one entry and choose the **Save** option from the shortcut menu. Now, specify the location, name, and format in which you want to save the image file in the **Render Output File** dialog box and choose the **Save** button.

7. Specify the **Color** and choose the **OK** button in the **BMP Image Options** dialog box.

8. Similarly, save the second history entry, as explained in Steps 6 and 7.

Note

You can render the model with the same rendered settings for all future references. To do so, select the history entry with that setting and choose the ***Make Render Settings Current*** *option from the shortcut menu.*

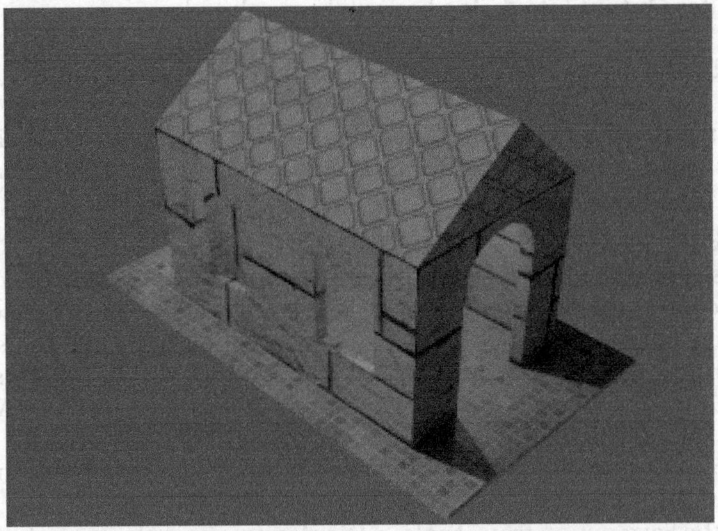

Figure 8-80 Rendered model with the effect of light 2

OBTAINING RENDERING INFORMATION

The bottom side area of the **Render** window is known as the statistics pane. This portion displays the details about the rendering and render settings in effect when the image was created. The information stated in the statistics pane is derived from the settings made in the **Render Presets Manager** window and the information that is generated at the time of the rendering.

SAVING A RENDERED IMAGE

A rendered image can be saved by rendering to a file or by rendering to the screen and then saving it. Redisplaying a saved rendering image requires very less time compared to the time involved in rendering. Various methods of saving the rendered image are discussed next.

Saving the Rendered Image to a File

You can save a rendered image directly to a file. One of the advantages of saving a rendered image to a file is that you can redisplay the rendered image in less time as compared to rendering the image again. Another advantage of saving a rendered image is that when you render a file in the viewport, the resolution of the image on rendering depends on the resolution of your current display. On the other hand, if you render the image to a file, you can specify a higher resolution. Later, you can display this rendered image that has a higher resolution. The rendered images can be saved in different formats, such as BMP, TGA, TIF, JPEG, and PNG. The following steps explain the procedure of saving a rendered image to a file.

1. Select the **More Output Settings** option from the **Render to Size** drop-down list in the **Render** panel of the **Visualize** tab.

2. Select the **Automatically save rendered image** check box and choose the **Browse** button; the **Render Output File** dialog box will be displayed.

3. Specify the file name and file type. Then, choose the **Save** button.

4. Choose the **Render to Size** tool from the **Render** panel of the **Visualize** tab. The rendered image is saved at the specified location.

Saving the Viewport Rendering

If you have selected the **Viewport** option from the **Render In** drop-down list, then the model will be rendered in the selected viewport. A rendered image in the viewport can be saved by using the **Save** option. To do so, choose the **Save** option from the **Tools > Display Image** in the menu bar; the **Render Output File** dialog box will be displayed. This dialog box is used to specify the file name and type. The valid output file formats are BMP, TGA, TIF, JPEG and PNG.

The steps given next explain the procedure of saving a viewport rendering.

1. Choose the **Save** option from **Tools > Display Image** in the menu bar to invoke the **Render Output File** dialog box.

2. Specify the file name and file type.Then, choose the **Save** button.

3. Specify the Color mode and choose the **OK** button in the **BMP Image Options** dialog box.

4. Choose the **Render to Size** tool from the **Render** panel in the **Visualize** tab; the rendered image is saved at the specified location.

Saving the Rendered Image from the Render Window

A rendered image in the **Render** window can be saved using the **Save** button of the **Render** window. In this case, the rendered image can be saved in any of these formats: BMP, TGA, TIF, JPEG, and PNG. The following steps explain the procedure for saving a render-window image:

1. Choose the **Render to Size** tool from the **Visualize** tab; the rendered image will be displayed in the **Render** window.

2. Choose the **Save** option from the shortcut menu displayed on right-clicking on the temporary image. Alternatively, use the **Save** button of the **Render** window to save the rendered image; the **Render Output File** dialog box is displayed.

3. Specify the file name and file type. Then, choose the **Save** button.

4. Specify the Color mode and choose the **OK** button in the **BMP Image Options** dialog box.

PLOTTING RENDERED IMAGES

To plot a rendered design, use the following steps:

1. Open the design to be plotted and then invoke the **Plot** dialog box. Remember that you do not need to first render the design and then invoke the **Plot** dialog box. You can also render the design while plotting. However, the render settings should be specified in advance.

2. Select the printer that supports rendered printing from the **Printer/plotter** area and select the other options.

3. Select the **Rendered** option from the **Shade plot** drop-down list in the **Shaded viewport options** area. If this area is not available by default, then choose **More Options** from the bottom right corner of the **Plot** dialog box.

4. Set the other options in this dialog box and then plot the design. The design will be first rendered and then plotted in the rendered form.

Note

*If the **Rendered** option is used for a highly complex set of objects, the hardcopy output might contain only the viewport border.*

UNLOADING AutoCAD RENDER

When you invoke any AutoCAD Render tool, AutoCAD Render is loaded automatically.

If you do not need AutoCAD Render, you can unload it by entering the **ARX** at the Command prompt. You can reload AutoCAD Render by invoking the **RENDER** command or any other command associated with rendering (such as **RENDERENVIRONMENT**, **LIGHT**, and so on).

Command: **ARX**
Enter an option [Files/Groups/Commands/CLasses/Services/Load/Unload]: **U**
Enter ARX/DBX file name to unload: **acrender**
acrender successfully unloaded.

WORKING WITH CAMERAS

Cameras are used to define the 3d perspective view of a model. In AutoCAD, you can place a camera, edit camera settings, turn on/off the camera, and save the perspective view. The options in the **Camera** panel are discussed next.

Create Camera

Ribbon: Visualize > Camera > Create Camera
Command: CAM(CAMERA)

To place a camera, choose the **Create Camera** tool from the **Camera** panel in the **Visualize** tab; you will be prompted to specify the camera location. Specify the camera position; the preview of the camera focus will be displayed and you will be prompted to specify the target location. Click in the drawing area to specify the required target location; the **Enter an option [?/Name/LOcation/Height/Target/LEns/Clipping/View/eXit]<eXit>:** prompt will be displayed. The options in the prompt are discussed next.

?

This option lists all cameras created in the current drawing.

Name

This option is used to specify a name for the camera.

LOcation

This option is used to change the location of the camera.

Height

This option is used to specify the height of the camera.

Target

This option is used to modify the target of the camera.

LEns

This option is used to define the magnification length or zoom factor of camera lens. Note that greater the lens length, narrower will be the view.

Clipping

Clipping planes define the boundaries for a view. On choosing this option, you can specify the location of the front and back clipping planes. On defining the front and back clipping planes, everything between the camera and front clipping plane and the target and back clipping plane will be hidden.

If you choose this option, a message prompting you to enable the front clipping plane will be displayed. If you choose **Yes**, then you will be prompted to specify the offset distance of the clipping plane from the target plane. Specify the required distance and press ENTER; a message will be displayed prompting you to enable the back clipping plane. If you choose **Yes**, you will be prompted to specify the offset distance of the clipping plane from the target plane.

Figure 8-81 shows the model with the front and back clipping planes defined at 25 units from the target point. Figure 8-82 shows the preview of the resultant model.

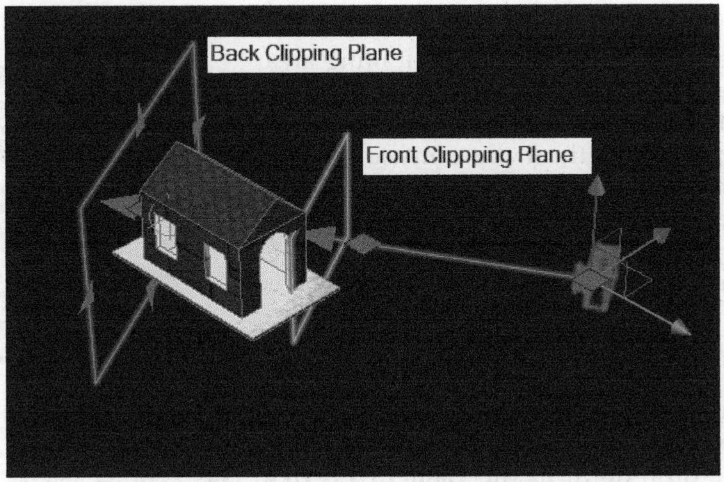

Figure 8-81 The front and back clipping planes

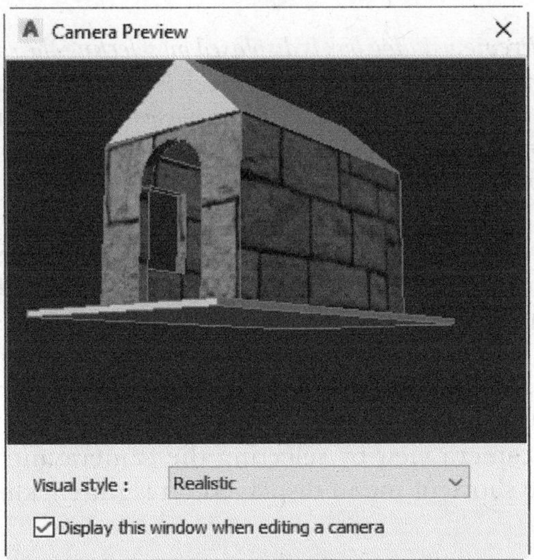

Figure 8-82 The preview of the model

You can turn off the display of front, back, or both clipping planes, display both the clipping planes, or adjust the offset values of the clipping planes using the **Properties** palette. To invoke the **Properties** palette, select the camera, right-click, and then choose the **Properties** option. You can also dynamically adjust the position of the clipping planes by using the grips displayed on selecting the camera.

View

This option is used to set the current view as the camera view.

eXit

This option is used to exit the tool.

Editing the Cameras

To edit a camera, select it from the drawing area; the **Camera Preview** window will be displayed, as shown in Figure 8-83. Also, the grips will be displayed on the length of the camera. You can adjust the focus of the camera by dragging these grips. The move gizmo will also be displayed when you move your cursor toward the source or target grip. You can use this gizmo to move the camera in the desired direction. The corresponding changes can also be viewed in the **Camera Preview** window. By default, the preview of the model will be displayed in the Wireframe mode, but we can change it to other visual styles. You can do so by using the **Visual style** drop-down in the **Camera Preview** window.

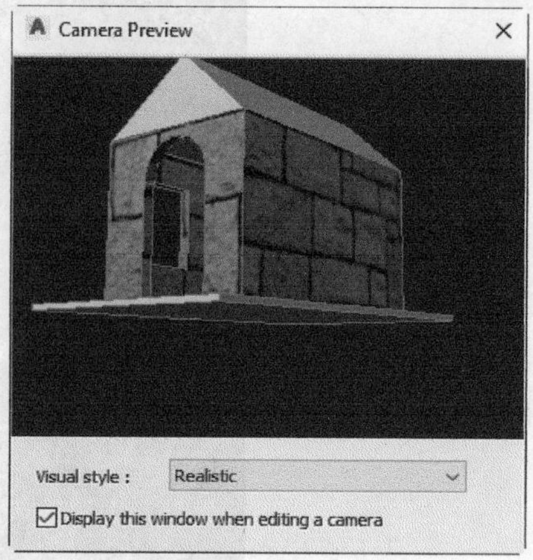

Figure 8-83 *The* ***Camera Preview*** *window*

Note

The ***Camera Preview*** *dialog box is displayed on selecting the camera because by default the* ***Display this window when editing a camera*** *check box is selected in the* ***Camera Preview*** *dialog box. If you do not want the dialog box to be displayed, you need to clear this check box. If you want to view it later, then select the camera, right-click, and then choose* ***View Camera Preview****; the* ***Camera Preview*** *dialog box will be displayed.*

Note that you can have more than one camera in one drawing. You can edit the camera properties by using the **Properties** palette. Using this palette, you can modify a camera's lens length, change its front and back clipping planes, and change the name of the camera.

You can set the camera view as the current view by selecting the camera from the **Views** drop-down list in the **Visualize** tab. Then, you can save the view by using the **View Manager** dialog box. You can also set the camera view by selecting the camera and then choosing the **Set Camera View** option from the shortcut menu displayed on right-clicking.

Note

To toggle the display of camera glyph, choose the ***Camera Display*** *button from the* ***Camera*** *panel of the* ***Visualize*** *tab.*

You can set the camera template from the **TOOL PALETTES**. To do so, invoke the **TOOL PALETTES** and right-click on its title bar; a shortcut menu will be displayed. Choose **Cameras** from the shortcut menu and then select the required option. The three camera options available in the menu are: **Normal Camera**, **Wide-angle Camera**, and **Extreme Wide-angle camera**.

CREATING ANIMATIONS

You can create a walk-through or fly-through animation by using the motion path animation. You can record and play back these presentations whenever required. This helps you communicate your design intent dynamically and with more impact. The tools to create an animation are not displayed in the **Ribbon** by default. To display them, choose the **Visualize** tab and right-click on any one of the buttons; a shortcut menu will be displayed. Choose **Show Panels > Animations** from the shortcut menu; the **Animations** panel will be added to the **Ribbon**. The methods of creating animations are discussed next.

Creating Animation of 3D Navigations

You can create, record, playback, and save animations of any of the 3D navigation modes, such as **Walk** and **Fly**. Before creating animations, you should specify the animation settings. To do so, choose the **Walk** or **Fly** button and right-click. Next, choose **Animation Settings** from the shortcut menu; the **Animation Settings** dialog box will be displayed, refer to Figure 8-84. In this dialog box, you can specify the visual style in which you want to view the model in animation, resolution of the frames, number of frames to be captured in one second, and the format (AVI, MPG, or WMV) in which you want to save the file while creating the animation of the 3D navigation.

Recording Animation

To create an animation, start any of the 3D navigation tool; the **Record Animation** button in the **Animations** panel in the **Visualize** tab will be enabled. Choose this button to start recording, refer to Figure 8-85. Navigate through the drawing model and all navigations will get recorded. You can also change the navigation mode while recording. To do so, choose the **Pause Animation** button from the **Animations** panel of the **Ribbon**. Next, right-click in the drawing area and choose an option from the **Other Navigation Modes**. Choose the **Record Animation** button again and the recording will start with the changed 3D navigation mode without any break in recording. If you are in the **Walk** or **Fly** navigation mode, you can also adjust the settings from the **POSITION LOCATOR** window, in the same way as explained above.

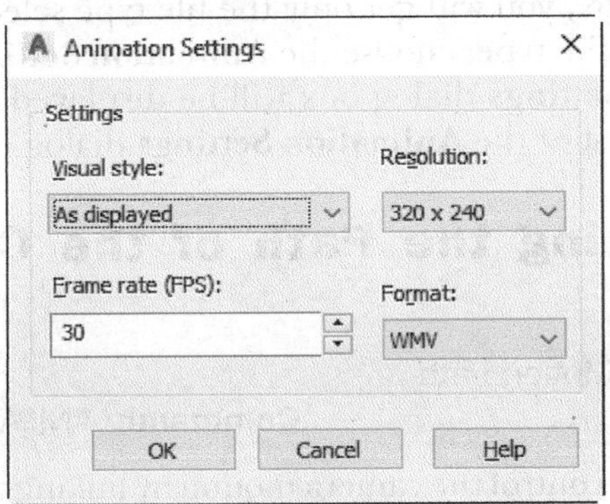

*Figure 8-84 The **Animation Settings** dialog box*

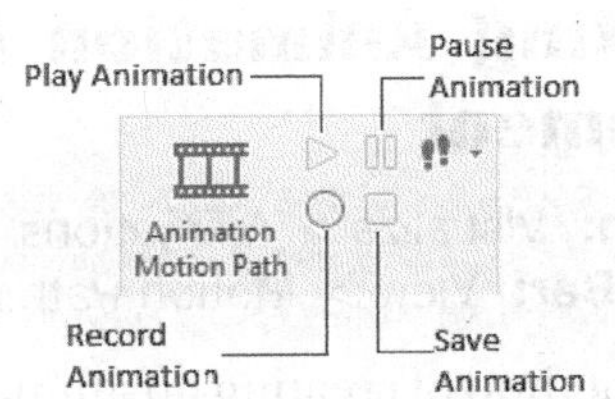

*Figure 8-85 The **Animations** panel in the **Visualize** tab*

Playing Animation

To preview a recorded animation, choose the **Play Animation** tool from the **Animations** panel in the **Visualize** tab; the recording will pause and the **Animation Preview** window will be displayed, refer to Figure 8-86. The **Animation Preview** window displays the animation. If you want to preview the animation in a different visual style, you can select another style from the drop-down list. The options in the **Visual Style** drop-down list are **Current**, **Hidden**, **Wireframe**, **Conceptual**, **Realistic**, **Shaded**, **Shaded with edges**, **Shades of Gray**, **Sketchy** and **X-Ray**. After playing the animation, you can also resume the recording by choosing the **Record** button displayed in red color in the **Animation Preview** window.

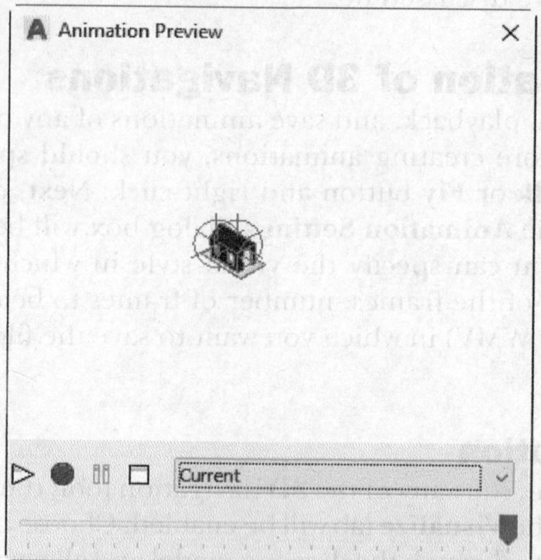

Figure 8-86 The Animation Preview window

Saving Animation

If you are satisfied with the animation playback, choose the **Save** button in the **Animation Preview** dialog box or the **Animations** panel; the **Save As** dialog box will be displayed on the screen. Select the file location, file name, type of file and then choose the **Save** button. In **Files of type** drop-down list of the **Save As** dialog box, you will get only the file type selected in the **Animation Settings** dialog box. To change the file type, choose the **Animation Settings** button from the **Save As** dialog box; the **Animation Settings** dialog box will be displayed. Select the desired file type from the **Format** drop-down list of the **Animation Settings** dialog box.

Creating Animation by Defining the Path of the Camera Movement

Ribbon: Visualize > Animations > Animation Motion Path
Menu Bar: View > Motion Path Animations **Command:** ANIPATH

In this method of creating an animation, you can control the camera motion by linking the camera movement and its target to a point or a path. If you want the camera or target to remain still while creating animation, link the camera or target to a point. However, if you want the camera or target to move along a path while creating animation, link the camera or target to a path. To create a motion path animation, choose the **Animation Motion Path** tool from the **Animations** panel in the **Visualize** tab; the **Motion Path Animation** dialog box will be displayed, refer to Figure 8-87. Using this dialog box, specify the settings for the camera motion path and create the animation file. The options in the **Motion Path Animation** dialog box are discussed next.

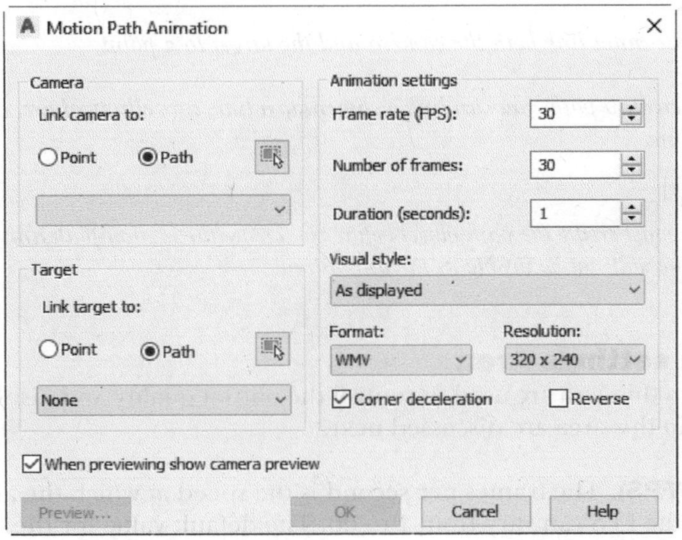

Figure 8-87 The ***Motion Path Animation*** *dialog box*

Camera Area

The options in this area are used to specify the camera movement. Select the **Point** or **Path** radio button, based on your requirement. Select the **Point** radio button, if you want the camera to remain stationary at the specified point in the drawing throughout the animation. Select the **Path** radio button, if you want the camera to move along the specified path in the drawing. Next, choose the **Pick Point / Select Path** button available next to the radio buttons to select the point/path in the drawing. Specify the point/path in the drawing; the **Point Name** or **Path Name** dialog box will be displayed, depending on whether the **Point** or **Path** radio button is selected as the camera link, respectively, refer to Figure 8-88. Specify a name for the point/path and choose the **OK** button. You can also select a previously created point/path from the drop-down list that displays the list of named points or paths.

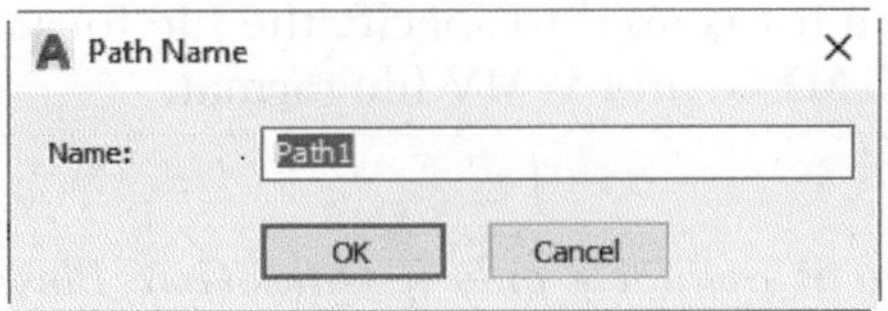

Figure 8-88 The ***Path Name*** *dialog box*

Target Area

The options in this area are used to specify the movement of the target with the movement of the camera. Select the **Point** or **Path** radio button, based on your requirement. To specify a target point, choose the **Pick Point** button and specify a point in the drawing. Enter a name for the point and choose the **OK** button in the **Point Name** dialog box. To specify a target path, choose the **Select Path** button and specify a path in the drawing. Enter a name for the path and choose the **OK** button in the **Path Name** dialog box. To specify an existing target point or path, select it from the drop-down list.

Note

1. You cannot link both the camera and the target to a point.

2. To create a path, you can link a camera to a line, arc, elliptical arc, circle, polyline, 3D polyline, or spline.

Tip

You must create the path object before you create the motion path animation. The path that you create will not be visible in the animation.

Animation settings Area

The options in this area are used to control the output quality and display of the animation file. The options in this area are discussed next.

Frame rate (FPS). The frames per second is the speed at which the animation will be played. The value of the FPS can vary from 1 to 60. The default value for the FPS is 30.

Number of frames. This option is used to specify the total number of frames to be created in the animation. This value divided by the FPS determines the duration of the animation file.

Duration (seconds). This option specifies the duration of the animation in seconds. Any change in the duration automatically resets the **Number of frames** value.

Visual style. This option displays a drop-down list of the visual styles and the render presets that can be applied to an animation file.

Note

You cannot create an animation of 3D navigation with a rendered model, however, you can create it by using a motion path.

Format. This drop-down list is used to specify the file format for the animation. You can save an animation to an **AVI**, **MPG**, and **WMV** file format.

Note

*The **MOV** format is available only if QuickTime Player is installed. The **WMV** format is available only if Microsoft Windows Media Player is installed. Otherwise, the **AVI** format is the default selection.*

Resolution. This drop-down list is used to specify the resolution of the resulting animation in terms of the width and height. The default value is 320 x 240.

Corner deceleration. This check box is used to specify the speed of the camera movement at the corners. If this check box is selected, the camera will move at a slower rate as it turns at a corner.

Reverse. This check box, if selected, will reverse the direction of the animation display.

When previewing show camera preview. This check box, if selected, will display the **Animation Preview** dialog box when you choose the **Preview** button so that you can preview the animation before you save it.

Preview. This button is used to get a preview of the animation in the **Animation Preview** dialog box, before saving it.

After you have finished adjusting the points, paths, and settings, choose **Preview** to view the animation, Next, choose the **OK** button to save the animation; the **Save As** dialog box will be displayed. Specify the location, file name, and file type of the animation to save and then choose the **Save** button.

Example 5

In this example, you will download the drawing file of the model shown in Figure 8-89 from *https://www.cadcim.com*. The path of the file is as follows: *Textbooks > CAD/CAM > AutoCAD Advanced > Advanced AutoCAD 2021: A Problem-Solving Approach (3D and Advanced) > Input Files*. Next, you will animate the downloaded model and then save this animation to a file.

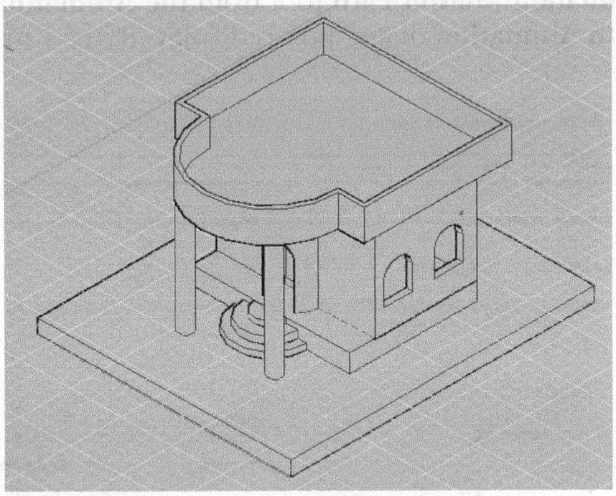

Figure 8-89 *Model for Example 5*

1. Download the model shown in Figure 8-89 using the path mentioned above.

2. Select the materials of your choice and attach them to the model, as described in Example 1. The rendered image of the model is shown in Figure 8-90.

3. Change the view of the model to the top view and create the path to attach the camera, refer to Figure 8-91.

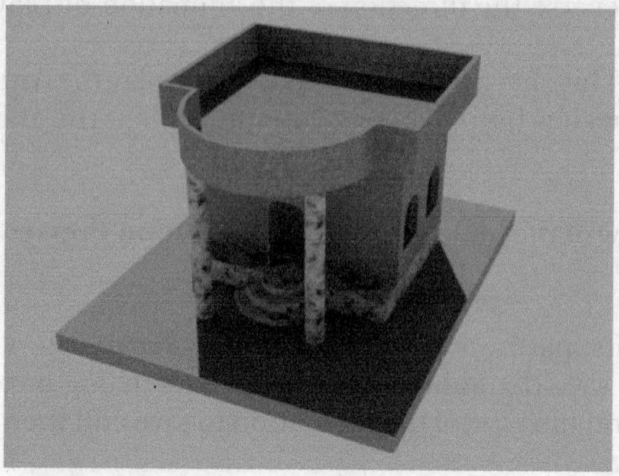

Figure 8-90 Rendered model for Example 5

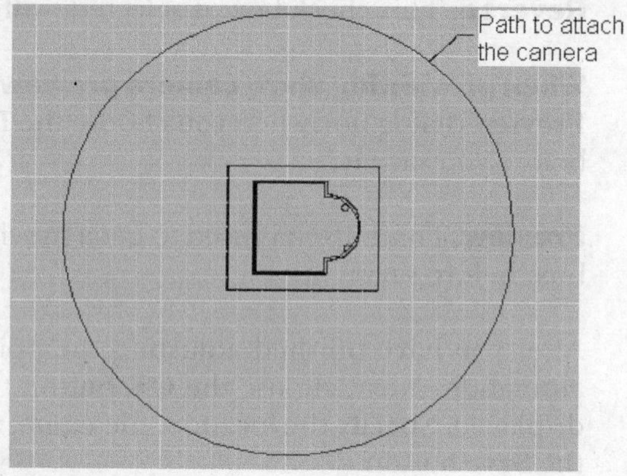

Figure 8-91 Top view of the model displaying the path to attach the camera

4. Move the path created in the previous step along the Z axis by a distance equal to half the height of the model.

5. Invoke the **Animation Motion Path** tool from the **Animations** panel in the **Visualize** tab; the **Motion Path Animation** dialog box is displayed, refer to Figure 8-92.

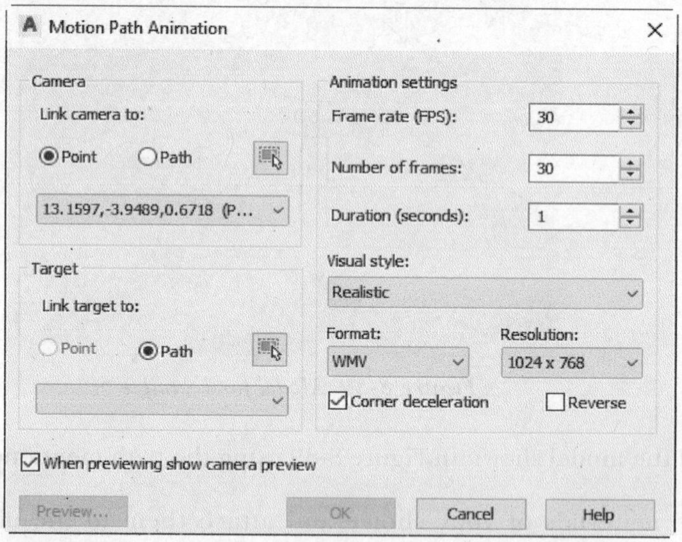

*Figure 8-92 The **Motion Path Animation** dialog box for Example 5*

6. Select the **Path** radio button and choose the **Select Path** button in the **Camera** area of the **Motion Path Animation** dialog box. Next, select the path created in the previous step; the **Path Name** dialog box is displayed. Enter the name of the path as **Path1**.

7. Select the **Point** radio button and choose the **Select Point** button in the **Target** area of the **Motion Path Animation** dialog box. Next, specify a point in the middle of the model, which will act as the target of the camera. On doing so, the **Point Name** dialog box is displayed. In this dialog box, enter the name as **Point1**.

8. Change the values of the **Animation settings** area to the values shown in Figure 8-92.

9. Choose the **Preview** button to take a preview of the animation in the **Animation Preview** dialog box. Next, close the **Animation Preview** dialog box.

10. Choose the **OK** button to save the animation; the **Save As** dialog box is displayed. Specify the location, file name, and file type of the animation to save and then choose the **Save** button from the **Save As** dialog box.

Self-Evaluation Test

Answer the following questions and then compare them to those given at the end of this chapter:

1. The __________ tool is used to attach material to a layer in a drawing.

2. The __________ source emits a focused beam of light in the defined direction.

3. The __________ and __________ commands are used to adjust the coordinates and the bitmap of the pattern of the material attached to the solid model.

4. The __________ tool is used to set exposure in the rendered image.

5. A __________ light source emits light in all directions, and the intensity of the emitted light is uniform.

6. A rendered image makes it easier to visualize the shape and size of a 3D object. (T/F)

7. You can unload AutoCAD Render by invoking the **ARX** command. (T/F)

8. The falloff occurs with a distant source of light. (T/F)

9. You can change the color of the ambient light. (T/F)

10. You cannot take the printout of a model without rendering it. (T/F)

Review Questions

Answer the following questions:

1. Which of the following light does not have a source, and therefore, no location or direction?

(a) **Default** (b) **Point**
(c) **Spot** (d) **Distant**

2. The intensity of light decreases as the distance increases. This phenomenon is called:

(a) **Attenuation** (b) **Frequency**
(c) **Light Effect** (d) None of these

3. Which of the following lights allows you to define the geographic location?

(a) **Sun** (b) **Point**
(c) **Spot** (d) **Distant**

4. Which of the following commands can be used to define the background of an object while it is being rendered?

(a) **RENDER** (b) **ARX**
(c) **BACKGROUND** (d) **VIEW**

5. Which of the following commands is used to create a motion path animation?

(a) **ANIMAP** (b) **ANITRAC**
(c) **ANIPATH** (d) **ANIMATION**

6. In the __________ source, the brightness of the incident light on an object is inversely proportional to the distance of the object from the light source.

7. The __________ palette allows you to set the rendering preferences for the rendering.

8. A spotlight source emits a __________ beam of light in one direction only.

9. Redisplaying a saved rendered image takes __________ time as compared to the time involved in rendering.

10. The __________ command is used to render only the selected portion of a drawing.

11. Attenuation is defined as __________.

12. You can assign materials to an object using the AutoCAD Color Index. (T/F)

13. The phenomenon of attenuation occurs in case of direction lights. (T/F)

14. You can link both the camera and the target to a point. (T/F)

Exercise 1

In this exercise, you will download the drawing file of the model shown in Figure 8-93 from *https://www.cadcim.com*. The path of the file is as follows: *Textbooks > CAD/CAM > AutoCAD Advanced > Advanced AutoCAD 2021: A Problem-Solving Approach (3D and Advanced) > Input Files*. Next, render the drawing after applying materials and inserting lights at appropriate locations to get a realistic model.

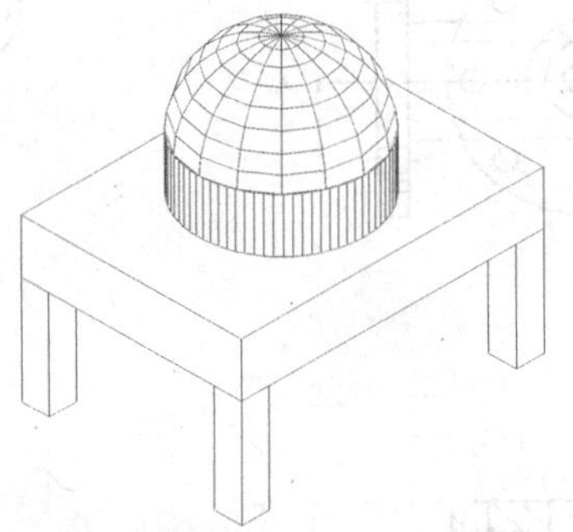

Figure 8-93 *Model for Exercise 1*

Exercise 2

In this exercise, you will download the drawing file of the model shown in Figure 8-94 from *https://www.cadcim.com*. The path of the file is as follows: *Textbooks > CAD/CAM > AutoCAD Advanced > Advanced AutoCAD 2021: A Problem-Solving Approach (3D and Advanced) > Input Files*. Next, you will apply materials of your choice to the downloaded model. Also, you will apply the Point light and the Spotlight at the sill of the window and at bottom of the door. Also, attach a background image to it and then render the model. If you want to create the model yourself, you can use the reference dimensions shown in Figure 8-94(Assume the missing dimensions).

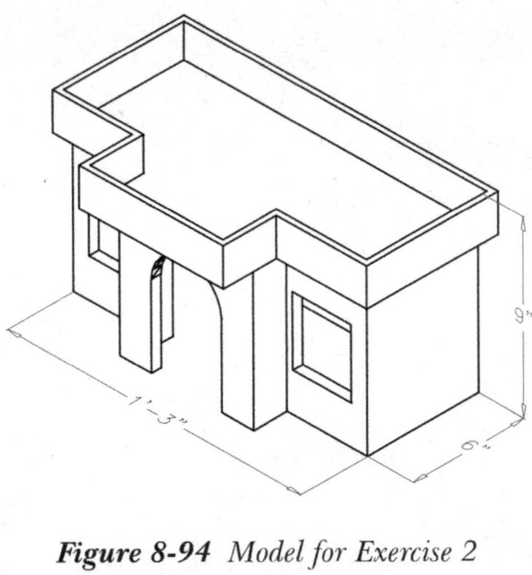

Figure 8-94 *Model for Exercise 2*

Exercise 3

Create the solid model shown in Figure 8-95. Also, assign brass material to the solid and render it.

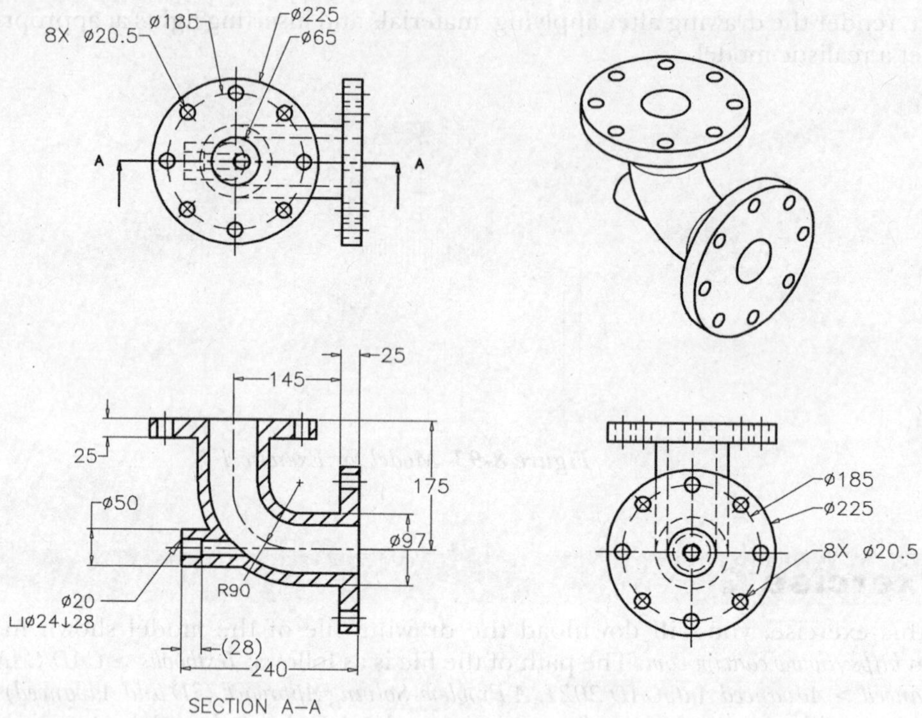

Figure 8-95 Views and dimensions of the model for Exercise 3

Exercise 4

In this exercise, you will download the drawing file of the model shown in Figure 8-96 from *https://www.cadcim.com*. The path of the file is as follows: *Textbooks > CAD/CAM > AutoCAD Advanced > Advanced AutoCAD 2021: A Problem-Solving Approach (3D and Advanced)> Input Files*. Also, you will assign materials and textures to different parts of the model and then render it.

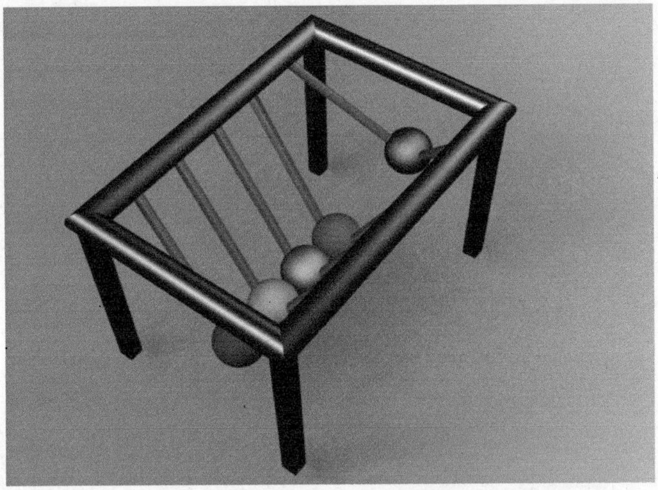

Figure 8-96 *Rendered image of the model*

Answers to Self-Evaluation Test

1. Attach By Layer, **2.** spotlight, **3.** **MATERIALMAP**, **SETUV**, **4.** **Environment**, **5.** distant, **6.** T, **7.** T, **8.** F, **9.** F, **10.** F

Chapter 9

AutoCAD on Internet and 3D Printing

Learning Objectives

After completing this chapter, you will be able to:

- *Launch a Web browser from AutoCAD*
- *Open and save drawings to and from the Internet*
- *Place hyperlinks in a drawing*
- *View DWF files with a Web browser*
- *Convert drawings into the DWF file format*
- *Share drawings on Autodesk account and on mobile*
- *Customize the synchronization settings*
- *Share and collaborate the DWG files*
- *3D Printing*

Key Terms

- *Browser*
- *URL*
- *Hyperlink*
- *i-Drop*
- *DWF*
- *Export to DWF*

INTRODUCTION

The Internet has become the most important and the fastest way to exchange information in the world. AutoCAD allows you to interact with the Internet in several ways. In AutoCAD, you can open and save files located on Internet, launch a web browser, and create Drawing Web that can be opened using the web browser. For using the Internet features in AutoCAD 2021, some components of Microsoft Internet Explorer must be present in your computer. If Internet Explorer version 6.1 (or later) is already installed, then you have these required components. If not, then the components are installed automatically during the installation of AutoCAD 2021 when you select: (1) the **Full Install**; or (2) the **Internet Tools** option during the **Custom** installation.

This chapter introduces the following Web-related commands:

BROWSER
Launches a Web browser from within AutoCAD.

HYPERLINK
Attaches and removes a uniform resource locator (URL) from an object or an area in the drawing.

HYPERLINKFWD
Moves to the next hyperlink (an undocumented command).

HYPERLINKBACK
Moves back to the previous hyperlink (an undocumented command).

HYPERLINKSTOP
Stops the hyperlink access action (an undocumented command).

PASTEASHYPERLINK
Attaches a URL to an object in the drawing from text stored in the Windows Clipboard (an undocumented command).

HYPERLINKBASE
A system variable for setting the path used for relative hyperlinks in the drawing.

Note
In AutoCAD, all file-related dialog boxes are "Web enabled".

INTERNET COMMANDS

The Internet related commands of AutoCAD are discussed next.

BROWSER: This command launches a Web browser from within AutoCAD. The default URL is now *http://www.autodesk.com*. However, you can type the URL without *http*. Also, you can specify the FTP location.

ATTACHURL: This command attaches a URL to an object or an area in the drawing. The **-HYPERLINK** command's **Insert** option supersedes this command.

GOTOURL: This command opens the URL attached to the selected object. Select an object that has a hyperlink; the file or web page that is associated with the hyperlink will open.

DETACHURL: This command removes the URL from an object. The **-HYPERLINK** command's **Remove** option supersedes this command.

DWFOUT: This command exports the drawing and embedded URLs as a DWF file. The **Plot** dialog box's **ePlot** option and the **Publish** tool supersedes this command. You can also choose the **DWF** tool from **Output > Export to DWF/PDF > Export** drop-down or **Export > DWF** from the **Application Menu** to export the drawing to DWF.

INSERTURL: This command inserts a block from Internet into the drawing. This command automatically invokes the **Insert** tool. As a result, the **Insert** dialog box is displayed. In this dialog box, choose the **Browse** and the **Search the Web** buttons and then type a URL for the block name.

OPENURL: This command opens a drawing from the Internet. This command automatically invokes the **Open** tool, thus displaying the **Select File** dialog box. You may type a URL for the file name.

SAVEURL: This command saves the drawing to the Internet. This command automatically executes the **Save** tool, thus displaying the **Save Drawing As** dialog box. You may type a URL for the file name.

You are probably already familiar with the best-known uses of the Internet: e-mail and the www (short for "World Wide Web"). E-mail allows the user to quickly exchange messages and data at very low cost. The Web brings together text, graphics, audio, and movies in an easy-to-use format. You can also use file transfer protocol (FTP) for effortless binary file transfer.

AutoCAD allows you to interact with the Internet in several ways. It can launch a Web browser from within AutoCAD with the **BROWSER** command. Hyperlinks can be inserted in drawings with the **HYPERLINK** command, which lets you link the drawing with the other documents on your computer and the Internet. With the **Plot** tool's ePlot option (short for "electronic plot), AutoCAD creates DWF files for viewing drawings in two-dimensional (2D) format on Web pages. AutoCAD can open, insert, and save drawings to and from the Internet through the **Open**, **Insert**, and **Save As** tools.

UNDERSTANDING URLS

The **Uniform Resource Locator**, known as URL, is the file naming system of the Internet. The URL system allows you to find any resource (a file) on the Internet. For example, resources include a text file, Web page, program file, an audio or movie clip, in short, anything you might also find on your own computer. The primary difference is that these resources are located on somebody else's computer. Various examples of URLs with their meanings are listed below:

Example of URL	Meaning
http://www.autodesk.com	Autodesk Primary Web site
news.autodesk.com	Autodesk Newsroom Web site

Note that the **http://** prefix is not required. Most of today's Web browsers automatically add it in the *routing* prefix, which saves you a few keystrokes.

URLs can access several different kinds of resources such as Web sites, e-mail, and news groups, but they always take the same general format as follows:

scheme://netloc

The scheme accesses the following specific resources on Internet:

Scheme	Meaning
file://	File is located on your computer's hard drive or local network
ftp://	File Transfer Protocol (used for downloading files)
http://	Hyper Text Transfer Protocol (the basis of Web sites)
mailto://	Electronic mail (e-mail)
news://	Usenet news (news groups)
telnet://	Telnet protocol
gopher://	Gopher protocol

The **://** characters indicate a network address. Autodesk recommends the following format for specifying URL-style file names with AutoCAD:

<table>
<tr><th>Resource</th><th>URL Format</th></tr>
<tr><td>Web Site</td><td>http://servername/pathname/filename</td></tr>
<tr><td>FTP Site</td><td>ftp://servername/pathname/filename</td></tr>
<tr><td>Local File</td><td>file:///drive:/pathname/filename</td></tr>
<tr><td>or</td><td>drive:\pathname\filename</td></tr>
<tr><td>or</td><td>file:///drive |/pathname/filename</td></tr>
<tr><td>or</td><td>file://\\localPC\pathname\filename</td></tr>
<tr><td>or</td><td>file:////localPC/pathname/filename</td></tr>
<tr><td>Network File</td><td>file://localhost/drive:/pathname/filename</td></tr>
<tr><td>or</td><td>\\localhost\drive: \pathname\filename</td></tr>
<tr><td>or</td><td>file://localhost/drive |/pathname/filename</td></tr>
</table>

The terminology can be confusing. The following definitions will help you clarify these terms:

Term	Meaning
server name	The name or location of a computer on the Internet, for example: *www.autodesk.com*
path name	The same as a subdirectory or folder name
drive	The driver letter such as C: or D:
local pc	A file located on your computer
local host	The name of the network host computer

If you are not sure of the name of the network host computer, use Windows Explorer to check the Network Neighborhood for the network names of computers.

Launching a Web Browser

The **BROWSER** command lets you start a Web browser from within AutoCAD. The commonly used Web browsers are Microsoft Internet Explorer, Google Chrome, and Mozilla Firefox.

By default, the **BROWSER** command uses whatever brand of Web browser program is registered in your computer's Windows operating system. AutoCAD prompts you for the URL such as *http://www.autodesk.com*. The **BROWSER** command can be used in scripts, toolbars, or menu macros, and AutoLISP routines to automatically access the Internet.

Command: **BROWSER**
Enter Web location (URL) <http://www.autodesk.com>: *Enter a URL*

The default URL is an HTML file added to your computer during AutoCAD's installation. After you type the URL and press ENTER, AutoCAD launches the Web browser and contacts the Web site. Figure 9-1 shows the Internet Explorer with the Autodesk's primary Web site.

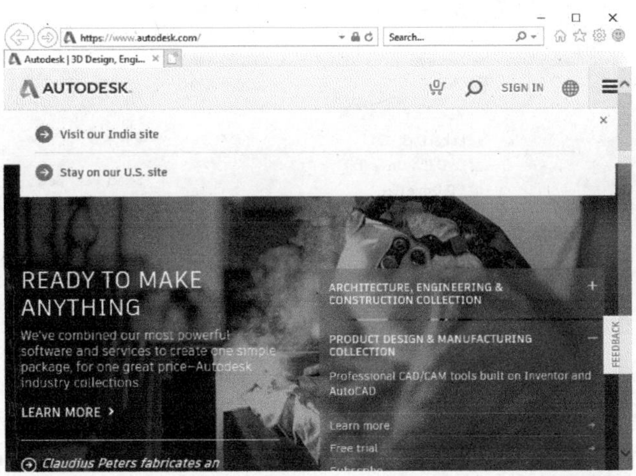

Figure 9-1 Google Chrome displaying the Autodesk website

Changing the Default Website

To change the default Web page that your browser starts from within AutoCAD, you need to change the setting in the **INETLOCATION** system variable. The variable stores the URL used by the last executed **BROWSER** command and the **Browse the Web** dialog box. Make the following change:

Command: **INETLOCATION**
Enter new value for INETLOCATION <"http://www.autodesk.com">: *Type URL.*

DRAWINGS ON THE INTERNET

When a drawing is stored on the Internet, you can access it from within AutoCAD using the standard **Open**, **Insert**, and **Save** tools. Instead of specifying the file's location with the usual drive-subdirectory-file name format such as *c:\acad 2021\filename.dwg*, use the URL format. (Recall that the URL is the universal file-naming system used by the Internet to access any file located on any computer hooked up to the Internet).

Opening Drawings from the Internet

Drawings from the Internet can easily be opened using the **Select File** dialog box, which can be displayed by invoking the **Open** tool. To do so, choose the **Search the Web** button from the **Select File** dialog box, refer to Figure 9-2.

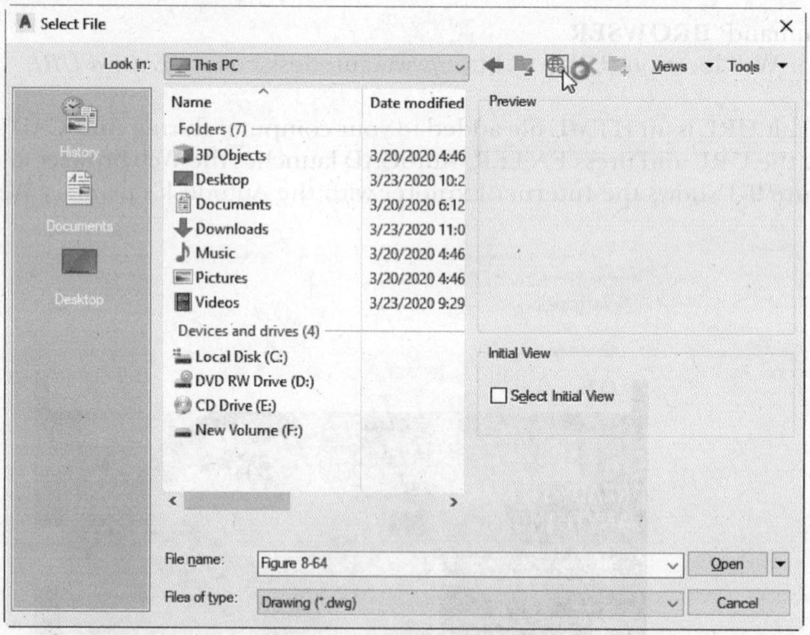

Figure 9-2 *Choosing the* ***Search the Web*** *button from the* ***Select File*** *dialog box*

When you choose the **Search the Web** button, AutoCAD opens the **Browse the Web** dialog box, refer to Figure 9-3. This dialog box is a simplified version of the Microsoft brand of Web browser. Its purpose is to allow you to browse the files in a Website.

By default, the **Browse the Web** dialog box displays the contents of the URL stored in the **INETLOCATION** system variable. You can easily change this to another folder or website by entering the required URL in the **Look in** edit box.

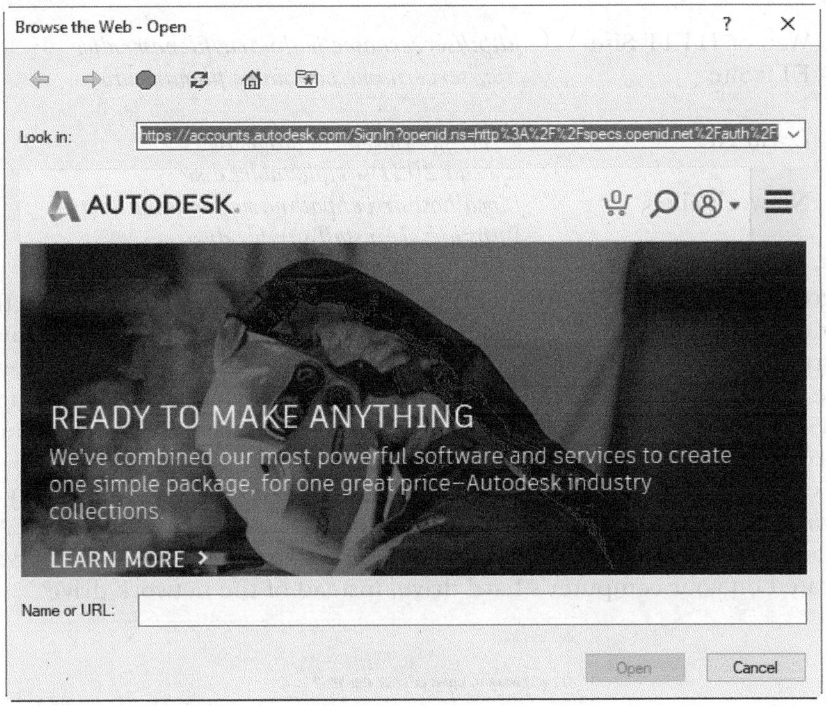

*Figure 9-3 The **Browse the Web** dialog box*

At the top of the dialog box, there are six buttons which are discussed next:

Back: This button takes you back to the previous URL.

Forward: This button takes you forward to the next URL.

Stop: This button halts the display of the Web page (useful if the connection is slow or the page is very large).

Refresh: This button redisplays the current Web page.

Home: This button takes you back to the location specified by the **INETLOCATION** system variable.

Favorites: This button lists the stored URLs (hyperlinks) or bookmarks. If you have previously used Google Chrome or Internet Explorer, you will find all your favorites listed here. Favorites are stored in the *C:\Users\Adminstrator\Favorites* folder on your computer.

The **Look in** field allows you to type the URL. Alternatively, click the down arrow to select the previous destination. If you have stored Website addresses in the Favorites folder, then select a URL from that list.

You can either double-click on the name of the file in the window, or type a URL in the **Name or URL** edit box. The following table shows the templates for typing the URL to open a drawing file:

Drawing Location	Template URL
Web or HTTP Site	*http://servername/pathname/filename.dwg*
FTP Site	*ftp://servername/pathname/filename.dwg*
Local File	*drive:\pathname\filename.dwg*
	c:\acad 2021\sample\tablet.dwg
Network File	*\\localhost\drive:\pathname\filename.dwg*
	\\upstairs\d:\install\sample.dwg

When you open a drawing from the Internet, it will probably take more time than opening a file on your computer. During the transfer of file, AutoCAD displays the **File Download** dialog box to report the progress, refer to Figure 9-4. If your computer uses a slow internet connection, it will take some time to download the drawing file. But if you have access to a faster connection, you can expect lesser time to download the drawing file. It may be helpful to understand that the **OPEN** command does not copy the file from the Internet location directly into AutoCAD. Instead, it copies the file from the Internet to your computer's designated **Temporary** subdirectory such as *C:\Windows\Temp* (and then loads the drawing from the hard drive into AutoCAD). This is known as caching. It helps to speed up the processing of the drawing, since the drawing file is now located on your computer's hard drive, instead of the network drive.

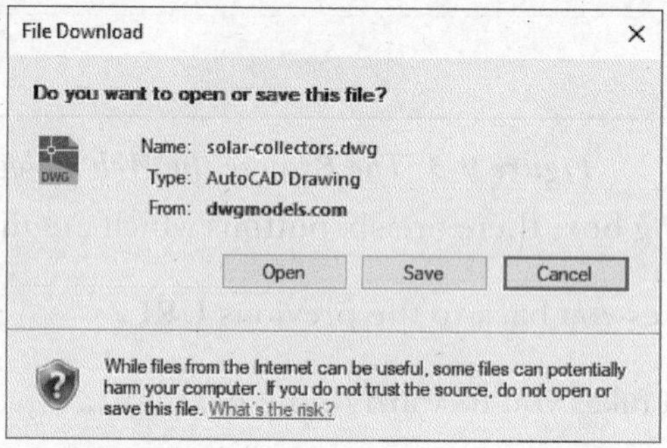

***Figure 9-4** The **File Download** dialog box*

Note
*You cannot use the **Locate** and **Find** options available in the **Tools** drop-down list of the **Select File** dialog box to locate files on the Internet.*

Example 1

The author's website has an area with a link that allows you to open a drawing in AutoCAD using the Internet. In this example, you will open a drawing file located at the author's website.

1. Start a new AutoCAD 2021 session.

2. Ensure that you have a live Internet connectivity. If you normally access the Internet via a telephone (modem) connection, dial your Internet service provider now.

3. Choose the **Open** button from the **Quick Access Toolbar**; the **Select File** dialog box is displayed.

4. Choose the **Search the Web** button to display the **Browse the Web** window.

5. In the **Look in** field, type **www.cadcim.com** and press ENTER; CADCIM Technologies website is opened.

6. Next, follow this path sequence: *Textbooks > CAD/CAM > AutoCAD Advanced > Advanced AutoCAD 2021: A Problem-Solving Approach (3D and Advanced)> Input Files*.

7. Click on the **Figure1** option in the **Input Files** area; the **File Download** will be initiated.

8. Once the file has been downloaded completely, the drawing will be displayed in the drawing area, refer to Figure 9-5.

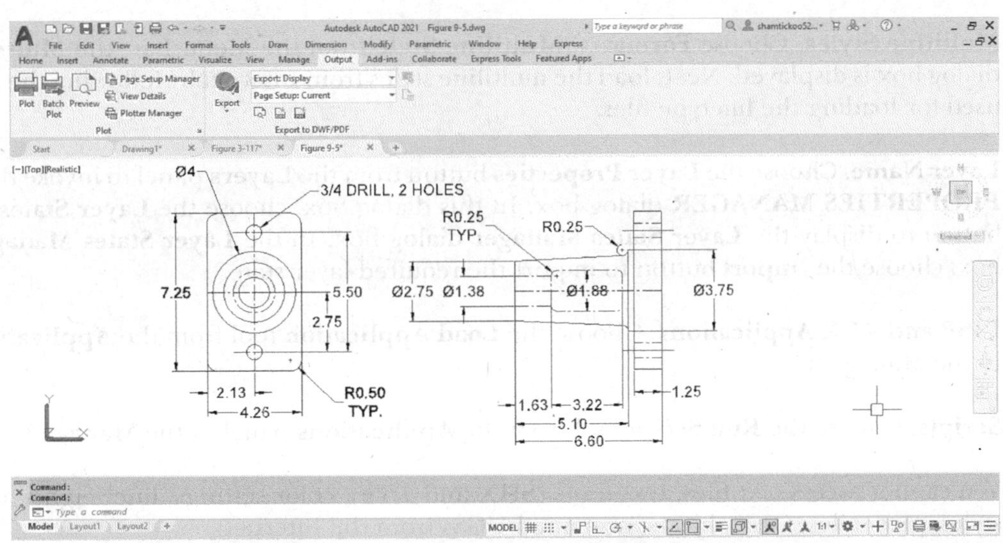

Figure 9-5 Drawing displayed in AutoCAD

INSERTING A BLOCK FROM THE INTERNET

When a block (symbol) is stored on the Internet, you can access it from within AutoCAD using the **INSERT** command. When the **Insert** dialog box appears, choose the **Browse** button to display the **Select Drawing File** dialog box. This is identical to the dialog box discussed earlier. After you select the file, AutoCAD downloads the file and continues with the prompt sequence of the **INSERT** command.

The process is identical for accessing external reference (xref) and raster image files. Other files that AutoCAD can access over the Internet include 3D Studio, ACIS, DXB (drawing exchange binary), Point Cloud, and WMF (Windows metafile). All these options are found in the **Insert** menu in the menu bar.

ACCESSING OTHER FILES ON THE INTERNET

Most of the other file-related dialog boxes allow you to access files from the Internet or the Intranet. This allows your firm or agency to have a central location that stores drawing standards. If you need to use a linetype or a hatch pattern, you can access the LIN or PAT file over the Internet. More than likely, you will have the location of these files stored in the Favorites list. Some examples include the following:

Linetypes. Invoke the **Drafting & Annotation** workspace. Next, choose the **Other** option from **Home > Properties > Linetype** drop-down list or **Format > Linetype** from the Menu Bar; the **Linetype Manager** dialog box will be displayed. Choose the **Load** button to invoke the **Load or Reload Linetypes** dialog box. Next, choose the **File** button to invoke the **Select Linetype File** dialog box. From this dialog box, choose the **Search the Web** button; the **Browse the Web** window is displayed. This window can be used to load the linetype files from Internet.

Hatch Patterns. Use the Web browser to copy *.pat* files from a remote location to your computer.

Multiline Styles. Choose **Format > Multiline Style** from the Menu Bar; the **Multiline Style** dialog box is displayed. Next, load the multiline styles from Internet by following the procedure used for loading the linetype files.

Layer Name. Choose the **Layer Properties** button from the **Layers** panel to invoke the **LAYER PROPERTIES MANAGER** dialog box. In this dialog box, choose the **Layer States Manager** button to display the **Layer States Manager** dialog box. In the **Layer States Manager** dialog box, choose the **Import** button to import the required layer state.

LISP and ARX Applications. Choose the **Load Application** tool from the **Applications** panel in the **Manage** tab.

Scripts. Choose the **Run Script** tool from the **Applications** panel in the **Manage** tab.

You cannot access text files, text fonts (SHX and TTF), color settings, lineweights, dimension styles, plot styles, OLE objects, or named UCSs from the Internet.

Note

The drawings that are inserted using the i-drop (SETIDROPHANDLER command) are inserted as a block and the ***INSERT*** *command is executed automatically when you drop the drawing in the main window of AutoCAD.*

SAVING A DRAWING ON THE INTERNET

When you are finished with editing a drawing in AutoCAD, you can save it to a file server on the Internet with the **SAVE** command. If you insert the drawing from the Internet (using **INSERT**) into the default *Drawing.dwg* drawing, AutoCAD insists you to first save the drawing on your computer's hard drive.

When a drawing of the same name already exists at that URL, AutoCAD warns you, just as it does when you use the **SAVEAS** command.

ONLINE RESOURCES

To access online resources, choose **Help > Additional Resources** from the menu bar; a cascading menu will be displayed. The options available in this menu are **Support Knowledge Base**, **Online Training Resources**, **Online Developer Center**, **Developer Help**, and **Autodesk User Group International**. Their functions are discussed next.

Support Knowledge Base

When you choose this option, the AutoCAD Services and Support Web page is displayed in the Web browser. Use the search box to search the database.

Note

*To obtain more information on the related topics in **Product Support** and the other **Online Training Resources** option, it is recommended to connect to the Internet and then choose the **Online Training Resources** option.*

Online Training Resources

When you choose this option, the Web page of training is displayed in the Web browser. The information on the following can be obtained by selecting this option.

- Information on Autodesk authorized training centers
- General training centers
- Autodesk Certification
- Learning tools

Online Developer Center

When you choose this option, the Web page is displayed with the following information:

- Answers to the questions that were asked by the users
- Sample applications
- Discussion groups
- Documentation

Developer Help

When you choose this button, the **Autodesk AutoCAD 2021 Help** window will be displayed containing developers help. You need not to be connected to internet for accessing this option.

Autodesk User Group International

When you choose this window, **Autodesk User Group International** Web browser window is displayed. This Web browser gives information about the AutoCAD user groups.

USING HYPERLINKS WITH AutoCAD

AutoCAD allows you to employ URLs in two ways:

1. Directly within an AutoCAD drawing.

2. Indirectly in DWF files displayed by a Web browser.

URLs are also known as hyperlinks. The term is used throughout this book. Hyperlinks are created, edited, and removed with the **HYPERLINK** command. You can also use the command line with the help of the **-HYPERLINK** command.

HYPERLINK Command

Ribbon: Insert > Data > Hyperlink **Menu Bar:** Insert > Hyperlink
Command: HYPERLINK

When you invoke this command, you will be prompted to select objects. Select the object(s) and press ENTER; the **Insert Hyperlink** dialog box will be displayed, refer to Figure 9-6.

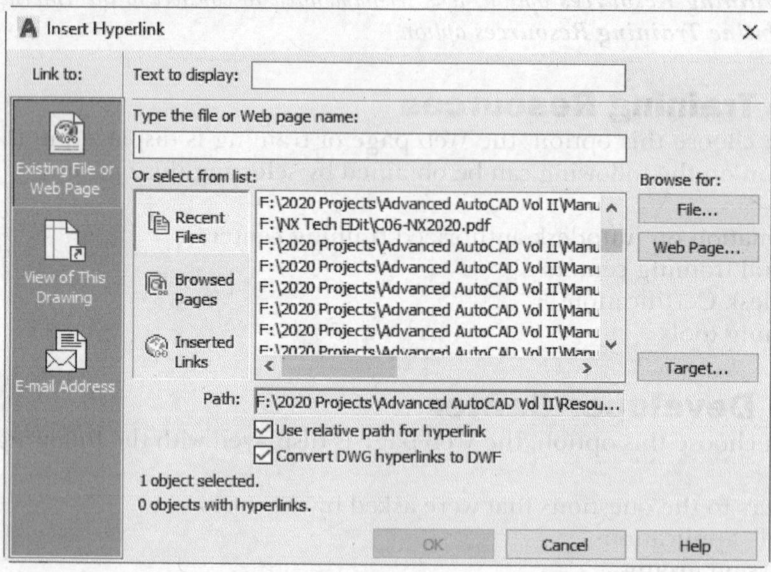

*Figure 9-6 The **Insert Hyperlink** dialog box*

If you select an object that has a hyperlink already attached to it, choose the swatch displayed on the right of the **Hyperlink** edit box from the **PROPERTIES** palette to display the **Edit Hyperlink** dialog box, as shown in Figure 9-7. The **Remove Link** button available in the dialog box is used to remove the hyperlink from an object.

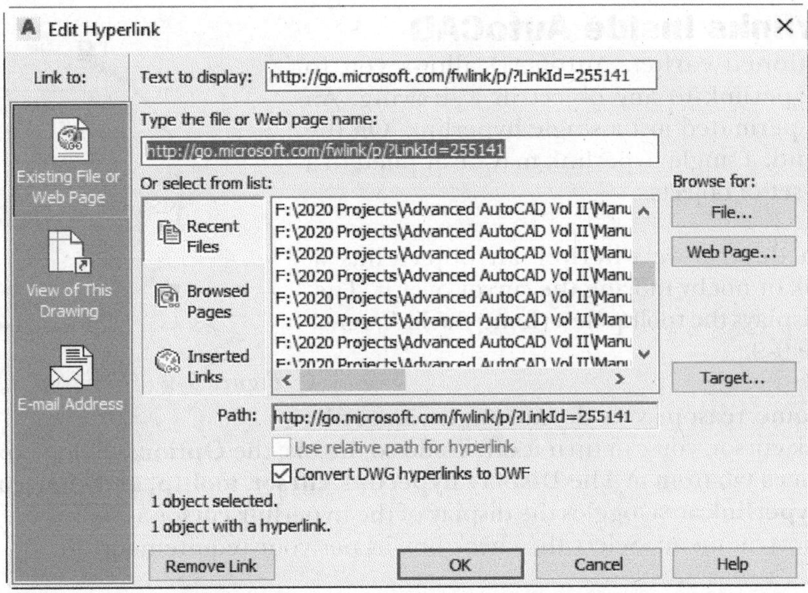

*Figure 9-7 The **Edit Hyperlink** dialog box*

If you use the Command line for inserting hyperlinks (**-HYPERLINK** command), you are also allowed to create hyperlink areas. A hyperlink area is a rectangular area that can be thought of as a 2D hyperlink (the dialog box-based **HYPERLINK** command does not create hyperlink areas). When you select the **Area** option from the Command line, a rectangular boundary object is placed automatically on the layer URLLAYER and it turns red, refer to Figure 9-8.

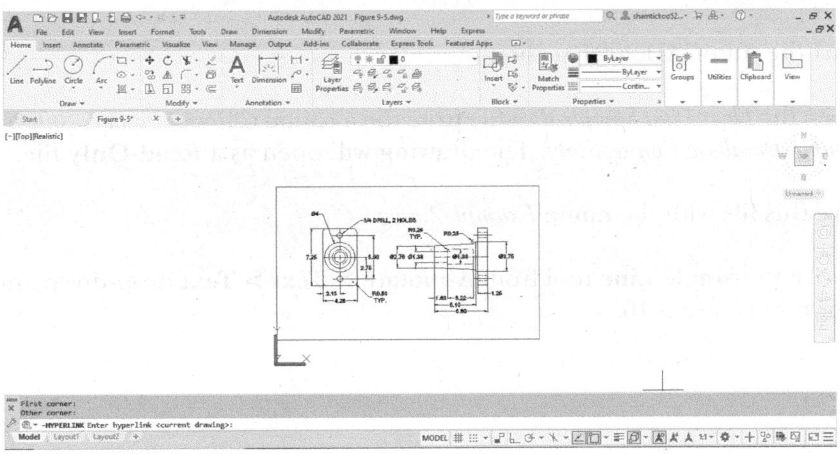

Figure 9-8 The rectangular hyperlink area

In the following sections, you will learn to apply and use hyperlinks in an AutoCAD drawing and in a Web browser through the dialog box-based **HYPERLINK** command.

Hyperlinks Inside AutoCAD

As mentioned earlier, AutoCAD allows you to add a hyperlink to any object in a drawing. An object is permitted just a single hyperlink. On the other hand, a single hyperlink may be applied to a selected set of objects.

You can determine whether an object has a hyperlink or not by moving the cursor over it. The cursor displays the tooltip describing the link, refer to Figure 9-9.

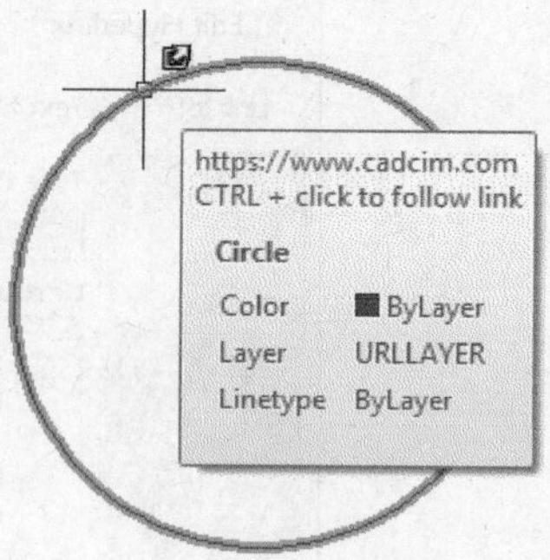

Figure 9-9 *The cursor displaying a hyperlink*

If, for some reason, you do not want to see the hyperlink cursor, you can turn it off. To do so, invoke the **Options** dialog box, choose the **User Preferences** tab from it. The **Display hyperlink cursor, tooltip, and shortcut menu** check box in the **Hyperlink** area toggles the display of the hyperlink cursor as well as the **Hyperlink** option in the shortcut menu. Select the check box as per your requirement.

Attaching Hyperlinks

The following example explains the method of attaching hyperlinks.

Example 2

In this example, you are given the drawing of a floor plan to which you will add hyperlinks of other AutoCAD drawing. They must be attached to objects. For this reason, you will place some text in the drawing and then attach hyperlinks to it.

1. Start the AutoCAD 2021 session.

2. Open the *Floor Plan Sample.dwg* file from the location *C:\Program Files\Autodesk\AutoCAD 2021\Sample\Database Connectivity*. The drawing will open as a **Read-Only** file.

3. Save this file with the name *Example2.dwg*.

4. Invoke the **Single Line** tool from **Annotate > Text > Text** drop-down and write the text as shown in Figure 9-10.

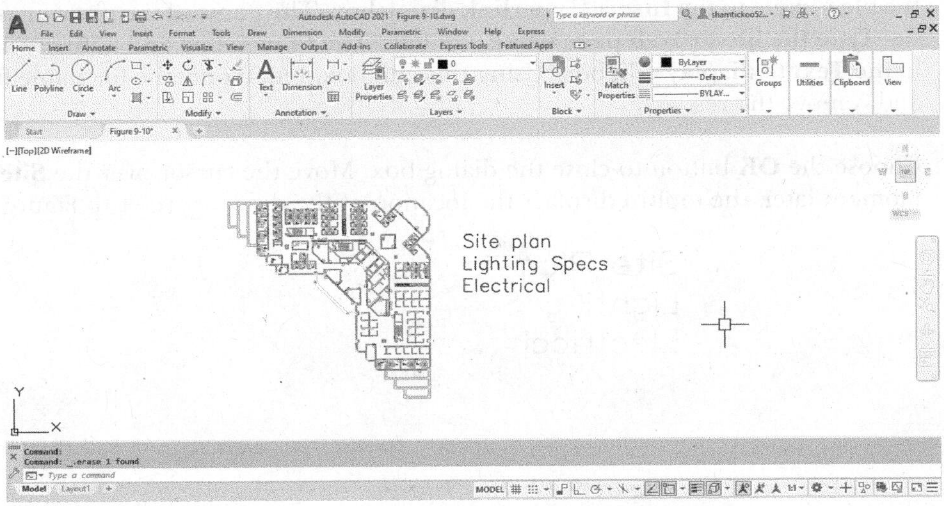

Figure 9-10 Text placed in a drawing

5. Choose the **Hyperlink** tool from the **Data** panel in the **Insert** tab; you are prompted to select objects. Select the text **Site Plan** and press ENTER to display the **Insert Hyperlink** dialog box.

6. Choose the **File** button from the **Insert Hyperlink** dialog box to display the **Browse the Web – Select Hyperlink** dialog box. Browse to *C:\Program Files\Autodesk\AutoCAD 2021\Sample\en-us\DesignCenter* folder, if it is not already opened, and select the *Home - Space Planner.dwg* file, refer to Figure 9-11.

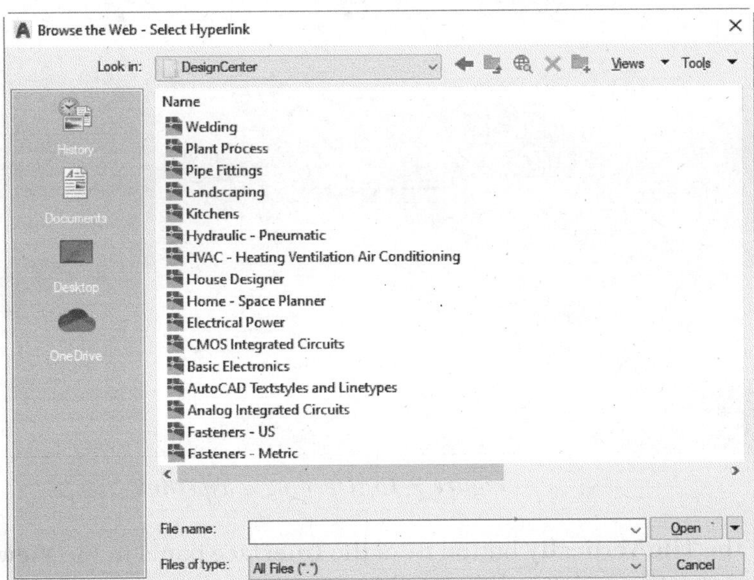

*Figure 9-11 The **Browse the Web - Select Hyperlink** dialog box*

7. Choose **Open** from the dialog box. AutoCAD does not open the drawing; rather, it copies the file's name to the **Insert Hyperlink** dialog box. The name of the drawing is displayed in the **Type the file or Web page name** edit box. The same name and path are also displayed in the **Text to display** edit box. Using this edit box, retain only the file name from the path and remove the rest.

8. Choose the **OK** button to close the dialog box. Move the cursor over the **Site Plan** text. A moment later, the tooltip displays the location of the drawing, refer to Figure 9-12.

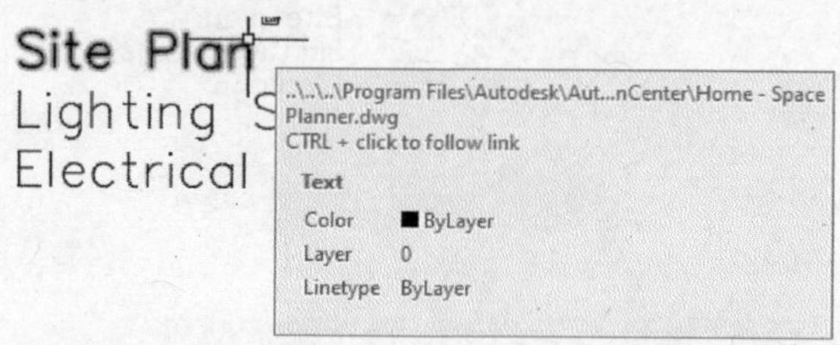

Figure 9-12 The Hyperlink cursor and tooltip

9. Connect to the Internet and then connect the URL *www.autodesk.com* to **Lighting Specs** using the **Web Page** button of the **Insert Hyperlink** dialog box.

10. You can directly open the file attached as hyperlink to the object by using the linked object. To do so, select the object to which the file is linked and then right-click to display the shortcut menu. In the shortcut menu, choose **Hyperlink > Open "file path'**. In this case, the file name is *Home - Space Planner.dwg*. Therefore, right-click and then choose **Hyperlink > Open "Home - Space Planner"** from the shortcut menu, refer to Figure 9-13.

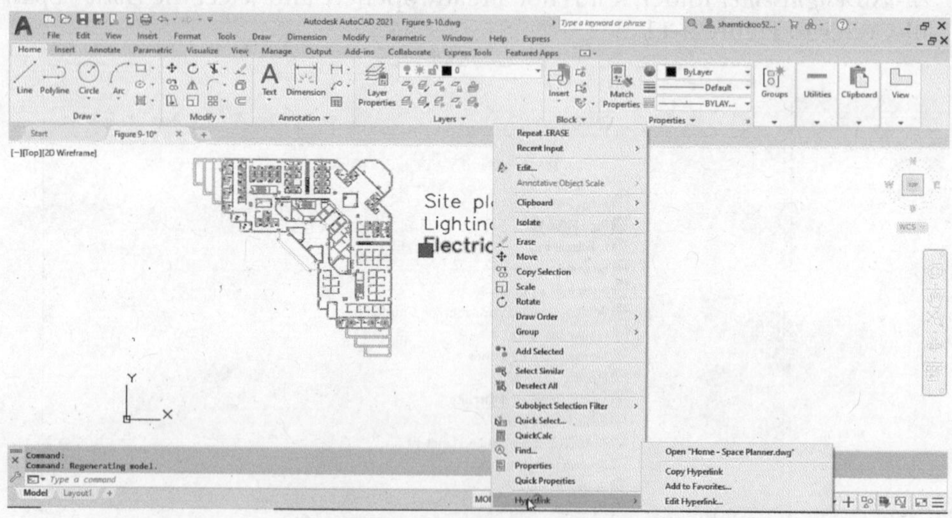

Figure 9-13 Opening a hyperlink

11. Choose the **Tile Vertically** button from the **Interface** panel in the **View** tab to view both the drawings together, refer to Figure 9-14.

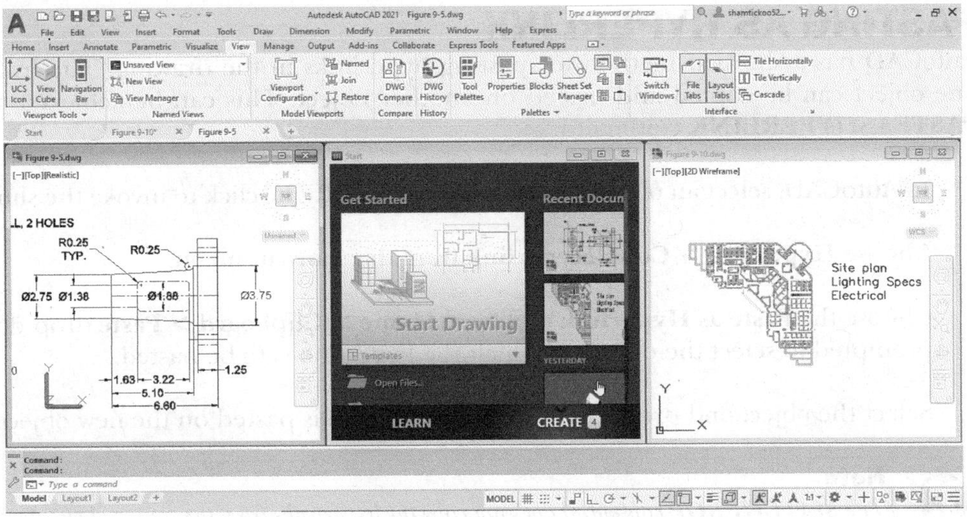

Figure 9-14 *Displaying both drawings in the drawing window*

12. Select the Lighting Specs text and then right-click on it. Choose *Hyperlink > Open "http://www.autodesk.com"* from the shortcut menu; the URL *www.autodesk.com* is launched in the web browser, refer to Figure 9-15. Make sure you are connected to the Internet before opening this URL.

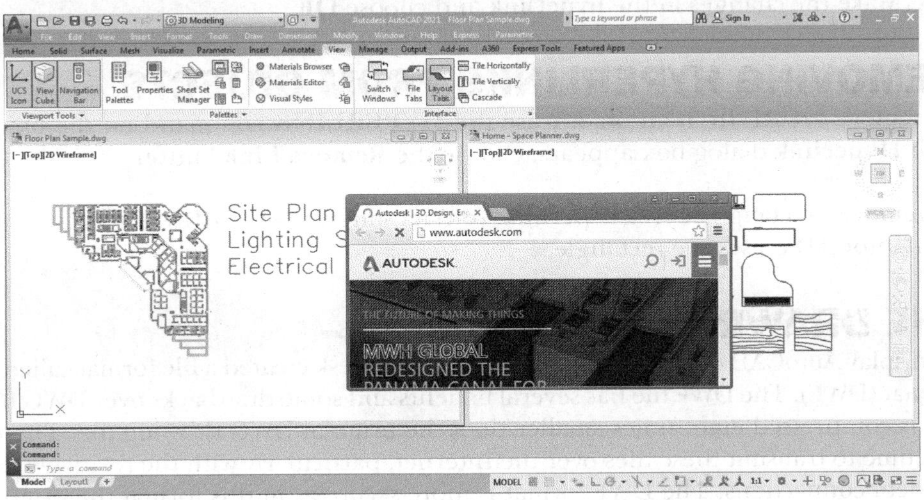

Figure 9-15 *Web browser opens the URL that was hyperlinked to the selected text*

13. Save the drawing.

PASTING AS HYPERLINK

AutoCAD has a shortcut method for pasting hyperlinks in the drawing. The hyperlink from one object can be copied and pasted on another object. This can be achieved by using the **PASTEASHYPERLINK** command.

1. In AutoCAD, select an object that has a hyperlink. Right-click to invoke the shortcut menu.

2. Choose **Hyperlink > Copy Hyperlink** from the shortcut menu.

3. Choose the **Paste as Hyperlink** tool from **Home > Clipboard > Paste** drop-down; you are prompted to select the object on which the hyperlink is to be pasted.

4. Select the object and press ENTER. The hyperlink is pasted on the new object.

Note

*The **MATCHPROP** command does not copy the hyperlinks from the source objects to the destination objects.*

EDITING HYPERLINKS

AutoCAD allows you to edit the hyperlinks attached to an object. To do so, select the hyperlinked object and right-click. Choose **Hyperlink > Edit Hyperlink** from the shortcut menu; the **Edit Hyperlink** dialog box will be displayed, which looks identical to the **Insert Hyperlink** dialog box. Make the changes in the hyperlink and choose **OK**.

REMOVING HYPERLINKS FROM OBJECTS

To remove a URL from an object, use the **HYPERLINK** command on the object. When the **Edit Hyperlink** dialog box appears, choose the **Remove Link** button.

To remove a rectangular area hyperlink, you can simply use the **ERASE** tool; select the rectangle and AutoCAD erases the rectangle.

THE DRAWING WEB FORMAT

To display AutoCAD drawings on the Internet, Autodesk created a file format called Drawing Web format (DWF). The DWF file has several benefits and some drawbacks over DWG files. The DWF file is compressed eight times smaller than the original DWG drawing file. Therefore, it takes less time to transmit these files over the Internet, particularly with the relatively slow telephone modem connections. The DWF format is more secure as in this format the original drawing is not being displayed, therefore, another user cannot tamper with the original DWG file.

However, the DWF format has some drawbacks, which are mentioned below:

- You must go through the extra step of translating from DWG to DWF.
- DWF files cannot display rendered or shaded drawings.
- DWF is a flat 2D-file format; therefore, it does not preserve 3D data, although you can export a 3D view.
- AutoCAD itself cannot display DWF files.

- DWF files cannot be converted back to DWG format without using file translation software from a third-party vendor.
- Earlier versions of DWF did not handle paper space objects (version 2.x and earlier), or line widths, lineweights, and non-rectangular viewports (version 3.x and earlier).

To view a DWF file on the Internet, your Web browser needs to have a *plug-in* software extension called **Autodesk DWF Viewer**. This viewer is installed on your system with AutoCAD 2021 installation. **Autodesk DWF Viewer** allows Internet Explorer 5.01 (or later) to handle a variety of file formats. Autodesk makes this DWF Viewer plug-in freely available from its Web site at *http://www.autodesk.com*. It is a good idea to regularly check for updates of the DWF plug-in, which is updated frequently.

CREATING A DWF FILE

You can use two methods to create DWF files in AutoCAD. The first method is to use the **PLOT** command and the second method is to use the **PUBLISH** command.

Creating a DWF File Using the PLOT Command

The following steps explain the procedure to create a DWF file using the **PLOT** tool:

1. Open the file to be converted into a DWF file. Choose the **Plot** tool from the **Quick Access Toolbar**; the **Batch Plot** message box will be displayed, refer to Figure 9-16.

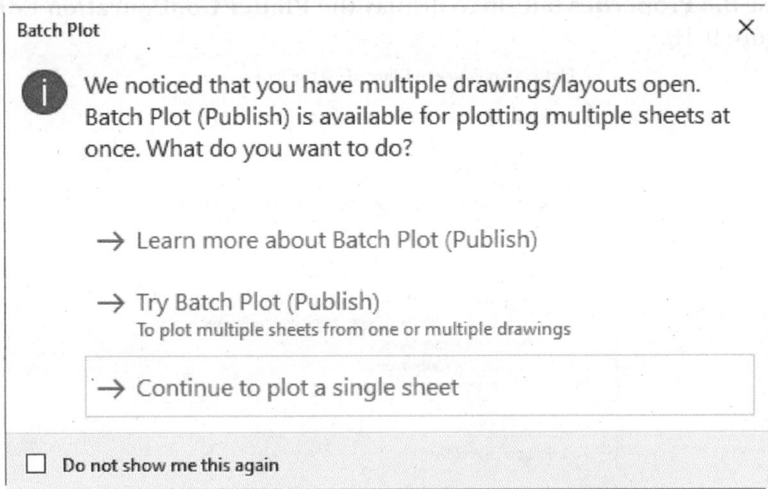

***Figure 9-16** The **Batch Plot** message box*

2. If you want to plot multiple sheets from one or multiple drawings, then choose the **Try Batch Plot (Publish)** option from the message box. Otherwise, choose **Continue to plot a single sheet** from the message box; the **Plot - Model** dialog box will be displayed, refer to Figure 9-17.

3. Select **DWF6 ePlot.pc3** from the **Name** drop-down list in the **Printer/plotter** area, refer to Figure 9-17.

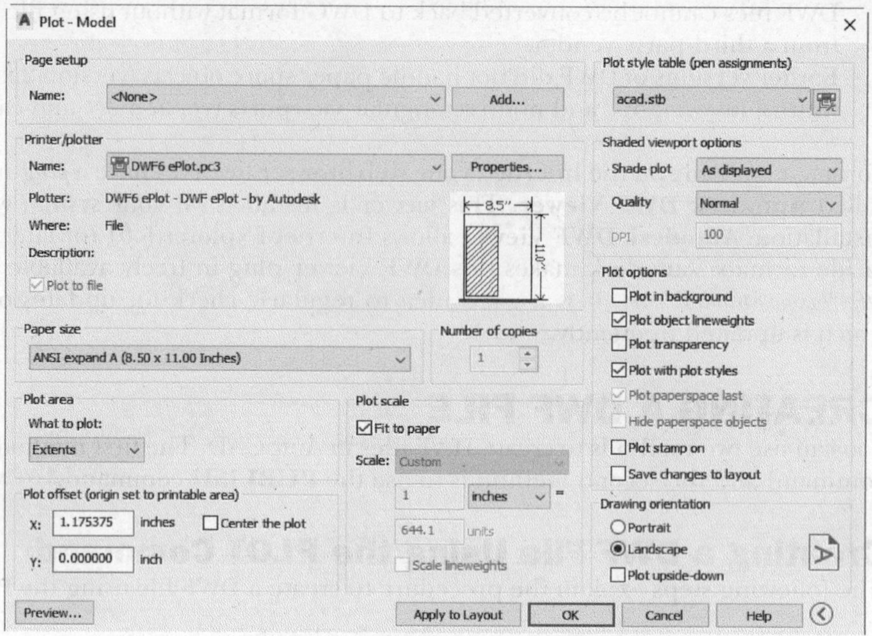

*Figure 9-17 The **Plot-Model** dialog box*

4. Choose the **Properties** button to display the **Plotter Configuration Editor** dialog box, refer to Figure 9-18.

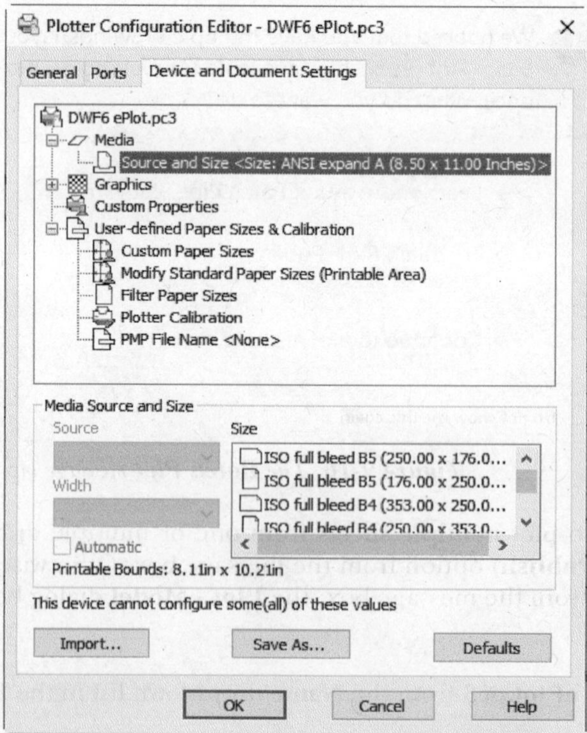

*Figure 9-18 The **Plotter Configuration Editor** dialog box*

5. In the **Device and Document Settings** tab of this dialog box, select **Custom Properties** in the tree view; the **Access Custom Dialog** area is displayed in the lower half of the dialog box.

6. Choose the **Custom Properties** button from the **Access Custom Dialog** area to display the **DWF6 ePlot Properties** dialog box, refer to Figure 9-19.

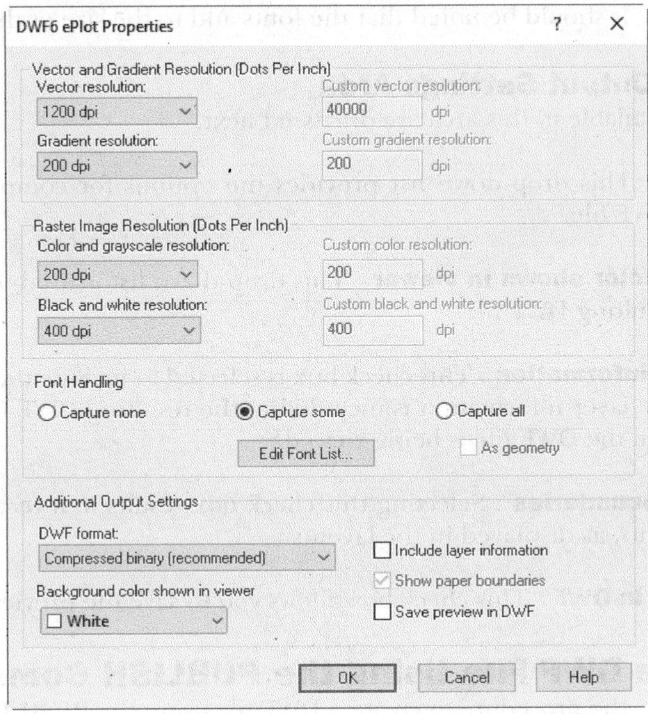

*Figure 9-19 The **DWF6 ePlot Properties** dialog box*

7. Set the required options in these dialog boxes and choose **OK** three times to return to the **Plot - Model** dialog box.

8. In the **Plot - Model** dialog box, use the required options to create the DWF file. Choose **OK** from the **Plot** dialog box; the **Browse for Plot File** dialog box will be displayed.

9. Specify the name of the DWF file in the **File name** edit box. If necessary, change the location where the file is to be stored.

DWF6 ePlot Properties Dialog Box Options

The options in this dialog box are discussed next.

Vector and Gradient Resolution (Dots Per Inch) Area

This area allows you to set the resolution for the vector information and gradients. Unlike AutoCAD DWG files that are based on real numbers, DWF files are saved using integer numbers. The higher the resolution, the better the quality of the DWF files. However, the size of the files also increases with the resolution.

Raster Image Resolution (Dots Per Inch) Area

This area allows you to set the resolution for the raster images in the DWF files.

Font Handling

This area of the **DWF6 ePlot Properties** dialog box is used to select the fonts that you need to include in the DWF file. You can choose the **Edit Font List** button from this area to display the list of the fonts. It should be noted that the fonts add to the size of the DWF file.

Additional Output Settings Area

The options available in this area are discussed next.

DWF format : This drop-down list provides the options for compressing or zipping while creating the DWF file.

Background color shown in viewer : This drop-down list is used to specify the background color of the resulting DWF file.

Include layer information : This check box is selected to include the layer information in the DWF file. If the layer information is included in the resulting DWF file, you can toggle layers off and on when the DWF file is being viewed.

Show paper boundaries : Selecting this check box results in a rectangular boundary at the drawing's extents, as displayed in the layouts.

Save preview in DWF : This check box allows you to save the preview in DWF file.

Creating a DWF File Using the PUBLISH Command

The following is the procedure to create a DWF file using the **PUBLISH** command:

Choose the **Batch Plot** tool from the **Plot** panel in the **Output** tab; the **Publish** dialog box will be displayed, refer to Figure 9-20. The options in this dialog box are discussed next.

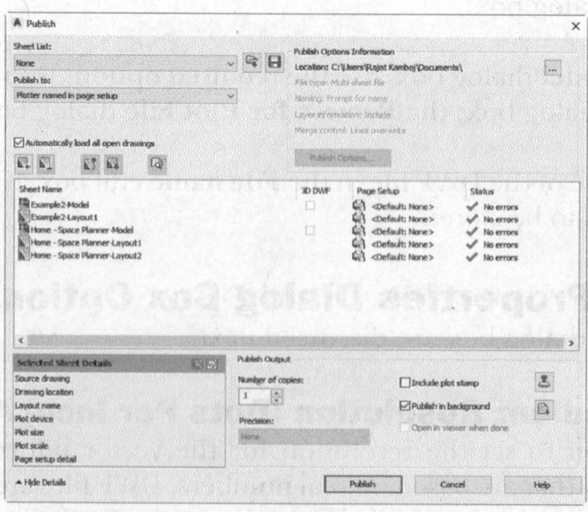

*Figure 9-20 The **Publish** dialog box*

The list box in the **Publish** dialog box lists the model and paper space layouts that will be included for publishing. Right-click on any of the sheets in the **Sheet Name** column to display a shortcut menu. The options in it can be used on the drawings listed in this area. You can change the page setup option of the sheets using the field in the **Page Setup/3D DWF** column. You can also import a page setup using the drop-down list that is displayed when you click on the field in this column. The remaining options in this area are discussed next.

Note

*If you have not saved the drawing before invoking the **PUBLISH** command, the sheet names in the list box will have prefix as **Unsaved**. Also, the status of the layouts that are not initialized will show **Layout not initialized**.*

Add Sheets. This button, when chosen, displays the **Select Drawings** dialog box. Using this dialog box, you can select the drawing files (*.dwg*). These files are then included in the creation of the DWF file.

Remove Sheets. This button is chosen to remove the sheet selected from the **Sheet Name** column.

Move Sheet Up. This button is chosen to move the selected sheet up by one position in the list.

Move Sheet Down. This button is chosen to move the selected sheet down by one position in the list.

Save Sheet List. This button, when chosen, displays the **Save List As** dialog box. This dialog box allows you to save the current list of drawing files as DSD files.

Load Sheet List. After saving a list, if you choose this button, the **Load List of Sheets** dialog box will be displayed with the saved list in the **Name** area of the **Load List of Sheets** dialog box. You can select the *.dsd* or *.bp3* file format from this dialog box and select the list to load. After selecting the list, you can proceed to publish the selected sheet list. But if you want to publish a different list, select the required list from the **Load List of Sheets** dialog box. On doing so, the **Publish - Load Sheet List** message box will be displayed. Choose the required option from this message box to continue with the publishing list.

Preview. This button is chosen to preview the sheet selected from the **Sheet Name** column.

Publish to

This drop-down list provides the options for specifying whether the output of the **PUBLISH** command should be plotted on a sheet using the printer mentioned in the page setup of the selected sheet or as a DWF or DWFx or PDF file.

Publish Output Area

This area provides the additional options while publishing the sheets. The **Number of copies** spinner is used to specify the number of copies to be published. Note that if you want the output in the form of a DWF file, the number of copies can only be one. The button below the **Plot Stamp Settings** button is used to reverse the default order of publishing the drawings listed in the list box. Select the **Include plot stamp** check box to include a plot stamp while publishing.

The **Plot Stamp Settings** button is chosen to invoke the **Plot Stamp** dialog box for configuring the settings of the plot stamp. The **Publish in background** check box is used to publish the selected drawings in background, while you can continue working with AutoCAD. Select the **Open in viewer when done** check box to open the published file in a new window.

Publish Options

When you choose this button, the **DWF Publish Options** dialog box is displayed, as shown in Figure 9-21. It provides you with the options to publish the drawings. These options are discussed next.

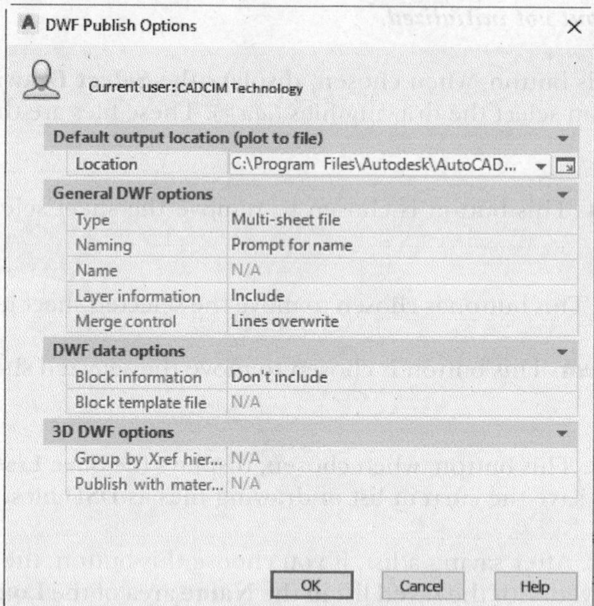

*Figure 9-21 The **DWF Publish Options** dialog box*

Default output location (plot-to-file) rollout. The options in this rollout are used to specify the location of the output of the **PUBLISH** command. By default, the sheets are published locally on the hard drive of your computer. You can modify the default location of the file using the edit box or the swatch button which is displayed when you click on the field that shows the name and location of the file.

General DWF options. The options in this rollout are used to specify DWF files. Click the particular field and specify the appropriate options.

DWF data options. The options in this area are used to specify the password protection. You can also specify whether the block information should be included in the resulting DWF file or not.

3D DWF options. The options in this area are used to specify the data that you can include in the 3D DWF publishing. When only 2D DWF files are listed for publishing, all of the **3D DWF options** are set to **N/A** and cannot be modified.

This completes the explanation of the options in the **DWF Publish Options** dialog box. The remaining options of the **Publish** dialog box are discussed next.

Show Details

When you choose this button, the **Publish** dialog box expands and shows the details related to the sheet selected from the **Sheet Name** list box.

Publish

This button is used to start the process of publishing or creating the DWF file.

Note

*You may need to set the value of the **BACKGROUNDPLOT** system variable to **0** if AutoCAD gives an error while publishing.*

Export to DWF Files

You can export a drawing to a DWF file by choosing the **DWF** tool from **Output > Export to DWF/PDF > Export** drop-down; the **Save As DWF** dialog box will be displayed, as shown in Figure 9-22. In this dialog box, the current settings for the DWF file will be displayed in the **Current Settings** area. To edit the current settings, choose the **Options** button; the **Export to DWF Options** dialog box will be displayed. In this dialog box, you can change the general information for the DWF file like file location, password protection, layer information, and so on. You can also invoke this dialog box by choosing the **Export to DWF Options** tool from the **Export to DWF/PDF** panel.

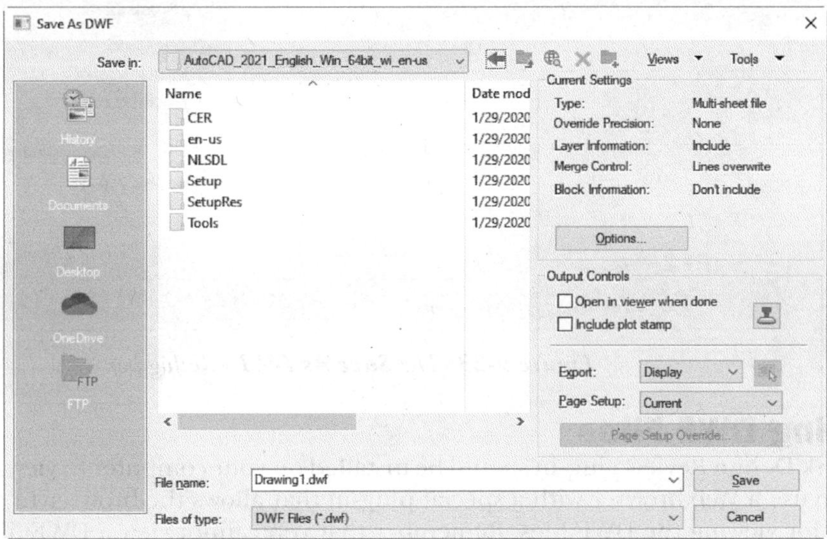

*Figure 9-22 The **Save As DWF** dialog box*

You can also select the portion of the drawing that is to be exported from the **Export** drop-down list in the **Save As DWF** dialog box. If you are in the **Model** tab, you can select the **Display** (objects currently displayed on the screen), **Extents** (drawing extents) or **Window** (selected area from the drawing) option and if you are in the **Layout** tab, you can select between the active layout or all layouts. These options are also available in the **What to Export** drop-down list of the **Export to DWF/PDF** panel in the **Output** tab of the **Ribbon**. You can also specify the page settings for the DWF file such as paper size, scale, and plot area. If you want to use the current settings of the **Page Setup Manager**, select the **Current** option from the **Page Setup** drop-down list in the **Save As DWF** dialog box or the **Export to DWF/PDF** panel. To override the current setting, choose the **Override** button. If you want to view the DWF in the Autodesk Design Review, select the **Open in viewer when done** check box. Select the **Include plot stamp** check box to include drawing name, paper size, date and time, and so on to the DWF file. After setting the parameters, choose **Save** from the **Save As DWF** dialog box; the drawing is exported.

Generating DWF Files for 3D Models

To create DWF files for 3D models, it is necessary to install 3D DWF Publish feature while installing AutoCAD 2021. Choose the **DWFx** tool from the **Export** drop-down of the **Export to DWF/PDF** panel in the **Output** tab to open the **Save As DWFx** dialog box, as shown in Figure 9-23. Browse to the location where you want to save the DWFx file, and then specify the name of the file. Next, choose the **Save** button to publish the drawing.

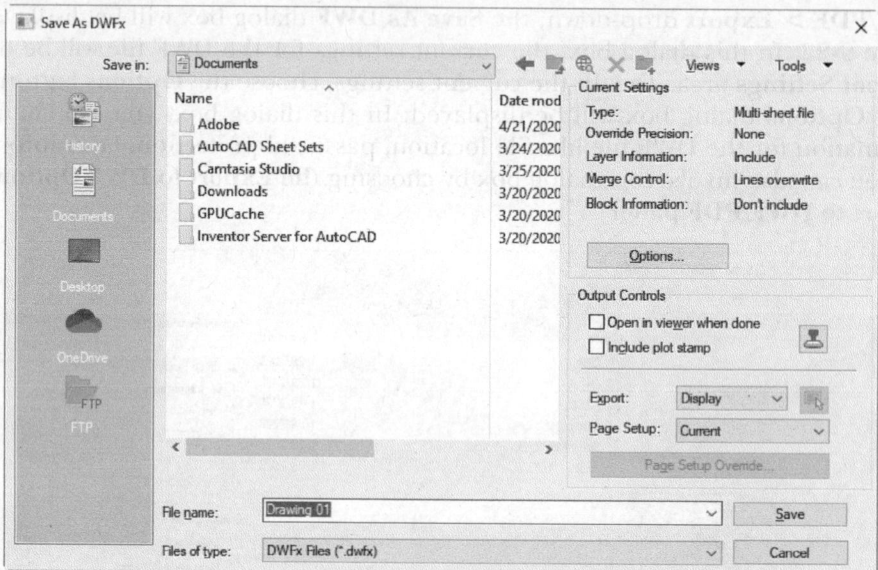

Figure 9-23 The ***Save As DWFx*** *dialog box*

Viewing DWF Files

Autodesk Design Review plug-in should be installed on your computer to view the DWF files. You can also use a Web browser with a special plug-in that allows the browser to correctly interpret the file for viewing the DWF files. Remember that you cannot view a DWF file with AutoCAD.

You can use various buttons provided in the Autodesk Design Review to manipulate the view of a DWF file. However, remember that the original objects of a DWF file cannot be modified. You can also right-click on the display screen to display a shortcut menu. The shortcut menu provides you with the options such as **Cut**, **Copy**, **Paste**, **Pan**, **Zoom**, **Steering Wheels**, and so on, refer to Figure 9-24. Choose an option from this shortcut menu to invoke the corresponding operation.

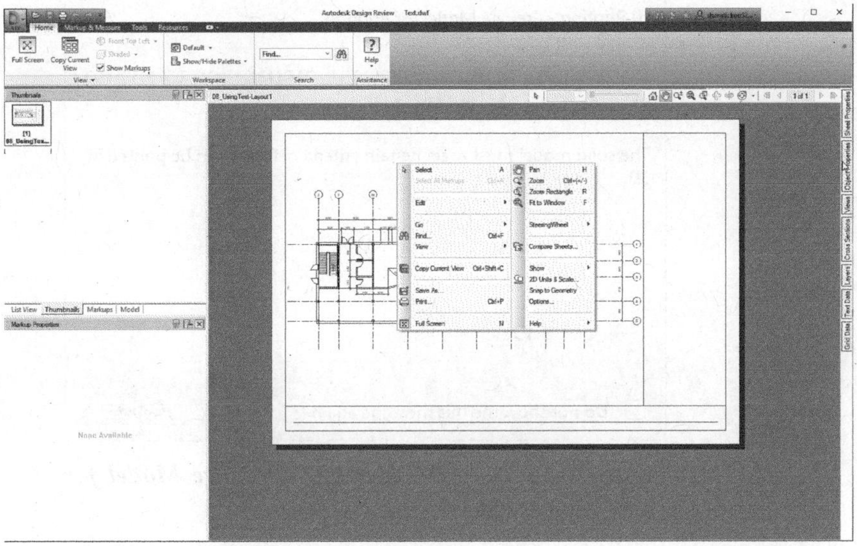

*Figure 9-24 The **Autodesk Design Review** with the shortcut menu*

Note

*To publish a sheet, the **DWF6 ePlot.pc3** plotter should be selected from the **Page Setup Manager** dialog box.*

3D PRINTING

3D printing or additive manufacturing is a process of making three dimensional solid objects from a digital file.

In AutoCAD 2021, the 3D printing tools are available in the **3D Print** panel of the **Output** tab in the **Ribbon**, refer to Figure 9-25. AutoCAD provides two tools for sending a 3D model to a 3D printer. On choosing the **Send to 3D Print Service** tool, the **3DPRINTSERVICE** command(formerly **3DPRINT**) will be activated. Alternatively, you can choose the **Print Studio** tool to activate the **3DPRINT** command.

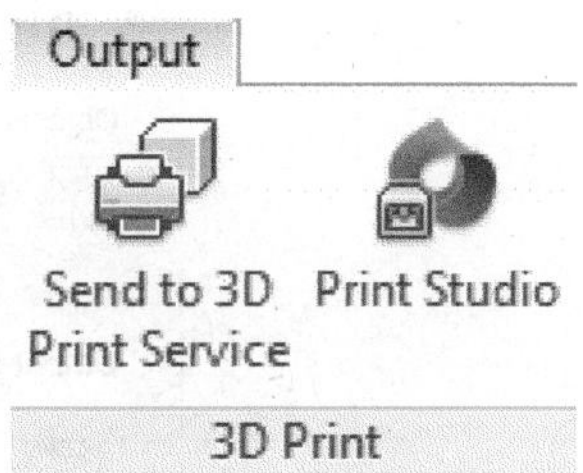

*Figure 9-25 The **3D Print** panel in the **Output** tab*

When you invoke the **Send to 3D Print Service** tool, the **3D Printing - Prepare Model for Printing** message box is displayed, refer to Figure 9-26.

Tip

*You can also access the 3D printing tools from the flyouts displayed on choosing the **Publish** and **Print** options available in the **Application Menu**.*

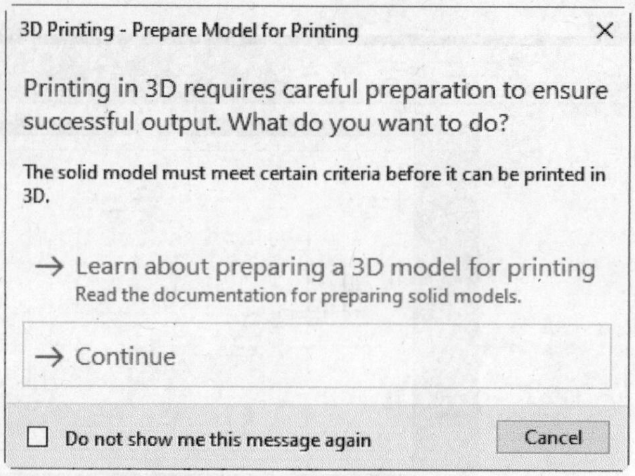

Figure 9-26 The ***3D Printing - Prepare Model for Printing*** *message box*

If you want to read the documentation for preparing a 3D model for printing, select **Learn about preparing a 3D model for printing** option from the message box. Otherwise, select **Continue** to proceed further. On selecting **Continue** from the message box, **3DPRINTSERVICE** command becomes active. The prompt sequence that will be followed is given next.

3DPRINTSERVICE Select solids or watertight meshes : *Select the solid(s) or watertight mesh(es) you want to send for 3D printing and press ENTER.*

On pressing ENTER, the **3D Print Options** dialog box will be displayed, refer to Figure 9-27. In this dialog box, you can view and edit various settings including the output dimensions.

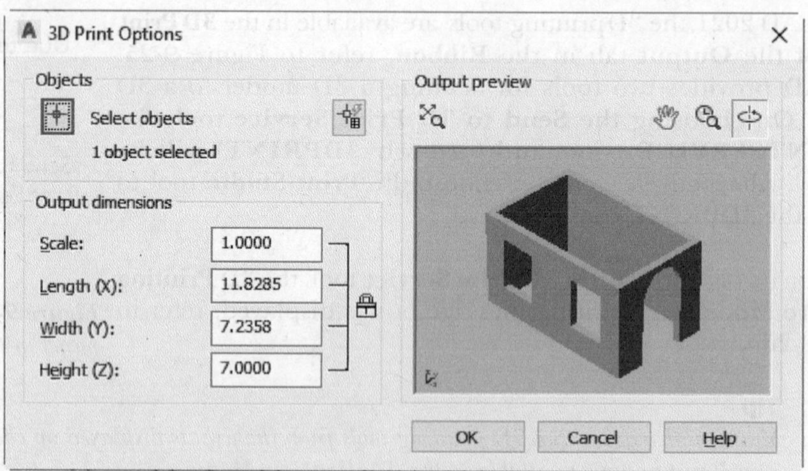

Figure 9-27 The ***3D Print Options*** *dialog box*

The options in the **3D Print Options** dialog box are discussed next.

Objects

The options in this area are discussed next.

Select objects

This button enables you to select the objects that you want to get 3D printed. When you choose the **Select objects** button, the **3D Print Options** dialog box disappears and allows you to select the objects. Once you select the objects and press ENTER, the dialog box reappears with the selected objects displayed in the **Output preview** area.

Quick Select

On choosing this button, the **Quick Select** dialog box is invoked which enables you to create a new selection set that will either include or exclude all objects whose object type and property criteria match as specified for the selection set.

Output dimensions

In this area, you can set the scale, length, width, and height of the 3D model to be sent for 3D printing.

Output Preview

In this area, four buttons namely **Zoom Extents**, **Pan**, **Zoom**, and **Orbit** are available along with a preview pane for the display of selected objects.

Once you have made all the required settings, choose the **OK** button to exit the dialog box. On choosing the **OK** button, the **Create STL File** dialog box will be displayed, refer to Figure 9-28, and you will be prompted to save the output file to STL format. After saving the file in the STL format, you can send it to the 3D printer for printing.

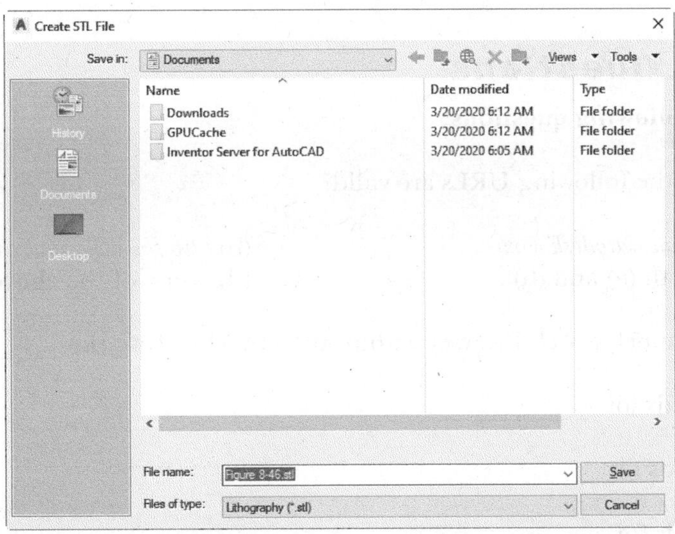

Figure 9-28 *The* ***Create STL File*** *dialog box*

Self-Evaluation Test

Answer the following questions and then compare them to those given at the end of this chapter:

1. Compression in a DWF file helps transmit the file in ____________ time to Internet.
2. Rectangular area hyperlinks are stored in the ________ layer.
3. To see the location of hyperlinks in a drawing, use the __________ command.
4. The ______ is an HTML tag that is used to embed objects in a webpage.
5. If you attach a hyperlink to a block, the hyperlink data is _________ when you scale the block unevenly, stretch the block, or explode it.
6. To access online resources, choose **Help > Additional Resources > Online Training Resources** from the menu bar. (T/F)
7. You cannot find out whether an object has a hyperlink or not. (T/F)
8. By default, the **Browse the Web** dialog box displays the contents of the URL stored in the **INETLOCATION** system variable. (T/F)
9. URLs are also known as hyperlinks. (T/F)
10. You can select text in an AutoCAD drawing which has hyperlink attached to it to paste it as a hyperlink. (T/F)

Review Questions

Answer the following questions:

1. Which of the following URLs are valid?

   (a) *www.autodesk.com* (b) *http://www.autodesk.com*
   (c) Both (a) and (b) (d) None of the above

2. You can launch a Web Browser within AutoCAD by using the _________ command.
3. DWF stands for ____________.
4. URL stands for ____________.
5. FTP stands for ____________.

6. Hyperlinks are created, edited, and removed with the __________ command.

7. The purpose of URLs is to let you create __________ between files.

8. Hyperlinks are active in AutoCAD 2021. (T/F)

9. URL can be attached to any object. (T/F)

10. AutoCAD provides the tools to share the documents online. (T/F)

Answers to Self-Evaluation Test

1. less, **2.** URLLAYER, **3.** **HYPERLINK**, **4.** <embed>, **5.** lost, **6.** T, **7.** F, **8.** T, **9.** T, **10.** T

Chapter 10

Script Files and Slide Shows

Learning Objectives

After completing this chapter, you will be able to:

- ***Write script files and use the Run Script option to run script files***
- ***Use the RSCRIPT and DELAY commands in script files***
- ***Run script files while loading AutoCAD***
- ***Create a slide show***
- ***Preload slides while running a slide show***

Key Terms

- ***Script Files***
- ***RESUME***
- ***Run Script***
- ***Switches***
- ***Preloading Slide***
- ***Slide Library***
- ***RSCRIPT***
- ***Slides***
- ***Delay Time***
- ***Slide Show***

WHAT ARE SCRIPT FILES?

AutoCAD has provides a facility called script files that allow you to combine different AutoCAD commands and execute them in a predetermined sequence. The commands can be written as a text file using any text editor like Notepad. These files, generally known as script files, have an extension *.scr* (example: *plot1.scr*). A script file is executed with the AutoCAD **Run Script** tool.

Script files can be used to generate a slide show, do the initial drawing setup, or plot a drawing to a predefined specification. They can also be used to automate certain command sequences that are used frequently in generating, editing, or viewing drawings. Remember that the script files cannot access dialog boxes or menus. When commands that open dialog boxes are issued from a script file, AutoCAD runs the command line version of the command instead of opening the dialog box.

Example 1 — *Initial Setup of Drawing*

Write a script file that will perform the following initial setup for a drawing (file name *script1.scr*). It is assumed that the drawing will be plotted on 12x9 size paper (Scale factor for plotting = 4).

Ortho	On		Zoom	All
Grid	2.0		Text height	0.125
Snap	0.5		LTSCALE	4.0
Limits	0,0	48.0,36.0	DIMSCALE	4.0

Step 1: Understanding commands and prompt entries

Before writing a script file, you need to know the AutoCAD commands and the entries required in response to the Command prompts. To find out the sequence of the Command prompt entries, you can type the command and then respond to different Command prompts. The following is the list of AutoCAD commands and prompt entries for Example 1:

Command: **ORTHO**
Enter mode [ON/OFF] <OFF>: **ON**

Command: **GRID**
Specify grid spacing(X) or [ON/OFF/Snap/Major/aDaptive/Limits/Follow/Aspect] <0.5000>: **2.0**

Command: **SNAP**
Specify snap spacing or [ON/OFF/Aspect/Legacy/Style/Type]<0.5000>: **0.5**

Command: **LIMITS**
Reset Model space limits:
Specify lower left corner or [ON/OFF] <0.0,0.0>: **0,0**
Specify upper right corner <12.0,9.0>: **48.0,36.0**

Command: **ZOOM**
Specify corner of window, enter a scale factor (nX or nXP), or
[All/Center/Dynamic/Extents/Previous/Scale/Window/Object] <real time>: **A**

Command: **TEXTSIZE**
Enter new value for TEXTSIZE <0.02>: **0.125**

Command: **LTSCALE**
Enter new linetype scale factor <1.0000>: **4.0**

Command: **DIMSCALE**
Enter new value for DIMSCALE <1.0000>: **4.0**

Step 2: Writing the script file

Once you know the commands and the required prompt entries, you can write a script file using any text editor such as the Notepad.

As you invoke the **NOTEPAD** command, AutoCAD prompts you to enter the file to be edited. Press ENTER in response to the prompt to display the **Notepad** editor. Write the script file in the **Notepad** editor. Given below is the listing of the script file for Example 1:

```
ORTHO
ON
GRID
2.0
SNAP
0.5
LIMITS
0,0
48.0,36.0
ZOOM
ALL
TEXTSIZE
0.125
LTSCALE
4.0
DIMSCALE 4.0
```

(Blank line for Return.)

Note that the commands and the prompt entries in this file are in the same sequence as mentioned earlier. You can also combine several statements in one line, as shown in the following list:

```
;This is my first script file, SCRIPT1.SCR
ORTHO ON
GRID 2.0
SNAP 0.5
LIMITS 0,0 48.0,36.0
ZOOM
ALL
TEXTSIZE 0.125
LTSCALE 4.0
DIMSCALE 4.0
```

(Blank line for Return.)

Save the script file as *SCRIPT1.scr* and exit the text editor. Remember that if you do not save the file in the *.scr* format, it will not work as a script file. Notice the space between the commands and the prompt entries. For example, between the **ORTHO** command and the **ON** command, there is a space. Similarly, there is a space between **GRID** and **2.0**.

Note

1. In the script file, a space is used to terminate a command or a prompt entry. Therefore, spaces are very important in these files. Make sure there are no extra spaces, unless they are required.

*2. After you change the limits, it is a good practice to use the **ZOOM** tool with the **All** option to increase the drawing display area.*

3. Keyboard shortcuts are not allowed in the script files. Therefore, make sure not to use them in the script files.

Tip

AutoCAD ignores and does not process any lines that begin with a semicolon (;). This allows you to put comments in the related file or line.

RUNNING SCRIPT FILES

The **Run Script** tool allows you to run a script file while you are in the drawing editor. Choose the **Run Script** tool from the **Applications** panel of the **Manage** tab; the **Select Script File** dialog box will be invoked, refer to Figure 10-1. You can enter the name of the script file or you can accept the default file name. The default script file name is the same as the drawing name. If you want to enter a new file name, type the name of the script file without the file extension (**.SCR**). (The file extension is assumed and need not be included with the file name.)

Step 3: Running the script file

To run the script file of Example 1, invoke the **Run Script** tool, select the file **SCRIPT1**, and then choose the **Open** button in the **Select Script File** dialog box, refer to Figure 10-1. You will notice the changes taking place on the screen as the script file commands are executed.

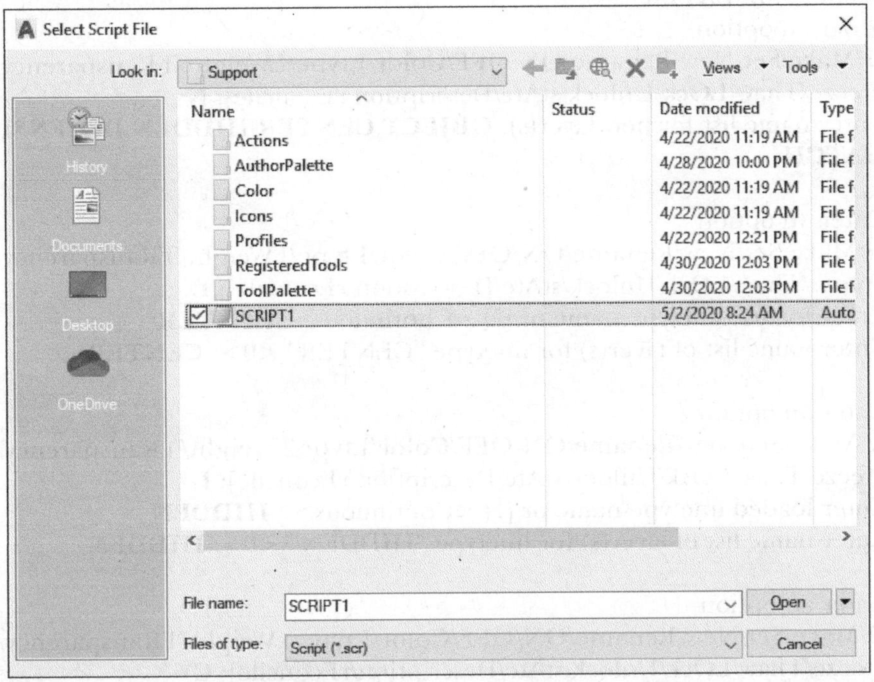

***Figure 10-1** The **Select Script File** dialog box*

You can also enter the name of the script file at the Command prompt by setting **FILEDIA**=0. The sequence for invoking the script using the Command line is given next.

Command: **FILEDIA**
Enter new value for FILEDIA <1>: **0**
Command: **SCRIPT**
Enter script file name <current>: *Specify the script file name.*

Example 2 — *Layers*

Write a script file that will set up the following layers with given colors and linetypes (file name *script2.scr*).

Layer Names	Color	Linetype	Line Weight
OBJECT	Red	Continuous	default
CENTER	Yellow	Center	default
HIDDEN	Blue	Hidden	default
DIMENSION	Green	Continuous	default
BORDER	Magenta	Continuous	default
HATCH	Cyan	Continuous	0.05

Step 1: Understanding commands and prompt entries

You need to know the AutoCAD commands and the required prompt entries before writing a script file. You need the following commands to create the layers with the given colors and linetypes.

Command: **-LAYER**
Enter an option
[?/Make/Set/New/Rename/ON/OFF/Color/Ltype/LWeight/TRansparency/MATerial/Plot/Freeze/Thaw/LOck/Unlock/stAte/Description/rEconcile]: **N**
Enter name list for new layer(s): **OBJECT,CENTER,HIDDEN,DIMENSION, BORDER, HATCH**

Enter an option
[?/Make/Set/New/Rename/ON/OFF/Color/Ltype/LWeight/TRansparency/MATerial/Plot/Freeze/Thaw/LOck/Unlock/stAte/Description/rEconcile]: **L**
Enter loaded linetype name or [?] <Continuous>: **CENTER**
Enter name list of layer(s) for linetype "CENTER" <0>: **CENTER**

Enter an option
[?/Make/Set/New/Rename/ON/OFF/Color/Ltype/LWeight/TRansparency/MATerial/Plot/Freeze/Thaw/LOck/Unlock/stAte/Description/rEconcile]: **L**
Enter loaded linetype name or [?] <Continuous>: **HIDDEN**
Enter name list of layer(s) for linetype "HIDDEN" <0>: **HIDDEN**

Enter an option
[?/Make/Set/New/Rename/ON/OFF/Color/Ltype/LWeight/TRansparency/MATerial/Plot/Freeze/Thaw/LOck/Unlock/stAte/Description/rEconcile]: **C**
New color [Truecolor/COlorbook]: **RED**
Enter name list of layer(s) for color 1 (red) <0>: **OBJECT**
Enter an option
[?/Make/Set/New/Rename/ON/OFF/Color/Ltype/LWeight/TRansparency/MATerial/Plot/Freeze/Thaw/LOck/Unlock/stAte/Description/rEconcile]: **C**
New color [Truecolor/COlorbook]: **YELLOW**
Enter name list of layer(s) for color 2 (yellow) <0>: **CENTER**

Enter an option
[?/Make/Set/New/Rename/ON/OFF/Color/Ltype/LWeight/TRansparency/MATerial/Plot/Freeze/Thaw/LOck/Unlock/stAte/Description/rEconcile]: **C**
New color [Truecolor/COlorbook]: **BLUE**
Enter name list of layer(s) for color 5 (blue)<0>: **HIDDEN**

Enter an option
[?/Make/Set/New/Rename/ON/OFF/Color/Ltype/LWeight/TRansparency/MATerial/Plot/Freeze/Thaw/LOck/Unlock/stAte/Description/rEconcile]: **C**
New color [Truecolor/COlorbook]: **GREEN**
Enter name list of layer(s) for color 3 (green)<0>: **DIMENSION**

Enter an option
[?/Make/Set/New/Rename/ON/OFF/Color/Ltype/LWeight/TRansparency/MATerial/Plot/Freeze/Thaw/LOck/Unlock/stAte/Description/rEconcile]: **C**
New color [Truecolor/COlorbook]: **MAGENTA**
Enter name list of layer(s) for color 6 (magenta)<0>: **BORDER**

Enter an option
[?/Make/Set/New/Rename/ON/OFF/Color/Ltype/LWeight/TRansparency/MATerial/Plot/
Freeze/Thaw/LOck/Unlock/stAte/Description/rEconcile]: **C**
New color [Truecolor/COlorbook]: **CYAN**
Enter name list of layer(s) for color 4 (cyan)<0>: **HATCH**

Enter an option
[?/Make/Set/New/Rename/ON/OFF/Color/Ltype/LWeight/TRansparency/MATerial/Plot/
Freeze/Thaw/LOck/Unlock/stAte/Description/rEconcile]: **LW**
Enter lineweight (0.0mm - 2.11mm): **0.05**
Enter name list of layers(s) for lineweight 0.05mm <0>: **HATCH**
[?/Make/Set/New/Rename/ON/OFF/Color/Ltype/LWeight/TRansparency/MATerial/Plot/
Freeze/Thaw/LOck/Unlock/stAte/Description/rEconcile]: Enter

Step 2: Writing the script file

The following file is a listing of the script file that creates different layers and assigns the given colors and linetypes to them:

```
;This script file will create new layers and
;assign different colors and linetypes to layers
LAYER
NEW
OBJECT,CENTER,HIDDEN,DIMENSION,BORDER,HATCH
L
CENTER
CENTER
L
HIDDEN
HIDDEN
C
RED
OBJECT
C
YELLOW
CENTER
C
BLUE
HIDDEN
C
GREEN
DIMENSION
C
MAGENTA
BORDER
C
CYAN
HATCH
                    (This is a blank line to terminate the LAYER command. End of script file.)
```

Save the script file as *script2.scr*.

Step 3: Running the script file

To run the script file of Example 2, choose the **Run Script** tool from the **Applications** panel of the **Manage** tab or enter **SCRIPT** at the Command prompt to invoke the **Select Script File** dialog box. Select **script2.scr** and then choose **Open**. You can also enter the **SCRIPT** command and the name of the script file at the Command prompt by setting **FILEDIA**=0.

Example 3 — *Rotating the Objects*

Write a script file that will rotate the line and the circle, as shown in Figure 10-2, around the lower endpoint of the line through 45 degree increments. The script file should be able to produce a continuous rotation of the given objects with a delay of two seconds after every 45 degree rotation (file name *script3.scr*). It is assumed that the line and circle are already drawn on the screen.

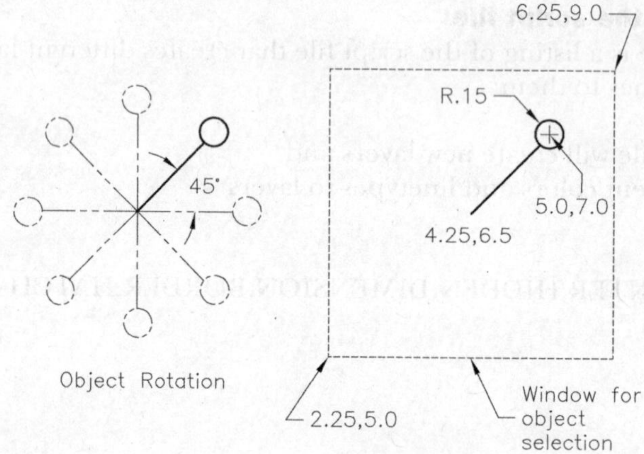

***Figure 10-2** Line and circle rotated through 45 degree increments*

Step 1: Understanding commands and prompt entries

Before writing the script file, enter the required commands and prompt entries. Write down the exact sequence of the entries in which they have been entered to perform the given operations. The following is the list of the AutoCAD command sequences needed to rotate the circle and the line around the lower endpoint of the line:

Command: **ROTATE**
Current positive angle in UCS: ANGDIR=counterclockwise ANGBASE=0
Select objects: **W** *(Window option to select object)*
Specify first corner: **2.25, 5.0**
Specify opposite corner: **6.25, 9.0**
Select objects: Enter
Specify base point: **4.25,6.5**
Specify rotation angle or [Reference]: **45**

Step 2: Writing the script file

Once the AutoCAD commands, command options, and their sequences are known, you can write a script file. You can use any text editor to write a script file. The following is a listing of the script file that will create the required rotation of the circle and line of Example 3. The line numbers on the right and the text written as '(Blank line for Return)' are not a part of the file; they are shown here for reference only.

```
1 ROTATE
2 W
3 2.25,5.0
4 6.25,9.0
5           (Blank line for Return.)
6 4.25,6.5
7 45
```

Line 1
ROTATE
In this line, **ROTATE** is an AutoCAD command that rotates the objects.

Line 2
W
In this line, **W** is the **Window** option for selecting the objects that need to be edited.

Line 3
2.25,5.0
In this line, 2.25 defines the *X* coordinate and 5.0 defines the *Y* coordinate of the lower left corner of the object selection window.

Line 4
6.25,9.0
In this line, 6.25 defines the *X* coordinate and 9.0 defines the *Y* coordinate of the upper right corner of the object selection window.

Line 5
Line 5 is a blank line that terminates the object selection process.

Line 6
4.25,6.5
In this line, 4.25 defines the *X* coordinate and 6.5 defines the *Y* coordinate of the base point for rotation.

Line 7
45
In this line, 45 is the incremental angle of rotation.

Note

One of the limitations of the script file is that all the information has to be contained within the same file. Such files do not let you enter any other information. For instance, in Example 3, if you want to use the ***Window*** *option to select the objects, the* ***Window*** *option (W) and the two points that define this window must be contained within the script file. The same is true for the base point and all other information that is entered in a script file. There is no way that a script file can prompt you to enter a particular piece of information and then resume the script file, unless you embed AutoLISP commands to prompt for user input.*

Step 3: Saving the script file

Save the script file with the name *script3.scr*.

Step 4: Running the script file

Choose **Tools > Run Script** from the menu bar, or choose the **Run Script** tool from the **Applications** panel of the **Manage** tab, or enter **SCRIPT** at the Command prompt to invoke the **Select Script File** dialog box. Select **script3.scr** and then choose **Open**. You will notice that the line and circle that were drawn on the screen are rotated once through an angle of 45 degrees. However, there will be no continuous rotation of the sketched entities. The next section (Repeating Script Files) explains how to continue the steps mentioned in the script file. You will also learn how to add a time delay between the continuous cycles in later sections of this chapter.

REPEATING SCRIPT FILES

The **RSCRIPT** command allows the user to execute the script file indefinitely until canceled. It is a very desirable feature when the user wants to run the same file continuously. For example, in the case of a slide show for a product demonstration, the **RSCRIPT** command can be used to run the script file repeatedly until it is terminated by pressing the ESC key. Similarly, in Example 3, the rotation command needs to be repeated indefinitely to create a continuous rotation of the objects. This can be accomplished by adding **RSCRIPT** at the end of the file, as shown in the following listing of the script file:

```
ROTATE
    W
    2.25,5.0
    6.25,9.0
                    (Blank line for Return.)
    4.25,6.5
    45
    RSCRIPT
```

The **RSCRIPT** command in line 8 will repeat the commands from line 1 to line 7, and thus set the script file in an indefinite loop. If you run the *script3.scr* file now, you will notice that there is a continuous rotation of the line and circle around the specified base point. However, the speed at which the entities rotate makes it difficult to view the objects. As a result, you need to add time delay between every repetition. The script file can be stopped by pressing the ESC or the BACKSPACE key.

Note

You cannot provide conditional statements in a script file to terminate the file when a particular condition is satisfied unless you use the AutoLISP functions in the script file.

INTRODUCING TIME DELAY IN SCRIPT FILES

As mentioned earlier, some of the operations in the script files are performed very quickly thereby making it difficult to observe them on the screen. It might be necessary to intentionally introduce a pause between certain operations in a script file. For example, in a slide show for a product demonstration, there must be a time delay between different slides so that the audience have enough time to see each slide. This is accomplished by using the **DELAY** command, which introduces a delay before the next command is executed. The general format of the **DELAY** command is given next.

Command: **DELAY Time**
Where **Command** -----AutoCAD Command prompt
DELAY ---------**DELAY** command
Time ------------Time in milliseconds

The **DELAY** command is to be followed by the delay time in milliseconds. For example, a delay of 500 milliseconds means that AutoCAD will pause for approximately half a second before executing the next command. It is approximately half a second because computer processing speeds vary. The maximum time delay you can enter is 32,767 milliseconds (about 33 seconds). In Example 3, half a second delay can be introduced by inserting a **DELAY** command line between line 7 and line 8, as in the following file listing:

ROTATE
W
2.25,5.0
6.25,9.0
(Blank line for Return.)
4.25,6.5
45
DELAY 500
RSCRIPT

The first seven lines of this file rotate the objects through a 45 degree angle. Before the **RSCRIPT** command on line 8 is executed, there is a delay of 500 milliseconds (about half a second). The **RSCRIPT** command will repeat the script file that rotates the objects through another 45 degree angle. Thus, a slide show is created with a time delay of half a second after every 45 degree increment.

RESUMING SCRIPT FILES

If you cancel a script file and then want to resume it, you can use the **RESUME** command.
Command: **RESUME**

The **RESUME** command can also be used if the script file has encountered an error that suspends its function. The **RESUME** command will skip the command that caused the error and continue with the rest of the script file. If the error occurs when the command is in progress, use a leading apostrophe with the **RESUME** command (**'RESUME**) to invoke the **RESUME** command in the transparent mode.

Command: **'RESUME**

COMMAND LINE SWITCHES

The command line switches can be used as arguments to the *acad.exe* file that launches AutoCAD. You can also use the **Options** dialog box to set the environment or by adding a set of environment variables in the *autoexec.bat* file. The command line switches and environment variables override the values set in the **Options** dialog box for the current session only. These switches do not alter the system registry. The following is the list of the command line switches:

Switch	Function
/c	Controls where AutoCAD stores and searches for the hardware configuration file. The default file is *acad 2021.cfg*
/s	Specifies which directories to search for support files if they are not in the current directory
/b	Designates a script to run after AutoCAD starts
/t	Specifies a template to use while creating a new drawing
/nologo	Starts AutoCAD without first displaying the logo screen
/v	Designates a particular view of the drawing to be displayed on start-up of AutoCAD
/r	Reconfigures AutoCAD with the default device configuration settings
/p	Specifies the profile to use on start-up

RUNNING A SCRIPT FILE WHILE LOADING AutoCAD

The script files can also be run while loading AutoCAD, before it is actually started. The following is the format of the command for running a script file while loading AutoCAD.

"Drive\Program Files\Autodesk\AutoCAD 2021\acad.exe" [existing-drawing] [/t template] [/v view] /b Script-file

In the following example, AutoCAD will open the existing drawing (MYdwg1) and then run the script file (Setup) through the **Run** dialog box, as shown in Figure 10-3.

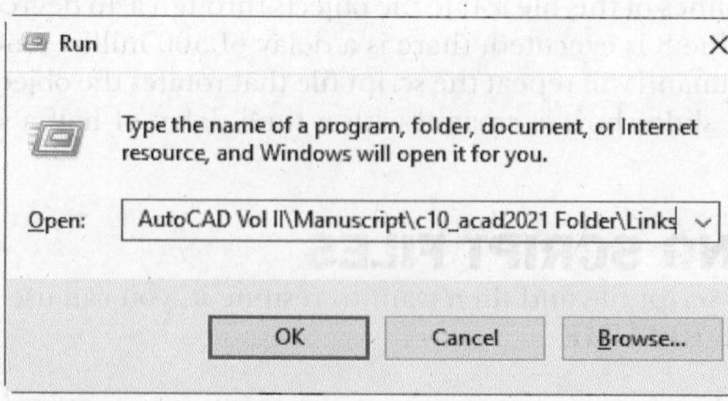

***Figure 10-3** Invoking the script file while loading AutoCAD using the **Run** dialog box*

Example:
"C:\Program Files\Autodesk\AutoCAD 2021\acad.exe" MYdwg1 /b Setup
Where, **AutoCAD** 2021 -------------AutoCAD 2021 subdirectory containing
---------------------AutoCAD system files
acad.exe --------ACAD command to start AutoCAD
MYDwg1 -------Existing drawing file name
Setup -----------Name of the script file

Note
Make sure that the drawing file that you want to open is saved in the C drive of your system. Also, you must have administrative privileges to save and open the drawing files from the C drive.

In the following example, AutoCAD will start a new drawing with the default name (Drawing), using the template file temp1, and then run the script file (Setup).

Example:
"C:\Program Files\Autodesk\AutoCAD 2021\acad.exe" /t temp1 /b Setup
Where **temp1** -----------Existing template file name
Setup -----------Name of the script file

or

"C:\ProgramFiles\Autodesk\AutoCAD 2021\acad.exe"/t temp1 "C:\MyFolder"/b Setup
Where **C:\Program Files\AutoCAD 2021\acad.exe** Path name for acad.exe
C:\MyFolder ---Path name for the Setup script file

In the following example, AutoCAD will start a new drawing with the default name (Drawing), and then run the script file (Setup).

Example:
"C:\Program Files\Autodesk\AutoCAD 2021\acad.exe" /b Setup
Where **Setup** ------------Name of the script file
Here, it is assumed that the AutoCAD system files are loaded in the AutoCAD 2021 directory.

Note
To invoke a script file while loading AutoCAD, the drawing file or the template file specified in the command must exist in the search path. You cannot start a new drawing with a given name. You can also use any template drawing file that is found in the template directory to run a script file through the ***Run*** *dialog box.*

Tip
You should avoid abbreviations to prevent any confusion. For example, C can be used as a close option when you are drawing lines. It can also be used as a command alias for drawing a circle. If you use both of them in a script file, it might be confusing.

Example 4 *Running a Script File while Loading AutoCAD*

Write a script file that can be invoked while loading AutoCAD and create a drawing with the following setup (filename *script4.scr*).

Grid	3.0
Snap	0.5
Limits	0,0
	36.0,24.0
Zoom	All
Text height	0.25
LTSCALE	3.0
DIMSCALE	3.0

Layers

Name	Color	Linetype
OBJ	Red	Continuous
CEN	Yellow	Center
HID	Blue	Hidden
DIM	Green	Continuous

Step 1: Writing the script file

Write a script file and save the file under the name *script4.scr*. The following is the listing of the script file that performs the initial setup for a drawing:

```
GRID 3.0
SNAP 0.5
LIMITS 0,0 36.0,24.0 ZOOM ALL
TEXTSIZE 0.25
LTSCALE 3
DIMSCALE 3.0
LAYER NEW
OBJ,CEN,HID,DIM
L CENTER CEN
L HIDDEN HID
C RED OBJ
C YELLOW CEN
C BLUE HID
C GREEN DIM
```

(Blank line for ENTER.)

Step 2: Loading the script file through the Run dialog box

After you have written and saved the file, quit the text editor. To run the script file, *script4*, select **Start > Run** and then enter the following command line.

"C:\Program Files\Autodesk\AutoCAD 2021\acad.exe" /t EX4 /b script4

Where **acad.exe** --------ACAD to load AutoCAD
EX4 -------------Template file name
SCRIPT4 ------Name of the script file

Here, it is assumed that the template file (EX4) and the script file (script4) is on C drive. When you enter this line, AutoCAD is loaded and the file *ex4.dwt* is opened. The script file, script4, is then automatically loaded and the commands defined in the file are executed.

In the following example, AutoCAD will start a new drawing with the default name (Drawing), and then run the script file (script4), refer to Figure 10-4.

Example:
"C:\Program Files\Autodesk\AutoCAD 2021\acad.exe" /b script4
Where **script4** ----------Name of the script file

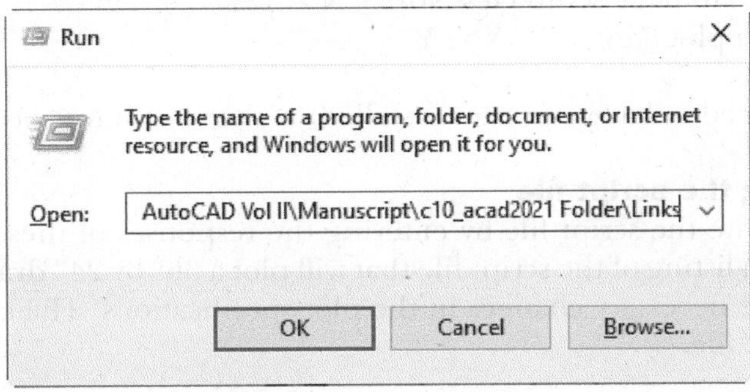

***Figure 10-4** Invoking the script file while loading AutoCAD using the **Run** dialog box*

Here, it is assumed that the AutoCAD system files are loaded in the AutoCAD 2021 directory.

Example 5 — *Plotting a Drawing*

Write a script file that will plot a 36" by 24" drawing to the maximum plot size on a 8.5" by 11" paper, using your system printer/plotter. Use the **Window** option to select the drawing to be plotted.

Step 1: Understanding commands and prompt entries

Before writing a script file to plot a drawing, find out the plotter specifications that must be entered in the script file to obtain the desired output. To determine the prompt entries and their sequence to set up the plotter specifications, enter the **-PLOT** command. Note the entries you make and their sequence (the entries for your printer or plotter will probably be different). The following is a listing of the plotter specifications with the new entries:

Command: **-PLOT**
Detailed plot configuration? [Yes/No] <No>: **Y**
Enter a layout name or [?] <Model>: Enter
Enter an output device name or [?] <Default Printer name>: *Name of printer or plotter* Enter
Enter paper size or [?] <Letter>: Enter

Enter paper units [Inches/Millimeters] <Inches>: **I**
Enter drawing orientation [Portrait/Landscape] <Landscape>: **P**
Plot upside down? [Yes/No] <No>: **N**
Enter plot area [Display/Extents/Limits/View/Window] <Display>: **W**
Enter lower left corner of window <0.000000,0.000000>: **0,0**
Enter upper right corner of window <0.000000,0.000000>: **36,24**
Enter plot scale (Plotted Inches=Drawing Units) or [Fit] <Fit>: **F**
Enter plot offset (x,y) or [Center] <0.00,0.00>: **0,0**
Plot with plot styles? [Yes/No] <Yes>: **Yes**
Enter plot style table name or [?] (enter . for none) <>: **.**
Plot with lineweights? [Yes/No] <Yes>: **Y**
Enter shade plot setting [As displayed/Wireframe/Hidden/Visual styles/Rendered] <As displayed>: Enter
Write the plot to a file [Yes/No] <N>: **N**
Save changes to page setup [Yes/No]? <N>: Enter
Proceed with plot [Yes/No] <Y>: **Y**

Note that you need to have a printer installed on the system for successful execution of script.

Step 2: Writing the script file

Now you can write the script file by entering the responses of these prompts in the file. The following file is a listing of the script file that will plot a 36" by 24" drawing on 8.5" by 11" paper after making the necessary changes in the plot specifications. The comments on the right are not a part of the file.

PLOT
Y
 (Blank line for ENTER, selects default layout.)
DWG TO PDF.pc3
 (Blank line for ENTER, selects the default paper size.)
I
P
N
w
0,0
36,24
F
0,0
Y
. *(Enter . for none)*
Y
A
N
N
Y

The method of saving and running the script file for this example is the same as that described in the previous examples. You can use a blank line to accept the default value for a prompt. A blank line in the script file will cause a Return. However, you must not accept the default plot specifications because the file may have been altered by another user or by another script file. Therefore, always enter the actual values in the file so that when you run a script file, it does not take the default values.

Example 6 — Animating a Clock

Write a script file to animate a clock with continuous rotation of the second hand (longer needle) through 5 degrees and the minutes hand (shorter needle) through 2 degrees clockwise around the center of the clock, refer to Figure 10-5.

***Figure 10-5** Drawing for Example 6*

The specifications are given next.

Specifications for the rim made of donut.

Color of Donut	Blue
Inner diameter of Donut	8.0
Outer diameter of Donut	8.4
Center point of Donut	5,5

Specifications for the digit mark made of polyline.

Color of the digit mark	Green
Start point of Pline	5,8.5
Initial width of Pline	0.25
Final width of Pline	0.25
Height of Pline	0.25

Specifications for second hand (long needle) made of polyline.

Color of the second hand	Red
Start point of Pline	5,5
Initial width of Pline	0.5
Final width of Pline	0.0
Length of Pline	3.5
Rotation of the second hand	5 degree clockwise

Specifications for minute hand (shorter needle) made of polyline.

Color of the minute hand	Cyan
Start point of Pline	5,5

Initial width of Pline	0.35
Final width of Pline	0.0
Length of Pline	3.0
Rotation of the minute hand	2 degree clockwise

Step 1: Understanding the commands and prompt entries for creation of the clock

For this example, you can create two script files and then link them. The first script file will demonstrate the creation of the clock on the screen. The next script file will demonstrate the rotation of the needles of the clock.

First write a script file to create the clock as follows and save the file under the name *clock.scr*. The following is the listing of this file:

Command: **-COLOR**
Enter default object color [Truecolor/COlorbook] <BYLAYER>: **Blue**
Command: **DONUT**
Specify inside diameter of donut<0.5>: **8.0**
Specify outside diameter of donut<0.5>: **8.4**
Specify center of donut or <exit>: **5,5**
Specify center of donut or <exit>: Enter
Command: **-COLOR**
Enter default object color [Truecolor/COlorbook] <BYLAYER>: **Green**
Command: **PLINE**
Specify start point: **5,8.5**
Specify next point or [Arc/Halfwidth/Length/Undo/Width]: **Width**
Specify starting width<0.00>: **0.25**
Specify ending width<0.25>: **0.25**
Specify next point or [Arc/Halfwidth/Length/Undo/Width]: **@0.25<270**
Specify next point or [Arc/Halfwidth/Length/Undo/Width]: Enter
Command: **-ARRAY**
Select objects: **Last**
Select objects: Enter
Enter the type of array[Rectangular/PAth/Polar]<R>: **Polar**
Specify center point of array or [Base]: **5,5**
Enter the number of items in the array: **12**
Specify the angle to fill(+= ccw, -=cw)<360>: **360**
Rotate arrayed objects ? [Yes/No]<Y>: **Y**
Command: **-COLOR**
Enter default object color [Truecolor/COlorbook] <BYLAYER>: **RED**
Command: **PLINE**
Specify start point: **5,5**
Specify next point or [Arc/Close/Halfwidth/Length/Undo/Width]: **Width**
Specify starting width<.25>: **0.5**
Specify ending width<0.5>: **0**
Specify next point or [Arc/Halfwidth/Length/Undo/Width]: **@3.5<0**
Specify next point or [Arc/Close/Halfwidth/Length/Undo/Width]: Enter
Command: **-COLOR**
Enter default object color [Truecolor/COlorbook] <BYLAYER>: **Cyan**

Command: **PLINE**
Specify start point: **5,5**
Specify next point or [Arc/Halfwidth/Length/Undo/Width]: **Width**
Specify starting width<0.0000>: **0.35**
Specify ending width<0.35>: **0**
Specify next point or [Arc/Halfwidth/Length/Undo/Width]: **@3<90**
Specify next point or [Arc/Close/Halfwidth/Length/Undo/Width]: Enter
Command: **SCRIPT**
ROTATE.SCR

Now you will write the script file by entering the responses to these prompts in the file *clock.scr*.

Next, you will write the script to rotate the clock hands and save the file with the name *ROTATE.scr*. Remember that while entering the commands in the script files, you do not need to add a hyphen (-) as a prefix to the command name to execute them from the command line. When a command is entered using the script file, the dialog box is not displayed and it is executed using the command line. For example, in this script file, the **COLOR** and **ARRAY** commands will be executed using the command line. Listing of the script file is given next.

```
Color
Blue
Donut
8.0
8.4
5,5
                    (Blank line for ENTER.)
Color
Green
Pline
5,8.5
W
0.25
0.25
@0.25<270
                    (Blank line for ENTER.)
Array
L
                    (Blank line for ENTER.)
P
5,5
12
360
Y
Color
Red
Pline
5,5
W
```

```
0.5
0
@3.5<0
                    (Blank line for ENTER.)
Color
Cyan
Pline
5,5
w
0.35
0
@3<90
                    (Blank line for ENTER.)
Script
ROTATE.scr          (Name of the script file that will cause rotation)
                    (Blank line for ENTER.)
```

Save this file as *clock.scr* in a directory that is specified in the AutoCAD support file search path. It is recommended that the *ROTATE.scr* file should also be saved in the same directory. Remember that if the files are not saved in the directory that is specified in the AutoCAD support file search path using the **Options** dialog box, the linked script file (*ROTATE.scr*) may not run.

Step 2: Understanding the commands and sequences for rotation of the needles

The last line in the above script file is *ROTATE.scr*. This is the name of the script file that will rotate the clock hands. Before writing the script file, enter the **ROTATE** command and respond to the command prompts that will cause the desired rotation. The following is the listing of the AutoCAD command sequences needed to rotate the objects:

Command: **ROTATE**
Select objects: **L**
Select objects: Enter
Specify base point: 5,5
Specify rotation angle or [Copy/Reference] <0>: -2
Command: **ROTATE**
Select objects: **C**
Specify first corner: 3,3
Specify other corner: 7,7
Select objects: **Remove**
Remove objects: **L**
Remove objects: Enter
Specify base point: 5,5
Specify rotation angle or [Copy/Reference]: -5

Now you can write the script file by entering the responses to these prompts in the file *ROTATE.scr*. The following is the listing of the script file that will rotate the clock hands:

```
Rotate
L
                    (Blank line for ENTER.)
5,5
-2
Rotate
c
3,3
7,7
R
L
                    (Blank line for ENTER.)
5,5
-5
Rscript
                    (Blank line for ENTER.)
```

Save the above script file as *ROTATE.scr*. Now, run the script file *clock.scr*. Since this file is linked with *ROTATE.scr*, it will automatically run *ROTATE.scr* after running *clock.scr*. Note that if the linked file is not saved in a directory specified in the AutoCAD support file search path, the last line of the *clock.scr* must include a fully-resolved path to *ROTATE.scr*, or AutoCAD would not be able to locate the file.

Exercise 1 ***Plotting a Drawing***

Write a script file that will plot a 288' by 192' drawing on a 36" x 24" sheet of paper. The drawing scale is 1/8" = 1'. (The filename is *script9.scr*. In this exercise, assume that AutoCAD is configured for the HPGL plotter and the plotter description is HPGL-Plotter.)

WHAT IS A SLIDE SHOW?

AutoCAD provides a facility of using script files to combine the slides in a text file and display them in a predetermined sequence. In this way, you can generate a slide show for a slide presentation. You can also introduce a time delay in the display so that the viewer has enough time to view each slide.

A drawing or parts of a drawing can also be displayed using the AutoCAD display commands. For example, you can use **ZOOM**, **PAN**, or other commands to display the details you want to show. If the drawing is very complicated, it takes time to display the desired information and it may not be possible to get the desired views in the right sequence. However, with slide shows you can arrange the slides in any order and present them in a definite sequence. In addition to saving time, this also helps to minimize the distraction that might be caused by constantly changing the drawing display. Also, some drawings are confidential in nature and you may not want to display some portions or views of them. You can send a slide show to a client without losing control of the drawings and the information that is contained in them.

WHAT ARE SLIDES?

A slide is the snapshot of a screen display; it is like taking a picture of a display with a camera. The slides do not contain any vector information like AutoCAD drawings, this means that the entities do not have any information associated with them. For example, the slides do not retain any information about the layers, colors, linetypes, start point, or endpoint of a line or viewpoint. Therefore, slides cannot be edited like drawings. If you want to make any changes in the slide, you need to edit the drawing and then make a new slide from the edited drawing.

CREATING SLIDES

In AutoCAD, slides are created using the **MSLIDE** command. If **FILEDIA** is set to 1, the **MSLIDE** command displays the **Create Slide File** dialog box, refer to Figure 10-6 on the screen. You can enter the slide file name in this dialog box. If **FILEDIA** is set to 0, the command will prompt you to enter the slide file name.

Command: **MSLIDE**
Enter name of slide file to create <Default>: *Slide file name.*

Example:
Command: **MSLIDE**
Slide File: <Drawing1> **SLIDE1**
Where **Drawing1** ------Default slide file name
SLIDE1 --------Slide file name

In this example, AutoCAD will save the slide file as *slide1.sld*.

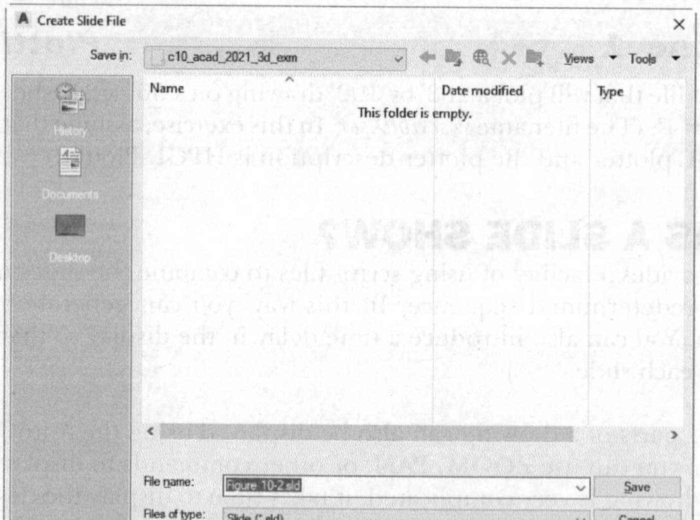

*Figure 10-6 The **Create Slide File** dialog box*

Note

*In model space, you can use the **MSLIDE** command to make a slide of the existing display in the current viewport. If you are in the paper space viewport, you can make a slide of the display in the paper space that includes all floating viewports created in it. When the viewports are not active, the **MSLIDE** command will make a slide of the current screen display.*

VIEWING SLIDES

To view a slide, enter the **VSLIDE** command at the Command prompt; the **Select Slide File** dialog box will be displayed, as shown in Figure 10-7. Choose the file that you want to view and then click **Open** button to exit the dialog box. The corresponding slide will be displayed on the screen. If **FILEDIA** is 0, the slide that you want to view can be directly entered at the Command prompt.

Command: **VSLIDE**
Enter name of slide file to view<Default>: *Name*.

Example:
Command: **VSLIDE**
Slide file <Drawing1>: SLIDE1
Where **Drawing1** ------Default slide file name
SLIDE1 --------Name of slide file

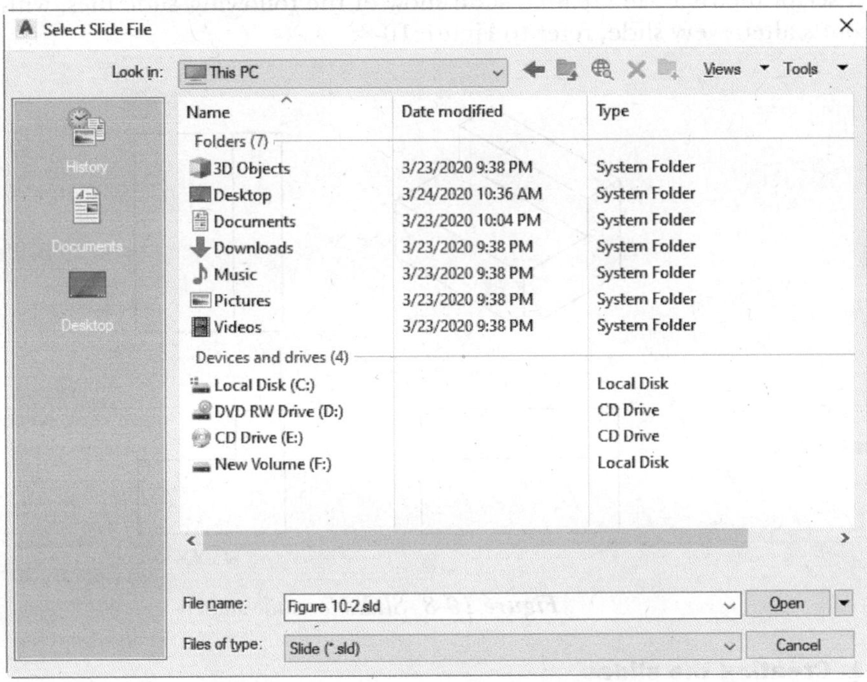

Figure 10-7 *The* ***Select Slide File*** *dialog box*

Note

1. After viewing a slide, you can use the ***REDRAW*** *command, roll the wheel, or pan with a mouse to remove the slide display and return to the existing drawing on the screen.*

2. Any command that is automatically followed by the ***REDRAW*** *command will also display the existing drawing. For example, AutoCAD* ***GRID, ZOOM ALL,*** *and* ***REGEN*** *commands will automatically return to the existing drawing on the screen.*

3. You can view the slides on a high-resolution or a low-resolution monitor. Depending on the resolution of the monitor, AutoCAD automatically adjusts the image. However, if you are using a high-resolution monitor, it is better to make the slides using the same monitor to take full advantage of that monitor.

Example 7 — *Slide Show*

Write a script file that will create a slide show of the following slide files, with a time delay of 15 seconds after every slide, refer to Figure 10-8.

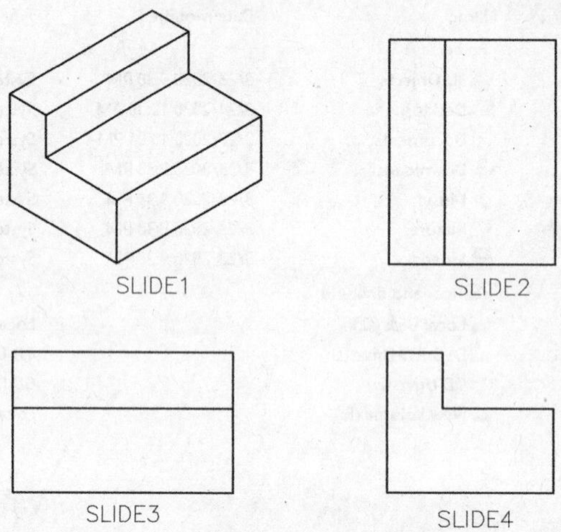

Figure 10-8 *Slides for slide show*

Step 1: Creating the slides

The first step in a slide show is to create the slides using the **MSLIDE** command. The **MSLIDE** command will invoke the **Create Slide File** dialog box. Enter the name of the slide as **SLIDE1** and choose the **Save** button to exit the dialog box. Similarly, other slides can be created and saved. Figure 10-8 shows the drawings that have been saved as slide files **SLIDE1**, **SLIDE2**, **SLIDE3**, and **SLIDE4**. The slides must be saved to a directory in AutoCAD's search path, otherwise, the script will not find the slides.

Step 2: Writing the script file

The second step is to find out the sequence, in which you want these slides to be displayed, with the necessary time delay, if any, between slides. Then you can use any text editor or the AutoCAD **EDIT** command (provided the *acad.pgp* file is present and **EDIT** is defined in the file) to write the script file with the extension *.scr*.

The following is the listing of the script file that will create a slide show of the slides in Figure 10-8. The name of the script file is **SLDSHOW1.scr**.

```
VSLIDE SLIDE1
DELAY 15000
VSLIDE SLIDE2
DELAY 15000
VSLIDE SLIDE3
DELAY 15000
VSLIDE SLIDE4
DELAY 15000
```

Step 3: Running the script file

To run this script file, choose the **Run Script** tool from **Manage > Applications** or enter **SCRIPT** at the Command prompt to invoke the **Select Script File** dialog box. Choose **SLDSHOW1** and then choose the **Open** button from the **Select Script File** dialog box. You can see the changes taking place on the screen.

PRELOADING SLIDES

In the script file of Example 7, VSLIDE SLIDE1 in line 1 loads the slide file, **SLIDE1**, and displays it on the screen. After a pause of 15,000 milliseconds, it starts loading the second slide file, **SLIDE2**. Depending on the computer and the disk access time, you will notice that it takes some time to load the second slide file. The same is true for the other slides. To avoid the delay in loading the slide files, AutoCAD has provided a facility to preload a slide while viewing the previous slide. This is accomplished by placing an asterisk (*) in front of the slide file name.

```
VSLIDE SLIDE1          (View slide, SLIDE1.)
VSLIDE *SLIDE2         (Preload slide, SLIDE2.)
DELAY 15000            (Delay of 15 seconds.)
VSLIDE                 (Display slide, SLIDE2.)
VSLIDE *SLIDE3         (Preload slide, SLIDE3.)
DELAY 15000            (Delay of 15 seconds.)
VSLIDE                 (Display slide, SLIDE3.)
VSLIDE *SLIDE4
DELAY 15000
VSLIDE
DELAY 15000
RSCRIPT                (Restart the script file.)
```

Example 8 *Preloading Slides*

Write a script file to generate a continuous slide show of the SLD1, SLD2, and SLD3 slide files, with a time delay of two seconds between slides.

The slide files are located in different subdirectories, as shown in Figure 10-9.

C:

Program Files

Autodesk

AutoCAD 2021

SUBDIR1(SLD1) SUBDIR2(SLD2) SUBDIR3(SLD3)

***Figure 10-9** Subdirectories of the C drive*

Where **C:** --------------------*Root directory.*
Program Files -------------*Root directory.*
Autodesk ------------------*Root directory.*
AutoCAD 2021---------- *Subdirectory where the AutoCAD files are loaded.*
SUBDIR1 ----------------- *Drawing subdirectory.*
SUBDIR2 ----------------- *Drawing subdirectory.*
SUBDIR3 ----------------- *Drawing subdirectory.*
SLD1 ---------------------*Slide file in SUBDIR1 subdirectory.*
SLD2 ---------------------*Slide file in SUBDIR2 subdirectory.*
SLD3 ---------------------*Slide file in SUBDIR3 subdirectory.*

The following is the listing of the script files that will generate a slide show for the slides in Example 8:

```
1 VSLIDE "C:/Program Files/Autodesk/AutoCAD 2021/SUBDIR1/SLD1.SLD"
2 DELAY  2000
3 VSLIDE "C:/Program Files/Autodesk/AutoCAD 2021/SUBDIR2/SLD2.SLD"
4 DELAY 2000
5 VSLIDE "C:/Program Files/Autodesk/AutoCAD 2021/SUBDIR3/SLD3.SLD"
6 DELAY 2000
7 RSCRIPT
```

Line 1
VSLIDE "C:/Program Files/Autodesk/AutoCAD 2021/SUBDIR1/SLD1.SLD"
In this line, the AutoCAD command **VSLIDE** loads the slide file **SLD1**. The path name is mentioned along with the command **VSLIDE**. If the path name directory contains spaces, then the path name must be enclosed in quotes.

Line 2
DELAY 2000

This line uses the AutoCAD **DELAY** command to create a pause of approximately two seconds before the next slide is loaded.

Line 3
VSLIDE "C:/Program Files/Autodesk/AutoCAD 2021/SUBDIR2/SLD2.SLD"
In this line, the AutoCAD command **VSLIDE** loads the slide file **SLD2**, located in the subdirectory **SUBDIR2**. If the slide file is located in a different subdirectory, you need to define the path with the slide file.

Line 5
VSLIDE "C:/Program Files/Autodesk/AutoCAD 2021/SUBDIR3/SLD3.SLD"
In this line, the **VSLIDE** command loads the slide file SLD3, located in the subdirectory **SUBDIR3**.

Line 7
RSCRIPT
In this line, the **RSCRIPT** command executes the script file again and displays the slides on the screen. This process continues indefinitely until the script file is canceled by pressing the ESC key or the BACKSPACE key.

SLIDE LIBRARIES

AutoCAD provides a utility, SLIDELIB, which constructs a library of the slide files. The format of the **SLIDELIB** utility command is as follows:

SLIDELIB (Library filename) <(Slide list filename)
Example:
SLIDELIB SLDLIB <SLDLIST
Where **SLIDELIB** -----AutoCAD's SLIDELIB utility
SLDLIB --------Slide library filename
SLDLIST ------List of slide filenames

The **SLIDELIB** utility is supplied with the AutoCAD software package. You can find this utility (SLIDELIB.EXE) in the *C:\Program Files\Autodesk\AutoCAD 2021* subdirectory. The slide file list is a list of the slide file names that you want in a slide show. It is a text file that can be written by using any text editor like Notepad.

C:

AutoCAD 2021

SUPPORT SLIDES

The slide file list can also be created by using the following command, if you have a DOS version 5.0 or above. You can use the make directory (md) or change directory (cd) commands in the DOS mode while making or changing directories.

C:\AutoCAD 2021\SLIDES>DIR *.SLD/B>SLDLIST

In this example, assume that the name of the slide file list is **SLDLIST** and all slide files are in the SLIDES subdirectory. To use this command to create a slide file list, all slide files must be in the same directory.

When you use the SLIDELIB utility, it reads the slide file names from the file that is specified in the slide list and the file is then written to the file specified by the library. In Example 9, the SLIDELIB utility reads the slide filenames from the file SLDLIST and writes them to the library file SLDSHOW1:

C:\AutoCAD 2021\SLIDES\ SLIDELIB SLDSHOW1 <SLDLIST

Note

1. You cannot edit a slide library file. If you want to change anything, you have to create a new list of the slide files and then use the SLIDELIB utility to create a new slide library.

*2. If you edit a slide while it is being displayed on the screen, the slide will not be edited. Instead, the current drawing that is behind the slide gets edited. Therefore, do not use any editing commands while you are viewing a slide. Use the **VSLIDE** and **DELAY** commands only while viewing a slide.*

3. The path name is not saved in the slide library. This is the reason if you have more than one slide with the same name, even though they are in different subdirectories, only one slide will be saved in the slide library.

Example 9 — *Slide Library*

Use AutoCAD's SLIDELIB utility to generate a continuous slide show of the following slide files with a time delay of 2.5 seconds between the slides. (The filenames are: SLDLIST for slide list file, SLDSHOW1 for slide library, SHOW1 for script file.)

front, top, rside, 3dview, isoview

The slide files are located in different subdirectories, as shown in Figure 10-10.

C

Dwg-Files

Proj-A	***Proj-B***	***Slide-Files***
front	*3dview*	*sldlist*
top	*isoview*	*slidelib.exe*
rside		

Figure 10-10 *Subdirectories to be created in C drive*

Where **C** ---------------- *(C drive.)*
Dwg-Files ---- *(Subdirectory where drawing files are located)*
Proj-A -------- *(Subdirectory where the slide files are located)*

Proj-B --------- *(Subdirectory where the slide files are located)*
Slide-Files --- *(Directory where Slidelib.exe and sldlist are copied)*

Step 1: Creating a list of the slide file names

The first step is to create a list of the slide file names with the drive and the directory information. Assume that you are in the **Slide-Files** subdirectory. You can use a text editor like Notepad to create a list of the slide files that you want to include in the slide show. After creating the list, save the text file and then remove its file extension. The following file is a listing of the file SLDLIST for Example 9:

```
c:\Dwg-Files\Proj-A\front
c:\Dwg-Files\Proj-A\top
c:\Dwg-Files\Proj-A\rside
c:\Dwg-Files\Proj-B\3dview
c:\Dwg-Files\Proj-B\isoview
```

Step 2: Copying the SLIDELIB utility

The **SLIDELIB** utility is supplied with the AutoCAD software package. You can find this utility (SLIDELIB.EXE) in the *C:\Program Files\Autodesk\AutoCAD 2021* subdirectory. Copy it to the **Slide-Files** folder.

Note
All related directories should be added in the AutoCAD's support files search path.

Step 3: Running the SLIDELIB utility

The third step is to use AutoCAD's SLIDELIB utility program to create the slide library. The name of the slide library is assumed to be **sldshow1** for this example. Before creating the slide library, copy the slide list file (SLDLIST) and the SLIDELIB utility from the support directory to the Slide-Files directory. This ensures that all the required files are in one directory. Enter the **SHELL** command at AutoCAD Command prompt and then press the ENTER key at the OS Command prompt. The **AutoCAD Shell Active** Command window will be displayed on the screen, refer to Figure 10-11. You can also use Windows DOS box instead of **AutoCAD Shell Active** Command window by choosing **All Programs > Accessories > Command Prompt**. Make sure that the drawing file is saved before using the **SHELL** command.

Command: **SHELL**
OS Command: Enter

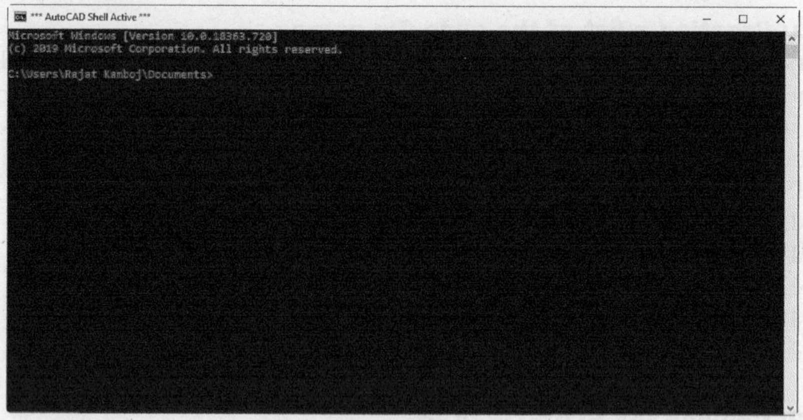

***Figure 10-11** The **AutoCAD Shell Active** Command window*

Now, enter the following command in the Command window to run the SLIDELIB utility and create the slide library. Here it is assumed that **Slide-Files** directory is the current directory. Use the **cd** command in the Command window to change the directory.

C:\Dwg-Files\Slide-Files>SLIDELIB sldshow1 <sldlist

Where **SLIDELIB** -----AutoCAD's SLIDELIB utility
sldshow1 -------Slide library
sldlist -----------Slide file list

Step 4: Writing the script file

Now, you can write a script file for the slide show that will use the slides in the slide library. The name of the script file for this example is assumed to be SHOW1.

```
VSLIDE C:\Dwg-Files\Slide-Files\sldshow1(front)
DELAY 2500
VSLIDE C:\Dwg-Files\Slide-Files\sldshow1(top)
DELAY 2500
VSLIDE C:\Dwg-Files\Slide-Files\sldshow1(rside)
DELAY 2500
VSLIDE C:\Dwg-Files\Slide-Files\sldshow1(3dview)
DELAY 2500
VSLIDE C:\Dwg-Files\Slide-Files\sldshow1(isoview)
DELAY 2500
RSCRIPT
```

Step 5: Running the script file

Invoke the **Select Script File** dialog box, as shown in Figure 10-12, by choosing the **Run Script** tool from **Manage > Applications**. You can also enter the **SCRIPT** command at the Command prompt after setting the system variable FILEDIA to 0.

Command: **SCRIPT**
Enter script file name<default>: **SHOW1**

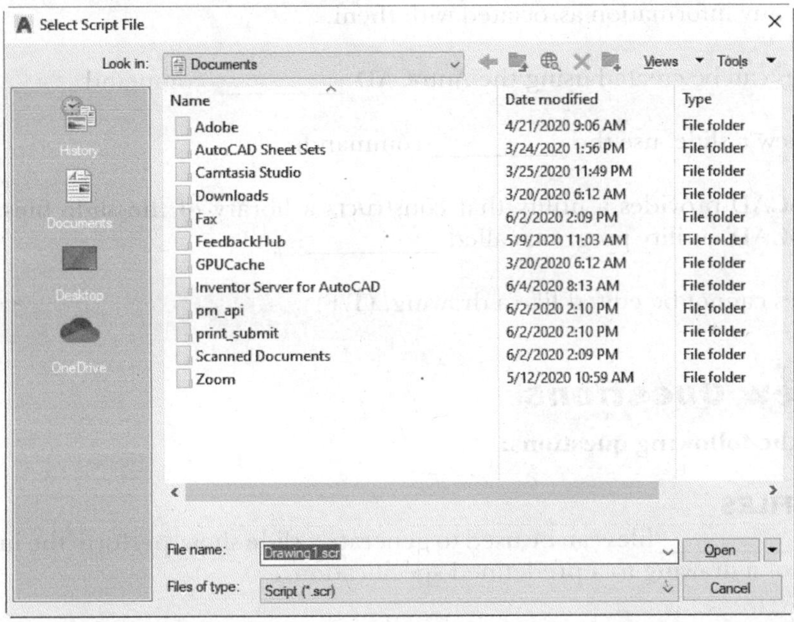

***Figure 10-12** Selecting the script file from the **Select Script File** dialog box*

Self-Evaluation Test

Answer the following questions and then compare them to those given at the end of this chapter:

SCRIPT FILES

1. In AutoCAD, you can use the __________ to combine different AutoCAD commands and execute them in a predetermined sequence.

2. Before writing a script file, you need to know the AutoCAD __________ and the __________ required in response to the command prompts.

3. In AutoCAD, the __________ command is used to run a script file.

4. In a script file, the __________ is used to terminate a command or a prompt entry.

5. The **DELAY** command is to be followed by __________ in milliseconds.

SLIDE SHOW

6. Slides do not contain any __________ information, which means that the entities do not have any information associated with them.

7. Slides can be created using the AutoCAD __________ command.

8. To view a slide, use the __________ command.

9. AutoCAD provides a utility that constructs a library of the slide files. This is done with AutoCAD's utility program called __________.

10. Slides cannot be edited like a drawing. (T/F)

Review Questions

Answer the following questions:

SCRIPT FILES

1. The __________ files can be used to generate a slide show, perform the initial drawing setup, or plot a drawing to a predefined specification.

2. In a script file, you can __________ several statements in one line.

3. When you run a script file, the default script file name is the same as the __________ name.

4. Type the name of the script file without the __________ file, when you run a script file.

5. One of the limitations of script files is that all the information has to be contained __________ the file.

6. The AutoCAD __________ command allows you to re-execute a script file indefinitely until the command is canceled.

7. You cannot provide a __________ statement in a script file to terminate the file when a particular condition is satisfied.

8. The AutoCAD __________ command schedules a delay before the next command is executed.

9. If the script file is canceled and you want to resume the script file, you need to use the __________ command.

SLIDE SHOW

10. A __________ can also be introduced in the script file so that the viewer has enough time to view a slide.

11. Slides are the __________ of a screen display.

12. In model space, you can use the __________ command to make a slide of the existing display in the current viewport.

13. If you want to make any changes in the slide, you need to __________ the drawing, then make a new slide from the edited drawing.

14. If the slide is in the slide library and you want to view it, the slide library name has to be __________ with the slide filename.

15. You cannot __________ a slide library file. If you want to change anything, you have to create a new list of the slide files and then use the __________ utility to create a new slide library.

16. If you are in paper space viewport, you can make a slide of the display in paper space that includes all floating viewports created in it. (T/F)

Exercise 2 — *Script Files*

Write a script file that will perform the following initial setup for a drawing.

Grid	2.0
Snap	0.5
Limits	0,0
	18.0,12.0
Zoom	All
Text height	0.25
LTSCALE	2.0

Overall dimension scale factor is 2
Aligned dimension text with the dimension line
Dimension text above the dimension line
Size of the center mark is 0.75

Exercise 3 — *Script Files*

Write a script file that will set up the following layers with the given colors and linetypes.

Layers

Name	Color	Linetype
Contour	Red	Continuous
SPipes	Yellow	Center
WPipes	Blue	Hidden
Power	Green	Continuous
Manholes	Magenta	Continuous
Trees	Cyan	Continuous

Exercise 4 — *Script Files*

Write a script file that will perform the following initial setup for a new drawing.

Limits	0,0 24,18
Grid	1.0
Snap	0.25
Ortho	On
Snap	On
Zoom	All
Pline width	0.02
PLine	0,0 24,0 24,18 0,18 0,0
Ltscale	1.5
Units	Decimal units Precision 0.00 Decimal degrees Precision 0 Base angle East (0.00) Angle measured counterclockwise

Layers

Name	Color	Linetype
Obj	Red	Continuous
Cen	Yellow	Center
Hid	Blue	Hidden
Dim	Green	Continuous

Exercise 5 — *Script Files*

Write a script file that will plot a given drawing according to the following specifications. (Use the plotter for which your system is configured and adjust the values accordingly.)

Plot, using the Window option
Window size (0,0 24,18)
Do not write the plot to file
Size in inch units
Plot origin (0.0,0.0)
Maximum plot size (8.5,11 or the smallest size available on your printer/plotter)
90° plot rotation
No removal of hidden lines
Plotting scale (Fit)

Exercise 6 — *Script Files*

Write a script file that will rotate a line continuously in 10 degrees increments around its midpoint, refer to Figure 10-13. The time delay between increments is one second.

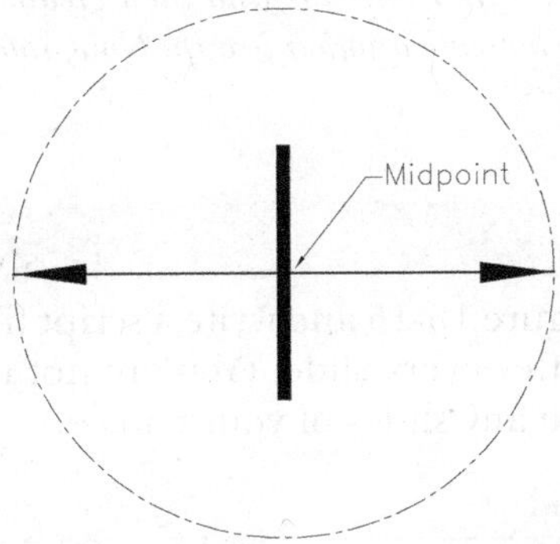

Figure 10-13 Drawing for Exercise 6

Exercise 7 — Script Files

Write a script file that will continuously rotate the arrangement shown in Figure 10-14 as per the following instructions:

One set of two circles and one line should rotate clockwise, while the other set of two circles and the other line should rotate counterclockwise. Assume the rotation to be 5 degrees around the intersection of the lines for both sets of arrangements.

Specifications are given below:

Start point of the horizontal line	2,4
End point of the horizontal line	8,4
Center point of circle at the start point of horizontal line	2,4
Diameter of the circle	1.0
Center point of circle at the end point of horizontal line	8,4
Diameter of circle	1.0
Start point of the vertical line	5,1
End point of the vertical line	5,7
Center point of circle at the start point of the vertical line	5,1
Diameter of the circle	1.0
Center point of circle at the end point of the vertical line	5,7
Diameter of the circle	1.0

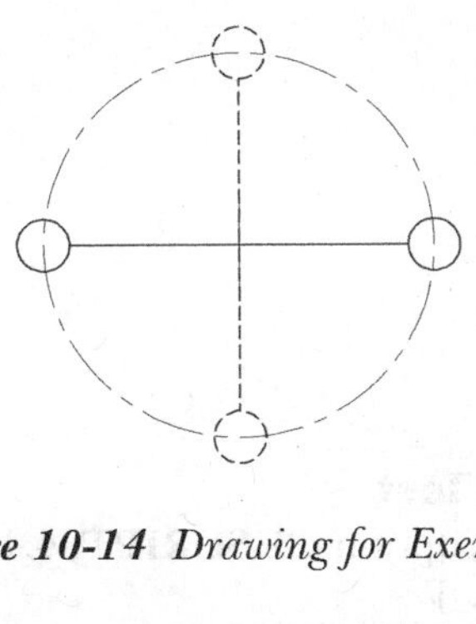

Figure 10-14 Drawing for Exercise 7

Hint: *Select one set of two circles and one line and then create one group. Similarly, select another set of two circles and one line and then create another group. Now, rotate one group clockwise and another group counterclockwise.*

Exercise 8 — *Slide Show*

Make the slides shown in Figure 10-15 and write a script file for a continuous slide show. Provide a time delay of 5 seconds after every slide. (You are not restricted to use only the slides shown in Figure 10-15; you can use any slides of your choice.)

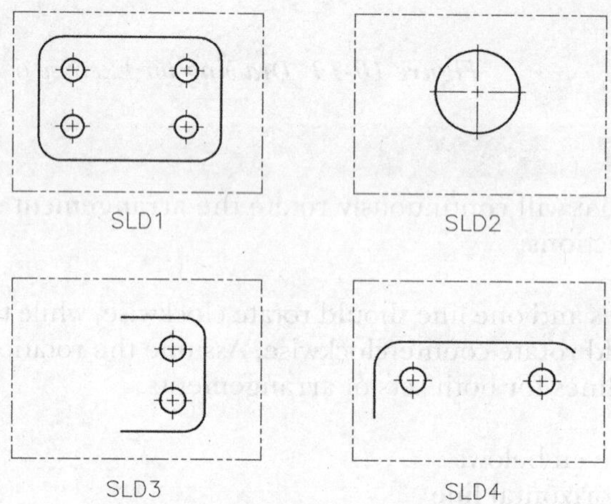

Figure 10-15 Slides for slide show

Exercise 9 — *Slide Library*

List the slides used in Exercise 8 in a file SLDLIST2 and create a slide library file SLDLIB2. Then write a script file SHOW2 using the slide library with a time delay of 5 seconds after every slide.

Answers to Self-Evaluation Test

1. SCRIPT files, **2.** Commands, options, **3. SCRIPT**, **4.** blank space, **5.** time, **6.** vector, **7. MSLIDE**, **8. VSLIDE**, **9. SLIDELIB**, **10.** T

Chapter 11

Creating Linetypes and Hatch Patterns

Learning Objectives

After completing this chapter, you will be able to:

- *Write linetype definitions*
- *Create different linetypes*
- *Create linetype files*
- *Determine LTSCALE for plotting the drawing to given specifications*
- *Define alternate linetypes and modify existing linetypes*
- *Create string and shape complex linetypes*
- *Understand hatch pattern definition*
- *Create new hatch patterns*
- *Determine the effect of angle and scale factor on hatch*
- *Create hatch patterns with multiple descriptors*
- *Save hatch patterns in a separate file*
- *Customize hatch pattern file*

Key Terms

- *Linetype*
- **.lin Files*
- *Header Line*
- *Pattern Line*
- *LTSCALE*
- *CELTSCALE*
- *String Complex Linetypes*
- *Shape Complex Linetypes*
- *Hatch Descriptors*
- **.pat Files*

STANDARD LINETYPES

The AutoCAD software package comes with a library comprising 59 different standard linetypes, including ISO linetypes and seven complex linetypes. These linetypes are saved in the *acad.lin* and *acadiso.lin* file. You can modify existing linetypes or create new ones.

LINETYPE DEFINITIONS

All linetype definitions consist of two parts: **header line** and **pattern line**.

Header Line

The **header line** consists of an asterisk (*) followed by the name of the linetype and the linetype description. The name and the linetype description should be separated by a comma. If there is no description, the comma that separates the linetype name and the description is not required.

The format of the header line is:

*** Linetype Name, Description**

Example:
*HIDDEN,__ __ __ __ __ __

Where	*	------------------Asterisk sign
	HIDDEN	------Linetype name
	,	------------------Comma
	__ __ __ __	----Linetype description

All linetype definitions require a linetype name. When you load a linetype or assign a linetype to an object, AutoCAD recognizes the linetype by the name you have assigned to the linetype definition. The names of the linetype definition should be selected to help the user recognize the linetype by its name. For example, the linetype name LINEFCX does not give the user any idea about the type of line. However, a linetype name like DASHDOT gives a better idea about the type of line that a user can expect.

The linetype description is a textual representation of the line. This representation can be generated by using dashes, dots, and spaces at the keyboard. The graphic given in the code is used for displaying preview of the linetypes. The linetype description cannot exceed 47 characters.

Pattern Line

The **pattern line** contains the definition of the line pattern consisting of the alignment field specification and the linetype specification separated by a comma.

The format of the pattern line is:
Alignment Field Specification, Linetype Specification

Example:

A,.75,-.25,.75

Where **A** ----------------Alignment field specification
, -------------------Comma
.75,-.25,.75 ----Linetype specification

The letter used for alignment field specification is A. This is the only alignment field supported by AutoCAD; therefore, the pattern line will always start with the letter A. The linetype specification defines the configuration of the dash-dot pattern to generate a line. The maximum number for dash length specification in the linetype is 12, provided the linetype pattern definition fits on one 80-character line.

ELEMENTS OF LINETYPE SPECIFICATION

All linetypes are created by combining the basic elements in a desired configuration. There are three basic elements that can be used to define a linetype specification.

Dash (Pen down)
Dot (Pen down, 0 length)
Space (Pen up)

Example:

_______ . _______ . _______ . _______

Where **.** -------------------Dot (pen down with 0 length)
Blank space ----------------Space (pen up)
_______ ------------------------------Dash (pen down with specified length)

The dashes are generated by defining a positive number. For example, .5 will generate a 0.5 units long dash. Similarly, spaces are generated by defining a negative number. For example, -.2 will generate a 0.2 units long space. The dot is generated by defining 0 length.

Example:

A,.5,-.2,0,-.2,.5

Where **0** ---------------Dot (zero length)
-.2 ----------------Length of space (pen up)
.5 ----------------Length of dash (pen down)

CREATING LINETYPES

Before creating a linetype, you need to decide the type of line that you want to generate. Draw the line on a piece of paper and measure the length of each element that constitutes the line. You need to define only one segment of the line because the pattern is repeated when you draw a line. Linetypes can be created or modified by any one of the following methods:

1. Using a text editor such as Notepad
2. Adding a new linetype in the *acad.lin* or *acadiso.lin* file
3. Using the **-LINETYPE** command

The following example explains how to create a new linetype using the three methods mentioned above.

Example 1 — *Linetype*

Create a linetype DASH3DOT, refer to Figure 11-1 with the following specifications:

Length of the first dash 0.5
Blank space 0.125
Dot
Blank space 0.125
Dot
Blank space 0.125
Dot
Blank space 0.125

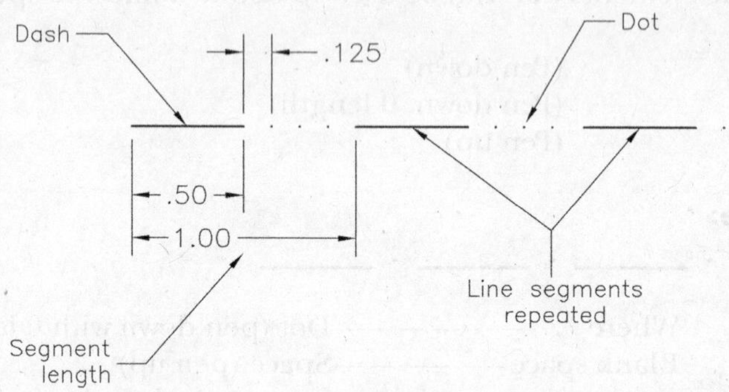

Figure 11-1 Linetype specifications of DASH3DOT

Using a Text Editor

Step 1: Writing Definition of Linetype

You can start a new linetype file and then add line definitions to this file. To do so, use any text editor such as Notepad to start a new file (*newlt.lin*) and then add the linetype definition of the DASH3DOT linetype. The name and the description must be separated by a comma (,). The description is optional. If you decide not to give one, omit the comma after the linetype name DASH3DOT.

***DASH3DOT,____ . . . ____ . . . ____**
A,.5,-.125,0,-.125,0,-.125,0,-.125

Save it as *newlt.lin* in AutoCAD's Support directory;
C:\Users\CADCIM\AppData\Roaming\Autodesk\AutoCAD 2021\ R24.0\enu\Support

Step 2: Loading the Linetype

To load this linetype, choose the **Other** option from **Properties > Linetype** drop-down list in the **Drafting & Annotation** workspace to display the **Linetype Manager** dialog box. Next, choose the **Load** button in the **Linetype Manager** dialog box to display the **Load or Reload**

Linetypes dialog box. Choose the **File** button in the **Load or Reload Linetypes** dialog box to display the **Select Linetype File** dialog box, as shown in Figure 11-2. Select the *newlt.lin* file from the location where you have saved it and then choose **Open**. Again, the **Load or Reload Linetypes** dialog box will be displayed. Choose the **DASH3DOT** linetype in the **Available Linetypes** area and then choose **OK**; the **Linetype Manager** dialog box is displayed. Select the **DASH3DOT** linetype and then choose the **Current** button to make the selected linetype as the current linetype. Then, choose **OK**. Now, if you draw any object, then the new linetype will be used to draw that object.

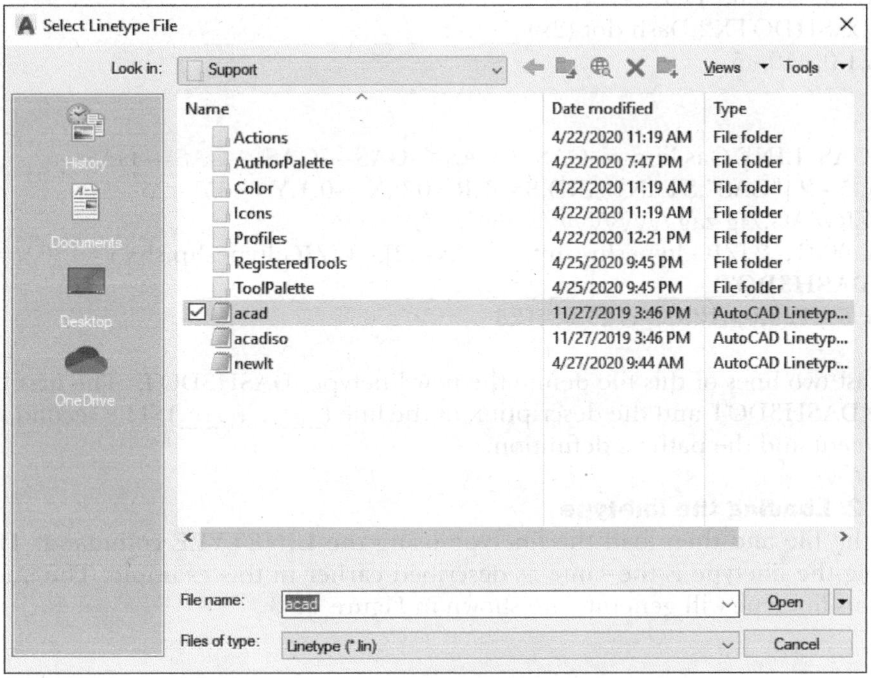

***Figure 11-2** The **Select Linetype File** dialog box*

Adding a New Linetype in the *acad.lin* File

Step 1: Adding a new linetype in the *acad.lin*

Browse to the *acad.lin* file and double-click on it; the *acad.lin* file opens in Notepad. In this text editor, you can insert the line definition that defines the new linetype. Given next is the partial listing of the *acad.lin* file after adding a new linetype to it:

```
*BORDER,Border __ __ . __ __ . __ __ . __ __ . __ __ .
A,.5,-.25,.5,-.25,0,-.25
*BORDER2,Border (.5x) __.__.__.__.__.__.__.__.__.__.__.
A,.25,-.125,.25,-.125,0,-.125
*BORDERX2,Border (2x) ____  ____  .  ____  ____  .  ___
A,1.0,-.5,1.0,-.5,0,-.5
*CENTER,Center ____ _ ____ _ ____ _ ____ _ ____ _ ____
A,1.25,-.25,.25,-.25
```

```
*CENTER2,Center (.5x) ___ _ ___ _ ___ _ ___ _ ___
A,.75,-.125,.125,-.125
*CENTERX2,Center (2x) ________ __ ________
A,2.5,-.5,.5,-.5
*DASHDOT,Dash dot __ . __ . __ . __ . __ . __
A,.5,-.25,0,-.25
*DASHDOT2,Dash dot (.5x) _._._._._._._._._._._._.
A,.25,-.125,0,-.125
*DASHDOTX2,Dash dot (2x) ____ . ____ . ____ . ___
A,1.0,-.50,-.5
|
|
*GAS_LINE,Gas line ----GAS----GAS----GAS----GAS----GAS----GAS--
A,.5,-.2,["GAS",STANDARD,S=.1,R=0.0,X=-0.1,Y=-.05],-.25
*ZIGZAG,Zig zag /\/\/\/\/\/\/\/\/\/\/\/\/\/\/\/\/\/\/\/\
A,.0001,-.2,[ZIG,ltypeshp.shx,x=-.2,s=.2],-.4,[ZIG,ltypeshp.shx,r=180,x=.2,s=.2],-.2
*DASH3DOT,____ . . . ____ . . . ____
A,.5,-.125,0,-.125,0,-.125,0,-.125
```

The last two lines of this file define the new linetype, DASH3DOT. The first line contains the name DASH3DOT and the description of the line (___ . . . ___). The second line contains the alignment and the pattern definition.

Step 2: Loading the linetype

Save the file and then load the linetype using the **LINETYPE** command. The procedure of loading the linetype is the same as described earlier in this example. The lines and polylines that this linetype will generate are shown in Figure 11-3.

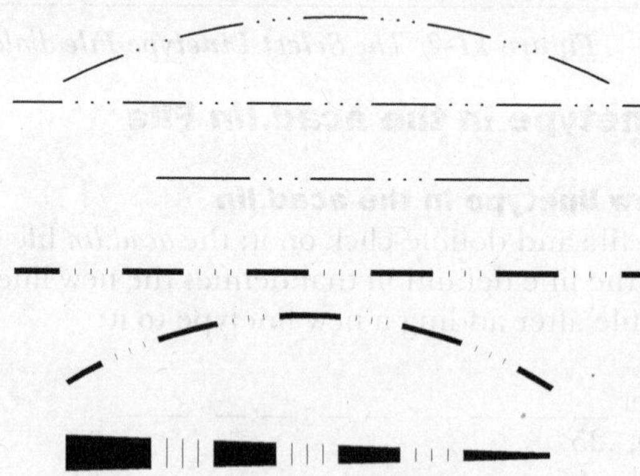

Figure 11-3 Lines created by the linetype DASH3DOT

Note

If you change the LTSCALE factor, all the lines in the drawing are affected by the new ratio.

Using the LINETYPE Command

Step 1: Creating a linetype

To create a linetype using the **LINETYPE** command, first make sure that you are in the drawing editor. Then enter the **-LINETYPE** command and choose the **Create** option to create a linetype.

Command: **-LINETYPE**
Enter an option [?/Create/Load/Set]: **C**

Enter the name of the linetype and the name of the library file in which you want to store the definition of the new linetype.

Enter name of linetype to create: **DASH3DOT**

If **FILEDIA**=1, the **Create or Append Linetype File** dialog box, refer to Figure 11-4, will appear on the screen. If **FILEDIA**=0, you are prompted to enter the name of the file.

Enter linetype file name for new linetype definition <default>: **Acad**

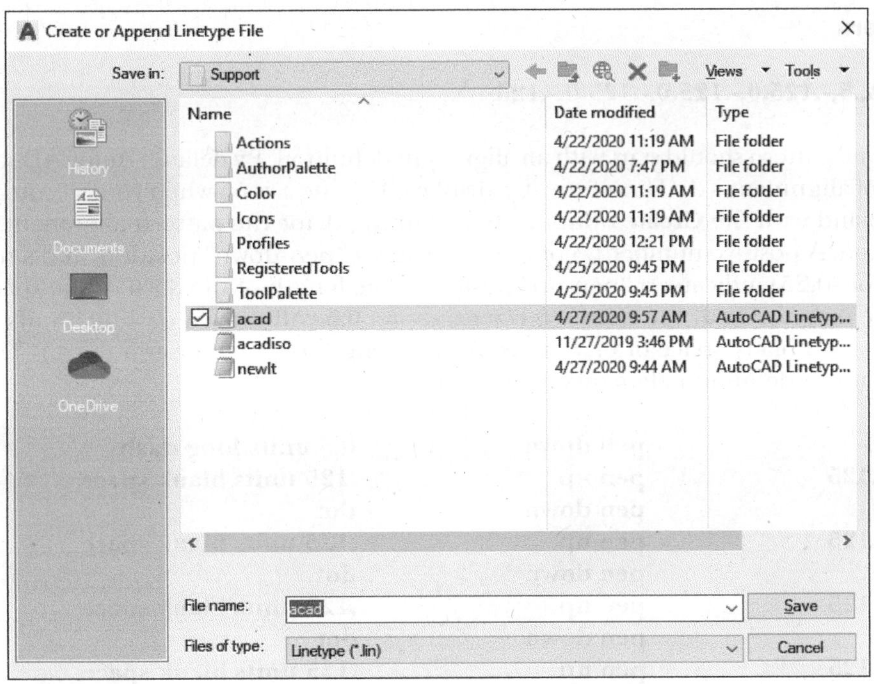

***Figure 11-4** The **Create or Append Linetype File** dialog box*

If the linetype already exists, the following message will be displayed on the screen:
Wait, checking if linetype already defined...
"Linetype" already exists in this file. Current definition is:
alignment, dash-1, dash-2, _____.
Overwrite?<N>

If you want to redefine the existing line style, enter **Y**. Otherwise, type **N** or press ENTER to choose the default value of N. You can then repeat the process with a different linetype name. After entering the name of the linetype and the library file name, you are prompted to enter the descriptive text and the pattern of the line.

Descriptive text: ***DASH3DOT,____ . . . ____ . . . ____**
Enter linetype pattern (on next line):
A,.5,-.125,0,-.125,0,-.125,0,-.125

Descriptive Text

***DASH3DOT,____ . . . ____ . . . ____**

For the descriptive text, you have to type an asterisk (*) followed by the name of the linetype. For Example 1, the name of the linetype is DASH3DOT. The name *DASH3DOT can be followed by the description of the linetype; the length of this description cannot exceed 47 characters. In this example, the description is dashes and dots ____ . . . ____. It could be any text or alphanumeric string. The description is displayed on the screen when you list the linetypes.

Pattern

A,.5,-.125,0,-.125,0,-.125,0,-.125

The line pattern should start with an alignment definition. By default, AutoCAD supports only one type of alignment—A. Therefore, it is displayed on the screen when you execute the **LINETYPE** command with the **Create** option. After entering **A** for the pattern alignment, define the pen position. A positive number (.5 or 0.5) indicates a "pen-down" position, and a negative number (-.25 or -0.25) indicates a "pen-up" position. The length of the dash or the space is designated by the magnitude of the number. For example, 0.5 will draw a dash 0.5 units long, and -0.25 will leave a blank space of 0.25 units. A dash length of 0 will draw a dot (.). The following are the pattern definition elements for Example 1:

.5	**pen down**	**0.5 units long dash**
-.125	**pen up**	**.125 units blank space**
0	**pen down**	**dot**
-.125	**pen up**	**.125 units blank space**
0	**pen down**	**dot**
-.125	**pen up**	**.125 units blank space**
0	**pen down**	**dot**
-.125	**pen up**	**.125 units blank space**

After you enter the pattern definition, the linetype (DASH3DOT) is automatically saved in the *acad.lin* file.

Step 2: Loading the linetype

Choose the **Other** option from **Home > Properties > Linetype** drop-down list to load the linetype or use the **LINETYPE** command. The linetype (DASH3DOT) can also be loaded using the **-LINETYPE** command and selecting the **Load** option.

ALIGNMENT SPECIFICATION

As the name suggests, the alignment specifies the pattern alignment at the start and the end of a line, circle, or arc. In other words, the line always starts and ends with the dash (___). The alignment definition "A" requires the first element to be a dash or dot (pen down), followed by a negative (pen up) segment. The minimum number of dash segments for alignment A is two. If the space is not enough for the line, a continuous line is drawn.

For example, in the linetype DASH3DOT of Example 1, the length of each line segment is 1.0 (.5 + .125 + .125 + .125 + .125 = 1.0). If the length of the line drawn is less than 1.00, a single line is drawn that looks like a continuous line, refer to Figure 11-5. If the length of the line is 1.00 or greater, the line will be drawn according to DASH3DOT linetype. AutoCAD automatically adjusts the length of the dashes and the line always starts and ends with a dash. The length of the starting and ending dashes is at least half the length of the dash as specified in the file. If the length of the dash as specified in the file is 0.5, the length of the starting and ending dashes is at least 0.25. To fit a line that starts and ends with a dash, the length of these dashes can also increase, as shown in Figure 11-5.

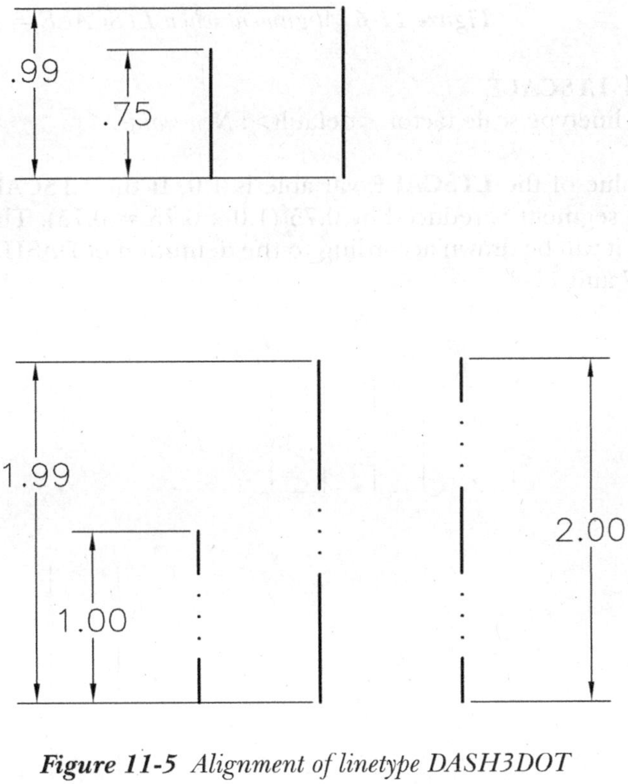

Figure 11-5 Alignment of linetype DASH3DOT

LTSCALE COMMAND

As mentioned earlier, the length of each line segment in the DASH3DOT linetype is 1.0 (.5 + .125 + .125 + .125 + .125 = 1.0). If you draw a line that is less than 1.0 unit long, a single dash is drawn that looks like a continuous line, refer to Figure 11-6. This problem can be rectified by changing the linetype scale factor variable **LTSCALE** to a smaller value. This can be accomplished using the **LTSCALE** command.

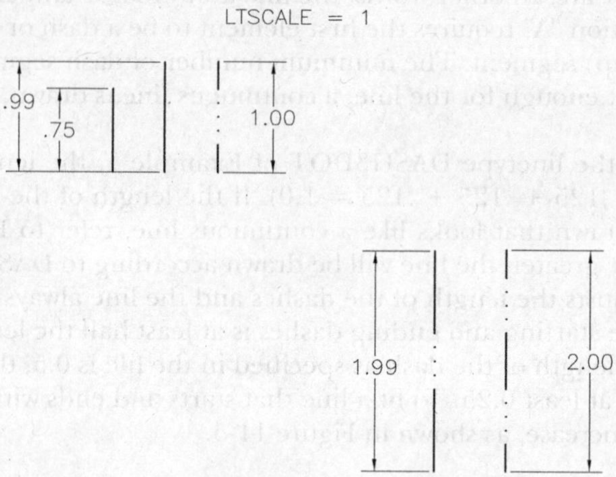

Figure 11-6 *Alignment when LTSCALE= 1*

Command: **LTSCALE**
Enter new linetype scale factor <default>: *New value.*

The default value of the **LTSCALE** variable is 1.0. If the LTSCALE is changed to 0.75, the length of each segment is reduced by 0.75 (1.0 x 0.75 = 0.75). Then, if you draw a line 0.75 unit or longer, it will be drawn according to the definition of DASH3DOT (___ . . . ___), refer to Figures 11-7 and 11-8.

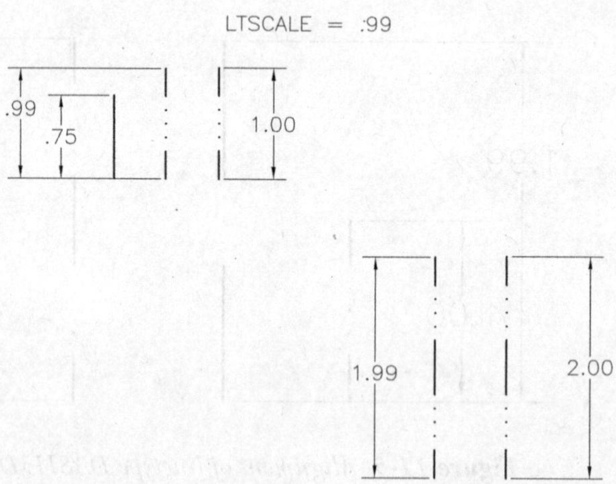

Figure 11-7 *Alignment when LTSCALE = 0.99*

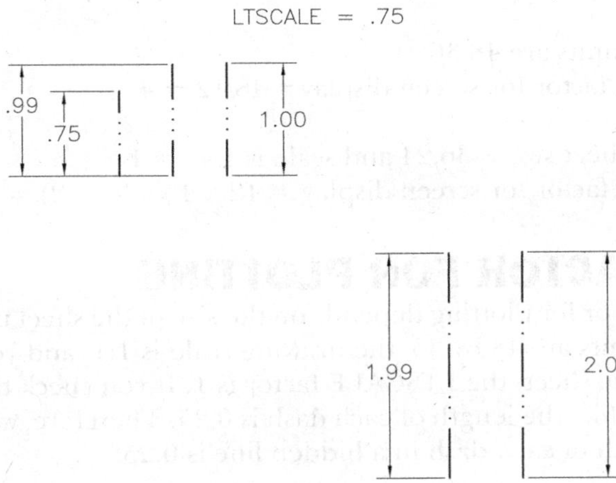

***Figure 11-8** Alignment when LTSCALE = 0.75*

The appearance of the lines is also affected by the limits of the drawing. Most of the AutoCAD linetypes work fine for drawings that have the limits 12,9. Figure 11-9 shows a line of linetype DASH3DOT that is four units long and the limits of the drawing are 12,9. If you increase the limits to 48,36 the lines will appear as continuous lines. If you want the line to appear the same as before on the screen, the LTSCALE needs to be changed. Since the limits of the drawing have increased four times, the LTSCALE should also be increased by the same proportion. If you change the scale factor to four, the line segments will also increase by a factor of four. As shown in Figure 11-9, the length of the starting and the ending dash has increased to one unit.

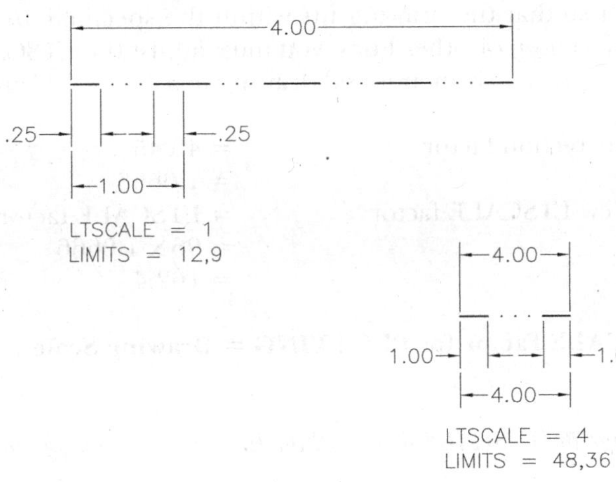

***Figure 11-9** Linetype DASH3DOT before and after changing the LTSCALE factor*

In general, the approximate LTSCALE factor for screen display can be obtained by dividing the X -limit of the drawing by the default X -limit (12.00). However, it is recommended that the linetype scale must be set according to plot scale discussed in the next section.

LTSCALE factor for SCREEN DISPLAY = X -limits of the drawing/12.00
Example:
Drawing limits are 48,36
LTSCALE factor for screen display= 48/12 = 4

Drawing sheet size is 36,24 and scale is 1/4" = 1'
LTSCALE factor for screen display = 12 x 4 x (36 / 12) = 144

LTSCALE FACTOR FOR PLOTTING

The LTSCALE factor for plotting depends on the size of the sheet used to plot the drawing. For example, if the limits are 48 by 36, the drawing scale is 1:1, and you want to plot the drawing on a 48" by 36" size sheet, the LTSCALE factor is 1. If you check the specification of a hidden line in the *acad.lin* file, the length of each dash is 0.25. Therefore, when you plot a drawing with 1:1 scale, the length of each dash in a hidden line is 0.25.

However, if the drawing scale is 1/8" = 1' and you want to plot the drawing on a 48" by 36" paper, the LTSCALE factor must be 96 (8 x 12 = 96). If you increase the LTSCALE factor to 96, the length of each dash in the hidden line will increase by a factor of 96. As a result, the length of each dash will be 24 units (0.25 x 96 = 24). At the time of plotting, the scale factor must be 1:96 to plot the 384' by 288' drawing on a 48" by 36" size paper. Each dash of the hidden line that was 24" long on the drawing will be 0.25 (24/96 = 0.25) inch long when plotted. Similarly, if the desired text size on the paper is 1/8", the text height in the drawing must be 12" (1/8 x 96 = 12").

Ltscale Factor for PLOTTING = Drawing Scale

Sometimes your plotter may not be able to plot a 48" by 36" drawing or you may like to decrease the size of the plot so that the drawing fits within the specified area. To get the correct dash lengths for hidden, center, or other lines, you must adjust the LTSCALE factor. For example, if you want to plot the previously mentioned drawing in a 45" by 34" area, the correction factor is:

Correction factor	= 48/45
	= 1.0666
New LTSCALE factor	= LTSCALE factor x Correction factor
	= 96 x 1.0666
	= 102.4

New LTSCALE Factor for PLOTTING = Drawing Scale x Correction Factor

Note
If you change the LTSCALE factor, all the lines in the drawing will be affected by the new ratio.

CURRENT LINETYPE SCALING (CELTSCALE)

Like **LTSCALE**, the **CELTSCALE** system variable controls the linetype scaling. The difference is that **CELTSCALE** determines the current linetype scaling. For example, if you set the **CELTSCALE** to 0.5, all the lines drawn after setting the new value for **CELTSCALE** will have the linetype scaling factor of 0.5. The value is retained in the **CELTSCALE** system variable. The first line (a) in Figure 11-10 is drawn with the **CELTSCALE** factor of 1 and the second line (b) is drawn with the **CELTSCALE** factor of 0.5. The length of the dashes is reduced by a factor of 0.5 when the **CELTSCALE** is 0.5.

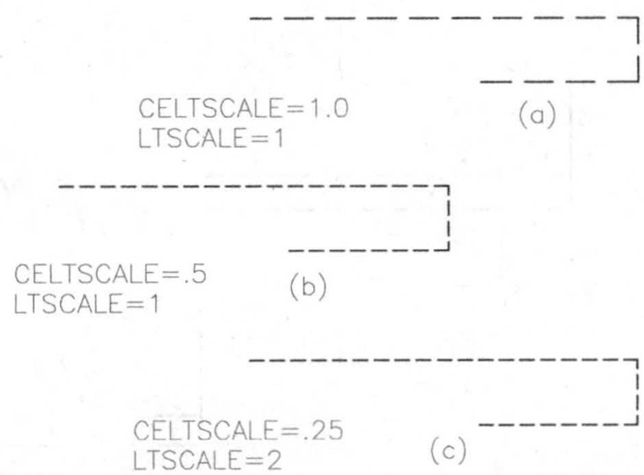

Figure 11-10 *Using **CELTSCALE** to control current linetype scaling*

The **LTSCALE** system variable controls the global scale factor. For example, if **LTSCALE** is set to 2, all the lines in the drawing will be affected by a factor of 2. The net scale factor is equal to the product of **CELTSCALE** and **LTSCALE**. Figure 11-10(c) shows a line that is drawn with **LTSCALE** of 2 and **CELTSCALE** of 0.25. The net scale factor is = **LTSCALE** x **CELTSCALE** = 2 x 0.25 = 0.5.

Note

*You can change the current linetype scale factor of a line by using the **Properties** palette that can be invoked by choosing the **Properties** tool from the **Quick Access** Toolbar (Customize to add).*

ALTERNATE LINETYPES

One of the problems with the LTSCALE factor is that it affects all the lines in a drawing. As shown in Figure 11-11(a), the length of each segment in all DASH3DOT type lines is approximately equal, no matter how long the lines are. You may want to have a small segment length if the lines are small and a longer segment length if the lines are long. You can accomplish this by using CELTSCALE (discussed later in this chapter) or by defining an alternate linetype with a different segment length. For example, you can define a linetype DASH3DOT and DASH3DOTX with different line pattern specifications.

```
*DASH3DOT,____ . . . ____ . . . ____ . . . ____
A,0.5,-.125,0,-.125,0,-.125,0,-.125
*DASH3DOTX,________ . . . __________
A,1.0,-.25,0,-.25,0,-.25,0,-.25
```

In the DASH3DOT linetype, the segment length is one unit; whereas, in the DASH3DOTX linetype the segment length is two units. You can have several alternate linetypes to produce the lines with different segment lengths. Figure 11-11(b) shows the lines generated by DASH3DOT and DASH3DOTX.

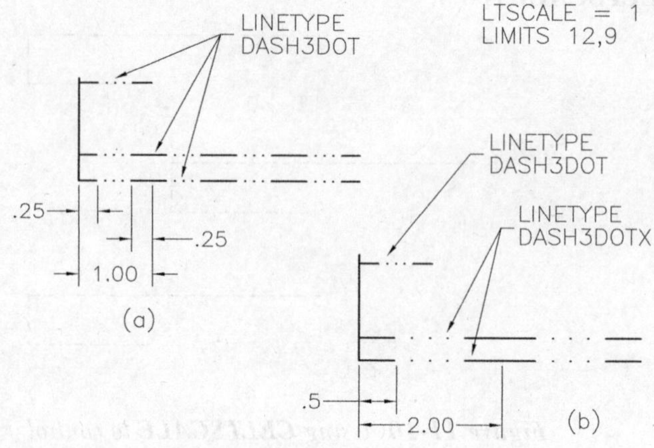

***Figure 11-11** Linetypes generated by DASH3DOT and DASH3DOTX*

Note

Although you may have used various linetypes with different segment lengths, the lines will be affected equally when you change the LTSCALE factor. For example, if the LTSCALE factor is 0.5, the segment length of DASH3DOT line will be 0.5 unit and the segment length of DASH3DOTX will be 1.0 unit.

MODIFYING LINETYPES

You can also modify the linetypes that are defined in the *acad.lin* or *acadiso.lin* file. You must save a copy of the original *acad.lin* or *acadiso.lin* file before making any changes to it. You need a text editor, such as Notepad, to modify the linetype. You can also use the **EDIT** function of DOS, or the **EDIT** command (provided the *acad.pgp* file is present and **EDIT** is defined in the file). For example, if you want to change the dash length of the border linetype from 0.5 to 0.75, load the file, and then edit the pattern line of the border linetype. The following file is a partial listing of the *acad.lin* file after changing the BORDER and CENTERX2 linetypes.

```
;; AutoCAD Linetype Definition file
;; Version 3.0

;; Copyright 2020 Autodesk, Inc. All rights reserved.

*BORDER,Border __ __ . __ __ . __ __ . __ __ . __ __ .
A,.5,-.25,.5,-.25,0,-.25
*BORDER2,Border (.5x) __.__.__.__.__.__.__.__.__.__.__.
A,.25,-.125,.25,-.125,0,-.125
*BORDERX2,Border (2x) ____ ____ . ____ ____ . __
A,1.0,-.5,1.0,-.5,0,-.5
*CENTER,Center ____ _ ____ _ ____ _ ____ _ ____ _ ____
A,1.25,-.25,.25,-.25
```

```
*CENTER2,Center (.5x) ___ _ ___ _ ___ _ ___ _ ___ _ ___
A,.75,-.125,.125,-.125
*CENTERX2,Center (2x) ________ __ ________ __ _____
A,2.5,-.5,.5,-.5

*DASHDOT,Dash dot __ . __ . __ . __ . __ . __ . __ . __
A,.5,-.25,0,-.25
*DASHDOT2,Dash dot (.5x) _._._._._._._._._._._._._._.
A,.25,-.125,0,-.125
*DASHDOTX2,Dash dot (2x) ____  .  ____  .  ____  .  ___
A,1.0,-.5,0,-.5

*DASHED,Dashed __ __ __ __ __ __ __ __ __ __ __ __ __ _
A,.5,-.25
*DASHED2,Dashed (.5x) _ _ _ _ _ _ _ _ _ _ _ _ _ _ _ _ _ _ _
A,.25,-.125
*DASHEDX2,Dashed (2x) ____  ____  ____  ____  ____  ___
A,1.0,-.5

*DIVIDE,Divide ____ . . ____ . . ____ . . ____ . . ____
A,.5,-.25,0,-.25,0,-.25
*DIVIDE2,Divide (.5x) __..__..__..__..__..__..__..__.._
A,.25,-.125,0,-.125,0,-.125
*DIVIDEX2,Divide (2x) ________  .  .  ________  .  .  _
A,1.0,-.5,0,-.5,0,-.5

*DOT,Dot . . . . . . . . . . . . . . . . . . . . . . . .
A,0,-.25
*DOT2,Dot (.5x) ........................................
A,0,-.125
*DOTX2,Dot (2x) .  .  .  .  .  .  .  .  .  .  .  .  .  .
A,0,-.5

*HIDDEN,Hidden __ __ __ __ __ __ __ __ __ __ __ __ __ __
A,.25,-.125
*HIDDEN2,Hidden (.5x) _ _ _ _ _ _ _ _ _ _ _ _ _ _ _ _ _ _ _
A,.125,-.0625
*HIDDENX2,Hidden (2x) ____ ____ ____ ____ ____ ____ ____
A,.5,-.25

*PHANTOM,Phantom ______ __ __ ______ __ __ ______
A,1.25,-.25,.25,-.25,.25,-.25
*PHANTOM2,Phantom (.5x) ___ _ _ ___ _ _ ___ _ _ ___ _ _
A,.625,-.125,.125,-.125,.125,-.125
*PHANTOMX2,Phantom (2x) ____________    ____    ____   _
A,2.5,-.5,.5,-.5,.5,-.5

;;
```

```
;; ISO 128 (ISO/DIS 12011) linetypes
;;
;; The size of the line segments for each defined ISO line is
;; defined for usage with a pen width of 1 mm. To use them with
;; the other ISO predefined pen widths, the line has to be scaled
;; with the appropriate value (e.g. pen width 0,5 mm -> ltscale 0.5).
;;
*ACAD_ISO02W100,ISO dash __ __ __ __ __ __ __ __ __ __ __ __ __
A,12,-3
|
|
*ACAD_ISO15W100,ISO double-dash triple-dot __ __ . . . __ __ . .
A,12,-3,12,-3,0,-3,0,-3,0,-3

;; Complex linetypes
;; Complex linetypes have been added to this file.
;; These linetypes were defined in LTYPESHP.LIN in
;; Release 13, and are incorporated in ACAD.LIN in
;; Release 14.
;;
;; These linetype definitions use LTYPESHP.SHX.
;;
*FENCELINE1,Fenceline circle ----0-----0----0-----0----0-----0--
A,.25,-.1,[CIRC1,ltypeshp.shx,x=-.1,s=.1],-.1,1
*FENCELINE2,Fenceline square ----[]-----[]----[]-----[]----[]---
A,.25,-.1,[BOX,ltypeshp.shx,x=-.1,s=.1],-.1,1
*TRACKS,Tracks -|-|-|-|-|-|-|-|-|-|-|-|-|-|-|-|-|-|-|-|-|-|-|-|-
A,.15,[TRACK1,ltypeshp.shx,s=.25],.15
*BATTING,Batting SSSSSSSSSSSSSSSSSSSSSSSSSSSSSSSSSSSSSSSSSSSSSS
A,.0001,-.1,[BAT,ltypeshp.shx,x=-.1,s=.1],-.2,[BAT,ltypeshp.shx,r=180,x=.1,s=.1],-.1
*HOT_WATER_SUPPLY,Hot water supply ---- HW ---- HW ---- HW ----
A,.5,-.2,["HW",STANDARD,S=.1,R=0.0,X=-0.1,Y=-.05],-.2
*GAS_LINE,Gas line ----GAS----GAS----GAS----GAS----GAS----GAS--
A,.5,-.2,["GAS",STANDARD,S=.1,R=0.0,X=-0.1,Y=-.05],-.25
*ZIGZAG,Zig zag /\/\/\/\/\/\/\/\/\/\/\/\/\/\/\/\/\/\/\/\/\/\/
A,.0001,-.2,[ZIG,ltypeshp.shx,x=-.2,s=.2],-.4,[ZIG,ltypeshp.shx,r=180,x=.2,s=.2],-.2
```

Example 2 — Linetype

Create a new file, *newlint.lin*, and define a linetype VARDASH with the following specifications:

Length of first dash 1.0
Blank space 0.25
Length of second dash 0.75
Blank space 0.25
Length of third dash 0.5
Blank space 0.25

Dot
Blank space 0.25
Length of next dash 0.5
Blank space 0.25
Length of next dash 0.75

Step 1: Writing definition of linetype

Use a text editor and insert the following lines to define the new linetype **VARDASH**.

***VARDASH,———— —— — . — —— ————**
A,1,-.25,.75,-.25,.5,-.25,0,-.25,.5,-.25,.75,-.25

Now, save this file with the name *newlint.lin*.

Step 2: Loading the linetype

You can use the **LINETYPE** command or choose **Home > Properties > Linetype > Other** from the **Ribbon** to load the linetype. The types of lines that this linetype will generate are shown in Figure 11-12.

Figure 11-12 *Lines generated by linetype VARDASH*

COMPLEX LINETYPES

In AutoCAD, you can create complex linetypes. The complex linetypes can be classified into two groups: string complex linetype and shape complex linetype. The difference between these line type is that the string complex linetype has a text string inserted in the line whereas the shape complex linetype has a shape inserted in the line. The facility of creating complex linetypes increases the functionality of lines. For example, if you want to draw a line around a building that indicates the fence line, you can do it by defining a complex linetype that will automatically give you the desired line with the text string (Fence). Similarly, you can define a complex linetype that will insert a shape (symbol) at predefined distances along the line.

CREATING A STRING COMPLEX LINETYPE

While writing the definition of a string complex linetype, the actual text and its attributes must be included in the linetype definition, refer to Figure 11-13.
The format of the string complex linetype is:

["String", Text Style, Text Height, Rotation, X-Offset, Y-Offset]

String. It is the actual text that you want to insert along the line. The text string must be enclosed in quotation marks (" ").

Text Style. This is the name of the text style file that you want to use for generating the text string. The text style must be predefined.

Text Height. This is the actual height of the text, if the text height defined in the text style is 0. Otherwise, it acts as a scale factor for the text height specified in the text style. In Figure 11-13, the height of the text is 0.1 units.

Rotation. The rotation can be specified as an absolute or relative angle. In the absolute rotation, the angle is always measured with respect to the positive *X* axis, no matter what AutoCAD's direction setting is. The absolute angle is represented by the letter "a".

In relative rotation, the angle is always measured with respect to orientation of dashes in the linetype. The relative angle is represented by the letter "r". The angle can be specified in radians (r), grads (g), or degrees (d). The default is degrees.

X-Offset. This is the distance of the lower left corner of the text string from the endpoint of the line segment measured along the line. If the line is horizontal, then the X-Offset distance is measured along the *X* axis. In Figure 11-13, the X-Offset distance is 0.05.

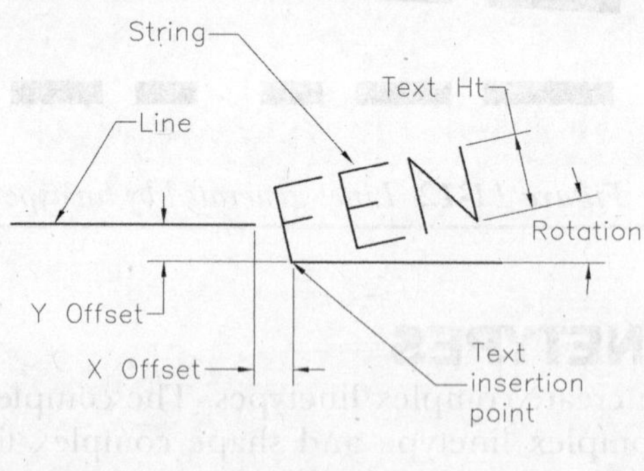

***Figure 11-13** Attributes of a string complex linetype*

Y-Offset. This is the distance of the lower left corner of the text string from the endpoint of the line segment measured perpendicular to the line. If the line is horizontal, then the Y-Offset distance is measured along the *Y* axis. In Figure 11-13, the Y-Offset distance is -0.05. The distance is negative because the start point of the text string is 0.05 units below the endpoint of the first line segment.

Example 3 *String Complex Linetype*

In this example, you will write definition of a string complex linetype that consists of the text string "Fence" and line segments. The length of each line segment is 0.75. The height of the text string is 0.1 units, and the space between the end of the text string and the following line segment is 0.05, refer to Figure 11-14.

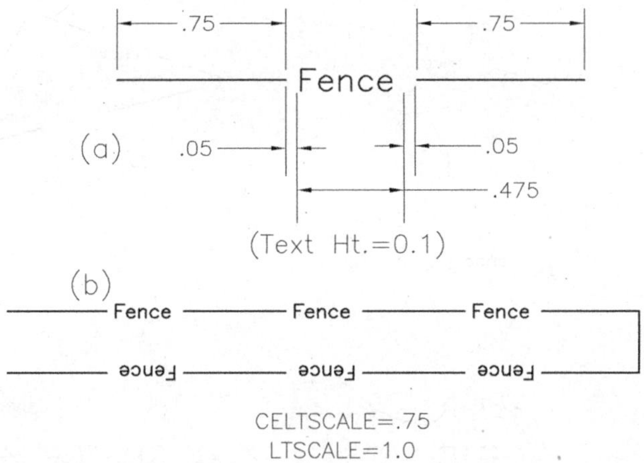

Figure 11-14 *The attributes of a string complex linetype and line specifications for Example 3*

Step 1: Determining the line specifications

Before writing the definition of a new linetype, it is important to determine the line specification. One of the ways to do this is to actually draw the lines and the text the way you want them to appear in the drawing. Once you have drawn the line and the text to your satisfaction, measure the distances needed to define the string complex linetype. The values are given as follows:

Text string	=Fence
Text style	=Standard
Text height	=0.1
Text rotation	=0
X-Offset	=0.05
Y-Offset	=-0.05
Length of the first line segment	=0.75
Distance between the line segments	=0.575

Step 2: Writing the definition of string complex linetype

Use a text editor to write the definition of the string complex linetype. You can add the definition to the *acad.lin* or *acadiso.lin* file or create a separate file. The extension of the file must be *.lin*. The following file is the listing of the *fence.lin* file for Example 3. The name of the linetype is NEWFence1.

```
*NEWFence1,New fence boundary line
A,.75,-.05,["Fence",STANDARD,S=.1,A=0.0,X=0,Y=-.05],-.575
```

Step 3: Loading the linetype

Choose the **Other** option from **Properties > Linetype** drop-down list to load the linetype or use the **LINETYPE** command. Now, draw a line or any object to check if the line is drawn as per given specifications, as shown in Figure 11-15. Notice that the text is always drawn along the X axis. Also, when you draw a line at an angle, polyline, circle, or spline, the text string does not align with the object, refer to Figure 11-15.

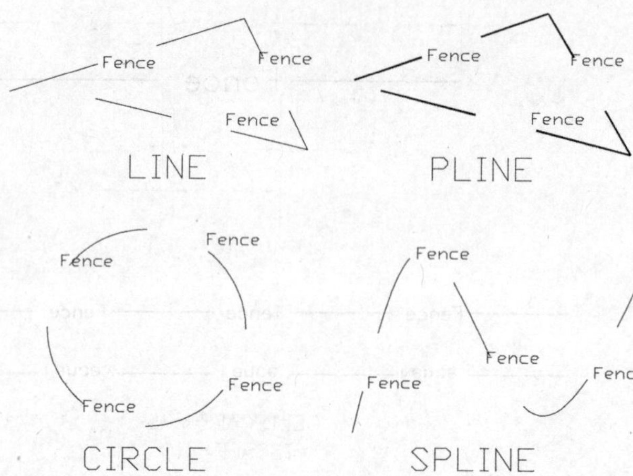

Figure 11-15 *Using string complex linetype with angle A=0*

Step 4: Aligning the text with the line

In the NEWFence linetype definition, the specified angle is 0° (Absolute angle A = 0). Therefore, when you use the NEWFence linetype to draw a line, circle, polyline, or spline, the text string (Fence) will be at zero degrees. If you want the text string (Fence) to align with the polyline, refer to Figure 11-16, spline, or circle, specify the angle as relative angle (R = 0) in the NEWFence linetype definition. The following is the linetype definition for NEWFence linetype with relative angle R = 0:

```
*NEWFence2,New fence boundary line
A,0.75,["Fence",Standard,S=0.1,R=0,X=0.05,Y=-0.05],-0.575
```

Note

You have to load the linetype again to get the changes updated.

Step 5: Aligning the midpoint of text with the line

In Figure 11-16, you will notice that the text string is not properly aligned with the circumference of the circle. This is because AutoCAD draws the text string in a direction that is tangent to the circle at the text insertion point.

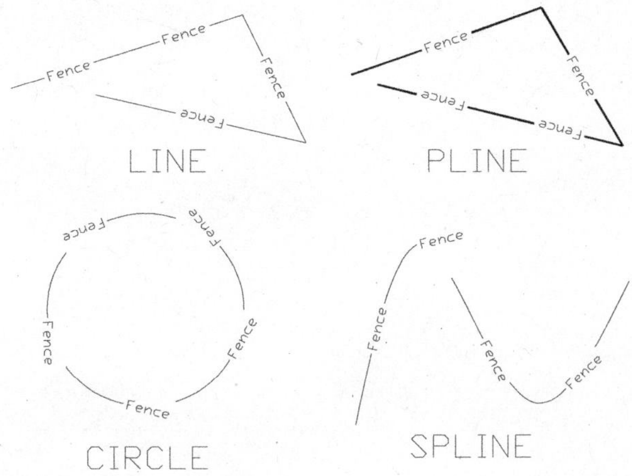

Figure 11-16 Using a string complex linetype with angle R = 0

To resolve this problem, you must define the mid point as the insertion point for the text string. Also, the line specifications should be assigned accordingly. Figure 11-17 shows the measurements of the NEWFence linetype with the mid point of the text as the insertion point and Figure 11-18 shows the entities sketched with the selected linetype.

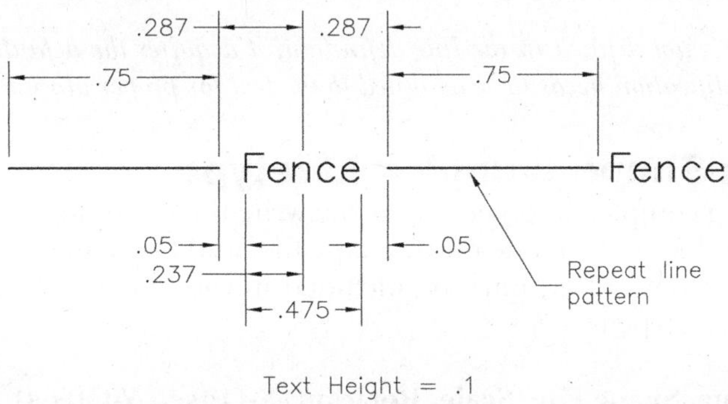

Figure 11-17 Specifications of a string complex linetype with the middle point of the text string as the text insertion point

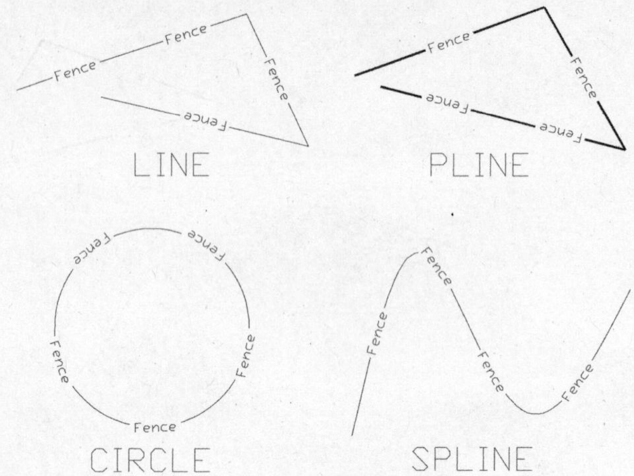

Figure 11-18 Using a string complex linetype with the middle point of the text string as the text insertion point

The following is the linetype definition for NEWFence linetype:

```
*NEWFence3,New fence boundary line
A,.75,-.287,["Fence",STANDARD,S=.1,X=-0.237,Y=.05],-.287
```

Note

If angle is not defined in the line definition, it acquires the default value of angle R = 0. But MID justification needs to be assigned to the text for proper alignment.

Creating a Shape Complex Linetype

As with the string complex linetype, when you write the definition of a shape complex linetype, the name of the shape, the name of the shape file, and other shape attributes such as rotation, scale, X-Offset, and Y-Offset, must be included in the linetype definition. The format of the shape complex linetype is:

[Shape Name, Shape File, Scale, Rotation, X-Offset, Y-Offset]

The following is the description of the attributes of Shape Complex Linetype, refer to Figure 11-19.

Shape Name. This is the name of the shape that you want to insert along the line. The shape name must exist; otherwise, no shape will be generated along the line.

Shape File. This is the name of the compiled shape file (*.shx*) that contains the definition of the shape being inserted in the line. The name of the subdirectory where the shape file is located must be in the AutoCAD search path. The shape files (*.shp*) must be compiled before using the **SHAPE** command to load the shape.

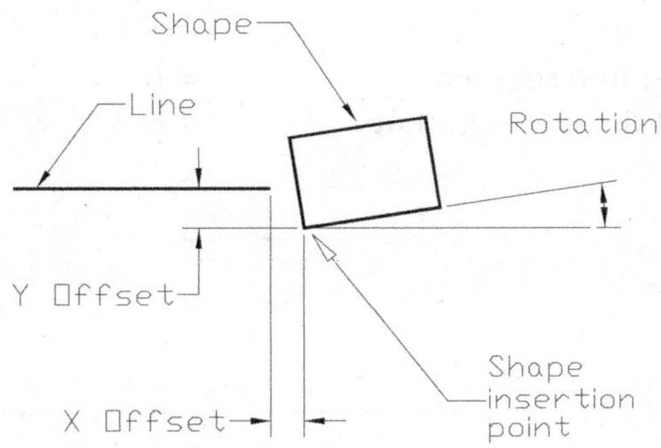

***Figure 11-19** The attributes of a shape complex linetype*

Scale. This is the scale factor by which the defined shape size is to be scaled. If the scale is 1, the size of the shape will be the same as defined in the shape definition (*.shp* file).

Rotation. The rotation can be specified as an absolute or relative angle. In absolute rotation, the angle is always measured with respect to the positive *X* axis, no matter what AutoCAD's direction setting. The absolute angle is represented by letter "a." In relative rotation, the angle is always measured with respect to the orientation of dashes in the linetype. The relative angle is represented by the letter "r." The angle can be specified in radians (r), grads (g), or degrees (d). The default is degrees.

X-Offset. This is the distance of the shape insertion point from the endpoint of the line segment measured along the line. If the line is horizontal, then the X-Offset distance is measured along the *X* axis.

Y-Offset. This is the distance of the shape insertion point from the endpoint of the line segment measured perpendicular to the line. If the line is horizontal, then the Y-Offset distance is measured along the *Y* axis.

Example 4 — Shape Complex Linetype

Write the definition of a shape complex linetype that consists of a shape (Manhole; the name of the shape is MH) and a line. The scale of the shape is 0.1, the length of each line segment is 0.75, and the space between line segments is 0.2.

Step 1: Determining the line specifications

Before writing the definition of a new linetype, it is important to determine the line specifications. One of the ways to do this is to actually draw the lines and the shape the way you want them to appear in the drawing, refer to Figure 11-20. Once you have drawn the line and the shape to your satisfaction, measure the distances needed to define the shape complex linetype. In this example, the values are as follows:

Shape name	=MH
Shape file name	=*mhole.shx* (Name of the compiled shape file.)
Scale	=0.1
Rotation	=0

X-Offset	=0.2
Y-Offset	=0
Length of the first line segment	= 0.75
Distance between the line segments	= 0.2

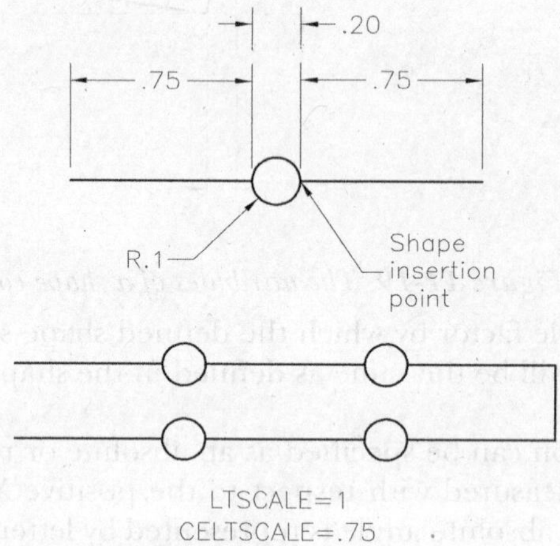

Figure 11-20 The attributes of the shape complex linetype and line specifications for Example 4

Step 2: Writing the definition of the shape

Use a text editor to write the definition of the shape file. The extension of the file must be *.shp*. The following file is the listing of the *mhole.shp* file for Example 4. The name of the shape is MH.

```
*215,9,MH
001,10,(1,007),
001,10,(1,071),0 Enter
```

Step 3: Compiling the shape

Use the **COMPILE** command to compile the shape file (*.shp* file). Remember that the path of the folder in which you save the shape file should be specified in the AutoCAD support file search path. When you use this command, the **Select Shape or Font File** dialog box will be displayed, refer to Figure 11-21. If **FILEDIA** = 0, this command will be executed using the command line. The following is the command sequence for compiling the shape file:

Command: **COMPILE**
Enter shape (.SHP) or PostScript font (.PFB) file name: **MHOLE**

Step 4: Writing the definition of the shape complex linetype

Use a text editor to write the definition of the shape complex linetype. You can add the definition to the *acad.lin* file or create a separate file. The extension of the file must be *.lin*. The following file is the listing of the *mhole.lin* file for Example 4. The name of the linetype is MHOLE.

```
*MHOLE,Line with Manholes
A,0.75,[MH,MHOLE.SHX,S=0.10,X=0.2,Y=0],-0.2 Enter
```

Step 5: Loading the linetype

To test the linetype, load the linetype using the **LINETYPE** command. Assign the linetype to a layer. Draw a line or any object to check if the line is drawn to the given specifications. The shape is drawn upside down when you draw a line from right to left. Figure 11-22 shows the execution of the linetype *mhole.lin* using line, pline, and spline. Figure 11-23 displays the region hatched using the string complex and shape complex line types, respectively.

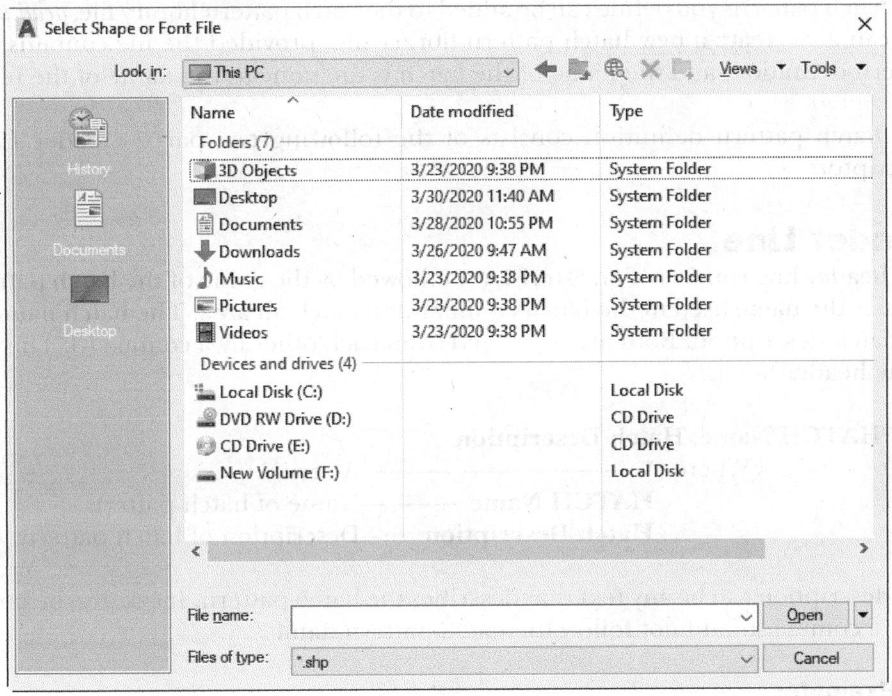

*Figure 11-21 The **Select Shape or Font File** dialog box*

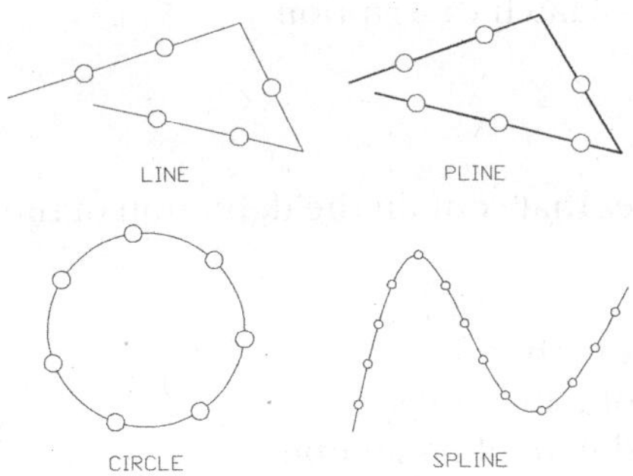

Figure 11-22 Using a shape complex linetype

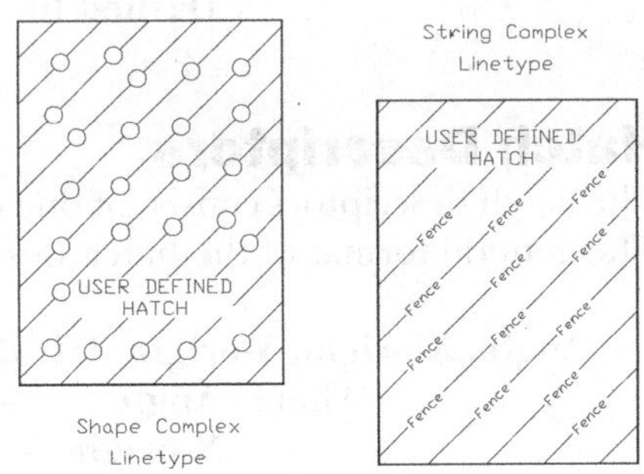

Figure 11-23 Using shape and string complex linetypes to create custom hatch

HATCH PATTERN DEFINITION

AutoCAD has a default hatch pattern library file, *acad.pat* and *acadiso.pat*, that contains 72 hatch patterns. Generally, you can hatch all the drawings using these default hatch patterns. However, if you need a different hatch pattern, AutoCAD allows you to create your own hatch patterns. There is no limit to the number of hatch patterns you can define.

The hatch patterns you define can be added to the hatch pattern library file, *acad.pat or acadiso.pat*. You can also create a new hatch pattern library file, provided the file contains only one hatch pattern definition, and the name of the hatch is the same as the name of the file.

The hatch pattern definition consists of the following two parts: Header Line and Hatch Descriptors.

Header Line

The header line consists of an asterisk (*) followed by the name of the hatch pattern. The hatch name is the name used in the hatch command to hatch an area. The hatch name is followed by the hatch description. Both are separated from each other by a comma (,). The general format of the header line is:

***HATCH Name, Hatch Description**

Where ***** -----------------------------Asterisk
HATCH Name -----------Name of hatch pattern
Hatch Description --Description of hatch pattern

The description can be any text that describes the hatch pattern. It can also be omitted, in which case, a comma should not follow the hatch pattern name.

Example:
***DASH45, Dashed lines at 45°**

Where **DASH45** --------Hatch name
Dashed lines at 45° --Hatch description

Hatch Descriptors

The hatch descriptors consist of one or more lines that contain the definition of the hatch lines. The general format of the hatch descriptor is:

Angle, X-origin, Y-origin, D1, D2 [,Dash Length.....]

Where **Angle** -----------Angle of hatch lines
X-origin --------*X* coordinate of hatch line
Y-origin --------*Y* coordinate of hatch line
D1 ---------------Displacement of second line (Delta-X)
D2 ---------------Distance between hatch lines (Delta-Y)
Length Length of dashes and spaces (Pattern line definition)

Example:
45,0,0,0,0.5,0.5,-0.125,0,-0.125

Where **45** ----------------Angle of hatch line
0 ------------------X-Origin
0 ------------------Y-Origin
0 ------------------Delta-X
0.5 ----------------Delta-Y
0.5 ----------------Dash (pen down)
-0.125 -----------Space (pen up)
0 ------------------Dot (pen down)
-0.125 -----------Space (pen up)
0.5,-0.125,0,-0.125 Pattern line definition

Hatch Angle

X-origin and Y-origin. The hatch angle is the angle that the hatch lines make with the positive *X* axis. The angle is positive if measured counterclockwise, refer to Figure 11-24, and negative if measured clockwise. When you draw a hatch pattern, the first hatch line starts from the point defined by X-origin and Y-origin.

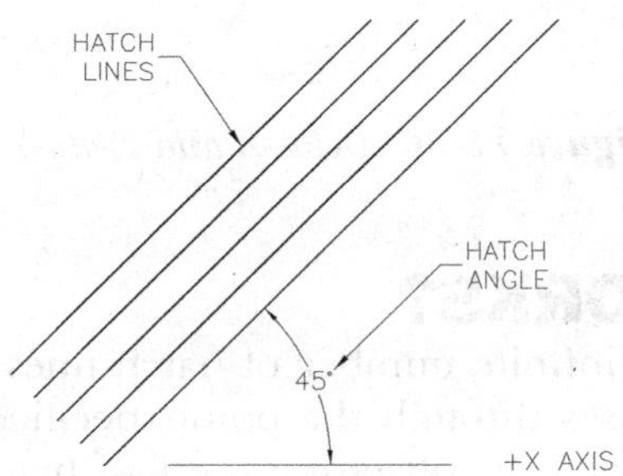

Figure 11-24 *Hatch angle*

The remaining lines are generated by offsetting the first hatch line by a distance specified by delta-X and delta-Y. In Figure 11-25(a), the first hatch line starts from the point with the coordinates X = 0 and Y = 0. In Figure 11-25(b), the first line of hatch starts from a point with the coordinates X = 0 and Y = 0.25.

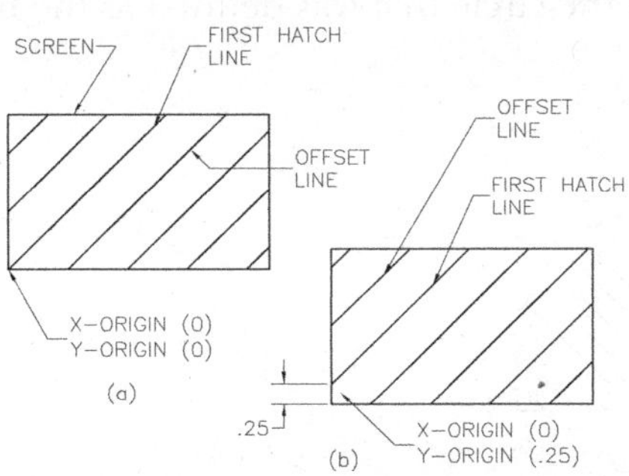

Figure 11-25 *X-origin and Y-origin of hatch lines*

Delta-X and Delta-Y. Delta-X is the displacement of the offset line in the direction in which the hatch lines are generated. For example, if the lines are drawn at a 0° angle and delta-X = 0.5, the offset line will be displaced by a distance delta-X (0.5) along the 0-angle direction. Similarly, if the hatch lines are drawn at a 45° angle, the offset line will be displaced by a distance delta-X (0.5) along a 45° direction, refer to Figure 11-26. Delta-Y is the displacement of the offset lines measured perpendicular to the hatch lines. For example, if delta-Y = 1.0, the space between any two hatch lines will be 1.0, refer to Figure 11-26.

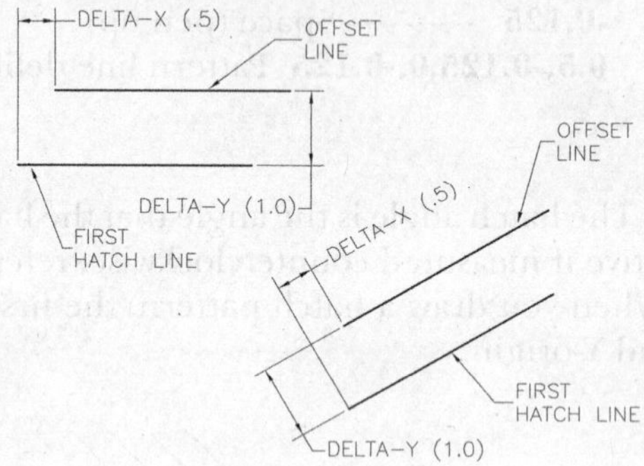

Figure 11-26 Delta-X and Delta-Y of hatch lines

HOW HATCH WORKS?

When you hatch an area, infinite number of hatch lines of infinite length is generated. The first hatch line always passes through the point specified by the X-origin and Y-origin. The remaining lines are generated by offsetting the first hatch line in both directions. The offset distance is determined by delta-X and delta-Y, refer to Figure 11-26. All selected entities that form the boundary of the hatch area are then checked for intersection with these lines. Any hatch lines found within the defined hatch boundaries are turned on, and the hatch lines outside the hatch boundary are turned off, as shown in Figure 11-27. Since the hatch lines are generated by offsetting, the hatch lines in all areas of drawing are automatically aligned relative to the drawing's snap origin. Figure 11-27(a) shows the hatch lines computed by AutoCAD. These lines are not drawn on the screen and are shown here for illustration only. Figure 11-27(b) shows the hatch lines generated in the circle that was defined as the hatch boundary.

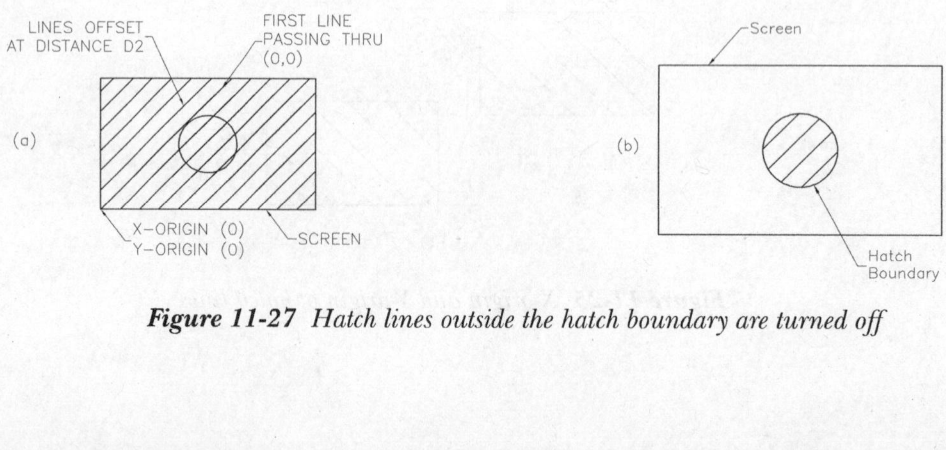

Figure 11-27 Hatch lines outside the hatch boundary are turned off

SIMPLE HATCH PATTERN

It is a good practice to develop the hatch pattern specification before writing a hatch pattern definition. For simple hatch patterns, it may not be that important. However for more complicated hatch patterns, you should know the detailed specifications. Example 5 illustrates the procedure for developing a simple hatch pattern.

Example 5 — *Hatch Pattern*

Write a hatch pattern definition for the hatch pattern shown in Figure 11-28, with the following specifications:

Name of the hatch pattern	=HATCH1
X-Origin	=0
Y-Origin	=0
Distance between hatch lines	=0.5
Displacement of hatch lines	=0
Hatch line pattern	=Continuous

Step 1: Creating the hatch pattern file

This hatch pattern definition can be added to the existing *acad.pat* hatch file. You can use any text editor (like Notepad) to write the file. Load the *acad.pat* file that is located in the *C:\Users\CADCIM\AppData\Roaming\Autodesk\AutoCAD 2021\ R24.0\enu\Support* directory and insert the following two lines at the end of the file.

***HATCH1,Hatch Pattern for Example 5**
45,0,0,0,.5

Where **45** ----------------Hatch angle
0 ------------------X-origin
0 ------------------Y-origin
0 ------------------Displacement of second hatch line
.5 -----------------Distance between hatch lines

The first field of hatch descriptors contains the angle of the hatch lines and the value of this angle in this particular case with respect to the positive *X* axis is 45°. The second and third fields describe the *X* and *Y* coordinates of the first hatch line origin. The first line of the hatch pattern will pass through this point. If the values of the X-origin and Y-origin were 0.5 and 1.0, respectively, then the first line would pass through the point with the *X* coordinate of 0.5 and the *Y* coordinate of 1.0, with respect to the drawing origin 0,0. The remaining lines are generated by offsetting the first line, as shown in Figure 11-28.

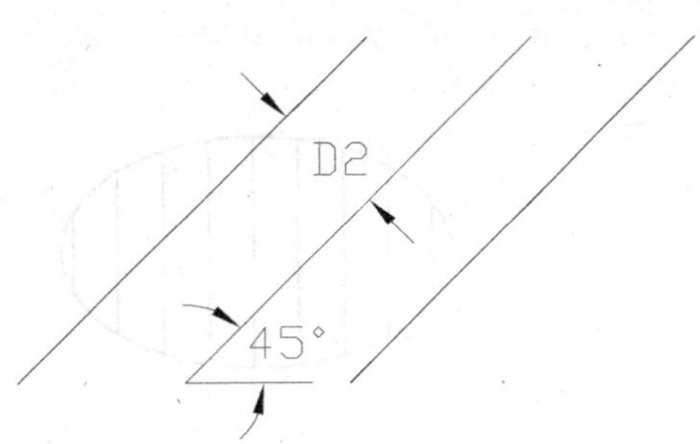

Figure 11-28 *Hatch pattern angle and offset distance*

Step 2: Applying the hatch pattern

Choose the **Hatch** tool from the **Draw** panel; the **Hatch Creation** context tab will get added to the **Ribbon**. Select the **HATCH1** pattern from **Pattern > Hatch Creation** context tab. If needed, change the **Scale** and **Angle** from the **Properties** panel of the **Hatch Creation** tab. Next, hatch a circle to test the hatch pattern.

EFFECT OF ANGLE AND SCALE FACTOR ON HATCH

When you hatch an area, to get the desired hatch spacing, you can alter the angle and displacement of hatch lines you have specified in the hatch pattern definition. You can do this by entering an appropriate value for angle and scale factor in the **HATCH** command.

To understand how the angle and the displacement can be changed, hatch an area with the hatch pattern HATCH1 in Example 5. You will notice that the hatch lines have been generated according to the definition of hatch pattern HATCH1. Notice the effect of hatch angle and scale factor on the hatch. Figure 11-29(a) shows a hatch with a 0° angle and a scale factor of 1.0. If the angle is 0, the hatch will be generated with the same angle as defined in the hatch pattern definition (45° in Example 5). Similarly, if the scale factor is 1.0, the distance between the hatch lines will be the same as defined in the hatch pattern definition. Figure 11-29(b) shows a hatch that is generated when the hatch scale factor is 0.5. If you measure the distance between the successive hatch lines, it will be 0.5 x 0.5 = 0.25. Figures 11-29(c) and (d) show the hatch when the angle is 45° and the scale factors are 1.0 and 0.5, respectively.

Scale and Angle can also be set by entering **-HATCH** at the Command prompt.

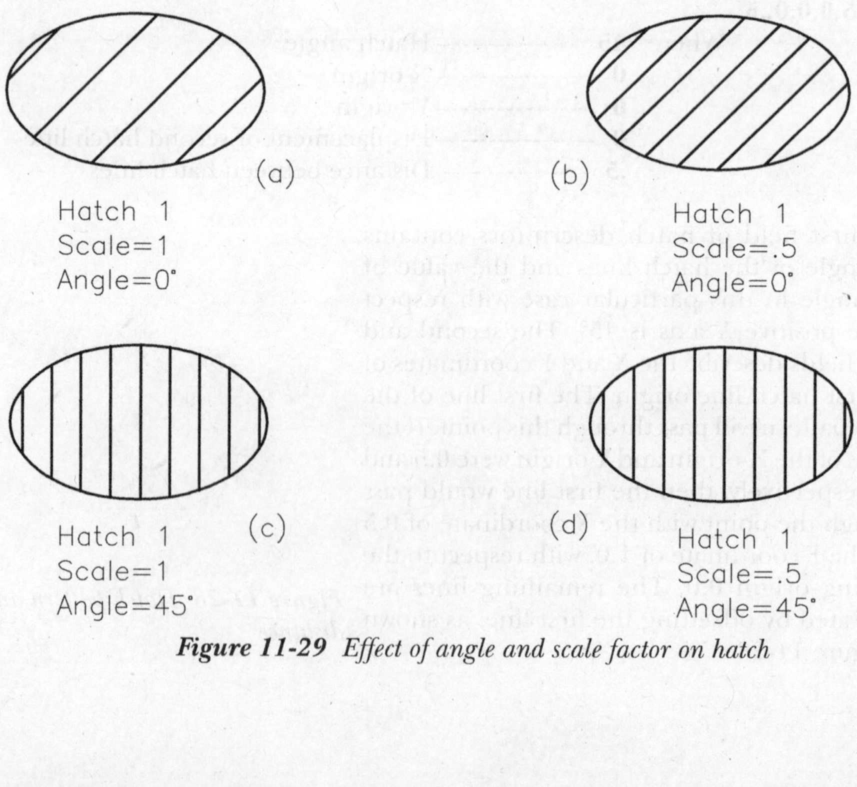

***Figure 11-29** Effect of angle and scale factor on hatch*

HATCH PATTERN WITH DASHES AND DOTS

The lines that you can use in a hatch pattern definition are not restricted to continuous lines. You can define any line pattern to generate a hatch pattern. The lines can be a combination of dashes, dots, and spaces in any configuration. However, the maximum number of dashes you can specify in the line pattern definition of a hatch pattern is six. Example 6 uses a dash-dot linetype to create a hatch pattern.

Example 6 — *Hatch Pattern*

Write a hatch pattern definition for the hatch pattern shown in Figure 11-30, with the following specifications. Define a new path such as *C:\Program Files\Hatch1* and save the hatch pattern in that path.

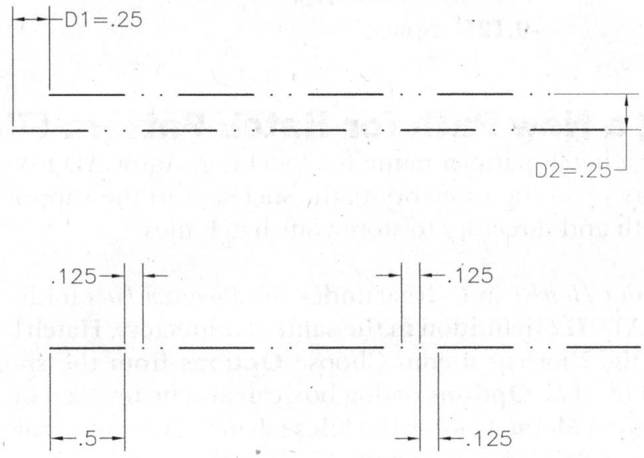

Figure 11-30 *Hatch lines made of dashes and dots*

Name of the hatch pattern =	HATCH2
Hatch angle =	0
X-origin =	0
Y-origin =	0
Displacement of lines (D1) =	0.25
Distance between lines (D2) =	0.25
Length of each dash =	0.5
Space between dashes and dots =	0.125
Space between dots =	0.125

Writing the definition of a hatch pattern

You can use any text editor (Notepad) to edit the *acad.pat* file. The general format of the header line and the hatch descriptors is:

***HATCH NAME, Hatch Description**
Angle, X-Origin, Y-Origin, D1, D2 [,Dash Length.....]

Substitute the values from Example 6 in the corresponding fields of the header line and field descriptor:

*HATCH2,Hatch with dashes and dots

0,0,0,0.25,0.25,0.5,-0.125,0,-0.125,0,-0.125

Where **0** ------------------Angle
0 -------------------X-origin
0 ------------------Y-origin
0.25 --------------Delta-X
0.25 --------------Delta-Y
0.5 ---------------Length of dash
-0.125 -----------Space (pen up)
0 ------------------Dot (pen down)
-0.125 -----------Space (pen up)
0 -------------------Dot
-0.125 Space

Specifying a New Path for Hatch Pattern Files

When you enter a hatch pattern name for hatching, AutoCAD looks for that file name in the **Support** directory or in the directory paths specified in the support file search path. You can specify a new path and directory to store your hatch files.

Create a new folder *Hatch1* in *C* drive under the *Program Files* folder. Save the *acad.pat* file with hatch pattern **HATCH2** definition in the same subdirectory, Hatch1. Right-click in the drawing area to activate the shortcut menu. Choose **Options** from the shortcut menu to display the **Options** dialog box. The **Options** dialog box can also be invoked by choosing the **Options** tool from the **Application Menu**. Choose the **Files** tab in the **Options** dialog box to display the **Search paths, file names and file locations** area. Click on the **+** sign of the **Support File Search Path** to display the different subdirectories of the **Support File Search Path**, as shown in Figure 11-31. Now, choose the **Add** button to display the space to add a new subdirectory. Enter the location of the new subdirectory, **C:\Program Files\Hatch1** or click on the **Browse** button to specify the path. Choose the **Apply** button and then choose **OK** to exit the **Options** dialog box. You have created a subdirectory and specified the search path for the hatch files.

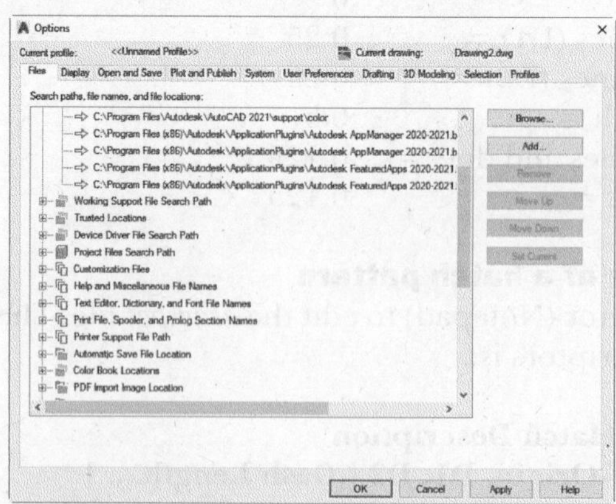

***Figure 11-31** The **Options** dialog box*

Follow the procedure as described in Example 5 to activate the hatch pattern. The hatch thus generated is shown in Figure 11-32. Figure 11-32(a) shows the hatch with a 0° angle and a scale factor of 1.0. Figure 11-32(b) shows the hatch with a 45° angle and a scale factor of 0.5.

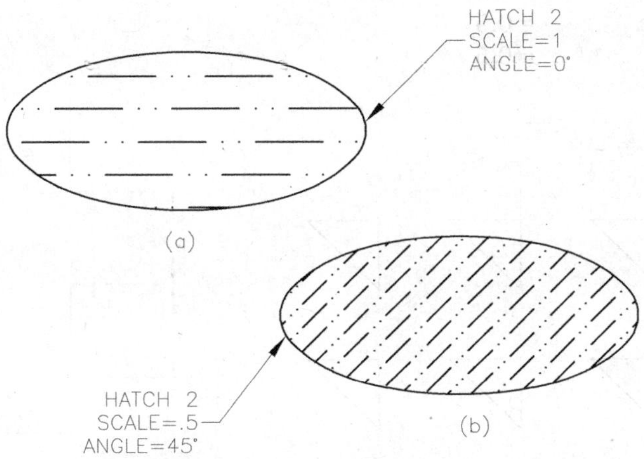

***Figure 11-32** Hatch pattern at different angles and scales*

HATCH WITH MULTIPLE DESCRIPTORS

Some hatch patterns require multiple lines to generate a shape. For example, if you want to create a hatch pattern of a brick wall, you need four hatch descriptors to generate rectangular shape. You can have any number of hatch descriptor lines in a hatch pattern definition. It is up to the user to combine them in any conceivable order. However, there are some shapes you can not generate. A shape that has a nonlinear element, such as an arc, cannot be generated by hatch pattern definition. However, you can simulate an arc by defining short line segments because you can use only straight lines to generate a hatch pattern. Example 7 uses three lines to define a triangular hatch pattern.

Example 7 — *Hatch Pattern*

Write a hatch pattern definition for the hatch pattern shown in Figure 11-33, with the following specifications:

Name of the hatch pattern	=HATCH3
Vertical height of the triangle	=0.5
Horizontal length of the triangle	=0.5
Vertical distance between the triangles	=0.5
Horizontal distance between the triangles	=0.5

Each triangle in this hatch pattern consists of the following three elements: a vertical line, a horizontal line, and a line inclined at 45°.

Step 1: Defining specifications for vertical line

For the vertical line, refer to Figure 11-34, the specifications are:

Hatch angle	=90°
X-origin	=0
Y-origin	=0
Delta-X (D1)	=0
Delta-Y (D2)	=1.0
Dash length	=0.5
Space	=0.5

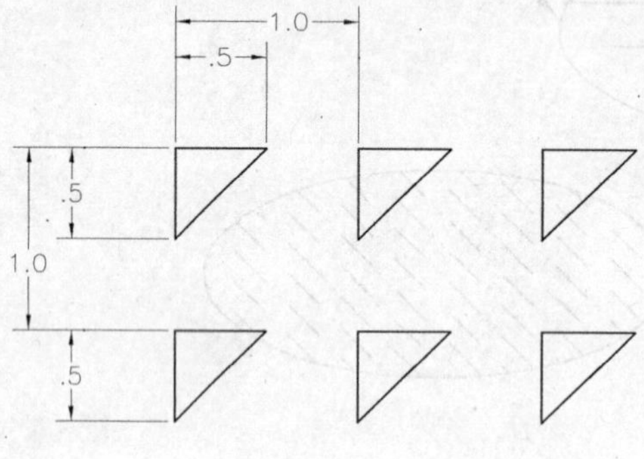

Figure 11-33 Triangle hatch pattern

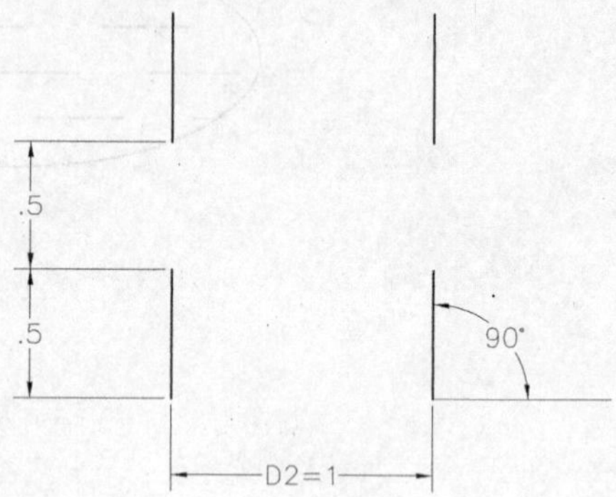

Figure 11-34 Vertical line

Substitute the values from the vertical line specification in various fields of the hatch descriptor to get the following line:

90,0,0,0,1,.5,-.5

Where **90** ------------------Hatch angle
0 ------------------X-origin
0 ------------------Y-origin
0 ------------------Delta-X
1 ------------------Delta-Y
.5 ------------------Dash (pen down)
-.5 ------------------Space (pen up)

Step 2: Defining specifications of horizontal line

For the horizontal line, refer to Figure 11-35, the specifications are:

Hatch angle	=0°
X-origin	=0
Y-origin	=0.5
Delta-X (D1)	=0
Delta-Y (D2)	=1.0
Dash length	=0.5
Space	=0.5

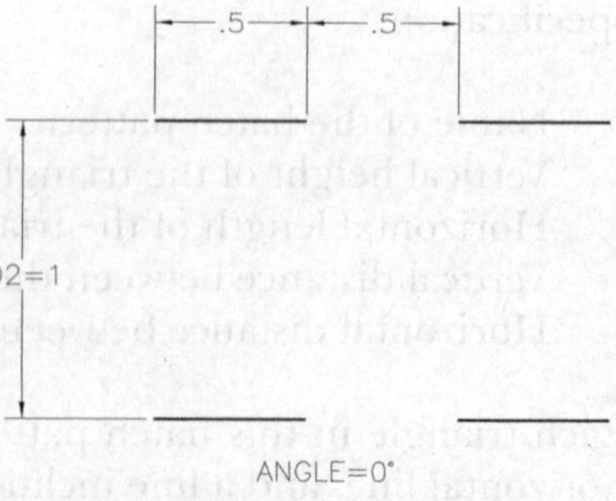

Figure 11-35 Horizontal line

The only difference between the vertical line and the horizontal line is the angle. For the horizontal line, the angle is 0°, whereas for the vertical line, the angle is 90°. Substitute the values from the vertical line specification to obtain the following line:

0,0,0.5,0,1,.5,-.5

Where **0** -----------------Hatch angle
0 -----------------X-origin
0.5 ---------------Y-origin
0 -----------------Delta-X
1 -----------------Delta-Y
.5 ----------------Dash (pen down)
-.5 ---------------Space (pen up)

Step 3: Defining specifications of the inclined line

This line is at an angle; therefore, you need to calculate the distances delta-X (D1) and delta-Y (D2), the length of the dashed line, and the length of the blank space. Figure 11-36 shows the calculations to find these values.

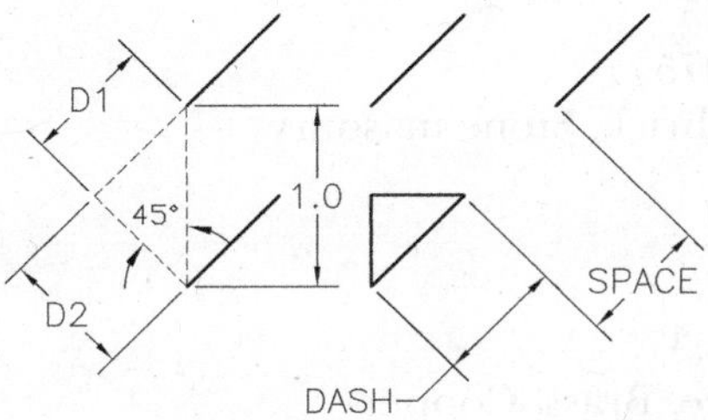

D1 = 1.0 x COS 45   D2 = 1.0 x SIN 45
D1 = .7071   D2 = .7071

DASH = SQRT(0.5^2 +0.5^2)
= .7071
SPACE = DASH = .7071

Figure 11-36 Line inclined at 45°

Hatch angle	=45°
X-Origin	=0
Y-Origin	=0
Delta-X (D1)	=0.7071
Delta-Y (D2)	=0.7071
Dash length	=0.7071
Space	=0.7071

After substituting the values in the general format of the hatch descriptor, you will obtain the following line:

45,0,0,.7071,.7071,.7071,-.7071

Where **45** ---------------Hatch angle
0 -----------------X-origin

0 ------------------Y-origin
.7071 -------------Delta-X
.7071 -------------Delta-Y
.7071 ------------Dash (pen down)
-.7071 -----------Space (pen up)

Step 4: Loading the hatch pattern

Now, you can combine three lines and insert them at the end of the *acad.pat* file or you can enter the values in a separate hatch file and save it. You can also use any text editor and insert the line definition.

The following file is a partial listing of the *acad.pat* file, after adding the hatch pattern definitions from Examples 5, 6, and 7.

```
*SOLID, Solid fill
45, 0,0, 0,.125
*Angle,Angle steel
0, 0,0, 0,.275, .2,-.075
90, 0,0, 0,.275, .2,-.075
*Ansi31,ANSI Iron, Brick, Stone masonry
45, 0,0, 0,.125
*Ansi32,ANSI Steel
45, 0,0, 0,.375
45, .176776695,0, 0,.375
*Ansi33,ANSI Bronze, Brass, Copper
45, 0,0, 0,.25
45, .176776695,0, 0,.25, .125,-.0625
*Ansi34,ANSI Plastic, Rubber
45, 0,0, 0,.75
45, .176776695,0, 0,.75
45, .353553391,0, 0,.75
45, .530330086,0, 0,.75
*Ansi35,ANSI Fire brick, Refractory material
45, 0,0, 0,.25
45, .176776695,0, 0,.25, .3125,-.0625,0,-.0625
*Ansi36,ANSI Marble, Slate, Glass
45, 0,0, .21875,.125, .3125,-.0625,0,-.0625

*Swamp,Swampy area
0, 0,0, .5,.866025403, .125,-.875
90, .0625,0, .866025403,.5, .0625,-1.669550806
90, .078125,0, .866025403,.5, .05,-1.682050806
90, .046875,0, .66025403,.5, .05,-1.682050806
|
|
0, 0,0, .125,.125, .125,-.125
90, .125,0, .125,.125, .125,-.125
*HATCH1,Hatch at 45 Degree Angle
```

```
45,0,0,0,.5
*HATCH2,Hatch with Dashes & Dots:
0,0,0,.25,.25,0.5,-.125,0,-.125,0,-.125
*HATCH3,Triangle Hatch:
90,0,0,0,1,.5,-.5
0,0,0.5,0,1,.5,-.5
45,0,0,.7071,.7071,.7071,-.7071
```

Load the hatch pattern as described in Example 5 and test the hatch. Figure 11-37 shows the hatch pattern that will be generated by this hatch pattern (HATCH3). In Figure 11-37(a) the hatch pattern is at a 0° angle and the scale factor is 0.5. In Figure 11-37(b) the hatch pattern is at a -45° angle and the scale factor is 0.5.

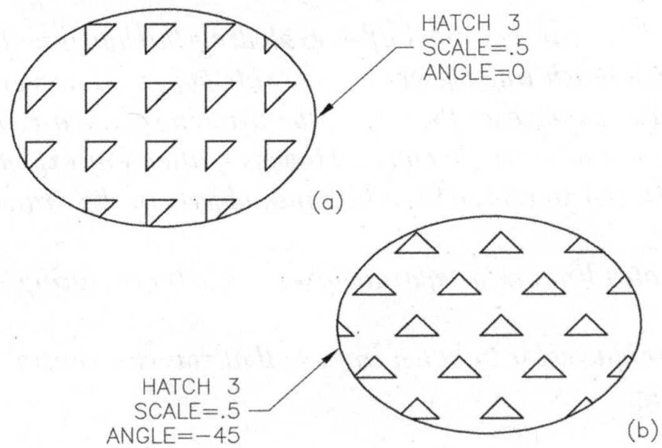

Figure 11-37 Hatch generated by HATCH3 pattern

SAVING HATCH PATTERNS IN A SEPARATE FILE

When you load a hatch pattern, AutoCAD looks for that definition in the *acad.pat* or *acadiso.pat* file. This is the reason the hatch pattern definitions must be in that file. However, you can add the new pattern definition to a different file and then copy that file to *acad.pat* or *acadiso.pat*. Be sure to make a copy of the original *acad.pat* or *acadiso.pat* file so that you can copy that file back when needed. Assume the name of the file that contains your custom hatch pattern definitions is *customh.pat*.

1. Copy *acad.pat* or *acadiso.pat* file to *acadorg.pat*
2. Copy *customh.pat* to *acad.pat* or *acadiso.pat*

If you want to use the original hatch pattern file, copy the *acadorg.pat* file to *acad.pat* or *acadiso.pat*.

CUSTOM HATCH PATTERN FILE

As mentioned earlier, you can add the new hatch pattern definitions to the *acad.pat* or *acadiso.pat* file. There is no limit to the number of hatch pattern definitions you can add to this file. However, if you have only one hatch pattern definition, you can define a separate file. It has the following requirements:

1. The name of the file has to be the same as the hatch pattern name.
2. The file can contain only one hatch pattern definition.
3. The hatch pattern name and the hatch file name should be unique.
4. If you use the hatch patterns saved on the removable drive quite often to hatch the drawings, you can add removable drive to the AutoCAD search path using the **Options** dialog box. AutoCAD will automatically search the file on the removable drive and will display it in the **Hatch Creation** tab of the **Ribbon**.

```
*HATCH3,Triangle Hatch:
90,0,0,0,1,.5,-.5
0,0,0.5,0,1,.5,-.5
45,0,0,.7071,.7071,.7071,-.7071
```

Note

*1. The hatch lines can be edited after exploding the hatch with the **EXPLODE** command. After exploding, each hatch line becomes a separate object. However, it is recommended not to explode a hatch because it increases the size of the drawing database. For example, if a hatch consists of 100 lines, save it as a single object. However, after you explode the hatch, every line becomes a separate object and you have 99 additional objects in the drawing.*

2. Keep the hatch lines in a separate layer to facilitate editing of the hatch lines.

3. Assign a unique color to hatch lines so that you can control the width of the hatch lines at the time of plotting.

Tip

*1. The file or the subdirectory in which hatch patterns have been saved must be defined in the **Support File Search Path** in the **Files** tab of the **Options** dialog box.*

*2. The hatch patterns that you create automatically get added to AutoCAD's slide library as an integral part of AutoCAD and are displayed in the **Preview Area** in the **Hatch Pattern Palette** dialog box under the **Hatch Creation** tab of the **Ribbon**. Hence, there is no need to create a slide library.*

Self-Evaluation Test

Answer the following questions and then compare them to those given at the end of this chapter:

1. The __________ command can be used to change the linetype scale factor.

2. The linetype description should not be more than ________ characters long.

3. A positive number denotes a pen ________ segment.

4. __________ segment length generates a dot.

5. A negative number denotes a pen __________ segment.

6. The __________ option of the **LINETYPE** command is used to generate a new linetype.

7. The description in the case of header line is __________.

8. The standard linetypes are stored in the __________ file.

9. The __________ determines the current linetype scaling.

10. The header line consists of an asterisk, the pattern name, and the __________.

11. The *acad.pat* or *acadiso.pat* file contains __________ number of hatch pattern definitions.

12. The standard hatch patterns are stored in the __________ file.

13. The first hatch line passes through a point whose coordinates are specified by __________ and __________.

Review Questions

Answer the following questions:

1. The __________ command can be used to create a new linetype.

2. The __________ command can be used to load a linetype.

3. In AutoCAD, the linetypes are saved in the __________ file.

4. AutoCAD supports only __________ alignment field specification.

5. A line pattern definition always starts with __________.

6. A header line definition always starts with __________.

7. The perpendicular distance between the hatch lines in a hatch pattern definition is specified by __________.

8. The displacement of the second hatch line in a hatch pattern definition is specified by __________.

9. The maximum number of dash lengths that can be specified in the line pattern definition of a hatch pattern is __________.

10. The hatch lines in different areas of the drawing will automatically __________ because the hatch lines are generated by offsetting.

11. The hatch angle as defined in the hatch pattern definition can be changed further when you use the __________ command.

12. When you load a hatch pattern, AutoCAD looks for that hatch pattern in the __________ file.

13. The hatch lines can be edited after __________ the hatch by using the __________ command.

Exercise 1 — Linetype

Using the **LINETYPE** command, create a new linetype "DASH3DASH" with the following specifications:

Length of the first dash 0.75
Blank space 0.125
Dash length 0.25
Blank space 0.125
Dash length 0.25
Blank space 0.125
Dash length 0.25
Blank space 0.125

Exercise 2 — Linetype

Use a text editor to create a new file, *newlt2.lin*, and a new linetype, DASH2DASH, with the following specifications:

Length of the first dash 0.5
Blank space 0.1
Dash length 0.2
Blank space 0.1
Dash length 0.2
Blank space 0.1

Exercise 3 — String Complex Linetype

a. Write the definition of a string complex linetype (hot water line), as shown in Figure 11-38(a). To determine the length of the HW text string, you should first draw the text (HW) using any text command and then measure its length.

b. Write the definition of a string complex linetype (gas line), as shown in Figure 11-38(b). Determine the length of the text string as mentioned in part a.

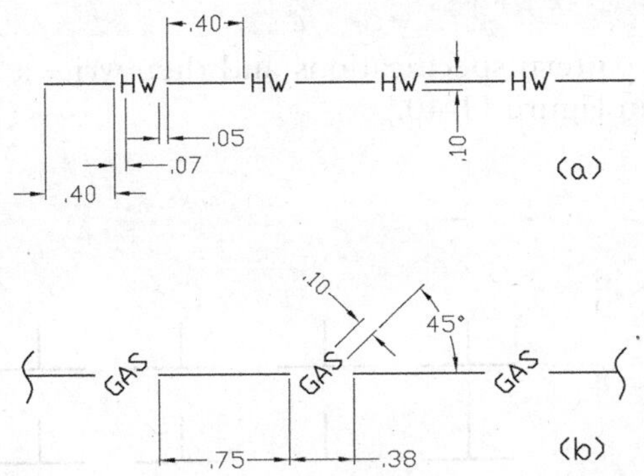

Figure 11-38 Specifications for a string complex linetype

Exercise 4 — Hatch Pattern

Determine the hatch pattern specifications and then write a hatch pattern definition for the hatch pattern shown in Figure 11-39.

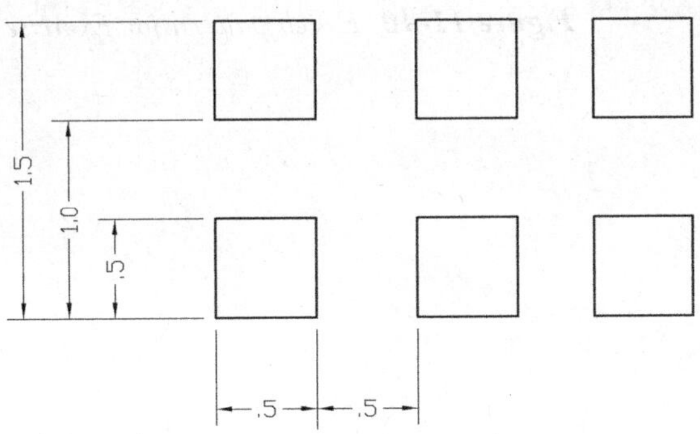

Figure 11-39 Drawing for Exercise 4

Exercise 5 — *Hatch Pattern*

Determine the hatch pattern specifications and then write a hatch pattern definition for the hatch pattern shown in Figure 11-40.

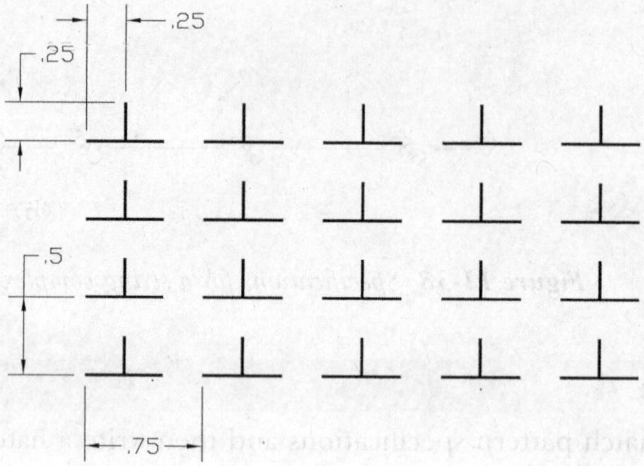

***Figure 11-40** Hatch pattern for Exercise 5*

Answers to Self-Evaluation Test

1. LTSCALE, **2.** 47, **3.** down, **4.** Zero, **5.** up, **6. Create**, **7.** optional, **8.** *acad.lin* or *acadiso.lin*, **9. CELTSCALE**, **10.** Pattern Description, **11.** 72, **12.** *acad.pat* or *acadiso.pat*, **13.** X-origin, Y-origin

Chapter 12

Customizing the acad.pgp File

Learning Objectives

After completing this chapter, you will be able to:

- *Customize the acad.pgp file*
- *Edit different sections of the acad.pgp file*
- *Abbreviate commands by defining command aliases*
- *Use the REINIT command to reinitialize the PGP file*

Key Terms

- *acad.pgp file*
- *Command Name*
- *OS Command Name*
- *Bit Flag*
- *Command Aliases*

WHAT IS THE acad.pgp FILE?

AutoCAD software comes with the program parameters file *acad.pgp*, which defines aliases for the operating system commands and some of the AutoCAD commands. When you install AutoCAD on a computer that runs on Windows 2000 or later versions, this file is automatically copied on to the *C:\Users\CADCIM\AppData\Roaming\Autodesk\AutoCAD 2021\R21.0\enu\Support* subdirectory of the hard drive. The *acad.pgp* file lets you access the commands of operating system from the drawing editor. For example, if you want to delete a file, all you need to do is enter **DEL** at the Command prompt (Command: **DEL**), and AutoCAD will prompt you to enter the name of the file that you want to delete.

The file also contains command aliases of some frequently used AutoCAD commands. For example, the command alias for the **LINE** command is L. This is the reason if you enter **L** at the Command prompt **(Command: L)**, AutoCAD will treat it as the **LINE** command. The *acad.pgp* file also contains comment lines that give you some information about different sections of the file. The *acad.pgp* file can be opened by choosing the **Edit Aliases** tool from the **Edit Aliases** drop-down of **Customization** panel in the **Manage** tab. You can also open the *acad.pgp* file by choosing the **Edit Program Parameters (acad.pgp)** tool from **Tools > Customize** in the menu bar. The following file shows the content of the standard *acad.pgp* file. Some of the lines have been deleted to make the file shorter.

```
;
;
; Program Parameters File For AutoCAD 2021
; External Command and Command Alias Definitions

; Copyright 2020 by Autodesk, Inc.  All Rights Reserved.
;
; Use of this software is subject to the terms of the Autodesk license
; agreement provided at the time of installation or download, or which
; otherwise accompanies this software in either electronic or hard copy form.

; Each time you open a new or existing drawing, AutoCAD searches
; the support path and reads the first acad.pgp file that it finds.

; -- External Commands --
; While AutoCAD is running, you can invoke other programs or utilities
; such Windows system commands, utilities, and applications.
; You define external commands by specifying a command name to be used
; from the AutoCAD command prompt and an executable command string
; that is passed to the operating system.

; -- Command Aliases --
; The Command Aliases section of this file provides default settings for
; AutoCAD command shortcuts.  Note: It is not recommended that you directly
; modify this section of the PGP file., as any changes you make to this section of the
; file will not migrate successfully if you upgrade your AutoCAD to a
```

```
; newer version. Instead, make changes to the new
; User Defined Command Aliases
; section towards the end of this file.

; -- User Defined Command Aliases --
; You can abbreviate frequently used AutoCAD commands by defining
; aliases for them in the User Defined Command Aliases section of acad.pgp.
; You can create a command alias for any AutoCAD command,
; device driver command, or external command.

; Recommendation: back up this file before editing it. To ensure that
; any changes you make to PGP settings can successfully be migrated
; when you upgrade to the next version of AutoCAD, it is suggested that
; you make any changes to the default settings in the User Defined Command
; Aliases section at the end of this file.

; External command format:
; <Command name>,[<Shell request>],<Bit flag>,[*]<Prompt>,

; The bits of the bit flag have the following meanings:
; Bit 1: if set, don't wait for the application to finish
; Bit 2: if set, run the application minimized
; Bit 4: if set, run the application "hidden"
; Bit 8: if set, put the argument string in quotes
;
; Fill the "bit flag" field with the sum of the desired bits.
; Bits 2 and 4 are mutually exclusive; if both are specified, only
; the 2 bit is used. The most useful values are likely to be 0
; (start the application and wait for it to finish), 1 (start the
; application and don't wait), 3 (minimize and don't wait), and 5
; (hide and don't wait). Values of 2 and 4 should normally be avoided,
; as they make AutoCAD unavailable until the application has completed.
;
; Bit 8 allows commands like DEL to work properly with filenames that
; have spaces such as "long filename.dwg". Note that this will interfere
; with passing space delimited lists of file names to these same commands.
; If you prefer multiplefile support to using long file names, turn off
; the "8" bit in those commands.

; Examples of external commands for command windows

DEL,      DEL,      8,File to delete: ,
DIR,      DIR,      8,File specification: ,
SH,       ,         1,*OS Command: ,
SHELL,    ,         1,*OS Command: ,
START,    START,    1,*Application to start: ,
TYPE,     TYPE,     8,File to list: ,
```

External commands area

```
; Examples of external commands for Windows
; See also the (STARTAPP) AutoLISP function for an alternative method.

EXPLORER,  START EXPLORER, 1,,
NOTEPAD,          START NOTEPAD,  1,*File to edit: ,
PBRUSH,           START PBRUSH,   1,,

; Command alias format:
;   <Alias>,*<Full command name>

;  The following are guidelines for creating new command aliases.
;  1. An alias should reduce a command by at least two characters.
;     Commands with a control key equivalent, status bar button,
;     or function key do not require a command alias.
;     Examples: Control N, O, P, and S for New, Open, Print, Save.
;  2. Try the first character of the command, then try the first two,
;     then the first three.
;  3. Once an alias is defined, add suffixes for related aliases:
;     Examples: R for Redraw, RA for Redrawall, L for Line, LT for
;     Linetype.
;  4. Use a hyphen to differentiate between command line and dialog
;     box commands.
;     Example: B for Block, -B for -Block.
;
; Exceptions to the rules include AA for Area, T for Mtext, X for Explode.

;  -- Sample aliases for AutoCAD commands --
;  These examples include most frequently used commands.  NOTE: It is recommended
;  that you not make any changes to this section of the PGP file to ensure the
;  proper migration of your customizations when you upgrade to the next version of
;  AutoCAD.  The aliases listed in this section are repeated in the User Custom
;  Settings section at the end of this file, which can safely be edited while
;  ensuring your changes will successfully migrate.

3A,             *3DARRAY
3DMIRROR,       *MIRROR3D
3DNavigate,     *3DWALK
3DO,            *3DORBIT
3DP,            *3DPRINT
3DPLOT,         *3DPRINT
3DW,            *3DWALK
3F,             *3DFACE
3M,             *3DMOVE
3P,             *3DPOLY
3R,             *3DROTATE
3S,             *3DSCALE
A,              *ARC
AC,             *BACTION
```

External commands

```
ADC,                   *ADCENTER
AECTOACAD,             *-ExportToAutoCAD
AA,                    *AREA
AL,                    *ALIGN
3AL,                   *3DALIGN
AP,                    *APPLOAD
APLAY,                 *ALLPLAY
AR,                    *ARRAY
-AR,                   *-ARRAY
ARR,                   *ACTRECORD
ARM,                   *ACTUSERMESSAGE
-ARM,                  *-ACTUSERMESSAGE
ARU,                   *ACTUSERINPUT
ARS,                   *ACTSTOP
-ARS,                  *-ACTSTOP
ATI,                   *ATTIPEDIT
ATT,                   *ATTDEF
-ATT,                  *-ATTDEF
ATE,                   *ATTEDIT
-ATE,                  *-ATTEDIT
ATTE,                  *-ATTEDIT
B,                     *BLOCK
|
|
|
|
HE,                    *HATCHEDIT
HB,                    *HATCHTOBACK
HI,                    *HIDE
I,                     *INSERT
-I,                    *-INSERT
IAD,                   *IMAGEADJUST
IAT,                   *IMAGEATTACH
ICL,                   *IMAGECLIP
IM,                    *IMAGE
-IM,                   *-IMAGE
IMP,                   *IMPORT
IN,                    *INTERSECT
INSERTCONTROLPOINT,    *CVADD
INF,                   *INTERFERE
IO,                    *INSERTOBJ
ISOLATE,               *ISOLATEOBJECTS
QVD,                   *QVDRAWING
QVDC,                  *QVDRAWINGCLOSE
QVL,                   *QVLAYOUT
QVLC,                  *QVLAYOUTCLOSE
J,                     *JOIN
L,                     *LINE
```

```
LA,                       *LAYER
-LA,                      *-LAYER
LAS,                      *LAYERSTATE
LE,                       *QLEADER
LEN,                      *LENGTHEN
LESS,                     *MESHSMOOTHLESS
LI,                       *LIST
LINEWEIGHT,               *LWEIGHT
LMAN,                     *LAYERSTATE
LO,                       *-LAYOUT
LS,                       *LIST
LT,                       *LINETYPE
-LT,                      *-LINETYPE
LTYPE,                    *LINETYPE
-LTYPE,                   *-LINETYPE
LTS,                      *LTSCALE
LW,                       *LWEIGHT
M,                        *MOVE
MA,                       *MATCHPROP
MAT,                      *MATERIALS
ME,                       *MEASURE
MEA,                      *MEASUREGEOM
MI,                       *MIRROR
ML,                       *MLINE
MLA,                      *MLEADERALIGN
MLC,                      *MLEADERCOLLECT
MLD,                      *MLEADER
|
|
|
R,                          *REDRAW
RA,                         *REDRAWALL
RC,                         *RENDERCROP
RE,                         *REGEN
REA,                        *REGENALL
REBUILD,                    *CVREBUILD
REC,                        *RECTANG
REFINE,                     *MESHREFINE
REG,                        *REGION
REMOVECONTROLPOINT,         *CVREMOVE
REN,                        *RENAME
-REN,                       *-RENAME
REV,                        *REVOLVE
RO,                         *ROTATE
|
|
|
; The following are alternative aliases and aliases as supplied
```

```
; in AutoCAD Release 13.
AV,                      *DSVIEWER
CP,                      *COPY
DIMALI,                  *DIMALIGNED
DIMANG,                  *DIMANGULAR
DIMBASE,                 *DIMBASELINE
DIMCONT,                 *DIMCONTINUE
DIMDIA,                  *DIMDIAMETER
DIMED,                   *DIMEDIT
DIMTED,                  *DIMTEDIT
DIMLIN,                  *DIMLINEAR
DIMORD,                  *DIMORDINATE
DIMRAD,                  *DIMRADIUS
DIMSTY,                  *DIMSTYLE
DIMOVER,                 *DIMOVERRIDE
LEAD,                    *LEADER
TM,                      *TILEMODE

; Aliases for Hyperlink/URL Release 14 compatibility
SAVEURL,                 *SAVE
OPENURL,                 *OPEN
INSERTURL,               *INSERT

; Aliases for commands discontinued in AutoCAD 2000:
AAD,                     *DBCONNECT
AEX,                     *DBCONNECT
ALI,                     *DBCONNECT
ASQ,                     *DBCONNECT
ARO,                     *DBCONNECT
ASE,                     *DBCONNECT
DDATTDEF,                *ATTDEF
DDATTEXT,                *ATTEXT
DDCHPROP,                *PROPERTIES
DDCOLOR,                 *COLOR
DDLMODES,                *LAYER
DDLTYPE,                 *LINETYPE
DDMODIFY,                *PROPERTIES
DDOSNAP,                 *OSNAP
DDUCS,                   *UCS

; Aliases for commands discontinued in AutoCAD 2004:
ACADBLOCKDIALOG,         *BLOCK
ACADWBLOCKDIALOG,        *WBLOCK
ADCENTER,                *ADCENTER
BMAKE,                   *BLOCK
BMOD,                    *BLOCK
BPOLY,                   *BOUNDARY
|
```

```
|
|
PAINTER,              *MATCHPROP
PREFERENCES,          *OPTIONS
RECTANGLE,            *RECTANG
SHADE,                *SHADEMODE
VIEWPORTS,            *VPORTS
|
|
|
; Aliases for commands discontinued in AutoCAD 2007:
RMAT,                 *MATBROWSEROPEN
FOG,                  *RENDERENVIRONMENT
FINISH,               *MATERIALS
SETUV,                *MATERIALMAP
SHOWMAT,              *LIST
RFILEOPT,             *RENDERPRESETS
RENDSCR,              *RENDERWIN

; Aliases for sysvars discontinued in AutoCAD 2013:
RASTERPREVIEW,        *THUMBSAVE
AUTOCOMPLETE,         *-INPUTSEARCHOPTIONS
AUTOCOMPLETEMODE,     *-INPUTSEARCHOPTIONS
AUTOCOMPLETEDELAY,    *INPUTSEARCHDELAY

; Aliases for commands discontinued in AutoCAD 2014:
3DCONFIG,        *GRAPHICSCONFIG
-3DCONFIG,       *-GRAPHICSCONFIG


;  -- User Defined Command Aliases --
;  Make any changes or additions to the default AutoCAD command aliases in
;  this section to ensure successful migration of these settings when you
;  upgrade to the next version of AutoCAD.  If a command alias appears more
;  than once in this file, items in the User Defined Command Alias take
;  precedence over duplicates that appear earlier in the file.
;  **********----------**********  ; No xlate ; DO NOT REMOVE
```

SECTIONS OF THE acad.pgp FILE

The contents of the AutoCAD program parameters file (*acad.pgp*) can be categorized into three sections based on the information that is defined in the *acad.pgp* file. They do not appear in any definite order in the file, and have no section headings. For example, the comment lines can be entered anywhere in the file and the same is true with external commands and AutoCAD command aliases. The *acad.pgp* file can be divided into three sections: comments, external commands, and command aliases.

Comments

The comments of *acad.pgp* file can contain any number of comment lines and can occur anywhere in the file. Every comment line must start with a semicolon (;) (This is a comment line). Any line that is preceded by a semicolon is ignored by AutoCAD. You should use the comment line to give some relevant information about the file that will help other AutoCAD users to understand, edit, or update the file.

External Command

In the external command section, you can define any valid external command that is supported by your system. The information must be entered in the following format:

<Command name>, [OS Command name],<Bit flag>, [*]<Command prompt>,

Command Name. This is the name you want to use to activate the external command from the AutoCAD drawing editor. For example, you can use **GOWORD** as a command name to load the Word program (Command: **GOWORD**). The command name must not be an AutoCAD command name or an AutoCAD system variable name. If the name is an AutoCAD command name, the command name in the **PGP** file will be ignored. Also, if the name is an AutoCAD system variable name, the system variable will be ignored. You should use the command names that reflect the expected result of the external commands. (For example, **HELLO** is not a good command name for a directory file.) The command names can be in uppercase or lowercase.

OS Command Name. The OS Command name is the name of a valid system command that is supported by an operating system. For example, in DOS, the command to delete files is DEL and therefore, the OS Command name used in the *acad.pgp* file must be DEL. The following is a list of the type of commands that can be used in the PGP file:

OS Commands (DEL, DIR, TYPE, COPY, RENAME, etc.)
Commands for starting a word processor, or a text editor (WORD, SHELL, etc.)
Name of the user-defined programs and batch files

Bit Flag. This field must contain a number, preferably 8 or 1. The following are the bit flag values and their meaning:

Bit flag set to	Meaning
0	Starts the application and waits for it to finish
1	Does not wait for the application to finish
2	Runs the application in minimized mode
4	Runs the application hidden
8	Puts the argument string in quotes

Command Prompt. The Command prompt field of the command line contains the prompt you want to display on the screen. It is an optional field that must be replaced by a comma if there is no prompt. If the operating system (OS) command that you want to use contains spaces, the prompt must be preceded by an asterisk (*). For example, the DOS command **EDIT NEW.PGP** contains a space between EDIT and NEW; therefore, the prompt used in this command line must be preceded by an asterisk. The command can be terminated by pressing ENTER. If the OS command consists of a single word (DIR, DEL, TYPE), the preceding asterisk must be omitted. In this case, you can terminate the command by pressing the SPACEBAR or the ENTER key.

Command Aliases

It is time-consuming to enter AutoCAD commands at the keyboard because it requires typing the complete command name before pressing ENTER. AutoCAD provides a facility that can be used to abbreviate the commands by defining aliases for the commands. This is made possible by the AutoCAD program parameters file (*acad.pgp* file). Each command alias line consists of two fields **(L, *LINE)**. The first field **(L)** defines the alias of the command; the second field **(*LINE)** consists of the AutoCAD command. The command must be preceded by an asterisk for AutoCAD to recognize the command line as a command alias. The two fields must be separated by a comma. The blank lines and the spaces between the two fields are ignored. In addition to AutoCAD commands, you can also use aliases for AutoLISP command names, provided the programs that contain the definition of these commands are loaded.

REINITIALIZING THE acad.pgp FILE

When you make any changes in the *acad.pgp* file, there are two ways to reinitialize the *acad.pgp* file. One is to quit AutoCAD and then restart the AutoCAD program. When you start AutoCAD, the *acad.pgp* file is automatically loaded. You can also reinitialize the *acad.pgp* file by using the **REINIT** command. The **REINIT** command lets you reinitialize the I/O ports, digitizer, and AutoCAD program parameters file, *acad.pgp*. When you enter the **REINIT** command, AutoCAD will display the **Re-initialization** dialog box, refer to Figure 12-1. To reinitialize the *acad.pgp* file, select the corresponding check box, and then choose **OK**. AutoCAD will reinitialize the program parameters file (*acad.pgp*), and then you can use the command aliases defined in the file.

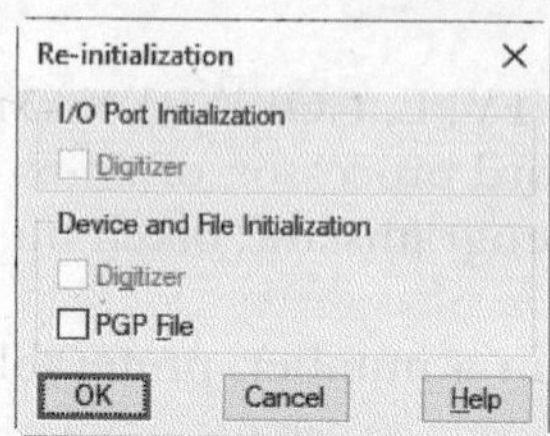

*Figure 12-1 The **Re-initialization** dialog box*

Tip

Copy and save the original acad.pgp file at some other location, so that after you have made changes in the acad.pgp file and used it, you could restore the default settings by copying and pasting the original acad.pgp file. This lets other users use the original, unedited file.

Example 1 — *Adding New Command Aliases*

Add the following external commands and AutoCAD command aliases to the AutoCAD program parameters file (*acad.pgp*).

External Commands

Abbreviation	Command Description
GOWORD	This command loads the word processor (Winword) program from *C:\Program Files\Winword*
RN	This command executes the rename command of DOS.
COP	This command executes the copy command of DOS.

Command Aliases Section

Abbreviation	Command	Abbreviation	Command
EL	Ellipse	T	Trim
CO	Copy	CH	Chamfer
O	Offset	ST	Stretch
S	Scale	MI	Mirror

The *acad.pgp* file is an ASCII text file. To edit this file, choose the **Edit Aliases** tool from the **Customization** panel in the **Manage** tab. You can also use text editor like notepad to edit the *acad.pgp* file. The following is a partial listing of the *acad.pgp* file after the insertion of the lines for the command aliases of Example 1. **The line numbers on the right are not a part of the file; they are given here for reference only.** The lines that have been added to the file are highlighted in bold face.

```
1  DEL,DEL,            8,File to delete: ,
2  DIR,DIR,            8,File specification ,
3  EDIT, START EDIT,   8,File to edit: ,
4  SH,                 1,*OS Command: ,
5  SHELL,              1,*OS Command: ,
6  START,START,        1,Application to start: ,
7  TYPE,TYPE,          8,File to list: ,
8
9  GOWORD, START WINWORD,1,,
10 RN, RENAME,8,File to rename:,
11 COP,COPY,8,File to copy:,
12 DIMLIN        *DIMLINEAR
13 DIMORD,       *DIMORDINATE
14 DIMRAD,       *DIMRADIUS
15 DIMSTY,       *DIMSTYLE
16 DIMOVER,      *DIMOVERRIDE
17 LEAD,         *LEADER
18 TM,           *TILEMODE
19 EL,           *ELLIPSE
20 CO,           *COPY
21 O,            *OFFSET
22 S,            *SCALE
23 MI,           *MIRROR
24 ST,           *STRETCH
```

Explanation

Line 9

GOWORD, START WINWORD,1,,

In line 9, **GOWORD** loads the word processor program **(WINWORD)**. The **winword.exe** program is located in the winword directory under Program Files.

Lines 10 and 11

RN, RENAME,8,File to rename:,

COP,COPY,8,File to copy:,

Line 10 defines the alias for the DOS command **RENAME**, and the next line defines the alias for the DOS command **COPY**. The **8** is a bit flag, and the Command prompt **File to rename and File to copy** is automatically displayed to let you know the format and the type of information that is expected.

Lines 19 and 20

EL, *ELLIPSE

CO, *COPY

Line 19 defines the alias (**EL**) for the **ELLIPSE** command, and the next line defines the alias (**CO**) for the **COPY** command. The commands must be preceded by an asterisk. You can put any number of spaces between the alias abbreviation and the command.

To reinitialize these commands, use the **REINIT** command or quit and restart AutoCAD.

Note

*If a command alias definition duplicates an existing one then the one that is lower down in the file is given preference and is allowed to work. For example, in a standard file, if you add S, *SCALE to the end of the file then your definition works and the one higher up in the file is ignored.*

Self-Evaluation Test

Answer the following questions and then compare them to those given at the end of this chapter:

1. One way of reinitializing the *acad.pgp* file is to __________ AutoCAD and then __________ it.

2. The command used to reinitialize the *acad.pgp* file is __________ .

3. In the command alias section, the AutoCAD command must be preceded by an __________ symbol.

4. Every comment line must start with a __________ .

5. The command alias and the AutoCAD command must be separated by a __________.

Review Questions

Answer the following questions.

1. The comment section can contain any number of lines. (T/F)
2. AutoCAD ignores any line that is preceded by a semicolon. (T/F)
3. The command alias must not be an AutoCAD command. (T/F)
4. The bit flag field must be set to 8. (T/F)
5. In the command alias section, the command alias must be preceded by a semicolon. (T/F)
6. You cannot use aliases for AutoLISP commands. (T/F)
7. The *acad.pgp* file does not come with AutoCAD software. (T/F)
8. The *acad.pgp* file is an ASCII file. (T/F)

Exercise 1 *Adding New Command Aliases*

Add the following external commands and AutoCAD command aliases to the AutoCAD program parameters file (*acad.pgp*):

External Command Section

Abbreviation	Command Description
MYWORDPAD	This command loads the WORDPAD program that resides in the **Program Files\Accessories** directory.
MYEXCEL	This command loads the EXCEL program that resides in the **Program Fies\Microsoft Office** directory.
CD	This command executes the CHKDSK command of DOS.
FORMAT	This command executes the FORMAT command of DOS.

Command Aliases Section

Abbreviation	Command	Abbreviation	Command
BL	**BLOCK**	LTS	**LTSCALE**
INS	**INSERT**	EXP	**EXPLODE**
DIS	**DISTANCE**	GR	**GRID**
TE	**TIME**		

Answers to Self-Evaluation Test

1. quit, restart, **2. REINIT**, **3.** asterisk, **4.** semicolon, **5.** comma

Chapter 13

Conventional Dimensioning and Projection Theory Using AutoCAD

Learning Objectives

After completing this chapter, you will be able to:

- *Understand the dimensioning units*
- *Understand about basic dimensioning rules*
- *Understand the dimensioning of cylindrical features, holes, rounds, fillets, chamfers, and repetitive features*
- *Understand reference dimensions*
- *Understand working drawings, detail drawings, and assembly drawings*
- *Understand the arrangement of projected views*
- *Understand about X, Y, and Z axes, XY, YZ and XZ planes, and parallel planes*
- *Draw orthographic projections and position views*
- *Dimension a drawing*
- *Draw sectional views using different types of sections*
- *Hatch sectioned surfaces*
- *Use and draw auxiliary views*

Key Terms

- *Dimensioning Rules*
- *Reference Dimensions*
- *Cylindrical Features*
- *Dimensioning fillets and chamfers*
- *Dimensioning Components*
- *Detail Drawing*
- *Assembly Drawing*
- *Bill of Materials*
- *Full Section*
- *Half Section*
- *Broken Section*
- *Revolved Section*
- *Offset Section*
- *Aligned Section*
- *Hatch Lines*
- *Auxiliary Views*

DIMENSIONING

Dimensioning is one of the most important elements in a drawing. When you dimension a drawing, you not only provide information of the size of a part, but also a series of instructions to a machinist, an engineer, or an architect. The way the part is positioned in a machine, the sequence of machining operations, and the location of different features of the part depend on how you dimension it. For example, the number of decimal places in a dimension (2.000) determines the type of machine to be used for the machining operation. The machining cost of such an operation is significantly higher than those that have dimension upto only one digit after the decimal (2.0). If you are using a computer numerical control (CNC) machine, then locating a feature may not be a problem, but the number of pieces that you can machine without changing the tool depends on the tolerance assigned to a dimension. A closer tolerance (+.0001, -.0005) will definitely increase the tooling cost and ultimately the cost of the product. Similarly, if a part is to be forged or cast, the radius of the edges and the tolerance you provide to these dimensions determine the cost of the product, the number of defective parts, and the number of parts you get from the die.

While dimensioning, you must consider the manufacturing process involved in making a part and the relationships that exist among different parts in an assembly. If you are not familiar with any operation, get help. You must not assume things when dimensioning or making a piece part drawing. The success of a product, to a large extent, depends on the way you dimension a part. Therefore, never underestimate the importance of dimensioning in a drawing.

DIMENSION UNITS

Generally, metric system of dimensioning is considered as the official standard of measurement for engineering drawings, but most of the drawings in North America are still dimensioned in decimal inches. So, you should be familiar with all dimensioning systems that are used in the interpretation of an engineering drawing. The dimensions used in this book are primarily decimal inch. However, metric dimensions are used very frequently. To make information more clear, engineering drawings should contain one of the following notes:

- Unless Otherwise Specified, All Dimensions Are in Millimeters
- Unless Otherwise Specified, All Dimensions Are in Inches

The Inch and Metric unit system is discussed next.

Inch Units

An inch is a unit of length in the imperial and United States customary systems of measurement. Historically, an inch was also used in a number of other systems of units. Traditional standards for the exact length of an inch have varied in the past, but since July 1959, when the international yard was defined as 0.9144 metres, the international inch has been exactly 25.4 mm. There are 12 inches in a foot and 36 inches in a yard.

The Decimal-Inch System

In the Decimal-Inch system, the parts are designed in basic decimal increments (preferably .02 inch) and the values are expressed as two numbers after the decimal, as shown in Figure 13-1. Using the .02 value as the increment the second value after the decimal will be an even number or zero. In some cases to meet the design requirements you can also use the values other than the increment of .02 inch, such as .25 inch or .29 inch. Whenever greater accuracy is required, the dimensions are expressed as values upto three or four decimal places, such as 1.6587 or 5.9876. In Decimal-Inch dimensioning system, the numbers to the right of the decimal point indicate the degree of precision. For the dimensions less than 1 there will not be a zero before the decimal point.

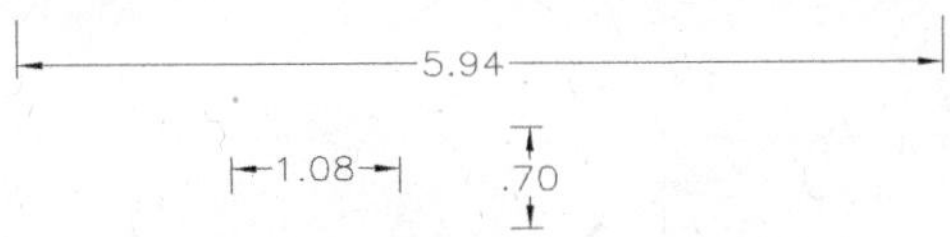

Figure 13-1 *Dimensions in the Decimal-Inch system*

The Fractional-Inch System

In the Fractional-Inch system, the parts are designed in common fractions, refer to Figure 13-2. The smallest fraction used is 1/256th of an inch. Sizes other than common fractions are expressed as decimals. This system of dimensioning was replaced by the Decimal-Inch dimensioning system of engineering drawings over 50 years ago. But you should be aware of this unit system because some tools like drills, reamers, and pipes are being manufactured using Fraction-Inch system.

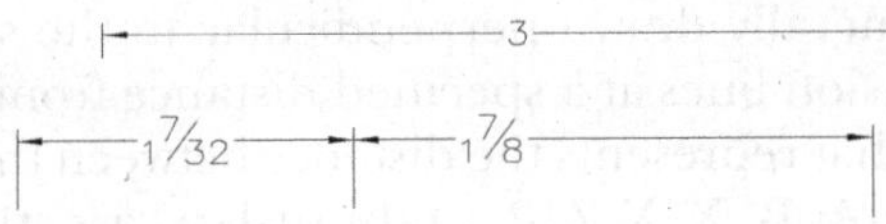

Figure 13-2 *Dimensions in the Fractional-Inch system*

SI (Metric) Units

The standard metric units used in an engineering drawing are the millimeters for linear measurements and the micrometers for surface roughness, refer to Figure 13-3. In the metric system of dimensioning, the numbers to the right of the decimal point indicate the degree of precision. Whole dimensions in a drawing do not require a zero to the right of the decimal point. For example, the dimension of 5 mm will be expressed as 5 not 5.0, unless and until the part to be manufactured requires that specific precision. For expressing large dimensions a space should be used to separate groups of three numbers in metric values, such as 54 487 or 4.524 47.

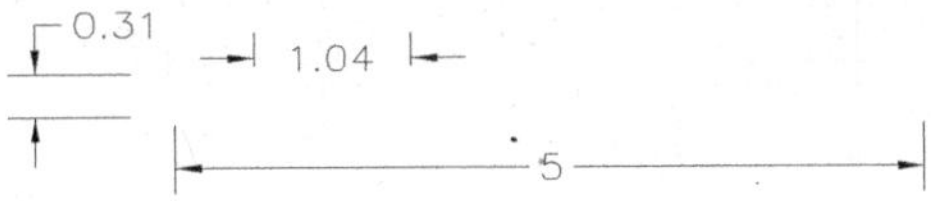

Figure 13-3 *Dimensions in the Metric (Millimeters) system*

DIMENSIONING COMPONENTS

A dimension consists of the following components, refer to Figure 13-4:

- Extension line
- Arrows or tick marks
- Dimension line

- Leader lines
- Dimension text

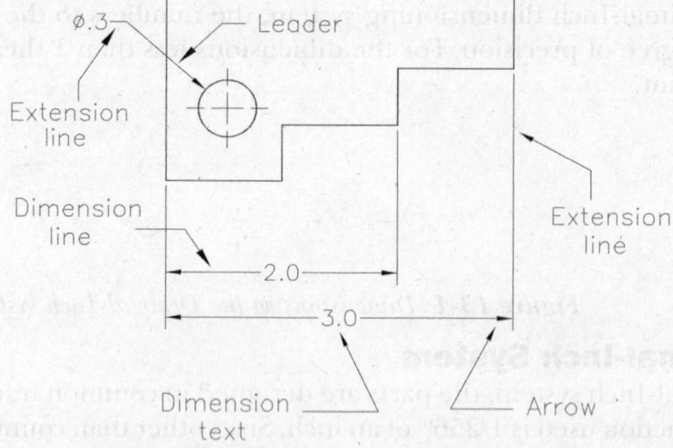

Figure 13-4 Dimensioning components

The extension lines are drawn to extend the points that are dimensioned. The length of the extension lines is determined by the number of dimensions and the placement of the dimension lines. These lines are generally drawn perpendicular to the surface. The dimension lines are drawn between the extension lines at a specified distance from the object lines. The dimension text is a numerical value that represents the distance between the points. The dimension text can also consist of a variable (A, B, X, Y, Z12,...). In such a case, the value assigned to it is defined in a separate table. The dimension text can be centered around or on the top of the dimension line. Arrows or tick marks are drawn at the end of the dimension line to indicate the start and end of the dimension. Leaders are used for dimensioning a circle, arc, or any nonlinear element of a drawing. They are also used to attach a note to a feature or to give the part numbers in an assembly drawing.

COMMON RULES FOR DIMENSIONING

1. Place dimensions in the view that best shows the shape of the object, refer to Figure 13-5. Sometimes dimensions can placed between views according to the availability of space between the views.

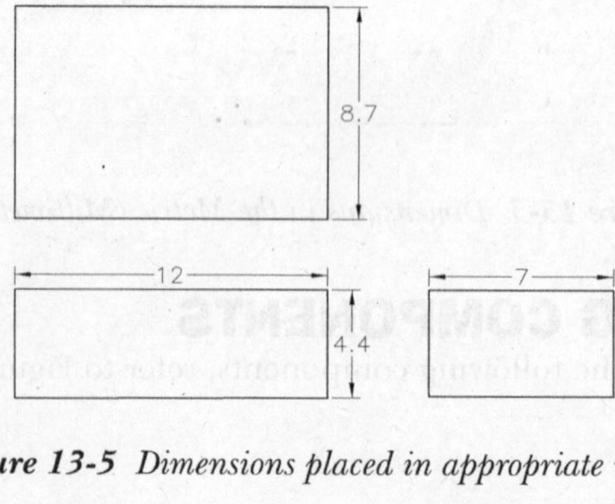

Figure 13-5 Dimensions placed in appropriate views

2. Place dimensions between the views when possible, refer to Figure 13-6.

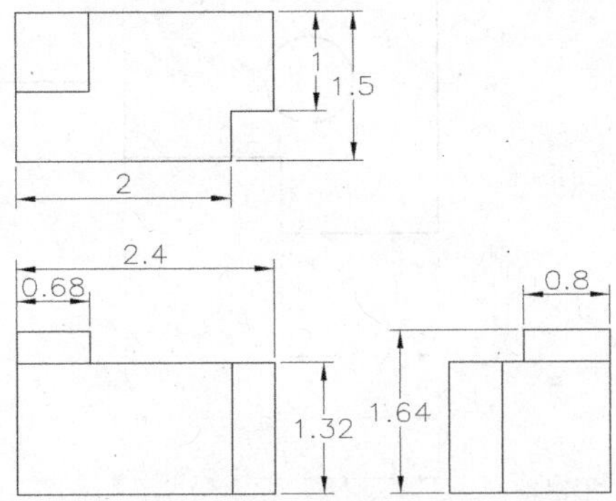

Figure 13-6 Place dimensions between views

3. You should make the dimensions in a separate layer/layers. This makes it easy to edit or control the display of dimensions (freeze, thaw, lock, and unlock). Also, the dimension layer/layers should be assigned a unique color so that at the time of plotting, you can assign the desired pen to plot the dimensions. This helps in controlling the line width and the contrast of dimensions at the time of plotting.

4. The distance of the first dimension line should be at least 0.375 units (10 units for metric drawing) from the object line. In CAD drawing, this distance may be 0.75 to 1.0 units (19 to 25 units for metric drawings). Once you decide on the spacing, it should be maintained throughout the drawing.

5. The distance between the first dimension line and the second dimension line must be at least 0.25 unit. In CAD drawings, this distance may be 0.25 to 0.5 unit (6 to 12 units for metric drawings). If there are more dimension lines (parallel dimensions), the distances between them must be the same (0.25 to 0.5 unit). Once you decide on the spacing (0.25 to 0.5), the same spacing should be maintained throughout the drawing. An appropriate snap setting is useful for maintaining this space. If you are using baseline dimensioning, you can use AutoCAD's **DIMDLI** variable to set the spacing. The dimensions must be placed in such a way so that they are not crowded, especially when there is not much space, refer to Figure 13-7.

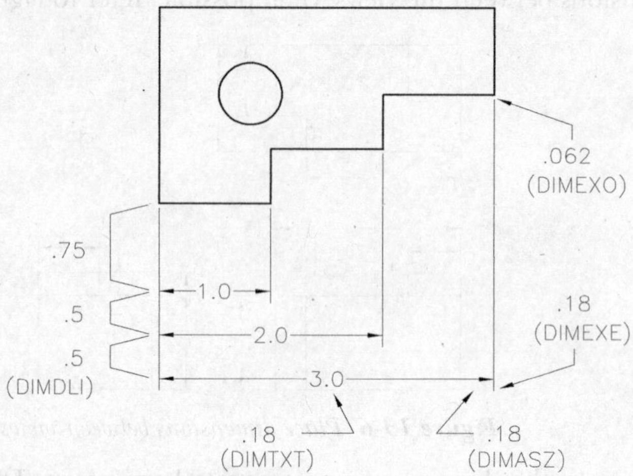

Figure 13-7 *Arrow size, text height, and spacing between dimension lines*

6. For parallel dimension lines, the dimension text can be staggered if there is not enough room between the dimension lines to place the dimension text. You can use the AutoCAD Object Grips feature or the **DIMTEDIT** command to stagger the dimension text, refer to Figure 13-8.

7. All dimensions should be given outside the view. However, the dimensions can be shown inside the view if they can be easily understood there and cause no confusion with the other dimensions or details, refer to Figure 13-9. In case of large drawings, dimensions can be placed on the view to improve clarity.

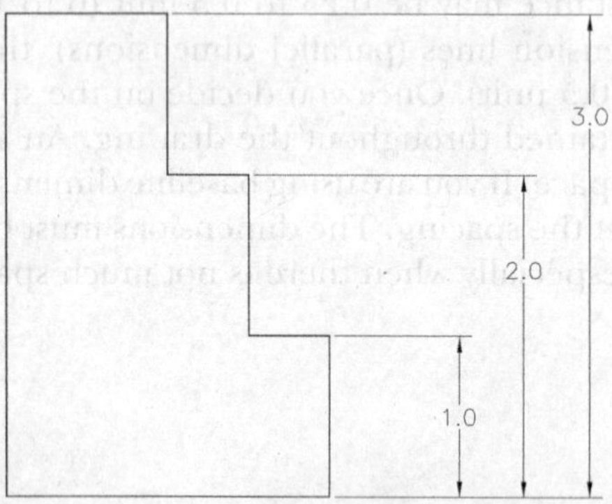

Figure 13-8 *Staggered dimensions*

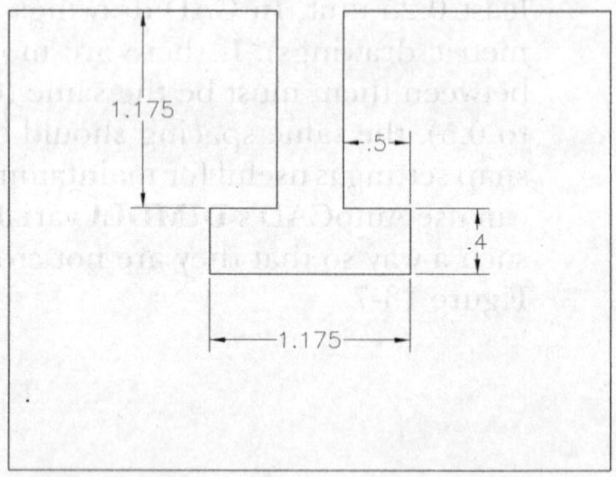

Figure 13-9 *Dimensions inside the view*

8. Dimension lines should not cross the extension lines, refer to Figure 13-10. You can accomplish this by giving the smallest dimension first and then the next largest dimension, refer to Figure 13-11.

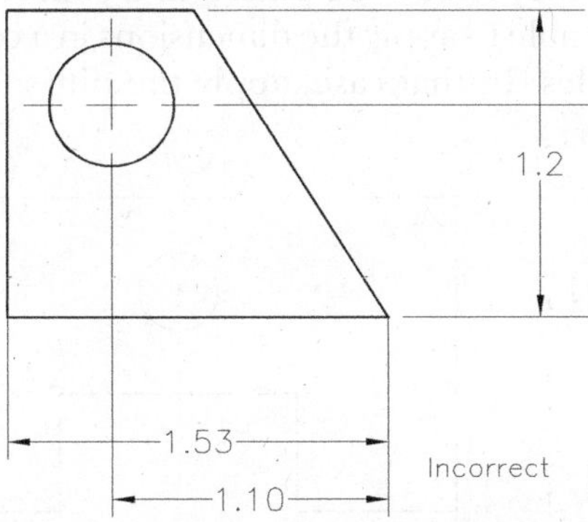

Figure 13-10 *Dimensions placed incorrectly*

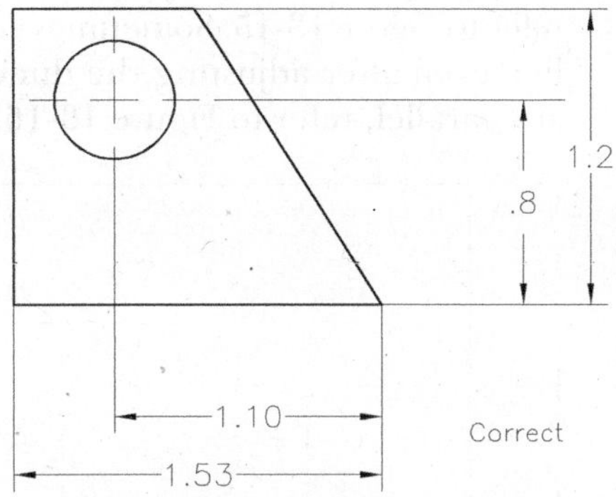

Figure 13-11 *Dimensions placed correctly*

9. If you decide to have the dimension text aligned with the dimension line, then the entire dimension text in the drawing must be aligned, refer to Figure 13-12. Similarly, if you decide to have the dimension text horizontal or above the dimension line, then to maintain uniformity in the drawing, the entire dimension text must be horizontal, refer to Figure 13-13 or above the dimension line, refer to Figure 13-14.

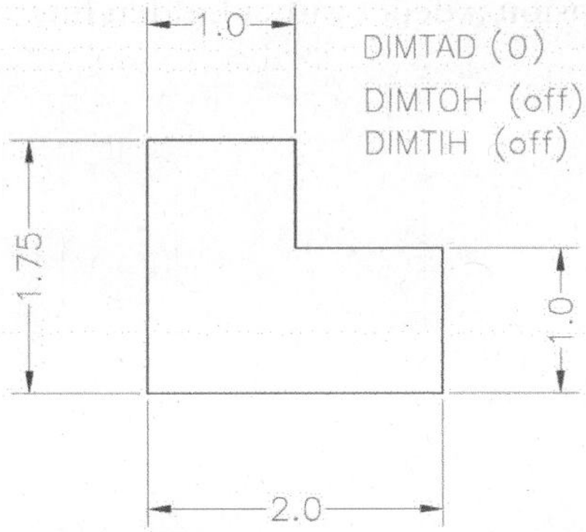

Figure 13-12 *Dimension text aligned with the dimension line*

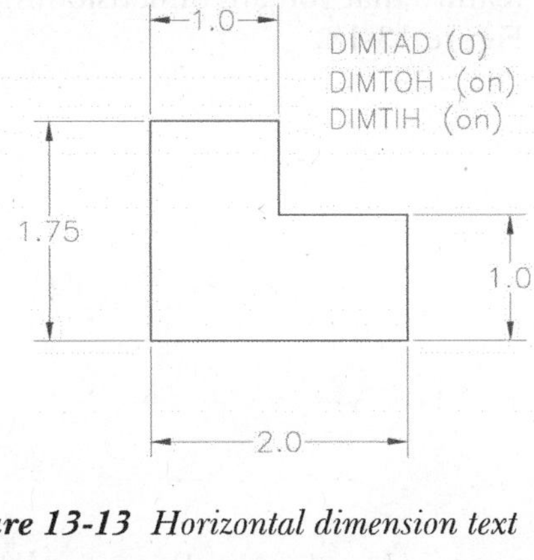

Figure 13-13 *Horizontal dimension text*

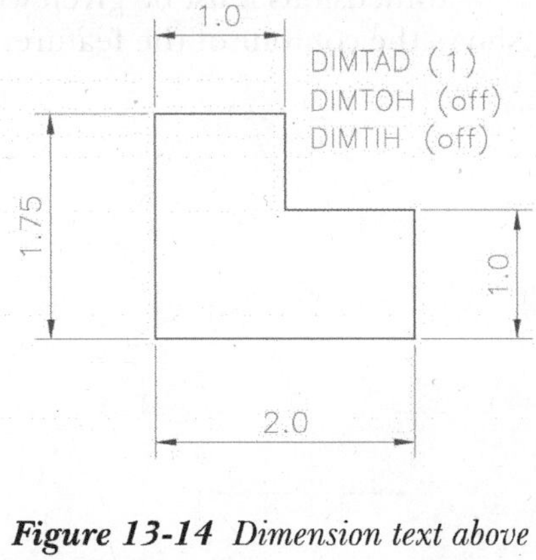

Figure 13-14 *Dimension text above the dimension line*

10. If you have a series of continuous dimensions, they should be placed in a continuous line, refer to Figure 13-15. Sometimes you may not be able to apply the dimensions in a continuous line even after adjusting the dimension variables. In that case, apply the dimensions that are parallel, refer to Figure 13-16.

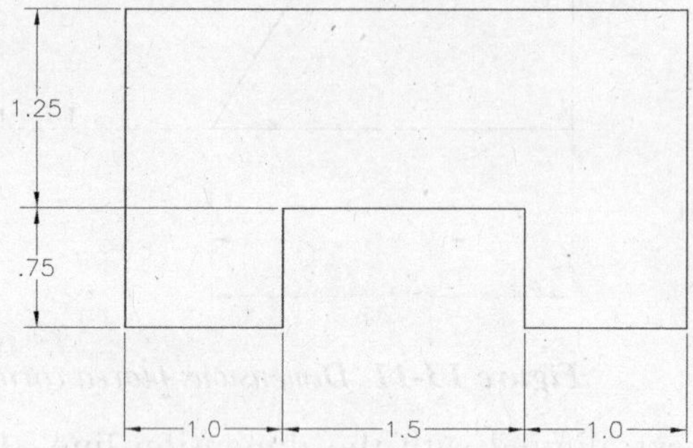

Figure 13-15 Continuous dimensions

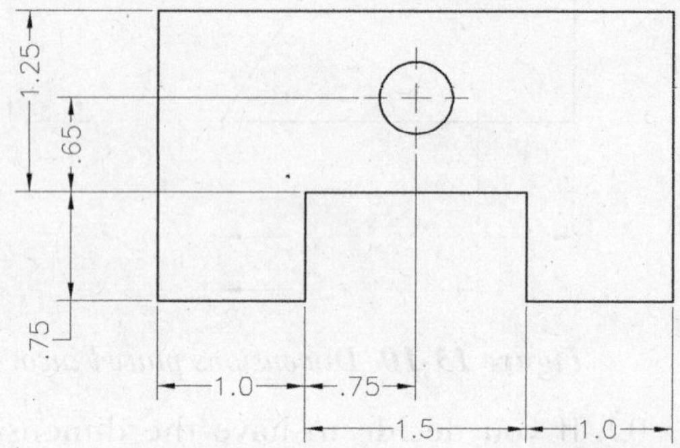

Figure 13-16 Parallel dimensions

11. You should not dimension with the hidden lines. The dimension should be given where the feature is visible, refer to Figure 13-17. However, in some complicated drawings, you might be justified to dimension a detail with a hidden line.

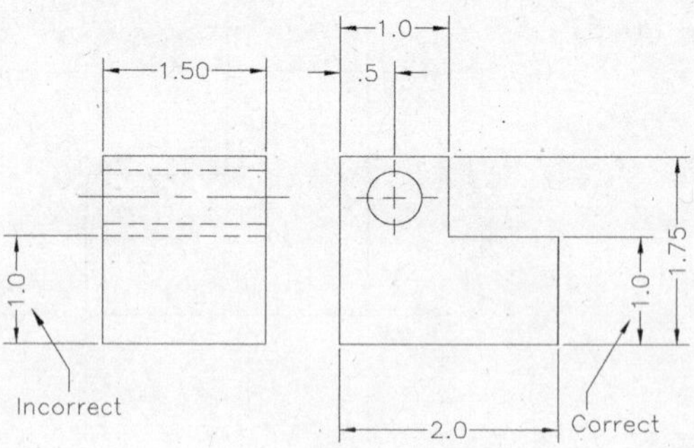

Figure 13-17 Undimensioned hidden lines

12. The dimensions must be given where the feature that you are dimensioning is obvious and shows the contour of the feature, refer to Figure 13-18.

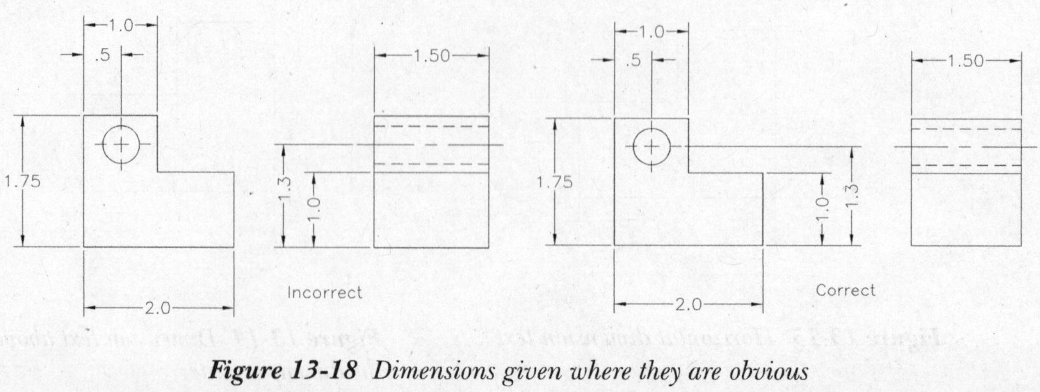

Figure 13-18 Dimensions given where they are obvious

13. The dimensions must not be repeated, as shown in Figure 13-19 as it makes difficult to update them.

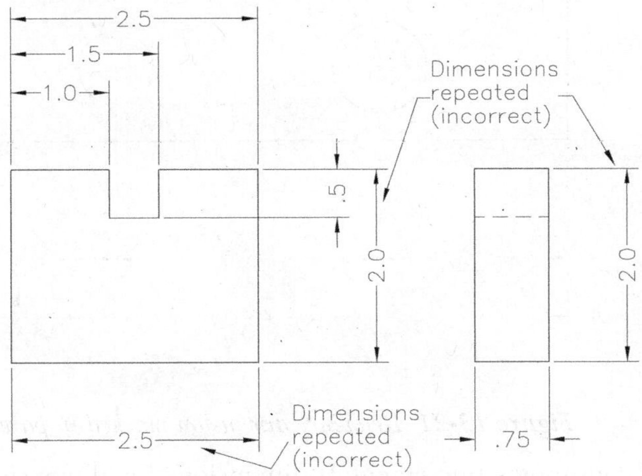

***Figure 13-19** incorrect method of dimensioning*

14. The dimensions must be given depending on how the part will be machined, and also on the relationship that exists between the different features of the part, refer to Figure 13-20.

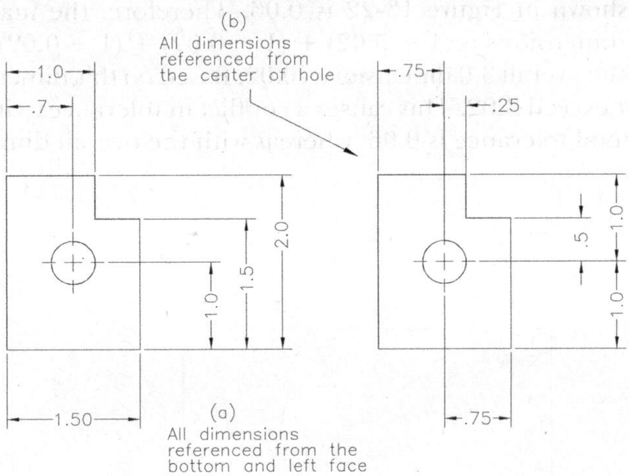

***Figure 13-20** Different dimensioning styles*

15. The dimensions enclosed in parenthesis can be identified as reference dimensions, refer to Figure 13-21. A reference dimension is placed on a drawing for information purpose only. Reference dimensions are not used for manufacturing of the part therefore it must be clearly labeled. Previously, reference dimensions were identified by placing the abbreviation REF after or below the dimension.

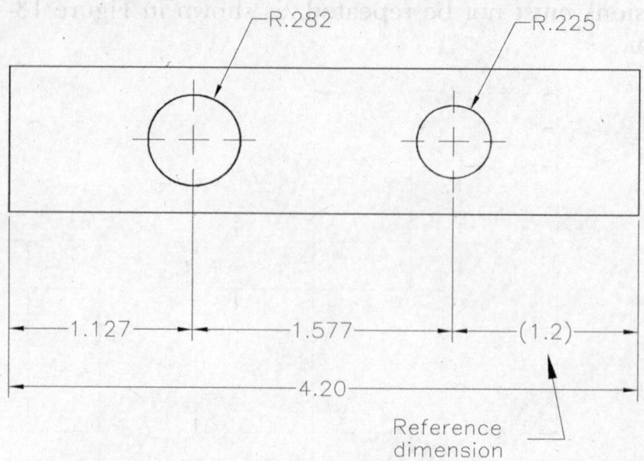

Figure 13-21 Reference dimension marked in parenthesis

16. If you give continuous (incremental) dimensions for dimensioning various features of a part, the overall dimension must be omitted or given as a reference dimension, refer to Figure 13-22. Similarly, if you give the overall dimension, one of the continuous (incremental) dimensions must be omitted or given as a reference dimension. Otherwise, there will be a conflict in tolerances. For example, the total positive tolerance on the three incremental dimensions shown in Figure 13-22 is 0.06. Therefore, the maximum size based on the incremental dimensions is (1 + 0.02) + (1 + 0.02) + (1 + 0.02) = 3.06. Also, the positive tolerance on the overall 3.0 dimension is 0.02. Based on this dimension, the overall size of the part must not exceed 3.02. This causes a conflict in tolerances with incremental dimensions because the total tolerance is 0.06, whereas with the overall dimension, the total tolerance is only 0.02.

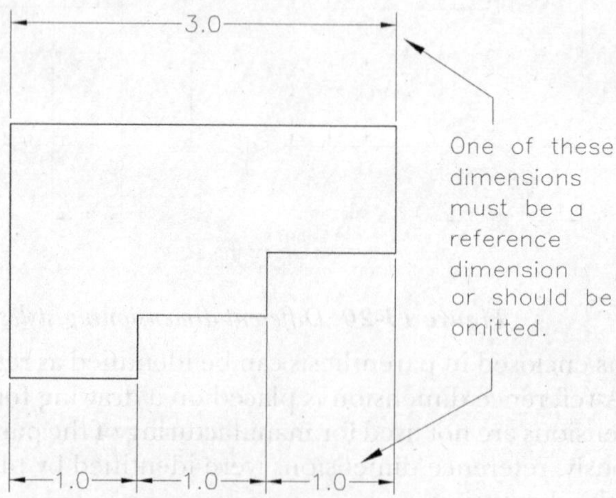

Figure 13-22 Referencing or omitting a dimension

17. If the dimension of a feature appears in a section view, you must not hatch the dimension text, refer to Figure 13-23. You can accomplish this task by selecting the dimension object while defining the hatch boundary. You can also accomplish this by drawing a rectangle

around the dimension text and then hatching the area after excluding the rectangle from the hatch boundary.

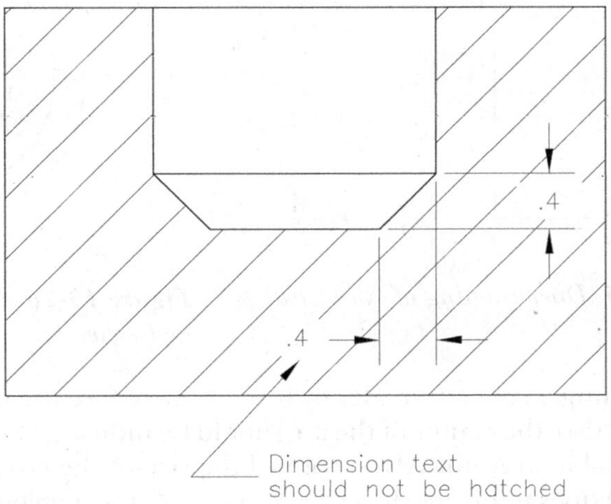

Figure 13-23 Dimension text excluded from hatching

18. While dimensioning a circle, the diameter should be preceded by the diameter symbol, refer to Figure 13-24. AutoCAD automatically puts the diameter symbol in front of the diameter value. However, if you override the default diameter value, you can use %%c followed by the value of the diameter (%%c1.00) to put the diameter symbol before the diameter dimension.

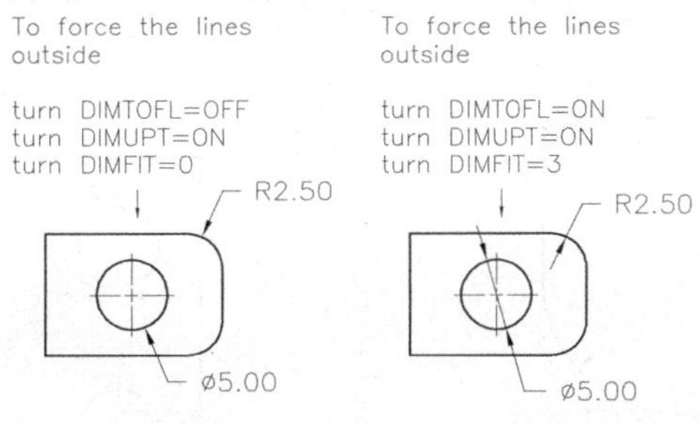

Figure 13-24 Diameter should be preceded by the diameter symbol

19. Cylindrical features should be dimensioned by the method shown in Figure 13-25. The circle must be dimensioned as a diameter, never as a radius. Where the diameters of a number of concentric cylinders are to be given, they must be shown on the end view, refer to Figure 13-26. For diameter dimensions, the diameter symbol Ø is used before the dimension.

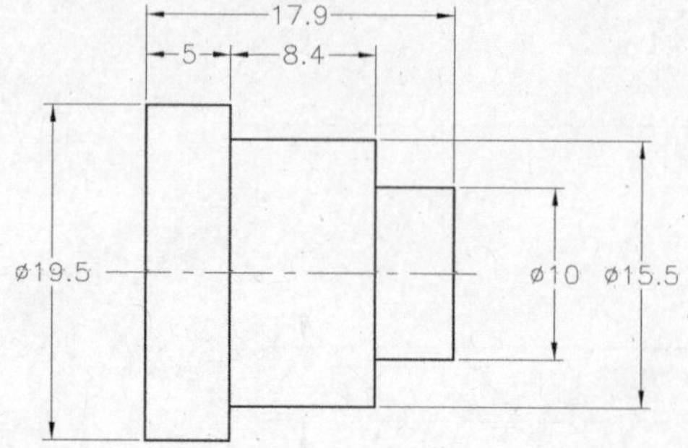

Figure 13-25 Dimensioning of cylindrical features

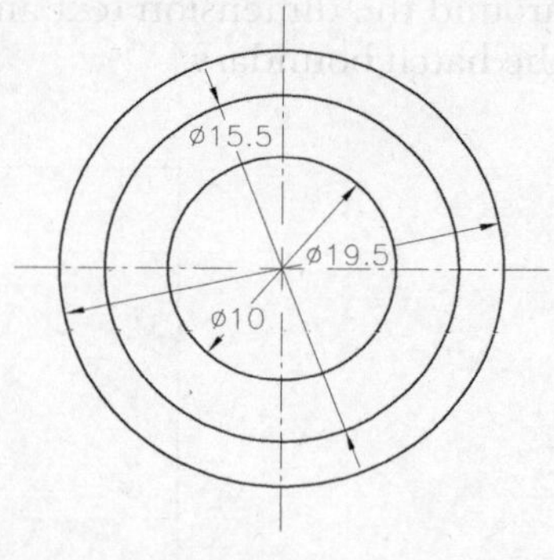

Figure 13-26 Dimensioning diameters on end view

20. For dimensioning a circular arc, letter R is added before the radius dimension, as shown in Figure 13-27. Also, the center of the arc should be indicated by a small cross. You can use the **DIMCEN** variable in AutoCAD to control the size of the cross. If the value of this variable is 0, AutoCAD does not draw the cross in the center when you dimension an arc or a circle.

21. The preferred method for designating the size of holes is shown in Figure 13–28. While dimensioning a hole feature a leader is used and the symbol Ø precedes the size of the hole. When two or more holes of the same size are required, the number of holes is specified. If a blind hole is required, the depth of the hole is specified by the depth symbol in the dimensioning note; otherwise, it is assumed that all holes shown are through holes. The degree of accuracy to which a hole is to be machined is specified on the drawing. The use of operational names such as *turn, bore, grind, ream, tap,* and *thread* with dimensions should be avoided.

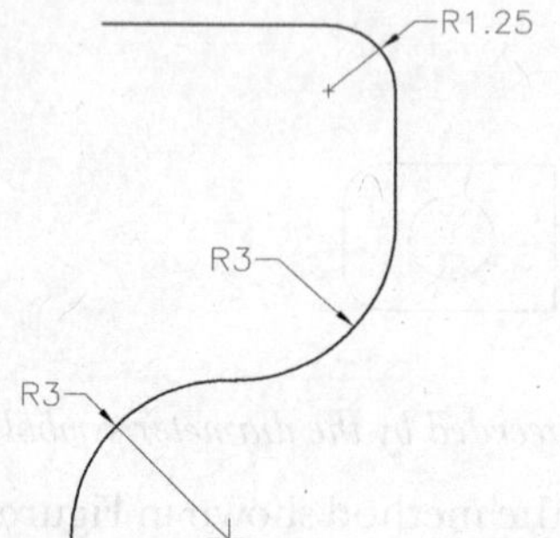

Figure 13-27 Dimensioning of arcs

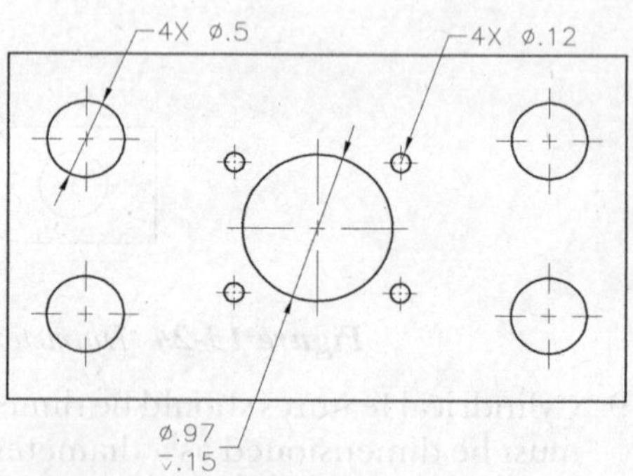

Figure 13-28 Dimensioning of holes

22. A dimension that is not to be scaled should be indicated by drawing a straight line under the dimension text, refer to Figure 13-29. This line can be drawn by using the **DDEDIT** command. If you invoke this command, AutoCAD will prompt you to select an annotative object. Select the object; the **Text Editor** will be displayed and a new **Text Editor** tab will be added to the **Ribbon**. Select the text (< >), and then choose the **U** button in the **Formatting** panel of the **Text Editor** tab to underline the text.

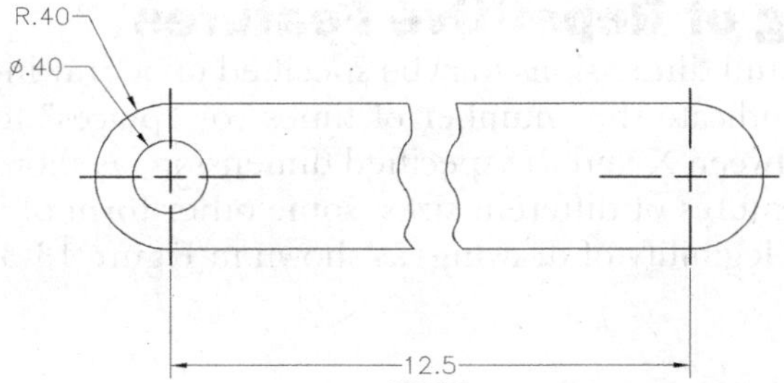

Figure 13-29 Specifying dimension that is not to be scaled

Dimensioning of Rounds and Fillets

A round, or radius, or chamfer is applied on the outer surface of a part to improve its appearance and to avoid formation of a sharp edge that might chip off under a sharp blow or cause interference. It is also a safety feature. In a fillet, additional material is allowed in the inner intersection of two surfaces, as shown in Figure 13-30. If all the fillets and rounds have equal dimension then a general note, such as ROUNDS AND FILLETS R10 or ROUNDS AND FILLETS R10 UNLESS OTHERWISE SPECIFIED, is normally used on the drawing instead of placing individual dimensions.

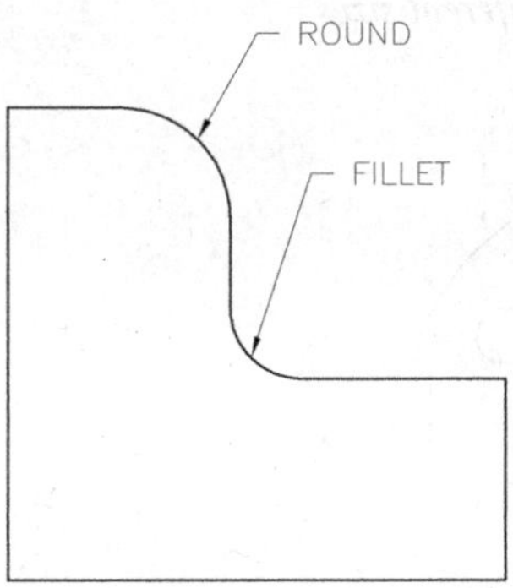

Figure 13-30 Fillets and rounds

A chamfer can be dimensioned by specifying the chamfer angle and the distance of the chamfer from the edge. It can also be dimensioned by specifying the distances, as shown in Figure 13-31.

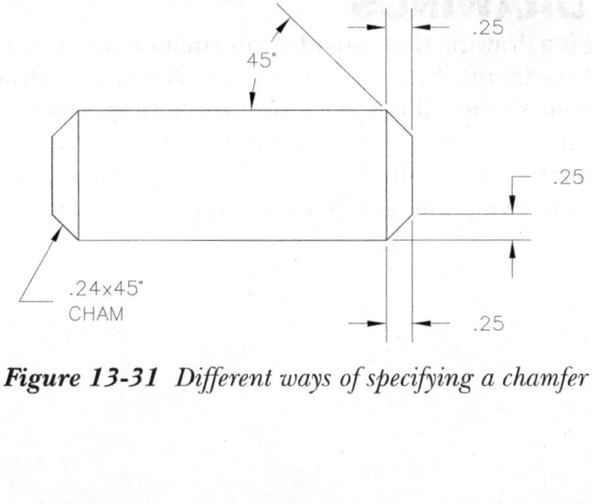

Figure 13-31 Different ways of specifying a chamfer

Dimensioning of Repetitive Features

Repetitive features and dimensions may be specified on a drawing by the use of an X preceded by the number to indicate the "number of times" or "places" for which they are required. A space is inserted between X and the specified dimension, as shown in Figure 13-32. If there are similar repetitive features of different sizes, some other form of indication may be required in order to ensure the legibility of drawing, as shown in Figure 13-33.

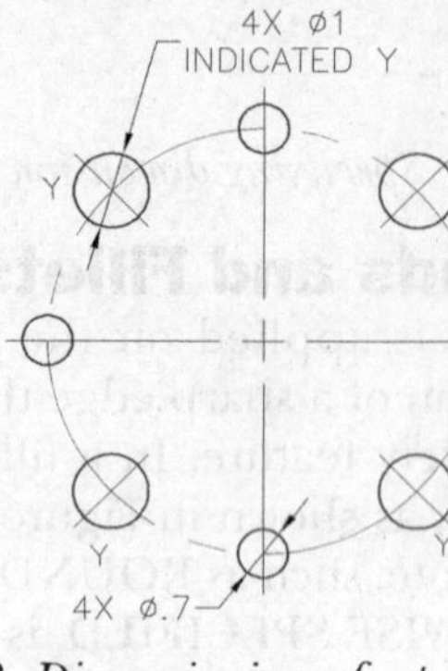

Figure 13-32 Dimensioning of repetitive features with different sizes

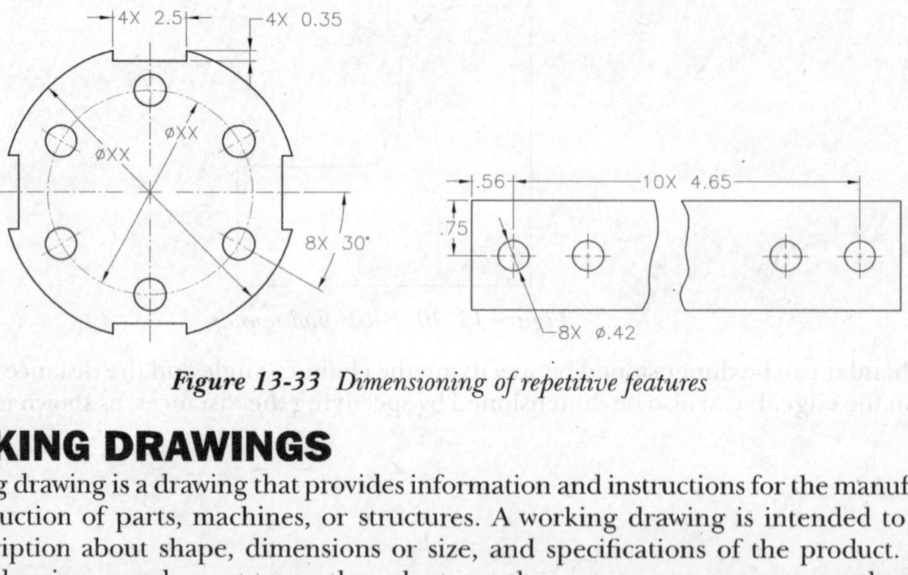

Figure 13-33 Dimensioning of repetitive features

WORKING DRAWINGS

A working drawing is a drawing that provides information and instructions for the manufacturing or construction of parts, machines, or structures. A working drawing is intended to provide the description about shape, dimensions or size, and specifications of the product. Because working drawings may be sent to another plant, another company, or even to another country to manufacture, construct, or assemble the final product, the drawing should qualify the drawing standards of the respective plant, company, or country.

Generally, working drawings are classified into two groups:

Detail Drawing

A detail drawing is the drawing of a single part that includes a complete and exact description of its form and shape. Detail drawings provide the necessary information for the manufacture of the parts for a specific product or structure, refer to Figure 13-34. Each detail drawing must be drawn and dimensioned to completely describe the size and shape of the part. It should also contain information that might be needed in manufacturing the part. The finished surfaces and all the necessary operations should be indicated by using symbols or notes on the drawing. The material of which the part is made and the number of parts that are required for the production of the assembled product must be given in the title block. Detail drawings should also contain part numbers. This information is used in the bill of materials and the assembly drawing. The part numbers make it easier to locate the drawing of a part. Regardless of the part's size, you should make a detail drawing of each part on a separate drawing. When required, these detail drawings can be inserted in the assembly drawing by using the **Attach** tool from the **Reference** panel of the **Insert** tab.

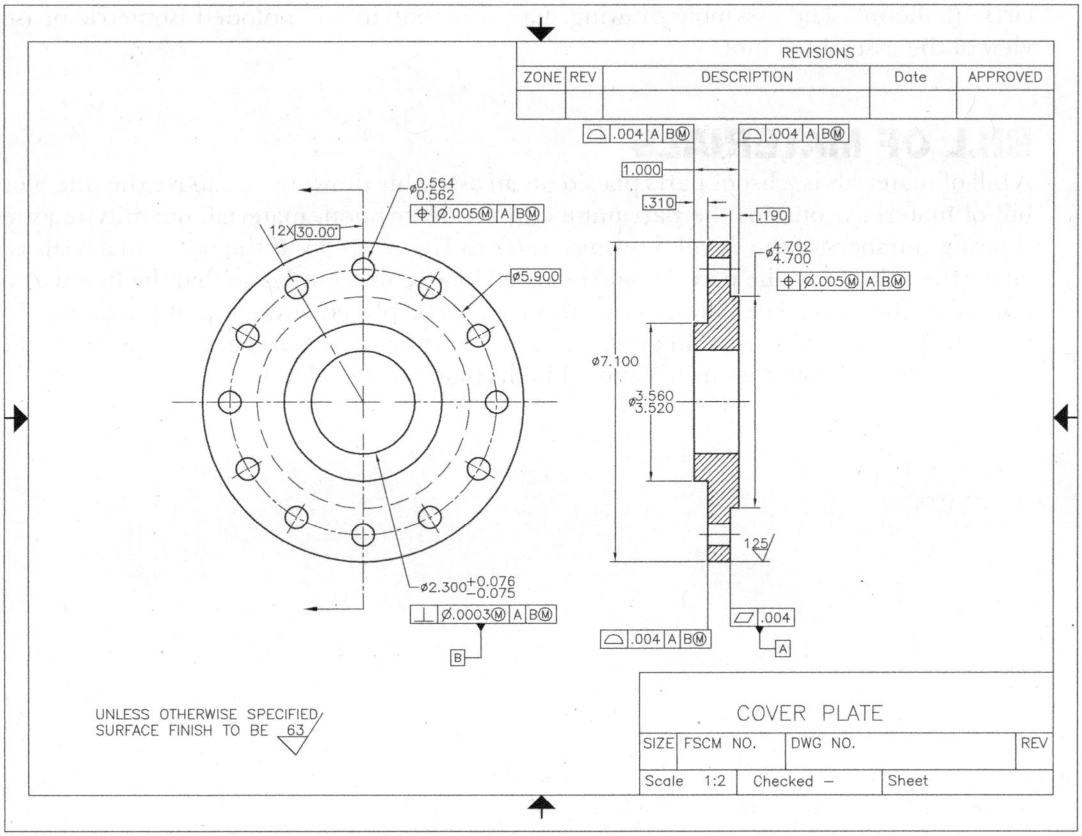

Figure 13-34 Detail drawing of Cover Plate

Assembly Drawing

An assembly drawing is the presentation of a product or structure put together, showing all parts in their operational positions. These drawings provide necessary information about the assembly of parts and structures, refer to Figure 13-35. Assembly drawings may include instructions, lists of component parts, reference numbers, references to detail drawings or shop drawings, and specifications. The main view may be drawn in full section so that the assembly drawing shows nearly all the individual parts and their locations. Additional views should be drawn only when some of the parts cannot be seen in the main view. The hidden lines, as far as possible, should be omitted from the assembly drawing because they clutter it and might cause confusion. However, a hidden line may be drawn if it helps to understand the product. Only assembly dimensions should be shown in the assembly drawing. Each part can be identified on the assembly drawing by the number used in the detail drawing and in the bill of materials. The part numbers should be given as shown in Figure 13-35. A part number consists of a text string for the detail number, a circle (balloon), a leader line, and an arrow or dot. The text should be made at least 0.2 inches (5 mm) high and enclosed in a 0.4 inch (10 mm) circle (balloon). The center of the circle must be located not less than 0.8 inches (20 mm) from the nearest line on the drawing. Also, the leader line should be radial with respect to the circle (balloon). The assembly drawing may also contain an exploded isometric or isometric view of the assembled unit.

BILL OF MATERIALS

A bill of materials is a list of parts placed on an assembly drawing just above the title block. The bill of materials contains the part number, part description, material, quantity required, and drawing numbers of the detail drawings, refer to Figure 13-35. If the bill of materials is placed above the title block, the parts should be listed in ascending order so that the first part is at the bottom of the table. The bill of materials may also be placed at the top of the drawing. In that case, the parts must be listed in descending order with the first part at the top of the table. This structure allows room for any additional items that may be added to the list.

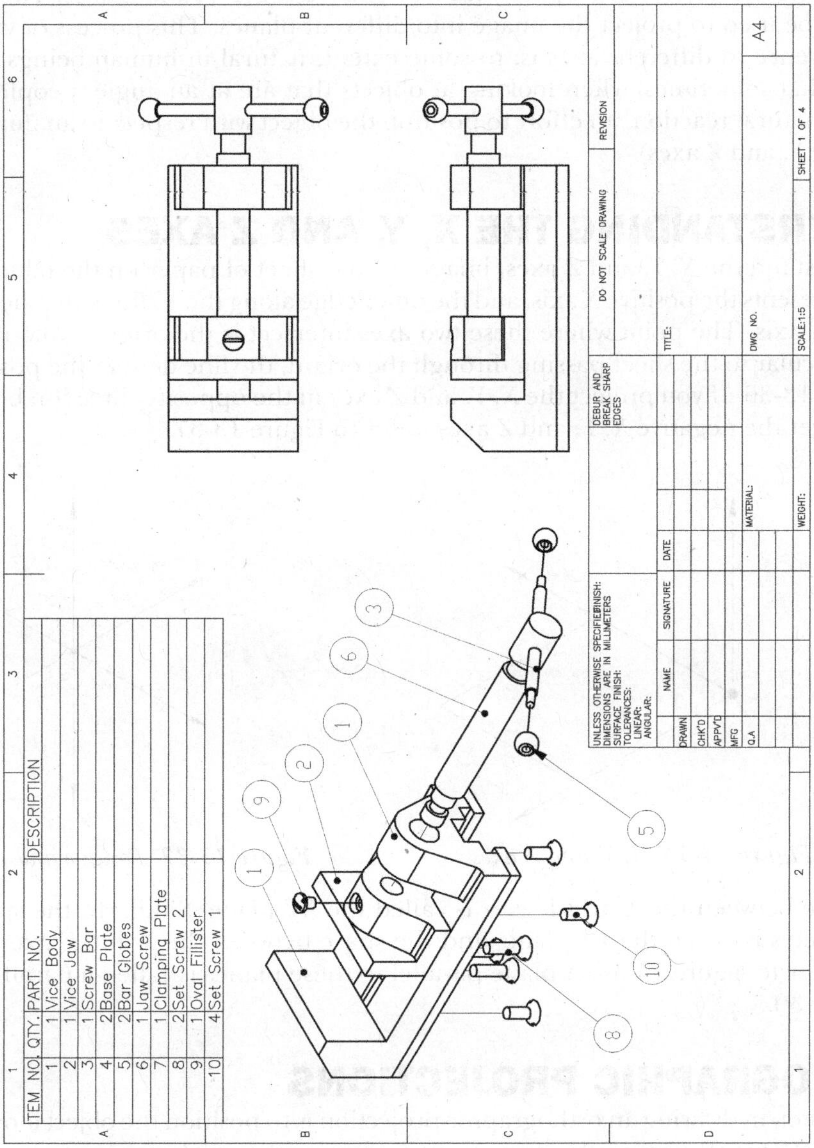

Figure 13-35 Assembly drawing with title block and bill of materials

MULTIVIEW DRAWINGS

When designers design a product, they visualize its shape in their minds. To represent that shape on paper or to communicate the idea to people, they must draw a picture of the product or its orthographic views. Pictorial drawings, such as isometric drawings, convey the shape of the object, but it is difficult to show all features and dimensions in an isometric drawing. Therefore, in industry, multiview drawings are the accepted standards for representing products. Multiview drawings are also known as orthographic projection drawings. To draw different views of an object, it is very important to visualize the shape of the product. The same is true when you look at different views of an object to determine its shape. To facilitate visualizing the shapes, you must picture the object in 3D space with reference to the *X*, *Y*, and *Z* axes. These reference axes can then be used to project the image into different planes. This process of visualizing objects with reference to different axes is, to some extent, natural in human beings. You might have noticed that sometimes, when looking at objects that are at an angle, people tilt their heads. This is a natural reaction, an effort to position the object with respect to an imaginary reference frame (*X*, *Y*, and *Z* axes).

UNDERSTANDING THE X, Y, AND Z AXES

To understand the *X*, *Y*, and *Z* axes, imagine a flat sheet of paper on the table. The horizontal edge represents the positive *X* axis, and the other edge along the width of the sheet, represents the positive *Y* axis. The point where these two axes intersect is the origin. Now, if you draw a line perpendicular to the sheet passing through the origin, the line defines the positive *Z* axis, refer to Figure 13-36. If you project the *X*, *Y*, and *Z* axes in the opposite direction beyond the origin, you will get the negative *X*, *Y*, and *Z* axes, refer to Figure 13-37.

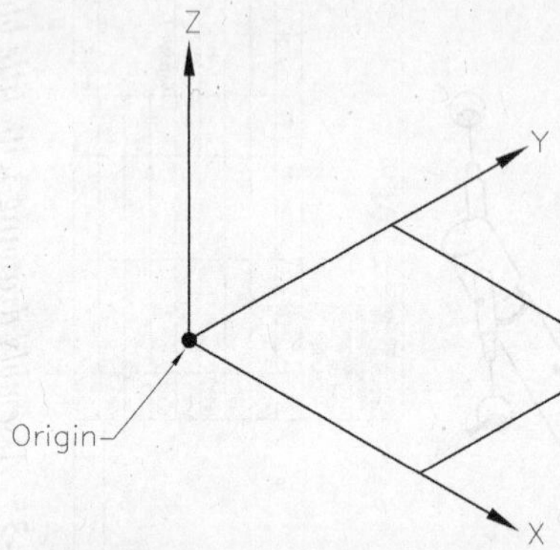

Figure 13-36 *X, Y, and Z axes*

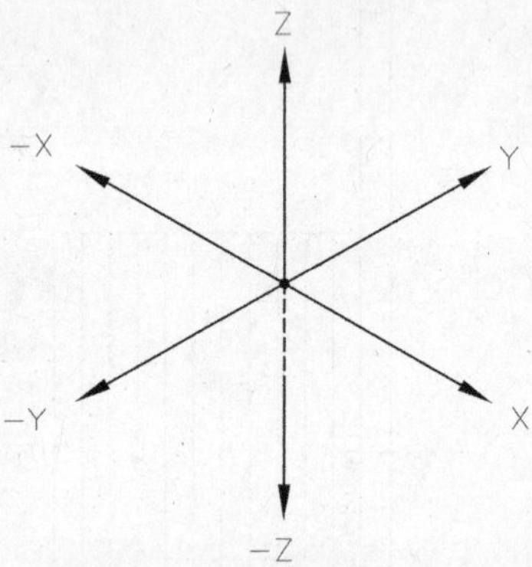

Figure 13-37 *Positive and negative axes*

The space between the *X* and *Y* axes is called the *XY* plane. Similarly, the space between the *Y* and *Z* axes is called the *YZ* plane, and the space between the *X* and *Z* axes is called the *XZ* plane, refer to Figure 13-38. A plane parallel to these planes is called a parallel plane, refer to Figure 13-39.

ORTHOGRAPHIC PROJECTIONS

The first step in drawing an orthographic projection is to position the object along the imaginary *X*, *Y*, and *Z* axes. For example, if you want to draw orthographic projections of the step block shown in Figure 13-40, position the block such that the far left corner coincides with the origin, and then align it with the *X*, *Y*, and *Z* axes.

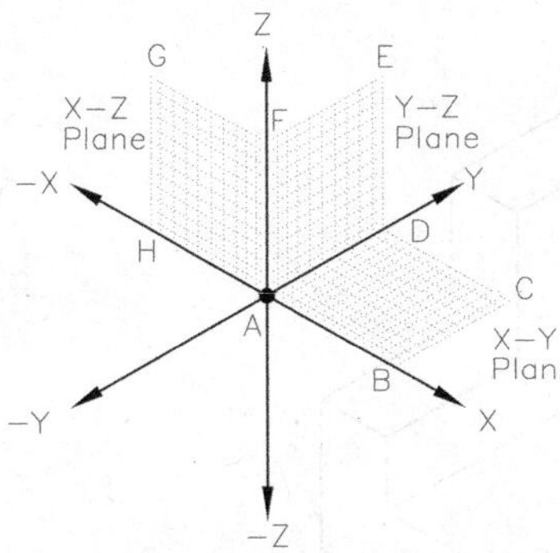

Figure 13-38 *XY, YZ, and XZ planes*

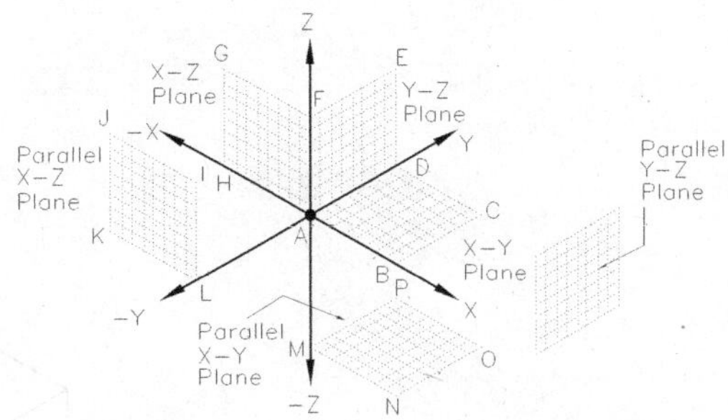

Figure 13-39 *Parallel planes*

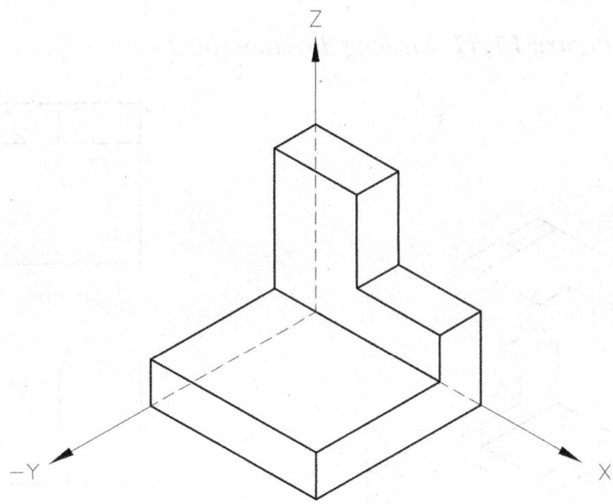

Figure 13-40 *Aligning the object with the X, Y, and Z axes*

Now, you can look at the object from different directions. Looking at the object along the negative *Y* axis and toward the origin is called the front view. Similarly, looking at it from the positive X direction is called the right side view. To get the top view, you can look at the object from the positive *Z* axis, refer to Figure 13-41.

To draw the front, side, and top views, project the points onto the parallel planes. For example, to draw the front view of the step block, imagine a plane parallel to the *XZ* plane located at a certain distance in front of the object. Now, project the points from the object onto the parallel plane, refer to Figure 13-42, and join them to complete the front view.

Repeat the same process for the side and top views. To represent these views on paper, position them, as shown in Figure 13-43.

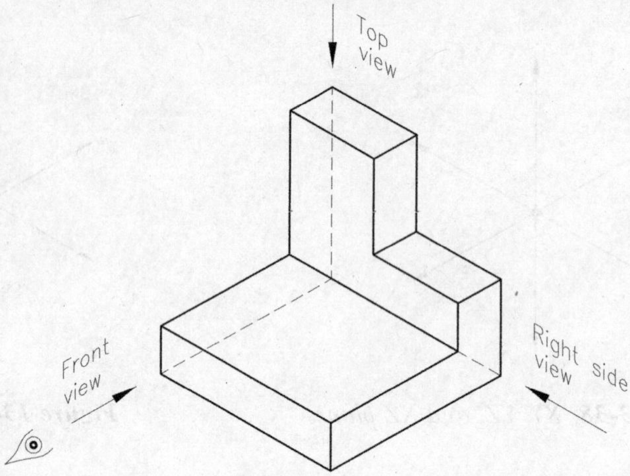

Figure 13-41 *Viewing directions for Front, Side, and Top views*

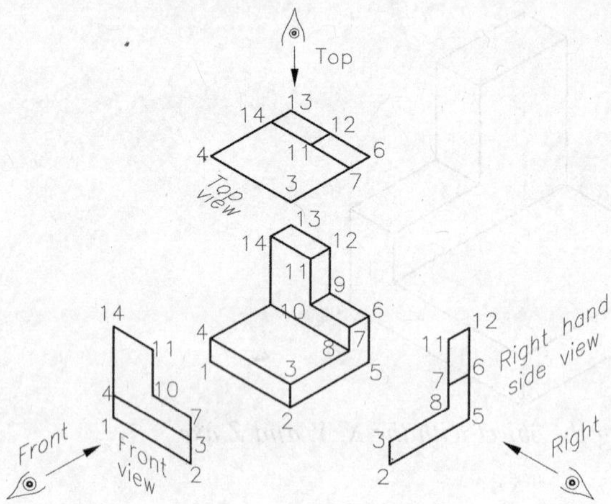

Figure 13-42 *Projecting points onto parallel planes*

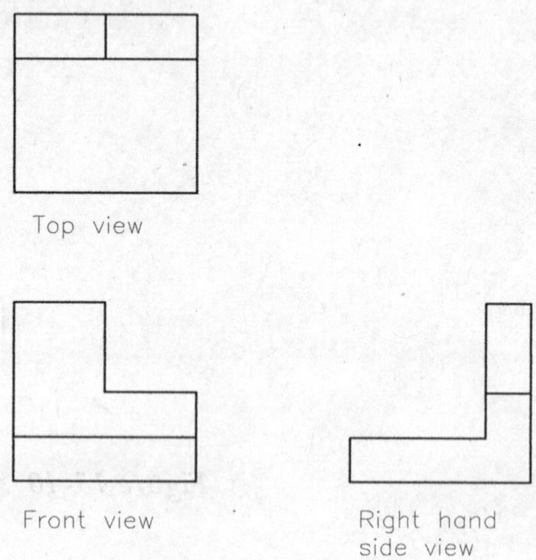

Figure 13-43 *Representing views on paper*

Another way of visualizing different views is to imagine the object enclosed in a glass box, refer to Figure 13-44.

Now, look at the object along the negative *Y* axis and draw the front view on the front glass panel. Repeat the process by looking along the positive *X* and *Z* axes, and draw the views on the right side and the top panel of the box, refer to Figure 13-45.

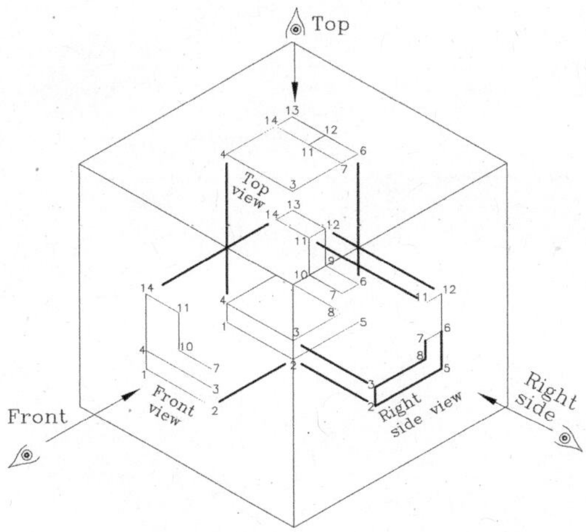

Figure 13-44 Objects inside a glass box

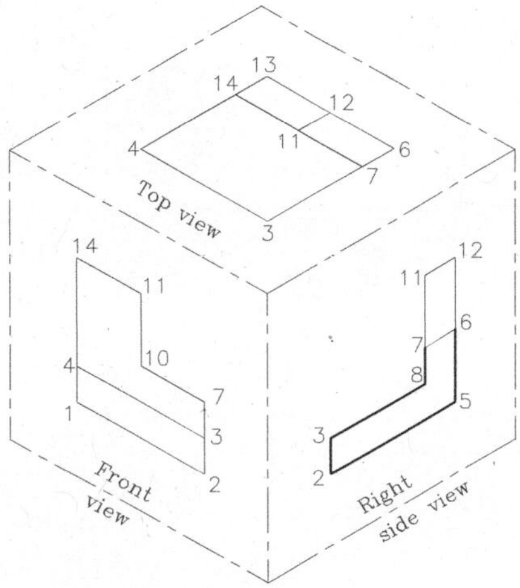

Figure 13-45 Front, top, and side views

To represent the front, side, and top views on paper, open the side and the top panels of the glass box, refer to Figure 13-46. The front panel is assumed to be stationary.

After opening the panels through 90 degree, the orthographic views will appear, as shown in Figure 13-47.

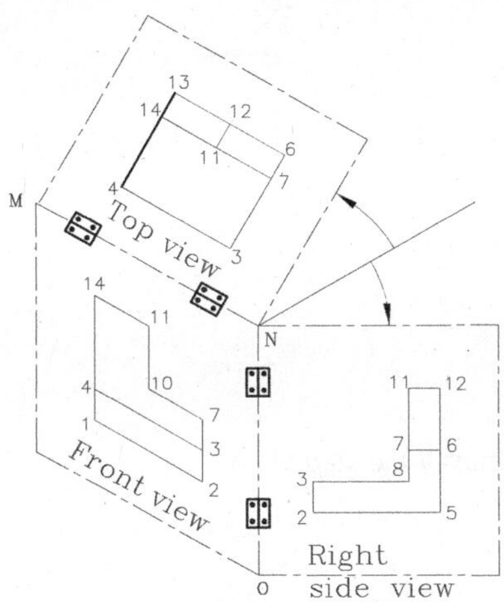

Figure 13-46 Opening the side and top panels

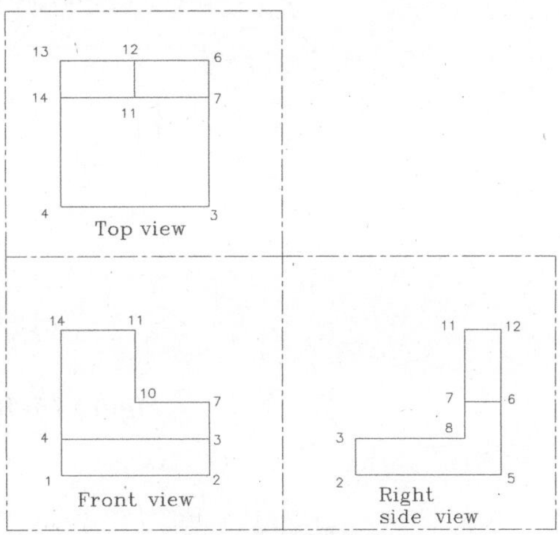

Figure 13-47 Views after opening the panels

POSITIONING ORTHOGRAPHIC VIEWS

Orthographic views must be positioned, as shown in Figure 13-48. The right side view must be positioned directly on the right side of the front view. Similarly, the top view must be directly above the front view. If the object requires additional views, they must be positioned, as shown in Figure 13-49.

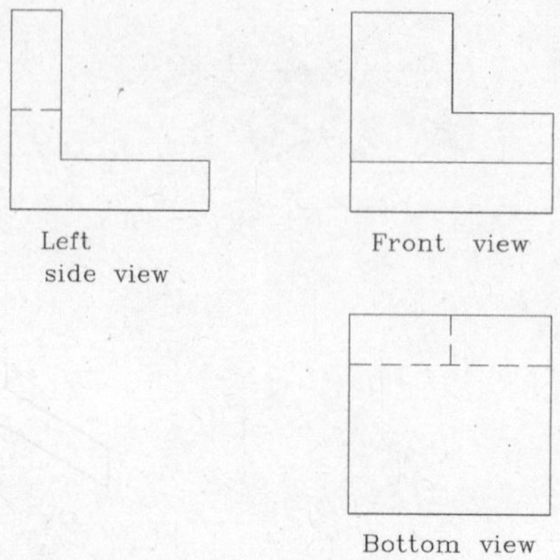

Figure 13-48 *Positioning orthographic views*

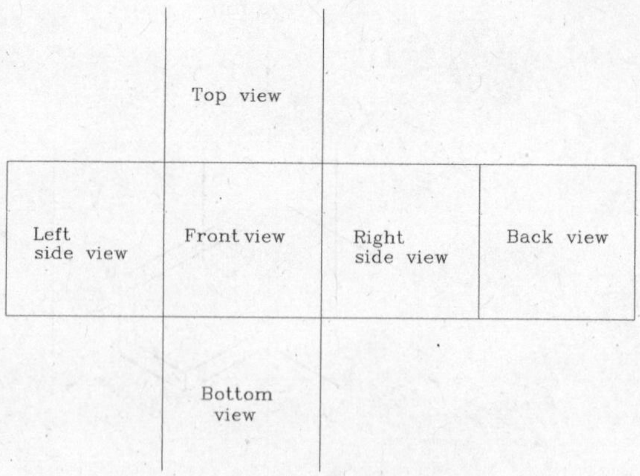

Figure 13-49 *Standard placement of orthographic views*

The different views of the step block are shown in Figure 13-50.

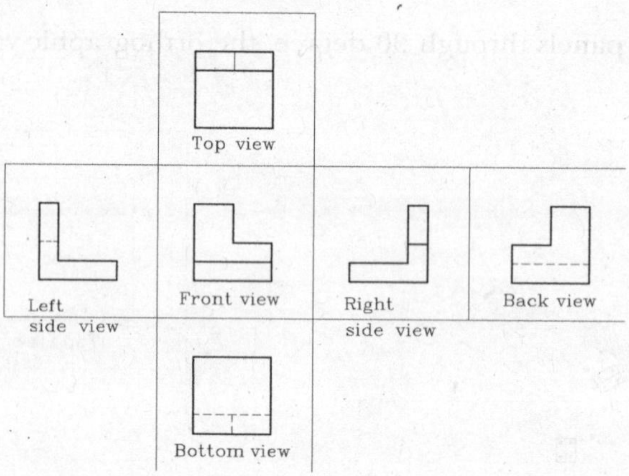

Figure 13-50 *Different views of the step block*

Example 1 — Orthographic Views

In this example, you will draw the required orthographic views of the object shown in Figure 13-51. Assume the dimensions of the drawing.

Drawing the orthographic views of an object involves the following steps:

1. Look at the object and determine the number of views required to show all its features. For example, the object in Figure 13-51 requires three views only (front, side, and top).

2. Based on the shape of the object, select the side that you want to show as the front view. In this example, the front view, i.e. the view along -y axis, is the one that shows the maximum number of features or that gives a better idea about the shape of the object. Sometimes, the front view is determined by how the part will be positioned in an assembly.

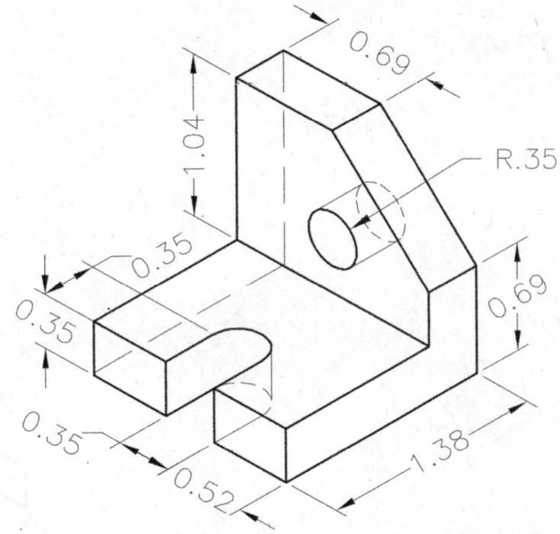

Figure 13-51 *Step block with hole and slot*

3. Picture the object in your mind and align it along the imaginary X, Y, and Z axes, refer to Figure 13-52.

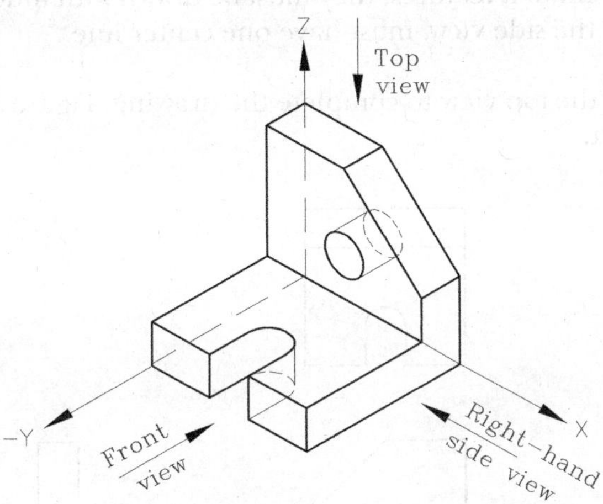

Figure 13-52 *Align the object with the imaginary X, Y, and Z axes*

4. Look at the object along the negative Y axis and project the image on the imaginary XZ parallel plane, refer to Figure 13-53.

5. Use the projection on imaginary XZ parallel plane to draw the front view of the object. If there are any hidden features, they must be drawn with hidden lines. The holes and slots must be shown with center lines.

6. To draw the right side view, look at the object along the positive X axis and project the image onto the imaginary YZ parallel plane.

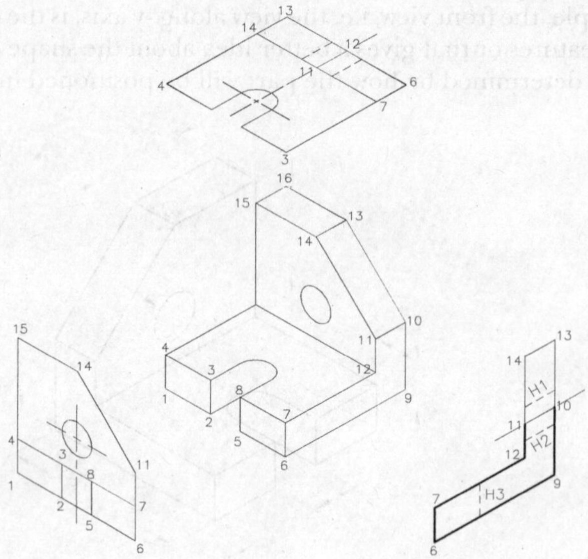

Figure 13-53 Project the image onto the parallel planes

7. Use the projection on imaginary YZ parallel plane to draw the right side view of the object. If there are any hidden features, they must be drawn with hidden lines. The holes and slots, when shown in the side view, must have one center line.

8. Similarly, draw the top view to complete the drawing. Figure 13-54 shows different views of the given object.

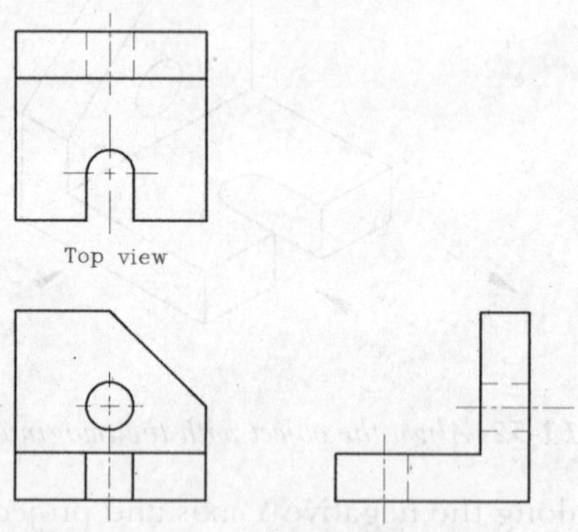

Figure 13-54 Front, side, and top views

Exercises 1 through 4 — Orthographic Views

Draw the required orthographic views of the objects shown in Figure 13-55 through Figure 13-58. The distance between the dotted lines is 1 unit.

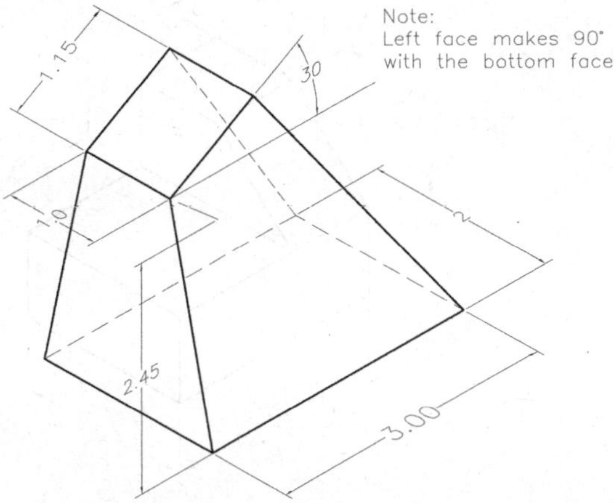

Figure 13-55 Drawing for Exercise 1 (the object is shown as a surface wireframe model)

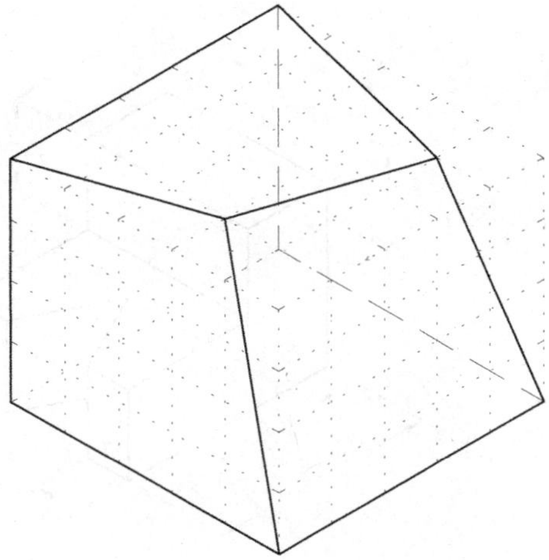

Figure 13-56 Drawing for Exercise 2

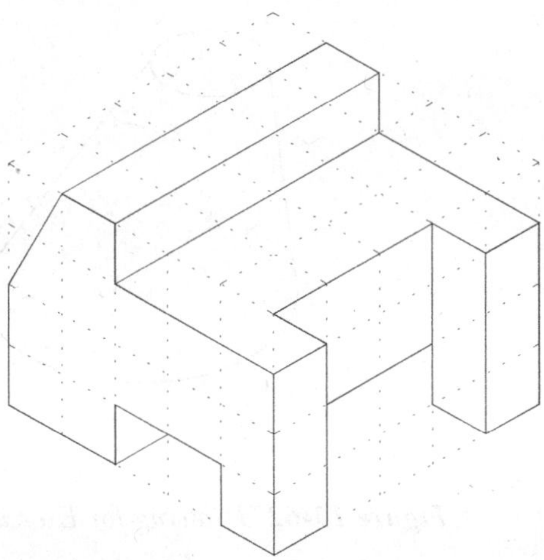

Figure 13-57 Drawing for Exercise 3

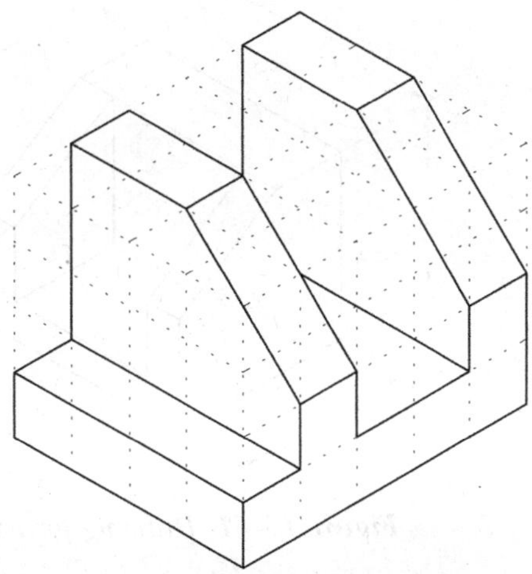

Figure 13-58 Drawing for Exercise 4

Exercises 5 through 10 *Orthographic Views*

Draw the required orthographic views of the following objects and then give the required dimensions, refer to Figures 13-59 through 13-64.

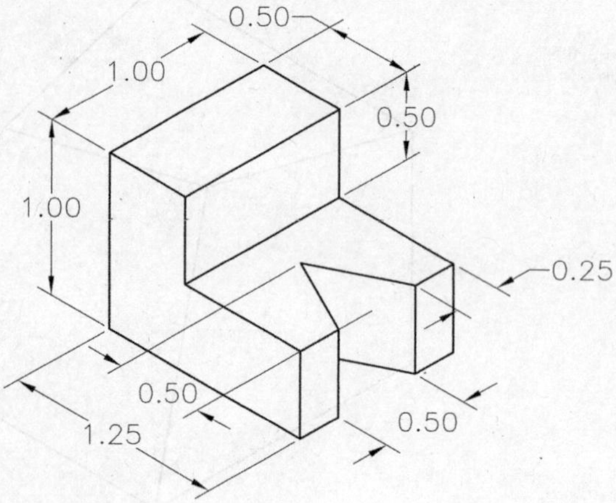

Figure 13-59 Drawing for Exercise 6

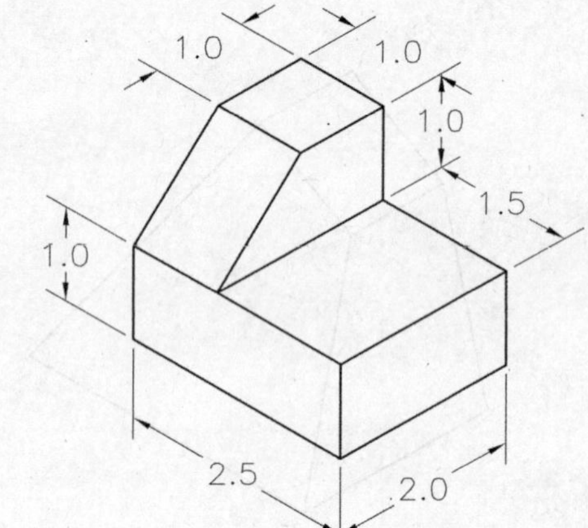

Figure 13-60 Drawing for Exercise 5

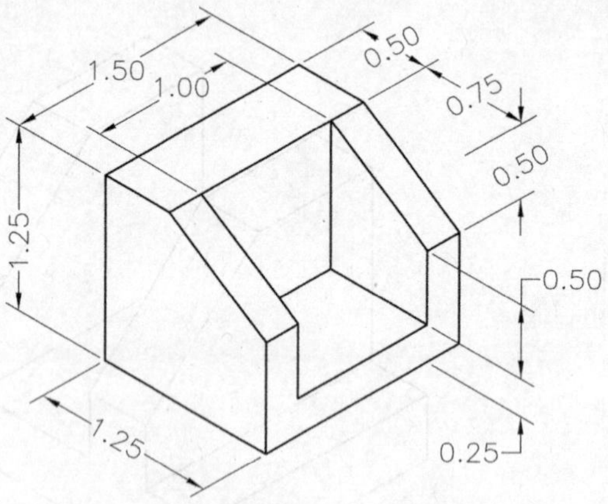

Figure 13-61 Drawing for Exercise 7

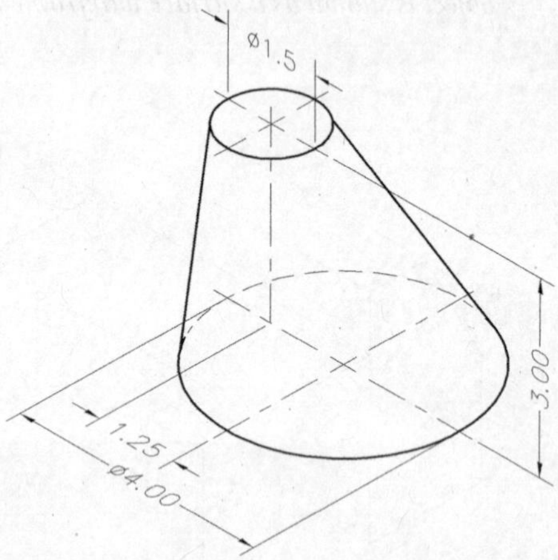

Figure 13-62 Drawing for Exercise 8

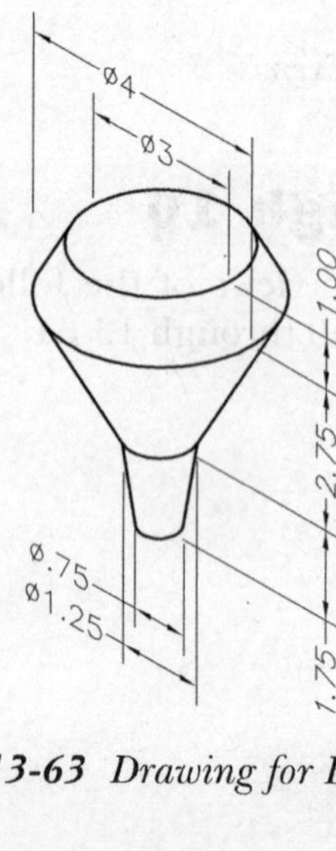

Figure 13-63 Drawing for Exercise 9

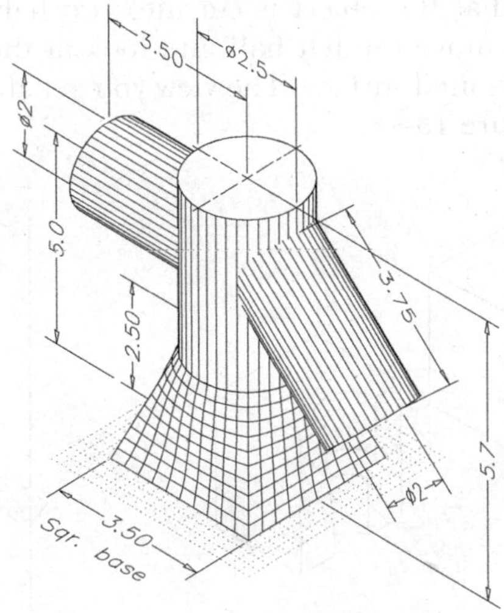

Figure 13-64 Drawing for Exercise 10 (assume the missing dimensions)

SECTIONAL VIEWS

In the principal orthographic views, the hidden features are generally shown by hidden lines. In some objects, the hidden lines may not be sufficient to represent the actual shape of the hidden feature. In such situations, sectional views can be used to show the features of the object that are not visible from outside. The location of the section and the direction of sight depend on the shape of the object and the features that need to be shown. Several ways to cut a section in the object are discussed next.

Full Section

Figure 13-65 shows an object that has a drilled counterbore hole, with taper. In the orthographic views, these features will be shown by the hidden lines, refer to Figure 13-66.

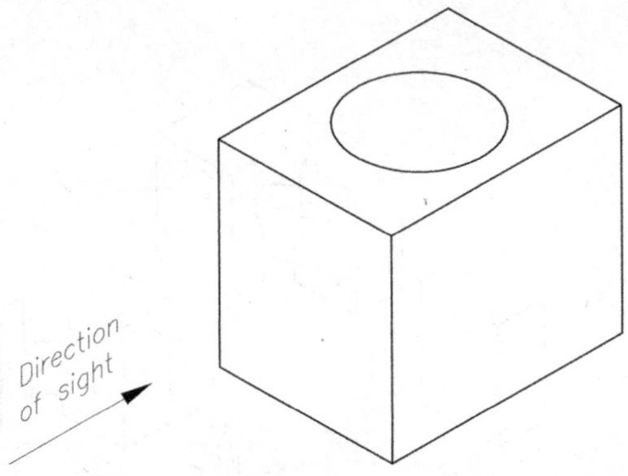

Figure 13-65 Rectangular object with hole

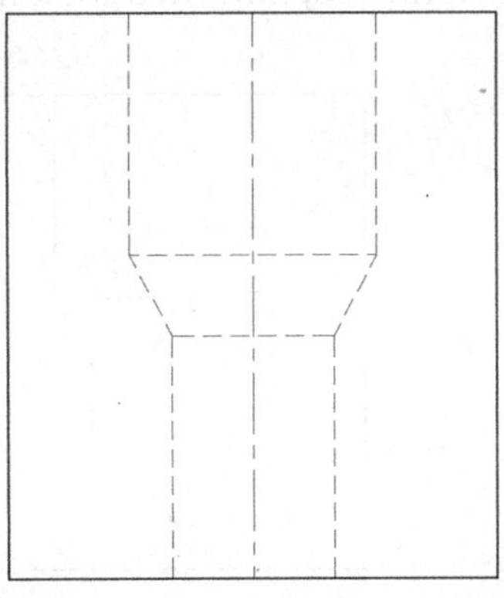

Figure 13-66 Feature shown with hidden lines

To better represent the hidden features, the object must be cut so that the hidden features are visible. In the full section, the object is cut along its entire length. To get a better idea of a full section, imagine that the object is cut into two halves along the centerline, as shown in Figure 13-67. Now, remove the left half and look at the right half in the direction that is perpendicular to the sectioned surface. The view you get after cutting the section is called a full section view, refer to Figure 13-68.

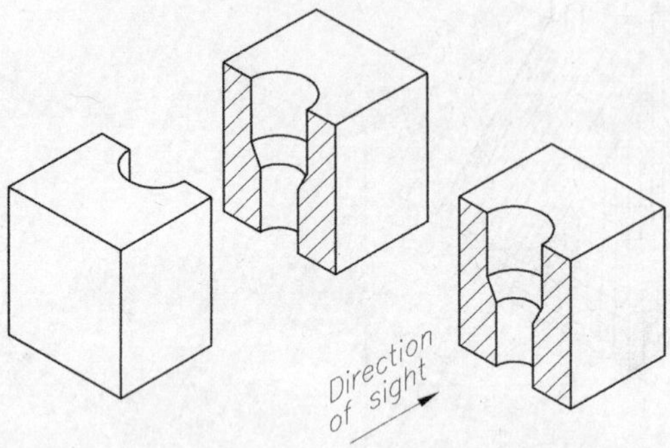

Figure 13-67 *One-half of the object removed*

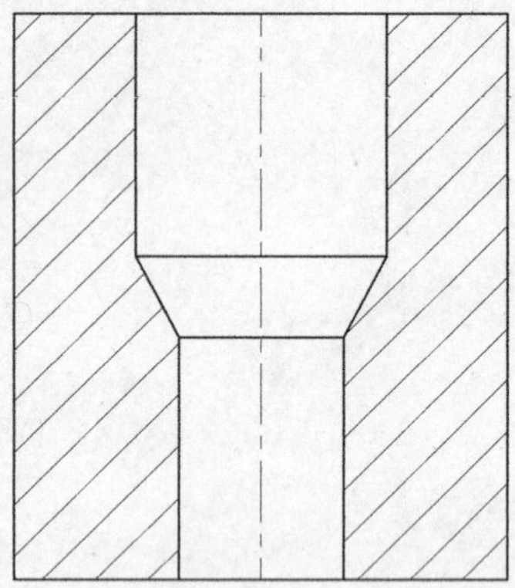

Figure 13-68 *Full section view*

In this section view, the features that would be hidden in a normal orthographic view are visible. Also, the part of the object where the material is actually cut is indicated by section lines. If the material is not cut, the section lines are not drawn. For example, if there is a hole, no material is cut when the part is sectioned, and so the section lines must not be drawn through that area of the section view.

Half Section

If the object is symmetrical, it is not necessary to draw a full section view. For example, in Figure 13-69, the object is symmetrical with respect to the centerline of the hole, so a full section is not required. But, in some objects it may help to understand and visualize the shape of the hidden details better to draw the view in half section. In half section, one-quarter of the object is removed, as shown in Figure 13-70. To draw a view in half section, imagine one-quarter of the object removed, and then look in the direction that is perpendicular to the sectioned surface.

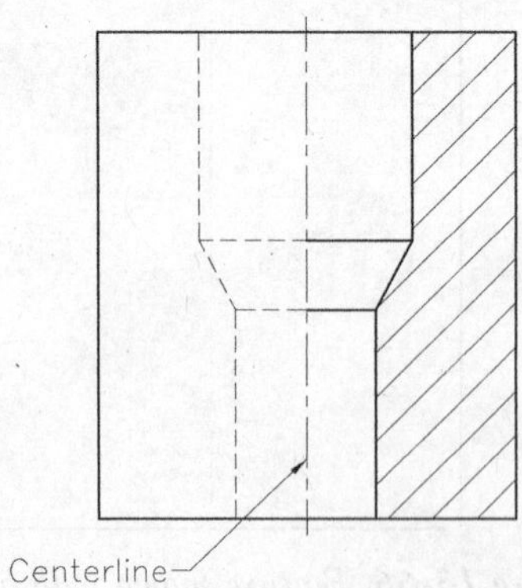

Figure 13-69 *Front view in half section*

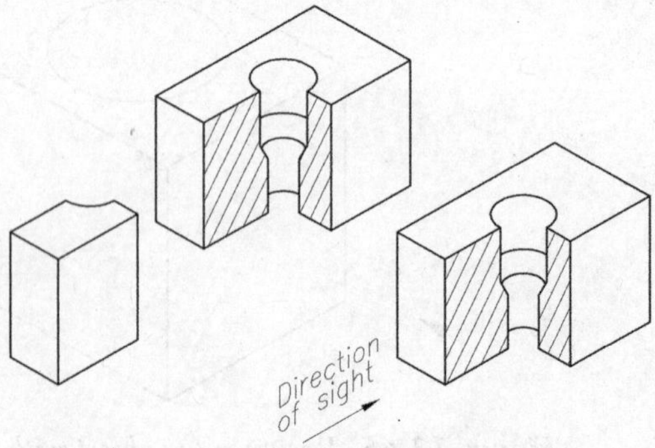

Figure 13-70 *One-quarter of the object removed*

You can also show the front view with a solid line in the middle, as shown in Figure 13-71. Sometimes the hidden lines, representing the remaining part of the hidden feature, are not drawn, refer to Figure 13-72.

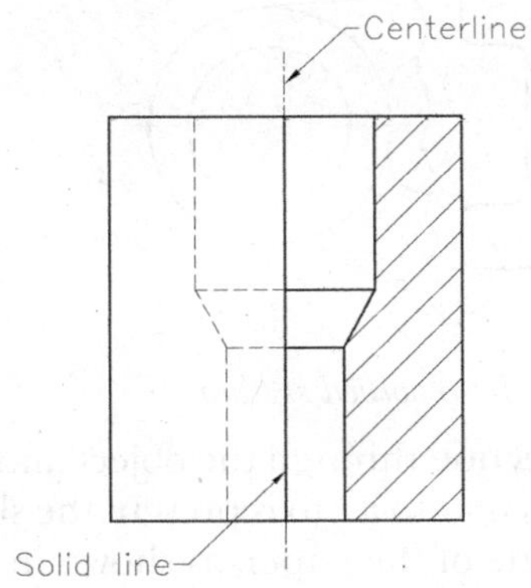

Figure 13-71 *Front view in half section*

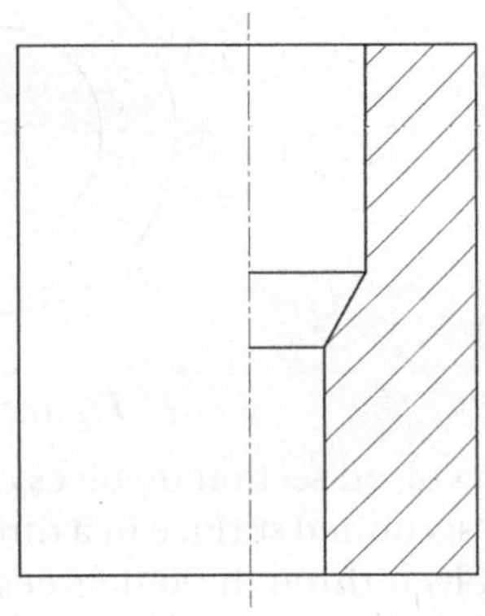

Figure 13-72 *Front view in half section with the hidden features not drawn*

Broken Section

In the broken section, only a small portion of the object is cut to expose the features that need to be drawn in the section. The broken section is designated by drawing a thick line in the section view, refer to Figure 13-73.

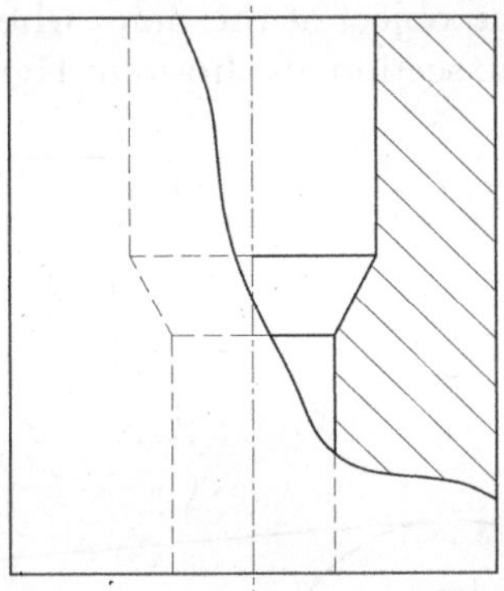

Figure 13-73 *Front view with broken section*

Revolved Section

The revolved section is used to show the true shape of the object at the point where the section is cut. The revolved section is used when it is not possible to show the features clearly in any principal view. For example, for the object shown in Figure 13-74, it is not possible to show the actual shape of the middle section in the front, side, or top view. Therefore, a revolved section is required to show the shape of the middle section.

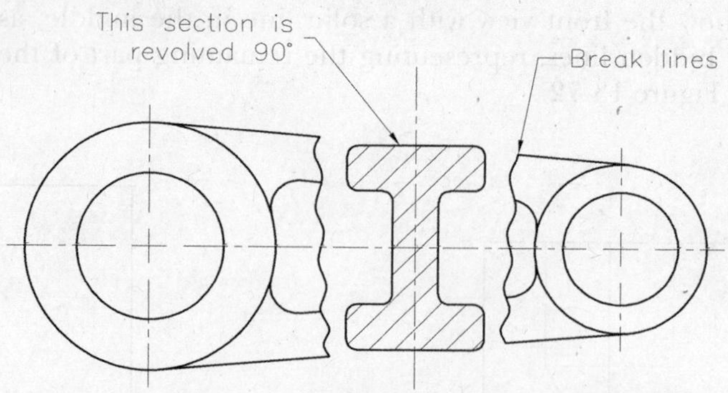

Figure 13-74 Front view with the revolved section

The revolved section involves cutting an imaginary section through the object and then looking at the sectioned surface in a direction that is perpendicular to it. To represent the shape, the view is revolved through 90 degrees and drawn in the plane of the paper, as shown in Figure 13-75. Depending on the shape of the object, and for clarity, it is recommended to provide a break in the object so that its lines do not interfere with the revolved section.

Removed Section

The removed section is similar to the revolved section, except that it is shown outside the object. The removed section is recommended when there is not enough space in the view to show it or if the scale of the section is different from the parent object. The removed section can be shown by drawing a line through the object at the point where the revolved section is required and then drawing the shape of the section, as shown in Figure 13-75.

Figure 13-75 Front view with the removed section

The other way of showing a removed section is to draw a cutting plane line through the object where you want to cut the section. The arrows should point in the direction, in which you are looking at the sectioned surface. The section can then be drawn at a convenient place in the drawing. The removed section must be labeled, as shown in Figure 13-76. If the scale has been changed, it must be mentioned with the view description.

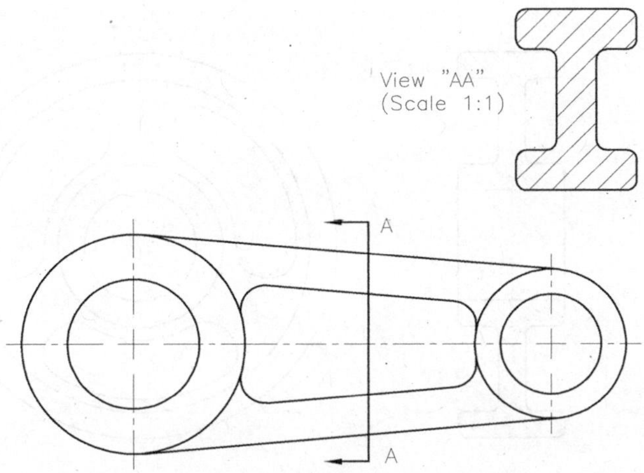

Figure 13-76 *Front view with the removed section drawn at a convenient place*

Offset Section

The offset section is used when the features of the object that you want to section are not in one plane. The offset section is designated by drawing a cutting plane line that is offset through the center of the features that need to be shown in the section, refer to Figure 13-77. The arrows indicate the direction in which the section is viewed.

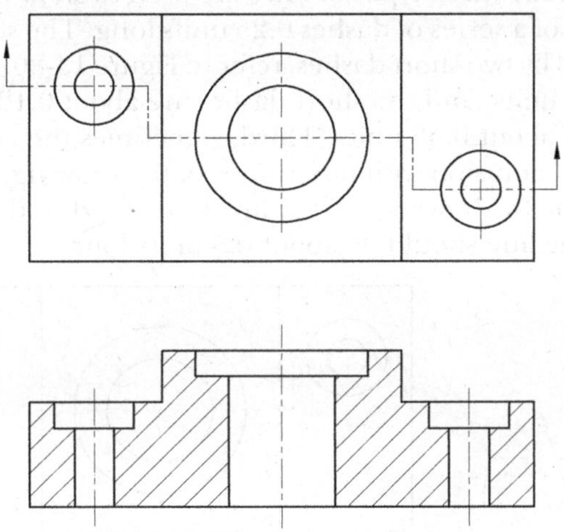

Figure 13-77 *Front view with offset section*

Aligned Section

In some objects, cutting a straight section might cause confusion in visualizing the shape of the section. Therefore, the aligned section is used to represent the shape along the cutting plane, refer to Figure 13-78. Such sections are widely used in circular objects that have spokes, ribs, or holes.

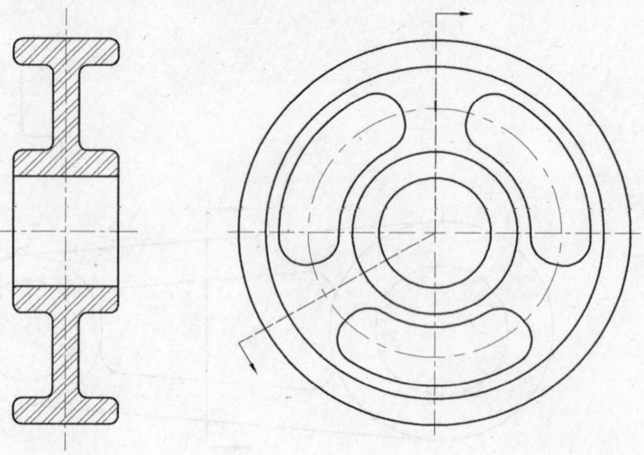

Figure 13-78 *Side view in section (aligned section)*

Cutting Plane Lines

Cutting plane lines are thicker than object lines, refer to Figure 13-79. You can use the **Polyline** tool to draw the polylines of the desired width, generally 0.005 to 0.01. However, for drawings that need to be plotted, you should assign a unique color to the cutting plane lines and then assign that color to the slot of the plotter that carries a pen of the required tip width.

In the industry, generally three types of lines are used to show the cutting plane for sectioning. The first line consists of a series of dashes 0.25 units long. The second type consists of a series of long dashes separated by two short dashes, refer to Figure 13-80. The length of the long dash can vary from 0.75 to 1.5 units, and the short dashes are about 0.12 units long. The space between the dashes should be about 0.03 units. Third, sometimes the cutting plane lines might clutter the drawing or cause confusion with other lines in the drawing. To avoid this problem, you can show the cutting plane by drawing a short line at the end of the section, refer to Figure 13-80 and Figure 13-81. The line should be about 0.5 units long.

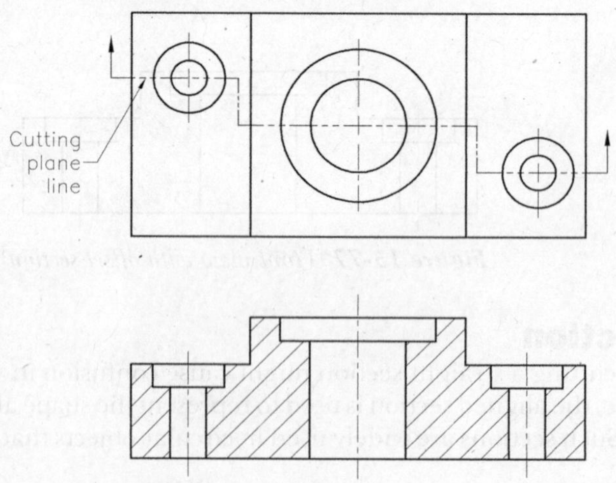

Figure 13-79 *Cutting plane lines*

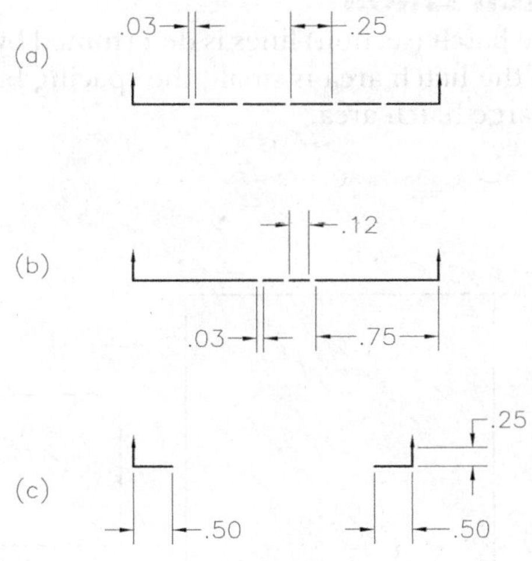

Figure 13-80 Cutting plane lines

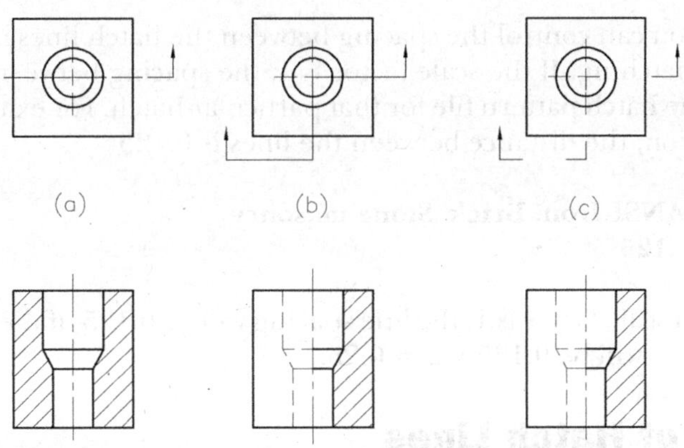

Figure 13-81 Application of cutting plane lines

Note

*In AutoCAD, you can define a new linetype that you can use to draw cutting plane lines. Refer to Chapter 11 (Creating Linetypes and Hatch Patterns) for more information on defining linetypes. Add the following lines to the **Aclt.lin** file, and then load the linetypes before assigning it to an object or a layer.*

```
*CPLANE1,___ ___ ___ ___
A,0.25,-0.03
*CPLANE2,___ ___ ___ ___
A,1.0,-0.03,0.12,-0.03,0.12,-0.03
```

Spacing for Hatch Lines

The spacing between the hatch (section) lines is determined by the space that is being hatched, refer to Figure 13-82. If the hatch area is small, the spacing between the hatch lines should be smaller compared to a large hatch area.

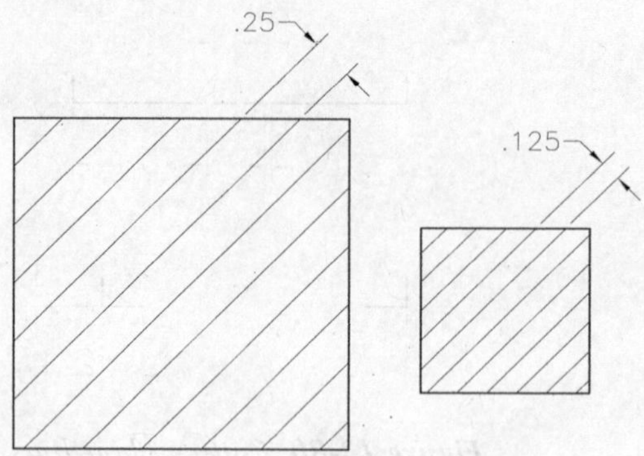

Figure 13-82 Hatch line spacing

In AutoCAD, you can control the spacing between the hatch lines by specifying the scale factor at the time of hatching. If the scale factor is 1, the spacing between the hatch lines is the same as defined in the hatch pattern file for that particular hatch. For example, in the following hatch pattern definition, the distance between the lines is 0.125.

***ANSI31, ANSI Iron, Brick, Stone masonry**
45, 0, 0, 0, .125

When the hatch scale factor is 1, the line spacing will be 0.125; if the scale factor is 2, the spacing between the lines will be 0.125 x 2 = 0.25.

Direction of Hatch Lines

The angle for the hatch lines should be 45 degrees. However, if there are two or more hatch areas next to one another representing different parts, the hatch angle must be changed so that the hatched areas look different, refer to Figure 13-83.

Also, if the hatch lines fall parallel to any edge of the hatch area, the hatch angle should be changed so that the lines are not parallel or perpendicular to any object line, refer to Figure 13-84.

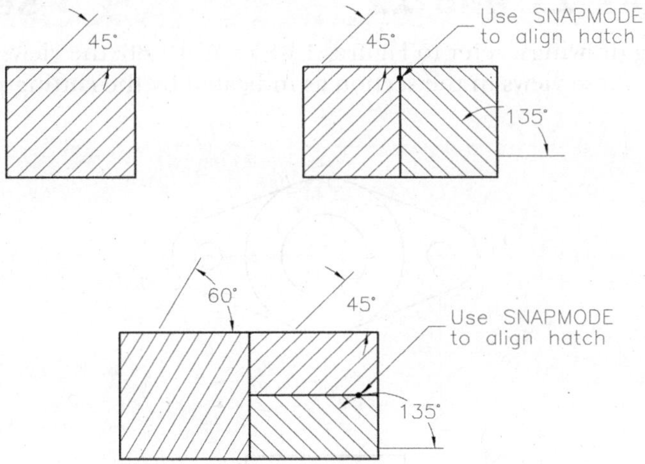

Figure 13-83 Hatch angle for adjacent parts

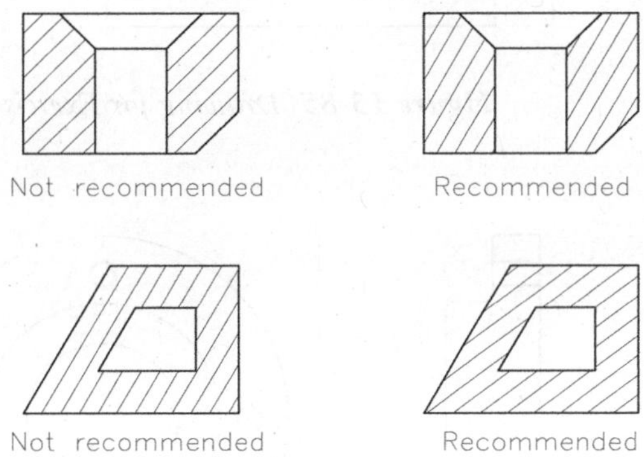

Figure 13-84 Hatch angle

Points to Remember

1. Some parts, such as bolts, nuts, shafts, ball bearings, fasteners, ribs, spokes, keys, and other similar items, if sectioned, should not be shown in the section. In case of ribs, if the cutting plane passes through the center plane of the feature, they should not be section-lined. If the cutting plane passes crosswise through ribs, they must be section-lined.

2. Hidden details should not be shown in the section view unless the hidden lines represent an important detail or help the viewer to understand the shape of the object.

3. The section lines (hatch lines) must be thinner than the object lines. You can accomplish this by assigning a unique color to the hatch lines and then assigning the color to that slot on the plotter that carries a pen with a thinner tip.

4. The section lines must be drawn on a separate layer for display and editing purposes.

Exercises 11 and 12 — *Section Views*

In the following drawings, refer to Figures 13-85 and 13-86, the views have been drawn without a section. Draw these views in the section as indicated by the cutting plane lines in each object.

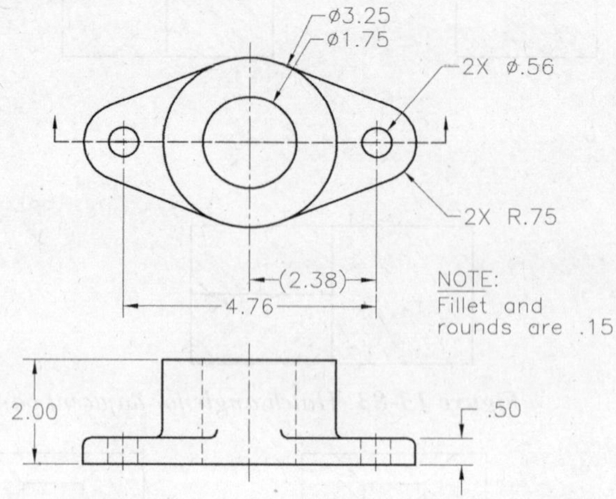

Figure 13-85 *Drawing for Exercise 11*

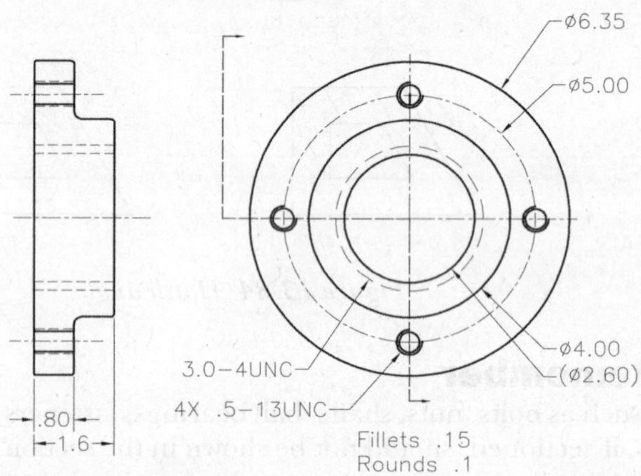

Figure 13-86 *Drawing for Exercise 12*

Exercises 13 and 14 — *Section Views*

Draw the orthographic views of the objects shown in Figures 13-87 and 13-88. The required view should be the front section view of the object such that the cutting plane passes through the holes. Also, draw the cutting plane lines in the top view.

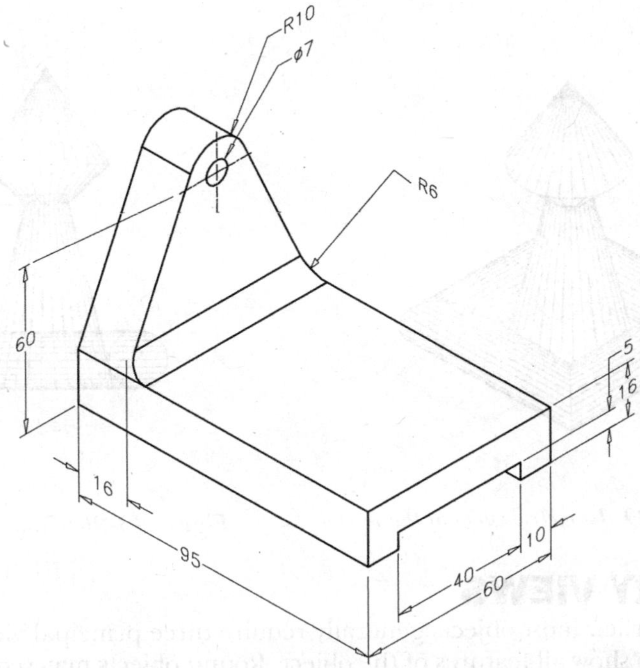

Figure 13-87 *Drawing for Exercise 13*

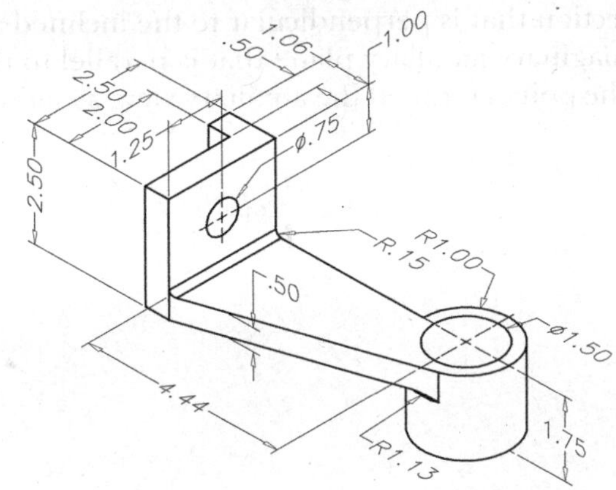

Figure 13-88 *Drawing for Exercise 14*

Exercise 15 — *Section View*

Draw the required orthographic views of the object shown in Figures 13-89 and 13-90 with the front view in the section. Also, draw the cutting plane lines in the top view to show the cutting plane. The material thickness is 0.25 units. (The object has been drawn as a surfaced 3D wiremesh model.)

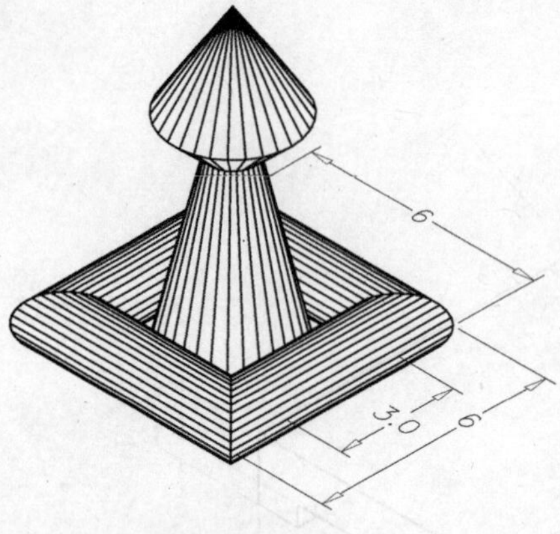

Figure 13-89 Isometric view of the model

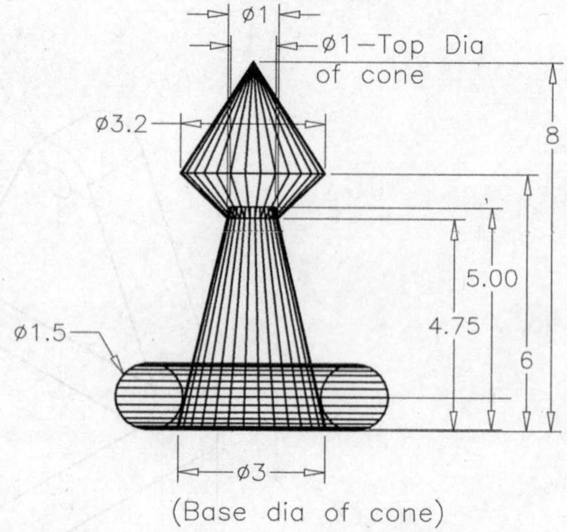

Figure 13-90 Front view of the model

AUXILIARY VIEWS

As discussed earlier, most objects generally require three principal views (front view, side view, and top view) to show all features of the object. Round objects may require just two views. Some objects have inclined surfaces. It may not be possible to show the actual shape of the inclined surface in one of the principal views. To get the true view of the inclined surface, you must look at the surface in a direction that is perpendicular to the inclined surface. Then you can project the points onto the imaginary auxiliary plane that is parallel to the inclined surface. The final view after projecting the points is called the auxiliary view, as shown in Figures 13-91 and 13-92.

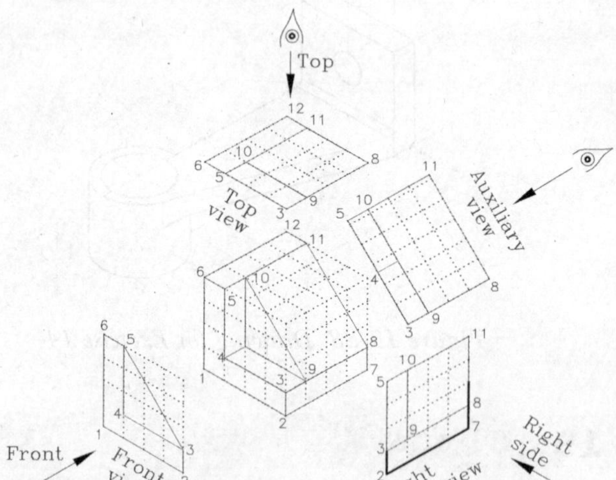

Figure 13-91 Points projected on the auxiliary plane

The auxiliary view in Figure 13-92 shows all the features of the object as seen from the auxiliary view direction. For example, the bottom left edge is shown as a hidden line. Similarly, the lower right and upper left edges are shown as continuous lines. Although these lines are technically correct, the purpose of the auxiliary view is to show the features of the inclined surface. Therefore, in the auxiliary plane, you should draw only those features that are on the inclined face, as shown in Figure 13-93. Other details that will help you to understand the shape of the object may also be included in the auxiliary view. The remaining lines should be ignored because they tend to cause confusion in visualizing the shape of the object.

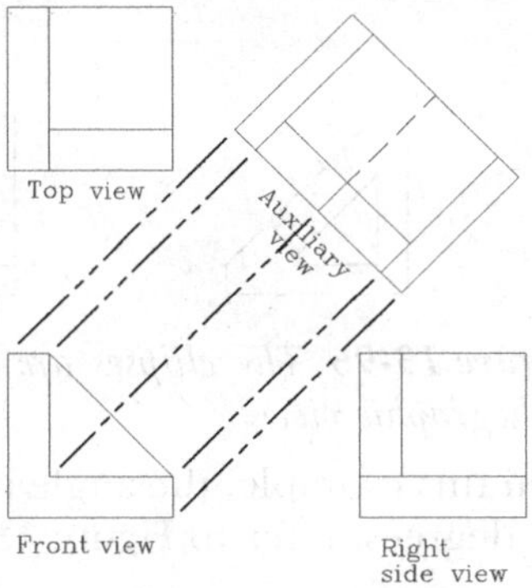

Figure 13-92 Auxiliary, front, and side views

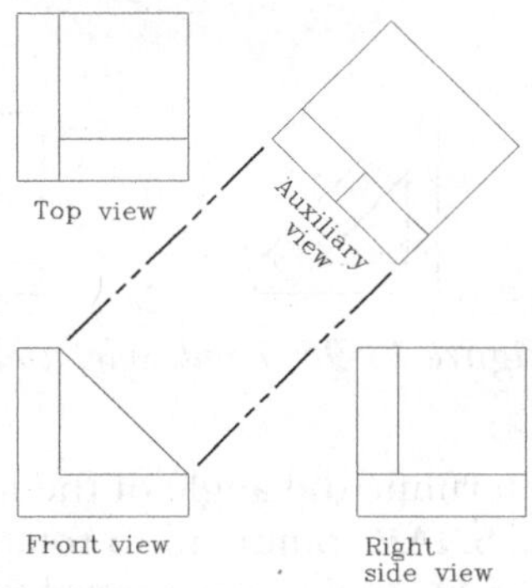

Figure 13-93 Features on the inclined plane in an auxiliary view

How to Draw Auxiliary Views

The following example illustrates how to use AutoCAD to generate an auxiliary view.

Draw the required views of the hollow triangular block that has a hole in the inclined face, as shown in Figure 13-94. (The block has been drawn as a solid model.)

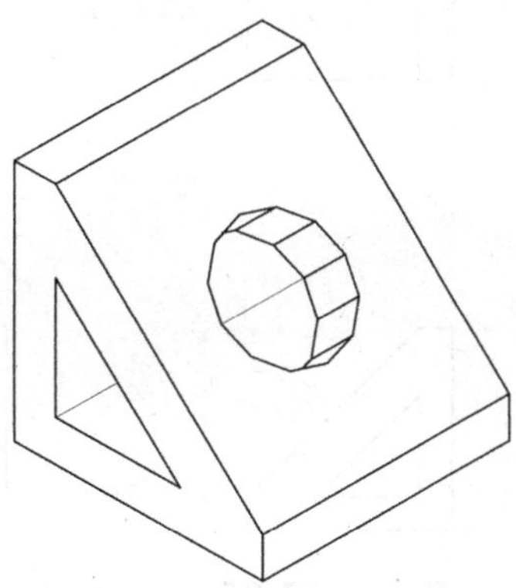

Figure 13-94 Hollow triangular block

The following steps are involved in drawing different views of this object.

1. Draw the required orthographic views: the front view, side view, and the top view as shown in Figure 13-95. The circles on the inclined surface appear like ellipses in the front and top views. These ellipses may not be shown in the orthographic views because they tend to clutter them, refer to Figure 13-96.

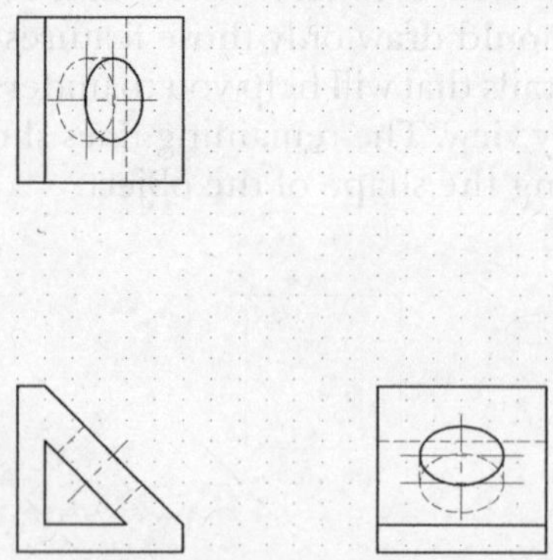

Figure 13-95 Front, side, and top views

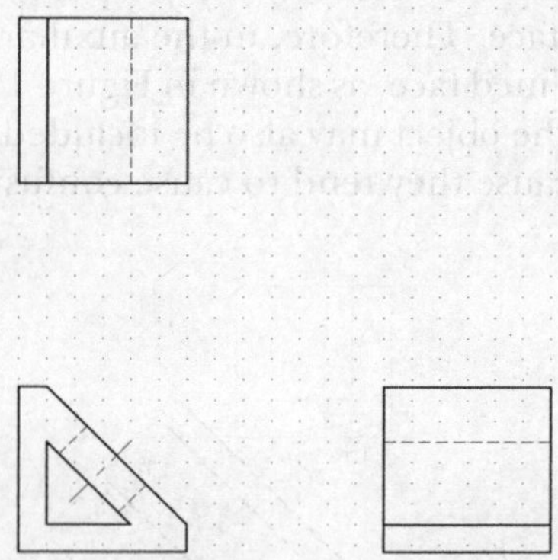

Figure 13-96 The ellipses are not visible in the orthographic views

2. Determine the angle of the inclined surface. In this example, the angle is 45 degrees. Use the **SNAP** command to rotate the snap by 45 degrees, refer to Figure 13-97 or rotate the UCS by 45 degrees around the *Z* axis.

Command: **SNAP** [Enter]
Specify snap spacing or [ON/OFF/Aspect/Style/Type] <0.5000>: **R** [Enter]
Specify base point <0.0000,0.0000>: *Select P1.*
Specify rotation angle <0>: **45** [Enter]

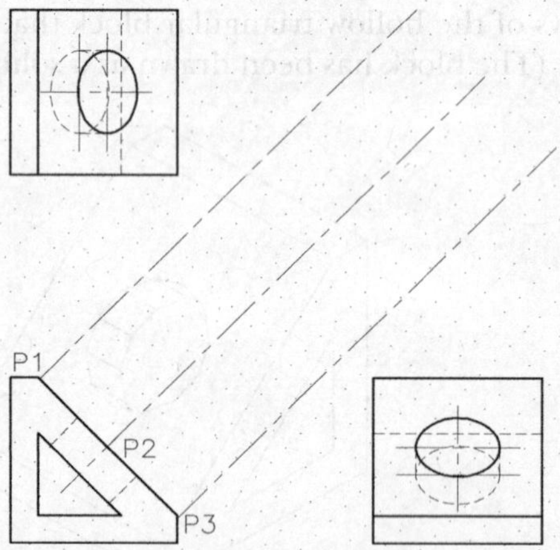

Figure 13-97 Grid lines at 45-degree

Using the rotate option, the snap will be rotated by 45 degrees and the grid lines will also be displayed at 45 degrees (if the **GRID** is on). Also, one of the grid lines will pass through point P1 because it was defined as the base point.

3. Turn **ORTHO** on, and project points P1, P2, and P3 from the front view onto the auxiliary plane. Now, you can complete the auxiliary view and give the dimensions. The projection lines can be erased after the auxiliary view is drawn, refer to Figure 13-98.

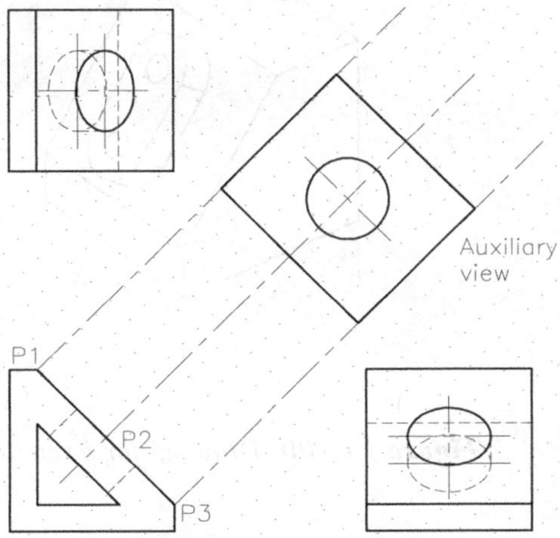

Figure 13-98 Auxiliary, front, side, and top views

Exercise 16 — Orthographic Views

Draw the orthographic and auxiliary views of the object shown in Figure 13-99. The object is drawn as a surfaced 3D wiremesh model.

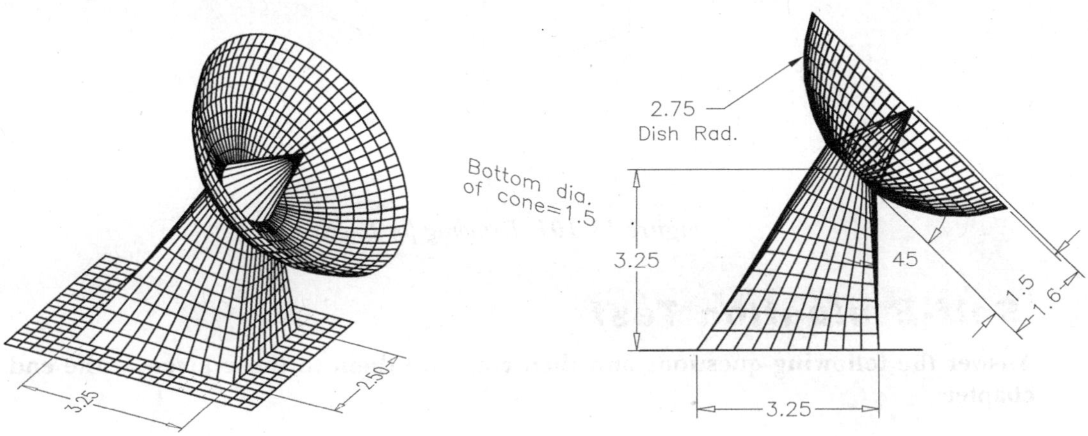

Figure 13-99 Dimensions for the mesh model

Exercises 17 and 18 — Orthographic Views

Draw the orthographic and auxiliary views of the objects shown in Figure 13-100 and Figure 13-101. The objects are drawn as 3D solid models and are shown at different angles (viewpoints are different).

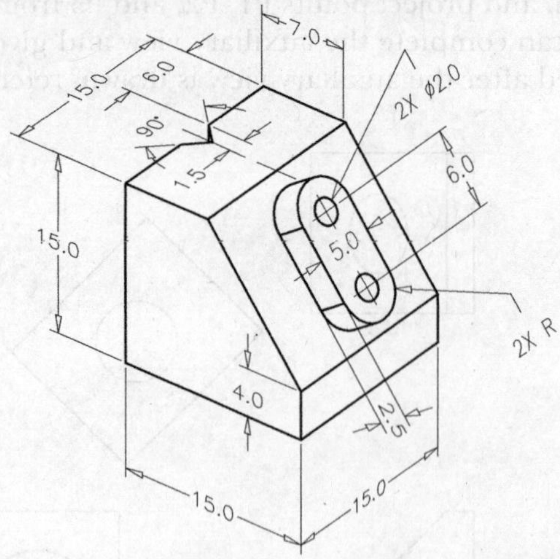

Figure 13-100 Drawing for Exercise 17

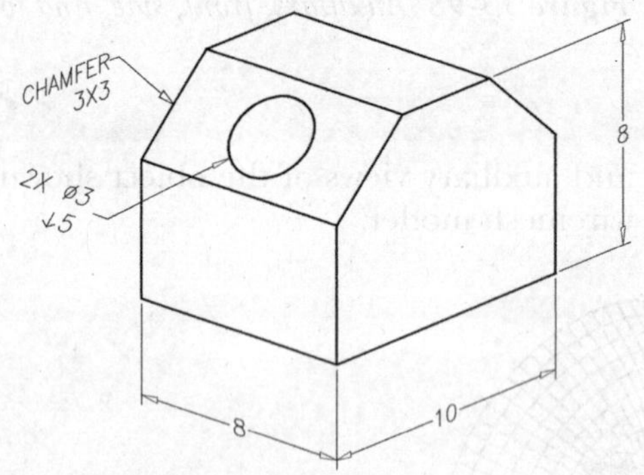

Figure 13-101 Drawing for Exercise 18

Self-Evaluation Test

Answer the following questions and then compare them to those given at the end of this chapter:

1. A line perpendicular to the *X* and *Y* axes defines the __________ axis.

2. The circle must be dimensioned as a __________, never as a radius.

3. If you give continuous (incremental) dimensioning for dimensioning various features of a part, the overall dimension must be omitted or given as a __________ dimension.

4. The removed section is similar to the __________ section except that it is shown outside the object.

5. In AutoCAD, you can control the spacing between hatch lines by specifying the _________ at the time of hatching.

6. The distance between the first dimension line and the second dimension line must be _________ to _________units.

7. The reference dimension must be enclosed in _________.

8. The front view shows the maximum number of features or gives a better idea about the shape of the object. (T/F)

9. The number of decimal places in a dimension (for example, 2.000) determines the type of machine that will be used for performing the machining operation. (T/F)

10. The dimension layer/layers should be assigned a unique color so that at the time of plotting you can assign a desired pen to plot the dimensions. (T/F)

11. All dimensions should be placed inside the view. (T/F)

12. The dimensions can be placed inside the view if they can be easily understood and cause no confusion with the other object lines. (T/F)

13. If the object is symmetrical, it is not necessary to draw a full section view. (T/F)

14. When dimensioning, you must consider the manufacturing process involved in making a part and the relationship that exists between different parts in an assembly. (T/F)

15. A dimension must be given where the feature is visible. However, in some complicated drawings, you might be justified to dimension a detail with a hidden line. (T/F)

Review Questions

Answer the following questions:

1. Multiview drawings are also known as _________ drawings.

2. The distance of the first dimension line should be _________ to _________ units from the object line.

3. For parallel dimension lines, the dimension text can be _________ if there is not enough room between the dimension lines to place the dimension text.

4. When dimensioning a circle, the diameter should be preceded by the _________.

5. When dimensioning an arc or a circle, the dimension line (leader) must be _________.

6. A bolt circle should be dimensioned by specifying the _________of the bolt circle, the_________ of the holes, and the _________ of the holes in the bolt circle.

7. In the __________ section, the object is cut along the entire length.

8. The part of the object where the material is actually cut is indicated by drawing __________ lines.

9. The __________ section is used to show the true shape of the object at the point where the section is cut.

10. The __________section is used when the features of the object that you want to section are not in one plane.

11. The section lines must be drawn on a separate layer for __________ and __________purposes.

12. In a broken section, only a __________ of the object is cut to __________ the features that need to be drawn in section.

13. The assembly drawing is used to show the __________ and their __________ in an assembled product or a machine unit.

14. The space between the *X* and *Y* axes is called the *XY* plane. (T/F)

15. A plane that is parallel to the *XY* plane is called a parallel plane. (T/F)

16. If you look at the object along the negative *Y* axis and toward the origin, you will get the side view. (T/F)

17. The top view must be directly below the front view. (T/F)

18. Before drawing orthographic views, you must look at the object and determine the number of views required to show all features of the object. (T/F)

19. By dimensioning, you not only modify the size of a part, but also give a series of instructions to a machinist, an engineer, or an architect. (T/F)

20. You can change grid, snap or UCS origin, and snap increments to make it easier to place the dimensions. (T/F)

21. You should not dimension with hidden lines. (T/F)

22. A dimension that is not to be scaled should be indicated by drawing a straight line under the dimension text. (T/F)

23. Dimensions must be given where the feature that you are dimensioning is obvious and shows the contour of the feature. (T/F)

24. In radial dimensioning, you should place the dimension text vertically. (T/F)

25. If the dimension of a feature appears in a section view, you must hatch the dimension text. (T/F)

26. Dimensions must not be repeated as it makes their updation difficult. (T/F)

27. Cutting plane lines are thinner than object lines. You can use the **Polyline** tool to draw the polylines of the desired width. (T/F)

28. The spacing between the hatch (section) lines is determined by the space being hatched. (T/F)

29. The angle for the hatch lines should be 45-degree. However, if there are two or more hatch areas next to one another representing different parts, the hatch angle must be changed so that the hatched areas look different. (T/F)

30. Some parts, such as bolts, nuts, shafts, ball bearings, fasteners, ribs, spokes, keys, and other similar items that do not show any important feature, if sectioned, must be shown in section. (T/F)

31. Section lines (hatch lines) must be thicker than object lines. (T/F)

Exercises 19 through 24

Draw the required orthographic views of the following objects (the isometric view of each object is given in Figures 13-102 through 13-107). The dimensions can be determined by counting the number of grid lines. The distance between the isometric grid lines is assumed to be 0.5 units. Also, dimension the drawings.

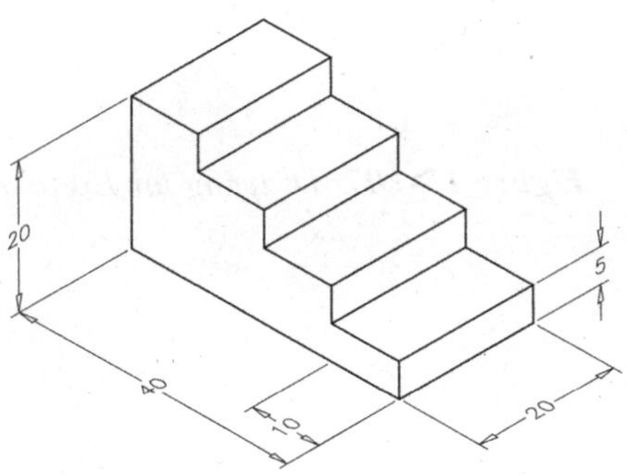

Figure 13-102 Drawing for Exercise 19

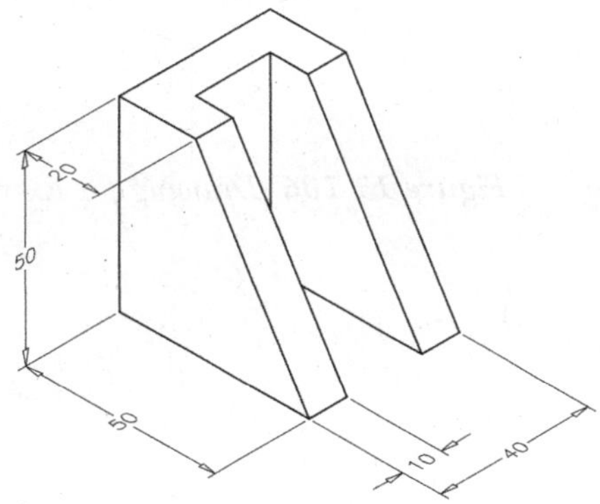

Figure 13-103 Drawing for Exercise 20

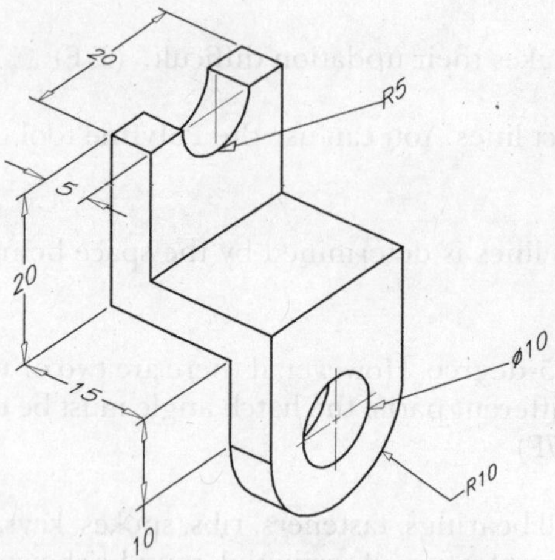

Figure 13-104 Drawing for Exercise 21

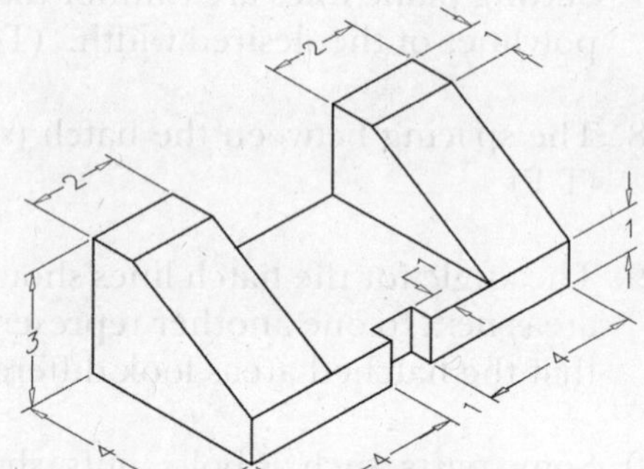

Figure 13-105 Drawing for Exercise 22

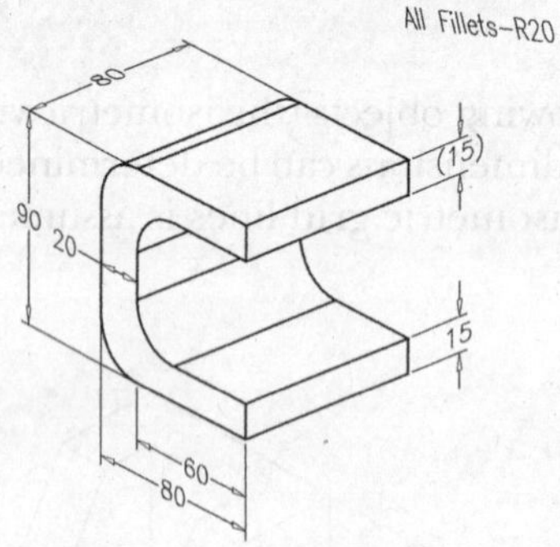

Figure 13-106 Drawing for Exercise 23

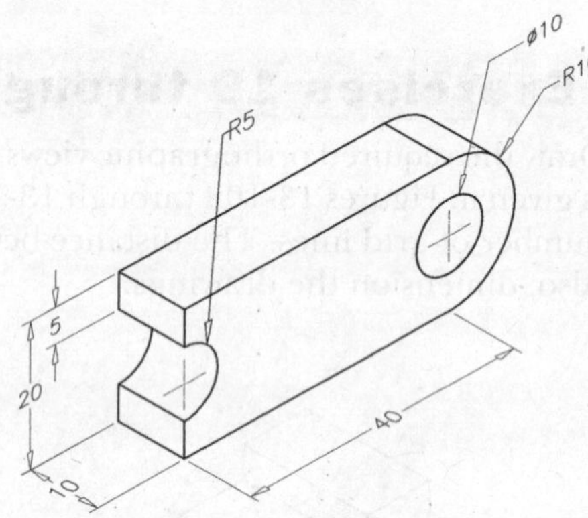

Figure 13-107 Drawing for Exercise 24

Answers to Self-Evaluation Test

1. Z, **2.** diameter, **3.** reference, **4.** revolved, **5.** scale factor, **6.** 0.25 to 0.5, **7.** parentheses, **8.** T, **9.** T, **10.** T, **11.** F, **12.** T, **13.** T, **14.** T, **15.**T

Chapter 14

Isometric Drawings

Learning Objectives

After completing this chapter, you will be able to:

- *Understand isometric drawings, isometric axes, and isometric planes*
- *Set isometric grid and snap*
- *Draw isometric circles in different isoplanes*
- *Dimension isometric objects*
- *Write text in isometric styles*

Key Terms

- *Isometric Planes*
- *Isometric Axes*
- *Isometric Snap*
- *Isometric Grid*
- *Iso Circles*
- *Isometric Text*

ISOMETRIC DRAWINGS

Isometric drawings are generally used to help visualize the shape of an object. For example, if you are given the orthographic views of an object, as shown in Figure 14-1, it takes time to put information together to visualize the shape. However, if an isometric drawing is given, as shown in Figure 14-2, it is much easier to understand the shape of the object. Thus, isometric drawings are widely used in industry to help in understanding products and their features.

Figure 14-1 Orthographic views of an object

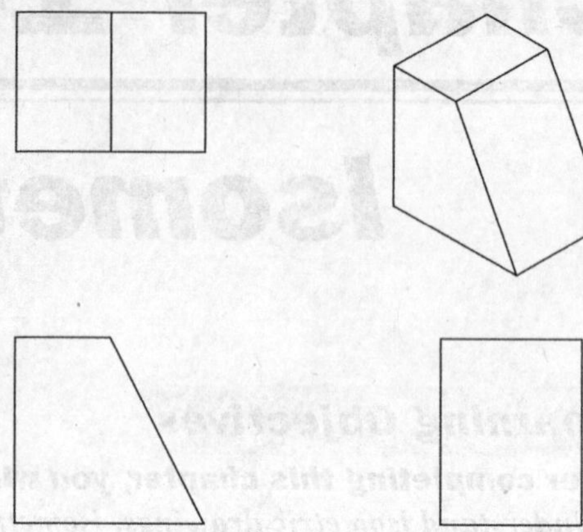

Figure 14-2 Orthographic views with an isometric drawing

An isometric drawing should not be confused with a three-dimensional (3D) drawing. An isometric drawing is just a two-dimensional (2D) representation of a 3D drawing on a 2D plane. A 3D drawing is the 3D model of an object on the X, Y, and Z axes. In other words, an isometric drawing is a 3D drawing on a 2D plane, whereas a 3D drawing is a true 3D model of the object. The model can be rotated and viewed from any direction. A 3D model can be a wireframe model, surface model, or solid model.

ISOMETRIC PROJECTIONS

The word "isometric" means equal measurement. The angle between any of the two principal axes of an isometric drawing is 120 degrees, refer to Figure 14-3. An isometric view is obtained by rotating the object by 45 degree angle around the imaginary vertical axis, and then tilting the object forward through a 35°16' angle. If you project the points and edges on the front plane, the projected length of the edges will be approximately 82 percent (isometric length/actual length = 9/11), which is shorter than the actual length of the edges. However, isometric drawings are always drawn to a full scale because their purpose is to help the user visualize the shape of the object. Isometric drawings are not meant to describe the actual size of the object. The actual dimensions, tolerances, and feature symbols must be shown in the orthographic views. Also, you should avoid showing any hidden lines in the isometric drawings unless they show an important feature of the object or help in understanding its shape.

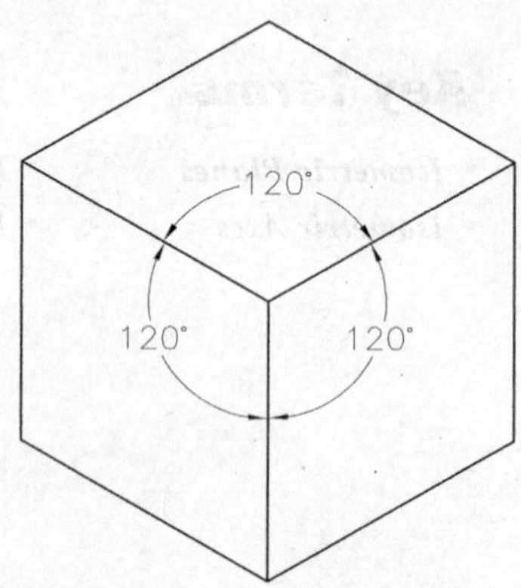

Figure 14-3 Principal axes of an isometric drawing

ISOMETRIC AXES AND PLANES

Isometric drawings have three axes: right horizontal axis (P0,P1), vertical axis (P0,P2), and left horizontal axis (P0,P3). The two horizontal axes are inclined at 30 degrees to the horizontal or X axis (X1,X2). The vertical axis is at 90 degrees, as shown in Figure 14-4.

When you draw an isometric drawing, the horizontal object lines are drawn along or parallel to the horizontal axis. Similarly, the vertical lines are drawn along or parallel to the vertical axis. For example, to make an isometric drawing of a rectangular block, the vertical edges of the block are drawn parallel to the vertical axis. The horizontal edges on the right side of the block are drawn parallel to the right horizontal axis (P0,P1), and the horizontal edges on the left side of the block are drawn parallel to the left horizontal axis (P0,P3). It is important to remember that the angles do not appear true in isometric drawings. Therefore, the edges or surfaces that are at an angle are drawn by locating their endpoints. The lines that are parallel to the isometric axes are called isometric lines. The lines that are not parallel to the isometric axes are called non isometric lines.

Similarly, the planes can be isometric planes or non isometric planes.

Isometric drawings have three principal planes, namely isoplane right, isoplane top, and isoplane left, as shown in Figure 14-5. The isoplane right (P0,P4,P10,P6) is defined by the vertical axis and the right horizontal axis. The isoplane top (P6,P10,P9,P7) is defined by the right and left horizontal axes. Similarly, the isoplane left (P0,P6,P7,P8) is defined by the vertical axis and the left horizontal axis.

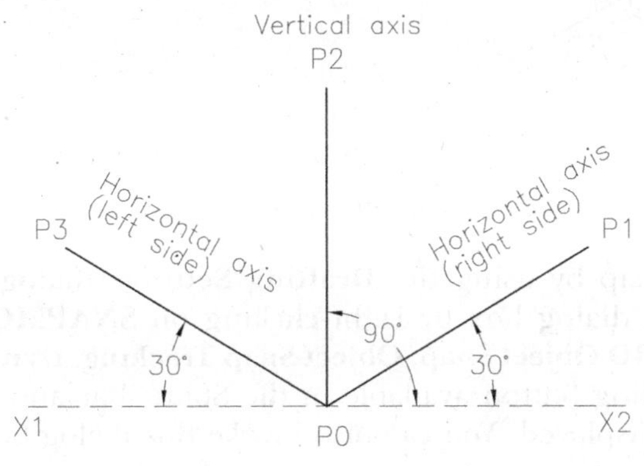

Figure 14-4 Isometric axes

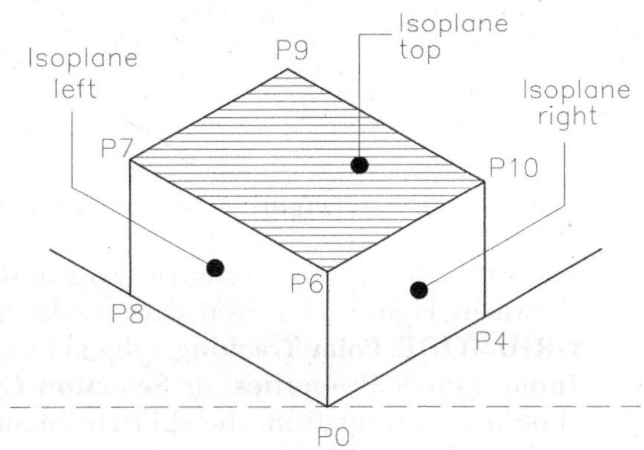

Figure 14-5 Isometric planes

SETTING THE ISOMETRIC GRID AND SNAP

You can use the **SNAP** command to set the isometric grid and snap. The isometric grid lines are displayed at 30 degree angle to the horizontal axis. Also, the distance between the grid lines is determined by the vertical spacing, which can be specified by using the **GRID** or **SNAP** command. The grid lines coincide with three isometric axes, which make it easier to create isometric drawings. The following command sequence and figure 14-6 illustrate the use of the **SNAP** command to set the isometric grid and snap of 0.5 unit:

Command: **SNAP**
Specify snap spacing or [ON/OFF/Aspect/Legacy/Style/Type] <0.5000>: **S**
Enter snap grid style [Standard/Isometric] <S>: **I**
Specify vertical spacing <0.5000>: *Enter a new snap distance.*

Note

*1. When you use the **SNAP** command to set the isometric grid, the grid lines may not be displayed. To display the grid lines, turn the grid on by choosing the **Grid Display** button from the Status Bar or press F7.*

2. You cannot set the aspect ratio for the isometric grid. Therefore, the spacing between the isometric grid lines will be the same.

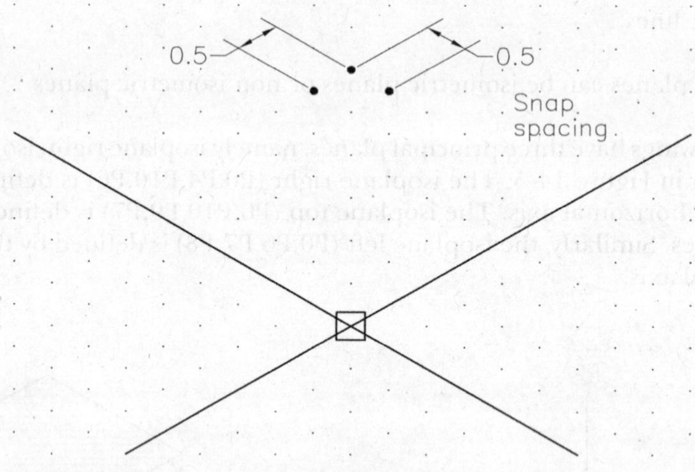

***Figure 14-6** Setting the isometric grid and snap in dotted grid*

You can also set the isometric grid and snap by using the **Drafting Settings** dialog box shown in Figure 14-7. You can invoke this dialog box by right-clicking on **SNAPMODE**, **GRIDMODE**, **Polar Tracking**, **Object Snap**, **3D Object Snap**, **Object Snap Tracking**, **Dynamic Input**, **Quick Properties**, or **Selection Cycling** button available in the Status Bar and then choosing **Settings** from the shortcut menu displayed. You can also invoke this dialog box by entering **DSETTINGS** at the Command prompt.

The isometric snap and grid functions can be turned on/off by choosing the **Grid On (F7)** check box located in the **Snap and Grid** tab of the **Drafting Settings** dialog box. The **Snap and Grid** tab also contains the radio buttons to set the snap type and style. To display the grid on the screen, make sure the grid is turned on.

When you set the isometric grid, the display of crosshairs also changes. The crosshairs are displayed at an isometric angle and their orientation depends on current isoplane. You can toggle between isoplane right, isoplane left, and isoplane top by pressing the CTRL and E keys (CTRL+E) simultaneously or by using the function key, F5. You can also toggle among different isoplanes by using the **Drafting Settings** dialog box or by entering the **ISOPLANE** command at the Command prompt:

Command: **ISOPLANE**
Enter isometric plane setting [Left/Top/Right] <Top>: **T**
Current Isoplane: **Top**

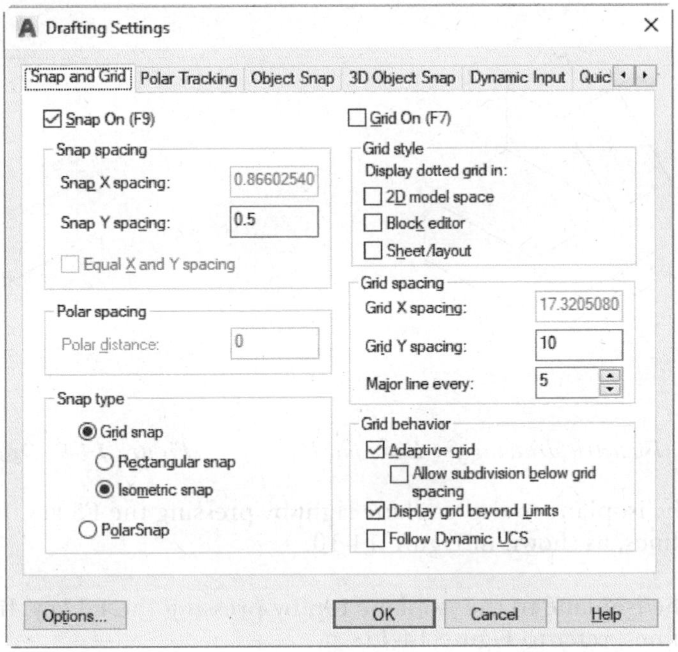

*Figure 14-7 The **Drafting Settings** dialog box*

The Ortho mode is useful when drawing in the Isometric mode. In the Isometric mode, Ortho aligns with the axes of the current isoplane.

Example 1 *Isometric Drawing*

In this example, you will create the isometric drawing shown in Figure 14-8.

1. Use the **SNAP** command to set the isometric grid and snap. The snap value is 0.5 unit.

   Command: **SNAP**
   Specify snap spacing or [ON/OFF/Aspect/Legacy/Style/Type] <0.5000>: **S**
   Enter snap grid style [Standard/Isometric] <S>: **I**
   Specify vertical spacing <0.5000>: **0.5** *(or press ENTER.)*

2. Change the isoplane to the isoplane left by pressing the F5 key. Choose the **Line** tool and draw lines between the points P1, P2, P3, P4, and P1, as shown in Figure 14-9.

Tip

*You can increase the size of the crosshairs using the **Crosshair size** slider bar in the **Display** tab of the **Options** dialog box.*

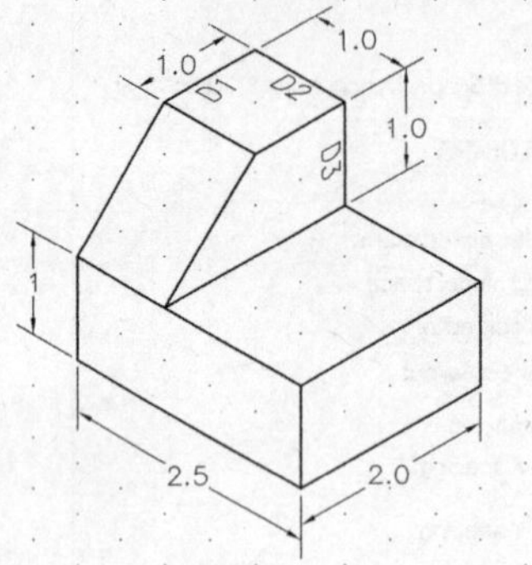

Figure 14-8 Isometric drawing for Example 1

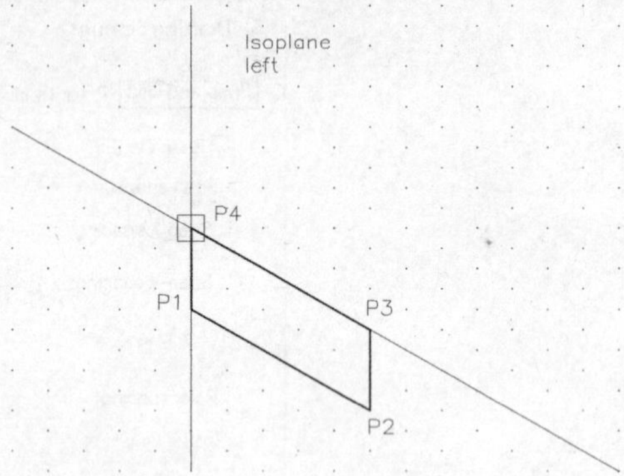

Figure 14-9 Drawing the bottom left face

3. Change the isoplane to the isoplane right by pressing the F5 key. Invoke the **Line** tool and draw the lines, as shown in Figure 14-10.

4. Change the isoplane to the isoplane top by pressing the F5 key. Invoke the **Line** tool and draw the lines, refer to Figure 14-11.

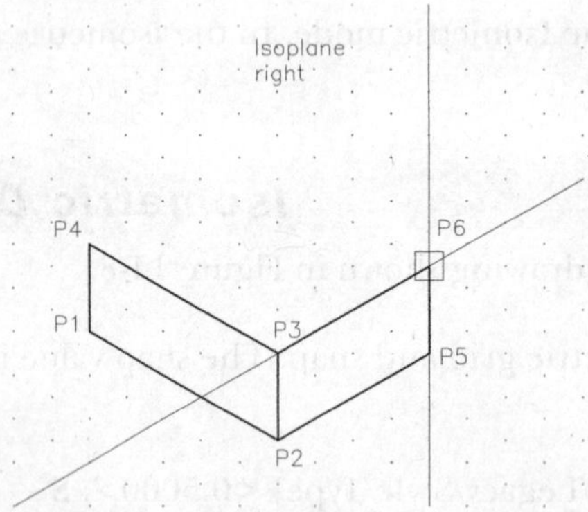

Figure 14-10 Drawing the bottom right face

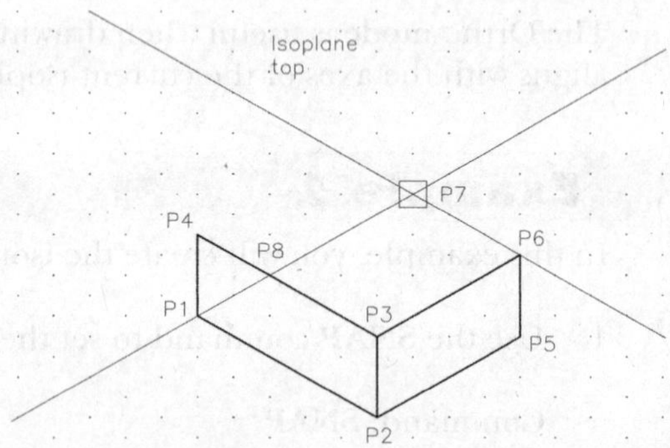

Figure 14-11 Drawing the top face

5. Similarly, draw the remaining lines, refer to Figure 14-12.

6. The front left end of the object is tapered at an angle. In isometric drawings, oblique surfaces (surfaces at an angle to the isometric axis) cannot be drawn like other lines. Make sure that the Endpoint Object Snap is on, and then locate the endpoints of the lines that define the oblique surface. Next, draw the lines between those points. To complete the drawing shown in Figure 14-8, draw a line from P10 to P8 and from P11 to P4, refer to Figure 14-13.

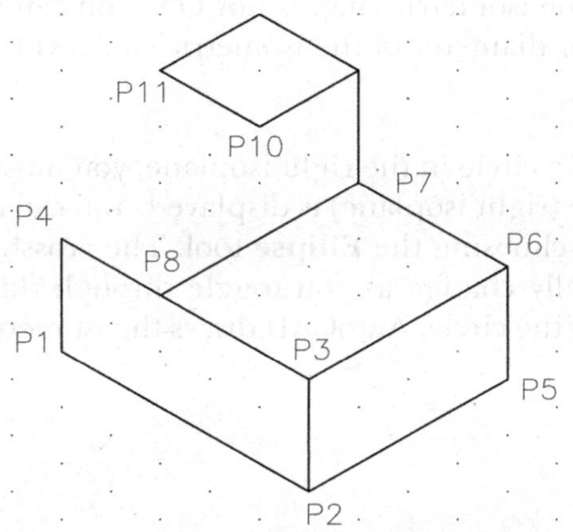

Figure 14-12 *Drawing the remaining lines*

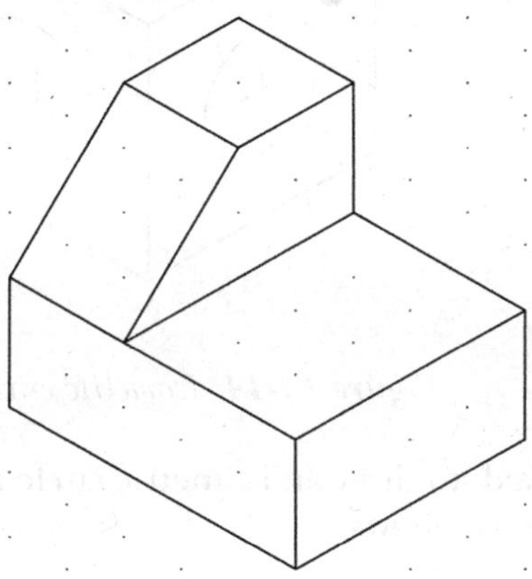

Figure 14-13 *Isometric drawing with the tapered face*

DRAWING ISOMETRIC CIRCLES

The isometric circles are drawn by using the tools available in the **Ellipse** drop-down and then selecting the **Isocircle** option. To draw an isometric circle, choose the **Axis**, **End,** or **Elliptical**

Arc tool from the **Ellipse** drop-down. As soon as you select any of these options, the **Isocircle** option will be available in the Command prompt. Select the **Isocircle** option from the Command prompt; you will be prompted to specify the center of isocircle. Specify the center of the isocircle. Next, you will be prompted to specify the radius of the isocircle. Once you specify the radius and press enter, isocircle will be created.

Note that you must have the Isometric Snap on while using the Ellipse tools to display the **Isocircle** option. If the isometric snap is not ON, you cannot draw an isometric circle. Before entering the radius or diameter of the isometric circle, you must make sure that you are in the required isoplane.

For example, to draw a circle in the right isoplane, you must toggle through the isoplanes until the required isoplane (right isoplane) is displayed. You can also set the required isoplane as the current plane before choosing the **Ellipse** tool. The crosshairs and the shape of the isometric circle will automatically change as you toggle through different isoplanes. As you enter the radius or diameter of the circle, AutoCAD draws the isometric circle in the selected plane, refer to Figure 14-14.

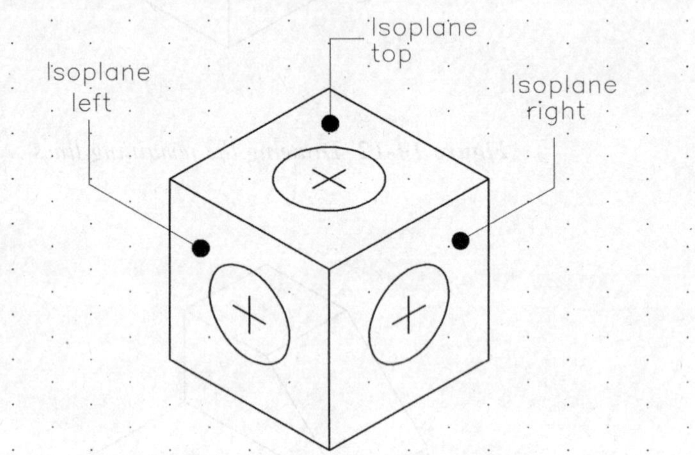

Figure 14-14 *Isometric circles drawn*

The prompt sequence used to draw an isometric circle after choosing the **Axis**, **End** tool from the **Ellipse** drop-down is as follows:

Specify axis endpoint of ellipse or [Arc/Center/Isocircle]: **I**
Specify center of isocircle: *Select a point.*
Specify radius of isocircle or [Diameter]: *Enter circle radius,* Enter

Creating Fillets in Isometric Drawings

To create fillets in isometric drawings, you first need to create an isometric circle and then trim its unwanted portion. Remember that there is no other method to directly create an isometric fillet.

Dimensioning Isometric Objects

Isometric dimensioning involves two steps: (1) dimensioning the drawing using the standard dimensioning tools, (2) editing the dimensions to change them to oblique dimensions.

Example 2 *Dimensioning*

The following example illustrates the process involved in dimensioning an isometric drawing. In this example, you will dimension the isometric drawing created in Example 1.

1. Dimension the drawing given in Example 1, as shown in Figure 14-15. You can use the aligned dimension to dimension the drawing. Remember that when you select the points, you must use the **Intersection** or **Endpoint** object snap to snap the endpoints of the object you are dimensioning. AutoCAD automatically leaves a gap between the object line and the extension line, as specified by the **DIMGAP** variable.

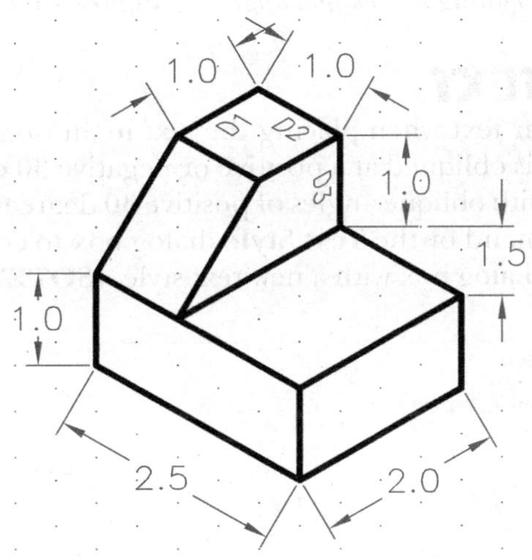

***Figure 14-15** The dimensioned isometric drawing before using the **Oblique** tool*

2. The next step is to edit the dimensions. You can choose the **Oblique** tool from the **Dimensions** panel of the **Annotate** tab. After selecting the dimension that you want to edit, you are prompted to enter the obliquing angle. The obliquing angle is determined by the angle that the extension line of the isometric dimension makes with the positive *X* axis. The following prompt sequence is displayed when you invoke this option from the **Ribbon**:
   Select objects: *Select the dimension (D1).*
   Select objects: *Press ENTER.*
   Enter obliquing angle (Press ENTER for none): **150**

For example, the extension line of the dimension labeled D1 makes a 150 degree angle with the positive X axis, refer to Figure 14-16(a), therefore, the oblique angle is 150 degrees. Similarly, the extension lines of the dimension labeled D2 and D3 make a 30 degree angle with the positive

X axis, refer to Figure 14-16(b) and (c) , therefore, the oblique angle is 30 degrees. After you edit all dimensions, the drawing should appear as shown in Figure 14-17.

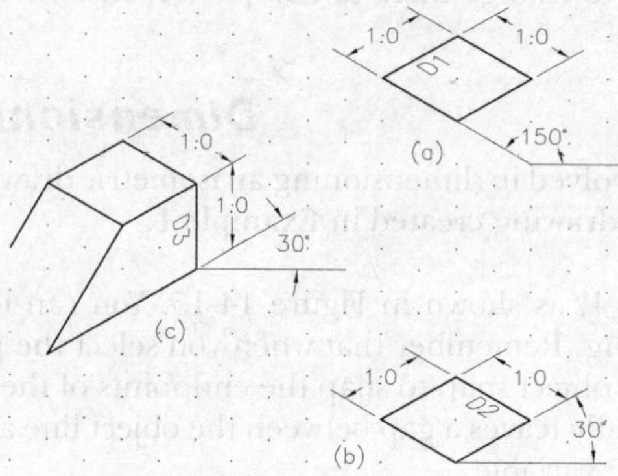

Figure 14-16 Determining the oblique angle

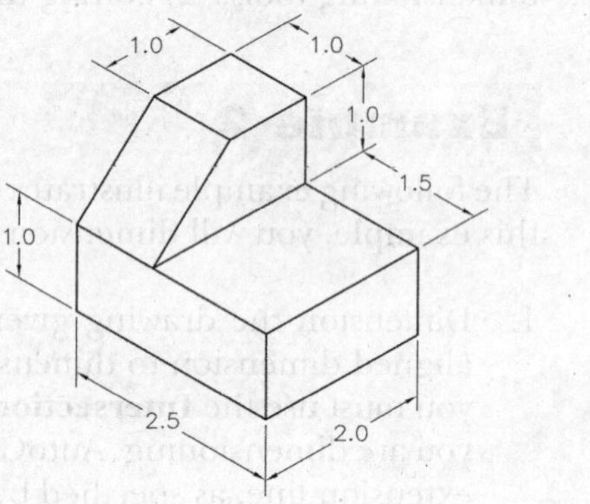

Figure 14-17 Object with isometric dimensions

ISOMETRIC TEXT

You cannot use regular text when placing the text in an isometric drawing because the text in an isometric drawing is obliqued at a positive or negative 30 degree angle. Therefore, you must create two text styles with oblique angles of positive 30 degrees and negative 30 degrees. You can use the **-STYLE** command or the **Text Style** dialog box to create a new text style. Figure 14-18 shows the **Text Style** dialog box with a new text style, **ISOTEXT1** and its corresponding values.

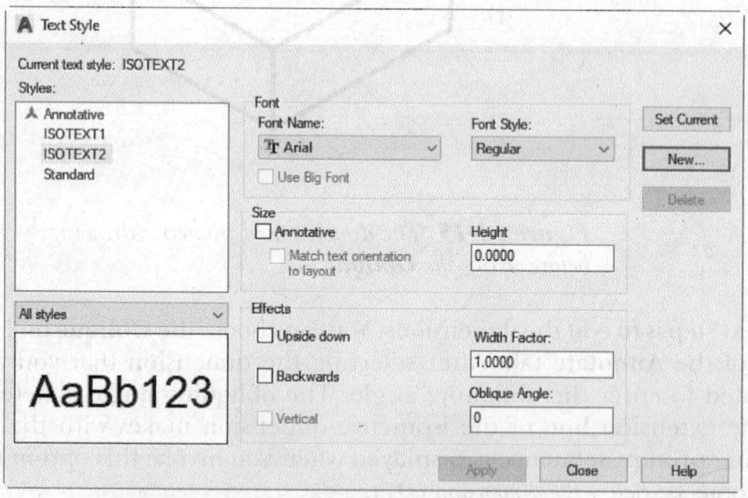

*Figure 14-18 The **Text Style** dialog box*

Similarly, you can create another text style, **ISOTEXT2**, with a negative 30 degrees oblique angle. When you place the text in an isometric drawing, you must also specify the rotation angle for the text. The text style and the text rotation angle depend on the placement of the text in the isometric drawing, as shown in Figure 14-19.

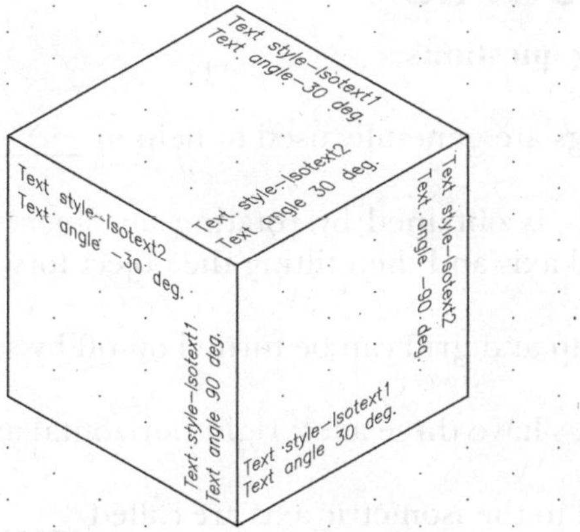

Figure 14-19 *Text style and rotation angle for isometric text*

Self-Evaluation Test

Answer the following questions and then compare them to those given at the end of this chapter:

1. The word "isometric" means __________. The three angles between the three principal axes of an isometric drawing measure __________ degree each.
2. The ratio of isometric length to the actual length in an isometric drawing is approximately __________.
3. The angle between the right isometric horizontal axis and the X axis is __________ degree.
4. Isometric drawings have three principal planes: isoplane right, isoplane top, and __________.
5. To toggle among isoplane right, isoplane left, and isoplane top, you can use __________ key combination or __________ function key.
6. The lines that are not parallel to the isometric axes are called __________.
7. You can only use the aligned dimension option to dimension an isometric drawing. (T/F)
8. The isometric snap must be turned on to display the **Isocircle** option while using the **Ellipse** tool. (T/F)
9. While placing text in an isometric drawing, you need to specify the rotation angles. (T/F)
10. You should avoid showing any hidden lines in isometric drawings. (T/F)

Review Questions

Answer the following questions:

1. Isometric drawings are generally used to help in __________ the shape of an object.

2. An isometric view is obtained by rotating an object by __________ degree around the imaginary vertical axis and then tilting the object forward through a __________ angle.

3. The isometric snap and grid can be turned on/off by selecting the __________ check box.

4. Isometric drawings have three axes: right horizontal axis, vertical axis, and __________.

5. The lines parallel to the isometric axis are called __________.

6. You can use the __________ command to set the isometric grid and snap.

7. Isometric grid lines are displayed at __________ degrees to the horizontal axis.

8. You can also set the isometric grid and snap by using the **Drafting Settings** dialog box, which can be invoked by entering __________ at the Command prompt.

9. Isometric circles are drawn by using the Ellipse tools and then selecting the __________ option.

10. To place text in an isometric drawing, you must create two text styles with oblique angles of __________ degree and __________ degree.

11. You should avoid showing hidden lines in isometric drawings unless they help in understanding its shape. (T/F)

12. Angles do not appear true in isometric drawings. (T/F)

13. You can set the aspect ratio for the isometric grid. (T/F)

14. You can draw an isometric circle without turning the isometric snap on. (T/F)

15. Only the aligned dimensions can be edited to change them to oblique dimensions. (T/F)

EXERCISES 1 through 4

Draw the following isometric drawings, refer to Figures 14-20 through 14-23. The dimensions can be determined by counting the number of grid lines. The distance between the isometric grid lines is assumed to be 0.5 unit. Dimension the drawing, as shown in Figure 14-23.

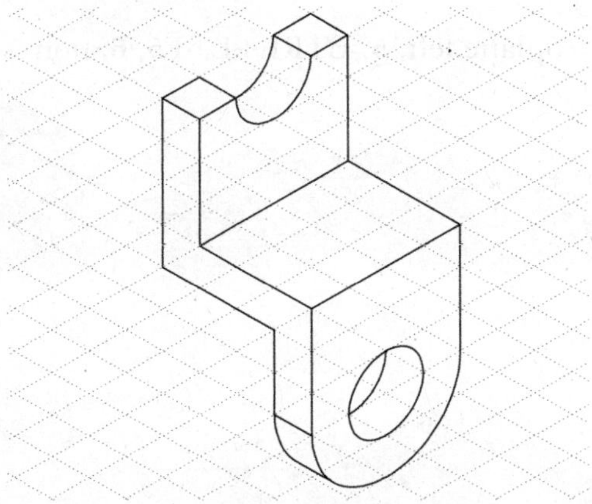

Figure 14-20 Drawing for Exercise 1

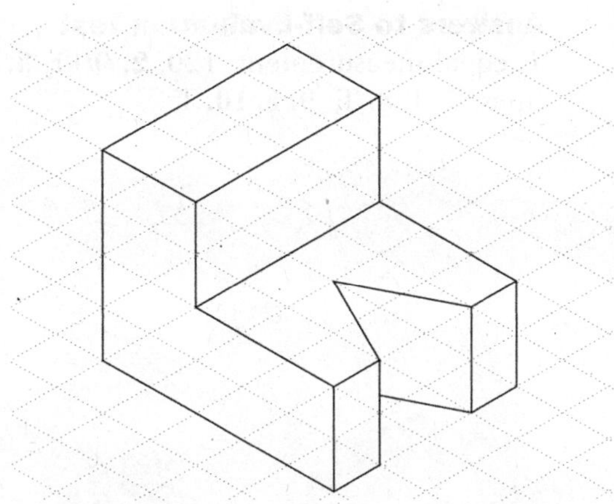

Figure 14-21 Drawing for Exercise 2

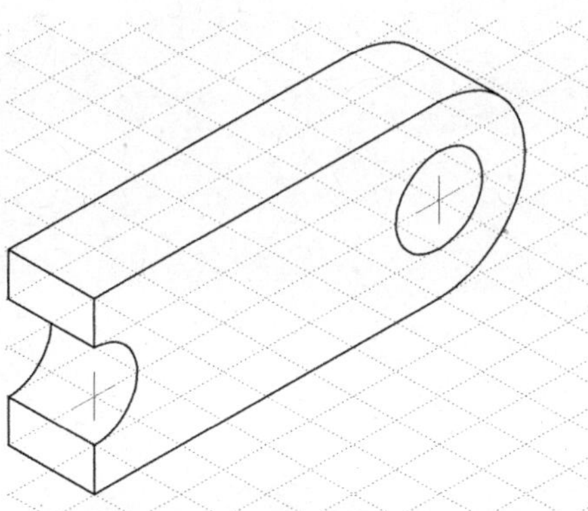

Figure 14-22 Drawing for Exercise 3

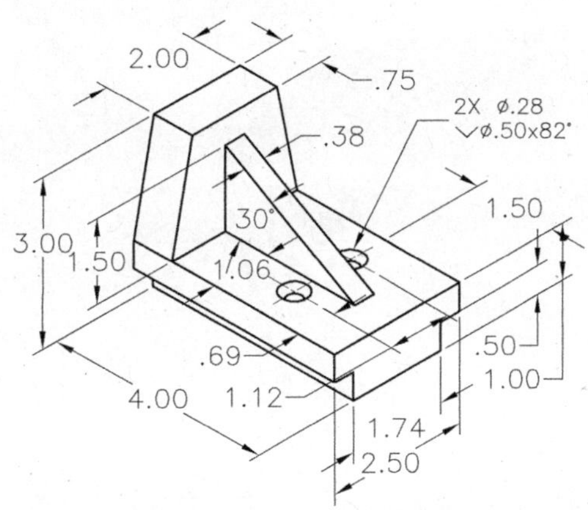

Figure 14-23 Drawing for Exercise 4

Answers to Self-Evaluation Test

1. equal measurement, 120, **2.** 9/11, **3.** 30, **4.** isoplane left, **5.** CTRL+E, F5, **6.** non isometric lines, **7.** T, **8.** T, **9.** F, **10.** T

Index

R

S

T

U

V

W

X

Y

Z

Other Titles of Interest - BPB/TICKOO Serires

Publication by BPB/TICKOO SERIES

The following is the list of some of the publications by BPB/TICKOO.

AutoCAD Textbooks

- AutoCAD 2021 for Engineers and Designers - Basic and Intermediate
- AutoCAD 2020 for Engineers and Designers - Basic and Intermediate
- AutoCAD 2020 Workbook

Autodesk Inventor Textbooks

- Autodesk Inventor Professional 2021 for Engineers and Designers
- Autodesk Inventor Professional 2020 for Engineers and Designers
- Inventor 2020 Workbook

AutoCAD MEP Textbooks

- AutoCAD MEP 2020 for Engineers and Designers
- AutoCAD MEP 2020 for Designers, 5th Edition

AutoCAD Plant 3D Textbooks

- AutoCAD Plant 3D 2020 for Designers, 5th Edition

Autodesk Fusion 360 Textbook

- Autodesk Fusion 360: A Tutorial Approach, 2nd Edition

Solid Edge Textbooks

- Solid Edge 2020 for Designers, 17th Edition
- Solid Edge 2019 for Engineers and Designers

NX Textbooks

- Siemens NX 2020 for Engineers and Designers
- Siemens NX 2019 for Engineers and Designers
- Siemens NX 2020 for Designers, 13th Edition
- Siemens NX 2019 Workbook

NX Mold Textbook

- Mold Design Using NX 11.0: A Tutorial Approach

NX Nastran Textbook

- NX Nastran 9.0 for Designers

SOLIDWORKS Textbooks
- SOLIDWORKS 2019 for Engineers and Designers
- SOLIDWORKS 2020 for Designers, 18th Edition

SOLIDWORKS Simulation Textbooks
- SOLIDWORKS Simulation 2018: A Tutorial Approach
- SOLIDWORKS Simulation 2016: A Tutorial Approach

CATIA Textbooks
- CATIA V5-6R2018 for Engineers and Designers
- CATIA V5-6R2019 for Designers, 17th Edition

Creo Parametric Textbooks
- Creo Parametric 6.0 for Engineers and Designers
- Creo Parametric 6.0 Workbook

ANSYS Textbooks
- Finite Element Analysis with ANSYS Workbench 2019 R2
- ANSYS Workbench 2019 R2: A Tutorial Approach

Creo Direct Textbook
- Creo Direct 2.0 and Beyond for Designers

Autodesk Alias Textbooks
- Learning Autodesk Alias Design 2016, 5th Edition
- Learning Autodesk Alias Design 2015, 4th Edition

AutoCAD LT Textbooks
- AutoCAD LT 2020 for Designers, 13th Edition
- AutoCAD LT 2017 for Designers, 12th Edition

AutoCAD Electrical Textbooks
- AutoCAD Electrical 2020: A Tutorial Approach for Engineers and Designers
- AutoCAD Electrical 2020 for Engineers and Designers
- AutoCAD Electrical 2019 for Engineers and Designers
- AutoCAD Electrical 2018 for Electrical Control Designers, 9th Edition

Autodesk Revit MEP Textbooks
- Exploring Autodesk Revit 2019 for MEP, 6th Edition
- Exploring Autodesk Revit 2018 for MEP, 5th Edition

AutoCAD Civil 3D Textbooks
- Exploring AutoCAD Civil 3D 2020 for Engineers and Designers
- Exploring AutoCAD Civil 3D 2019 for Engineers and Designers
- Exploring AutoCAD Civil 3D 2020, 10th Edition

AutoCAD Map 3D Textbooks
- Exploring AutoCAD Map 3D 2018, 8th Edition
- Exploring AutoCAD Map 3D 2017, 7th Edition

RISA-3D Textbook
- Exploring RISA-3D 14.0

Autodesk Navisworks Textbooks
- Exploring Autodesk Navisworks 2020 for BIM
- Exploring Autodesk Navisworks 2019 for BIM

AutoCAD Raster Design Textbooks
- Exploring AutoCAD Raster Design 2017

Bentley STAAD.Pro Textbooks
- Exploring Bentley STAAD.Pro (CONNECT Edition), 3rd Edition
- Exploring Bentley STAAD.Pro V8i (SELECTseries 6)

Autodesk 3ds Max Textbooks
- Autodesk 3ds Max 2021 for 3D Designers
- Autodesk 3ds Max 2020 for 3D Designers
- Autodesk 3ds Max 2019: A Comprehensive Guide, 19th Edition
- Autodesk 3ds Max 2018: A Comprehensive Guide, 18th Edition

Autodesk Maya Textbooks
- Autodesk Maya 2020 for 3D Artists
- Autodesk Maya 2019 for 3D Artists
- Autodesk Maya 2019 Workbook
- Autodesk Maya 2018: A Comprehensive Guide, 10th Edition

ZBrush Textbooks
- Pixologic ZBrush 2020 for Digital Artists
- Pixologic ZBrush 2018 for Digital Artists
- Pixologic ZBrush 4R8: A Comprehensive Guide, 4th Edition

Blender Textbook
- Blender 2.79 for Digital Artists

CINEMA 4D Textbooks
- MAXON CINEMA 4D R20 Studio for Digital Artists
- MAXON CINEMA 4D R20 Studio Workbook
- MAXON CINEMA 4D R19 Studio: A Tutorial Approach, 6th Edition